GUN
COLLECTOR'S
DIGEST

Edited by Joseph J. Schroeder, Jr.

DIGEST BOOKS, INC., NORTHFIELD, ILLINOIS

GUN COLLECTOR'S DIGEST STAFF

EDITOR
Joseph J. Schroeder, Jr.
ASSOCIATE EDITOR
Harold A. Murtz
ASSISTANT EDITOR
Lilo Anderson
ART DIRECTOR
Mary MacDonald
ASSOCIATE PUBLISHER
Sheldon L. Factor

Articles starting on pages 13, 74 and 147 are from *Gun World* through the courtesy and the permission of copyright holder—Gallant Publishing Co., Capistrano Beach, Calif. Articles starting on pages 79 and 200 are from *Guns* through the courtesy and the permission of copyright holder—Publishers' Development Corp., Skokie, Ill. Articles starting on pages 130, 136 and 280 are from *Shooting Times* through the courtesy and the permission of copyright holder—Peoria Journal Star, Inc., Peoria, Ill.

ISBN 0-695-80432-4   Library of Congress Catalog Card #73-83406

INTRODUCTION

Gun collectors are fortunate people in many respects. Theirs is a dynamic and worthwhile hobby, one that combines the study of history and politics with a recognition of fine craftsmanship and art. All this, and their guns are blue-chip investments whose potential for appreciation has been well established. Surely one could ask for little more from a hobby activity!

Gun collecting is a hobby whose fraternity has drawn its members from all walks of life. Most collectors judge each other *as collectors*, basing their respect on collecting astuteness rather than social position or bank account. Of course, the wealthy collector can out-bid one who is less affluent in direct competition, and the well-to-do collector often has dealers out looking for the things he needs. However, many truly fine collector's items turn up in the collections of low-budget collectors simply because the low-budget collector is willing to work harder at finding what he wants. Too, many collectors at all income levels support much or all of their activity by "horse trading" and part-time dealing, making enough profit on "sleeper" items (items that don't fit into or are duplicated in their own collections) that they never have to dip into the family sugar bowl when a new "jewel" comes their way. Dedicated people, these "gun nuts," but a finer group from which to choose one's friends would be hard to find!

GUN COLLECTOR'S DIGEST is aimed at every gun collector—anyone who collects guns or cartridges, or anyone who has ever thought of collecting guns or cartridges. Because of this broad direction it contains many articles on the how-to aspects of collecting, covering such subjects as building a library, photographing guns and cartridges, restoring guns, where to go to find worthwhile collector guns—and how to cope with gun control laws. The remainder of the book consists of articles on various collecting specialties, but even here we have included many that emphasize the choice of a collecting *direction* or philosophy to complement those that are concerned only with a special area.

The reader will find much in the subject matter of GUN COLLECTOR'S DIGEST that concerns "modern" guns—guns that were not considered to be true collector's items as recently as a decade ago. This has been done deliberately, as we feel that the whole complexion of gun collecting has changed in recent years. Interest in the classic guns of bygone eras still remains high, but as their supply dwindles and growing affluence brings new recruits to the field, the arms of recent conflicts and even recently discontinued sporting arms become more and more desirable in collector's eyes. Thus it is that you will find articles on self-loading pistols, bolt action rifles, flare pistols and even machine guns alongside the usual collector fare of Smith & Wessons, Civil War carbines and elegant flints. Our mix, unusual as it may seem to those familiar with previous books on gun collecting, didn't just happen. It is a planned mix, based on observations of what is happening in today's marketplace—the things we have seen at current gun shows and in collector-oriented periodicals.

There is some very valuable additional material to be found in GUN COLLECTOR'S DIGEST. Our "Gun Collector's Groups & Shows," for example, is probably the most complete such directory ever compiled. No matter what part of the United States, or, for that matter, any foreign country you live in, it can probably help you to find a friendly group of fellow collectors with whom to share your hobby. If information is—as it should be—your wish, you will find complete guides to both valuable collector's periodicals and books in "Periodicals for Collectors" and "The Gun Collector's Bookshelf," respectively. Finally, no collector—even one whose prime interest lies in pre-1899 antiques—should fail to familiarize himself with "The Gun Control Act of 1968," whose pertinent provisions we have also included.

In summary, then, GUN COLLECTOR'S DIGEST is *your* book—a book for collectors, written and edited by collectors. We who contributed to it have learned much about our hobby in the process. We trust that you will find it as valuable as we have.

Joseph J. Schroeder, Jr.

CONTENTS

Almost ideal for handgun display, case built into basement rec-room wall has sliding glass doors, lock. Built-in lighting provides fringe benefit, keeps case (and guns) warmer than room, preventing rust from condensation.

Random Advice on the Care and Feeding of a Gun Collection

by JOSEPH SCHROEDER

ACTUALLY, if you are reading this you have probably already started your gun (or cartridge) collection. That is, you've gathered whatever you could find from whatever sources you could think of and—lo and behold—you have a "collection."

However, such a collection—sometimes optimistically called a "general" collection—isn't really a collection at all. It's not a collection because its content wasn't planned—it just happened! This isn't to say that you don't get good collector's items from such obvious sources as friends, neighbors, relatives, business acquaintances and ads in local papers, because you can—and often very reasonably, too. The problem is that the content of such a collection is governed by availability, not planning. Your "collection" is likely to include a Garand, a 1911 Colt, an Enfield percussion musket with a broken hammer, a double barrel shotgun with a split stock and damascus barrels, three nickel plated 22 revolvers, and a near mint cased set of fine English duelling pistols! Some nice items, some junk—but no coherent collection, no *theme*.

So where do the experienced collectors go to build a real collection? Local gun shops are a good start. Most gun shop people are gun nuts just like you, and if they know you are seriously looking for specific items they'll be glad to bird-dog for you. If you make it a habit to visit the local shops often, you'll meet other collectors—not necessarily collectors of the same things you collect, but *active* collectors who'll also keep an eye open for your needs, while you watch out for theirs. They'll tell you about nearby gun

Long gun portion of the same display. Case is too large for glass doors, so the guns are exposed to curious fingers.

Handgun collectors do have it easier! This 30-drawer cabinet in a corner of the editor's den could hold nearly 100 auto pistols, supports bookcase to boot.

Corner of editor's den showing cabinet for pistols, parts of reference library. Note cased sets above, display award on wall.

Traditional rifle rack, useful where not too many long guns are to be displayed. A large collection is most easily arranged vertically in rows along a wall.

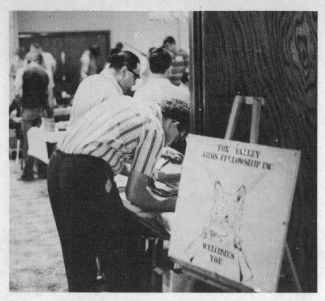

"Fox Valley Welcomes You"—Let's visit a typical regional gun show.

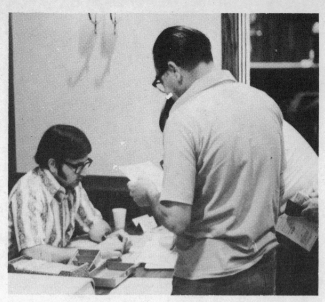

Well-run gun shows protect themselves and members by checking in visitors and require I.D. badges of members.

shows, too, maybe even a show we've overlooked in our complete Gun Show Directory in the back of this book. Watch the ads in the various gun publications (see our listing of these, too), both for availability and as a guide to prices. Don't be afraid to answer the classified ads you see, either. In over 20 years of active collecting and dealing by mail and telephone with other collectors and dealers, I've found by far the vast majority to be honest, responsible gentlemen, anxious to stand behind anything they sell. This is particularly true of the larger collector-oriented dealers whose ads you'll see in *Gun Report, Arms Gazette* and some of the other nationally distributed periodicals. Despite our bad media-created "gun nut" image, I'd be hard to put to name a hobby

that has as fine a bunch of participants as gun collecting!

What to Collect?

That's strictly personal—you collect what you collect because that's what you want to collect! Of course, unless your budget is unlimited you'd best steer clear of mint wheel-lock pistols or cased Colt dragoons. Just one of those is currently worth more than many a fair-sized collection of lesser fare. Or if you and your bride are sharing an efficiency apartment, a large rifle collection is not for you. But barring such obvious limitations, the collector who presents a comprehensive display of inexpensive suicide specials or military bolt action rifles, and knows

Variety is the story—choice Winchesters are offered here.

Typical horse-swapper bids two $500 cats for a $1000 dog.

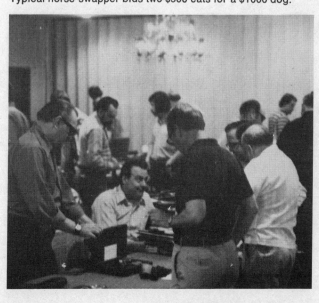

Fox Valley Arms President Paul Selley shows a choice Single Action from trophy-winning Colt display.

Research is the name of the game—is this like the one in the book, or do we have a rare variation? 1973 National Automatic Pistol Collector's Association convention.

what he has and what he still needs, merits a lot more respect than one who displays a few expensive but unrelated rarities and doesn't really know why they're good. It doesn't matter so much *what* you decide to collect, but *how* you decide to collect! Collecting is a form of education, and without intelligent direction it is not collecting but *gathering*. There is a tremendous amount of satisfaction in finding that you know things about your specialty that you can't find in books. Of course, it is easier to let someone else do the ground-work for you. Colts, Winchesters and Lugers are specialties in which a collector need only be able to read and write (in a checkbook, since there are lots like him competing for what's offered) to gather an interesting collection. But how much more pleasure there is in beating your own path—do a thorough job, and you may even find yourself the

noted author-expert that everyone quotes! Break your own ground, and prices won't be out of sight as they are in the more popular fields. This isn't to say that you should ignore gun literature, however. Jim White, a true gentleman and one of the old-time collector/dealers, told me when I was first getting started that to be a true *collector* I should buy a gun *book* everytime I bought a *gun*. Expand this to include everything in print covering your specialty —catalogs, manuals, ads—and you are on the right path.

Speaking of prices, what is a good collector's item worth? In simplest terms, it's worth exactly what someone is willing to pay for it. In practical terms, all but the rarest guns have "trading levels" that are reflected in gun show prices and the ads in the most active gun trading publications. Condition is

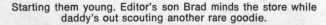

Starting them young. Editor's son Brad minds the store while daddy's out scouting another rare goodie.

Typical scene at a giant Ohio Gun Collectors Association meeting in Columbus. These 700-plus table shows usually attract over 5000 members and guests.

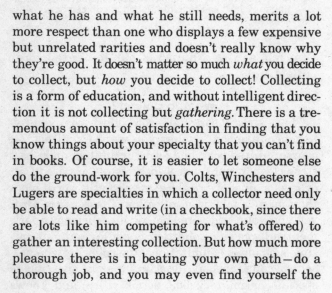

Specialized shows draw smaller attendance, but common interest keeps enthusiasm high. This scene from 1973 annual convention of National Automatic Pistol Collector's Association shows two of the prize-winning displays.

Shooting irons aren't the only fare at gun shows. Here author Frank Sellers complements his antique handguns with some outstanding Western bronzes.

very important, and most advertisers are reasonably accurate in descriptions. Just remember the old saw, "Rare junk is still junk"—though I've bought some pretty rare "junk" that competent restoration has made into choice collector's items! And true "mint" condition can add a hefty premium to the going price of a choice piece. Study prices and learn to judge condition—if you don't do this early in your collecting career, you're in for some expensive education. One thing is certain though—*intelligent* gun collecting is a heck of a good investment! Good collector guns only go up, and at a lot faster rate than inflation.

Caring for Your Collection

Some collectors immediately disassemble and clean every new gun, carefully oiling it in and out before putting it away in storage. Others remove any obvious rust or glop, squirt it with rust inhibit-

ing oil, and hang it on the wall. There are good arguments on both sides. *Don't* wire brush or even steel wool a gun with any original finish—unless you know what you are doing. Surface rust, soaked with oil, comes off easily with a sharpened brass scraper (no risk) or a dull knife blade (careful!). Oil-soaked, dirty grips can be boiled and/or bleached, dented stocks restored with a hot iron and damp cloth. *You* can improve the appearance of almost any gun you acquire, but you must know what you are doing.

To make sure your guns stay looking good, keep the metal oiled, keep humidity in your gun room under 50% (air conditioning on humid summer days is a *must*) and your guns should last forever. Many collectors keep a silicone impregnated mitt or an oily rag handy to their guns—the few moments spent wiping off metal surfaces after handling will prevent those heart-breaking rust-etched fingerprints.

Another highly specialized group is the cartridge collectors, whose annual three-day show is usually sold out. Here collector-dealer Jim Tillinghast examines a puzzling specimen.

The Editor's prize-winning display of Bergmann pistols and accessories at the NAPCA 1973 Annual Convention.

This is particularly important if you like to show your guns to non-gun collecting friends. Some people's perspiration is so corrosive that it will etch through blue in a few hours.

As to storage and display, every collector is faced with the decision as to whether security or the pleasure of enjoying his collection is paramount. Of course, if your collection is valuable enough, a sophisticated protection system such as the type offered by ADT or the automatic alarm systems that tie into the local police switchboard are well worth their high costs. But for the majority of collectors, many of whom spend little more on their hobby each year than such a system costs, other means are needed. One obvious way to help keep your collection *yours* is to restrict the number of people who know you have guns. Though being reticent may keep the news of your hobby from someone who's just dying to give you a choice goodie, it also keeps the word of your "arsenal" from the ears of those whose intentions aren't as charitable. If you must have a den or recreation room display, put it on a wall that can't be seen from the outside through a window or from an entrance used by casual visitors. A display case with lockable sliding glass panels keeps casual hands off your collection, and a removable fiberboard or plywood panel to cover the case when not on display might even cause a casual burglar to pass it by!

Every serious collector owes his collection the protection offered by an ultrasonic or other low-cost burglar alarm. These plug-in units will light lights and sound bells or horns when someone moves in the room in which they are installed, and that is often enough to drive many sneak thieves away. If you have a few (or more) very valuable handguns in your collection, a safe deposit box in a nearby bank is a great place to keep them when you're out of town — or even between sessions with visiting collectors or trips to shows. Some collectors (this one included)make it a practice to remove all handguns from the house when it will be empty overnight — a friend or neighbor is usually happy to put a suitcase or two in a closet or under a bed for you when you're going out of town.

Gun insurance is a good idea, since even though it can't replace a real rarity it can reduce the pain of loss! You will usually have some coverage from a standard homeowner's policy, but read the small print for limitations. The NRA gun insurance is one of the best buys available, and having the NRA to help you in case of a dispute is a big plus. Never lose sight of the fact that your collection is an investment, and a darned good one, too. Collector guns have been appreciating steadily since World War II, and a recent *Wall Street Journal* article rated them a close second to coins among hobbies with investment potential.

Gun Collecting and the Law

Gun collectors have more potential legal concerns than almost any other hobbyist. First and foremost is the Gun Control Act of 1968, which essentially forbids the interstate transfer of any firearm made after 1898 except to holders of Federal Firearms Licenses. GCA'68 has been modified by a number of Revenue Rulings, now called "ATF Rulings," many of which are very beneficial and vitally important to collectors. For this reason we are reproducing much of GCA'68 and *all* pertinent ATF Rulings in this book. Active collectors of post-1898 guns may wish to obtain a *Collector's License* ($10 per year), which permits an individual to deal in modern guns that are classified as "Curios and Relics" *across* state lines. The negative aspect of a collector's license is that you must keep a complete record of all firearms you own, no matter when obtained (this is good sense, anyway), and these records, along with your collection and licensed premises (home), are subject to inspection by Treasury agents at "any reasonable hour." Collectors of modern guns who don't wish to have a collector's license must make arrangements with a friendly local dealer to handle interstate transactions for them, a process that involves enough paperwork to justify the dealer's charging a few dollars for each gun handled. Each federal licensee receives a copy of *Published Ordinances Firearms* each year. This book includes pertinent parts of all state laws and local ordinances relating to the purchase of guns and ammunition, as well as the complete text of GCA'68 and all subsequent rulings. Ask your local dealer to let you look at his copy, or better yet, purchase your own from the Superintendent of Documents, U.S. Government Printing Office, Washington, D.C. 20402. Price of the 1973 edition is $2.60 postpaid; it can also be purchased over the counter in the government book stores in many cities. Another valuable publication is the *Alcohol, Tobacco and Firearms Bulletin,* a monthly booklet that provides current information on ATF Rulings and the like. Subscription rate for 1973 was $4.50 per year, but it will probably be raised to $5.25 a year in 1974. It is also available from the Superintendent of Documents.

However you choose to learn about them, you *must* obey *all* state, local and federal laws in your collecting activities. Not to do so is to jeopardize not only your investment but your entire future! It just isn't worth it! Buying or selling a modern gun across a state line without a license can result in confiscation of your entire collection and your indictment for a felony! DON'T DO IT!

In summary, gun collecting is a great hobby you are sharing with fine people. Approach it thoughtfully and stay within the law and you'll never regret having joined us.

●

Denmark, Norway and the United States have more in common than a love for long-legged blondes and sea food — all used the...

KRAG-JORGENSEN RIFLE

by COL. ROBERT H. RANKIN, USMC (RET.)

U.S. Marine in dress uniform of Spanish-American war period, armed with bayonet-equipped Model 1896 Krag rifle.

THE KRAG-JORGENSEN was used only for some fourteen years by our regular army. This is a comparatively short time indeed for a military rifle. Compare this, for instance, with the fabled Springfield '03, which reigned supreme in the United States fighting forces for the better part of half a century. The Krag did see some combat use during and immediately after that embroglio known as the Spanish-American War. Then it was turned over to the National Guard for a time. Finally, it was issued to cadet organizations and military schools.

In fact, the author's first contact with the Krag-Jorgensen, was when, as a young second lieutenant, he was assigned to duty as an instructor at a military school. That was shortly before World War II. Fresh from line duty with troops, the writer was little impressed with the Krag as compared to the rugged, reliable, accurate Model 1903 Springfield with which he was so familiar both as an enlisted man and as an officer. Interestingly enough, after the attack on Pearl Harbor Krags in the armories of military schools were recalled by Uncle Sam for reissue as training rifles.

Once a rather commonly seen weapon, due in no small part to the fact that great numbers were sold off by the U.S. government as surplus to civilian shooters at low prices, the Krag is now a desirable collector's item.

This bolt-operated magazine rifle is characterized to some extent by its unique gate-loading magazine. The entrance to the magazine is through a door or gate on the right side of the weapon, which is opened

Danish Krag-Jorgensen Rifles and Carbines

1. Original Model 1889 Infantry Rifle. Note metal jacket over barrel, similar to German M1888 Commision Rifle.

2. Model 1889 Cavalry Carbine, early style (introduced about 1912).

3. Model 1889/1924 Cavalry Carbine.

4. Infantry Carbine, Model 1889/1924. Bayonet is M1915.

5. Artillery Carbine, Model 1889/1924.

6. Engineer's Carbine, Model 1889/1924.

7. Model 1928 Sniper's Rifle. Note heavy barrel, special sights and sporter stock.

Above photographs all courtesy of Tojhusmuseet, Copenhagen.

to insert five rounds of ammunition. The gate then is closed. On the Danish model, this gate is hinged at the front end to swing forward, but on other models, it is hinged at the bottom to swing down. This latter arrangement is something of an advantage inasmuch as rounds are prevented from being dropped, since they are caught by the open gate.

The weapon was developed by Captain—later Colonel—Ole Herman Johannes Krag of the Norwegian Army and by Erik Jorgensen, an arms expert at the Danish government arsenal.

Krag, long interested in arms development, was first ordered to duty at the Kongsberg arsenal in 1870. In collaboration with Axel Peterson, a government arms expert, he developed the Krag-Peterson rifle. This incorporated a modified Martini falling block action with a tubular magazine which was located under the barrel. It fired a 12.77mm rimfire black powder cartridge. Krag then later joined Jorgensen in arms development work and during 1889 they were granted a Norwegian patent on the bolt action military rifle bearing their name.

That same year it was adopted by Denmark. It was not until some five years later that it was adopted by the United States.

The first Danish model, the 1889, appeared in several versions. The version known as the infantry rifle was standard in the Danish army until World War II. This piece also was used by some German occupation troops in Denmark in World War II.

The Danish Model 1889 infantry rifle weighs 9½ pounds, is 58.28 inches long over-all and has a barrel 32.78 inches long. The barrel has Metford rifling with six grooves with a twist to the right. In Denmark this is referred to as Rasmussen rifling for the individual who suggested its use. It is chambered for the 8mm Danish rimmed cartridge, has a barleycorn front sight and a leaf type rear sight. The magazine accommodates five rounds. As is the case in other Krag-Jorgensen designs, the magazine spring, lever and follower all are attached to the hinged loading gate. When this gate is opened the spring and the follower retract, allowing the magazine to be loaded with loose rounds. Originally a patented charger was provided. This charger consisted of a sheet metal box with a spring-loaded lever on one side to retain the cartridges. By depressing this lever the cartridges could be dumped into the magazine. This charger was heavy, expensive to manufacture and proved to be clumsy in operation. It was soon discarded.

Krags have the advantage of being capable of being loaded with the action either open or closed. A cutoff allows the gun to be used as a single-shot with the magazine in reserve.

The Model 1889 Danish Krag was produced in at least five variations. The infantry version of the Model 1889 rifle has a metal jacket surrounding the

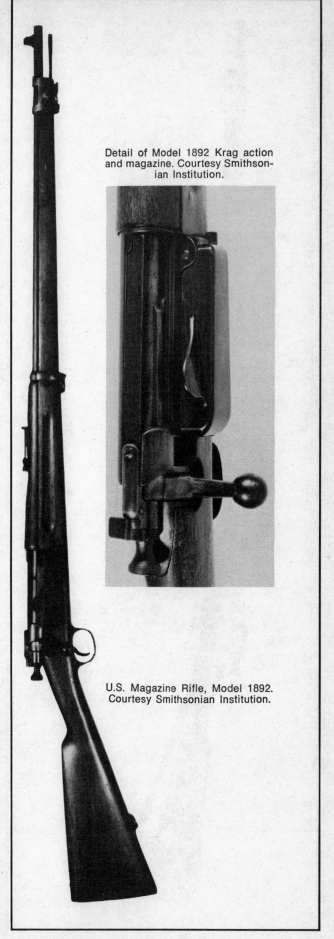

Detail of Model 1892 Krag action and magazine. Courtesy Smithsonian Institution.

U.S. Magazine Rifle, Model 1892. Courtesy Smithsonian Institution.

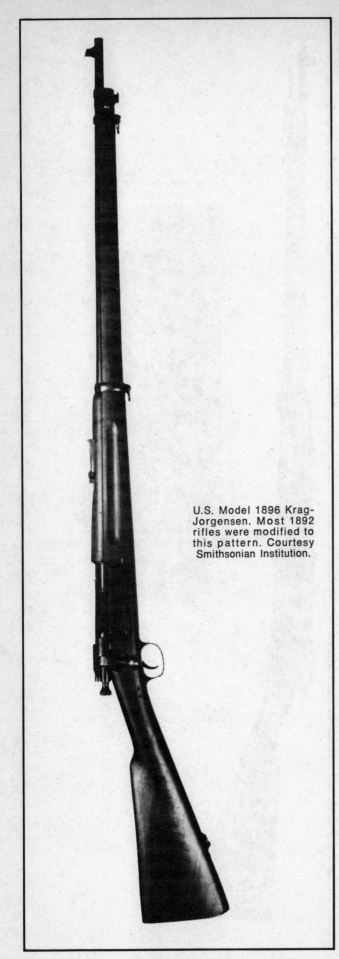

U.S. Model 1896 Krag-Jorgensen. Most 1892 rifles were modified to this pattern. Courtesy Smithsonian Institution.

barrel serving as a handguard. It is designed to accommodate a bayonet. The Fodfolkskarabin, or infantry carbine, also has a metal handguard. In 8mm caliber, it is 43.3 inches long over-all, with a barrel 24 inches long. It weighs 8.8 pounds. The bolt handle is straight as is the case with the infantry rifle.

The Model 1889 Artillerikarabin, or artillery carbine, introduced in 1924, is similar to the infantry carbine but has a turned down bolt handle. There is also a stud on the left side of the stock which is used in suspending the gun from a leather loop on the artilleryman's back.

The Model 1889 Ingeniorkarabin, or engineer carbine, also introduced in 1924, has a wood handguard whereas the previously noted carbines have a metal handguard. It is 43.25 inches long overall. The barrel is 23.63 inches long.

All of the above carbines are in 8mm caliber and accommodate a bayonet.

In 1914 a so-called cavalry rifle was introduced. This piece has the rear sling swivel on the left side just ahead of the trigger guard. The bolt handle is straight.

In 1928 the basic Krag rifle was modified to a sniper type with heavy barrel and wooden hand guard. It has a sporting type stock with pistol grip. There is a micrometer rear sight and hooded target-type front sight. This rifle weighs 11.7 pounds. It is 46 inches long over-all, with a 26.3 inch barrel. It has a turned down bolt handle.

Neither the 1914 cavalry rifle nor the Model 1928 sniper rifle are designed to accommodate a bayonet.

Beginning in 1925, the six-groove Metford rifling of the Danish Krags was changed to the four-groove concentric type.

The Danish Krags were manufactured in the government arsenal at Haerens Tojhus and at Gevaerfabrikan Kobenhavn. Until 1890 a black powder cartridge was used. After that a smokeless powder round was used.

The Krag story now switches to the United States. The advantages of a magazine rifle to the foot soldier had been apparent from the Civil War onward. Additional design impetus was given by the development of the bolt action. However, the development of a truly efficient magazine rifle was curtailed by the black powder cartridges then in use. It was not until 1884 that smokeless powder was developed in France and it was not until several years later, after considerable laborious research, that other nations were able to unravel the secret of manufacturing such a propellant.

By 1890 the process of making smokeless powder had become generally known internationally and this country moved ahead to adopt a magazine rifle using the new propellant. That same year, the U. S. Army appointed a board to inquire into such adoption. This board advertised trials and it was announced that competitors had until July 1, 1892, to submit their weapons. All in all, a total of fifty-three guns was submitted. These were from both American and foreign competitors. Foreign entries included several Mauser models, Lee magazine rifles, a Mannlicher and several versions of the Krag-Jorgensen.

After extended trials and considerable study of the results, the board determined that the weapon which was being sought should be capable of being used as a single loader as well as a magazine weapon and that it should be capable of adaption to either rimmed or rimless cartridges.

During the trials each gun was subjected to the firing of five hundred rounds without cleaning. The action then was blasted with sand dust for two minutes, after which another twenty rounds were fired. The gun then was fired with cartridges rendered defective by filing them across the head. Finally, each gun was artificially rusted and, after drying, was subjected to more firing. All of this was designed to simulate the rough treatment which the piece would receive in field service with troops.

At the conclusion of the trials, the Krag-Jorgensen system was recommended for adoption by the U.S. Army, the designers to be paid one dollar apiece for each gun manufactured. Final determination of the caliber, rifling and type of cleaning rod and bayonet were held in abeyance for the time being. The recommendations of the trial board were promptly approved successively by the Chief of Ordnance and acting Secretary of War.

Although the trial board had been fair and objective in its work and had certainly allowed adequate time for the submission of entries, some American gun designers were so disappointed that a foreign weapon had been selected that they cried "foul." These die-hards were influential enough to cause Congress to order new trials. Among those protesting the original findings of the board was the old firm of military relic dealers, Francis Bannerman, which submitted a Spencer-Lee pump-action rifle. This was a combination of the designs of Christopher Spencer and James Paris Lee, both well known arms designers. Other rifles submitted included three weapons offered by Major W. R. Livermore of the U.S. Army and U.S. Marine Lieutenant H. K. White.

On May 16, 1893 the board reported out that no American weapon could be recommended and the official decision was again made to adopt the Krag. Manufacture was begun at the Springfield Armory and the following year, 1894, the first Krags were issued to the troops.

The first U.S. Krag, designated the U.S. Magazine Rifle, Model 1892, weighs 9.3 pounds and is 49.1 inches long over-all, with a barrel 30 inches long. It is rifled with four grooves, right-hand twist. A long

cleaning rod is inserted into the stock from the muzzle end. The butt stock is straight with a thin butt plate without a trap and without a curve at the toe.

A knife-type bayonet was regular issue for use with the U.S. Krag. The spear-point blade is nearly 12 inches long. Some blades are blued. Others were issued bright. The grips are of walnut and the pommel is of birdshead pattern. The guard has a ring which passes over the muzzle. The metal scabbard is blued.

A carbine model was designed at this time, but was never manufactured. This was to be half stocked with the stock itself 7.85 inches shorter than the rifle stock. There would have been no provision for a bayonet. A sling swivel and a ring would have been attached to the left side of the stock.

Some twenty-odd thousand Model 1892 Krags were manufactured. These were later modified to Model 1896 rifles. They are chambered for the 30-40 rimmed Krag-Jorgensen cartridge with a round nose bullet weighing 220 grains. It was sped on its way by a charge of smokeless powder weighing an average of 40 grains.

In 1896, a modified Krag was adopted in both a rifle and a carbine version. Among other modifications, the long cleaning rod was removed from under the barrel. Instead, there is a jointed rod which is inserted in a recess in the butt stock. The thickened butt plate has a hinged trap over this recess. The toe of the butt is rounded. An improved rear sight was provided. The original rear sight had a sliding leaf and was graduated up to 1900 yards. The Model 1896 rear sight is capable of elevating adjustment with the leaf down by simply moving the slide up an included plane. It is graduated up to 1800 yards. The overall length of the rifle was shortened by a quarter of an inch. Around 30,000 Model 1896 rifles were manufactured.

The Model 1896 carbine was intended for cavalry use. It weighs approximately 8 pounds, has an overall length of some 40 inches. The barrel is 22 inches long. A sling ring is attached to the left side of the stock. The walnut stock is held to the barrel by one band. The sliding leaf rear sight is graduated up to 1900 yards. Like the rifle, the carbine is rifled with four grooves making one turn to the right in 10 inches. Some 20,000 Model 1896 Krag carbines were manufactured. These later were altered to improved Model 1898 and 1899 carbines.

In addition to the Model 1896 rifle and carbine, a modified Krag, known as the U.S. Cadet rifle, also was manufactured. The length over-all is 49.10 inches. The barrel is 30 inches long. Weight is approximately 9.1 pounds.

Two years later, the Model 1898 Krag rifle and carbine appeared. In these, the bolt handle seat was cut off flush with the receiver and did not project

U.S. Model 1898 Krag-Jorgensen. Note sight and detail differences. Courtesy Smithsonian Institution.

as in the earlier models. There was also a new rear sight. This has a solid center leaf and is adjustable for windage. This model was approved for manufacture on March 14, 1898, and was in production four months later, in July. Around 262,000 Model 1898 Krag rifles were made between 1898 and 1904, when their manufacture was terminated. Five thousand Model 1898 carbines were made, these in 1899.

In 1899, another version of the carbine appeared. This differed from the 1898 model in having the rear sight protected by a humped handguard. The stock was two inches longer than that of the previous models.

There was no provision for a bayonet on these carbines. However, for the rifles, in addition to the practical knife type Krag bayonet, two other types were issued. These were abortions of the worst sort. Designed to be used for brush cutting as well as for use as anti-personnel weapons, they were an abject failure in both departments. One of these odd-ball Krag bayonets has a Bowie knife blade slightly over nine inches long and 1¼ inches wide. The other bayonet has a bolo-type blade with a relatively straight back and a deeply bellied cutting edge. It is 10⅝ inches long and slightly over two inches wide. Both bayonets have metal scabbards. They are now collector's items.

Mention should be made at this time of the so-called Gallery Krag. This is in 22 caliber and was converted from the Model 1898 Krag by substituting a 22 caliber barrel for the 30 caliber barrel and making necessary changes in the breech action. It was a single shot affair. A limited standard weapon, it was introduced in 1907.

It is estimated that, all in all, some 442,000 rifles and 63,000 carbines of Krag-Jorgensen design were manufactured at the Springfield Armory. The vast majority of these were used by the U. S. Army. Some Model 1898 Krag rifles were used by the Navy, Marine Corps and Coast Guard.

The combat record of the Krag-Jorgensen in the U.S. services is somewhat limited, but is excellent nonetheless. During the Spanish-American War, regular army units were armed with it, as were a few volunteer outfits. The largest number of American troops, volunteers all, were armed with the old Springfield single-shot, black powder 45-70 rifle which belched out vast clouds of white smoke each time a shot was touched off. The Krag was also used by our troops in the Philippine Insurrection of 1899-1902 and during the Boxer Rebellion in China in 1900-1901.

During World War I and to a limited extent in World War II the Krag was used as a training rifle. It immediately became obsolete when this country adopted the Springfield '03, with its Mauser action.

Although invented by Norwegians, the Krag-Jorgensen was not adopted by Norway until 1894.

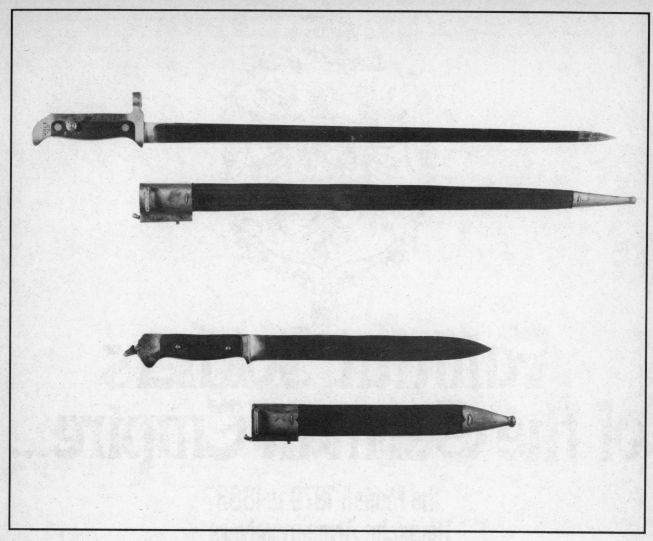

Danish (above) compared to U.S. bayonet. Courtesy Smithsonian Institution.

The Norwegian Model 1894 is similar to the American Model 1892, but is in 6.5mm caliber. It is 49.9 inches long with a barrel 29.9 inches long. It weighs 9.38 pounds. The barrel is rifled with four grooves with a twist to the left. The stock has a pistol grip. This rifle is designed to accommodate a bayonet.

Some Norwegian Model 1894s were manufactured in the government arsenal, Kongsberg Vapenfabrikk, Kongsberg, Norway, but around 30,000 were made by Osterreichische Waffenfabrik Gesellschaft, Steyr, Austria.

In 1895, a carbine model was adopted. This weighs 7.5 pounds, is 40 inches long, with a barrel 20.4 inches long. Known as a cavalry model, it was followed two years later by the mountain troop model of 1897. Both models have half-stocks. In 1904 an engineer carbine and in 1907 an artillery carbine were adopted. These basically are the 1895 cavalry carbine but with stock and hand guard extending nearly to the muzzle. In 1912 another carbine appeared. It is full-stocked and is similar to the 1894 rifle. It weighs 9 pounds, is 43.5 inches long, with a barrel 24.09 inches long. A variation with a 26.1 inch heavy barrel and special peep sight is known as the Model 1923 short sniper rifle.

Other variations of the Model 1894 Norwegian Krag-Jorgensen include a Model 1894 sniper rifle with telescopic sight, a Model 1925 sniper rifle with heavy barrel and micrometer sight and the Model 1930 sniper rifle. This last item weighs eleven pounds, and has a half-stock, micrometer rear sight and hooded front sight.

The Model 1930 sniper rifle and the 1895, 1897, 1904 and 1907 carbines are not designed to accommodate a bayonet.

All in all, the Krag-Jorgensen was a good rifle. Critics point out, however, that it was expensive to manufacture, not lending itself to modern mass production methods. It is also noted that the Krag does not use a charger to load the magazine. The loading gate protruding from the side of the piece is considered clumsy and unsightly. Additionally, the bolt is not held open when the magazine is empty to signal the shooter that it's time to reload. Despite these faults, however, the Krag served its users well. ●

Faithful Soldiers of the German Empire...

the Modell 1879 u. 1883 Deutsche Armeerevolvers

For nearly half a century and in the four corners of the world, these revolvers served the German Republic.

by William H.J. Chamberlain

THE SEPARATE or associated German states of 1870 came together to erect the *Deutsches Reich* in 1871. For the resulting *Reichsarmee* and the *Reichskriegsmarine* there was created a *Reichsrevolver* in 1879. The *Reichsrevolver Modell 1879* and improved *Modell 1883* replaced the various handguns of the national contingents of the imperial army, became the revolvers of the imperial navy, and served the empire until the *Reich* became a *Republik* in 1918 even though they had been officially relieved by the *Pistole '08*. In this article we shall consider these old soldiers first as mechanisms, then as collector's items and finally review some of the interesting civilian variations.

The Revolver as a Mechanism

The design was a product of the Spandau Arms Commission, which had been given the task of standardizing and improving the equipment of the imperial armed forces. For this reason, both the Modell 1879 and the Modell 1883 (M'79 and M'83) are often called "Commission Revolvers" by English-speaking writers and collectors, a designation that recognizes the effective origin of the design. German-speaking writers and collectors prefer to recognize the purpose of the design: to provide a uniform handgun for an imperial armed force. The design replaced several national weapons, such as the sturdy percussion pistol of 1850 and the practical adaptation of a Beaumont-Adams percussion revolver used by the Prussian army and navy; an impractical heavy caliber 5-shot copy of a Smith & Wesson No. 2 for the Saxon army; the mechanically brilliant

Fig. 1—A Modell 1879 Reichsrevolver, Mauser-contract serial 658, made in 1880 but not issued until 1882.

single shot Bavarian Werder cartridge pistol, and the array of pistols used by the Kingdom of Wuerttemburg, the Grand Duchy of Baden and all the other free states and cities. Roland K. Edelmann, writing in the *Deutsches Waffen-Journal,* has dealt extensively with this matter of nomenclature. Thus, today as in the 1880s, the proper name for the design is *Reichsrevolver.*

The M'79 and the M'83 differ very little from each other, mechanically. Both are uncomplicated single-action designs, with a massive loading gate on one side and a safety-lever on the other. The obvious visual differences are the shapes of the butts and the lengths of the barrels. The barrel of the M'79 specifically measured for this article (Fig. 1) is 7¼″ long; the M'83's barrel is 4⁹⁄₁₆″ (Fig. 2). Advertisements in German-language collectors' magazines often specify "Reichsrevolver, Langer Lauf" or "Reichsrevolver, Kurzer Lauf," so as not to miss an opportunity with someone who might not know the model year. An M'79 in collector's hands should show that it was originally given a brown finish on the main components, sometimes rather hard to distinguish from rust. The trigger and hammer were

pickled gray; the other external fittings were blued. The M'83s normally had a very dark blue or black finish, with the hammer, trigger and cylinder pin polished bright. Both models should have smooth wood grips, although some very low-numbered M'83s have been reported with checkered grips.

The cylinder latch is the basic mechanical difference between the M'79 and the M'83, considering the barrel length and butt shape differences to be merely superficial. The M'79's cylinder latch (Figs. 3,4) is a bolt which goes right through the frame and through a transverse semi-circular cut on the shaft of the cylinder pin. The bolt has a thumb-lever formed in one piece with its head. When that thumb lever is rotated 90 degrees downward from rest, it presents a semi-circular cut on its own shaft to the cylinder pin and frees the pin. The M'83 uses a spring-loaded pin, operating head to the right, which controls the cylinder pin through a similar system of interference and withdrawal.

There are two reasons for giving so much space here to such a seemingly minor detail. One reason is for the recognition of models. Heinz Lehner, writing in the *Deutsches Waffen-Journal* for January, 1972

Fig. 2—A regulation Reichsrevolver Modell 1883, made by F. vonDreyse, Soemmerda. This single-action revolver, serial 6636, was issued to the Light Ammunition Column supporting the 22nd Field Artillery Regiment.

has presented an 1879-barrel and 1883-butted revolver which he labels a "transitional" model because it has the 1883 cylinder-pin latch. He does not, however, state that this transitional type was officially recognized by the ordnance authorities.

Damage prevention is the other reason. That bolt on the M'79 is a true bolt, threaded into the frame on the right side. It cannot be driven out as though it were a pin when trying to disassemble a sticky specimen, although if a forceful attempt is made it may soon *become* a pin. Many have! Further, the thin strip of metal joining the thumb-piece to the bolt is a leaf spring formed of the same piece of metal. It serves to keep the stud on the thumb-piece in a detent on the frame when at rest, as well as to drive the bolt through that 90 degree turn downwards. The thread bottoms at the end of those 90 degrees and the spring breaks off with a few more pounds of pressure. Many have. This may be the reason why the Ordnance authorities changed the design in 1883.

Both models have the barrels screwed into the frames, where they are supported by a generously deep socket (Fig. 5). The flats on the frame and rear

of the barrel allowed a good purchase for wrench and vise. Considering that the front sights are integral to the barrel and were machined beforehand, a great deal of force must have been used very often to screw the barrel home. One M'83 examined for this article had had the barrel removed for some unknown reason in the past; the workman who did the job had had to saw a groove all around the joint in order to relieve the metal which had "flowed" when the barrel was first screwed home.

The M'79's barrel has a muzzle-ring. The German word "Mündungswulst" can be (freely) translated as "fat mouth" and that does indeed describe it. This metallic reenforcement defended the muzzle against external forces practically and against internal forces theoretically. It is a common enough feature on European military handguns of the mid-19th Century. The Prussian pistol of 1850 had it, as did the Mauser "Zig-zag" revolver of 1878, which was *not* a military weapon.

The frame includes the grip strap (and butt-cap, on the M'79) and is a solid piece of metal. The lock plate comes off easily to uncover the lock; there is no hook or dovetail to be jiggled. With the lock-plate

Fig. 3—Closeup of early type of Mauser contract markings on serial 658, dated 1880 for manufacture and 1882 for issue.

off, the trigger guard can be wriggled free and there's the lock work ready to be admired: uncomplicated, solid, with a smooth pull-off and a thumping positive hammer-blow. The design, however simple and reliable, was not an advance in European terms. It was better than the Adams revolvers in the British service in that it had a positive cylinder-bolt; it was behind the Adams and most other European service revolvers since it was not double-action. As for the lock recess itself, it seems well laid out to permit being formed with simple passes of mills and drills. All the curves have constant radii. While two issue M'83s were at hand for study, their lock-plates were deliberately exchanged. It

Fig. 4—Cylinder-pin release latch for an "M'79 in "release" position, pin partially withdrawn. The latch will break off if one attempts to swing it through any more of an arc.

was pleasant to discover that they *could* be exchanged. Both cylinder and cylinder-pins were then exchanged, again with success as to fit and function. This seems a good performance, since one revolver was made at Erfurt and the other by von Dreyse. It would be silly to make a general rule from this limited instance, but the writer hopes that someone will take up for specific study the whole question of "interchangeability" regarding European military service small arms of the 19th Century.

One should use caution when removing the lock-plate. The metal-to-metal seam is right-angled and free, but the metal-to-wood seam will occasionally have some interference so the grips should first be freed to prevent possible damage to them. After that, merely remove the three lock-plate screws and use the three slots cut into the seam (one top and two on bottom) to pry the plate straight up off the hammer and trigger trunion. The shaft of the safety catch will come with the plate and there seems little need to remove the safety catch separately. The bearing depth of the safety-catch shaft is greater than that of the trunnions so, in technical language, when the plate lifts off the trunnions, stop prying and start wriggling.

The cylinder recesses the cartridge heads, in keeping with the general solidity of the design (Fig. 6). Most European service revolvers embodied this feature in the 1870s; the British to compensate for the flimsy head of the Boxer cartridge base and the Germans to make room for the sturdy Mauser-type base. Does anyone recall when this was introduced as an important "new" safety innovation for 22 rimfire revolvers in the United States?

No ejector is fitted to either the M'79 or the M'83. I do not know why. One doubts that patent rights came into the question. Many 1883-pattern revolvers made for the civilian market in Belgium and Germany have a simple rod-and-tube ejector fitted to the frame and do not appear to have acknowledged any debt to Colt's for the idea. The nearest European patents had expired by 1883, as well. Some writers claim that fired cartridges were ejected by using the withdrawn cylinder-pin, which is mechanically possible. Herr Edelmann, however, has identified a separately-carried two-piece combination cleaning rod and ejector rod, which permitted the more sensible drill of ejecting the cartridges with the cylinder in place. Separately-carried rods were not uncommon in Europe. It is possible to cite percussion Belgian, Swiss and Prussian pistols as conceptual ancestors. The system was carried to its logical conclusion in Denmark, where the Model 1848 Dragoon pistol, if carried by a trooper also armed with a carbine, was required to be served by the carbine's loading rod. Among cartridge revolvers which lacked ejector rods, the Dutch M'74 was a contemporary. Of course no amount of examples can make its omission a good idea.

The chambers of the military revolvers and many of the civilian specimens are numbered clockwise 1 through 6. There is a good, military reason for that: range safety. The firer loaded chambers 5 through 1 at a loading table under supervision of a junior NCO. The revolver would be at half-cock, the cylinder-bolt free. The firer would then ease the hammer off half-cock and lower it so that the fixed hammer nose rested in the empty number 6 chamber, which would automatically be in that position if the loader had begun with number 5. The cylinder bolt would reengage. The firer would then apply the safety catch, locking the hammer, and proceeded to the firing point when commanded. The NCO at the firing point would inspect the revolver to verify that the hammer was fully down, safety applied and that chamber number 5 was positioned just to the left of the top strap, ready to lead off a five-round string. If not, well, as they sing in "Lilli Marlene," *Es kann drei Tage kosten!*

The safety catch on these and other European revolvers seems superfluous to many observers. It is useful on the Reichsrevolver M'79 and M'83 due to the sole fault of the lock design: the hammer does not rebound. To carry the revolver *fully* loaded,

Fig. 5—Construction details of a regulation M'83. The numbered pin below the barrel socket is the head of the cylinder-pin bolt. The supported length of the barrel extends from the "step" in the octagonal area to its rear face.

Fig. 6—The combination of a stepped-base cartridge and recessed chambers was applied to both the M'79 and M'83. Here, an M'83 open for loading. The ejector rod was a separately-carried accessory.

ready for action, rather than on the firing range, requires one either to try something exciting or to use the safety catch. It is possible to ease the hammer forward so that the hammer nose rests in the cut-outs between the cartridges. I have experimented with and do not prefer that method. The alternative is to use the safety catch. Half-cock the revolver; the notch is deep and the trigger sear is strong. Apply the safety catch; as shown in Fig. 7, it will prevent the hammer from moving back off the half-cock notch if the revolver should slop about in the holster. Place the revolver in its holster; the full leather flaps will keep it from falling out and firing by impact. Keep the lanyard attached to the lanyard ring and one's own body, so that if it does fall from the holster or hand it is less likely to fall far enough to fire by impact. Crude, but militarily effective and definitely a systematic way of treating the matter (Fig. 8).

The caliber of the revolvers is 10.6mm *Deutscher Reichsarmee Revolver*. That's the designation given it by DWM, who distinguish it from the *Revolver Mauser 10.6mm* and the *Russland Ordonnanz Revolver Kal. .44 S & W*, its nearest relatives, and it seems best to leave it that way, their way. There are numerous "synonyms" for the cartridge, especially in White and Munhall's book, and confusion is aided by the varying "caliber" stamps found on the revolver barrels. These stamps varied from "10,55" to "10,65" on revolvers examined for this article (Fig. 9). The stamps do not designate the caliber of the cartridge, but merely report the bore diameter of the revolver on which they appear. More precisely: they report that the bore diameter is

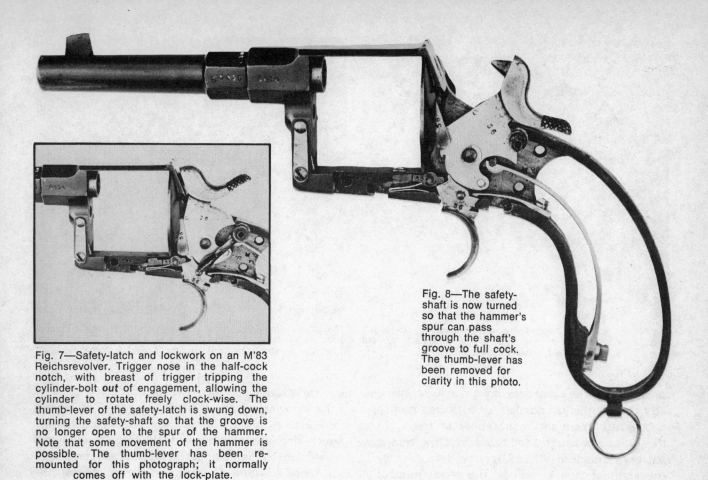

Fig. 7—Safety-latch and lockwork on an M'83 Reichsrevolver. Trigger nose in the half-cock notch, with breast of trigger tripping the cylinder-bolt *out* of engagement, allowing the cylinder to rotate freely clock-wise. The thumb-lever of the safety-latch is swung down, turning the safety-shaft so that the groove is no longer open to the spur of the hammer. Note that some movement of the hammer is possible. The thumb-lever has been re-mounted for this photograph; it normally comes off with the lock-plate.

Fig. 8—The safety-shaft is now turned so that the hammer's spur can pass through the shaft's groove to full cock. The thumb-lever has been removed for clarity in this photo.

near the lower or upper tolerance or that it is dead on the specification. One sees the same system used on many Lugers.

Collector points

Regimental marks are usually found on the butt crown plate for the M'79 and along the curve of the rear strap for the M'83. Locating them is simple; interpreting them is mildly complicated, except when it is impossible. There are some general rules which will help with the marks of regular and reserve regiments and it seems best to deal with them first.

First, seek out the largest-sized block capital letter, preferably near the center of the inscription. The letters and numbers flanking it are modifiers. An "A" is Field Artillery, distinct from Foot Artillery. An "R" is for Regiment of Infantry. Do not confuse Roman "ones" and Germanic "J"s for "I"s; indeed, forget about them for a while, remembering only that "R" is Infantry. Cavalry units will have the initial letters of *D*ragoon, *U*hlan, *H*ussar, *C*arabinier and *K*ürassier designations. "T" designates a support group, the military "train." The medical service is "S," for *Sanitatswache, -kolonne, -kompagnie* and the like. "M" is for *m*unitions supply units, not for medical.

Are you ready for the numbers? Arabic numerals

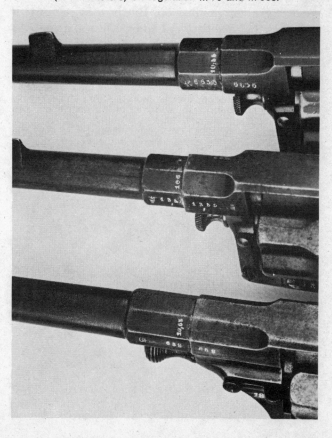

Fig. 9—Bore *diameter* marks, which are often mistaken for cartridge designations (top to bottom): 10,55; 10,6; and 10,55 (in millimeters) on regulation M'79 and M'83s.

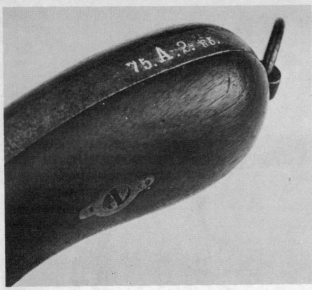

Fig. 10—Regimental markings as they appear on a Modell 1883 which was Revolver No. 65 of the 2nd Battery, 75th Field Artillery Regiment.

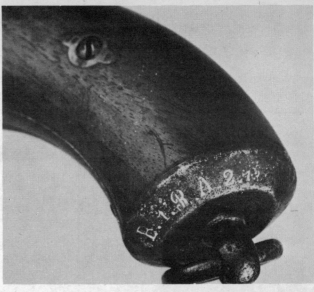

Fig. 11—Typical regimental markings on the butt of a Reichsrevolver Modell 1879. This pistol was issued to the 1st Royal Bavarian Reserve Artillery Regiment, 2nd Battery, Revolver No. 133.

to the left of the main arm or service letter are usually the regimental number, or battalion number if a separate train/battalion. Those to the right of the letter are usually the number of the company, battery, squadron (of cavalry) or detachment. To the right of that should be the serial number of the revolver in that specific company, in the form of a small-sized group of arabic numerals. Now we know, for example, that the M'83 in Fig. 10 is from the 2nd Battery of the 75th Field Artillery Regiment, revolver number 65. By the way, since it is unlikely that one battery had 65 officers, we should ignore the claim seen in other places that the M'83

Fig. 12—Regimental marking found inside flap of a M'81 holster for the Reischsrevolver Modell 1879. This style of marking differs from those described in the text. It denotes the 6th (Mounted) Battery, 5th Field Artillery Regiment, Revolver No. 1 as of 1901. The holster, made by "A.W.M." is dated 1900 on the exterior of the flap.

was exclusively an officers' revolver.

Now to muddy the waters. A large block-capital "B" denotes a unit of the Royal Bavarian Army, which declined the honor of having its elements tossed into the same imperial number sequence with all those lowland Germans. A *script* capital "R" denotes a Reserve unit. This means that the M'79 in Fig. 11 belonged to the 2nd battery of the 1st Royal Bavarian Reserve Field Artillery Regiment. A lower case "l" means "light."

Marching grimly along, we encounter lower-case "r"s and block-capital "E"s and "G"s. The first distinguishes the mounted (*reitende*) from the horse-drawn (*fahrende*) batteries of the field artillery, which was not the same as the foot artillery. The "G" denotes a unit of the guards, which, with their elite and traditional units, have their own variations. Among the simpler is the marking on an M'83: "GTS .2. 113." This revolver is from the second company of the medical battalion of the guards military train. The "E"! That's for the replacement or reserve (*Ersatz*) subcommands of a regular regiment, usually artillery.

This does not exhaust all the possibilities, but it does exhaust the writer and possibly the reader. A larger and intelligently organized selection of examples is given in Edelmann's article, and abstracted from the work of Jürgen Olmes. Even so, this writer has seen regimental marks that are yet puzzles, and the various machine-gun units, dispatch-rider regiments and detachments, and naval and coast artillery units will provide more puzzles. Therefore, the general rule deserves restating here. Locate the block capital letter denoting the colonel's command. Go left for the battalion or regimental number, right for the number of the captain's command. With light ammunition columns, the right-hand arabic numerals are usually for the number of the supported artillery regiment. The right-flank numerals give the number of the revolver in the captain's command. All other symbols are modifiers. All the rules have exceptions (Fig. 12).

Now let us turn to the makers' marks. The Mauser contract mark will be seen in two forms. The earliest is "Gebruder Mauser & Cie.-Oberndorf" shown in Fig. 3. This trading style was changed to "Waffenfabrik Mauser" in 1884, which will help with the few undated specimens to be found. M'79 revolvers made by Mauser are not "Mauser Revolvers!" Mauser did patent a revolver in 1878, when the firm was competing for the adoption of a military design. They failed, and a good thing, too, for their revolver was complicated and unhandy. It used a horizontally sliding rod slaved to the hammer to drive the cylinder around by means of a stud on that rod riding in grooves cut on the periphery of the cylinder. Now, that "Zig-zag" revolver *is* a Mauser revolver.

Franz Karl Rudolph von Dreyse, of Soemmerda, was the son of Nikolaus, the needle-gun designer. In keeping with his ancestry, the most wonderfully complex mechanism used on the civilian 1883 pattern revolvers came from his shop. His military contracts, however, were ordinary. His death in August, 1894, is, one assumes, a terminal date for the use of the mark illustrated in Fig. 13.

Two makers' marks not illustrated here must be dealt with together. The first indicates a consortium among the firms of Sauer & Sohn, V. Christian Schilling and C. G. Haenel, all of Suhl, and is formed by their initials. The second mark indicates that Sauer & Sohn had left the consortium or had not yet joined it. In point of logic, it could indicate both. The evidence presented by a respectable German author for the one view seems to admit of either view. In the absence of factory records, a great many more reports of M'79 and M'83 revolvers, correlated by maker, serial number, type and—when seen—date stamps are required before one can make a definite statement. Until then, the following scheme seems defensible. An M'79 with the mark of all three firms is "middle period." One with the mark of only Schilling and Haenel is "early" and one with the mark only of Sauer & Sohn may be either early or late. An M'83 made by the full consortium (Sauer, Schilling, Haenel) is early for *that* period; one by only Schilling and Haenel would be late and this writer is willing to accept a date in 1884 for this division. This scheme postulates that Sauer may have made up some M'79s after leaving the consortium. It does seem that the M'83s early period is rather short. I have seen only one M'83 made by the full consortium.

Dates appear on many M'79s and M'83s. Some-

Fig. 13—The contractor's mark for Franz K. R. vonDreyse, Soemmerda, as found on the Reichsrevolver Modell 1883, shown in Fig. 2.

times there are two dates. The date found below the Erfurt arsenal mark (Fig. 14) is the year of manufacture. That is also the case with the date stamped inside the maker's mark on Mauser contract revolvers. Two date stamps, one somewhere forward on the frame, may reasonably be taken to indicate both the year of manufacture and the year of delivery to troops from depot stores on Mauser or on any other maker's revolvers (Fig. 3). The picture is not yet clear with regard to the instance of only one date on Dreyse's or revolvers by any of the Sauer, Schilling, Haenel combinations. For example: there's an M'79 made by the full Sauer-Schilling-Haenel group and dated 1895. Its serial number is 218. Since it was initially issued to the first section of the light ammunition column for

Fig. 14—Another Modell 1883 with Erfurt Arsenal manufacture-mark and dated 1894. The leaf spring mounted vertically on the frame forward of the cylinder tensions one end of the bolt for the cylinder pin.

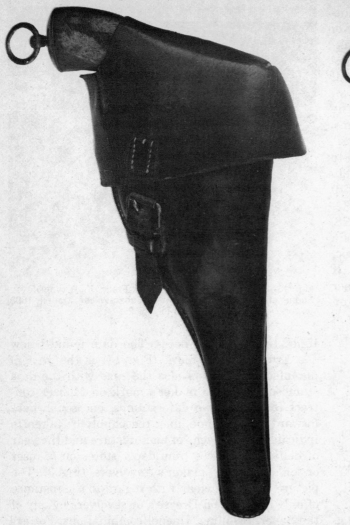

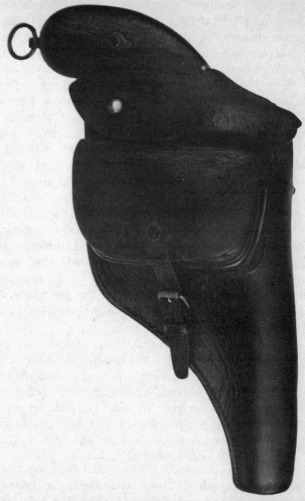

Fig. 15—The M'81 holster for the M'79 Reichsrevolver. The two belt loops for this brown leather holster are angled so that the revolver butt slopes front if worn on the left.

Fig. 16—The M'91 holster, with 12-round cartridge pouch sewn on, for the M'83 Reichsrevolver. The two belt loops on the back angle the butt forward when the holster is worn on the left side.

the 1st Field Artillery Regiment, we may consider that this was an early revolver issued rather late to a low priority unit.

Dating by proof marks or serial numbers is not yet reliable. Not enough data have been recorded to permit cross-referencing. (Indeed, one purpose of this lengthy section on marks—maker, regiment, serial and proof—is to point out the sort of data that must be collected.)

Serial numbers appear to have been applied independently by each individual arsenal or contractor. One can see how the shifting alliances among Sauer, Schilling and Haenel could complicate this aspect. Furthermore, the presence of lower-case script letters beneath some serial numbers raises not only the question of cyclical numbering but also of how many such subscripts have been unreported as "unimportant?" Nor are proof marks much use, on military arms. The Reichsrevolvers were marked with *Reichsadler* proof on the barrel—except in Bavaria—before and after the Proof Act of 1891

came into full force in 1893. These military weapons were not required to undergo civil proofing unless they were sold to the public as revolvers assembled from surplus parts. Brethren, I say unto you that if you have a dated Reichsrevolver, "cherish the date, and keep it holy."

The holsters illustrated here represent the basic types. The M'79 was first carried in a holster modified from the holster used for the Bavarian 1869 Werder single-shot pistol. The holster specifically made for the M'79 was designated the Holster M'81 by most of the Reich's military forces. The ultramontane Bavarians—bless 'em—considered the matter for a year and then called it the Holster M'82. This is the holster illustrated in Fig. 15: the M'81/82. The Reichsrevolver M'83s holster illustrated in Fig. 16 is the Holster M'91—in Bavaria, the M'93. Among the legitimate military variations of these holsters are ones for the M'83 without the 12-round cartridge pouch and one for the M'79 which has an extension to the back-piece making it more suitable for use by mounted troops.

The Reichsrevolver did see battlefield use. Theoretically, by WW I it had been relieved by the Pistole '08. Actually, increases in pre-war force strength authorizations as well as the process of mobilization in 1914 operated to keep both revolver models on duty. The first cause is obvious; the second requires explanation.

In the first place, mobilization brought out from armories and depots those revolvers which had been placed there directly from the manufacturer and held on specific allotment for reserve regiments, or which had been returned, also on allotment to reserve regiments, from regular units which had been rearmed with the Pistole '08. This applies to both the M'79 and the M'83s. Next to consider is the rapidly shifting army organization of the years 1900-1914 as military structure incorporated new military technology. This period saw the creation and abandonment of dispatch rider regiments in which each man was armed with an M'83; of machinegun regiments which were later distributed as separate companies to infantry regiments or as fortress artillery machinegunners, and on and on. There were new units which persisted: motorized radio battalions; motorized transport columns—66 of those—plus the air services, including 5 Zeppelin sections prior to August 1914. In other words, it is quite likely that the supply of pistols never caught up with the demand for handguns in the regular units; that reserve combat units drew revolvers from depots when called up and that some regular units, such as seacoast artillery, may have had to exchange weapons with mobile units.

There is evidence, also, that these revolvers were used in combat before and after the First World War. Germany had a colonial empire dating from 1884 and had had colonial wars. There was the Arabist Revolt in German East Africa in 1888, which was dealt with by Hauptmann Wissmann and one thousand troops. Those troops were mainly Sudanese, but there were both German military cadre and a German naval landing force with them. That last is important because the Reichsrevolver was issued to the Reichskreigsmarine on the same need standards as to Reichsarmee personnel. The Maji-Maji Rebellion in the same colony in 1905 required a larger force for two years; more Reichsrevolvers. It was in German South-West Africa that the hardest colonial fighting took place, during the complicated Herero Revolt, from 1903 through 1908. Major reinforcements for the *Schutztruppe* were sent out from home under Major-General von Trotha, who had 19,000 men in the field before it was all over. In 1914, there were yet 9 companies of Schutztruppe and 3 mountain batteries on duty there, nearly all of them German with around 1,500 men of all ranks. During the First World War itself, General Paul von Lettow-Vorbeck's splendid work held up the British in German East Africa for four years. Last, one should remember that there were German troops active in China during the Boxer Rebellion.

Germany, like most other colonial powers, did not issue handguns to the native troops of her colonial military and police forces, not even to senior native NCOs. Therefore, the percentage of revolver-armed men in any of these colonial wars is not directly related to the numbers involved. Yet, to the total of German colonial officers and NCOs who did carry revolvers—180 in Cameroon alone, for example—should be added the numbers of German police commanders and district police supervisors: over 550 in Africa, Samoa and New Guinea.

Freikorps and armed private guard units used the Reichsrevolver in armed domestic struggle in Germany from 1918-1922, and it is likely that the established *Reichswehr* did also. Admittedly, it will be more difficult to ascribe a specific Reichsrevolver to a specific Freikorps or guard unit than to a Reichswehr formation. The Freikorps, for example, and the "dissident elements" whom they frequently opposed such as the Eberhardt Brigade, armed themselves as best they could from whatever stocks had not been confiscated by the Allies. It would be a bit too much to suppose that they marked their weapons in a regulation manner that was also uniform to all. There is reason to believe that some organizations marked the revolvers by branding the wooden butts; railway guard sections, for example. The coincidental sale by Waffen-Frankonia, December, 1972, of a lot of Gew. '98s branded identically to a Reichsrevolver Modell '79 which had been in a United States collection for many years previously is fresh support for this notion.

The Regulation Cartridge and Two Close Relatives

Specifications	10.6mm Reichsrevolver	44 S&W Russian	10.6mm Mauser Revolver
Case Mouth dia.	10.70mm	11.0mm	10.90mm
Case Head dia.	11.55mm	11.58mm	11.62mm
Rim dia.	13.1mm	13.0mm	13.0mm
Case Length	24.9mm	24.5mm	24.9mm
Bullet Weight	262 gr.	255 gr.	N.A.
Powder Charge	20 grs.	23 grs.	N.A.
Muzzle Velocity	670 fps	770 fps	N.A.

Adapted from Datig's DWM Cartridges *and* White & Munhall's Pistol and Revolver Cartridges.

In summary, the combat use of the M'73 and M'83 is a window through which to view colonial policy and the confusions attendant upon both a rapidly changing military technology and post-war civil

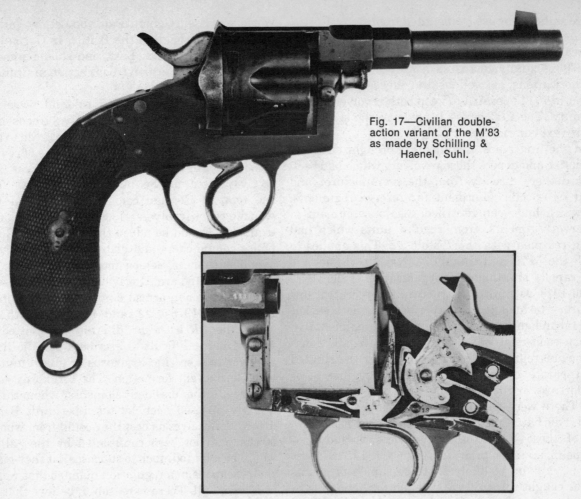

Fig. 17—Civilian double-action variant of the M'83 as made by Schilling & Haenel, Suhl.

Fig. 18—The double-action lock mechanism on the civilian "1883" revolver. The "cylinder locking bolt" of this design is a lump machined on the trigger and which protrudes through the wall of the lock recess when at full cock.

collapse. The attempt to link any one such revolver with the history of its using unit will be difficult but intellectually rewarding. In some cases, it will be very difficult. Japanese collections are the ones most likely to hold any revolvers captured from the German garrison at Tsingtao, while the Wahehe tribe, who wiped out Baron von Zelewski and his 350 men in Africa may have considered any Reichsrevolver with a proven record of colonial service with police, Schutztruppe or the regulars would be one worth having.

Civilian Variations

Civilian variations of the basic military design divide themselves into Belgian and German categories by manufacturer; only the German will be treated in this article. When revolvers made expressly for the civilian market are found, they either conform to the military specification in all respects save (usually) finish and grip checkering, or they have mechanical modifications aimed at supplying certain features whose lack made the Reichsrevolver quite old hat in the

civilian arms world of the day. These modifications include the addition of a tube-guided ejector rod fixed to the right of the frame, and a double-action or double-trigger lock mechanism. Contemporary evidence suggests that these revolvers should be called something other than Reichsrevolver in order to distinguish them from specific military models made under military contract to military specifications. The term *Deutscher Revolver Typ 1879* and *Typ 1883* is suggested without claim for originality. The variety of names used for the pattern 1873 Colt revolver in 45 caliber is analogous. These Typ 1879 and 1883 revolvers usually have checkered grips; the true M'79 and M'83 are rarely checkered.

The most common form of civilian modification to the lock is a straightforward double-action mechanism, which fits nicely into the standard frame as it requires only an elongation of the trigger slot to accommodate both the trigger motion and the driven end of the single-action sear lever. This lock's design was in the public domain at the time of its employment on these revolvers. The basic double-

Fig. 19—Another civilian variant, in double-trigger mechanism, of the 1883 revolver as made by vonDreyse, Suhl. Serial 2457. Single-action with the rear trigger; double-action **and** "hesitation-action" with the front trigger.

Fig. 20—Doing it the hard way. Lockwork detail of F. von-Dreyse's non-regulation variant of the M'83, at full cock for single-action fire by the rear trigger. The front trigger gives a heavy double-action pull, and, in combination with the rear trigger, a form of "hesitation" action.

action components follow in principle the design of Robert Adams, London, 1851. The single-action sear lever is exactly as used on the French naval revolver of 1870. Indeed, the design of specific components and the arrangement of the total mechanism—as distinct from its principle—is identical to that used on the French enlisted man's revolver, *Modelle 1873*. This lock design has been attributed to Eugene Lefaucheux and is commonly called the "Chamelot-Delvigne." Like any alley-cat, it had a wide range and an obscure ancestry. The German specimen shown in Figs. 17 and 18 is by the Schilling and Haenel group (without Sauer) and is numbered 113. Its proof marks place it after the Proof Act of 1891 came into full force in 1893, which seems a bit late for so simple a design with so low a number. However, an open resale after the Act of an item originally sold before the Act would have required a trip to the proof-house. The bore measure is given as "10,55" (mm) for a four-groove rifling, equal widths, clockwise twist. Finish is a dark blue; hammer, trigger cylinder-pin and lock are bright; the springs still show yellow. The 1911 Adolf Frank

("ALFA") catalog offered revolvers of this type, suspiciously Belgian-looking, at *Reichsmarks 53* in price and misleadingly labeled them as "military revolvers, model 1883." The regulation revolver was offered at RM60 on the preceding page of that catalog.

The most useful remark for the double-trigger mechanism at this writing is: "Ach! du lieber Strohsack!" The next most useful remark is that the two specimens known to me—and I'm sure more exist—are both by F. von Dreyse, in Soemmerda. The one shown in Fig. 19 is number 2457; the one in the Student's Collection at the Tower of London is number 2634, and that one has an ejector rod. It is apparent that von Dreyse used a standard military frame on which to arrange this charming mechanism. For example, the lock plate has the standard three slots for prying it up, yet two are useless since they are covered by the enlarged roots for the trigger guard. Further, there is a cut at the forward end of the lock recess which would be used by the standard single-action trigger spring but which is surplus here. Regrettably, the trigger spring that is used places force against the root of the trigger guard. Since the forward lock-plate screw threads through that root on its way to bed in the frame, one should take care to relieve tension on the trigger guard before turning the screw in or out.

Dimension Examples		
	M1879 (Mauser-1880)	M1883 (Erfurt 1894)
Length Over-All	341mm	255mm
Barrel Length	181mm	117mm
Number of Grooves	4 equal width	4 equal width
Direction of Twist	RH	RH
Weight Empty	1.05kg.	0.92kg.
Number of Shots	6	6

There are two locks present in this frame, as can be seen in Fig. 20. Single-action firing is done with the rear trigger, which operates the cylinder bolt and which gives a very smooth pull-off. The front trigger provides double-action firing by driving the hammer back by means of a long bar linked to the trigger and held against the hammer by one of the more fragile of the six springs used. The curve of the hammer cams the bar out of the driving notch on the hammer at the proper moment, which is just after the rear face of the double-action trigger has pushed the single-action trigger out of the full-cock notch. Indeed, it is possible to begin a double-action pull with the front trigger, feel the rear trigger engage the full-cock notch and then, after taking more deliberate aim, squeeze off the shot. This may have been von Dreyse's rationale for the design. The enormous theoretical advantage of this system seems of little practical worth, especially if one were sitting on a skittish horse. It is not surprising that there is no claim to patent protection anywhere on the weapon since the idea of a "hesitation" action had been embodied on a Robert Adams percussion revolver as early as 1854 and the Tranter two-trigger system, which is similar to von Dreyse's, had been marketed for nearly as long. Accepting as given the 1891 Proof Act marks on number 2457 and speculating that the maker's mark on it would have been abandoned after his death in 1894, I'll assign a date of 1893-1894 to this specimen.

There are only two more things to say before closing this article anent the Reichsrevolver Modell 1879 and Modell 1883 and their commercial counterparts. First, they require further study, which will be intellectually rewarding—at least to whomever does it. Second, I thank you for the interest that carried you to this point. ●

BIBLIOGRAPHY
Books
Datig, Fred A., *DWM Cartridges,* 1896-1956. Fadco, Beverly Hills, CA, 1960.

Hermann, Carl Hans, *Deutsche Militar Geschichte, Eine Einfuhrung.* Bernard u. Graefe Verlag für Wehrwesen, Frankfurt am Main, 1966.

Hogg, Ian V., *German Pistols And Revolvers,* 1871-1945. Arms & Armour Press, London, 1971.

Stockel, Johan F., *Handskydevaabens Bedommelse.* F. Hendryksens Reproduktions-Atelier, Kobenhaven 1964, Vol. I.

Taylerson, A.W.F., *Revolving Arms.* Herbert Jenkins, London, 1967.

_____, *The Revolver,* 1865 to 1888. Herbert Jenkins, London, 1966.

White, H.P. and B.D. Munhall, *Pistol And Revolver Cartridges.* 1967.

Periodicals
From *The American Rifleman,* National Rifle Association of America, Washington, DC:

Chamberlain, W.H.J., "Identifying John Adams' Revolvers," October 1971.

From the *Deutsches Waffen-Journal,* Verlag Schwend, GmbH, Schwabisch Hall, Bundesrepublik Deutschland:

Edelmann, Roland K., "Die Reichsrevolver" several numbers, 1968-69.

Englehardt, A. Baron (revised by Gerhard Wirnsberger) "Die Beschusszeichen der Europaischen Staaten," several numbers, 1972-73.

Lehner, Heinz, "Uebergangsmodell Reichsrevolvers Typ 1879/83" January 1972.

From the *Gun Digest,* Digest Books, Inc., Northfield, IL:

Stewart, James B., "Bergmann System Military Pistols" 1973 Edition.

Reprint
"Arms of the World, 1911" the *ALFA* Catalogue. Digest Books, Inc., Northfield, IL.

Acknowledgments
I have received useful assistance from: Mr. C.W.C. Brown, Boston University; Mr. Karl Bruemmer, Brook Park, Ohio; Mr. Ted Galvin, Jr., Medina, Ohio; Dr. Carlyle S. Smith, University of Kansas.

Photographs by Mr. Richard K. Halter, Columbus, Ohio. The revolvers illustrated are from the collection of Hamish T. MacFarlane, Esq.

Collector's cartridges, common or uncommon, aren't always what they seem to be…

Cartridge Variations

by GRAHAM BURNSIDE

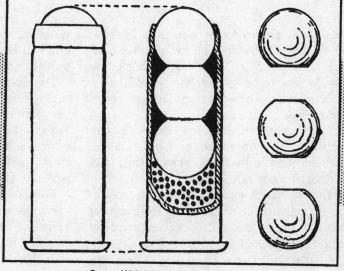

Capt. Wright's last design, from Report of Chief of Ordnance, 1879.

MANY COLLECTORS scorn variations. They either are smug and self-satisfied or they have fooled themselves into believing that variations are uninteresting and unimportant. To the truly advanced collector variations comprise the most interesting part of his hobby.

One time an eastern cartridge collector was visiting my home. He asked to see the 12mm Perrin cartridge. Not knowing which one he wanted I removed the tray containing the Perrin specimens and pointed out nine or ten variations. Although this collector felt familiar with the Perrin cartridge he was surprised to see three different inside-primed variations and twice as many externally-primed types employing Berdan primer, Boxer primer, battery cup primer and several French and Belgian types as yet not fully identified. To have a dozen variations of one cartridge is quite commonplace. In checking my files I find that I have twenty-four 12mm pinfires, forty-two 38 long centerfires, sixty-one 50-70s, and one hundred and eighteen 45-70s! If I had been specializing in military items undoubtedly I would have many more of the commoner issues than I have. I rather like 9mm Luger variations and have one hundred and four

different specimens, but a really top-notch display of Luger cartridges could probably be several times that size.

If some collectors scorn headstamp or bullet style variations I have no complaint, but too often their policy of avoiding variations precludes their obtaining some very choice and desirable items.

Pictured here are a few variations—some of which have never been illustrated to my knowledge. Possibly through this display some collectors will be stimulated to seek out variations that they have previously ignored

Three Ball Load

Practically every collector is familiar with the 45 Colt inside-primed center-fire with Benét cup-anvil (Fig. 1) but a much harder specimen to find is the experimental three-ball load (possibly the design of Captain E. M. Wright—*circa* 1878).

John E. Parsons, in his book *The Peacemaker and its Rivals,* shows a drawing of a three-ball load "for the Colt's *service* revolver." The drawing looks to be of a conventional brass centerfire case which undoubtedly came after the Benét cup-anvil type (see above).

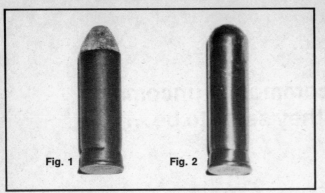

Fig. 1   Fig. 2

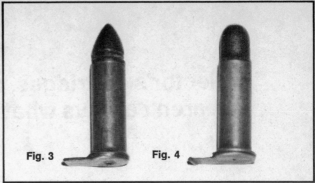

Fig. 3   Fig. 4

An X-ray of the pictured specimen (Fig. 2) shows it to have the three balls faced off in the same manner as are those seen in Mr. Parson's book. The top ball is flattened at its base; the second ball is flattened fore and aft, while the third ball is faced off on its forward end.

Since my specimen is the only one I have ever seen I'm assuming it is a rare variation. I have no idea of its incidence in collections across the land.

The 36 Sharps mule-ear cartridge is well known and while the two specimens shown seem to present merely bullet variations, micrometer examination shows them to be of quite different dimensions.

Although both specimens employ the same design in case construction, that's about where the similarity ceases. The specimen on the left (Fig. 3) has a smaller base diameter and is made from seamed brass tubing. The one with the rounded ball style (Fig. 4) was made from brass stock that was turned out before being soldered to the two piece base. It is my opinion that Christian Sharps made those guns that take the mule-ear cartridge as alterations from the arms (or parts remaining from the arms) that had used paper or combustible cartridges. Because Mr. Sharps did the conversions at slightly different times, and essentially by hand, these pistols and rifles fail to show a uniform set of specifications. I have handled three Sharps pistols altered for the

mule-ear cartridge and all had chambers that were quite different; only one of them would accept the mule-ear cartridge that I had at that time.

The specimen made from seamed brass tubing came from a cased Sharps pistol-carbine and could very well represent a fourth chamber. Thus it appears to me that all Sharps mule-ear cartridges, as made for different individual arms, vary one from another – if they are interchangeable it's a matter of shere coincidence.

Most of us know about the 52-70 Sharps rimfire cartridge (Fig. 5), but very few collectors know the existence of the same cartridge (Fig. 6) with a brass case and in centerfire, by UMC.

Just why the centerfire version was ever made is something of a mystery. We can safely assume that a conversion from rimfire to centerfire would be a sensible move back in the late 1860s or early 1870s, but this cartridge does not make good sense because it is practically the same as the well known 50-70-450 Gov't and Sharps cartridges. Indeed, the arms made for the 52-70 Sharps centerfire cartridge function quite well with 50-70 ammo.

Sharps to Chile?

There is a rumor that Chile or another South American government was interested in buying

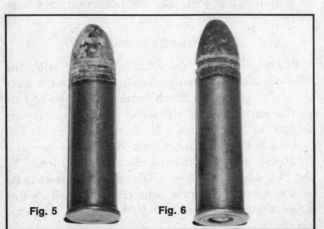

Fig. 5   Fig. 6

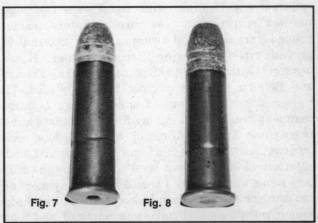

Fig. 7   Fig. 8

Sharps carbines chambered for a 52 caliber cartridge in centerfire. I have searched for evidence of such a situation but have been unsuccessful. The specimen of 52-70 that I have is the only one I know of, and it came to me from Chile. I also have a carbine of 52 bore with an original centerfire block. This Sharps carbine is in pristine condition; it has an unsleeved 52 caliber barrel of six grooves and an original spring-loaded striker.

Possibly the rarity of the 52-70 centerfire cartridge exists because the carbines *could* function with 50-70 ammo—so it was unnecessary to continue the manufacture of the 52-70. Groups fired with 50-70 ammo in my 52-70 carbine are slightly superior to those fired with 50-70 cartridges in a 50-70 sleeved barrel carbine of the same condition.

The 46 cal. Winchester cartridge is a desirable item these days for it was about the first really complete cartridge Winchester ever produced. Undoubtedly there was much experimentation done by the New Haven organization and the odds are that one of these is the result of those experiments.

The specimen on the right is, I believe, the commoner of the two (Fig. 8). The photograph clearly shows that these two have different bases, different case lengths, and different bullet styles. Also, as can be seen in the photograph, each has a different style of base indentation, where the internal primer is located. Both specimens conform to the specifications of the Oliver F. Winchester patent (Jan. 1st, 1867— No. 60814). I'm sure the specimen on the right is an improvement over the one on the left. The one on the left (Fig. 7) simply has an indentation where the internal primer is located and the striker would have to upset the fulminate of the primer through a full thickness of the base metal (copper). The improved version has the base metal cut thin or in some way formed thin so the striker did not have to buck a full thickness. This thinning of the base metal is only at the location of the internal primer and in no way is the strength of the case head impaired.

Most cartridge enthusiasts would be happy to have one 58 Maynard "flop ear," but to those who have one already—here is another one to look for. As can be seen by the photograph the cartridge on the left (Fig. 9) has a heavy brass case turned, probably, from solid stock, and the one on the right (Fig. 10) was made from relatively thin unseamed brass tubing. Both have an identical attached base in the sense that the attachment is the same. The thickness and style of the cases do vary, but both rounds are 58 caliber and I feel were made for the same arm. Edward Maynard was a man who designed and built arms and cartridges to suit his fancy or the fancy of his clientele. In this way so-called "models" came and went with almost

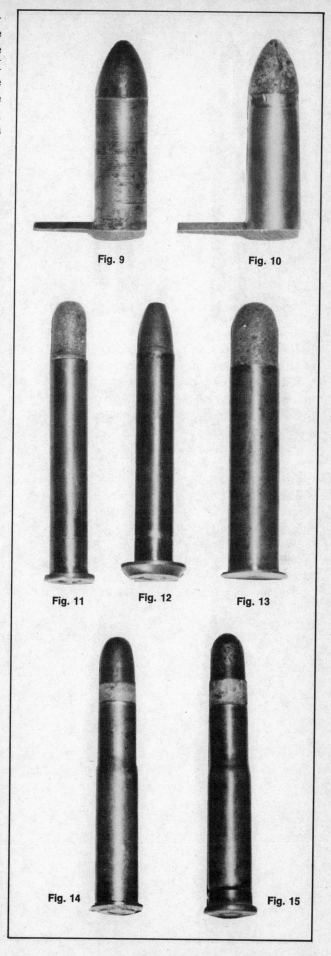

Fig. 9   Fig. 10

Fig. 11   Fig. 12   Fig. 13

Fig. 14   Fig. 15

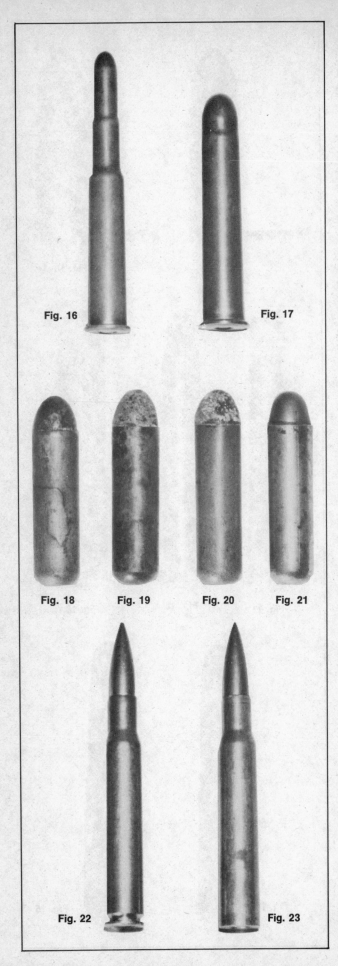

Fig. 16 Fig. 17

Fig. 18 Fig. 19 Fig. 20 Fig. 21

Fig. 22 Fig. 23

great rapidity. Unless a particular idea of Dr. Maynard's was lasting enough to gain more or less general acceptance it may well have appeared and then vanished with a single piece only made for a special customer or friend.

Here we have a trio of Maynard cartridges. The center item (Fig. 12) is familiar to all as the 40-70 Model of 1873, but the one on the left (Fig. 11) beclouds the normally accepted picture of Maynard evolution. The first item has the two-piece head construction of the 1873 Maynards, but the general contours of the 1882 style Maynard cartridges.

The easy way out is to call it a "transitional Maynard"—that's good as far as it goes, but it doesn't go anywhere! I only know of three of these specimens—and no one to my knowledge knows just where this variation fits into the Maynard story. The third Maynard shown (Fig. 13) is a ball load of the 55 caliber Maynard shotgun shell, Model of 1865. Actually it is 56 caliber, but then it is understandable that Dr. Maynard simply rifled a heavy 55 caliber shotgun bore and for that reason the ball cartridge would necessarily be of larger caliber. One such arm is known. It is a cased outfit complete with two barrels—one smoothbore and one rifled. The chambers take the same case. The cased outfit is also equipped with mould and loading tools. No such combination is listed in the Maynard catalogs—it must have been built to order.

The 44-77 Remington cartridge (Fig. 14) is a rather common item found in practically every collection. It is called 44-77 Sharps by most collectors. The 44-77 Remington and the 44-77 Sharps are interchangeable, but can be differentiated by noting the ball style (see the GUN DIGEST, 1957, pp. 100-105). Actually the Sharps catalog lists the 44-2¼ inch necked cases as loaded with 75 grains of black powder, so proper Sharps terminology would call such specimens "44-75 Sharps necked." The rare variation on the right (Fig. 15) is the 44-77 Remington cartridge with removable steel head for rapid reloading. The steel head was screwed off by hand and a fresh primer installed without the aid of tools of any kind. These reloadable cases were not available long, probably for two reasons. One, their obvious higher cost meant that few shooters could afford them and two, unless the unit was kept quite clean (a difficult feat with black powder) the screw-off head would become jammed tight—tight enough that it could not be removed by hand.

30-40 Krag and 45-70 cartridges (Figs. 16 and 17) are about as common as cartridges can get. Many collectors pass them by as a matter of habit. These two rare variations are truly worth looking for. Both are blank cartridges made from a continuous brass draw that extends the entire length. The ends are closed over smoothly and evenly, the tip ends of the case being formed into "petals" that evenly

Cartridge Variations and their Dimensions

Fig.	Cartridge	Case length, inches	Overall length, inches	Base diameter, inches	Head diameter, inches	Diameter at mouth, inches	Ignition or primer type
1	45 Colt	1⁹⁄₃₂	1³⁹⁄₆₄	.503	.483	.476	Benét cup anvil
2	45 Colt, 3-ball	1½	1⅝	.514	.478	.478	Benét cup anvil
3	36 Sharps mule ear	1⁵⁄₆₄	1³⁷⁄₆₄	.465	.411	.411	percussion
4	36 Sharps mule ear	1⁵⁄₆₄	1³³⁄₆₄	.495	.393	.385	percussion
5	52-70 Sharps	1¹⁵⁄₃₂	2⁵⁄₃₂	.642	.562	.538	rim fire
6	52-70 Sharps	1⁹⁄₁₆	2¼	.657	.565	.535	centerfire
7	46 O. F. Winchester	1¹⁵⁄₃₂	1⁶¹⁄₆₄	.619	.532	.471	inside primed
8	46 O. F. Winchester	1¹³⁄₃₂	1³¹⁄₃₂	.633	.534	.465	inside primed
9	58 Maynard	1¹³⁄₃₂	2¹⁄₃₂	——	.615	.612	percussion
10	58 Maynard	1⁷⁄₁₆	2¹⁄₃₂	——	.617	.603	percussion
11	40-70 Maynard	2¹³⁄₃₂	3¹⁄₁₆	.595	.454	.447	centerfire Berdan
12	40-70 Maynard '73	2⁷⁄₁₆	3¹⁄₃₂	.757	.453	.446	centerfire Berdan
13	56 Maynard '65	2¹⁷⁄₆₄	3	.766	.585	.580	percussion
14	44-77 Remington	2¼	3¹⁄₃₂	.624	.521	.463	centerfire
15	44-77 Remington	2¼	3³⁄₃₂	.618	.518	.468	centerfire
16	30-40 Krag	——	3⁵⁄₆₄	.540	.458	——	centerfire
17	45-70 Gov't.	——	2⁹⁄₁₆	.600	.501	——	centerfire
18	50 Gallager	1⁴¹⁄₆₄	2¹⁄₆₄	——	.530	.544	percussion
19	52 Gallager	1⁴³⁄₆₄	2¹⁄₁₆	——	.546	.552	percussion
20	54 Gallager	1¹¹⁄₁₆	2¹⁄₁₆	——	.549	.549	percussion
21	54 Gallager	1¹¹⁄₁₆	2¾	——	.547	.549	percussion
22	30-06 Gov't.	2³¹⁄₆₄	3⁵⁄₁₆	.470	.465	.332	centerfire
23	30-06 Gov't.	2³¹⁄₆₄	3²¹⁄₆₄	——	.464	.333	centerfire

meet one another. The 30-40 Krag all-brass blank has three such petals; the 45-70 has four. Both specimens have the same head style and are unhead-stamped. It is now known that both of these all-brass blanks were government issued for Gatling gun use about 1905, as improved versions of earlier open-mouthed types. The latter sometimes malfunctioned.

The 50 caliber drawn brass Gallager cartridge has been described many times. It seems that everyone assumes that the things are 50 caliber and that they are for the familiar Gallager carbine of Civil War vintage. It could be that all variations are for the same arm but they definitely are not all 50 caliber. The specimen on the left (Fig. 18) *is* 50 caliber, but the next one over is 52 caliber, and the next is 54 caliber (Figs. 19 and 20). These first three all differ in base style, size of flash hole, bullet crimp, and case length. The fourth specimen shown (Fig. 21) is the tinned version of the 54 caliber round.

44-60 Ballard!

The U.S. Ordnance Department is sometimes responsible for variations in arms and ammo. I have a record of a Civil War contract with Merwin and Bray (Nov. 24th, 1863) in which the government ordered six Ballard carbines, *all different.* Each was to be chambered for rimfire cartridges of varying lengths. All six were 44 caliber, but the copper cartridges were for: 1) 35 grains of powder; 2) 40 grains of powder; 3) 45 grains, and so on up to

number 6 for 60 grains of powder. (A 44-60 Ballard rimfire I would like to see!)

Another example is a contract with Sharps and Hankins that called for carbines of three different chamber diameters and in two different calibers (Dec. 15, 1867)! Strange variations are not limited to the olden days when the munitions industry was stumbling around looking for optimum specifications. The NATO 30 caliber cartridge is found in at least three different case lengths, all made in brass and aluminum.

The two 30-60 cartridges shown are both fully loaded by Frankford Arsenal. The one on the left (Fig. 22) is a standard ball load of 1952 (FA 52). The one on the right (Fig. 23) is a test load without extractor groove. It is headstamped "F.A.Test." I do not know what arm or mechanism used this rimless-grooveless version, but it would probably work to some degree in an autoloading or automatic arm. It could have been an experimental round developed for the sole purpose of determining just how much pressure the '06 case could withstand.

Undoubtedly there are literally tons of cartridge variations that I have never seen—fine! I'll have a whale of a lot of fun finding some of them in the months and years ahead. None of us will ever get them all—our horizons should be as unobtainable as the one we see every day. With faith, determination and enthusiasm we plunge ahead into the great unknown. ●

Four-shot 6.35mm Regnum repeater, serial number 789. This arm was August Menz' first entry into the handgun field.

Three-shot 12mm Scheintod Repetier-Pistole, serial number 367. Gas-pistol version of the Regnum. The upper barrel of this example has apparently burst and has been sleeved to about 9mm for some unknown cartridge.

6.35mm Menta automatic, serial number 5154. The grip pattern is typical of most Beholla-pattern pistols and was not peculiar to Menz. Note the takedown hole in the slide.

The Handguns of

August Menz

A comprehensive study of the products of a prolific but little-known German arms maker.

by JAMES B. STEWART

To HISTORIANS the significance of the German province of Thuringia is that it was the seat of the Weimar Republic, which existed from the end of the First World War until the rise of Hitler. It is doubtful, however, if many gun collectors are aware that the city of Weimar is located in this beautiful province of mountains and woods. To them the important cities of Thuringia are Erfurt, Sommerda, Zella-Mehlis, and Suhl. Here existed the largest concentration of German small arms manufacturers during the first half of the twentieth century.

Consider the neighboring cities of Zella-Mehlis and Suhl, located about five kilometers apart on a tributary of the Werra River. Zella-Mehlis was the location of the world-famous Walther Waffenwerke and several smaller manufacturers. In terms of sheer numbers, however, Zella-Mehlis was far overshadowed by Suhl. In that small city were the well-known arms manufactories of Pickert, JGA, Simson, Sauer & Sohn, Stenda, Bergmann-Lignose, Schmeisser, and Krieghoff, as well as a host of smaller workshops and custom gunbuilders.

One of the most interesting of the smaller operations was that of August Menz. Since German gunmakers were late to adopt the semi-automatic pocket pistol (the first of commercial significance being the 7.65mm Dreyse Model 1907, made in the Thuringian town of Sommerda), Menz' first essay into the handgun field was in the form of a repeater known as the Regnum. This arm appeared on the market about 1908 and was available until the First World War.

The Regnum employs four superposed barrels chambered for the 6.35mm Browning, or 25 ACP, cartridge. Sequential fire is accomplished by a rotating hammer shaped somewhat like an automotive engine crankshaft. The hammer is indexed by a pawl in the double-action lockwork so that successive pulls on the trigger result in the discharge of the barrels in sequence. For loading and unloading the hinged barrel block is tipped down; an automatic ejector is provided for the spent cartridges. The arm is equipped with a lever-type manual safety. The only ready identification comes from the "AM" monogram on the grips. The gun was apparently not very popular as serial numbers noted all are below 1000 and the arm is quite uncommon.

During the same period (and using much of the same tooling) Menz also produced a 12mm three-barrel-superposed repeating gas pistol known as the *Scheintod*. This arm is mechanically identical to the Regnum but fired a standard German 12mm gas cartridge (similar to a small shotgun shell). The cartridge contained a choking gas which rendered the recipient insensible, hence the name "Scheintod" or "appearance of death." It is unknown how many were made as examples are scarce and have low serial numbers, but it was carried in various catalogs until at least 1922. A similar design also found in catalogs is a modified version apparently made by the same firm that made the later German "Tomma" repeaters.

Menz' entry into the automatic pistol field came as a direct result of the First World War. It had proven impossible for DWM and the Erfurt arsenal to produce the officially adopted 9mm Luger in the quantities required by the Kaiser's armies. As a result the Prussian War Office authorized the use of 7.65mm (32 ACP) substitute-standard automatics such as the Dreyse, Langenhan, Mauser 1914, and Walther Model 4. Among those selected was a new pistol developed by the Becker & Hollander Waffenbau of Suhl.

This seven-shot pistol, trade named *Beholla,* was just ready for commercial production when the war broke out. Of extremely simple and rugged design,

Early production 6.35mm Liliput, serial 5623. This first variation shows the early slide markings and finger grooves. It also has the rare monogram grip inlays. Some few were even produced with a cameo-type portrait as an inlay.

Liliput-based Menz blank pistol for the special paper-bulleted 6.35mm cartridge. These arms were numbered in their own series, this late example being number 5518. Note slide legend, "barrel" top holes, and moulded-in monograms in the grips.

Prototype 4.25mm Nord Flug, not serialed. Only three or four of this design are known to survive. Note the typical metal caliber inlay in the grip.

it is striker fired and uses an open-top slide similar to the contemporary Walther Model 1. However, takedown was simpler than the Walther as the barrel was pinned to the frame and the pin was accessible through holes in the sides of the slide. Simple tools were required to strip the Beholla, unlike the Walther, but it made for rapid and low cost manufacture.

Realizing that Becker and Hollander were too small to supply the desired quantities the Prussian War Office had them send sample guns to several

trade name *Stenda*. Becker and Hollander themselves produced about 50,000 while Menz produced about 60,000.

Becker and Hollander apparently ceased production and sale of the arm with the termination of the war, but Stenda and Menz continued marketing it in modified form. The new model, which employed a sliding barrel-retaining catch let into the side of the frame rather than the previous transverse pin, was advertised until at least 1924. Interestingly, postwar Stenda numbering was apparently continued

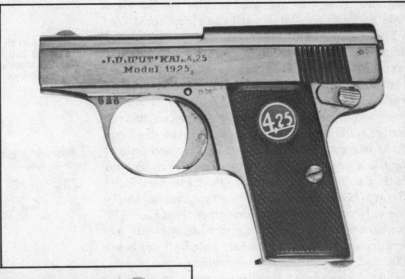

Early production version of the 4.25mm Menz Liliput, serial number 926. Note grip and frame similarity to non-production Nord Flug.

Right side of intermediate production 4.25mm Liliput, serial 1599. Note the revised caliber inlay and how the Nord Flug grips were ground at the top and rear to fit Liliput frame.

manufacturers, both in and out of Suhl, so that others might also produce the design. The firms selected were H. M. Gering & Co., of Arnstadt, Stenda Werke Waffenfabrik, of Suhl, and Waffenfabrik August Menz.

Serial numbers indicate that Gering produced about 40,000 of their *Leonhardt* trade-named version, but very few of them have the Prussian War Office acceptance stamp. The subcontract military pistols were produced by August Menz under the trade name *Menta* and by Stenda Werke under the

from the Beholla series: serials for the revised design run to better than 72,000. Still stranger, careful examination of several examples indicates that either Stenda Werke manufactured the postwar arms for sale by Menz under his trade name—or vice versa. In light of his other activities it seems probable that it was Menz who entered into this manufacturing arrangement for Stenda.

Starting about 1918 Menz produced a scaled-down six-shot version of the Menta pistol chambered for the 6.35mm *Browning* cartridge. This showed Menz' business acumen, for in postwar Germany 25 caliber automatics were to outsell 32 caliber five to one. Like its big brother, the 25 caliber Menta used the transverse pin takedown system. This was not as neat a system as was used in such competitors as Walther's Models 5 and 7, so when the new takedown latch system was applied to the Stenda and large Menta, Menz adapted it to his second 25 caliber automatic which he trade-named simply *Menz.*

The Menz used the same frame as the Menta, but with the addition of a turn lever on the frame

6.35mm Menz Modell II, serial number 2582. This increased-capacity model shows the later-style finger grooves as used on all Menz 6.35mm and 4.25mm automatics.

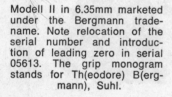

Modell II in 6.35mm marketed under the Bergmann trade-name. Note relocation of the serial number and introduction of leading zero in serial 05613. The grip monogram stands for Th(eodore) B(ergmann), Suhl.

compete head-on with giants such as Walther and Mauser. So, while producing Menzes and Mentas and low cost single-shot 22 caliber rifles, he was also searching for some non-competitive product with which to build his volume. During this search he came upon the two things which were to make him famous among gun collectors; the patent of Dipl. Ing. Franz Karpinski of Charlottenberg, and the diminutive 4.25mm Erika cartridge. Karpinski's design was for a rather ingenious takedown system incorporating a recoil spring and guide over the bar-

which locked the barrel in position. The slide rear hump was also reduced, rendering the arm more conventional in appearance. Since the frames were virtually identical the two guns were serial numbered in the same series. It is apparent that neither was very successful because serial numbers indicate that a total of less than 15,000, mostly Mentas, were produced before production terminated in 1924.

As commercial production of firearms resumed all over Germany after the war it became increasingly obvious to Menz that his small operation could not

rel, a removable rear sight, and a pushbutton on the rear of the breechblock which released it from the frame. Seeing a novelty pistol as a product with which he felt he could be competitive, Menz combined Karpinski's design with the 4.25mm Erika cartridge and produced a few hand made samples of a pistol which he called the *Nord Flug (north flight).*

While Menz was working with this design the Walther Waffenfabrik gave birth, in mid-1921, to a true vest pocket automatic—their now-famous Model 9. It was an instant success. Menz combined the best features of the Model 9 with the pushbutton take-down from his Nord Flug; the result looked like a miniature Model 9. It was originally named *Orzel,* Polish for eagle, but it is better known by its production name, *Liliput.*

Manufacture of the eight-shot 4.25mm Liliput started in late 1923, and before it terminated in 1929 more than 6000 pistols had been made. This may not seem like many until you realize that the Liliput in this caliber cost almost half again as much as a contemporary 25 caliber automatic. This miniature novelty pistol was available either in blue finish and black grips with a silver caliber inlay, or in nickel with white grips having a brass caliber inlay. These inlays were to become a virtual Menz trade-

paying the bills. Since the basic design was obviously sound Menz scaled it up and, trading on the now famous name, began production in early 1924 of a six-shot 6.35mm *Liliput.* This 6.35mm Liliput can be considered Menz' most successful design. By 1926 he had produced approximately 25,000, by 1927 serial numbers were in the mid-30,000s, and before production stopped they reached over 45,000. Private-label versions were also sold under the names *Bijou* (French for jewel) and *Orzel* (misread by one writer as "Okzet") as well as a fair number under the *Kaba* trade name for *Ka*rl *Ba*uer and Company of Berlin. There were also 4.25mm Liliputs made for Bauer.

Early 6.35mm pistols are marked with the Liliput

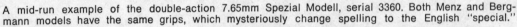

A mid-run example of the double-action 7.65mm Spezial Modell, serial 3360. Both Menz and Bergmann models have the same grips, which mysteriously change spelling to the English "special."

mark. It is interesting to note that before Menz developed the Liliput tooling had proceeded so far on the Nord Flug that the frames of the two pistols are nearly identical. The left grip on the Liliput is the one intended to be used on the Nord Flug, and the right grip was made in the Nord Flug molds but had the rear edge and top ground off to better fit the Liliput. So much better was the acceptance of the more conventional looking Liliput than of its 4.25mm competitor, the Erika, that the Erika soon went out of production (although it was offered for sale as a discontinued model until about 1929) and the cartridge is known today as the 4.25mm Liliput.

While the diminutive arm put Menz' name before the public it apparently didn't do enough toward

name on the slide but with the Menz name only on the side of the barrel, hidden by the slide. For some reason a few grip inlays have the AM monogram or a portrait bust in place of the caliber. Later pistols also carry date markings such as "Model 1925," "Model 1927," and so on. After 1928 this secondary marking was changed to "Model I."

Encouraged by the success of the 6.35mm Liliput, Menz scaled it up again and produced a six-shot 7.65mm Liliput. It apparently was not very successful as examples are rare. This too was later marked "Model I."

An extremely interesting and little-known version of the 25 caliber Liliput was produced in a separate numbering series during the later part of that pistol's production. This model is marked on the slide "Nur fur Schreckschuss-Patronen Cal 6.35." While seeming identical to the regular Liliput (except for moulded-in grip monograms rather than metal inserts) a close look at the arm will show that it is not in the usual sense a cartridge automatic. Early examples do indeed have what appears from the front to be a through-bored barrel, but which in fact extends only a fraction of an inch beyond the muzzle and does not connect with the chamber and remainder of the bore. Later versions merely have three small holes drilled in the front of what would be the muzzle. All have an angled hole drilled into the top of the barrel to meet the bore. Some also have a second hole bored vertically behind this.

Early examples were sometimes later erroneously described as "shoot around the corner pistols." An examination of the German marking indicates that these are starter or blank pistols. "Schreckschuss" translates as "loud shot" or "frightening shot." These interesting oddities were, then, another of Menz' attempts to bring in a little more revenue with minimum investment by using the existing parts of his production pistol. Because its parts were scaled to withstand the special paper-bulleted 6.35mm blank cartridge, the cost of this arm was about forty percent more than contemporary 22 Short caliber blank pistols such as the Walther and therefore not a financial success.

The Liliputs had apparently helped but Menz was still finding it difficult to make ends meet so in 1928 he brought out additional models. These were the eight-shot Model 2 in 6.35mm and a 7.65mm Model 2 which, while still six shot, adopted the appearance of the 25 caliber Model 2 in that the slide and frame were cut away under the muzzle. At this point the 7.65mm Model 1 was dropped from production so the Menz line now consisted of the Liliputs, the 25 caliber Model 2 and the 32 caliber Model 2. Results were disappointing. 25 caliber Menz Model 2 serial numbers run to only the 5000s and the 32 caliber Model 2 apparently sold fewer than 1000.

Menz was now in serious trouble. Although the Liliputs still plodded along with decent sales, something more was needed. Therefore in 1930 he worked up a series of four 7.65mm automatic pistols. His decision to concentrate on this caliber was probably due to the fantastic success that Walther was having with their 7.65mm Models PP and PPK, which had been introduced in late 1929.

The four pistols which Menz proposed all used the same frame and slide, with only minor modifications, so that tooling could be kept to a minimum. In general appearance and design philosophy these eight-shot pistols resembled the Walther. Takedown was accomplished by means of a stirrup block located at the front of the trigger guard, a modification of Walther's system in which the entire trigger guard

is pivoted to lower the securing block. The magazine release, unlike earlier Menz products but like the Walther, was behind the trigger rather than in the usual heel-of-the-butt position. All the Menzes except one had exposed hammers, again like Walther, and all had a cartridge indicator in the form of a pop-up blade on the top of the slide. Beyond that point they did differ somewhat among themselves.

The first type, continuing Menz' previous nomenclature, was known as the Model 3 or, more fully, as the *Menz P und B* (for Police und Behorden, or police and official use) *Caliber 7.65 Model III.* This arm had conventional single-action lockwork and therefore differed in appearance from the Walther having a normal "semi-sheath" trigger rather than the "free" trigger of double-action automatics. The Model 3 was extensively advertised in contemporary catalogs until the mid-30s but the lack of examples (one of the few known being numbered 019) and the fact that all catalog illustrations are line drawings makes one wonder how many were actually produced.

The second arm in the series was designated the Model 3a and differed from the others by being striker fired like earlier Menz pistols. Otherwise, except for the lack of a lanyard loop and a screwed-on extension to the front of the slide, it was identical to the Model 3. Due to its simplified construction the 3a was priced about twenty percent below the Model 3.

The third pistol in the series was designated the Model 4. It was an even more direct copy of the Walther product in that it had the typical "free" trigger of a double-action automatic. As a result it differed from the Models 3 and 3a by having the trigger guard opening extend further down the frame. It, like the 3a, had a screwed-on extension to the slide. Interestingly, while this pistol was double-action it was double-action *only*; that is, the hammer did not cock during the recoil cycle, so that all shots had to be fired with a full trigger pull like a double-action revolver. This feature was called "Revolver-abzug," revolver trigger.

This was modified in the last of the series, the Model 4a. This arm was identical in every respect to the Model 4 except that its lockwork combined single-action and double-action; it there y became an almost exact duplicate of the Walther PP (except for the safety location). Stainless steel barrels were available for the entire series at slight additional cost.

There is considerable question if this group of pistols ever actually reached production. Whether it was lack of financial resources or potential conflict with patentable features of the Walther series is conjectural, but only a few examples of each type survive. None except the 3 was ever illustrated in contemporary sales catalogs.

Catalog illustration, however, is not necessary for

6.35mm Menz, serial number 10179. Note similarity of grips and frame to the Menta in contrast to the modified slide. The front lever releases the barrel.

production; although it was not so illustrated Menz did produce, after 1936, an unusual eight-shot double-action 32 caliber automatic. The design differed considerably from the ill-fated Models 3 and 4 and enough from the Walthers that there should have been no question of patent conflicts.

This pistol is known as the *Menz PB Spezial*. Somewhat fewer than 1000 were made, all apparently numbered between 3000 and 4000. It retained the takedown system of the earlier 3 and 4 but moved the magazine release catch back to the butt. The blade-type cartridge indicator was dropped. The typical Menz safety catch at the rear end of the frame was exchanged for an ingenious one located on the slide, arranged so that it rotated the firing pin out of line of the hammer fall and interposed a block of steel in between—a very simple and secure system.

The greatest difference, though, was in the lockwork. While it was double-action it was, in fact, a two-stage double action. With the hammer down

(uncocked) an initial pull on the trigger merely cocked it. The trigger then had to be released momentarily and be repulled in order to drop the hammer. From then on operation was normal. The Spezial was also interesting in that it was the first pistol designed to be converted to other calibers with auxiliary barrels and recoil springs. These were to be available for the 9mm Browning Short (380) and a special 22 caliber center-fire cartridge. Apparently only the 9mm conversion was ever actually furnished.

Whether or not this design would have helped Menz in the long run is unknown, but money and time had run out. About 1938 Menz apparently sold out to the Lignose interests. The A.K.T. Lignose Gesellschaft revived the Bergmann tradename, which it had bought along with Bergmann's handgun production and facilities in Suhl about 1920, and applied it to the remaining Menz products. The late production of the Model 1 Liliput and the Model 2, both in 6.35mm, and the remaining PB Spezial pistols will be found marked "Theodore Bergmann Erben" which translates as "Theodore Bergmann's heirs." Grips, too, bear special moulded-in Bergmann markings. In the Liliput this break comes in the low 40,000 serial number range. In the Model 2 it apparently occurs between 5500 and 6000. For some reason in the PB Spezial the names seem to be intermixed within the serial range, and grips, which incidentally, are marked "Special," are not differentiated indicating that perhaps the frames and grips were all finished and the frames numbered before Lignose took over.

In any event, when the name Menz had to disappear from the market it is certainly fitting that the final products of such a prolific designer and experimenter should bear the famous name of another pioneering automatic pistol designer, Theodore Bergmann. ●

Right side of a late 6.35mm Liliput Modell I marketed under the Bergmann name. Note slide legend and special monogram grips. Serial number is one of the highest, 44709.

Odd-Ball Percussions!?!

by FRANK SELLERS

THE PERCUSSION period (1830-1870) saw many unusual firearms designs and patents. There were two main reasons for this. One, the industrial revolution, fostered by a warlike period of history, introduced new materials to be worked with; and two, existing patents forced people who wanted to go into the firearms business to invent arms to circumvent the earlier patents. Some of the arms invented during this period, especially the last ten years (after the expiration of Colt's patent), are fairly standard in function and appearance; others are very unusual. A few of the weird and wonderful are shown here.

Rollin White "Cartridge" Revolver

This odd appearing wooden model was made under Rollin White's patent 12,648, April 3, 1855. The box behind the chamber held paper cartridges which were loaded into the chamber *from the rear* when the hammer was cocked. This patent, more by accident than design, gave Smith & Wesson a virtual monopoly on the manufacture and sale of metallic cartridge revolvers until 1869. Only about a dozen percussion revolvers were made under this patent, mostly for use in the various patent infringement trials. None of the trial pieces bear more than a passing resemblance to the patent model. *(James Brook Collection)*

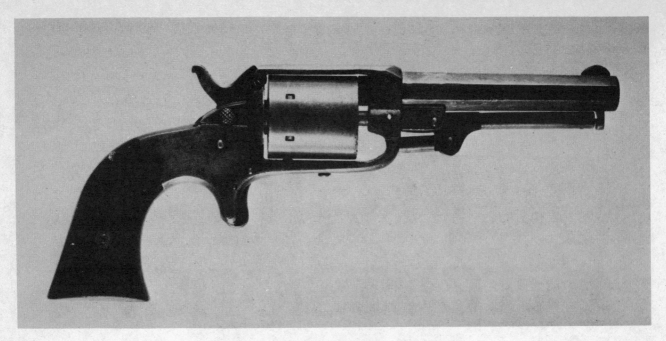

Reid Combination Rimfire/Percussion

James Reid of New York City achieved fame for his "knuckledusters." However, he did make several varieties of more "normal" revolvers before starting the manufacture of "My Friends." The last type of revolver made by Reid before leaving New York City was a combination percussion and rimfire revolver which was designed to get around the Rollin White patent on bored-through cylinders. It employed a removable nipple screwed into the rear of the chambers on very shallow threads. With the nipples in place, the revolver could be fired with loose powder and balls. With the nipples removed, regular 32 rimfire cartridges could be used. Judging from the number of guns with missing nipples found today, very few people used them as cap and ball revolvers. A total of 1650 were made, with barrel lengths ranging from 3¾ to 8 inches. Both brass and iron frames were made. *(Frank Sellers Collection)*

Linberg & Phillips Double Cylinder Revolver

The Linberg & Phillips revolver was one of many attempts to obtain more firepower with a single gun of ordinary size. Patented by Charles J. Linberg and William J. Phillips of St. Louis on December 6, 1870, it used two cylinders placed back to back on a single cylinder pin. The rear cylinder was locked in position with a firing pin under the nose of the hammer and the front cylinder was rotated by a hand in the barrel lug. The two cylinders were held together by a nipple shield and the unit was turned end for end to fire the second cylinder. Very few of these were made, for a very obvious reason: when fully loaded, six shots point directly toward the user! *(Smithsonian Institution Collection)*

John Gardner Double Cylinder

While similar in appearance to the Linberg & Phillips, the revolver of John Gardner works entirely differently. Both cylinders of the Gardner point forward and are locked together when fully loaded. A firing pin passes along the topstrap and strikes the nipples of the front cylinder to fire the first five shots. The firing pin is long enough to keep the hammer from striking the nipples of the rear cylinder. The sixth chamber in the front cylinder is bored through and is not loaded. As the hammer falls for the sixth shot, the firing pin is pushed forward (there being no nipple in the front cylinder to stop it), uncoupling the cylinders and locking the front cylinder into place. The hammer then is able to strike the nipples of the rear cylinder, which are discharged through the sixth chamber of the front cylinder, which acts as a barrel extension. The patent model was made on a Remington frame and is the only known specimen. *(Smithsonian Institution Collection)*

William Montgomery Storm Revolver

William Montgomery Storm held a great many firearms patents, none of them very successful in this country. A peculiarity in his signature has led many authors to refer to him as "Mont-Storm" or even "Montstorm." The revolver shown here is the patent model for U. S. Patent 14,420, issued March 11, 1856. Since this revolver was never produced commercially, it is of relatively little importance, except to demonstrate that some items in the collectors field were not always as highly valued as they are now. The barrel used to make this model, cut down and threaded to fit, was taken from a silver inlaid Texas Paterson Colt! *(Smithsonian Institution Collection)*

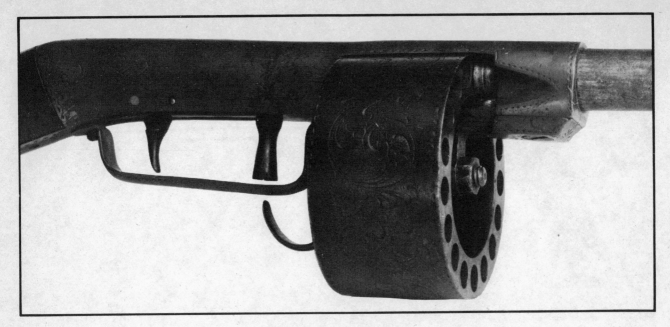

Hall's Hinged Cylinder

Alexander Hall's patent of June 10, 1856 (U. S. Patent 15,110) covered a cylinder which could not turn all the way around. In order to increase the number of shots in a cylinder without greatly increasing its weight, Hall devised a cylinder which was supported by a hinge. The cylinder could turn only from one side of the hinge to the other (approximately 340°). Most of the production model Hall rifles were 15 shot, but specimens capable of as many as 25 shots are known. *(Smithsonian Institution Collection)*

Jaquith Revolving Rifle

The Jaquith revolving rifle exhibits only one odd feature—the cylinder lies above the barrel instead of below. As Jaquith stated in his patent (U. S. Patent 832, July 12, 1838), "This arrangement, in case of any accidental ignition of the neighboring charges, renders the forward hand of the person using the gun more safe." The center of the cylinder was left open so the shooter could sight through it—in effect, a large peep sight. Less than 100 of these rifles were made, all handmade and following no particular pattern. Calibers on known specimens vary from 31 to 54, and barrel lengths from 18 to 40 inches. *(Joseph Desserick Collection)*

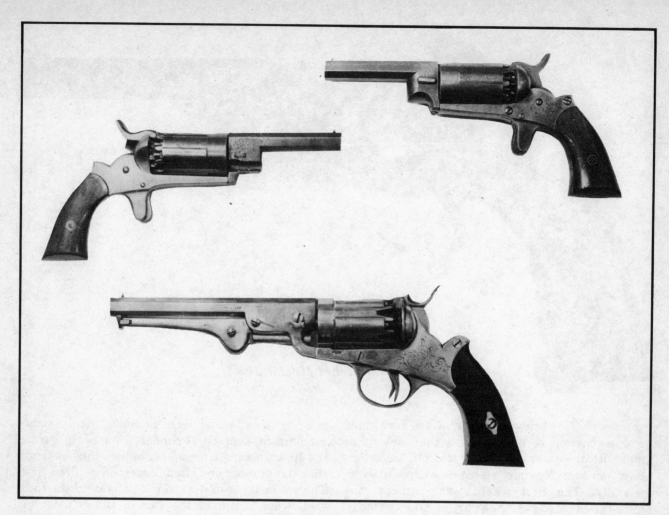

Walch Firearms Co.

Three production models of Walch revolvers were made: an iron frame 12 shot navy (36) revolver and both brass and iron frame pocket revolvers. Approximately 1500 each of the small frame and 200 of the large frame revolvers were made under John Walch's patent of February 9, 1859. The patented feature of these revolvers was the double loading of each chamber, as the small frames had five chambers and fired ten shots and the large frames had six chambers and fired twelve shots. To accomplish this two charges were loaded into each chamber, one on top of the other. The bullet for the rear charge acted as a recoil shield for the front charge. A flash groove for the front charge passed from the right nipple, along the side of the cylinder, and into the chamber about halfway along its length. When the trigger was pulled the right hammer fell, firing the front charge. A second pull on the trigger caused the left hammer to fall, firing the rear charge. (Early revolvers had two triggers, one for each hammer.) The single trigger mechanism was patented by John P. Lindsay, who made the 12 shot revolvers for Walch Firearms Co. The 10 shot variety were made by New Haven Arms Co. *(Samuel E. Smith Collection)*

Massachusetts Arms Co.

One of a dozen or so revolvers made under Rollin White's April 3, 1855 patent, this one was made by William McFarland and Smith Bruce of the Massachusetts Arms Company. It was made for D. B. Wesson and is one of four made by Mass. Arms Co. It was made from a standard production pocket revolver by cutting the back end off the cylinder and inserting a plate between the cylinder and the recoil shield to direct the fire from the nipple to the center of the paper cartridge. A spring deflector was also added to prevent the flame from the fired chamber from setting off other chambers. *(Frank Sellers Collection)*

Newbury Ratchet Mechanism

Frederick Newberry of Albany, New York, held more percussion revolver patents than any other man, with the exception of Samuel Colt. Unfortunately, none of Newbury's proved successful commercially. The first patent was, perhaps, the most complicated of Newbury's nine patents. For some reason he felt that it was necessary to always fire the number one chamber first. A series of pins and levers insured that the cylinder, which had to be removed from the gun for loading, was always placed back on the gun with the number one chamber under the hammer. The ratchet mechanism kept the cylinder from being turned the first time the trigger was pulled, thus assuring that the number one chamber would be fired first. Thereafter the gun worked normally until the sixth shot, when a pin in the side of the cylinder hit against the frame and jammed the whole thing. This prevented any attempt at firing an empty gun! The patent model is the only known specimen. *(Smithsonian Institution Collection)*

Albert Parker Revolver

Although the revolvers of Albert Parker are marked "Patent Secured," no patent has been found for them. Two revolving mechanisms are found on the Parker revolvers. One is a standard hand and bolt system, similar to the Allen pepper-boxes, and the other is the one shown here. A series of pins protrude from the outside of the cylinder. A revolving arm, shaped like a figure 7, rides over these pins and is operated by a long link attached to the hammer. As the hammer is cocked the slanted part of the revolving arm is drawn over a pin, causing the cylinder to turn. As the hammer falls, the straight arm keeps the cylinder lined up with the barrel. Very few of these were made and only three specimens are known today. *(William Locke Collection)*

Rupertus Priming Mechanism

The percussion revolvers of Jacob Rupertus were very well made, but somewhat frail. Based on Rupertus' patent of April 19, 1859, these revolvers were made in three sizes—the Army model or 44, Navy or 36, and pocket or 28. The pocket model was made in two types, the brass frame and the iron frame. It is estimated that less than a dozen of each size Rupertus was made. The feature patented by Rupertus was the priming mechanism mounted in the backstrap. This used priming pellets, similar to Sharps', which were fed into the face of the hammer at full cock. The hammer then carried the primer forward to discharge it against the specially constructed nipple or "safety tube" as it was called in the patent. This safety tube sealed the individual chamber at the moment of discharge. *(William M. Locke Collection)*

The basic patent for the Pettengill revolvers was held by Thomas K. Austin. Over a year elapsed from the time Austin filed for his patent (May 13, 1857) until it was issued (U. S. Patent 21,730, October 12, 1858). The mechanism employed a completely relaxed mainspring. Unlike most revolver mainsprings, Austin's is under no tension until the trigger is pulled. The first design shown here was quite complicated and used a Maynard tape primer instead of regular caps and nipples. Very few were made. *(Frank Sellers Collection)*

Aaron Vaughn 14-Shot Revolver

Aaron Vaughn received a patent for his 14-shot revolver on May 27, 1862. The advantages of his "improvement in revolvers" are not readily apparent since it requires twice as many parts and a proportionately larger and heavier weapon to double the number of shots. Two rows of chambers were discharged through two separate barrels. This required two hammers and two rammers, though only one trigger was used. The right hammer had a short sear notch and the left hammer a very long notch, thus insuring that the left hammer fell after the right one. Only a few of these were made—the highest known serial number is 16. *(Smithsonian Institution Collection)*

Hollingsworth & Mershon Revolving Rifle

John Hollingsworth and Ralph Mershon of Zanesville, Ohio, held three patents relating to spring-revolved pistols. Although revolvers made under the different patents bear no resemblance to each other, they are all the same in principle—a spring is wound up which will both cock the hammer and revolve the cylinder when the trigger is pulled. The revolving rifle shown was made under the first patent (U. S. Patent 12,470, February 27, 1855). It has a brass frame and is cocked (wound up) by a crank at the back of the receiver. The only practical feature of the gun is the brass tube around the barrel—as this is the same size as the cylinder, it allows the bullets from accidental multiple discharges to pass safely without harming the shooter. The specimen shown is the only known rifle by Hollingsworth & Mershon. *(Henry M. Stewart Collection)*

DeBrame Barrel

One of the more novel attempts at increasing the velocity of a fired projectile was that patented by J. A. DeBrame on July 2, 1861. DeBrame reasoned that, as all the velocity should have been imparted to the bullet by the initial explosion, the only function of the barrel (from the standpoint of velocity) would be to slow down the bullet through friction. Since the barrel was necessary both for sighting and to impart a stabilizing spin to the bullet, DeBrame devised a system in which only the lands of the rifling touched the bullet, thus reducing friction to a minimum. Though trials conducted by the army proved that his theory was correct, other considerations such as the unrestrained gas blast and fouling outweighed any advantages and the system was dropped. Only experimental pieces were made, the pistol shown being a Whitney 2 trigger model with a DeBrame barrel. *(Smithsonian Institution Collection)*

Bunsen Clockwork Revolving Rifle

George C. Bunsen of Belleville, Illinois patented a mechanically operated revolver on December 26, 1865 (U. S. Patent 51,690). The main feature of this revolving rifle is the clockwork mechanism mounted in the butt of the gun. The mechanism is first wound up, using a clock key on the earlier guns or a built-in winder on the later ones, and a loaded cylinder put in place. What appears to be a set trigger mechanism is actually two triggers. The forward trigger allows single shots to be fired while the rear trigger will fire the gun until the spring unwinds—an early attempt at automatic fire. Notice that the extra shotgun barrel has only a four-shot cylinder while the rifle cylinder has eight chambers. Since the mechanism is unchanged, regardless of the barrel-cylinder set used, the hammer would have to fall twice for each shot. This "click-bang, click-bang" sequence must have taken some getting used to! *(Milwaukee Public Museum Collection)* ●

Collecting

on a NATIONAL THEME

by JAMES B. HUGHES, JR.

PERHAPS the two most important decisions for a beginning collector are: where should I start my collection…and where should it end? Collecting today is wide open; one can choose rifles, pistols, other types of firearms, edged weapons, and/or all sorts of militaria! Some of us are interested in fine sporting arms, others in antique arms or only those that remain in unused condition, still others in engraved or presentation pieces, and yet others in arms produced by a single maker. After some years of collecting with no apparent purpose or aim, simply gathering in those weapons that interested me, I discovered that I was indeed collecting in a specific field: The Weapons Of A Nation.

Collecting on a *national theme* is to become an historian. A working knowledge of both arms and history is necessary to work in this area. If one sets out to collect on this national theme several guidelines should be established. Select a nation that has a history that you understand and find interesting and, preferably, uses a language you have some knowledge of.

Above: A random selection of Mexican military "blades" from the author's collection. Angular bayonet was used on the Remington and Whitney rolling block rifles, the Cadet Dress Dagger is from the Military Academy in Mexico City, the cavalry sabre standard from the 1870s to the 1920s, and the ubiquitous '98 system Mauser knife bayonet used from 1903 onwards.

Let's consider larger nations first. Large nations offer several advantages over small nations for our collecting purposes. Usually their ordnance for a given period is well defined and somewhat standardized. The Model X was adopted in 1898 and continued in service (albeit with variations and modifications) until it was replaced in 1935 by the Model Z. Such established facts enable you to look for specific additions for that most important collection, *yours*. At least some references of the types vital to the serious student of armaments will be available in English. These, too, will serve to point the way to necessary arms to complete a display or collection.

The larger nations have almost all participated in

For various reasons a small nation was my own selection. I heartily recommend this choice to the novice collector. A small nation is often a poor nation, whose tendency is to purchase either discards (obsolete or captured) or odd weapons from less popular manufacturers. Mexico, for example, had Spencer carbines, Remington rolling blocks, Peabodys, and Whitney rolling blocks all in service at the same time. Another example is Korea at the turn of the century, where the French Gras, the Japanese Murata, and the Russian Berdan all served together. While references abound on United States, German, and British military arms, original research is absolutely necessary to uncover the tangle of munitions

The Mexican Model 1924 Mauser, caliber 7mm, made by FN in Belgium. The coat of arms (inset) distinguishes it from those made for Argentina, Brazil, China, Columbia, Costa Rica, Iran, Liberia, Lithuania, Peru, Paraguay, Uruguay, Venezuela, Yemen, and Yugoslavia. Also pictured are the Mexican issue bayonet, cartridge pouch, canvas breech cover, and two clips of 7x57mm cartridges loaded in Mexico City.

a recent conflict, major or minor, which saw the expansion, as well as documentation, of munitions in use. After every such war the surplus and captured arms have been sold off. Now, of course, the GCA '68 has put an end to the importation of post-1898 war surplus firearms, and a crimp in some military collecting. One major disadvantage of collecting a larger nation's arms is that there are many other collectors who share your interest in the relics of a major nation. As new reference works become available, collector interest grows. A new book in the arms field often leads to price increases in the market place, as our fraternity competes for the now well defined and properly described pieces.

history for a small nation. A strange bolt-action single shot cavalry carbine turns up marked SISTEMA PERUANA MODELO 1873. What is it? There is no book on Peruvian military arms to turn to. The standard reference books list Remingtons, Winchesters, and later, Mausers for Peru. Only a diligent search through many sources reveals that this is a Bornmuller, made by Anton Schaler of Suhl, Germany for a Peruvian contract that was filled in 1875. Such research is, to me, one of the most pleasurable aspects of collecting. It is discovering new information that you, the collector, can bring to the light of day. Almost any collector can find information on a well known firearm in one of

Mexican revolvers all! From top left, counter-clockwise: Russian Model 44, made on contract in Spain by Orbea Hermanos (same early style crest as Whitney rifle); Remington Model 1875 Army revolver in 45 Colt; Colt Model 1895 revolver in 41 Long Colt, as issued to guards employed in the Mexican Mail Service; Colt Model 1878 Double Action Army in 45 Colt, 500 purchased in 1890 (crest inset); Pieper Model 1893 Double Action revolver, fitted with the gas seal cylinder found in the 1895 Russian revolver, 8mm Nagant, marked "Ejercito Mexicano" on top strap, side plate and cylinder. The epaulette is for a cavalry captain, about 1860; the eagle is from the Mexican "pickelhaube" as worn prior to the 1910 Revolution.

the standard references, but hand that collector a "maverick" and all is lost.

The need for original research is one of the reasons for my suggestion that the collector choose a country for whose native tongue he is knowledgeable. An additional advantage to collecting a small nation's arms is the probability that it has had internal conflicts, which usually result in an influx of "foreign" weapons. Guatemala in the late 1950s was faced with a series of such internal crises; at this time there was an influx of 1903 Springfields, Sten submachine guns, Garand rifles, and MG-34 machine guns. These add variety to your collecting.

Once you have selected a country, you should also decide how far you want to go. Your interests and your wallet will establish this limit. Several specific collection plans suggest themselves at this point. One can collect by span of years. One such period would be from "independence" through the present day. This will often encompass the three ignition systems: flint, percussion, and metallic cartridges. Two other logical periods would be pre-cartridge and metallic cartridge. Flintlocks and percussions, if

you are interested in antiques, fill the collection of the pre-cartridge period. The field is wide. A British surplus Brown Bess can turn up as far away as Argentina—they were once an item of issue there. Colt-made 58 muskets, marked on the barrel with the cryptic letters "SLP," were once the property of the Mexican State of San Luis Potosi. The smaller countries offer almost endless possibilities as the odds and ends of various wars were sold and resold to fill a current military need in a far-off part of the world.

The cartridge period offers just as wide a selection in weaponry. From single shot to automatic, all types of firearms have been used by all powers. The Remington rolling block has been an issue weapon in almost every country of the world. Even the Vatican purchased one lot to arm the Papal Guards! Siam (now Thailand) used a hodge-podge of cartridge weapons, including but not limited to Winchesters, Mausers, Arisakas, Martinis, Nambus and Webleys. The South African republics used Mausers, Martinis, and Wanzels.

Still another collection could be built on *types* of

This nickel plated Colt Double Action in 41 Long Colt was purchased for the Postal System of Mexico in 1902. The issue or ownership markings appear on the right side of the barrel: CORREOS R.M.

weapons used by a specific country. Mexico used rolling blocks, Mausers, Arisakas, Mondragons, and Winchesters among other long arms. Chile purchased Lugers and Steyr M-1911 automatic pistols and then made their own revolvers. Argentina purchased heavy weapons (machine guns) made by Maxim-Nordenfeldt, Vickers, Browning and Auto-Ordnance. Even light artillery can be collected, and, despite the restrictions of GCA '68, probably is!

The individual services present still another collecting field. One could choose Infantry arms, Cavalry weapons, or—usually a smaller field—Naval weaponry. Weapons of the Austrian Navy run the gamut from the KM Colt 1851 Navies to the Model 1895 Mannlicher rifles. Dress weapons, for example daggers, present another field for the national collector. The dress weapons of Nazi Germany embrace both military and political fields with swords, daggers, and bayonets. Cavalry carbines from the American Civil War are a widely shared collecting specialty. British infantry arms, even when restricted to the cartridge period, have many, many variations to challenge the collector. The English

penchant for modifying arms and adding "marks" "stars," etc. to the designation's makes for endless variations.

The arms of a specific conflict present an interesting variation on "National Theme" collecting. Many people now collect German World War II weapons. There is a similar interest in Japanese armament of that period. Arms of the Mexican Revolution is a field that involves both military and commercial arms. In many revolutions government forces utilized "military" arms while the rebels, at least at the start, are often in the field with sporting-type weapons.

Yet another collecting field would be a nation's military products which were designed or intended for export. Many countries, large and small, have depended heavily on foreign sources for their military hardware. Belgium has exported tens of thousands of Mauser-designed bolt rifles. The Fabrique Nationale SAFN auto-rifle has seen use by several countries, as has the M1935 High Power Pistol. Even the small Arabian states have purchased this well-

The arms of a mounted "Guard," the Pieper-Nagant revolving carbine and Revolver from 1893, the cavalry sword as issued until the 1920s, and a captain's epaulette from the Juarez era.

known pistol. At one time it was even made in Canada for the English, Russians, and Chinese. The United States has also acted as arms supplier to many countries. Remington sold their rolling block (or the rights to manufacture it) around the world: unauthorized copies were produced in local arsenals. During the Franco-Prussian War many then-surplus U.S. Civil War arms were exported to arm the French. During the First World War, Hopkins & Allen produced the Belgian Model 1889 Rifle, a Mauser, on contract for the Belgian army. Winchester made Model 1895 Muskets for the Tsar of Russia. Plumb Hardware Co. fabricated bayonets for our ally, Serbia. We were also the Allies arsenal between 1939-1945. This time it was on highest level,

with formal governmental assistance provided in the form of Lend-Lease. Private enterprise was also once again in the picture, with Johnson Automatics supplying many Model 1941 rifles to the Dutch Indies Forces.

Of course, the traditional "Arms Exporters To The World Market" should not be forgotten. Germany, Austria, Spain, and Czechoslovakia have long been suppliers of the entire range of munitions, new or second hand, to anxious foreign buyers. This collecting field calls for much research to discover who sold what to whom and when. Details of contracts, when available, do not always spell out the way the transaction was actually completed. If you enjoy research, this then is an area for you.

Old and new, the magazine rifle with smokeless cartridges and a short knife bayonet together with the single shot rifle, black powder cartridge, and angular bayonet. The Mexican Model 1924 Mauser in 7mm is in contrast with the Whitney Model 1872 Rifle in 11mm Spanish and its long (18") triangular socket bayonet. The Whitney bears an earlier style Mexican ownership marking (inset).

A selection of Mexican weapons for mounted troops: Remington Model 1897 Carbine in 7mm (crest same as Model 1924); Pieper-Nagant Model 1893 Carbine in 8mm Nagant, as issued to select troops who were also armed with a similar handgun using the same cartridge; Mauser Model 1895 Carbine in 7mm, as made by D.W.M. of Berlin (same crest with date of manufacture); Mexican Cavalry Sabre, patterned after our Model 1860, made by A. Combaluzier of Mexico City. These four pieces were in active service from 1893 through the end of the 1910 Revolution.

I have consistently mentioned research, and, for a reason. To collect in a specific field one must study that field and then use his knowledge. Research and *reference works* go hand in hand. The most important part of knowledge is to know were to find it! Become familiar with your own arms library. If you do not have an arms library, start one now—before you start your collection. A good library doesn't really cost you money, it makes or saves you money! Most serious collectors will have a good selection of the basic arms books. These provide a sound foundation for the library. To them should be added your own notebook, magazine clippings, newspaper items, etc., etc. A prime source of unusual information is an original contractor's catalogue. These books, when found, usually give detailed specifications. The C.Z. Sales/Order Catalogue, written in Spanish and issued circa 1930, details a CZ Mauser that can be made for "English Ammunition," i.e., 303 British. Where else would you find this unusual weapon recorded? Many of the Belgian gunmakers printed extensive export catalogues. These record both the original and imitation military arms of the period. There is an additional source of information—not as dependable as the producer's catalogues—but none-the-less valuable. These are military studies conducted by other countries, enemy or friendly. These

intelligence reports serve to identify many items of issue. They, too, are hard to find but are vital tools to the researcher.

The very last item for study is the weapon itself. Many things can be learned from the actual arm. Just remember that some things may be misleading. Nazi Germany used numeric, alphabetic, and alphanumeric codes to conceal the size and location of their arms industry. Serial numbers do not always reflect total production. Ownership of arms can change, but ownership markings may or may not be changed. Markings can be added or removed. The ordnance workshop is the collector's nightmare. Proceed with caution when using the firearm as a primary source of information.

Probably the greatest advantage to collecting in a national theme is that your fellow collectors, (after shaking their heads because you have been diverted from their true course, C--ts & Win----ters)may enter into the spirit of the chase and find all sorts of "goodies" for you to add to your collection. They, too, will delight in finding the odds and ends that enhance the collection. After all, they are stuck on a cut and dried course. You have the entire national history of a country, with all its victories and defeats, to collect. ●

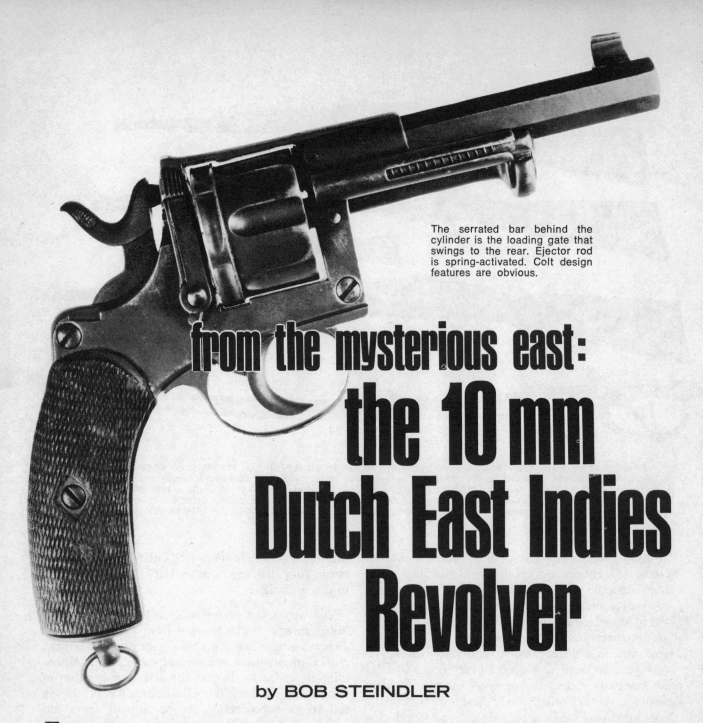

The serrated bar behind the cylinder is the loading gate that swings to the rear. Ejector rod is spring-activated. Colt design features are obvious.

from the mysterious east:
the 10 mm Dutch East Indies Revolver

by BOB STEINDLER

For BETTER than 10 years I had noted various references to something called the Chamelot-Delvigne system. This system, incorporated into a number of revolvers which appeared during the latter part of the 19th century, was an improvement of something or other. But none of the standard reference works I consulted spelled out just what this system consisted of or precisely how it improved anything. To make matters a bit more frustrating, none of the guns in my collection contained the Chamelot-Delvigne system; I was unable to study it or dope out its specific functions on my own.

The Chamelot-Delvigne design or system seems to have been used for the first time in the French army revolver of the late 1800s. Recently Century Arms of St. Albans, Vt., advertised the Dutch service revol-

ver of 1873. According to Taylerson and others, this revolver also incorporates the elusive Chamelot-Delvigne design, albeit in a somewhat modified form, and I therefore ordered one of these Dutch guns posthaste. While waiting for it to arrive, I studied several of the standard handgun text books. A total of four variations of the Dutch service revolver are known, and I was hoping that the gun I had ordered would be the standard Model 1873 six-shot revolver. When the gun finally arrived, I made a quick comparison between it and the one shown in W.H.B. Smith's *Book of Pistols and Revolvers*.

Aside from the shape of the trigger guard, the gun shown in this text and my gun were not at all alike. I then turned to several other texts on the subject of revolvers in general and old service revolvers in par-

Tracking down a newly-acquired gun can be rewarding and frustrating at the same time. Here's how one such search progressed from uncertainty to fruition and back.

The Dutch 10.4mm Colonial revolver, left view. "B" under crown marks are plentiful. The ejector rod handle has been moved out of its spring detent housing. The gun has no half-cock and can be fired either single- or double-action.

ticular. The more I studied the literature and the gun, the more certain I became that the gun sold to me as a Dutch service revolver was anything but that. But then, what was it? One thing was certain — the gun was more along the lines of the Colt design than the Chamelot-Delvigne system, which meant that I still did not have a gun with that design in my collection.

Hans Bert Lockhoven's *Waffen Bibliothek* and his monumental *Arms Archives* merely confirmed my previous findings, as did Bock and Weigel's *Handbuch der Faustfeuerwaffen*. In other words, my gun was *not* the Dutch service revolver of 1873.

The next logical step was to secure a round of the 9.4mm Dutch service ammo and see if that round would chamber in my revolver. Ten or 15 years ago

you could buy a whole case of it for next to nothing, but no more. Until quite recently no supplies of the Dutch service cartridge had been available for some years, but small quantities of this ammo, or what is said to be this ammo, have now become available through the same outlet — Century Arms. My quest for a sample round led me to dealers, surplus stores and to cartridge collectors who specialize in metric rounds or in metric military rounds — none of them could supply me with even one 9.4mm Dutch service round.

The 9.4mm round I was looking for is sometimes also called the 9.4mm Hembrug cartridge. Erlmeier-Brandt list no less than 23 synonyms for it. The cartridge was manufactured by numerous European and British ammunition manufacturers, and was

Under high-power magnification of a comparison microscope, the "34" on one case head is quite legible, while "32" on another is barely discernible. Other cases in the lot are not marked.

Even if the age of the brass is considered, these four rounds of 10.4mm Dutch ammo seem older than the dates on the bullets would indicate. This would tend to confirm the theory that the cases were reloaded by Pyrotechnische Werkplant. The lead in the bullets is quite soft, possibly indicating the use of pure lead rather than an alloy.

listed in catalogs as late as the last years of the 1930s.

After removing as much dirt, grime and fouling as possible from my mystery revolver, I began to look for proof marks or manufacturers' marks. While the meaning of Dutch proof marks has never been explored fully, the makers of the Dutch 1873 model were not bashful about marking their products. I found several marks on the gun which were obviously inspector's stamps, but nary a Dutch *proof* mark or the mark of any of the known gun companies of the period. A photograph obtained from Century Arms shows the identical gun to mine, but with an "A.U.R." stamp that obviously had been added much later.

Lee Kennett, who is continuing Baron Engelhardt's work on proof marks for the GUN DIGEST was unable to shed any light on the marks I had found on that revolver. He suggested that I write the Nederlands Leger-en Wappenmuseum "General Hoefer" in Leiden. I promptly wrote the director of the museum, K.B.C. Görlitz, enclosing a series of photographs and some rubbings I had taken from some of the marks on the gun. While waiting for an answer from Europe, I searched through a number of the catalogs of the largest European arms museums in the hope of finding the twin of my revolver — again, I found nothing.

A soft lead slug driven through the barrel showed that the rifling in the octagonal barrel was quite shallow. The slug miked .399"-.401". White and Munhall list the bullet diameter for the 9.4mm Dutch round as .378"-.401" and case length as .763"-.847". Erlmeier-Brandt give .380"-.401" as bullet diameter, listing case length as .785"-.826". Both

sources indicate that only round nose bullets were loaded. After several unsuccessful attempts, I managed to clobber together a dummy case based on the average case dimensions. This case was not only too short for the chambers of the cylinder, but there was also excessive play between the case wall and the walls of the six chambers. Obviously, either my dummy case was way off or the gun was *not* chambered for the 9.4 Dutch round.

The first lead to the true identity of my revolver came from Boothroyd's excellent book, *The Handgun.* He states: "The Dutch East Indies Police were issued with a 10mm revolver differing from the Model 1873. The cartridges for this were made at the Pyrotechnische Werkplants, Surabaja, Java."

Through an old friend who for many years had lived in that neck of the woods, I began the job of tracking down a sample round of the larger Dutch service cartridge. Erlmeier-Brandt list a 10mm Dutch East Indies cartridge and give four synonyms for the round: *10mm Holl. Ind. Polizei-Revolver* (Dutch East Indies Police revolver), *10mm Niederl.-Ind. Revolver* (Niederlandishe-Indien or Dutch East Indies), *10mm Sherpe Patroon No. 3,* and *P.S.W. No. 3.* The last designation stands for Pyrotechnische Werkplants Soerabaja (Dutch spelling), the "3" probably indicating plant number three.

It seems that this cartridge was primarily manufactured in Surabaja and Bandung, but European specimens of this cartridge are also known. The information about the Bandung facilities and the following case and bullet dimensions were furnished by Mynheer Görlitz of the Leiden arms museum. The slightly tapered, flat nose lead bullet carries two grease grooves, measures .295" at the nose and .374"

The brown cardboard box wih heavy wax coating carries 12 rounds, and the markings appear to be rubber stamped.

across the hollow base. The length of the bullet is .650″, and it weighs 172.1 grains. The powder charge is 2.8 grains of a smokeless powder.

According to museum sources, the rimmed case is 1.063″ long and measures .492″ at the head. The loaded round measures 1.319″ over-all and weighs 272.3 grains. The Erlmeier-Brandt data for this cartridge vary somewhat from the data supplied by the Leiden museum, and they also list a round nose bullet in a case that appears to be somewhat shorter.

With the help of the above case and bullet specifications and a Cerrosafe chamber cast, I was now cer-

tain that the mystery revolver had finally been identified—it is the 10.4mm Dutch colonial police revolver.

Here is some additional information that was supplied by the staff of the Leiden museum. "The revolver was originally issued to the Dutch Colonial Army under the designation 'Revolver KNIL Mod. 1873.' In contrast to the regular Dutch service revolver, this gun is based on the Colt system and when this revolver was replaced by a semi-automatic pistol, the guns were re-issued to the colonial police forces.

"After Indonesia attained independence, many of the old Dutch guns were put to use by the fledgling Indonesian military and police forces." Although the previously mentioned A.U.R. marking has not been explained fully, it appears probable that some of these guns had been issued to the revolutionary Indonesian air force after 1950. If this was the case, it is possible that the "R" is a badly stamped "I", with A.U.I. standing for Angkatan Udara Indonesia or Air Force of Indonesia."

As far as proof marks are concerned, I was informed that "most Dutch military arms of the prewar type bore the miniscule stamped crown above a capital letter, this being the proofmark with the letter initial of the arms inspector. For many revolvers this mark has been considered ample proof of the safety and reliability of the arm, so the stamping of the manufacturer's name was very often deemed unnecessary." Just for the record, the standard 9.4mm Dutch service revolver was manufactured by de Beaumont, by Stevens at Maastricht, and by Bar at Delft.

Shortly after receiving the above information

Right side of the "System Kuhn" revolver. The ejector system, front sight and round barrel differ from the 10.4mm Dutch revolver, but the trigger and hammer shape, as well as the shape of the grip, frame and trigger guard are identical to the Dutch East Indies gun.

Left side of the "System Kuhn" revolver. Despite abuse and careless handling, the finish and appearance of the gun are good. Interior parts such as the hand, trigger spring, etc. all appear to have been well polished before assembly.

Obviously someone went to a lot of trouble and cost to have the words "System Kuhn" inlaid in gold. But who was Kuhn and where did he work? The trigger spring hold-down appears unusual but does not seem to be a replacement.

Cylinder marking of the new mystery gun shows the crown marks with "U" above—or below. The exact meaning of these marks is yet unknown.

from Holland, I was able to secure four of the original 10.4mm Surabaja cartridges. The heavily waxed square cardboard box is made to contain 12 rounds and is marked "P.S. Nr. 3." and "P.W. 2-41." The flat-nose wadcutter bullets are stamped "41" on one side and "2" on the other side, thus indicating manufacture of these rounds during February of 1941. The cases are Berdan primed, and according to Mynheer Görlitz, cases were not headstamped. While two of the rounds in my collection show no evidence of ever having been headstamped, the other two rounds show very faint traces of markings under the 40X magnification of my Nikon comparison microscope. The marks, unfortunately, are so faint that they have defied attempts to reproduce them photographically.

One of these cases shows the number "34" fairly clearly under high magnification and with oblique illumination, while the other round, under the same conditions, reveals a very, very faint number "32." No other marks are visible on the straight, rimmed cases, and those numbers have not been explained. Similarly, I have been unable to explain the significance of the circled number 31 that appears on the box. The P.S. Nr. 3. is probably a reversal of "Scherpe Patroon No. 3."

Though unable to document this, it seems that this ammunition for the 10.4mm revolver is actually a factory reload, or, if you prefer, a re-manufactured round, since there is no evidence that there were any brass manufacturing facilities at either ammo plant. Just who made these cases and where remains unknown.

No more had I doped out what gun I had purchased and what ammunition the gun digested, when another Dutch revolver came to my attention. So far this one has defied my efforts to identify it. It not only is different than the four known Dutch issue revolvers and from the Dutch colonial gun in many structural and mechanical features, but it also bears the legend, inlaid in gold on the left side plate, "SYSTEM KUHN."

The round barrel carries the number eight with an arrow through it, and one flute in the cylinder carries a mark that somewhat resembles two crowns, bases facing each other, with a capital U above one of these crowns. Another search through the handgun literature has failed to reveal anything about the Kuhn system, and I was unable to find a single picture of an identical gun in any of my references. The gun will, however, chamber the 10.4mm Dutch round, while my 9.4mm Dutch dummy case fits but loosely in the chambers of this revolver. I have no idea where the gun was made or to what troops it was issued—and I only assume that it was a service revolver because of the lanyard ring.

After all the time and trouble I have gone through, I still don't have a revolver with the Chamelot-Delvigne system in my collection—nor do I fully comprehend what that system actually does. But I do have the satisfaction of having unearthed some heretofore unknown information and having identified one of the scarcer revolvers of yesteryear. And that is what gun collecting is all about. ●

COLT vs. WHITNEY

The little-known rivalry between the Colt-Burgess and the Whitney-Scharf.

by ROSS KENNEDY

COMPETITION has always played a major role in the firearms industry. Traditional rivalries include Colt and Smith & Wesson in the handgun field, and in the repeating lever-action rifle market Winchester, Whitney and Marlin are prominent. In the 1880s Colt and Winchester began to intrude on each other's marketing territory. Due to this conflict and the agreement that resulted from it production of the Colt-Burgess repeating rifle was terminated. The story of the Colt-Winchester conflict has been told and re-told. However, a rivalry between arms makers that is rarely mentioned is that between Colt and Whitney. The reason for this is that there never really was direct competition between these two firms for the production/marketing of any particular weapon. To resolve this rather redundant statement, it is necessary to start at the beginning—that beginning when firearms making in America first began to move from the hands of the local gunsmith and into those of the large manufacturer.

Let's begin with Eli Whitney. In 1798 he started America's first successful firearms manufactory, the Whitneyville Armory, in order to fulfill a contract with the U.S. Government. There he manufactured ten thousand stand of muskets modeled after the pattern 1763 French Charleville. Twenty-seven years later, in 1825, Eli Whitney died. He had invented the cotton gin and helped found the American firearms industry by fathering the concept of interchangeable parts. He left a booming firearms business to his three daughters and a son, Eli Whitney Jr.

Meanwhile, in 1814 a young Colt—Samuel—was born to Sarah and Christopher Colt. At the age of twenty-one Sam Colt was granted an American patent for his percussion revolver, which he was soon manufacturing in a converted silk mill on the Passaic River in Paterson, New Jersey. However,

Top: Early Colt-Burgess rifle, serial 31.

Below: Whitney-Scharf rifle, serial 1518. Courtesy Winchester Gun Museum.

sales of the new Paterson Colt were not great and, in 1842, Colt went bankrupt. However, with the advent of the Texas-Mexican War and through the influence of Colonel Samuel H. Walker, Colt secured a government contract to make one thousand improved revolvers. Without facilities of his own, Colt was forced to sublet the contract to an established arms maker, Whitney. The Whitneyville-Walker revolvers, which included the Government contract guns plus a small number of civilian models, were made in 1847. When the contract was completed, Colt and Whitney parted ways and Colt set up his own factory in Hartford, Connecticut.

The first real period of competition between Colt and Whitney occurred at the beginning of the Civil War. Whitney manufactured a percussion revolver which competed with both the Colt 1851 Navy and 1860 Army; Whitney called his 36 caliber revolver the "Whitney Navy Model." With the end of the war, Whitney ceased production of the Whitney-Navy and focused his attention on breech loading rifles and, ultimately, repeaters.

For the Colt Patent Firearms Company the 1860s was a decade of change, partially due to the death of Sam Colt in 1862. Elisha Root took over as president of the company and proved to be a very able successor, with his experience as a designer and patent holder of numerous machinery and firearms inventions. In 1865 Root was succeeded by Richard Jarvis, who brought the Colt Patent Firearms Company into the twentieth century. It was under Jarvis' leadership that the last "competition" between Colt and Whitney took place.

In the early 1880s rivalry between America's two foremost firearms makers was growing ever more keen. Although Winchester and Colt served different needs of the American firearms market, no working agreement had been reached by the two companies to stick to his own field. As early as 1876 Winchester had developed a prototype revolver which would be a direct competitor to the Colt Single Action Army.[1] Although this gun never went into production, its designer, Hugo Borchardt, was to design several other revolvers before leaving Winchester to work for Sharps. Later William Mason also designed a revolver for Winchester. With this growing threat to Colt's dominance of the revolver industry, Jarvis commissioned the services of another firearms genius, Andrew Burgess. After purchasing the rights to several Burgess patents for a lever action rifle, the engineers at Colt assembled a working prototype by 1883. Commercial production of the new Colt-Burgess repeating rifle commenced that same year.

The Colt-Burgess was manufactured only in 44-40, which cut production costs and did not affect revolver output. At the time Colt was also producing the SAA revolver in all its variations, the number one, two and three Derringers in 41 caliber rimfire, the Old Line 22 Single Action pocket revolver, the New Line Single Action pocket revolver in four calibers, the New Line Police Pistol, a variety of Double Action Lightning revolvers, the Double Action Army revolver in all its variations and calibers, both hammer and hammerless Colt shotguns in several gauges and barrel lengths and, in 1885, the Colt Lightning rifle in many calibers and models. This represents a huge volume of production above and beyond the production of the Colt-Burgess..

On the other hand, when Whitney put the Whitney-Scharf rifle on the market in early 1887, he had only two other arms already in production.[2] Whitney's main product was the Whitney Improved Rolling Block single shot rifle (similar to the Remington-Ryder rolling block), which proved to be the mainstay of his business; most of his rolling blocks were muskets made for various foreign governments.

Whitneyville Walker revolver, manufactured by Whitney under contract from Colt in 1487.

Colt First Model Dragoon. The first Hartford-made Colt, the Dragoon closely resembled the Whitney-made Walkers. Photo courtesy of the Winchester Gun Museum.

For the U.S. civilian market Whitney offered a modest number of Improved Rolling Block sporting and target rifles in several calibers, and a fair number of Whitney-Kennedy repeaters in seven different calibers and numerous barrel lengths and variations.[3]

The Whitney-Scharf seemed to have no specific reason for existence. It filled no void in the Whitney repeater line that was not already filled by the Whitney-Kennedy, although it did have a smaller frame and shorter throw at the lever. Eli Whitney and William C. Scharf together designed the new repeating rifle, and by December, 1886 they were granted a patent for it. Whitney introduced the new rifle in 1887, but it was in production for only one year when

the Whitney Arms Company was purchased by Winchester on February 8, 1888 and it was discontinued. The Whitney-Scharf never really had a chance to get established on the market, since less than 2,000 rifles and carbines were produced.

Similarly, Colt's production of the Colt-Burgess was terminated before it was really given a chance to compete with Winchester's Model 1873 and 1876, Marlin's Model 1881 and the Whitney-Kennedy. Considering the little promotion it was given and its scant two or three years of production, the Colt-Burgess was relatively successful. When production ceased some time in 1885 or 1886, 6,403 Colt-Burgess rifles and carbines had been made. In 1884 the Colt-Burgess repeater was selling well, which probably

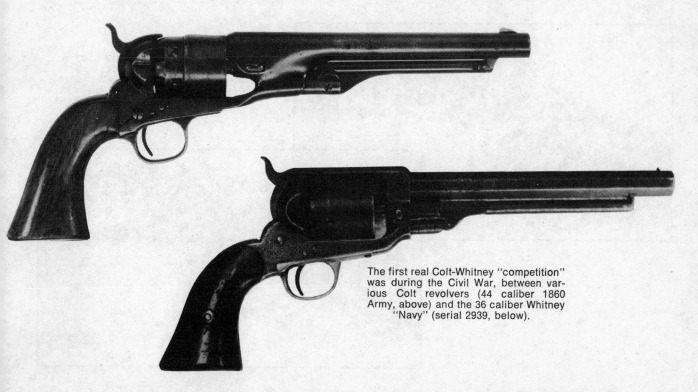

The first real Colt-Whitney "competition" was during the Civil War, between various Colt revolvers (44 caliber 1860 Army, above) and the 36 caliber Whitney "Navy" (serial 2939, below).

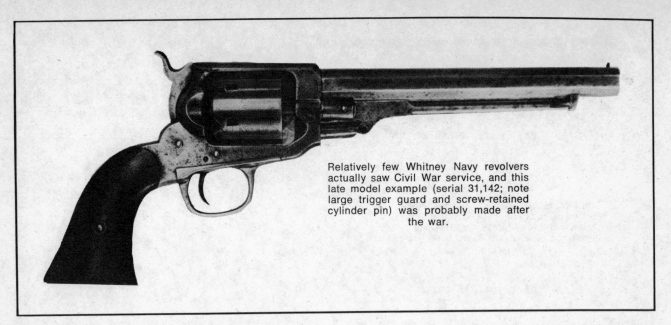

Relatively few Whitney Navy revolvers actually saw Civil War service, and this late model example (serial 31,142; note large trigger guard and screw-retained cylinder pin) was probably made after the war.

had a disturbing influence on Winchester. However, it was Winchester's development of two excellent revolvers, one each by Borchardt and Mason, that finally started the "fireworks." Production of the Colt-Burgess was stopped when Winchester and Colt arrived at an agreement to keep them from stepping on each other's toes.

The Colt-Burgess action was a composite of six different Andrew Burgess patents. The resultant action was compact, with a short-throw lever and a rigid, simple frame design. To keep the action as small as possible, the firing pin had a half-loop in its forward half to clear the lifter. The operating lever was linked to the breech-bolt by a toggle to which it was pinned. The lever forces the lifter up; tension is

exerted on the rear of the lifter by a small leaf spring in the side of the frame. The lever pivots on the bottom of the frame by means of a large pin with a rivet-type head on one end and a threaded socket in the other. A screw locks the pin in place by threading onto the socket. The loading gate on the Colt-Burgess is distinctly Burgess, of the type used on the Marlin Model 1881. It consists of a flat, spring-loaded gate which slides through a guide into the side of the fore-end. As on the Marlin, this thin part of the fore-end is very weak and susceptible to cracking.

The Colt-Burgess was made both as a rifle and as a carbine, but only in 44-40 caliber. The rifles were made with round, half-round and full-octagonal bar-

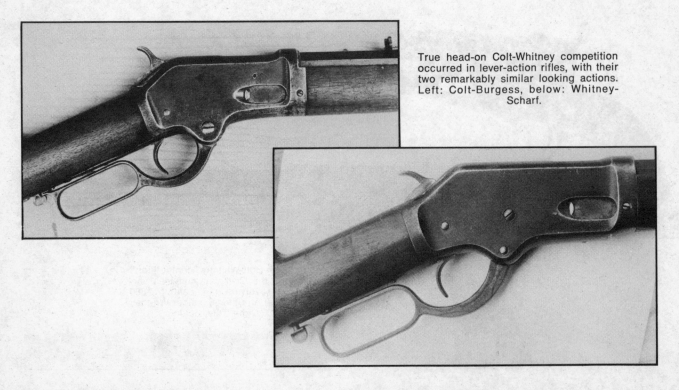

True head-on Colt-Whitney competition occurred in lever-action rifles, with their two remarkably similar looking actions. Left: Colt-Burgess, below: Whitney-Scharf.

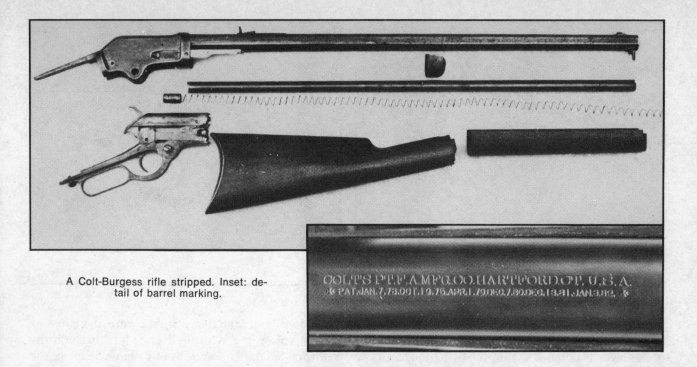

A Colt-Burgess rifle stripped. Inset: detail of barrel marking.

COLT'S PT F'A MFG.CO.HARTFORD.CT. U.S.A.
PAT.JAN.7,73.OCT.19,75.APR.1,79.DEC.7,80.DEC.13,81.JAN.3,82.

rels but only in 25½-inch length. The carbine had a round 20-inch barrel. All barrels were made with a groove on the under-side to enable the magazine tube to fit snugly. The magazine tube is held to the barrel by a unique catch, located at the muzzle end, which is dovetailed into the barrel. This catch replaces the traditional front magazine tube ring as used on the Winchester and Whitney. The magazine tube is also held by a screw near the muzzle end which threads into the barrel. Butt stocks for both the carbine and the rifle were the same, being fitted with a butt-trap to house cleaning rods.

The Whitney-Scharf, though resembling the Colt-Burgess, was a wholly different design with the exception of the loading gate system. The design is covered by a single patent specification granted jointly to Eli Whitney and William C. Scharf. However, no recognition was given to Andrew Burgess for use of his patented loading gate design. Like the Colt-Burgess, the Whitney-Scharf was made both as a carbine and as a rifle. However, the Whitney-Scharf frame was larger and internally quite different. The Whitney-Scharf breech-bolt houses a straight firing pin. Directly beneath the breech-bolt and pivoted through its front end is a spring-fed piece to control the upward movement of the lifter rear. Tension is maintained on the lifter by a hand screwed to the floor-plate. A spring-operated claw

WHITNEY-ARMS-CO-WHITNEYVILLE-CONN

A Whitney-Scharf rifle stripped. Note similarity of loading systems. Inset: barrel (above) and tang markings.

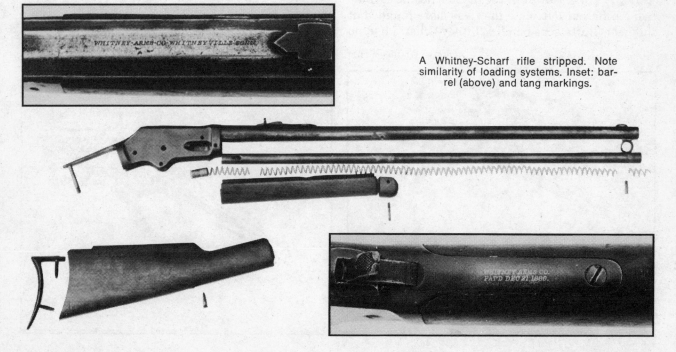

WHITNEY ARMS CO.
PAT'D DEC 21 1886.

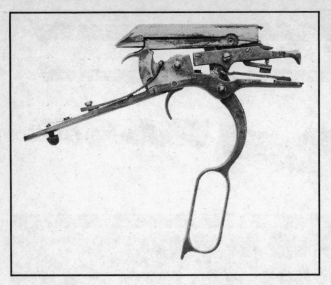

Action of Colt-Burgess, open (left) and closed.

exerts pressure on the cartridge as it is lifted in the carrier. The lever fits into a slot in the bolt; the tip of the lever is notched so that the firing pin can slide through it. As in the Colt-Burgess, the floor plate and lower tang are all one piece and shell ejection is through an oval hole in the top of the frame. The trigger and hammer assembly is a separate unit on the lower tang. The lever of the Whitney-Scharf pivots on a screw through the lower part of the frame.

Like the Colt-Burgess, the Whitney-Scharf was not manufactured long enough to warrant modifications to the original production model. However, unlike the Colt, it was made to chamber all three of the popular "short Winchester" cartridges: 32-20, 38-40 and 44-40. The rifle was available with a 24-, 26- or 28-inch barrel, either round or octagon. The saddle ring carbine was made only with a twenty-inch round barrel. Both carbine and rifle buttstocks were the same. However, the 32-20 rifle and carbine had a different buttplate that was more rounded at the heel. Buttstocks on all Whitney-Scharfs had no

provision for a trap door. Sights were the same as those used on the Whitney-Kennedy. Although the Whitney-Scharf is scarce in any shape or form, the carbine is a rare find indeed.

The Colt-Burgess and the Whitney-Scharf were not so much in competition with each other, but were rather in competition with Winchester—who put an end to both of them. For today's collector the Whitneyville-Walker is to the Colt Dragoon what the Whitney-Scharf is to the Colt-Burgess:competitors only in desirability. ●

Notes

1. Harold F. Williamson, *Winchester: The Gun That Won The West,* New York City, (A. S. Barnes & Co.) 1970, page 69.

2. Although there are no records available pertaining to production of the numerous Whitney pocket revolvers, it seems very unlikely that any of these revolvers were manufactured after 1880. Production of the Whitney-Phoenix sporting rifle and shotgun had terminated before 1886.

3. The production rate and particulars pertaining to the Whitney Improved Rolling Block rifle, musket and carbine along with information on the other Whitney breech-loading arms will be covered in detail in the publication *Whitney Repeating Rifles,* now in preparation, by author Kennedy.

Action of Whitney-Scharf, open (left) and closed.

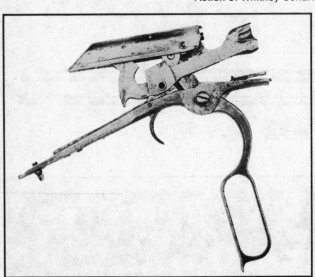

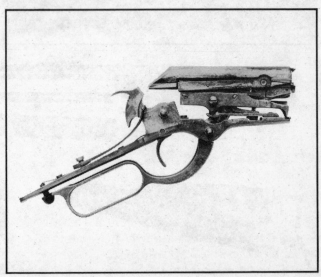

Part I
COLLECT MACHINE GUNS?

The original, classic Thompson Model 1921 with rare 100-round drum magazine.

SURE YOU CAN, BUT...

by JAMES BANNAN

Y OU COLLECT machine guns? That's against the law! At least, that's the response you usually get when you say you're interested in becoming a machine gun collector.

Let us take a closer look at the subject. Gun collecting is a fine and interesting hobby and with so many varieties of firearms, one must somehow limit his collecting if he wishes to try to assemble a meaningful collection. Hand guns, long guns, single shots, bolt actions, slide, clip, magazine, semi-auto or automatics are just some of the collecting possibilities.

I started collecting guns at an early age, buying or swapping for any gun that I could get my hands on. Soon I had a room full of odds, ends and junk, so I decided I'd better begin collecting one model and learn something about it. I started with the Luger, but it seemed like everyone else had the same idea and it wasn't long before I sold out and was looking for something more reasonable to collect. Then

I thought of my old "tommy gun"—a 1921 Thompson. Maybe I could collect Thompsons and Thompson accessories—there are only four models (I thought). It would be easy to get them all and their accessories. Well, that was 20 years ago and I am still trying to complete my collection! It has been a very rewarding experience, however, and I have met a thousand interesting people along the way.

The first decision the potential machine gun collector should make is what route to take—live (working) or dewat (deactivated)? First, if you go the live route you must consider federal, state, and local laws and regulations that limit machine gun ownership. There will be a one time Federal Transfer Tax of $200.00 on each weapon acquired, which could run into a large sum of money.

Under federal law, all machine guns, heavy, light, or sub, live or dewat must be registered with the Bureau of Alcohol, Tobacco and Firearms of the U.S.

Model 1927 Thompson, 45 ACP. This is the semi-automatic version of the Model 1921 and is marked on the receiver: "Thompson Semi-Automatic Carbine." It was manufactured by Colt in limited numbers. Even though the gun is capable of semi-auto fire only, it is still classified with machine guns by the Bureau of Alcohol, Tobacco and Firearms because of its short barrel and readily converted mechanism and must be registered.

Treasury Department. A firearm not registered cannot be transferred from individual to individual or to or from a dealer. Under the amnesty of 1968 all taxable weapons, live, dewat or unserviceable should have been registered. There are no provisions in the law to register an unregistered weapon now, except for new weapons from a federally licensed automatic weapons dealer, called a Class III dealer. A live weapon transfer from a dealer to an individual, from an individual to an individual, or from an individual to a dealer, requires payment of a transfer tax of $200.00 per weapon per transfer.

Suppose you decide to collect live machine guns. Your first step must be to check your state and local laws on live ownership. Some states have no provision for registering, other states do not allow an individual to possess a machine gun under any conditions, while still others may require you to be bonded by an insurance company. If your state does *not* allow machine gun ownership, permission

to transfer them will not be given by the Treasury.

Assuming you have overcome these obstacles, you are now ready to start your collection. A check with local gun clubs or dealers may provide you with the name of a nearby Class III (machine gun) dealer, or you may consult ads in the many gun publications for machine gun dealers listing guns for sale.

When you have located a weapon you want and an ATF application has been made and approved, the dealer can deliver your prize to you. Now what? You may want to try it out on the range (a somewhat costly deal at a dime or more a round). Out to the local target range you go, and there your trouble really begins. First, most ranges won't allow you to even have it around the range due to the lack of knowledge on registration and ownership of automatic weapons, let alone shoot it. They say you chew up their targets too much! Your best bet is to develop a friend on the police force, and offer to let him and his fellow officers shoot it with you on their range.

The Model 1928A1 Thompson was a simplification of the M1928 and was intended for the military. The vertical front grip was replaced by the horizontal-type fore-end making the gun less bulky and easier to handle. Made by Auto Ordnance Corp., the gun was produced in large quantities and was issued with a 20-round magazine. The 1921 Thompson barrel had more fins which were noticably thinner.

Many crude copies of different weapons have come out of the Orient, but this is one of the most interesting. It is a Chinese copy of the Thompson made prior to WW II. Note the method of sling attachment, fore-end and front sight.

This way you'll have use of a range and also will be helping your community by training the officers in a different type of weapon.

Dewat or unserviceable weapons are something different. You won't be shooting them so you won't be concerned with a range. However, they still must be registered by federal law. Even though a machine gun is welded up it is still looked upon as a danger- ous weapon by the uninformed. Further you will probably be the talk of your neighborhood as "that nut down the street with all those illegal weapons."

Becoming a machine gun collector may not be totally out of the question for you—it just has a lot of problems most gun collectors will never have to face. But if you find full auto weapons as fascinating as I have, the rewards are well worth the bother. ●

The U.S. M3 submachine gun was a WW II development to replace the costly-to-manufacture Thompson and appeared about 1942. It is made chiefly of cheap stampings. Note the telescoping wire stock, stamped trigger and cocking handle which is pulled to the rear to retract the bolt. It is substantially lighter and simpler than the Thompson and proved quite efficient. It saw wide use in tanks and armored vehicles during the war and is still serving as a secondary-standard weapon with the U.S. Army.

Part II
COLLECTOR'S MACHINE GUNS

an HISTORICAL Review

by DEAN GRENNELL

IT WAS Dr. Richard Jordan Gatling (1818-1903) whose quick-firing gun elevated his surname into a household word. Beginning work on his design in 1851, he obtained a patent in 1862: amply in time to catch his big chance. Alas, the Gatling gun foundered on the rocks of bureaucratic inertia, almost to the same extent as the ill-fated Ager. General Ben Butler used twelve Gatlings with good success at the siege of Petersburg, but failed to impress the higher-ups in charge of approval and purchasing.

The Gatling employed a number of barrels rotating around a common axis, loading, firing and extracting cartridges at appropriate points during rotation. The basic idea is a good one, as witness the fact that a similar principle still is in use in high-performance aircraft arms of the present day.

Appomattox had met its date with destiny by the time Gatling began getting it all together. He negotiated an arrangement with Colt in 1867 and

Father and son, side-by-side. The fast-firing 20mm Vulcan aircraft cannon is shown with its famous 19th century predecessor, the Gatling gun. Both guns have a rotating cluster of barrels and are externally powered—the Gatling gun by hand crank and the Vulcan either electrically or hydraulically.

Two famous Browning machine guns, the M1919A6 with bipod, carrying handle and buttstock, and the water-cooled 1917A1, both 30 caliber.

that firm continued to build the Gatling until it was displaced by more modern and effective designs around the turn of the century.

Ironically enough, Custer had four Gatlings in caliber 45-70 at his headquarters when his forces were wiped out of existence at Little Big Horn in 1876. Custer's troops carried 45-70 single-shot rifles and carbines while some of their Indian adversaries — by no means so slavish toward tradition — were armed with repeating Winchesters and Henrys and it seems likely that this made some significant amount of difference in the outcome of that notorious engagement.

The Gatling stammered its swan song during the Spanish-American fracas of 1898; that "splendid little war," as it was termed by some — probably those who did not sample such delights as tainted beef, malaria and the dubious joys of stacking obsolete, black powder single-shots against repeating Mausers firing high-velocity smokeless ammo that would not appear too archaic by standards of 1973. Even at the wilty end of its salad days, the Gatling found little favor in high places along the Potomac. Captain John Parker went to vast effort to obtain and use a battery of Gatlings and did much to pioneer the tactics for machine gun employment in future wars.

Part of the distaste for the Gatling in 1898 stemmed from the fact that Hiram Stevens Maxim

(1840-1915) had, by that time, developed the first true, self-powered machine gun in the sense that we use the term today. It was recoil-operated, but for good measure, Maxim had also dreamed up the principle of the gas-operated gun and set it aside. Later, John M. Browning would employ gas pressure to operate some of his designs, but Maxim is credited with recognizing both of the basic principles used in virtually all automatic arms down through the present day.

Those of us with ancestors who fought in and sur-

The first Colt machine gun, designed by Browning, affectionately known as the "potato digger."

Japanese Type 92 Hotchkiss-type heavy machine gun of WW II vintage. Note the heavy finned barrel and massive tripod.

vived the Civil War can feel grateful that rapid-fire weaponry played no more than a token role in that conflict. That was essentially the last war to emphasize the massed charge of unprotected troops, both mounted and afoot. The Crimean War, in which the legendary but hapless Six Hundred met their doom occurred a few years earlier, 1853-56.

By the final years of the so-called Gay Nineties, machine guns had demonstrated their awesome capabilities beyond overlooking by all but the most purblind strategists. Various police actions—to use a term not yet then invented—mostly in Africa, had pitted large hordes of hostile natives armed with spears against small forces of Europeans armed with machine guns. The ensuing carnage is best left undescribed.

The message should have been plain on the wall for all to see, as noted, but it wasn't. In the early years of the First World War the Allied high command flung numerous units of cavalry and infantry into eternity against the staccato sleet of steel-jacketed death from the German machine guns. The

Japanese Type 96 (6.5mm)/Type 99 (7.7mm) LMG saw wide use, resembles the British Bren gun slightly.

U.S. B.A.R. M1918A2 was used late in WW I and extensively in WW II. It has a 20-round box magazine, is gas-operated and weighs approximately 21 pounds, empty.

generals and field marshals of WWI showed notable disregard for the taking of risks and shedding of blood, so long as their own hide was not endangered.

Curiously enough, Maxims faced Maxims, muzzle to muzzle, across the pocked mud of No Man's Land in that bitter conflict. The British Vickers machine gun, famed in countless stories published after the Armistice of 1918, was basically a Maxim with minor modifications made after Maxim's patents had run out, about 1903. The German Spandau, made at Spandau arsenal in a city of that name that later was incorporated into Berlin, likewise was the Maxim design, for which they had purchased manufacturing rights in 1899, refining it into what they called the Model 08. It would appear that 1908 was a significant year for German weapons development since the legendary Luger also is known as the Pistole 08.

Germany had gone into the war in 1914 with something over twelve thousand of the Spandaus on hand,

having seen its tactical value quite clearly. Facilities for the production of further units and maintenance parts for existing guns were excellent.

Browning, in the meantime, had designed his gas-operated Model of 1895. You might describe it as resembling a length of gas-pipe fastened to the top edge of a piece of two-by-four, with a pistol grip and an unguarded trigger at the rear. This does not conjure up a particularly poetic sort of image but the actual gun has considerable charm and style in its appearance. Colloquially, it's referred to as "the old potato-digger." This stems from its rather singular actuating lever, which pivots over nearly 180 degrees during each firing cycle. The lever is located under the barrel, near the muzzle. A port in the lower circumference of the barrel directs a jet of high pressure powder gas against a steel plug on the end of the lever, driving it through its arc and actuating the mechanism to prepare for firing the next round.

If the tripod happens to be emplaced in loose dirt

Austrian Schwarzlose heavy machine gun of WW I, water-cooled, 7.92mm.

German Maxim 08/15 was widely used in WW I. It is water-cooled and fired the 7.92mm cartridge. The cocking handle moved with the bolt through each cycle and undoubtedly bruised more than a few knuckles, hands and arms in a fire-fight.

so that it settles from the vibration of firings, the shuttling lever can sag low enough to kick clumps of topsoil back into the gunner's eye. Thus that semi-affectionate nickname.

Browning went on to develop the BAR—Browning Automatic Rifle—and some of these went to France in 1918 as equipment for regiments of the U.S. Marines. For reasons never explained with much clarity, upon debarking, the Marines' BARs were replaced by the notorious French Chauchat. Often referred to in fictional works about that war as the "sho-sho gun," the Chauchat fired the 8mm Lebel, a rimmed round for which the French service rifle was chambered. It quickly became something of a by-word for contrary unreliability.

The standard Browning machine gun, in air-cooled and water-cooled versions, came into being so late in WWI as to see little use before the war was over. The Thompson submachine gun was not far behind. Both designs were refined over the next quarter-century or so to play major roles in WWII.

Books could be—and have been—written about the Thompson, alone. Though it seems incredible in terms of today's attitudes, it once could be purchased at the local hardware store with little more fuss and red tape than, for example, a pump shotgun. The going price was around $200, which was a fair piece of change in the Roaring Twenties. Advertisements of that time depicted a picturesque cowpoke standing on the porch of a ranch house, grimly hosing the hostility out of an attacking band of cattle rustlers with one of the capable contraptions.

Machine guns are not only fascinating mechanisms, they've seen a lot of history, too. Despite the legal problems they make a fabulous collecting specialty. ●

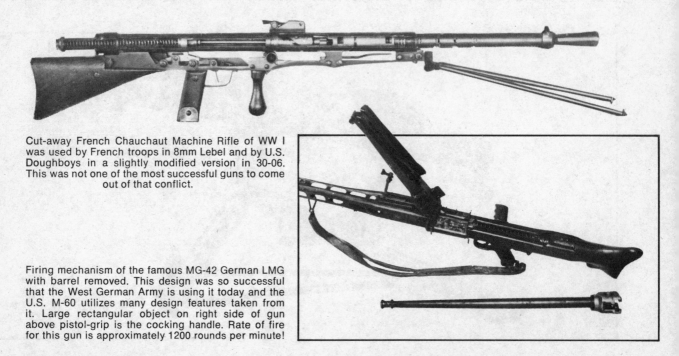

Cut-away French Chauchaut Machine Rifle of WW I was used by French troops in 8mm Lebel and by U.S. Doughboys in a slightly modified version in 30-06. This was not one of the most successful guns to come out of that conflict.

Firing mechanism of the famous MG-42 German LMG with barrel removed. This design was so successful that the West German Army is using it today and the U.S. M-60 utilizes many design features taken from it. Large rectangular object on right side of gun above pistol-grip is the cocking handle. Rate of fire for this gun is approximately 1200 rounds per minute!

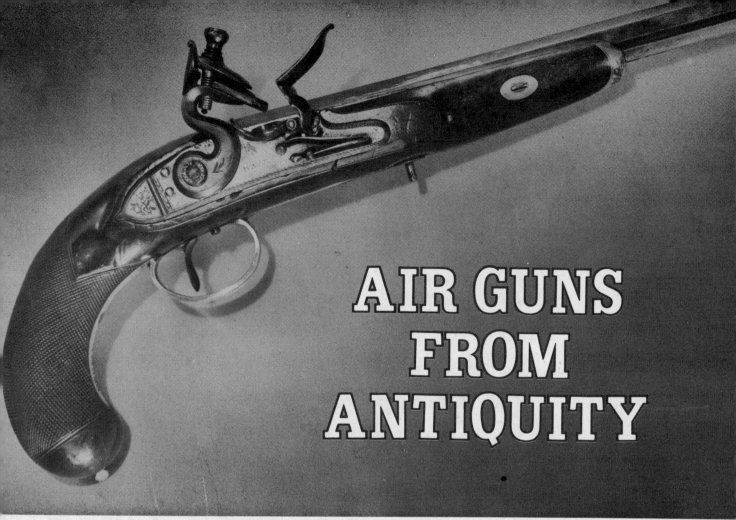

AIR GUNS FROM ANTIQUITY

"Air Gun" denotes a BB or pellet gun
in the minds of most collectors, yet these
air guns are as old, rare and desirable as any
powder burners a collector is likely to encounter.

by JAY CHARLES

AIR GUNS HAVE a long, though not always honorable, history. While today's air guns are frequently considered kid's guns, serious competitive target shooting with air guns is quite the adult sport in Europe, especially in Germany and Austria. But the historical use of air guns encompasses not only target shooting, but military usage as well as poaching.

One of the earliest, if not *the* earliest, air guns is credited to Güter of Nuremburg. Though the historic background of these guns is rather hazy and accurate records do not appear to exist, various gun historians believe that he worked between 1400 and 1560.

Whatever the actual date of origin, many early fine gun makers created beautiful specimens of "wind guns." Some of them, showing superior workmanship and obviously made by skilled artisans, are unsigned. Maker's names are a matter of conjecture, based to a large extent on certain similarities of workmanship on wood or steel.

The relative silence of the wind or air gun when discharging its projectile made these guns very popular with poachers. Since game belonged to the land owner and the gentry frowned on poaching and discouraged the practice with rather severe punishments, makers of air guns found it politic not to advertise their illicit skills. It appears likely that the assumption that the best air guns were made by the better gunsmiths is probably correct. Only skilled hands could produce a gun that contained such close tolerances as the pieces seen in today's collections. A poor gunsmith could never maintain those tolerances, thus only the best of the gun makers were also the producers of air guns.

But the game and game keepers were not the only

"Flintlock" air pistol by Thomas Bate, London. Except for dummy flint and air tank fitting on bottom, this could pass for the genuine article.

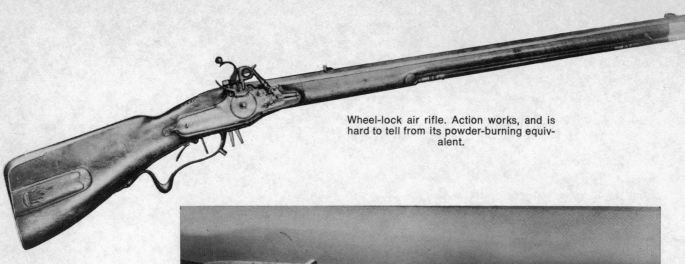

Wheel-lock air rifle. Action works, and is hard to tell from its powder-burning equivalent.

Detail of top of wheel-lock. Lack of ignition wheel is only clue to true action.

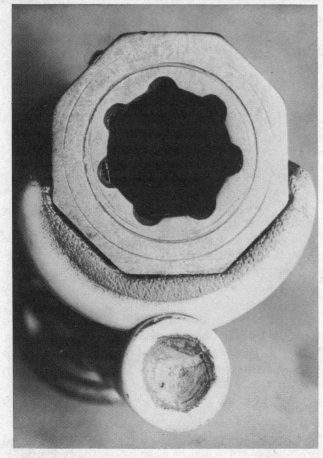

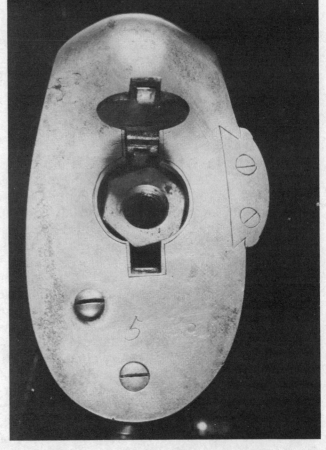

Close-up of muzzle (left) and butt of wheel-lock. Threaded hole is attachment for air pump.

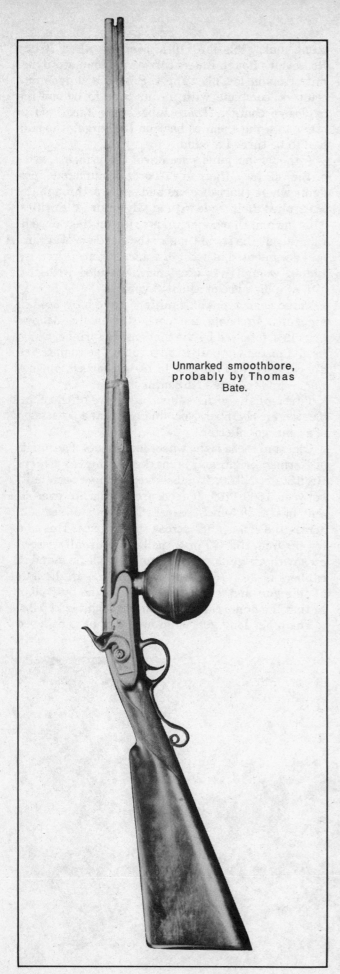

Unmarked smoothbore, probably by Thomas Bate.

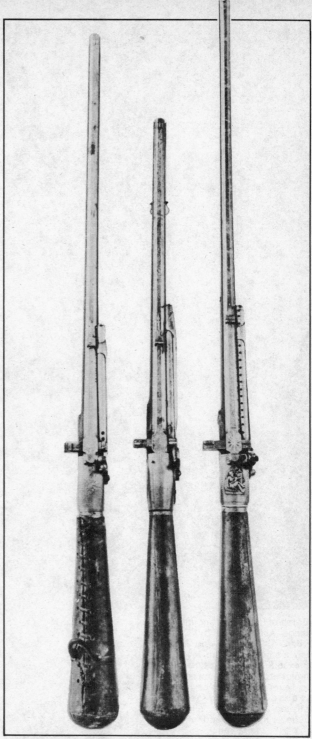

Top view of three repeating air rifles of the design of G. C. Girandoni of South Tirol (now Italy) and made between 1780 and 1810. Center rifle is military; others are hunting models.

targets of the early wind guns. A corps of Austrians at the Battle of Wagram during the first part of the 19th century was armed with repeating air rifles. These Austrian sharpshooters caused so much havoc among Napoleon's troops that he felt compelled to issue an edict, proclaiming the users of these guns as assassins—all prisoners taken with an air gun were to be executed!

Air powered guns did not reappear on the military

Detail of fancy sporting model made about 1810 by Coutriner, Vienna, showing loading method. Loading lever is pressed to right, letting one bullet drop into hollow recess in lever. When lever is released long leaf spring pushes lever back, aligning bullet with bore and air release vent.

Breech of rifle above, showing detachable air tank.

scene until the late 19th century when Teddy Roosevelt's Rough Riders carried a pneumatic dynamite cannon to Cuba. The U.S. also had dynamite cruisers, complete with an air tube to launch the explosive charges. These tubes were fixed, and in order to bring them to bear on the target, the ship had to be turned around.

Although air guns were never the principal arms of the military, there are records of numerous incidents where sharpshooters and snipers, through the ages, plied their trade with highly accurate air rifles.

Lewis and Clark took an air rifle on their expedition (about the same time as the Battle of Wagram) and documented at least one deer taken with it. An Indian woman was accidently wounded with this gun at a distance of some 40 yards.

Three basic types of "ignition" have been used in air guns. Probably the earliest was the bellows principle, followed by the condensing syringe, which used a piston close-fitted in a tube. The compressed air cylinder was the last to be introduced, appearing around the late 17th century.

Three of the guns shown here are of the compressed air chamber type, and are in the possession of a Chicago collector.

Oldest of these is the wheel-lock model. The gun is of German origin and is marked WentzLav Ehren-BreitStein, N 100. It is believed to have been built between 1680-1700. It measures 45 inches over-all and has a 30.5-inch barrel. The bore mikes .52" across the lands, .58" across the grooves. This is a far cry from the 177 or 22 pellet one usually associates with air guns, but air guns have been found in calibers up to .775". The air chamber is in the butt of this gun and a trapdoor opens in the butt plate so that the pump can be attached. Weight is 12.5 lbs.

The other long gun is unmarked, but is believed

to have been made by Bate around 1780. Smooth-bored in 38 caliber, the gun is equipped with a single set trigger, has a single screw take-down, and originally had a rifled tube which was inserted in place of the smooth barrel. Overall length is 49.5 inches and the barrel length is 33 inches. Weight without air cylinder is 5.75 lbs., and with it 8 lbs.

The real eye-catcher is the flintlock air pistol. Not too many of these were made, and most of them were custom jobs. Marked "Bate-London," it is elaborately engraved. Even the ferrule which attaches the air cylinder is ornate, although it can't be seen when the gun is assembled for use. Like the Bate long gun, the pistol was made between 1770 and 1780.

The 31 caliber barrel is 10 inches long, and the rifling strongly resembles Marlin's Micro-Groove. Over-all length is 19.5 inches, and without air cylinder the gun weighs 2.75 pounds; the cylinder alone weighs 1.75 pounds. Trigger is of the set variety.

The flintlock mechanism on the pistol works and looks like the real thing, but it does not strike sparks since a fake flint is used. The mechanism activates an eccentric which opens the valve momentarily to discharge a blast of compressed air. The system is probably a bit more elaborate than is necessary, but it is a pleasure to see the meticulous workmanship. The long guns shown also have working lock mechanisms. Seems that even in 1770 people wanted their air guns to look like real guns!

These old air guns are very accurate—and they are deadly as their history shows. Some of the low-powered plinking air guns have retained an astounding degree of their original accuracy, and considering their workmanship, it is really not too surprising to find that there is an increasing interest in those old wind guns! ●

Compressor for filling air tank. Tank is placed in container at top, which is water filled to prevent overheating. Crank is then turned 2000 revolutions (aided by centrifugal weights) to completely fill tank.

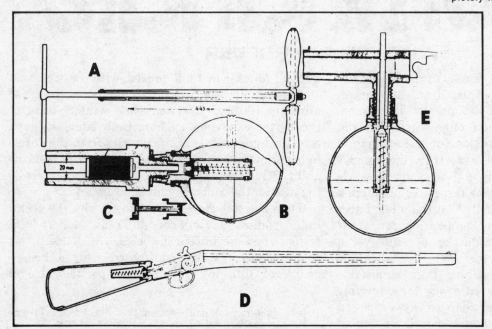

Valve and pump mechanisms of air rifles (from an early drawing).
A. Air pump used with balloon-type air containers.
B. Valve assembly and air pump fitted to balloon container.
C. Space in which sweep of piston compresses final volume of air.
D. Buttstock air chamber.
E. Air container which is screwed to bottom of air rifle.

Awkward looking and complicated as a Chinese puzzle, there's a certain fascination to...

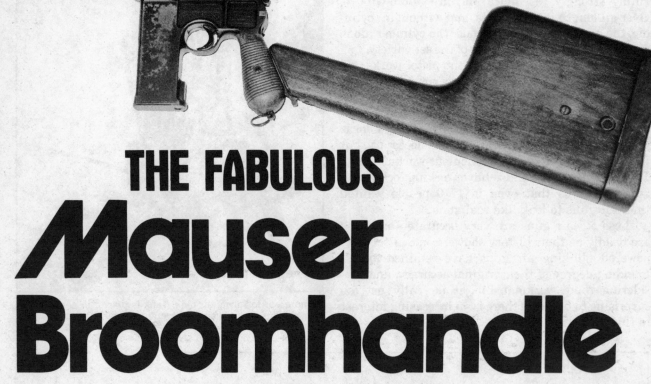

THE FABULOUS
Mauser Broomhandle

by JOSEPH SCHROEDER

MAUSER'S Model 1896 pistol was the first really *successful* self-loader to be placed on the market. While it was true that designs by Bergmann, Borchardt, Mannlicher and others preceded the Mauser product's introduction, only Bergmann's pistols and the Borchardt were truly marketed — and in quantities of only a few thousand each during the few years of their respective production lives. Mauser's "Broomhandle," on the other hand, survived as a commercial proposition for about 40 years, with a total production of well over a million pistols.

In the course of establishing this remarkable record the weapon underwent a very large number of changes. None of these changes, however, can be construed as altering the basic design patented by Paul Mauser in 1895. Indeed, with the exception of beefing up the locking lugs (between serial numbers 100 and 200) and some reinforcement of the barrel extension a short time later, all such changes appear to result primarily from the desire to lower manufacturing costs or to improve marketability. That these changes have created an interesting task for the collector cannot be disputed!

When the collector sets out to classify the seemingly endless variety of different Model 1896 pistols, he encounters no clear-cut pattern for them. Instead, he is confronted with a hodgepodge of differing magazine capacities, barrel

Rarest of the rare, an early Mauser 1896 with integral 20-shot magazine and matching wood holster-stock.

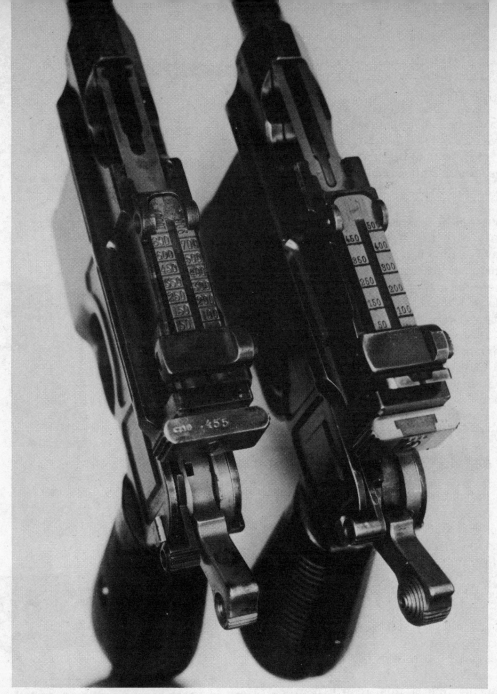

Close up showing principal differences between old (right) and later style Model 1896 pistols. Note hammers, firing pin retention, safeties, rear sight mounting and extractors.

lengths, rear sight mountings and markings, frame panel milling patterns, and so on. Serial numbers appear to offer some guidance, until one that is much too low to "fit" presents itself. There must be a logical pattern—but what is it?

In the past it has been popular to identify certain variations of the Model 1896 as "Model 1900," "Model 1905," and "Model 1912." These designations were *not* used by the factory, and are not accurate. On the contrary, with the one exception of the experimental hammer-safety equipped Model 1902, Mauser simply identified *all* variations as the Model 1896 until the introduction of the slightly updated Model 1930. When you realize that about two-thirds of the 100 or so variations of the Model

1896 recognized by collectors date from the first eight years of production, the futility of model designation by year becomes obvious.

Perhaps the best way to attack the identification problem is by classification of the many differences, major and minor, with respect to their origins. Taking this approach, changes can be categorized as being either *evolutionary*, those modifications occurring as a natural result of field or manufacturing experience, or *style*, where a basic characteristic is changed to improve the apparent suitability for a specific application. Let us first examine those differences that fall under the classification of changes in style.

A somewhat arbitrary listing of the major *styles*

of the Model 1896 must include: standard 10-shot pistol; 6-shot pistol; 20-shot pistol; Carbine; "Bolo" model; Schnellfeuer.

The basic Model 1896 pistol is a standard 10-shot pistol. It was probably the first type to be introduced, and was the only style to be continued (with evolutionary modification) till production ceased in the 1930s. As about a million Mausers were made in this style, more variations of it are to be found than of any other.

The 6-shot style pistol was probably introduced simultaneously with the 10-shot, as the earliest 1896 thus far recorded is a 6-shot, serial 21, with a spur-type hammer. Someone at Mauser must have felt that there was a market somewhere for a "trimmed down" Model 1896, as small groups of 6-shot pistols were made up periodically till 1905 or so. Most 6 shots have short barrels and fixed rear sights; a few exceptions have been observed. All 6 shots except those of the cone hammer era have the small "Bolo" type grip. Any one of the more than 15 recorded 6-shot variations is a highly prized collector's item.

To a Mauser pistol collector an early 20-shot 1896 is a find comparable to that of a Walker for the lover of old Colts. Its elongated magazine provided the user with unparalleled fire power, but apparently the additional weight and increased awkwardness doomed this style to failure. Only two very limited production serial ranges have been recorded, and their narrow spread indicates that perhaps as few as 20 or 25 of the 20-shot pistols were made as production items. All were cone-hammer types. In addition, a few very unusual "flat-side" 20 shots have also turned up. These may have been military test pieces as they are numbered in a separate series.

Though not nearly so rare as the 20-shot pistol, the carbine ranks very high in collector desirability. Production life of this weapon paralleled that of the 6-shot pistol, and most of the early evolutionary variations seen on pistols are also found among the carbines. Unfortunately, most of the thousand or so carbines that were made had barrels shorter than the magical 16 inches that used to differentiate a rifle from a "sawed-off shotgun" in the eyes of the United States Treasury Department. As a result, many of the examples found in this country have been made legal by welding an extension to the barrel to make it the required length. Happily, Revenue Rulings made possible by the Gun Control Act of 1968 have removed the Mauser 1896 pistol-carbine—along with early Mauser cone-hammer and large-ring transitional pistols with holster-stocks—from the controls they formerly shared with machine guns and sawed-off shotguns, so there is now no more legal restriction on their ownership or transfer than

Very early cone hammer with step barrel and "SYSTEM MAUSER" chamber marking. Serial 107.

Slightly later example with very rare 20-shot integral magazine. Barrel is tapered rather than stepped, but panel and barrel extension milling follows early style. Serial 757.

Still later cone hammer short barrel six-shot with fixed sights. 10-shots with this style barrel and a very few six shots with standard barrels and adjustable rear sights are also found. Serial 7776.

Large-ring-hammer transitional, a conventional cone hammer but using the later style hammer. Note "Von Lengerke & Detmold, New York" marking—many early Mausers bear importer's or retailer's marks. Serial 13288.

there is on any other rifle or pistol of like vintage.

The so-called "Bolo" style pistol, named from its supposed use in the Russian revolution, seems to have originated as a combination of the shorter 6-shot pistol barrel and the 10-shot frame. The post World War I Bolos, of which several hundred thousand were made, are quite well known. What is less common knowledge is that a number of Bolo variations were made before the war, though only in very small quantity. Not to be confused with the true Bolo are the 1920 reworks, standard 10-shot style pistols of various vintages that were altered after the war to conform with the provisions of the Treaty of Versailles. These have had their barrels shortened to 4 inches, and their adjustable rear sights replaced with a fixed V.

In the 1920s several Spanish manufacturers came out with copies of the Model 1896, and some of these were equipped with a selector switch to permit full-automatic fire. In response to this competitive pressure Mauser introduced the *Schnellfeuer* model in 1932. To take the pounding that occurred during fully automatic fire, the barrel extension and action were modified and beefed up. The frame and trigger were also changed to accommodate the selector switch, and the magazine well was opened up to permit insertion of a 10- or 20-shot removable magazine. The *Schnellfeuer* style pistol met with immediate success, and nearly 100,000 were marketed—many in China—before production ceased just before the start of the Second World War. A very rare and valuable *Schnellfeuer* variation is the semi-automatic only version, which used a *Schnellfeuer* frame with its removable magazine but had no provision in the frame or lockwork for the selector switch.

As many of the above types were produced over a period of years, some, particularly the earlier styles, exhibit a variety of evolutionary changes. For the most part these changes are common to all styles of the Model 1896 produced during the period that they were in effect. By far the greater number of the evolutionary changes occurred during the production of the first 45,000 pistols, as at this point (ca. 1905) the design finally stabilized into the form recognized as the most common version of the 10-shot pistol.

Among the early pistols the areas in which the *evolutionary* changes are most frequently noted are outlined below.

Hammers

Three basic hammer types are found on the Model 1896. The earliest is the "cone," which features a thick, large boss pierced by a small hole. The cone hammer was used on all pistols up to about serial 12,000, and on most of the remainder to

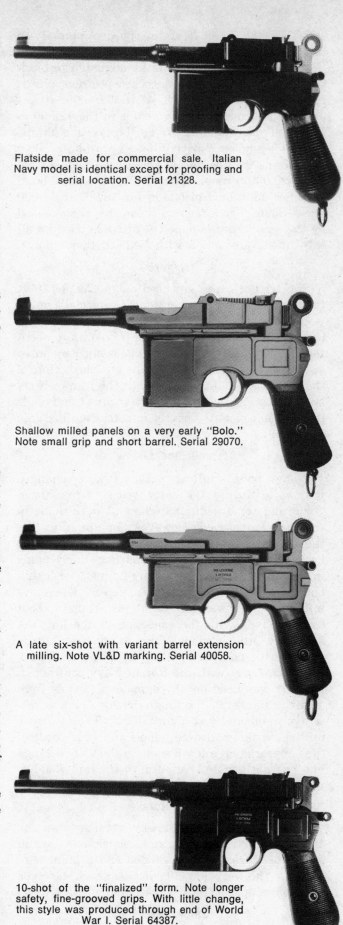

Flatside made for commercial sale. Italian Navy model is identical except for proofing and serial location. Serial 21328.

Shallow milled panels on a very early "Bolo." Note small grip and short barrel. Serial 29070.

A late six-shot with variant barrel extension milling. Note VL&D marking. Serial 40058.

10-shot of the "finalized" form. Note longer safety, fine-grooved grips. With little change, this style was produced through end of World War I. Serial 64387.

serial 15,000, when it was dropped completely in favor of the large ring hammer.

The large ring hammer is high enough to block the sight picture in the uncocked position, and it is pierced by a hole almost ⅜" in diameter. It was used on a number of early pistols in the 12,000 to 15,000 serial range (known as "Large Ring Transitionals") and exclusively on the Italian Navy contract as well as on all commercial pistols from serial 20,000 through about 35,000. It is also found on a few additional pistols in the 40,000 to 41,000 serial range. The large ring hammer was succeeded by the small ring hammer, which was used on all subsequent production with little further change.

Triggers

Two trigger types are used on the Model 1896, though as previously mentioned a special trigger was used on the later *Schnellfeuer*. The early type trigger, used on all commercial pistols up to about serial 21,000, is quite broad in shape and is mounted in a separate block that dovetails into the bottom of the frame. The late type, used on the Italian Navy and all commercial pistols from about 21,000 on, is thinner and mounts directly in notches milled into the frame.

Frame Panel Milling

Frame panel milling patterns were changed frequently during the early years of the Model 1896, and some additional changes were made in the post-war period. However, for simplification the many variants are usually lumped into three broad classes, *early, flatside* and *late*. Early panel milling is characterized by large panels with thin borders, relatively shallow in depth. The early milling pattern was used on all pistols up to about serial 35,000, with the exception of the flatsides and a few other variants noted below. The flatside model, with no panel milling at all on its frame, was introduced with the Italian Navy contract in 1899. It was used on all commercial pistols from about serial 21,000 through 29,200, plus a few strays numbered just above 30,000. The late type milling, with small deep panels and wide borders, first appeared on a few 6 shots in the 29,500 range but was not generally used until the mid 30,000s, when it reappeared for good.

Extractors

Only two types of extractors were used on the 1896. The early type, long and slender, was used on all pistols through about 35,000 and a number of guns in the very low 40,000s. A short, fat type with "ears" appears on all subsequent guns.

Safety Levers

The early safety lever pulls down through an arc of only a few degrees to place the gun on "safe."

Interesting contract pistol, one of 1,000 made for Persia just before World War I. Serial 154187.

Post-war "Bolo." Note lanyard ring stud is rotated 90°. Many thousands of these were imported into U.S. during 1920s. Serial 458786.

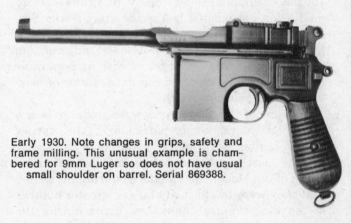
Early 1930. Note changes in grips, safety and frame milling. This unusual example is chambered for 9mm Luger so does not have usual small shoulder on barrel. Serial 869388.

Model "711," a semi-auto version of Schnellfeuer with removable magazine. Serial 84672.

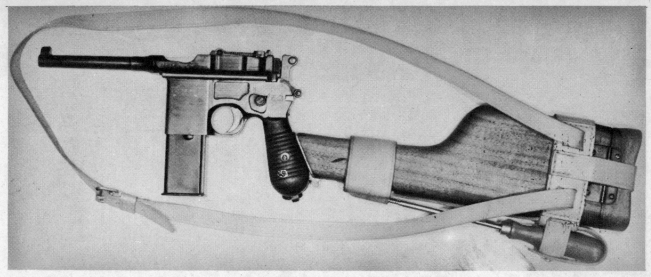

Complete Schnellfeuer rig with holster-stock and 20-shot removable magazine. Illegal unless registered with Treasury during 1968 amnesty.

At around serial number 35,000 a new safety, pushing up through an arc of 60 degrees for "safe," was introduced. Pistols in the 40,000 to 41,000 range mostly have the earlier safety, but all later production carries the late type. Two subsequent modifications were made to the late type safety, however. The first, introduced just before WW I was the *Neue Sicherung* or new safety, which prevented the safety from being applied accidentally while the gun was cocked. New safety equipped guns, which start at serial number 290,000, can be identified by the letters "NS" stamped on the back of the hammer. With the introduction of the Model 1930 the safety function, though not appearance, was again changed. On this model the safety merely prevents the hammer from striking the firing pin, so the trigger can be used to safely drop the hammer on a loaded chamber.

Sights

Early Model 1896s are found with both adjustable tangent and fixed rear sights. Early tangent sights were fastened to the top of the barrel extension by means of a separate pin. This was changed to integral lugs milled into the sides of the sight leaf, which were then slipped into matching undercut notches on the barrel extension, with the Italian Navy contract in 1899. However, both types of rear sight mounting were used through most of the commercial flatside production. All subsequent pistols used the later type.

Leaf sight markings also show a great variety. The earliest examples were marked from 1 to 10 (for 100 to 1000 meters), and 50-500 and 50-1000 marked sights followed. Some unusual sights found on early 1896s marketed in England were

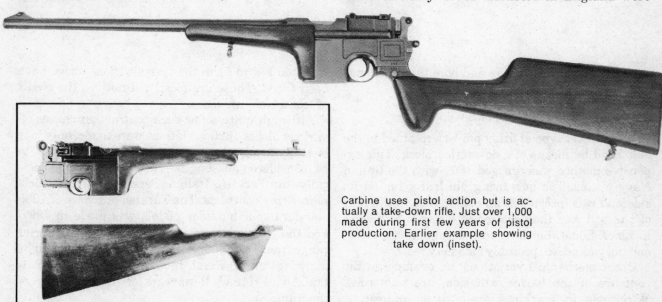

Carbine uses pistol action but is actually a take-down rifle. Just over 1,000 made during first few years of pistol production. Earlier example showing take down (inset).

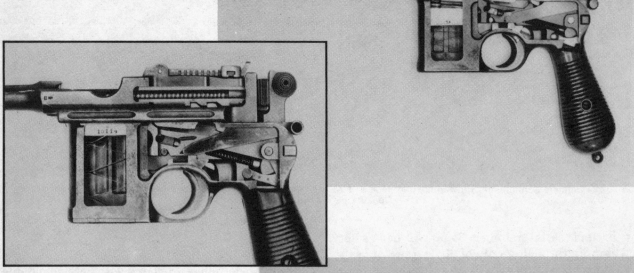

Very early **"System Mauser"** (at right) marked factory cutaway for salesman's sample or demonstration. Note single locking lug. Serial 24.

Detail of later cone hammer cutaway. Note double locking lugs.

Most successful competitor to Mauser was Astra 900. This example, sectioned for use in factory instruction, demonstrates difference in construction.

marked to only 300 meters and bore the additional legend "Mauser Cartridge 303."

Firing Pins

The earliest type of firing pin was retained in the bolt head by means of a dovetailed block. This expensive method was dropped 1899 with the Italian Navy pistols. The new firing pin had a lug on its side and was inserted in an oblong hole in the rear of the bolt and then rotated 90 degrees to hold it in place. Somewhat later (ca. serial 35,000), a second lug was added, probably for safety reasons.

Other mechanical variations, for example in the contours of the barrel extension, are numerous. Variations in markings are also of interest. A number of pistols with unusual markings and se-

rials too low to fit in the classifications above have been found. These are mostly, if not all, the result of "contract" purchases.

Although quite a few such contract purchases of various Model 1896 variations were made, only four of these involved a sufficient number of pistols to be considered at length. These were, chronologically, the Turkish, Italian, Persian, and 1916 German Army contracts. The Turkish purchase of 1000 standard cone-hammer pistols was made in 1897, and the guns supplied were given their own serial range from 1 to 1000. Both serial numbers and sight markings are in Farsi. In addition, the seal of Sultan Abdul-Hamid II appears on the left side of the frame.

The Italian Navy purchase of 1899 involved 5000

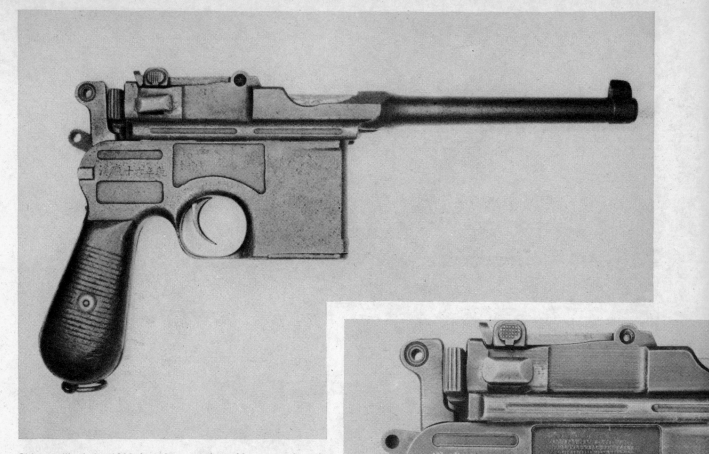

Chinese liked the 1896, bought many from Mauser and made many copies. These hand-made examples are not mechanically identical, but bear same markings (inset).

pistols, and is particularly interesting as these weapons marked the introduction of a number of evolutionary type changes. The pistol itself is a flatside with late type trigger, rear sight, and firing pin. It would be interesting to know whether these radical changes were adapted as a result of suggestions made by the customer. Serial numbers range from 1 to 5000, and it is apparent that these 5000 pistols account for the gap that exists in the early commercial serial numbers between 15,000 and 20,000. No special marking is provided, but the pistols are proofed with the letters DV on the left side of the chamber and a crown over AV under it instead of the usual crown over U German proof.

The Persian contract pistols were produced much later, probably in 1910 or 1911. Unlike the previous contract models the Persian pistols are serialled in the commercial number series, but a special block of numbers, from 154,001 through 155,000, was set aside for them. The Persian pistols are standard pre-war commercial pistols, except for the Persian crest on the rear panel on the left side of the frame and a Persian proof mark on the left side of the barrel extension. This model has been frequently faked in the past, but aside from the improper serial number range a phoney is usually obvious from the crudeness of the crest.

Early in 1916, the German government realized that the output of Luger pistols from DWM and the Erfurt arsenal were inadequate to satisfy the military demand for sidearms. Rather than attempt to set up a third source to manufacture Lugers they contracted with Mauser to supply Model 1896 pistols chambered for the 9mm Parabellum cartridge. 150,000 pistols were ordered, and by the end of the war about 135,000 had been delivered. Since

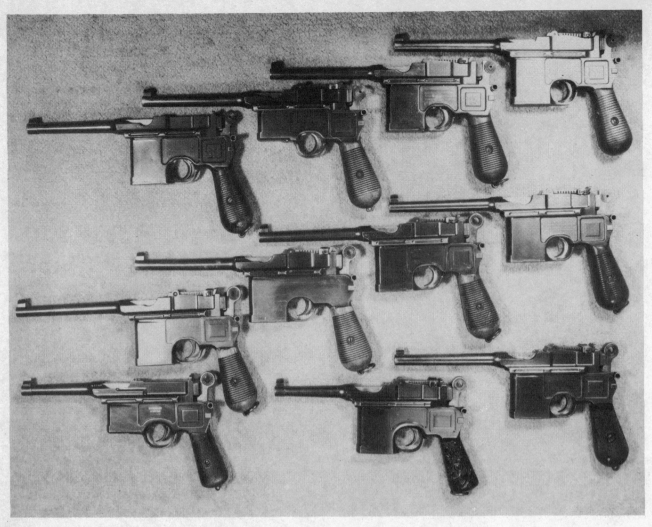

Final exam time! Now you've been through the evolution of Mauser's 1896, you should be able to put this group
—all different—in proper sequence. Good luck!

a number of Model 1896s in 7.63mm were already in use by the army, most of the 9mm pistols supplied bore a large number 9, cut into the grips and filled with red paint, to indicate their caliber.

In addition to the above contracts, in which enough pistols were involved that there can be no question that they saw official service, there were a number of other government purchases of the Model 1896 for evaluation purposes. Most of the pistols involved were early variations, and can be distinguished from their commercial counterparts by their very low serial numbers and nonstandard proof marks. Examples are known in both 6 and 10-shot versions.

Though most 1896s were chambered for the 7.63mm Mauser shell, a souped-up version of the 7.65mm Borchardt cartridge, pistols chambered for two other calibers beside the 9mm Parabellum are sometimes found. Earliest is the 9mm Mauser Export, a powerful round with considerably better ballistics than the Luger shell. Relatively few

pistols seem to have been produced in this caliber, with a few stray examples appearing in the 40 and 50 thousands, one group in the 88,000 serial range and the other at about 176,000. The 9mm Export cartridge is actually better known than its pistol, as a number of European submachine guns were chambered for it. The second unusual caliber is 8.15mm, for which a few Model 1930 pistols have been found—but no examples of the cartridge are known! It *is* legitimate, however, as DWM shows the cartridge in their record books as case number 580.

There can be no really "simple" system for classifying the Mauser Broomhandle variations. There are simply too many possible combinations of the different styles and the various evolutionary changes. However, separating the two types of changes and putting those that are a result of evolution in their proper chronological order does provide a basis for reducing much of the traditional confusion associated with this fascinating weapon. ●

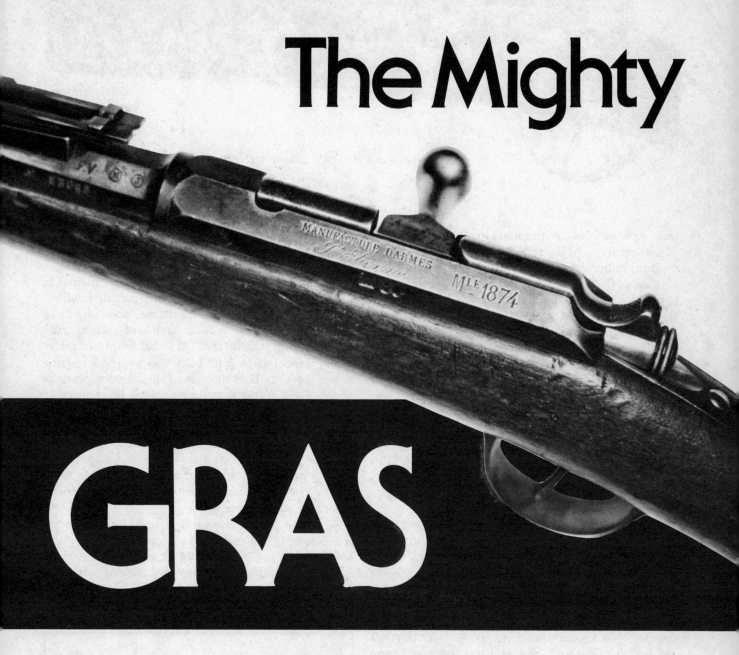

The Mighty

GRAS

by JAMES B. HUGHES, JR.

THE BASIC Gras rifle was designed as a cartridge alternation to the needlefire M-1866 Chassepot. It was named after Captain Basile Gras (born 1836, died 1901), the head of the French Artillery Commission appointed to the task of modernizing the Chassepot. Prussia, the old enemy of France, had earlier adopted the cartridge-firing 1871 Mauser. The adoption by the French of the M-1874 ended the era of the needle gun in Europe as a military arm.

In addition to the rifle, which has a 32½" barrel and weighs 9⅓ pounds, two short barreled versions of the Gras were made: the carbine with a 20" barrel and a musketoon having a 28" barrel. They are fitted with turned-down bolts for mounted service and have brass furniture. The carbine is 39" long and weighs 7⅓ pounds; the musketoon, while not fitted with a bayonet lug, is almost of rifle dimensions: 45¾" long and 8¼ pounds. All iron fittings are blued except the bolt and trigger, which are left bright.

Those arms submitted for cartridge conversion

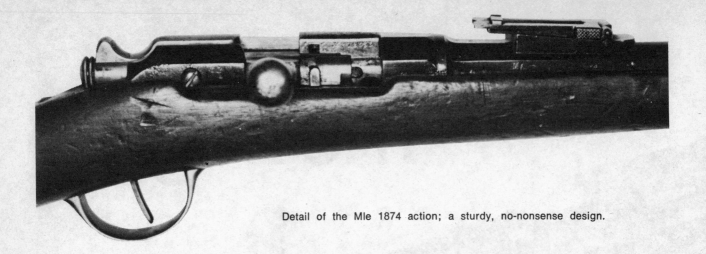

Detail of the Mle 1874 action; a sturdy, no-nonsense design.

may be identified by the markings on the left flat of the receiver, "Mle 1866-74," and the arsenal of original manufacture. Some of the conversion work was done in England on contract. These arms are marked "Kynoch-Gun-Factory-Aston" on the top flat of the barrel in addition to "Musket-43-77-380" on the right barrel flat. This English conversion uses a bolt of slightly different design that has no provision for recocking and will not interchange with the standard French bolt. The conversion work in both England and France entailed the alteration of the bolt to cock on the upstroke, since the 1866 Chassepot had required manual cocking before the bolt could be opened. The addition of an extractor to the bolt face was also necessary. The date of conversion is marked on the barrel (right side) near the breech. The actual cost of the cartridge alteration was then about 10 Francs.

Those arms newly manufactured for the 11mm Gras cartridge were made at the French arsenals of St. Etienne, Chatellerault and Tulle. These arms are marked on the left side of the receiver with "Mle 1874" and the arsenal name. The year of production is marked on the right flat of the barrel near the receiver. Barrels are proofed on the left flat. Serial numbers appear on the left vertical flat of the barrel and the bolt parts, and repeated on the bayonet lug. Inspector's marks appear on most parts.

In 1880 the rear sight leaf was changed to agree with the ballistics of the M-1878 bullet. At the same time the cleaning rod was also changed. Those arms with these changes are marked "M80" on the vertical flat of the receiver in addition to the standard markings.

Additional variations of the Gras were manufactured in limited numbers throughout the 1880s. One was a musketoon, chambered for a special reduced load cartridge, for the "Battalion Ecole" or Military Academy. This cadet arm was chambered for a cartridge using 41 grains of black powder

and a 363 grain paper-patched lead bullet. Another variation was the "petit Gras" or small Gras in 8mm caliber. The 8mm Gras cartridge, produced experimentally, utilized 72 grains of black powder to propel a 235-gr. jacketed bullet. The last version used in France was the "Mle 1874 M80 M14," which was a standard 11mm rifle altered to fire the M-1886/93 Lebel 8mm cartridge.

The Model 1874 M80 M14 was a product of the arms shortage that developed in the opening days of the First World War. To equip the large number of newly recruited men the long-obsolete Gras was once again called into service. The original barrel was shortened by 6 inches and reamed out to take a liner that was bored and chambered for 8mm Lebel. A handguard was added, as were Mannlicher-Berthier pattern sights. These sleeved arms saw only limited service.

Since the Gras had been developed as a cartridge conversion of the needlefire Chassepot, either the 1866 Chassepot or the 1874 Gras bayonet will fit it. The 1866 Chassepot bayonet, issued with the first conversions, is 27½" over-all with 22½"

Specifications

Caliber: 11mm Gras (11mm x 60R)
Cartridge: DWM #38, ROTH #69, English: .43-77-380
Charge: 81-gr. black rifle powder (1874)
Bullet: 388-gr. lead, paper patched (DWM #18)
Capacity: Single shot
Sights: Rear—Adjustable leaf, 200 to 1800 meters
      Front—Barleycorn
Safety: None
Length of Barrel: 32½"
Rifling: 4 Grooves, 1 turn in 21½"
Length w/o Bayonet: 51¼"   **With Bayonet:** 71¾"
Weight w/o Bayonet: 9⅓ lbs.   **With Bayonet:** 10½ lbs.
Locked: Turn bolt, split bridge receiver
Rate of Fire: 15 rounds per minute

Militärgewehre deutscher und fremder Staaten.

Fusils militaires allemands et étrangers.

German and Foreign Military Rifles.

Fusiles de los ejércitos de Alemania y las demás Naciones extranjeras.

19/27

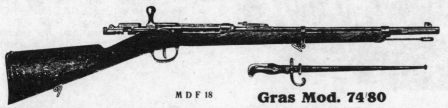

MDF 18
a

Gras Mod. 66/74

| Vorrat
Approvisionnement
Supply
Existencia | 6000 |

Original französisches Armee-Gewehr „Gras", Mod. 66/74, Cal. 11 mm, ohne Bajonett, Länge 1,30 m, Gewicht 4,250 Kilo.

Fusil de guerre francais Original „Gras", Mod. 66/74, Cal. 11 mm, sans bayonette, longueur 1,30 m, poids 4,250 Kilo.

Original French army rifle „Gras", model 66/74, cal. 11 mm, without bayonet, length 1,30 m, weight 4,250 Kilo.

Fusil de guerra francés original „Gras", Mod. 66/74, cal. 11 mm, sin bayoneta, longitud 1,30 m, peso 4,250 Kilos.

MDF 18

Gras Mod. 74/80

| Vorrat
Approvisionnement
Supply
Existencia | 6000 |

Original französisches Armee-Gewehr „Gras", Mod. 74/80, cal. 11 mm, Länge 1,30 m, Gewicht 4,250 Kilo, mit Bajonett, welches 0,66 m lang und 0,750 Kilo schwer ist.

Fusil de guerre „Gras" Original, Mod. 74/80, cal. 11 mm, longueur 1,30 m, poids 4,250 Kilo, et avec bayonette longue de 0,66 m, pesant 0,750 Kilo.

Original French Army Rifle „Gras", model 74/80, cal. 11 mm, length 1,30 m, weight 4,250 Kilo, with bayonet, which is 0,66 m long and weighs 0,750 Kilos.

Fusil original del ejercito francés „Gras", Modelo 74/80, cal. 11 mm, longitud con bayoneta 1,30 m, peso 4,250 Kilos. — Bayoneta 0,66 m y 0,750 Kilos.

MDF 19

Gras Car.

| Vorrat
Approvisionnement
Supply
Existencia | 500 |

„Gras"-Carabiner, ganze Länge 0,99 m, Gewicht 3,300 Kilo.

carabine „Gras", longueur totale 0,99 m, poids 3,300 Kilo.

„Gras" Carbine, entire length 0,99 m, weight 3,300 Kilos.

Carabina „Gras", longitud total 0,99 m, peso 3,300 Kilos.

MDF 19
a

Gras Gend. Car.

| Vorrat
Approvisionnement
Supply
Existencia | 300 |

Französischer Gendarmerie-Karabiner „Gras", hergestellt aus MDF 18, Mod. 66/74, Gewicht 3,700 Kilo, ganze Länge 1,15 m.

Carabine française „Gras" de Gendarmerie, faite du MDF 18, Mod. 66/74, poids 3,700 Kilo, longueur totale 1,15 m.

French gendarme carbine „Gras", made from rifle MDF 18, mod. 66/74, weight 3,700 Kilos, entire length 1,15 m.

Carabina francesa „Gras" de gendarmeria, formada del MDF 18, Mod. 66/74, peso 3,700 Kilos, longitud total 1,15 m.

MDF 19
b

Gras Kav. Car.

| Vorrat
Approvisionnement
Supply
Existencia | 455 |

Französischer „Gras"-Kavallerie-Karabiner, Mod. 74/80, hergestellt aus MDF 18, Gewicht 3,750 Kilo, ganze Länge 1,16 m.

Carabine française „Gras" de cavalerie, Mod. 74/80, faite du MDF 18, poids 3,750 Kilos, longueur totale 1,16 m.

French „Gras" cavalry carbine, mod. 74/80, made from MDF 18, weight 3,750 Kilos, entire length 1,16 m.

Carabina francesa „Gras" de caballeria, mod. 74/80, formada del MDF 18, peso 3,750 Kilos, longitud total 1,16 m.

MDF 18 a	MDF 18	MDF 19	MDF 19 a	MDF 19 b
† Netlas	† Nedulg	† Nostrem	† Nogend	† Graska
Mark 20.—	Mark 22.—	Mark 28.—	Mark 32.—	Mark 32.—

Gras rifles and carbines offered by the Adolph Frank firm of Hamburg, Germany in their "ALFA" catalog of 1911. Note the prices in Deutschmarks in the table at the bottom; 20 Deutschmarks was equal to $4.75 in 1911—hardly a cheap price for the time!

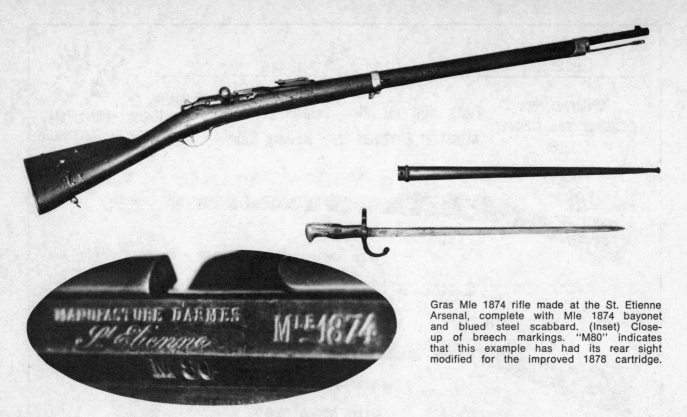

Gras Mle 1874 rifle made at the St. Etienne Arsenal, complete with Mle 1874 bayonet and blued steel scabbard. (Inset) Close-up of breech markings. "M80" indicates that this example has had its rear sight modified for the improved 1878 cartridge.

sword blade and a blued steel scabbard. The Model 1874 Gras bayonet is of the *epee* pattern ("T" backed blade); it was produced in several French arsenals and at Steyr in Austria. Each bayonet is marked with the model (1874), the arsenal of manufacture, and the date of fabrication. Those bayonets made at Steyr have the markings in both French and German. The hilt pommel is of brass with wood grip plates. The epee blade is 21″ long, the entire bayonet, 25½″. The scabbard is blued steel.

The Gras was adopted by France in 1874 to replace the 1866 Chassepot and the 1857 Rifle which had been converted in 1867 "a Tabatierre." It was in turn replaced by the 1886 Lebel rifle, the first French gun designed for smokeless powder. In addition to its French government use, the Gras saw service around the world. It was used by Greece (rifle and carbine adopted circa 1880) and other Balkan nations. At least 2,000 were purchased by the government of Columbia. In 1904, the Korean military had 10,000 Gras rifles in service plus an outstanding order for 20,000 new rifles placed the year before. However, they could not take delivery on these additional arms as they could find no purchasers for the variety of weapons then in service that they wished to replace. In 1915 the French Republic delivered some 450,000 Gras to the hard-pressed Tsar of Russia, for use against the Kaiser's troops. A. M. Chobert of the Sidarme firm in France patented a conversion of the Gras action to a signal or Very gun in 1916. The Adolf Frank Co. (ALFA) of Hamburg, Germany offered 13,255 rifles and car-

bines for sale in 1911, together with cartridges, bayonets, and other accessories. Gras 1874 pattern bayonets were altered by the Greeks to fit their 1903 Mannlicher rifles by bushing the muzzle ring. Even the cartridge was pressed into WW I service: during the First World War it was loaded with an incendiary bullet as an anti-balloon cartridge, and Vickers machine guns were altered to use it against the Germans.

Almost 50 years after its introduction into French service the Gras and its cartridge were still in military use. As late as the Italian invasion of Ethiopia the rifle was pressed into service—Ethiopian troops armed with the old black powder Gras defended their land against the invaders in 1935. Chile used Gras rifles until their government replaced them with the M-1888 Mannlicher from Steyr in Austria. These Chilean Gras rifles were made at Chatellerault, and are so marked but also bear the additional markings of *Henry Entrepreneur* and are without model designation. At least 2,500 were purchased from M. Henry, who had the arsenal run them off to fill his export contract. Chilean ownership is indicated by the Chilean crest, a shield surrounding a star over "M DEL E," impressed into the buttstock.

Early military cartridge rifles like the Gras have long been neglected by the vast majority of collectors. All too often even the knowledgeable dealers have overlooked their historical and evolutionary value, classifying them "en masse" as decorators to be heaped in a dusty corner and forgotten. They deserve better! ●

An enthusiastic cartridge collector
offers some valuable insights in his...

Cartridge Collecting Considerations

by BOB TREMAINE

Old powder cans are not only of historical interest but also are valuable collector's items.

FOR A GOOD MANY YEARS I accumulated cartridges. I picked up variations in headstamps, sundry military rounds that came my way, hunting cartridges from all over the world, shotshells from here and abroad, box lots of unusual ammo and stuff that had been discontinued when I was still in knee pants.

At first this accumulation of stuff—it could hardly be called anything but that—was housed in shoe boxes. Then I began sorting through it, separating cartridges first into United States, British, European, and miscellaneous other countries of origin. These groups were further broken down into military rifle and handgun ammo, sporting rifle ammo, target cartridges for rifle and pistol. Shotshells were separated by country and maker, and also by gauges and shot size.

Not really rare but unusual enough to cause comment are these six boxes of foreign 22 rimfire ammo.

This clean-up process took over two years and gave me a large quantity of trading stock. In the process I discovered that I had accumulated a whole mess of early rimfires as well as late rimfire rounds, both as single specimens and box lots. During my accumulation period I had also picked up specimens that fit into the special ignition periods, for example pinfire, and a couple of rare lipfire rounds. There also was a cigarbox of wholly unidentifiable U.S.-made rounds with U.S. headstamps that didn't look like any of the standard factory rounds. Later I was to discover that I had the start of a very good wildcat cartridge collection!

At this point I was faced with the prospects of having to move, so I set about the task of cleaning house and packing up my "collection." Why didn't I simply unload the whole mess onto a cartridge collector? A rough count revealed that I had accumulated better than 2,000 specimens, some of them fairly unusual, with even a few choice rarities here and there in the drawers.

I had found that certain areas and eras in the history of cartridge evolution interested me especially. The first thing to do, then, was to weed out—see what I had that really held my interest, and then limit my collecting to those areas.

For many years, whenever I had met an honest-to-gosh cartridge collector and proclaimed myself to be one too, most of these gents—hearing of my non-directed interest in cartridges—soon lost their interest in me. Heck, I was a general "collector" and there ain't nothing lower than one of them critters in the eyes of the specialist. Now, some 10 years

Box lots of sundry ammo. Some are so old that boxes crumble, others are only a couple of decades old but already are quite scarce.

after that first raised eyebrow, I tend to agree with them. Cartridge collecting is a vast field, and nobody can possibly do such an undertaking complete justice.

But what area of collecting should the novice collector consider, or what areas should the accumulator concentrate on? How about the question of housing your collection?

Let's start with the problems of storing your collection and identifying your specimens—problems common to all cartridge collectors. Dumping your collectible cartridges in a shoe box or the like is the best and fastest way to ruin a couple of rare rounds. Old timers in the cartridge collecting game have by now cornered the market on the scarce and costly spool cabinets that were used to display spools of thread in general stores and yard goods shops. I am glad they did, for spool cabinets, although handy, have a built-in drawback.

The shallow drawers, often divided into neat compartments that would hold one to four cartridges, are usually made of oak. Oak contains tannic acid and a couple of other natural chemicals that are enemies of brass cartridge cases and lead bullets. Store your collection in one of those cabinets long enough and your brass cases will be stained by the acids retained by the wood. Lead bullets will oxidize, turning white with a powdery residue.

A shallow-drawered cabinet is still the best way to house a cartridge collection. If you have a power saw, you can build your own cabinet with suitable drawers. An excellent source for shallow-drawered

cabinets is a used furniture outlet. The cabinets that hold standard legal forms are often discarded by law offices for newer and better equipment; blue print cabinets are another excellent choice for housing your cartridge collection.

There are two means of stopping the rounds from rolling hither and yon in the drawers and being damaged. Find a photographer who uses 4" x 5" sheet film and ask him for the empty film boxes. Each pack of film comes in shallow three-box packages, and these three boxes make excellent tray separators. Or use corrugated cardboard cut to fit each drawer.

How you arrange the collection will, of course, depend on the direction your collecting interest takes. For instance, variations in headstamps need not be identified further on each cartridge since the variation is there to see. But if you collect, for instance, 9mm Luger (Parabellum) rounds, you will find that the same factory produced a number of identical-looking cartridges—but they use different primers, powders, or bullets. You'll want to mark these cartridges for future identification. Maybe you have a "silent" 9mm Luger round—one that is loaded to deliver sub-sonic velocities—designed for a silenced, or rather silencer-equipped, gun.

Marking a round with an electric etcher or diamond-tipped scribe will do the job, but it will also detract from the round's collector value. Some collectors are able to recall every last detail about every single round in their collection—I cannot do that. So I mark the not readily identified rounds with a felt tipped pen, then cover the marking with a small piece of Scotch tape. If the need arises the tape comes off easily, and the ink markings simply rub off. Since the smaller rounds don't give you enough space for all the pertinent information, you may have to devise a coding system.

Let's consider U.S. military 30-06 ammo for a

Military and commercial stripper clips, loaded or empty, are part and parcel of the cartridge collection. While some collectors don't want dummy rounds (upper right) in their collections, author feels it is better to have any representative sample, even dummy or inactivated, than to have none.

Shadow photo should present little problem for the dedicated cartridge buff. Can you identify them? (L to R: 2.7mm Kolibri, 475 No. 2 Nitro-Express, and "Kwazy Kat" made from '06 blank round run through 228 sizing dies during idle moments.)

How many of these shotshells can you identify? Some of these shells were bought in Europe, others found here and there during scrounging trips. Shotshells make an especially colorful display.

minute. Most of these cartridges are marked according to manufacturing plant and year of manufacture. Assign a number to each plant, then give each round from that plant a number. Thus, you'll have #3 for Lake City, and a tracer round from WW II might have the number 47, while a later tracer round with a different bullet or headstamp (*hs* for short) may get the number 125. Thus, you'd have 3-47 and 3-125.

This means record keeping. Years ago Warren Horn, a very savvy cartridge collector from Burlington, VT, copyrighted a cartridge information sheet that contains everything you need or want to know about a cartridge. His sheets sell for $3.50 per 100 plus postage. It would be hard to develop a better system of gathering all the info about one round on one sheet of paper. Gathered in a ringbook or two, you can amass a fantastic amount of ammo information and data with relative ease. Record each round as you acquire it and details are still fresh in your mind. You might even want to put down how much you paid for that particular cartridge.

It is amazing how some cartridges increase in value—almost while you are watching. Not long ago I bought some specimens I needed to complete one set in my collection from an old collecting acquaintance. What had started as a casual hobby with him had become a very profitable business when he decided to sell his trading stock as well as his collection before retiring to sunny Florida.

When it comes to storing and displaying your cartridge collection, there are a few other points to consider. Some time ago it was popular to mount cartridges with wire on display boards. To keep them nice and shiny the cartridges were cleaned, either chemically or mechanically, and then sprayed with a clear lacquer. I fell heir to such a display and have been cursing the day that the original owner decided to use lacquer to keep his rounds appearing new. The lacquer sticks to everything, and the just-sprayed rounds peeled all the green paint from the board. So far I have not found a solvent that will dissolve that thick layer of 20 year old lacquer.

Collectors handy with tools often make display boxes or shelves with foam padding that nestles each cartridge, or each round may be arranged in a cutout bed in styrofoam. This is a neat way of displaying cartridges—but every time you add one to the collection you either have to rearrange everything or start with a new styrofoam sheet.

As already pointed out, brass will undergo changes due to external chemical influences. Old cartridges with cracked cases or split case mouths must often be included in your collection until better specimens can be found. Other ammo that comes your way is often dirty, greasy, oily and generally a mess. One question that has never been fully resolved is how much cleaning should I do, and what is the best way to go about it?

Combustible cartridges and such special ignition systems as pinfires are best left alone and housed in plastic pill bottles. The combustibles cannot be cleaned readily and some pinfires, when cleaned too vigorously, have been known to be ruined. Plated cases and cartridges should not be cleaned either, since the plating is often only a very thin washcoat barely 0.0002" thick and scrubbing or tumbling will invariably destroy it.

Rounds that contain paper patched bullets should be cleaned with special care, and the paper patching must be protected. Some collectors use a special paper collar, others use clear lacquer to protect the patch. Personally I prefer the paper collar, since a member of my family is allergic to lacquer fumes.

Sundry fine-grit cleaning compounds have found favor with collectors for cleaning cartridges. Brillo pads will do, but they require wiping off the soapy grime— a tedious and not very pleasant job. I have found that the J-B Bore Cleaning Compound, used very sparingly, does as fine a job as anything else, and the cases polish brightly without too much rubbing. The compound leaves a slightly greasy film on the cartridges that seems to help preserve them. One jar of J-B will do many cartridges, and even old copper cases clean up easily with it.

Most cartridge collectors try to preserve their specimens in such a fashion that the round will look the same way 20 years after it left the plant as it did the day it popped out of the machine. I have tried lacquering the rounds, but for previously mentioned reasons I don't like lacquer. It is also a tedious job that often needs redoing, and lacquered cartridges pose somewhat of a problem to photograph.

As with all other collecting hobbies, there are different schools of thought on maintaining the collection. For instance, should an old rimfire round that has acquired years of honest patina be cleaned? Some purists object to any cleaning, others want the round to appear new. I have no strong feelings on the subject one way or the other, and since it is your collection I suggest that you follow your own inclination.

Many collectors not only try to accumulate individual specimens but will also collect boxes—either full or empty. Full boxes often pose a serious dilemma. Let's say you have obtained a scarce box, still factory sealed. Of course you know what the cartridge looks like, but you don't know the condition of the cartridges in the box, nor do you know what kind of headstamp is on the cases. Should you carefully break the seal and open the box, look at a round and maybe add it to your specimen collection? I follow that school of thought, but also have some good arguments in favor of leaving the box as it is and wrapping it in plastic film for future safekeeping.

Lead bullets gradually turn gray and then white with a powdery lead salt which flakes off. Oaken

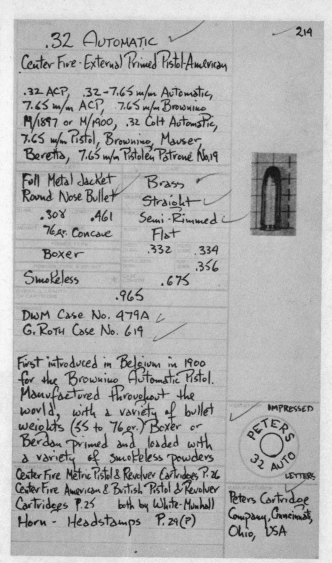

This data sheet is the best author has found, can be bought for less money than it costs you to make up and print your own. Note photo of cartridge.

Assortment of foreign and domestic shotshells, housed in metal Cardex file. No order has yet been brought into this portion of author's cartridge collection!

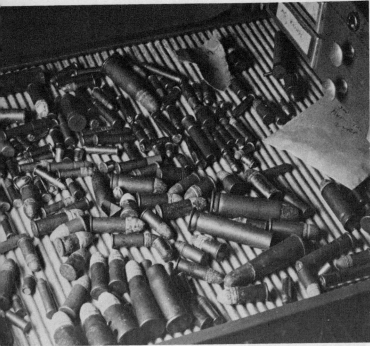

Used Cardex metal file, bought for $2, makes ideal cartridge storage cabinet. Note corrugated cardboard cut to fit drawer prevents cartridges from rolling around. This is part of author's unclassified rimfire section.

This simple home-made cabinet contains author's wildcat collection. This arrangement makes possible expansion of collection since it only entails moving a few cartridges from tray to tray as collection grows.

cabinets with free acid in the wood speed lead deterioration. One way to lick the problem of acid exuding from the wood is to apply several wash-coats of shellac to all exposed wood surfaces. Gently clean oxidized lead bullets as much as possible with a stiff bristle brush. Then clean them with J-B Compound, polish and leave them bare—or lacquer them after removing the greasy J-B residue with a clean-

This shows how cartridges ride in the wooden trays. These are British sporting cartridges.

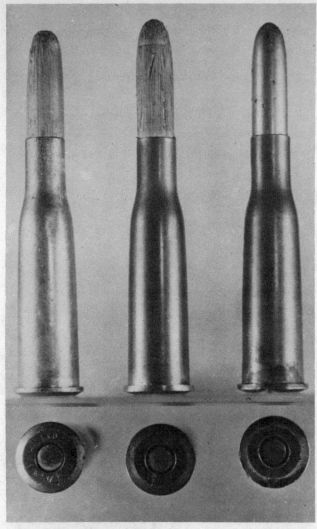

Can you identify these military rounds from Europe? No? Well, these are Portuguese Kropatschek 8x60 rounds, the two on the left with wooden bullets while one at right has steel jacketed bullet—note headstamp variations.

Wooden trays in drawers are made from pine board, routed on saw router. Finish is coat of wash shellac, a very thin dilution of commercial shellac that dries hard and fast.

ing patch soaked in denatured alcohol.

As your collection improves you may want to replace deteriorated examples with better specimens. Every cartridge collector has his own way of keeping a want list. Often you can make an even trade for a cartridge that you want to replace with one or more duplicates from your trading stock.

Now that you are about to undergo the change from cartridge *accumulator* to cartridge *collector*, what should you collect? If your interest lies in hunting, for instance, you may want to collect U.S.-made rifle cartridges, not only by makers, but also by calibers. A friend of mine collects 5.56mm military ammo—not only by countries and arsenals, but also the various special purpose rounds. These include experimental rounds and sanitized rounds, that is, ammo without hs to prevent tracing its origin. Incidentally, sanitized ammo is not new—it seems to have been used even before WW I.

You might collect the various types of U.S. military 30-06 rounds, or Lend-Lease ammo from WW II, or German military rounds of the same period. Another possibility is military clips (chargers), and stripper clips complete with ammo make a fascinating sideline for the cartridge collector.

If you take your cartridge collecting seriously you should invest $5 for an annual membership in the International Cartridge Collectors Association. Write to Don Amesbury, 4065 Montecito Ave., Tucson, AZ 85711 for an application blank. The monthly *Cartridge Trader,* issued by the ICCA, is itself worth the membership fee. Their shows are where you can see some of the finest collections in the country, and where some really rare specimens are on display.

There are a number of books that will help you identify cartridges. John Amber and Frank Barnes combined talents to produce *Cartridges of the World.*[1] Warren Horn has an excellent paper-bound volume that is invaluable for identification of cartridges (64 Ridgewood Dr., Burlington, VT, 05401, $5.00). Some of the better cartridge books are out of print, but once in a while a collector offers some of his books in the *Cartridge Trader.* Lists of cartridges for sale or trade are offered in every issue of *CT,* and they, too, are another source of cartridge information. Since the White-Munhall books have been out of print for some time, the Erlmeier-Brandt *Manual of Pistol and Revolver Cartridges* has become the standard reference for centerfire metric calibers in this area of collecting.

So—now that you are on your way to changing your social status from accumulator to collector—whatcha got to trade? ●

---

[1] Available from Digest Books, Inc., 540 Frontage Road, Northfield, IL 60093, $6.95 post paid.

THOSE LO-O-ONG BARREL 25s

"Gun Control" is nothing new—the Austro-Hungarian turn-of-the-century idea was a ban on snub-noses.

by JAMES B. STEWART

THE COMMON BELIEF that the right to bear arms and attacks on this right are both purely American phenomena is considerably in error. In fact the right of Americans to bear arms has its roots in English Common Law. As early as 1765 in his famous commentaries on law Sir William Blackstone wrote in England that the right to have and use arms for self-preservation and defense is one of the essential rights and liberties of Englishmen. There is considerable evidence to support the theory that the Second Amendment to the U.S. Constitution was an attempt to set down in writing that part of the English Common Law which the forces of the Crown had suppressed in the colonies. Because of the long duration of the frontier in this country and the attendant continuing necessity for personal

Above: M1920 Steyr with integral extended barrel to meet the Czechoslovak 18 cm law. Although grips, serial, and markings are of early 1920 vintage, the arm was proofed in 1932. Below: M1912 Clement with long interchangeable barrel. Note the Austro-Hungarian re-proofing dated 1913. Shown with original holster.

armament, the first attacks on the right to bear arms came elsewhere.

In the early years of the nineteenth century the industrial revolution was under way in England and the government was concerned that the resultant social upheaval would cause a popular revolution as well. There were rumors of armed groups drilling and the government became so concerned that they rushed six restrictive acts through Parliament. One of these was the Seizure of Arms Act, an act so unpopular that it was in force for less than two years. One member of Parliament, during the debate concerning repeal of this act, argued, "The distinctive difference between a free man and a slave is the right to possess arms, not so much as has been stated, for the purpose of defending his property, as his liberty. Neither can he do, if deprived of those arms, in the hour of need."

So strong were the feelings of the English in this matter that it took the world-wide unsettled and turbulent conditions of the early twentieth century to again attack the right to bear arms. This came in the form of the English 1903 Pistols Act, a weak measure which applied only to pistols with barrels less than nine inches in length. It was, among other things, a subterfuge to raise revenues. Before you went into a gun shop to buy a pistol you first went into the post office, often next door, and purchased a gun license which you got immediately without much question.

There is evidence to support the opinion that this attempt to control arms of short barrel length was occasioned by the advent of the easily concealable pocket revolver and its too frequent use, particularly on the Continent, in political assassinations. Politicians are ever zealous in causes which might affect their personal longevity!

The act does not state that it is intended to control crime, only to prevent incompetents from obtaining weapons and thereby to reduce the number of accidents. It is somewhat surprising, therefore, that the first legislative complaints regarding the measure were that there was no discernible effect on the crime rate and that there was suddenly a great

Illustration of long-barrel FN M1906 Baby Browning from a 1927 German arms catalog. Note that the model is specified as for Czechoslovakia and stated as being 18 cm long.

interest in sales of pistols with slightly more than nine-inch barrels.

Some officials became even more uneasy with the 1906 introduction of the 25 caliber, or 6.35mm, Browning cartridge and its accompanying diminutive automatic by Fabrique Nationale d'Armes de Guerre of Belgium. In Russia the Czar had his personal secret police equipped with the pistol. On the other hand, in the Austro-Hungarian Empire, a law went into effect which stated that no firearms with an over-all length of less than 18 cm could be purchased by a citizen without special permission. In effect the law restricted sale of short-barrel weapons to a few highly placed government employees.

The theory was that this restriction would effectively prevent the sale of the 25 automatic and therefore keep it, or any other of similar size, out of the hands of potential anarchists and assassins. As with all laws which attempt to control the instrument rather than its misuse, it was doomed to failure.

An early attempt to circumvent the 18 cm law appears in the 1914 catalog of Buchel of Zella-Mehlis, Germany, which carries an advertisement for the Walther Model 1 in 25 caliber and lists it as alternatively available for Austria with an overall length of 18 cm. This modification was easily accomplished in the Walther as it has a concentric sleeve around the barrel; the Austrian version merely has this sleeve extended to protrude several inches in front of the frame. This suitably lengthened the arm without affecting its true barrel length, and incidentally provided a very effective flash hider! Several of

these pistols are known to have survived.

Manufacturers within the Empire were no less adroit at sidestepping the law. The 1909 "Steyr," based on the patents of Nicholas Pieper of Liege, Belgium, became available from the Osterreichische Waffenfabrik-Gesellschaft, Steyr, in a special domestic version which had the barrel suitably extended to satisfy the 18 cm requirement. This was a costly undertaking with the Steyr because the barrel is integral with the recoil spring guide housing and the longer version required special tooling to manufacture. Alois Tomiska of Vienna also produced during this period his pioneering double action "Little Tom" with a special long barrel, an easier matter for Tomiska as the Little Tom has an easily-removable barrel mounted similarly to that of the Beretta.

The two countries which were the largest manufacturers of 25 caliber automatics during this period were Spain and Belgium and, predictably, entrepreneurs in these countries produced models for consumption in Austria-Hungary. Charles P. H. Clement of Liege, Belgium, was first with his modified Model 1909 — the design later bought by Smith & Wesson for their ill-fated 35 caliber auto. The 25 caliber Clement had a barrel and recoil spring housing similar to the Steyr, but Clement opted to extend the recoil spring housing as well as the barrel thereby simplifying his tooling problem. He also produced his 1911 and 1912 models for Austria-Hungary. This was a somewhat easier matter as, after the sale of the 1909 to Smith & Wesson, the later Clement pistols were made similarly to the

Browning and had easily removable barrels; thus barrel substitutions were simple and economical.

Not to be outdone by its minor competition, Fabrique Nationale also introduced a special long-barrel version of its famous "Baby Browning" for sale in Austria-Hungary. They also produced long-barreled versions of their 32 and 380 caliber Model 1910, which was also too short for that market.

Spain, the great copier, produced an amazing variety of Browning-pattern 25 and 32 automatics. Among these several were made available with the longer barrels. The firm that most avidly pursued this market was that of Arizmendi in its various organizational forms. Long-barreled versions are known of the "Wallman," the "Roland," the "Ydeal," and the "Singer," all products of that manufacturer. There were also long-barreled versions of the Spanish made "Looking Glass," "Bufalo" (sic), "Union I" "Vesta," "Tiwa," and "Victoria," which was the fore-

Waffenfabrik. Long-barreled Spanish 25s were again listed in most catalogs. And when the Manufacture d'Armes Bayonne, in Bayonne, France, went into production on their "MAB Model A," a long-barreled version of it was slated for the Czechoslovak market.

The real burden of the law fell on the Czech arms firms that made small automatics. They either had to sell all their product outside the country, as was the case with the "Praga," the "Fox," and the "CZ 22," or to produce a compromise design that allowed for easy interchangeability of barrels so that long-barreled versions could be produced for domestic sale.

The ludicrous situation brought about by this totally ineffective law continued until the invasion of Czechoslovakia by Nazi Germany in the opening days of the Second World War. For example, the 1939-40 edition of the Czech arms catalog Cenik Cis. lists nine 25 caliber automatics available with

M1913 Spanish Walman, one of many Browning copies. This example is shown with a matching, interchangeable, long barrel to allow it to meet the 18 cm law. The knurled button on the right side is a barrel release for quick takedown.

runner of the famous "Astra." There were probably others. These are often erroneously referred to as "target models" but they were simply pistols made to conform to Austro-Hungarian law.

With the outbreak of the First World War in 1914, importation and manufacture of commercial arms in the Austro-Hungarian Empire ceased. She allied herself with Germany and all of her resources were dedicated to the production of war materiel. At the end of the war, as a result of the Versailles Treaty, the Austro-Hungarian Empire was broken up. Strangely, despite the obvious failure of the 18 cm law, it was retained by that portion of the Empire which became the Czechoslovak Republic.

Predictably, as soon as commercial arms production resumed so did manufacture of the evasions. The Steyr went back into production at the renamed Steyr Werke as did the Little Tom at the Wiener

long barrels for domestic consumption, as well as a great variety of normal-sized imports which theoretically could not be purchased by any but military and official personnel. The 18 cm arms listed include three of Czech manufacture, all basically Browning copies, the "Slavia," the "Mars," and the "Duo," two Spanish, the Ydeal and the Singer, the French MAB A, the Austrian Steyr, and the Belgian "Melior II" and ubiquitous FN Baby Browning.

Like all ill-considered firearms laws this one had no perceptible effect on crime. After the turmoil following the Second World War, when Russia took over Czechoslovakia, the law was considered unnecessary and was apparently stricken from the books. Although many models of 25 automatic have been made in Czechoslovakia since that time none, as far as is known, has had other than a normal barrel length. ●

Skill, the right equipment,
and knowledge...lots of it...
are musts for

RESTORING RARE GUNS

by JOHN KAUFIELD

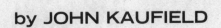

GUN *restoration* is an exact and complicated process. Its desirability is obvious in many cases. The hesitancy to refinish a firearm shown by some collectors is caused by confusion between what is meant by the terms *reblue* and *restore*. The intention here is to acquaint the reader with the processes involved in both.

Rebluing is generally frowned on by gun collectors. This is because a large majority of the firearms that are reblued lose 20% to 50% of the value they had prior to the "average" bluing job. This depreciation results from rounded corners, dished screw holes, and incorrect surface texture, all created by improper polishing. In addition, wrong bluing methods will rarely look correct on a collector-type gun. The result of the average gunsmith rebluing job is a gun that is black and shiny, but one that looks different than it did when new.

Restoration of a gun's finish is the returning of

(Above) "Before and after" pictures of a Mars pistol, a prime example of an extensive restoration. Prior to restoration this "Walker" of the auto pistol field was of little value to any collector. After careful restoration it sold for the price of a new compact car.

This is typical of the more extensive restoration of very valuable firearms. In the "before" condition rust had eaten through the forward part of the frame. Because of this and extensive pitting of the barrel, it was decided to sever the frame just forward of the trigger guard. The barrel was cut off even with the front of the frame. A new recoil spring housing was machined and welded to the frame. The same procedure was used on the barrel. Other pitted areas were filled with welding. After major repairs were made to the metal surface itself, polishing was completed. Missing parts such as the magazine, grips and some minor parts were made.

A well-used Luger artillery prior to restoration. Welding is required to correct the deep pitting and to fill in a non-original sight dovetail milled in the rear toggle.

that gun to its original condition. In order to *restore* a gun, your gunsmith should have full knowledge of the procedures and materials that were used to produce the original finish. A restored gun should have all original markings sharp and contours intact. The surface texture and brightness of polish should be the same as they originally were. The type of finish, or combination of finishes, should be selected to duplicate that, or those, of the original gun.

Though proper restoration can return a gun to fine condition, there are collectors who insist that a firearm retain the scratches and dents that result from years of faithful service. These people usually refer to the even rust color of the gun as being a "nice patina." The fact remains, however, that with more people collecting guns, and the supply of collectable guns remaining constant, firearms in fine condition, or properly restored, are more desirable and appreciate faster than guns in poor condition.

Because the process of restoration is much more

involved than a simple blue job, it is much more expensive. Therefore, restoration is generally restricted to the more rare and/or valuable firearms. A $25 Iver Johnson revolver restored for $100 would still be nothing more than a $35 Iver Johnson. However, if a rough pre-war Colt Single Action valued at $150 is restored properly, it will compare very favorably in value with an excellent $500 S.A. in original condition.

The restoration process begins with disassembly. Guns to be restored are stripped to their basic component parts, including removal of the barrel. This is not always as easy as it sounds. The Borchardt pistol, for example, has a rear frame assembly that is attached by a combination lanyard loop and rivet. To effect disassembly the head of the rivet has to be cut off, then weld-added and re-riveted later on in reassembly. Regardless of the work involved, complete disassembly is important so that a complete new polish can be done without interference from projecting surfaces.

The Luger artillery barrel and rear toggle shown after welding, but prior to final polishing.

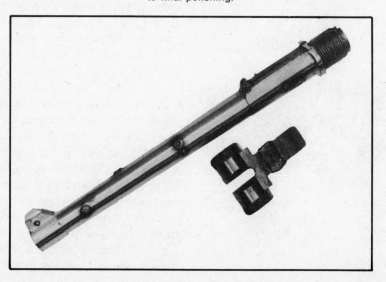

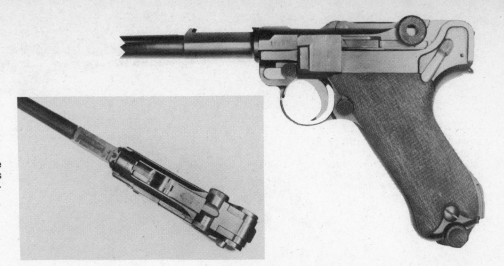

Top and side views of same Luger after finishing. Needs only rear sight leaf to be complete.

Once disassembly is complete, attention has to be focused on such seriously damaged areas as those where major pitting has occurred or where there are non-factory alterations. If pitting has reached a depth where it cannot be removed by polishing, welding is necessary. The type of welding used is heliarc, which deposits a clean weld without excessive heat. Knowledge of the type of steel used in the gun to be welded is helpful here. A welding rod should be selected which approximates the base metal so the weld cannot be seen through the final finish. Welding can also be used to extend a barrel that has been shortened, or to fill a non-factory sight slot. Scope mount holes, however, are usually plugged instead of welded because many times the interior as well as the exterior of an action has to be finished.

If the firearm to be restored has been plated, it is necessary to strip the old finish before polishing. Chrome offers a problem because it has to be electro-stripped, and care has to be exerted because the stripping solution used attacks the base metal. Nickel plating can be chemically stripped without causing any problems to the base metal. Silver and

Colt Single Action damaged by fire. Fire damaged guns are a common job in my shop. Normally a gun in this price range would not be worth the amount of work as needed on this Colt. However, this one had some historical significance.

gold plating are removed by dissolving them in a mixture of acids. Here, as with chrome, the base metal will be etched and requires extra polishing to be smooth again.

When major repairs are completed, the next and most important consideration in restoring a firearm is polishing the metal. Polishing is one area in the refinishing of guns that usually leaves a gun collector cold. The reason is obvious when one looks at the average reblued gun. Corners are rounded off, screw holes dished, and important markings blurred or removed completely. This is caused by the polisher using a soft muslin wheel.

At the other extreme is the false belief that a firearm can be restored to original condition by careful hand polishing alone. Hand polishing can produce a finely finished firearm, but the result is usually a gun that looks "too good." To produce a finish that really duplicates the original, it is necessary to use equipment similar to that used in the factory.

If a good deal of pitting is located near markings, the only solution is to remove the pitting and re-stamp or re-engrave them. If the original markings were stamped or roll-engraved, it is preferable to restamp them using steel stamps made to duplicate the original markings. Should stamps not be available, careful engraving will pass.

If a gun has missing parts replacements should be carefully made to duplicate the original; even tool marks should match. Of course, every attempt should be made to locate an original part—both for authenticity and because it would be much less expensive than hours of machine work would be.

Decorative engraved firearms present problems of their own. If pitting is present in engraved areas, the engraving can be polished, then recut. If inlays are present, restoration is even more complicated. Engraved guns can be restored, but extensive restoration is best performed on non-engraved guns.

Most collectors who consider restoring a firearm do not intend to shoot it. Some, of course, like to shoot the guns in their collections. Unfortunately, most guns that are in need of restoration have badly shot out bores. Several possibilities exist in renewing the barrel.

Relining is the first option to consider. This method allows the original barrel and its markings to remain intact. Reboring to a larger caliber is possible in many guns; e.g., 38-40 to 44-40. If neither of these are practical, a new barrel can be made which duplicates the original—even to the rifling and markings.

In considering restoration of the wood, it should be decided if the old stock is worth restoring or if a new one should be made. If the old stock is sound the finish can be removed and the wood degreased and bleached. Once the wood is clean, any checkering can be recut and a finish applied which approxi-

Rust bluing is the finest quality blue that can be applied to a gun. It is an old process, used well before the turn of the century. Most large gun factories used this method until after World War II, when rising labor costs prohibited its continued use. The bluing solution is applied to the gun metal by swabbing, and the part then placed in a steam chamber. After many applications a thick red rust is formed which is then carded off with a wire wheel. Wear resistance is excellent. Colors range from blue-black to black, depending on the steel and solution used. Rust blue produces finishes that tend to be of a satin texture.

Heat bluing produces a smooth blue to black finish, depending on the process used and the temperature (which can be as high as 800°). Heat bluing includes the processes of charcoal bluing, niter

The same fire damaged SA Colt after restoration. Nickel plating was confirmed by the factory as the original finish.

mates the original.

After all the metal and woodwork has been accomplished and the polishing completed, the firearm is ready for application of the finish.

There are many misconceptions concerning what is necessary to place a durable and pleasing color on steel. To fully describe the techniques and problems of chemical and heat coloring of steel would require a full-length book on the subject. The following summaries will serve as brief introductions to those that most concern us.

Salt bluing is the most popular finish in current use. Salt blues are sold under various trade names such as Lynx-Blu-Blak, Houghto-Blue and Oxynate No. 7. They all involve immersing the metal in a hot caustic solution. Actually black oxide a few mills thick is the resulting finish. Color ranges from a dull blue-black to a mirror-black, depending on the preliminary polish. Wear resistance is good to very good.

bluing, and carbonia bluing. Wear resistance of most heat blues is only fair, as they have the tendency to flake off.

Parkerizing is basically a military finish which uses phosphoric acid to build a rust-resistant finish on steel. There are several Parkerizing processes, each giving a slightly different color ranging from green to black.

Browning was the predecessor to rust bluing; both are similar in process. Browning leaves a rust brown finish. Twist or Damascus steel barrels are usually browned, as the wavy figure in the steel is enhanced due to the unequal action of the browning solution on it. Some browning formulas do require further treatment after finishing to bring out the twist pattern.

Color case hardening causes more misconceptions among collectors than any other type of finish. The theories I hear about how case colors are produced

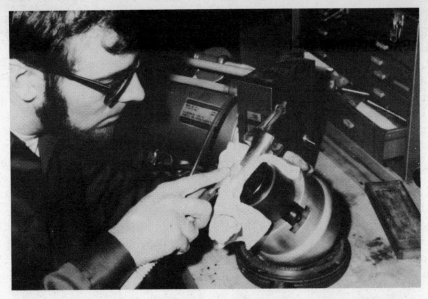

Engraving and re-engraving is a part of restoration. This shows a double barrel shotgun receiver having the engraving "chased" or deepened after polishing. This is sometimes necessary if the metal has pitting extending below the depth of engraving. In extreme cases where welding and extensive polishing are required, a latex cast of the original engraving is taken before restoration is begun. After the metal surface is returned to satisfactory condition, it is engraved to duplicate the original.

never cease to amaze me. True case hardening is produced by heating a steel part to a red heat while it is packed in a bed of carbonaceous material, then quenching it. This produces both colors and surface hardness. The colors produced by pack-hardening range from light blue to dark blue, gray, brown, and — occasionally — red. Patterns are determined by the quench and the mass of the part. Case hardening can also be accomplished by dipping the part in molten cyanide, then quenching. This is a faster method, but the colors produced are not as pretty nor is the case as deep as the method above. Quality guns are seldom cyanide hardened, except for an occasional small part.

Other methods can be used to produce only colors — the acetylene torch and oil is one. These methods, however, should not be used in the restoration of quality guns.

Plated finishes. The most common types of plating used on firearms are nickel and silver. Nickel is generally preferred over chrome, because it has less tendency to peel and produces a better looking finish. The silver plating process is more costly than nickel or chrome because it is necessary to polish the silver after plating to bring it to a high gloss.

Probably the most important consideration in restoring a gun is duplicating the original finish. This statement is worth repeating, *because quality restoration depends on this knowledge.* Your gunsmith must know what the original finish on a firearm is before he can select the process to duplicate it. Here are the finishes that appear to have been used on some of the more common candidates for restoration.

Colts. Throughout its history, the Colt factory has used many different finishes on its products. From percussion Colts through very early Single Actions a charcoal blue was used, usually combined with color case hardening. Nickel and silver were used occasionally, either as full finishes, or on backstraps and trigger guards. Around the 1900s, Colt changed

Polishing a Luger barrel extension. Older firearms are noted for their excellent finishes. These fine finishes were produced by skilled craftsmen who painstakingly polished each part to perfection. The time and labor involved were considerable. This kind of effort is also necessary in restoring a firearm, but is further complicated by pitting and trade stampings. Correct polish is the single most important factor in judging the quality of a restored gun. Without proper polish, the value of correct metal coloring will be lost.

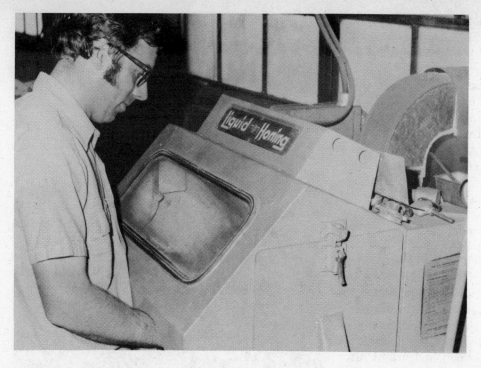

Liquid honing—also known as sand blasting. This operation is used to put a matte finish on steel. Generally this process was not used on commercial firearms until the late 1920s. Sand blasting is useful in removing the buildup of years of rust, prior to polishing.

from charcoal blue to carbonia blue, which produced a "bluer" finish. Carbonia blue was used almost exclusively until World War II. Based on examination of some pre-war Colt automatic pistols, I believe they also used salt blue but only on a limited basis. Nickel plating was available as an optional finish from about 1870 to the present. During the very early 1900s, Colt nickel plating was changed by adding brightners to the nickel bath. This produced a whiter color. After World War II carbonia bluing was eliminated in favor of immersion salt bluing. Case hardening was reintroduced when Colt brought back the Single Action in 1955.

Winchesters. The first of the 1866 Winchesters used a charcoal blue on the barrels. This was later changed to a rust blue. From the 1873 Model up to pre World War II guns, Winchester barrels were almost exclusively rust blued. The actions of all, except Models 54 and 70, were carbonia blued. The finish was darker that that of Colt because they used a higher temperature in the process. From shortly after World War II to the present, all Winchester bluing has been done by the immersion salt process. Color case hardening was used from the first Winchesters to about 1920, but was usually limited to hammers, levers and butt plates. However, until the early 1900s color case hardening was the standard finish for the receivers of Models 1886, 1887 and High- and Low-Wall single shots. Case hardened receivers could also be had by special

Checking surface texture and proof marks. A surface comparator is being used here to determine the correct polishing method needed to duplicate the original surface texture on a pre-war Winchester receiver. When restoring unfamiliar or seldom seen firearms, I generally make a complete inspection on a comparator prior to polishing on unfamiliar guns.

order on 1873, 1876, and 1894 rifles. The color case hardening process used by Winchester was basically the same as Colt; both used pack hardening. Gold, silver and nickel plating were also used by Winchester as decorative finishes.

Lugers. Luger finishes can be divided into two basic categories, rust blue and salt blue. The color of the 1900 Model was a medium blue to blue-black. From the 1902 to the 1908 Commercial, the color was black with a slightly bluish cast. Many well-used Lugers will show a definite blue color due to the aging of the finish. Examination of mint unfired Lugers, however, show the blacker finish previously mentioned. Rust blues were used until the mid 30s, when salt blues were introduced.

The salt blues are of two types, Mauser and Kreighoff. Kreighoff's salt process is more blue and has a high polish, while Mauser's is blue-black. In addition, Lugers prior to the 30s had certain parts such as the trigger, safety, ejectors and toggle pins strawed or temper (heat) blued. Certain areas of rust blued Lugers were also polished bright after bluing. The inside of frames, forks and muzzles were finished in this manner. Of equal importance as the application of the correct finish when restoring Lugers, is duplicating the surface texture of the particular Luger being restored. Tool marks should be replaced if they were removed in polishing. These are usually located around the take-down lever, in the frame ears and on the left side of the frame. The exception to this would be the 1900 Models, which are usually free of tool marks.

Mauser Broomhandles. Mauser used rust and salt blues very similar to those found on Lugers. Rust blues were used until the 30s when they were replaced by the faster salt process. Surface texture duplication, as explained above, applies to the Mauser as well.

Parker Shotguns. The early Parker barrels were browned and showed the Damascus pattern. As fluid steel barrels were developed, browning was eliminated in favor of rust blue. Rust blue remained as the barrel finish until the end of Parker production. All receivers were color case hardened and the colors were typically Parker; i.e., gray, and a light translucent blue with some red.

L. C. Smith Shotguns. The finishes used by L. C. Smith for their barrels were very similar to Parker's. The case hardening colors differ from Parker in that they were more gray and brown, with less blue. Also, the colors were not translucent, but more of a satin texture.

Antique Firearms 1750-1850. Most guns of this era were browned using a variety of formulas which gave many different results. Colors ranged from a plum brown to rust colored brown. In some cases, especially on pistols, barrels were left white. Usually the lockwork and fittings were color case hardened.

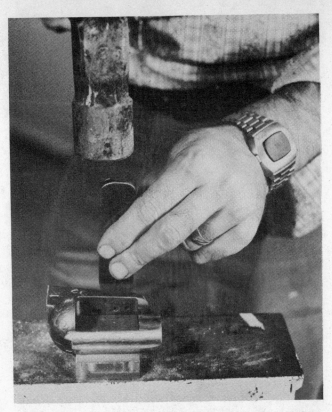

Stamping patent dates on a single action frame. When serious pitting is located near trade stampings it is necessary to polish off the original markings and then restamp or re-engrave them.

It is difficult to list specific finishes for this class of firearms because the finishes varied from maker to maker within the same country, or even within the region he was located.

Gunsmiths who specialize exclusively in *restoring* guns using techniques described in this article are

Rust bluing of a Winchester barrel. This is the old rust and rub method of bluing. Although only one of many methods of coloring metal, it is probably the most used finish on 1860 to World War II fireams.

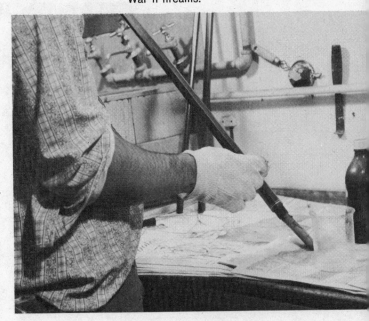

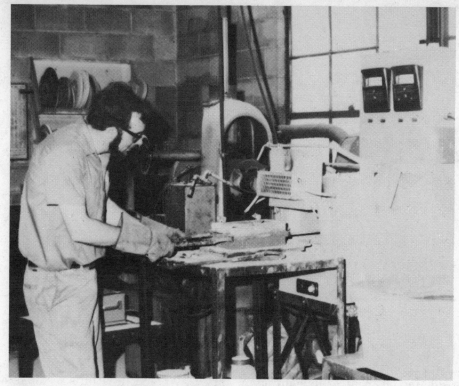

Color case hardening. Shown in this photo is the carbonizing box as it is withdrawn from the furnace. Color hardening is somewhat of an "art," as final colors and patterns cannot be accurately predicted before quenching. Bcause case hardening takes place at a "red heat" certain precautions should be taken to reduce the possibility of warpage. The furnace pictured was ordered with dual electronic temperature controllers. One controller is used as a backup to guard against overheating the part. In addition, close fitting blocks should be used inside receivers to further reduce warpage. Occasionally, after all precautions are taken, warpage still occurs. It is then necessary to refire the working parts.

Recheckering a Parker stock. If stocks have been refinished it is necessary to recut the checkering. It is important to use the same cutter angle as used in the factory. This angle can vary from 60° to 90°. It is also important to recut the diamonds to a point or flat-topped, following the original style.

Milling set up for cutting away Lugers. This set up is also used to machine pitted areas where polishing is impossible or where a tool marked instead of polished surface is needed.

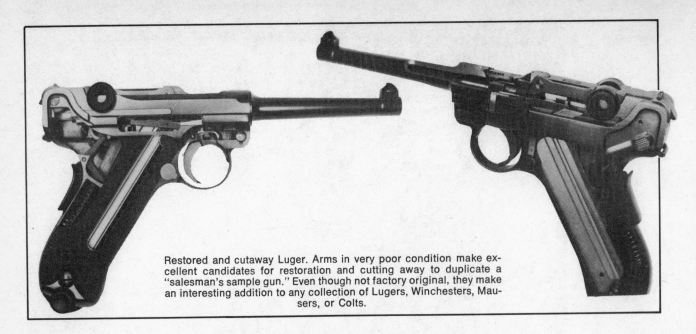

Restored and cutaway Luger. Arms in very poor condition make excellent candidates for restoration and cutting away to duplicate a "salesman's sample gun." Even though not factory original, they make an interesting addition to any collection of Lugers, Winchesters, Mausers, or Colts.

difficult to locate. I personally know of fewer than half a dozen of this type of craftsman. However, there are a number of competent gunsmiths who do restoration as a sideline business, or in addition to general gunsmithing.

Considering the limited number of gunsmiths who claim to be able to restore that old gun, how should a collector select, or even locate, one? The best way is by attending gun shows and requesting recommendations from other collectors, particularly those with collecting interests similar to yours. Advertisements in various firearms publications are often helpful as well. If you would like to solicit information regarding a specific restoration job from a gunsmith once you have his name, by all means do so. Just use consideration in your correspondence, brevity being much appreciated since he makes his living by gun restoration, not letter writing! In addition, it is unfair to ask for a quote on "restoring my Colt S.A. in 'nice' condition, except for the pitting on the left side." The work involved in restoring a particular gun varies considerably according to its condition. The *only* way a gunsmith can quote a price on restoring a specific gun, is by examining it.

Of primary importance to a collector is the opportunity to examine a restorer's work before sending him a valuable firearm for restoration. If this is not possible, a fellow collector's recommendation is usually reliable. Asking a gunsmith to provide references is generally considered bad form, as well as not being very helpful to you. A smart gunsmith would send you names of customers who are his friends. Worse, this practice would be unfair to his customers by making them accessible to strangers.

A good alternative, if the collector is a first time customer without access to a sample piece to inspect, is to send the gunsmith a lower priced firearm to restore. This way the risk is limited, and you are able to inspect the quality of his work from a "before and after" point of view.

Finally, the sticky question of collector ethics arises. When a firearm is restored for the sole purpose of selling it, should the seller inform the buyer that the gun has been restored? In all cases in which the buyer *asks* if the finish is original, he should be informed that the gun was restored to original condition. On the other hand, the author feels that ethics do not require that one hang a sign on a gun reading "restored." If a gun is *correctly* restored, it should stand on its own merit. The buyer will not find it necessary to inquire about its authenticity.

We have presented some definitions, procedures, and problems you may encounter when you consider upgrading a gun in your collection...there is a wide range of possibilities and options open to a collector. The choices are interesting and the results can be gratifying. If you are offered a scarce firearm in poor condition, but at a reasonable price, you need not let condition prohibit its purchase. It can be restored, and if purchase price plus restoration costs are less than current market value you've made a good buy! Just decide what you want done, and find the right man for the job. ●

Editor's Note: Two sources for this highly specialized work that the editor can recommend from personal experience are:
Small Arms Engineering
(John Kaufield)
Box 306
Des Plaines, Illinois 60016
and
J. J. Jenkins
467 Stanford Pl.
Santa Barbara, California 93105

controversial but highly collectable ...

the COLT BUNTLINE

by GEORGE E. VIRGINES

PERHAPS one of the most controversial of the rare Colts in the Single Action Army series is the "Buntline Special." This Colt received its ostentatious name from an oft-repeated legend created by author Stuart N. Lake in his book, "Wyatt Earp, Frontier Marshal." He credits the "Buntline Specials" to a "Ned Buntline," real name Edward Z. C. Judson, a writer of western tales. According to the Earp biography, Ned Buntline presented five special long-barreled Colts to five lawmen; Wyatt Earp, Bat Masterson, Neal Brown, Charlie Bassett, and Bill Tilghman. All had allegedly been law officers in and around Dodge City circa 1876.

This event and the description of the presentation pieces captured the imaginations and challenged researchers of frontier history. The exalted Colts that triggered such controversy were described as: "Five special 45 caliber six-guns of regulation single-action types, but with barrels of a foot long. Each gun had a demountable walnut stock, thumb screw arrangement to fit the weapon for a shoulder piece, a buckskin thong to enable to sling the stock to the belt or saddle horn. The walnut butt of each gun has the word 'Ned' carved deeply in the wood and each was accompanied by a hand tooled holster modeled for the weapon."

Through the years historians and gun collectors

A modern "Colt Buntline Special 45," beautifully engraved by E. C. Prudhomme.

The unique standard frame 16-inch barrel Colt, serial 25922, in the Gaines de Graffenried collection.

have diligently researched this alleged presentation, yet absolutely no evidence has been uncovered to substantiate that these particular "Buntline Specials" ever existed or were presented by Ned Buntline. However, after the publication of Lake's book all long-barreled single action Colts have been tagged "Buntline Specials" by the gun collecting fraternity.

The idea of long barrels on Colt handguns is not restricted to the single actions. Sam Colt installed long barrels on his Paterson models; both holster and belt types were produced with 9½- and 12-inch barrels. The Model 1851 Navy is known to have been produced on special order with barrels of 10 and 12 inches. Even a Colt New House pistol of 32 caliber had been noted with a 10-inch barrel. The Colt Double Action Lightning M1877, the Double Action Frontier and Camp Perry model pistols have been found with long barrels from 8- to 12-inches. But the most publicized and popular long-barreled Colts were the "Buntline Specials."

It was at the Great Exposition of 1876 in Philadelphia that these long-barreled, attachable-stock Colt pistols were first introduced to the public. A rare photograph of Colt's display cases at the Exposition shows a variety of Colt firearms including the first long-barreled Colt Single Action and two different size skeleton stocks.

These new Colts differed from the standard Single Action by having flat-topped frames with a folding leaf rear sight. A variety of front sights was available. Finish was commercial blue with case-hardened frame and hammer; grips were varnished walnut. A large stock-attachment screw replaced the conventional hammer screw in the frame. Original skeleton stocks, now as rare as "Buntline Specials," were made of cast bronze with a nickel plated finish. A hook-on portion fitted into the long hammer screw and a knurled nut was tightened to hold the other hook to the base of the butt. They bore no markings. Skeleton stocks were advertised in London price lists and also by B. Kittredge Company at $5.00.

The serial number range of the first long-barreled Colts was from 28800 to 28830. According to factory records 11 guns were listed with 16-inch barrels, one with 12-inch, three with 10-inch, and two not identified as to barrel length. All were 45 except for two in 44-40, and all were shipped between 1877 and 1884. One of the main wholesalers for Colt was the B. Kittredge Co. of Cincinnati, Ohio, who ordered four 16-inch barreled Colts on December 1, 1877 and in March of 1890 placed another order for five.

The survival rate of these extraordinary Colts is limited and the earliest reported example is in the famous Robert Q. Sutherland collection. This rare Colt, serial 28802, has a 16-inch barrel and is 45 caliber. Complete with the rare skeleton stock, and with original finish, it was purchased from the

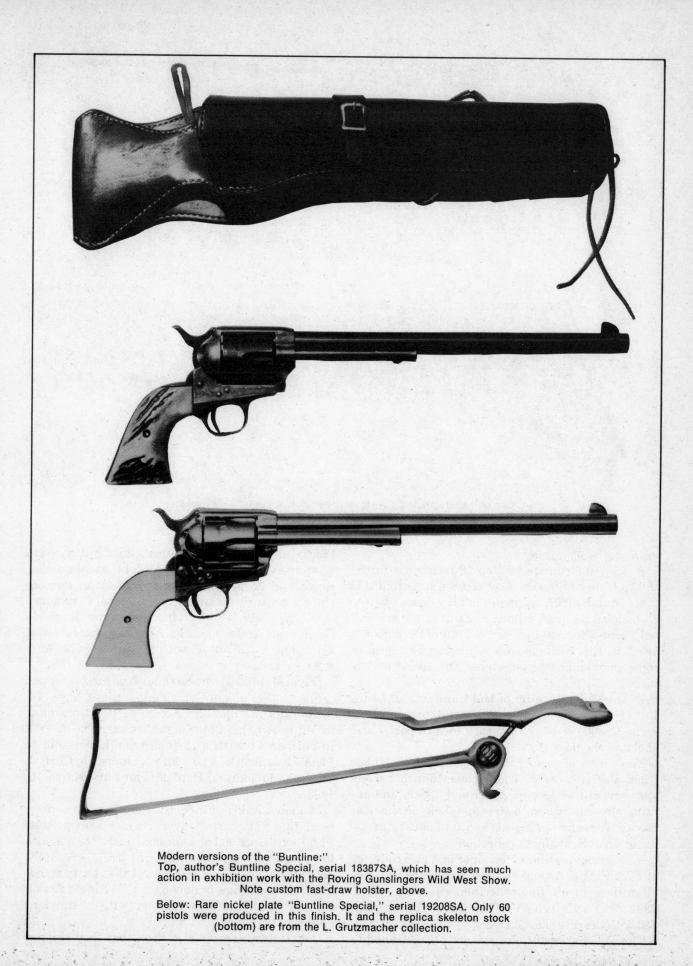

Modern versions of the ''Buntline:''
Top, author's Buntline Special, serial 18387SA, which has seen much action in exhibition work with the Roving Gunslingers Wild West Show. Note custom fast-draw holster, above.

Below: Rare nickel plate ''Buntline Special,'' serial 19208SA. Only 60 pistols were produced in this finish. It and the replica skeleton stock (bottom) are from the L. Grutzmacher collection.

One of the rare original "Buntlines," complete with original skeleton
stock and holster, from the fine John S. DuMont collection.

grandson of Sam Colt.

A very unfortunate flat-top "Buntline" is in the Philip Fisher collection. Colt records state that this piece, serial 28807, originally left the factory with a 16-inch barrel in 45 caliber, and was in the original shipment of four 16-inch barrel Colts of December 1, 1877 to the Kittredge Co. Unfortunate, because some individual later shortened the barrel to 7½-inches!

In the Colt Museum of the Connecticut State Library is an exceptionally fine representative, serial 28809, in 45 caliber, with 16-inch barrel and skeleton shoulder stock.

The rarest of rare, a matched pair of 45 caliber "Specials," also exist. These have 16-inch barrels and consecutive serials, 28818 and 28819, and are complete with custom holsters and skeleton shoulder stocks. These fine pieces were once in noted gun collector John S. duMont's collection.

Mel Torme, popular entertainer and also collector of Colt Single Actions, boasts of a representative "Buntline" in his fine collection. His piece, serial 28822, has a 12-inch 45 caliber barrel and is equipped with the rare skeleton stock.

The long-barreled Colts are not all restricted to

the flat-top frame types. Others exist, but they are all in the Colt Single Action Model P serial number range and do not have a separate serial number block. One such specimen in the Model P standard frame type with a 16-inch barrel is in the Gaines de Graffenried collection. His rare Colt bears serial 25922 and is caliber 45, with the desirable skeleton stock.

David M. Brown, who has one of the most complete caliber collections of Colt Single Actions, has a 12-inch "Buntline Special." According to a Colt letter to Mr. Brown, his Colt Single Action, serial 150873 in caliber 44 with a 12-inch barrel, was sold to Fletcher Jenks Co.—no address; shipped to Chris J. Thorsen, no address; Date of shipment—March 16, 1893.

In their catalog of 1888, the Colt Company advertised that "all barrels over 7½-inches long (cost) $1.00 extra per each additional inch." It has also long been a Colt practice to sell barrels separately. An extremely rare 12-inch barrel that bears standard Colt markings is now on a Colt Single Action that originally left the factory with a standard length barrel.

Colt factory records also show that they shipped

Colt publicity photo showing factory cased set of both Frontier and Buntline Scouts.

Single Actions with 8½-, 9-, and 10-inch barrels. The first 10-inch barreled Colt was shipped on May 20, 1878.

Some unusual Single Action barrel lengths and their calibers that have been noted are as follows:

Serial 82402, cal. 44-40, 10-inch barrel, sold and shipped to Hartley & Graham, N.Y., Sept. 14, 1882.

Serial 143405, cal. 44-40, 10-inch barrel, sold and shipped to Colt San Francisco Agency, Calif., Oct. 15, 1891.

Serial 144267, cal. 38-40, 9-inch barrel, shipped to R. E. Latty & Sons, Dec. 1891.

Serial 130266, cal. 44-40, flat-top, shipped with 9-inch barrel.

Serial 127266, cal. 38-40, 8½-inch barrel, (circa 1884.)

To date there is no record of any pre-World War II long-barrel Colt Single Action ever being shipped from the factory engraved, cased, or as a presentation model. So very few of these unique Colts have come to light that a good possibility still exists for some lucky collector to discover one of these "Buntline Specials."

Through the years the myth of Wyatt Earp and the Buntline Special has become so entrenched that they have almost become inseparable. In 1957 the Colt Company decided rather than fight the myth to join it by producing a Colt Single Action with a 12-inch barrel. They not only re-introduced the long-barreled Colt but adopted the nickname of Ned Buntline's famous variation, marking the left side of the barrel "Colt Buntline Special 45."

All models are available in only 45 caliber; standard is case-hardened Model P type frame, with balance of gun blued with a choice of walnut or ebony checkered black grips. Front sight is fixed. Nickel plate is also available. Original price was $140.

The first serial number for this collector's item is 12207SA, and it was shipped November 20, 1957. Every Buntline barrel is marked "BB" with a number. However the numbers have no relationship to the serial number except to authenticate that the barrel and gun have been recorded as a "Buntline Special."

According to Colt records, between the first year of issue—1957—and April 1973 there have been a total of 3,975 Buntline Specials produced. Only 60 of these were finished in nickel plate. There have been no cased models other than the commemorative specimens and only approximately six that were

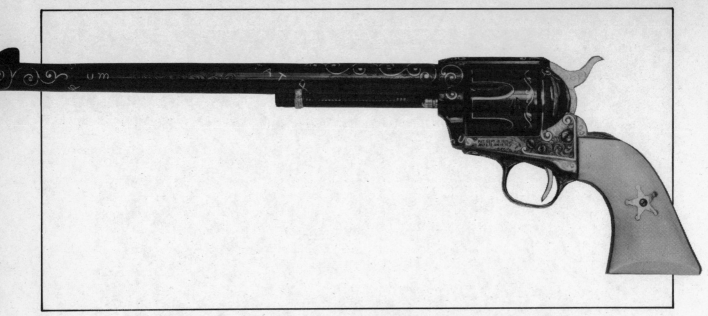

Alvin A. White engraved "Buntline Special," serial 36892SA, in the Colt company collection.

factory engraved.

A one-of-a-kind post-war Buntline with serial 36892SA was specially engraved as a road-show attraction. Herb Glass layed out the designs and master engraver Alvin A. White spent some 270 man hours in scroll-engraving the major parts of the gun. Inlaid in red gold on the backstrap is a rattlesnake and the word "Equalizer." On the barrel and frame are 14 different registered cattle brands. A silver cactus and skull are in high relief on the recoil shield and loading gate, trigger and hammer are gold plated, and the hammer is also engraved. Carved ivory grips, with a bull's head with gold horns on the right side and a gold star badge on the left side, complete the pistol. Several years ago when this fine piece was completed it was valued at $2,750 by Colt. No doubt the value would be much higher today.

The Buntline's long barrel gives plenty of room for artists and engravers to display their skills. The noted gun engraver E. C. Prudhomme embellished a modern version Buntline with his craftsmanship in scrolls and gold inlays. John Mecom, Jr. of Houston, Texas chose a Colt Buntline to be completely engraved "Texas Style" with inlays of gold, silver, and platinum. The history of Texas was the motif chosen, and the engraver spent more than 1,640 hours depicting scenes of the Alamo, Judge Roy Bean's saloon, the cowboy, railroad, covered wagon, oil well, longhorn steer, the State outline, Lone Star Memorial, and Texas State Seal.

One of the first Colt Buntline Specials was presented by Colt November 20, 1957 to Las Vegas Police Officer, Walter R. Earp, Jr., a grand-nephew of Wyatt Earp, by the then President of Colt, Fred A. Roff, Jr. This was a special serial 15349SA, with the inscription "Walter Raymond Earp, Jr." engraved on the back strap.

The new Buntline Special was a natural for a commemorative issue so in 1964 Colt issued 150 Buntline Specials, caliber 45, 12-inch barrels and completely gold plated. The markings on the left side of the barrel hailed it the "Wyatt Earp Buntline Special." It was equipped with black laminated rosewood grips and a gold plated rampant Colt medallion. To add to the attractiveness of this fine piece it was cased in a black finished wood case with a gold Wyatt Earp motif branded into the center of the lid and the gold Colt logo in the lower right. Green velvet lined the bottom and green satin in the lid made the interior most colorful. H. Cook Sporting Goods of Albuquerque, New Mexico was the sponsoring dealer. The original price was $250.

To cement the ties of Wyatt Earp and the "Buntline Special," the Colt factory issued a new version of the Earp commemorative in 1970. This was one of a series of commemoratives relating to famous lawmen of the old West. What made this particular collector's specimen unique was the 16⅛-inch barrel, long enough to satisfy government restrictions on "short-barreled rifles." This rare beauty came in 45 caliber with a case-hardened frame, nickeled hammer and trigger, walnut grips, and the very desirable skeleton shoulder stock. It was equipped with a fixed rear sight and an enlarged, squared-off, front sight. Barrel markings were "Lawmen Series— Wyatt Earp" and only 500 were produced. Original price $395.

The mate to the above Colt is the smaller Frontier Scout, in 22 Long Rifle with 12-inch barrel. The quantity produced was 3000, and original price $125. Barrel markings are the same as the 45. Each gun was offered cased in wood covered with black leatherette. The cover is imprinted in gold with a scene from the famed "Gunfight at the OK Corral." The case interiors were lined with red velvet on the bottom and red satin on the top. Accompanying each commemorative is a booklet, "Wyatt Earp" by E. B. Mann.

Listed in Colt advertisements from 1961 through 1964 was another "Buntline Special," this new version called the "New Frontier Single Action" revolver. It is a flat top with adjustable rear sight and ramp style front sight. The barrel is 12-inches and in caliber 45 only. Finish is a high-gloss Colt Royal Blue with case-hardened frame and walnut grips embellished with a gold-plated rampant Colt medallion. This model is in the same serial number series as the New Frontier Models and bears the prefix letters "NF" with the serial number. Original price $175. Production records for the New Frontier Buntline Special from 1962 to 1967 show only 48 were made.

To illustrate that imitation is still the highest form of flattery, a number of other gun manufacturers who make copies of the Single Action added the "Buntline Special" to their list of available models. Even Colt offers their scaled down version of the Single Action, the 22 caliber Frontier Scout, in "Buntline" versions with 7½-, 9½-, and 12-inch barrels.

In conclusion one must become convinced that no amount of research or documentation will ever diminish the myth of the "Buntline Special," but that does not lessen the desirability of these unusual pistols. ●

The gold plated Wyatt Earp Commemorative with 12-inch barrel. Only 150 produced.

"COLT BUNTLINE SPECIAL .45"

Appendix I—YEAR-BY-YEAR-PRODUCTION

Colt Buntline Special 45 Single Action production.

Year	Blued	Nickel Plated
1957	595	2
1958	1644	7
1959	277	27
1960	46	6
1961	50	8
1962	48	10
1963	10	
1964	30	
1965	62	
1966	95	
1967	47	
1968	46	
1969	143	
1970	129	
1971	295	
1972	313	
1973	85	
total production to April 1973: 3,975		

"COLT BUNTLINE SPECIAL .45"

Appendix II—Commemorative Models

Wyatt Earp Buntline Special Commemorative —1964 Production.
Caliber 45—Barrel length 12 inches.
Quantity—150
Separate serial number range from 0001-WE to 0150-WE.

Wyatt Earp Commemorative—Lawmen Series —1970 Production.
Caliber 45—Barrel length 16⅛ inches
Quantity—500
Separate serial number range from 1-WYE to 500-WYE.

Colt Buntline Special .45 Single Action New Frontier Model Production figures

Year	Blued	Nickel Plated
1962	23	0
1963	20	0
1964	0	0
1965	0	0
1966	4	0
1967	1	0
Total production: 48		

Hidden Values in English Guns

by CONRAD SUNDEEN

ONLY RECENTLY has the gun collecting fraternity begun to recognize the true value of British firearms. This is not to say that their interesting aspects have gone unrecognized but their value has, and there are reasons for this. First of all the American collector has cherished his own—the Revolutionary, the pioneer, the Civil War, the frontier weapons,—all tools of their times that have excited the imagination and won the dollar recognition they deserved. Secondly, the American collector feels that little outside his native shores can match the history, interest, and pure *American* quality of guns made and used in the United States. Both statements have truth. They explain the tremendous interest in and demand for American historical weapons, and the extravagant prices paid for fine examples. All this is as it should be, and this influence has been felt across the world. Because we

Part of the author's collection of British guns. Storing the guns muzzle down prevents any oil in the actions from seeping into the stocks. Note the collection of gun-makers signs hanging above the rack—a nice touch.

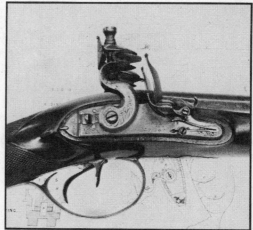

Double-barrel 20-bore flintlock manufactured in 1770 by "Twigg." Note the unusual shape of the trigger guard and the long, near-vertical frizzens.

This single-barrel percussion rifled musket in 12 bore is one of 22 such pieces built by Purdey in the 1830s. Even after years of hard use the fit of wood to metal is still excellent. The lock plate appears simple and uncluttered.

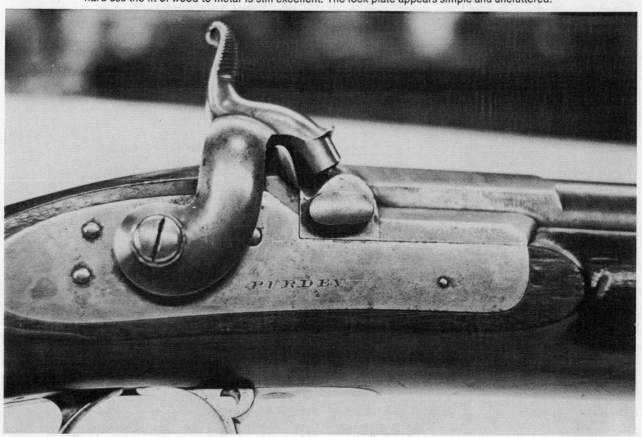

This double-barrel black powder express rifle was made by ''Manton & Co. London & Calcutta'' during the 1880s. Workmanship is impeccable. Note the unusual shape of the lockplate, graceful lines of the stock and under-lever.

A double-barrel black powder express rifle built by J. Beattie & Son, London in the 1860s.

''Snap Action'' double-barrel 12 bore game gun by James Purdey & Sons, London was made in 1868. Note the unusual barrel latch system incorporated into the trigger guard from which Purdey derived the name for this arrangement.

collected, because we valued certain things, so did later arrivals on the gun collecting scene value these same things. The result is that in a sense we have been distracted, have failed to accord the British gunmaker his proper recognition. And, you may say, it's too late—English guns are too expensive now.

They're not! They're good investments and certain to retain their value. Here's why.

Britain was the center and earliest winner of the fruits brought by the Industrial Revolution. The British made mechanical engineering a science, shaped it to compatibility with their craft heritage,

Unusual double-barrel 12 bore "Bar-In-Wood" top-lever game gun by James Purdey & Sons, London. Name for this piece comes from the fact that the frame is made of wood. Entire breech area is extensively engraved.

expanded it with their business knowledge and almost captured the world. In the best years, from 1750 to 1914, Britain led the world in quality manufacturing; only America challenged her with new techniques of automatic machinery and mass production. And this period was the heyday of the British gunmaker. He had the craft-apprentice system, the engineering *and* the market for his wares. This last was vital to the maker of fine guns because they were costly luxuries, to be sold only in a wealthy society. British society was wealthy and her gunmakers prospered, always in competion with themselves and always developing their skills to produce the absolute best that time and effort could produce. The British gunmaker reached his peak about 1900, when newer luxuries began to cut into his market, when the world began to shrink and when social changes robbed him of the skilled apprentice who had spent 60 hours a week making

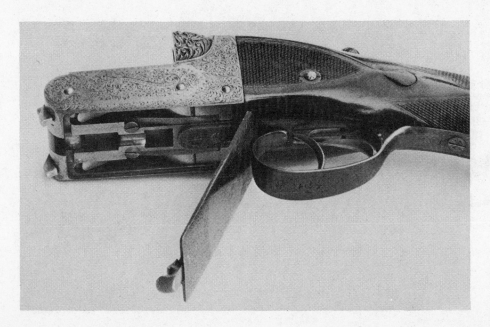

Double-barrel sporting rifle made by Westley Richards, Birmingham, with a unique bottom inspection plate and fixed locks. Manufactured in 1910.

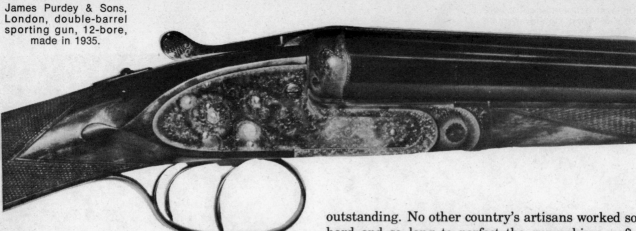

James Purdey & Sons, London, double-barrel sporting gun, 12-bore, made in 1935.

his product at very low hourly cost. Times have changed but no better guns have been made since. Only modern metallurgy makes a current English gun at all superior to its 1900 sister.

To the collector a fine gun is part design, part art and part hardware. On all counts the British gun is

outstanding. No other country's artisans worked so hard and so long to perfect the gunmaking craft. They succeeded. England had dozens of makers, all polishing their skills simultaneously, and the result is a wealth of superior quality firearms. Many, many of these remain for us today because they were always expensive, generally treasured and usually well cared for. As a result today's gun collector has an interesting area to explore. So does the shooter, because most of those gunmakers' output was designed for sporting use. The customer of the 1800s was prosperous—often a large land holder—and the guns he wanted were for sport shooting or hunting. Today these same guns have utility; they can be used on the American scene—for birds, for game and for competition.

Two other factors are pertinent. First is the fact that in pure numbers the bulk of the English guns available today were made before World War I. Those made since represent only a small portion of the total. And the total in existence is relatively fixed, limited by the few additions made at extreme cost since World War I. Second, is the world-wide awakening to fine craftsmanship. As we become more industrialized and more automated we cherish

Double-barrel sporting rifle manufactured in 1929 by Holland & Holland, London, with hand-detachable sidelocks.

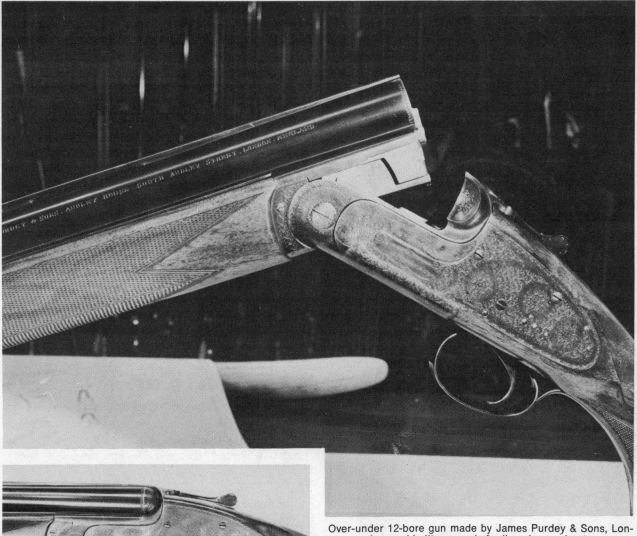

Over-under 12-bore gun made by James Purdey & Sons, London, and built expressly for live pigeon shoots.

Purdey's efforts were not confined to the long-gun field as is evidenced by this double-barrel 450-bore "Howdah" pistol, manufactured in 1874.

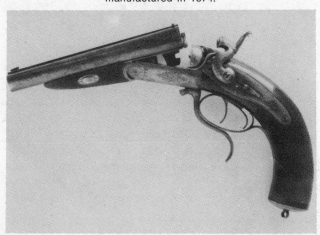

the craftsmanship of the past more and more. And this means that collectors who are not gun enthusiasts now search for and collect guns of quality workmanship.

To sum this all up it comes to these points: 1. The British gunmaker produced a superior product. It had design, craftmanship and utility. 2. These gunmakers' products are limited in number and that number will not be appreciably changed. 3. The public recognition of "craft," and the expanding ranks of collectors indicate an increasing interest in and demand for these British firearms.

Last but not least is the declining value of money which directs savings to "real" merchandise, the merchandise of art, antique, craft. Fine British firearms fall into all of these categories. They cannot avoid being more sought after, more valuable in time and therefore represent collecting pleasure *plus* investment attraction. They will achieve collector recognition, but before they do you can still buy interesting examples at reasonable prices with confidence that your money is safe. ●

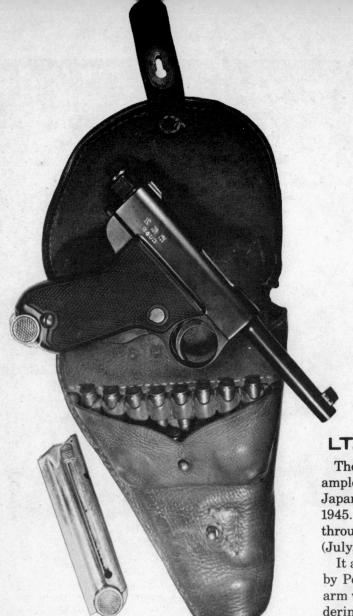

Japanese Military Arms
Part I
PISTOLS

by

LT. COL. BILL BROPHY (RET.)

THE MOST COMPLETE and finest collection of Japanese small arms in the United States is at the Infantry Museum at Fort Benning. The greatest part of this collection was donated to the U.S. Government by Major William B. Mozey; the Mozey collection is the most outstanding attraction among 2,500 or more items and artifacts on display at "The Home of the Infantry" Museum.

As a young man Major Mozey was introduced to military weapons through the war relics and souvenirs brought back by the military veterans in his family. By asking questions about type, origin, place of manufacture, quality and development, he found a general lack of technical information among the souvenir owners. His inherent inquisitiveness and interest for learning more about weapons resulted in his acquiring some pieces of his own. A search of the available literature on the subject of Japanese weapons revealed little or nothing that would satisfy his questions. This became a challenge and Major Mozey studied Japanese weapons and accumulated a wealth of knowledge.

The Mozey collection contains at least one example of each of the standard types and models of Japanese hand and shoulder arms up to the year 1945. It spans the early Japanese matchlocks through the late production guns of World War II (July, 1945).

It appears that firearms were introduced to Japan by Portuguese sailors in the mid 1500s. This early arm was the snapping matchlock which uses a smoldering wick lowered into a flash pan for ignition. Because of the Japanese stubborn isolationist stand, some of the refinements to this system of ignition never did enter Japan. It is not uncommon to find Oriental matchlocks that were made in the mid-1800s, while the rest of the world was making a major breakthrough in manufacturing of ammunition and firearms and successful breech-loading types were in the making. The Japanese were slow getting started, yet caught up quickly by adopting the good features of the Dutch, French, and British arms. As master copiers they were able to fight the Chinese and Russians with fair arms, and thanks to their experiences in China and Manchuria, were able to make additional improvements in their weaponry.

The Japanese system of model identification is not to give model numbers to their weapons, but to indicate model designation by the character "Shiki" which means type; it is not, therefore, technically correct to call Japanese weapons through World War II by a model number. To figure out the year of adoption of a Japanese weapon isn't always easy,

Above: "Baby" Nambu 7mm with original holster, spare magazine.

A very rare pair of consecutively numbered "Baby" Nambus from The Infantry Museum collection.

even if you know the type number. They changed the system several times, and in the interest of accuracy, this system should be explained. The first system was to use the year of reign of the Emperor as the type number. An example is the Type 38 rifle, which was adopted in the 38th year of the reign of Emperor Meiji (1905). This system changed with Emperor Taisho in 1925, and a second system became effective to mark Japanese ordnance. The new method was to use the last two digits of the year since the founding of the Japanese Empire in 660 B.C. Therefore, the Japanese year is our year plus 660. For example: our year 1939 would be their year 2599, and ordnance adopted in that year would be marked Type 99. Type 99 7.7mm rifle was adopted during this system. The third system became effective in Japanese year 2600 (our year 1940) when they started using only the last digit of their calendar year. A good example of this last system is the Type 2, 7.7mm paratrooper rifle which was adopted in their year 2602 (1942).

The first Japanese handguns were matchlocks which differed from the matchlock rifles only in the

Three versions of Type Nambu grip safety pistols. From top: 1) Rare first version of 8mm cut for shoulder stock. Note trigger shape and fixed lanyard loop. 2) Later model of 8mm. Note low line of sight, loose lanyard loop and aluminum finger piece of magazine. 3) Scarce "Baby" Nambu. This 7mm pistol is small version of 8mm except for the fixed rear sight. Do not confuse these with Type 14 (1925).

Showing Tokyo Gas & Electric markings (left) and the Tokyo Arsenal (right), 7mm "Baby" Nambus are well-made, much desired by collectors.

Top: Type 14 (1925) 8mm pistol produced at Tokyo Arsenal in May, 1928. Note small trigger guard. Below: May, 1945 production Type 14 (1925) pistol made at Nagoya Arsenal with larger trigger guard for use with gloved hand and a magazine friction spring in the lower front of the grip which prevents the magazine dropping out if the magazine catch is accidentally pushed. Note the very poor finish and simplified construction of this late model.

Numbered consecutively, these Type 14 (1925) 8mm pistols were made at the Nagoya Arsenal in 1945 and liberated by a G.I. in this unfinished state.

length of butt and barrel. Many matchlock arms were ornately inlaid with precious metals and became family heirlooms to be handed down from generation to generation. Some date back to the 16th Century, when they were first introduced into Japan by the Portuguese.

The first service pistol adopted was the Type 26 (1893) 9mm revolver, a double action, top break gun. It was originally made for the cavalry and was issued to many non-commissioned officers as late as 1940-45. It has 6 chambers, weighs 32 ounces, and is 9½ inches long. The Type 26 is crudely made and correct alignment of the cylinder with the barrel is almost impossible. This top-break revolver has frequently been identified as a copy of earlier Smith & Wesson revolvers.

The Japanese would have done well to copy more than the top-break system, as the Type 26 pistol is quite inferior to military revolvers of the world, and Smith & Wessons in particular.

Its 9mm rimmed cartridge has a lead bullet and develops a muzzle velocity of about 750 fps. The cartridges are quite rare today and were never made outside of Japan. No other handgun was ever chambered for this round.

A Colonel Kijiro Nambu created and developed

the pistol that replaced the Type 26 revolver. Well designed and made, his "Type Nambu" 8mm semi-automatic, recoil operated, magazine-fed pistol was introduced about 1914.

There are always exceptions to rules, and this pistol is one of them. It was not standardized as a service pistol and does not have a numerical type designation. Apparently it was made for commercial sale. The ideographs marked on the pistol read "Type Nambu" after its inventor Colonel Nambu, later General, who still later operated the Nambu

of World War II. It has a bottlenecked, semi-rimmed case, using a round-nosed, jacketed bullet of 102-gr. with a muzzle velocity of 950 fps.

Why the Japanese military chose this mediocre cartridge will probably never be known. It might have been a desire to have a 100 per cent Japanese developed pistol and cartridge to "show the world." There are a number of military pistol cartridges that would have been a better choice. The 7.63mm Mauser (30 Mauser) with an 86-gr. bullet at 1,420 fps would have been better, as would the 7.65mm Luger

Type 94 (1934) 8mm pistol (top) made at Nagoya Arsenal in December, 1937, and later Type 94 (1934) made during wartime in May, 1945.

Pair of consecutively numbered Type 94 (1934) pistols made by Nambu Arms Co. for Tokyo Arsenal in Dec., 1937.

Arms Company. The "Type Nambu" pistol has been referred to as the "Japanese Luger." The only similarity between this pistol and the German Luger is in the external appearance. It has a completely different locking system, incorporating a separate locking block which swings up from the receiver and locks securely into the underside of the breechblock. In conflict with general opinion, these early Nambus were well finished, show good workmanship and were excellently designed semi-automatic pistols. The gun weighs about 30 ounces, is about 9 inches long and the magazine holds 8 cartridges.

With the introduction of this pistol the Japanese standardized the 8mm cartridge for service use, and this cartridge was used in all pistols through the end

(30 Luger) with a 93-gr. bullet at 1,250 fps, or better than any, the 9mm Parabellum.

The early "Type Nambu," or "Grandpa" Nambu, was cut at the rear of the pistol grip to accept a wooden combination shoulder-stock/holster. Few of these shoulder-stocked pistols were made, and they are rare today. Examples of the shoulder stock occur in some U.S. collections, and some of these came from an order delivered to Siam in the early 'teens. Later Nambus, commonly called the "Papa" Nambu, are not cut for the stock.

A scaled down version of the "Type Nambu" pistol,

in 7mm caliber, was made about the same time. This pistol, commonly referred to as the "Baby Nambu," is of excellent workmanship and finish. It weighs about 23 ounces, is 6¾ inches long and the magazine holds 7 cartridges.

After handling a large number of Japanese weapons it is easy to recognize the "Baby Nambu" as the prestige weapon of modern Japanese ordnance. Like the "Papa Nambu," it was not a standardized service pistol and was not given a Type designation. Japanese officers were required to purchase their own handguns. The finish, workmanship, the special cartridge, the quality holsters and the fact that only about 6,000 guns were manufactured support the theory that the Baby Nambu was made for high

hands—the subsequent production had an ugly but practical, oval-shaped trigger guard. The workmanship of the Type 14 (1925) is usually poorer than in the earlier Nambu, and became worse as World War II pressure increased. The collection displays the various production changes, graphically showing the reduction in quality and workmanship as the war years advanced.

Available records do not reflect the reason for, or individuals behind, the next pistols displayed. Colonel Nambu had certainly developed well designed pistols in his "Type Nambu" and Type 14 (1925). Production by Tokyo, Nagoya, Kokura and Koishigawa arsenals, as well as Nambu Arms, Kayoba Manufacturing and Tokyo Gas and Electric

This very rare Type 1 (1941) 7.65mm Japanese semi-automatic was made around 1943, used by officers of a high rank.

ranking military officers and political figures. A rare pair of consecutively numbered "Baby Nambus" are displayed in the Mozey collection.

The 7mm Nambu is a bottle-necked, semi-rimmed cartridge with a 55 gr. jacketed bullet that has an MV of 1,050 fps.

The "Type Nambu" pistol was in production until a simplified, mass produced version was adopted as the standard service pistol in 1925—designated the Type 14 (1925). The major changes in this new pistol were: simplified grooved wooden grips; a round, grooved cocking piece, and the recoil spring housing, grip safety and leaf rear sight were eliminated. Until the mid-30s the trigger guard was round. Experience in cold regions dictated the need to enlarge the trigger guard to accommodate gloved

Companies had demonstrated their ability to produce weapons of sound design and good workmanship, yet an inferior and poorly made pistol designated the Type 94 (1934) was standardized as a second service pistol. It fires the 8mm cartridge, is recoil operated, weighs 27 ounces, is 7⅛ inches long and the magazine holds 6 rounds.

A civilian version of this pistol had been on the commercial market and exported to South America before standardization. It is speculated that during the build up of hostilities with China (1930s) the availability of the tooling and commercial production of this pistol brought about standardization, based purely on availability, not design.

The overall size of this pistol is smaller than the Type 14 with a ridiculous configuration and im-

Japanese officers had to pay for the pistols they used. This DWM 7.65mm Browning (.32 ACP) semi-automatic is such a gun. The holster was made at the Nagoya Arsenal and is made with good leather, workmanship.

unknown good points it might have. The weapon can be fired prior to complete locking of the breech, and when the striker is cocked the sear can be accidentally depressed from the outside without touching the trigger.

At the start of World War II, the Japanese adopted a 7.65mm semi-automatic pocket pistol for use by officers. It was designated Type 1 (1941) and had only limited production. A fine example of this scarce gun is included in the Mozey collection.

The fact that the Japanese officer had to buy his own pistol unquestionably resulted in various demands and requirements from "top-brass." The wearing of a pistol by officers in many countries is considered a badge of authority rather than an item of utilitarian use. The higher the rank, the more important quality and appearance would be, which is supported by the use of fine pistols like the DWM (original maker of the Luger) 7.65mm (32 ACP) pocket pistol, fitted with a holster by Nagoya Arsenal, for use by general officers.

You can determine the officer's rank by the type pistol he carried.

General Officer – "Baby Nambu" or quality foreign commercial

Colonel – "Type Nambu" or Type 1 (1941)

Lt. Col., Major – Early Type 14 (1925)

Captain – Early Type 94 (1934) or late Type 14 (1925)

Lieutenant – Late Type 14 (1925) and 94 (1934)

NCO – Type 26 (1893) revolver

Somehow the Nambu pistols, their development, and their history have been neglected by arms students. Most collectors have glossed over them, and, in many cases, Japanese pistols were unjustly labeled "junk"... except the Baby Nambu which is justly famed for its scarcity. ●

practical grip shape. The grip is too small and poorly placed – even for the small Japanese hand. The pistol has a strange appearance and is certainly "different" from any other military pistol of the world.

Besides its poor lines and shape, the Type 94 has safety deficiencies that would over-ride any

At far left is a 7mm rimless bottleneck cartridge used in "Baby" Nambu; next is an 8mm semi-rim, bottleneck, low-velocity (950 fps) cartridge for Type Nambu (1914), Type 14 (1925) and Type 94 (1934) pistols; third is 9mm rimmed, lead bullet cartridge to be used in Type 26 (1893) cavalry revolver, last is 45 ACP (M1911 Ball) U.S. cartridge shown for comparison.

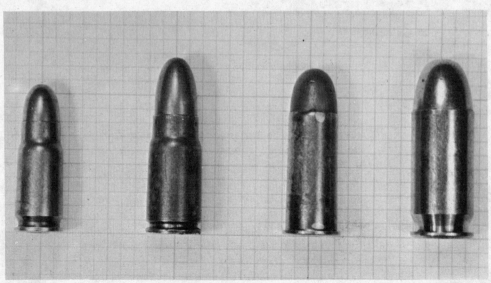

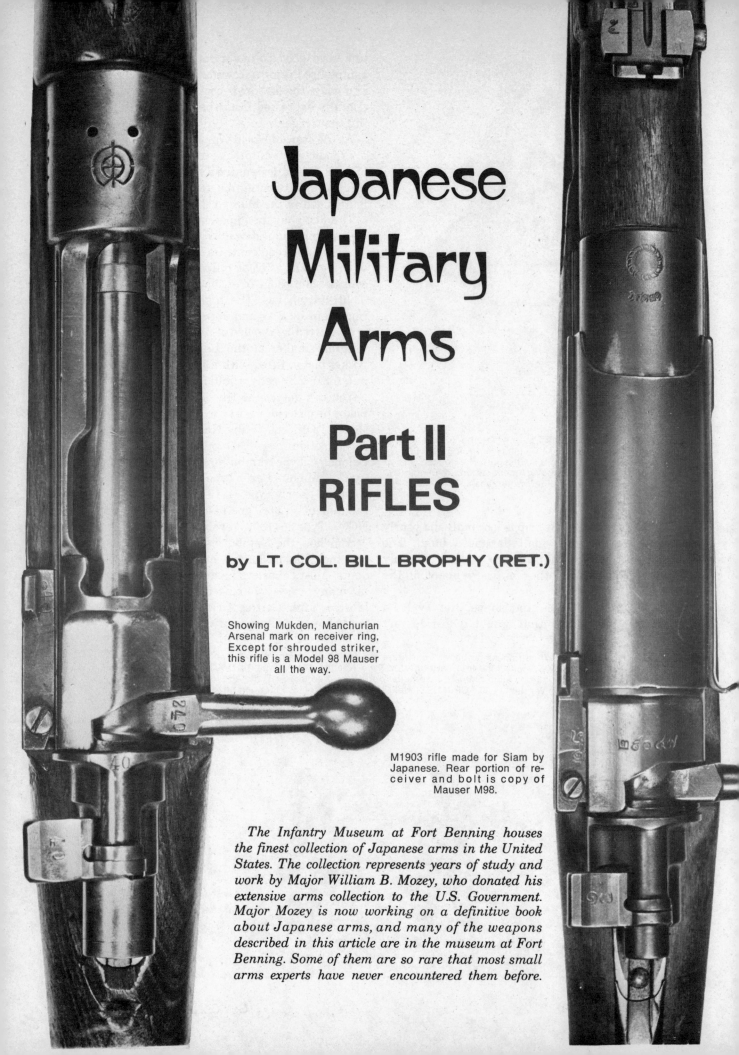

Japanese Military Arms

Part II
RIFLES

by LT. COL. BILL BROPHY (RET.)

Showing Mukden, Manchurian Arsenal mark on receiver ring, Except for shrouded striker, this rifle is a Model 98 Mauser all the way.

M1903 rifle made for Siam by Japanese. Rear portion of receiver and bolt is copy of Mauser M98.

The Infantry Museum at Fort Benning houses the finest collection of Japanese arms in the United States. The collection represents years of study and work by Major William B. Mozey, who donated his extensive arms collection to the U.S. Government. Major Mozey is now working on a definitive book about Japanese arms, and many of the weapons described in this article are in the museum at Fort Benning. Some of them are so rare that most small arms experts have never encountered them before.

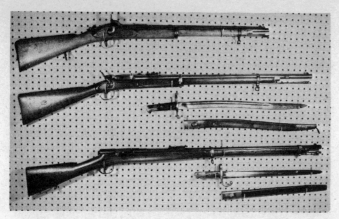

Top: Copy of Westley-Richards breech loading carbine. Middle: Copy of Enfield musket converted to breechloader. Bottom: Single-shot Type 18, 11mm Murata.

Top: Type 22 (Pattern B) with original bayonet and scabbard. Middle: Rare Murata Type 22 8mm bolt-action, tube loading, repeater. Bottom: Type 22 carbine.

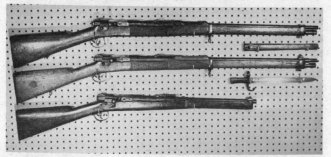

Left: Type 30 (1897), 6.5mm Arisaka bolt action, magazine-fed long rifle. Right: Type 30 (1897) carbine is the same as Type 30 except barrel length. The bayonet, scabbard and frog shown here is used on both guns.

THE FIRST JAPANESE service rifle was invented by Major Murata Tsuneyoshi. This was a copy of the French Chassepot rifle and is identified as the Type 3 (1880) Murata, 11mm single shot rifle. With some minor modifications it became the Type 22 (1889) rifle, which is an 8mm version of the 11mm rifle, and has a tubular magazine holding eight cartridges. The Type 22 carbine differs from the rifle by having a shorter barrel and stock.

It was the war with China (1894) that made the Japanese realize that there were some deficiencies in their weapons. Colonel Arisaka was named to head a commission which brought into being the Type 30 (1897) Arisaka Rifle. This rifle copied the turning bolt of the Mauser design, and loaded, with a clip from above, a new 6.5mm cartridge.

With some additional improvements a slightly modified version of the Type 30 rifle became the Type 35 (1902) rifle. Type 35 rifles are very rare and this collection displays an original and unmodified piece that has a squeeze-type rear sight not identified with any other Japanese weapon.

Colonel Arisaka also gave his name to the Type 38 (1905) Arisaka 6.5mm rifle which incorporated features of the Mauser rifle and the Type 35 rifle. It is considered by many arms students as a leading design for simplicity, and is one of the strongest rifle actions when in good condition.

It is not always easy to recognize the good from the bad among Japanese weapons, as they have not produced many weapons of obvious quality. The poor finish on metal and wood during WW II and the cheap looking stock, dovetailed from two pieces of poor wood, don't help the impression.

The general opinion of Japanese weapons has been developed from the hoard of late WW II production arms that came back as souvenirs from the Pacific Theater with our returning servicemen. Most of these weapons had the scars of battle upon them, and when it was found that some had cast iron receivers, the "junk" label became fixed. Strangely, the pre-war Japanese weapons are well made and utilize one of the strongest breeching systems used in military rifles. When the bolt of the 1905 and after rifle is closed with a round in the chamber, the head of the case is surrounded by metal. If a cartridge case ruptures, the escaping gas is contained or diverted away, doing little or no damage. During tests after WW II, it was found that this system of gas sealing the chamber made it literally impossible to blow up well-made Japanese rifles, while most U.S. and European weapons were destroyed under identical conditions. Many of today's commercial U.S. rifles use a modified form of this system.

One thing must be said for Japanese arms: they worked under adverse conditions and gave the best

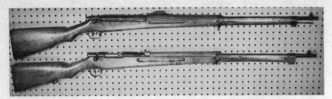

Top: Rare Type 35 (1902) 6.5 magazine-fed Arisaka rifle. Slightly modified, it became Type 38 in 1905. Bottom: 1902/45 had '02 receivers and '45 components.

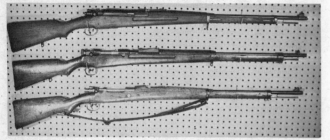

Top: Siamese 8mm M1903 rifle from Tokyo Arsenal. Middle: Unknown Jap. model made for Siam. Bottom: Jap. Mauser M1898 marked Mukden Arsenal, Manchuria.

Type 38 Pressure Test rifles. Top: Tokyo Arsenal, serial 1. Middle: Type 38 from Nagoya Arsenal, serial 1. Bottom: Type 99 (1939), Kokura Arsenal, serial 3.

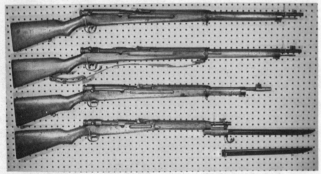

Type 38 Arisakas are 6.5mm, magazine-fed, bolt action. From top: Tokyo Arsenal long rifle, WW II long rifle, Tokyo Arsenal short rifle, and Tokyo Arsenal carbine.

Top: Type 38 carbine hit by shell fragment, "sporterized" by Gen. Stilwell. Below: Rare Type 38 carbines modified for paratroopers by hinging the stock.

fighting men in the world many a tough time. By our standards they look like they are made from inferior material, although most were well designed and effective.

The Type 38 6.5mm rifle came in three different barrel lengths: the infantry, medium and carbine versions, and were official Japanese rifles from 1906 to 1945. The Type 38 6.5mm carbine was in wide use, principally by engineer and transportation troops, and is only different from the rifle in having a short carbine-length barrel. A few Type 38 carbines were modified to paratrooper configuration by hinging the stock at the pistol grip — a rare conversion seldom encountered today.

Different variations of all these weapons are displayed as well as examples made at different arsenals. Most weapons are displayed with their bayonets, slings, muzzle covers etc. which contribute to the complete and authentic display.

General Joseph W. Stillwell's personal Type 38 carbine is on display in the collection. The stock was whittled by the General and customized to his liking. He didn't help its appearance a great deal, but neither did the old campaign hat he wore help his appearance, except to the troops of the China-Burma-India Campaign.

A special carbine, Type 44 (1911), was developed for the cavalry. It differs from the Type 38 carbine in having a permanently attached bayonet which, when not in use, folds under the fore-end. This carbine was originally to be used by mounted troops. During WW II mounted troops were not important, and, when the pressure was on the Japanese logistic system, the cavalry carbines were used where needed.

The sniper rifle of most countries is generally a warmed-over service rifle with a telescopic sight installed. The Japanese were no different. The Type 38 rifle, when equipped with a telescope on the left side of the rifle, a turned-down bolt, a wire monopod pivoted at the lower band and with a little better finish, became the Type 97 (1937), 6.5mm sniper rifle.

Examples of some of the rare weapons not available to public viewing, except in this collection, are the Type 35 (1902) rifles made by Japan, modified to take the 7.9 x 57 cartridge and sold to Russia; a rifle locally designated the Type 1902/45, utilizing a receiver that had been in storage since 1902 and made into rifles during the last ditch effort in 1945; 7mm rifles that were made in Japan and sold to Mexico; rifles similar to the Type 38 (1905) that were made for Siam and carry the National Crest or the Crest of the Royal Army on the receivers; numerous training rifles not designed to fire live ammunition, made to conserve material and time during the last years of World War II; and scarce models of a 6.5mm rifle made by Beretta which used Italian Model

1891 type receivers and bolts and Mauser type magazines.

There are a number of Type 99 (1939) 7.7mm rifles. This rifle is a variation of the Type 38 rifle which some writers refer to as an improved version. The bolt is not as smooth in operation and many parts are stampings. This rifle was not in general use at the start of WW II, but as it became available was used side-by-side with the Type 38 6.5mm rifle until the end of the war. The 7.7mm cartridge was developed as a result of combat experience with the 6.5mm during war with China and Russia when the light cartridge was found to be inadequate. The Japanese wanted to standardize ammunition with the already adopted (1932) 7.7mm semi-rimmed heavy machine-gun cartridge.

As the pressure of WW II increased, Japanese weapons suffered in quality. The Type 99 rifle was simplified during 1940-45 and various production changes can be found. Some of the basic changes were: elimination of the monopod, no cleaning rod in fore-end, fixed aperture rear sights, elimination of the handguard, wooden buttplate, rough machining, cast iron receivers, bores not chrome-plated and tangs made part of the receiver.

The Navy had a special Type 99 rifle with a cast iron receiver, built much different than the receiver of the standard Type 99 rifle. The use of cast iron in this rifle was due to the shortage of manpower and material. It was adopted as an expedient to produce weapons faster at a time when heavy bombing of industrial centers and military losses were having an effect on the production capability of the whole country. These special Type 99 rifles are marked with the navy anchor and can be identified primarily by rough, unmachined surfaces. The barrel breech has an integral extension that contains the locking recesses for the bolt lugs. Thus the receiver does not need a great deal of strength, as it only supports the bolt and magazine with the pressure of the burning powder being held by the barrel and bolt. This system is used in various weapons of the world today. The M60 machine gun, now standard in the U.S. Army, uses the principle very successfully.

In 1939 the Type 99 rifle was also adopted for sniper use by installation of a telescope. The power of the telescope was increased from 2.5x of the Type 97 to 4x, and the combination designated the Type 99 sniper rifle.

The Type 99 service rifle was modified for paratrooper use by altering the receiver and fitting a barrel with interrupted threads which permitted easy disassembly into two compact pieces — the barrel and the stocked action. These early modified rifles are scarce, as few were made and the system was soon changed to a tapered wedge held in place with a screw. The wedge system of take-down was simpler to manufacture and made a better union of

Close-up Type 38 Pressure Test rifle from the Tokyo Arsenal showing massive breach ring that houses piston and crusher for determining chamber pressure.

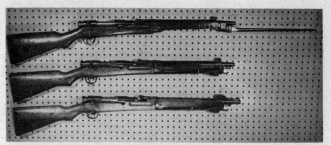

Three variations of Type 44 (1911) cavalry carbine; Top: With short front band. Middle: With long front band. Bottom: With long front band plus extension.

Top: Type 97 (1937) 6.5mm sniper rifle, developed from Type 38, with 2.5x scope installed. Middle: Type 99 (1939) 7.7mm sniper rifle with 4x scope. Bottom: Late Type 99. Different mount, separate from scope.

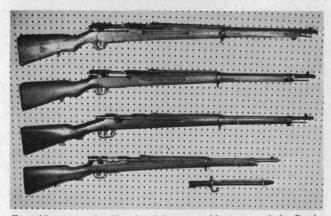

Two rifles at top are Naval training guns. Most can only be fired with blanks. Third is 6.5mm Japanese rifle by Beretta. Bottom is child's training rifle.

Cutaway of Type 38 rifle. Striker spring, floorplate, follower, and follower spring are missing.

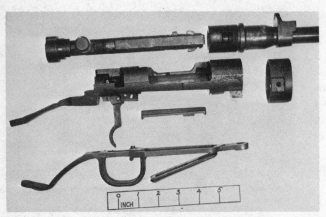

Special Type 99 action shows barrel and bolt relationship. Locking recess is visible in barrel extension and locking lugs on bolt are in locked position.

Special Type 99 receiver shows barrel end and locking recesses for bolt lugs to rotate into.

Breech end of special Type 99 rifle barrel. This gun, not to be confused with Navy training rifles, is identified by Navy anchor, steel barrel extension.

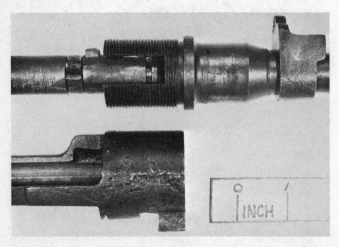

In this view of the special Type 99, the cast-iron receiver is shown in the locked position (the extractor has been removed to show position of the bolt).

barrel and receiver when assembled. It became standard and was designated the Type 2 (1942) rifle for paratrooper use.

Most collectors try and obtain representative pieces that show the general evolution of weapons of a country. About 15 different Japanese long-arms would show most of the different types of carbines and rifles. The Mozey collection has specialized to the degree of collecting specimens by arsenal of manufacture, commercial manufacture and period of manufacture with production changes of each. The collection totals over 300 Japanese shoulder weapons of all different types.

Rare arsenal pressure guns used in the development of ammunition and during production control in the manufacture of ammunition are also included. These pressure guns were made in very limited

Top: Type 99 modified for take down by interrupted screw system at barrel and receiver juncture, paratrooper use. Middle: Early Type 2. Bottom: Late Type 2.

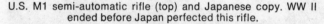

U.S. M1 semi-automatic rifle (top) and Japanese copy. WW II ended before Japan perfected this rifle.

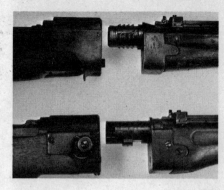

Top: Type 99 modified for paratrooper use. Barrel and receiver are locked in place by spring loaded plunger. Bottom: Type 2 (1942). Barrel is locked to receiver by tapered wedge, engaging lug on barrel.

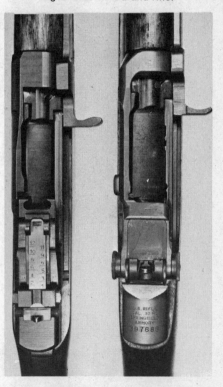

Left: Japanese copy of U.S. Garand rifle shows Mauser-type sliding rear sight. Right: U.S. M1 Garand rifle.

Top: U.S. M1 Garand rifle. Bottom: Type 5, 7.7mm Japanese copy holds 10 rounds loaded from two 5-round clips. Trigger does not separate from the stock when the rifle is taken down.

numbers and are extremely scarce.

It is strange that a collection as complete as this one should be lacking one weapon that is in my collection. Some years ago I obtained for my Springfield collection one of the Japanese copies of the U.S. M1 rifle. It is referred to in some texts as the Type 5 (1945) 7.7mm semi-automatic rifle. My specimen of this poor copy of the M1 is unfired, shows evidence of being a tool room job and has the number 15 marked on the receiver and most parts.

While most Japanese service rifles appear to be made of inferior materials and workmanship is not all it could be, they are basically sound, reliable firearms that have been unjustly maligned. There are many variations of the basic models—enough so that the collector of these interesting guns will have his hands full trying to find them all. ●

GUN COLLECTING IN

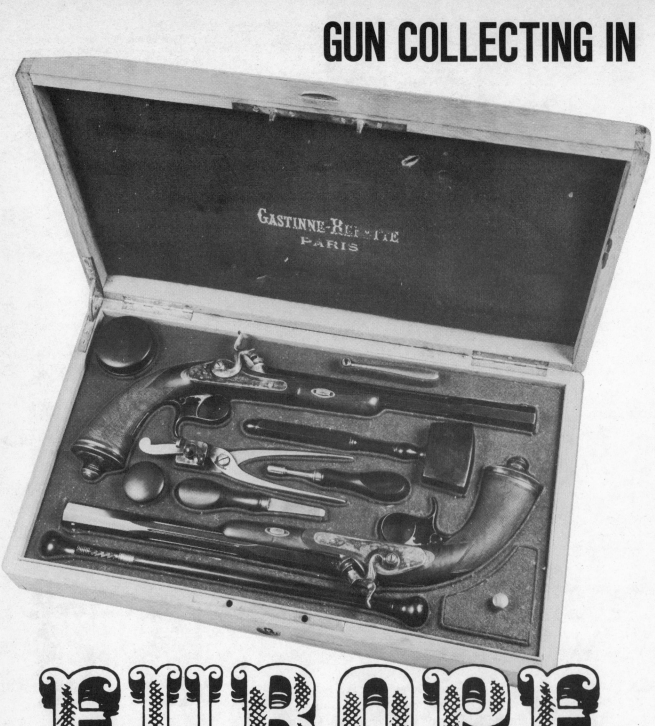

EUROPE

by FRED A. DATIG

THREE OR FOUR little old men with long grey beards, their Lodencloth jackets and Tyrolean hats hanging nearby, sitting at a back table in a dimly lit Gasthaus drinking beer, wine and schnapps and smoking their old fashioned pipes . . . this is the picture which comes to mind when the subject of a Continental European gun collectors' meeting is brought up.

Not too many years ago that was about the size and shape of it. Recently, however, while the surroundings and refreshments have remained much the same, the number of collectors has greatly increased and their average age has dropped decidedly. Today, instead of that single back-room table, medium-sized banquet rooms are rented from some centrally located restaurant, hotel or, that's

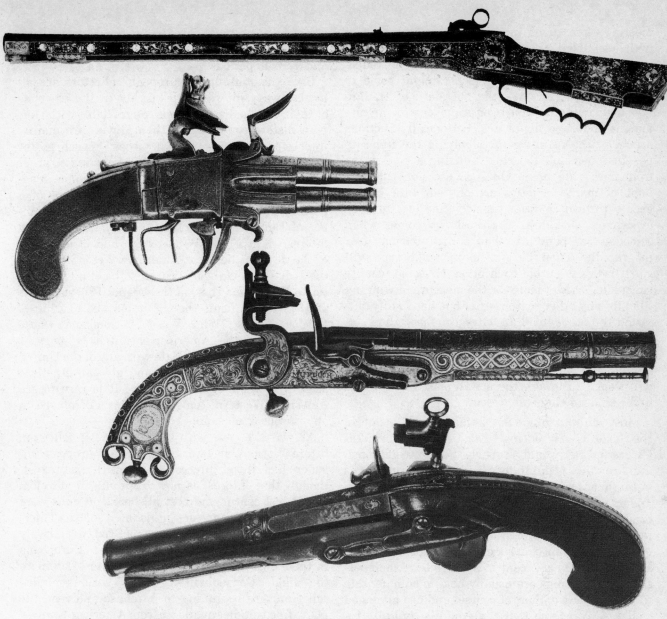

Traditionally, gun collecting in Europe has been restricted to a relatively few very wealthy enthusiasts whose interests lay in early and high art guns, such as those above. This is no longer the case, according to author Datig.

right, Gasthaus. Meetings are usually held one evening per month, with attendance averaging between 25 and 60 members; if it's summer, of course, many are off on their vacations. One or two of the fabled "little old men" are usually present among the younger, well-dressed doctors, lawyers, policemen, engineers, students and middle and upper-middle class businessmen, but the old timers stay pretty much to themselves, say little and drink more. When one of them does have something to say, though, you can bet it's well worth hearing; the room becomes as still as a mouse with *everyone* paying attention and almost without exception learning something worth knowing.

Typical seating arrangements are in the form of a "U," with the club's officers seated at the base and all other members facing half-sideways toward them. Officers are elected by the club membership not necessarily for their knowledge or efficiency

but rather because they are the ones who prefer talking to listening and/or because the majority would much rather let someone else do the dirty work. True "gun nuts" in the American sense of the word are few and far between. This is not meant to infer that there are *no* knowledgeable members but they are a much smaller percentage of the total membership than one finds in the U.S.A. While some European collectors can boast medium or even large collections by any standards, the actual knowledge of or interest in the individual or collective pieces seldom ever reaches the point of "fanaticism" to be found in the U.S.A. Of course, there are some European gun club members who join clubs and eagerly look forward to the monthly meetings merely as an excuse to get out of the house and down a few — well, perhaps more than a few — with the boys.

Once the formal club business has been dispensed with — which sometimes takes 2 or 3 hours — the meeting then turns into a veritable flea market with just about anything even vaguely connected with gun collecting being bought, sold or traded. Once in a great while a sleeper might come to light but generally it's the old story of trading two 500 dollar (or mark or franc or crown) cats for one thousand dollar dog. Periodically auctions are held, the membership supplying the items to be auctioned and the club realizing a percentage from each sale price. On such occasions piles of junk of many varieties are offered, with a real goodie thrown in from time to time just to keep everyone's attention. The most fun comes when someone has bent his elbow a little too much or too rapidly. Then he and another like type will start trying to outbid each other for some usually ridiculous article, more for the pleasure of winning than for any other reason. After one has finally outlasted the other, paid an outrageous price and collected his treasure, you can almost bet that the very next item offered will be identical to the one just having been sold. More often than not the same two will then go through the act all over again, much to the amusement of all present.

Most clubs arrange an annual social event in the form of an outing. Picnics or weeniebakes ("wurstbakes" would probably be more appropriate) are quite popular, as are junkets to some arms museum or private collection known for its quantity and/or quality. Oftentimes members' wives will accompany them on a 2 or 3 day club tour to a famous museum in some foreign country and, surprisingly enough, attendance on such an excursion may reach as high as fifty per cent of a club's total membership. Such outings are usually held in summer due to the better weather, of course, and are arranged well in advance so that the group is cordially received by the museum staff and given a real guided tour in the best sense of the word. Unlike their counterparts in the U.S.A., most European collectors will go to great lengths in order to be able to visit museums which boast fine arms collections. For this there are two basic reasons; first of all, the average European collector may never get a chance to see real rarities unless he visits a museum — real goodies simply aren't floating around Europe like they are in the States. There are probably more fine guns at any large U.S. gun show than the average European collector would have the chance to see in his whole life were it not for the museums! Secondly, Europe contains some of the world's oldest and finest museum collections, some dating back for many centuries, so it stands to reason that an avid enthusiast has a great wealth of knowledge available by simply studying the fine displays most European museums have to offer. Quite naturally, most museums specialize in the military and commercial arms of their own country, but most also house representative collections of arms and armor of many nations and from all periods.

Like the museums, European collectors are almost always interested primarily in the weapons of their own lands. Germans collect items with German history connected to them; Swiss are mainly interested in Swiss martial pieces; French go for items made by famous French makers and so on. It is the exception rather than the rule to come across a European whose interest lies in the arms of a country not his own, though there are now a number of European "Western fanatics" who are only interested in Colts, Winchesters and other relics of the days of the great American West. Similarly, the U.S. Civil War has proven to be of more interest to Europeans than is the Franco-Prussian War of 1870-71. Difficult though it may be to believe, Europe boasts "Wild West" enthusiasts whose knowledge of the American Frontier is so great that they could surely debate with any of the United States' foremost authorities and give an excellent account of themselves. However, it is rare to see American Western items prominently displayed in any European museum.

As was the case with most American collectors before World War Two, the average European collector has little interest in arms literature although that interest is now beginning to develop. In the last century, almost all books on guns were penned by Europeans or Englishmen such as Thierbach, Wille, Schmidt and Greener. Today relatively few technical arms books are available to Europeans in their own languages, and U.S. writers dominate the field. Consequently, really serious-minded collectors are beginning to purchase and read the many fine volumes available from American sources. Some dedicated contemporary Europeans have compiled valuable data dealing with European arms, however. The six volumes by the Frenchman Boudriot, for instance, are classics in the field of French military weapons. At present a small group of Swiss collectors is turning out what will surely be an outstanding series of volumes on Swiss ordnance material of all types, covering 1817 to the present. Lesser ambitious attempts have recently appeared from Denmark, Italy, Germany and other European countries, and the trend seems to be leaning more and more towards making information available to all by means of the printed word. A few years ago the average European collector was content to receive his information by word of mouth but recently even the standard complaint "why isn't it available in my language; I can't read English" is heard less and less, while more and more copies of English-language gun books are being purchased by collectors of all nationalities. Imagine that the only book available in America on Colts had been written in

Tremendous interest in the American West has developed in Europe in recent years. As a result some U.S. guns, like this Winchester '73 and factory engraved Colt Bisley, are selling for at least as much in Europe as they are here!

Hungarian, and that you must either buy that one or do without, and it is not difficult to see the handicap under which the average European collector labors in his quest for knowledge on his chosen subject. However, if the current trend in Europe continues to develop it's only a matter of time until American collectors will be faced with the problem of having to suffer through technical texts in German, French or other foreign languages if they want to learn all that is to be known about European military arms.

Most European enthusiasts are greatly interested in shooting anything they get their hands on, whether it be flintlock or machine gun. Consequently, most clubs hold shooting events from time to time in which all club members are invited to participate. The Finns and Swedes are fortunate in having government programs which allow them the opportunity of shooting military weapons not normally available to shooters in other countries,

namely machine pistols (submachine guns). Swiss nationals may, of course, shoot their personal military small arms, including assault rifles, on just about any given weekend the year 'round. Even crossbow matches are held in Switzerland and some of the fabled "little old men" can outshoot an expert rifleman at 50 or 100 yards with those traditional, unwieldy yet precise, shooting machines. Muzzle-loading shooting is also quite popular throughout Europe, thanks now mainly to the availability of the numerous replica firearms on today's market. The most enthusiastic muzzle-loading rifle shooters, however, prefer using authentic period pieces—most of which are well over 100 years old. Recently a match was held in France in which teams from various countries competed on the 150 and 200 yard ranges. Interestingly enough, the top scorers used French Chassepot needle rifles with homemade needlefire paper cartridges—a fact which greatly surprised the Swiss team armed with

Though it bears little resemblance to the American Legion Hall or high school gym that houses a typical American gun show, the "Golden Bear" (left) is the kind of spot one would go for a European gun collectors' meeting.

super-precise Swiss "Federal" rifles, noted for their extreme accuracy.

Collecting enthusiasm varies greatly from country to country, depending almost entirely on the gun laws of the land in question. Therefore, Switzerland with Europe's (if not the world's) most liberal and sensible gun laws (and lowest gun/crime rate) can boast the largest number of gun collectors by far, a very small percentage of whom are members of any club, however. On the other hand, Belgium and Denmark have very strict gun laws (and also low gun/crime rates) and relatively few collectors. Germany has a large gun fraternity, as does France. Some very large and impressive collections are also to be found in Finland and Sweden, and some very fine and valuable collections are located in Italy. For the average European, however, gun collecting is either too expensive or poses more problems than it's worth.

European gun clubs aren't always all that they could be, either, democratically speaking. A good example is a very recent one concerning a club member in good standing whose case you may judge for yourself. The member in question was paid a visit by the country's customs investigators who, without benefit of a legal search or seizure warrant, confiscated a number of firearms from him simply because he could not prove on the spot that the guns

had been legally imported into the country within the past 2 year period. The member's club, instead of aiding him in obtaining his legal rights, and upon hearing vague rumors that he had had undefined "difficulties with the authorities," hastened to notify him by word of mouth (not in writing) that he must resign his membership or be suspended until such time as he was able to prove his innocence. Despite the fact that no charges were brought against the member, he was nevertheless suspended after deciding that resignation would look like an admission of guilt. Notice of the suspension was also conveyed to him by word of mouth, the club's officers apparently preferring not to put anything in writing. As of this writing close to a year has passed. The member has still had no charges brought against him, while the authorities completely ignore his demands that the guns they illegally seized be returned to him. He is not only still on suspension from his club, but its members consider him guilty until he can prove his own innocence. Nazi Germany in the 1930s? No. Western Europe in the 1970s!

So, no matter how black things may look in America with all the new gun laws and threats of even more to come, the American gun collector still enjoys many times the freedoms and advantages of his European counterpart. All things considered the U.S.A. is still the "Promised Land" for the gun collector. ●

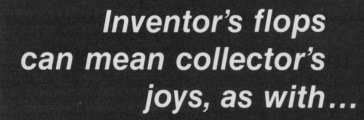

Inventor's flops can mean collector's joys, as with...

ELGIN'S KNIFE PISTOL

This 54 caliber Navy Elgin, serial number 5, is from the Mariners Museum at Newport News, Virginia. It is almost 17 inches long and weighs two pounds, six ounces.

by COL. ROBERT H. RANKIN, USMC (Ret.)

OF ALL FIELDS of human activity, arms design probably has produced more weird creations than any other. There appears to be a certain fascination about weapons that keeps drawing forth the most idiotic proposals.

Time after time, down through the years, some individual will have what he believes is the strikingly brilliant idea of combining two successful arms to produce a new version, with all the best characteristics of both in a single piece. For the most part, these combinations turn out to be nothing better than unsuccessful improvisations, hybrid monstrosities which bring heartbreak and financial disaster to the inventor.

Although many of these weapons were costly failures during the life of their inventors, they have survived to become extremely high priced collector items today. A prime example of all this is George

Elgin's brain storm, described in his patent papers as a "pistol knife" and as a "pistol cutlass."

Both of the above tags are descriptive of his weapons which combine a pistol with a fixed blade. The following is taken from Elgin's application for a patent for an "Improvement in the Pistol Knife or Cutlass:"

"The nature of my invention consists in combining the pistol and the Bowie knife, or the pistol and cutlass, in such manner that it can be used with as much ease and facility as either the pistol, knife, or cutlass could be if separate, and in an engagement, when the pistol is discharged, the knife (or cutlass) can be brought into immediate use without changing or drawing, as the two instruments are in the hand at the same time."

Although Elgin was granted a United States patent for his device on July 5, 1837, the basic idea couldn't have been at all original with him. In fact, Samuel Colt, somewhat more than a year earlier, on February 25, 1836, was granted a patent for a revolver incorporating a short dagger blade which folded back under the barrel with a hilt-like guard protecting the hand. At least one model of this Colt combination weapon was made as early as 1832. Colt also made, as a one-only item, a revolver with a large, fixed blade under the barrel and with a guard protecting the hand. Wisely enough Colt, who was a practical type, didn't think enough of the idea to put the design into production.

Actually the idea of combining a firearm with a less sophisticated weapon is hundreds of years old. Almost from the advent of gunpowder there have been attempts along this line. Firearms history is indeed replete with reference to these hybrids, while museum and private collections contain many examples.

In the Metropolitan Museum of Art in New York City, for example, is a combination shield and matchlock pistol, with the barrel of the pistol protruding through the center of the shield. There is a small shuttered window in the top of the shield through which the user can peek at his enemy. This weirdo dates from the early 1500s.

In this museum is also a mace or war club with protruding spikes, called a holy water sprinkler by reason of the drops of blood which it drew from its victim, fitted with four matchlock barrels which fired along the long axis of the piece. In other museums and in private collections are found firearms combined with pikes, swords, knives, battleaxes and even crossbows. Just why anyone would want to combine an inaccurate, limited range matchlock with an accurate, long range, efficient crossbow is a mystery indeed!

That the idea of the combination weapon was not exactly new with Elgin also is apparent in official records which reveal that the United States Patent Office, on March 17, 1837, gave notice that Elgin's claim was at odds with that filed by R. B. Lawton for a weapon combining a pistol with a blade. However, following a hearing in June, 1837, the official decision was handed down that Elgin had "priority of invention."

In any event, Elgin's pistols bring a fancy price on the modern collectors' market. At the present writing, a specimen can easily bring as much as $1500. The wide variations in specifications and markings of the extremely small number of surviving weapons make them interesting to the arms historian and exceedingly valuable to the collector.

Elgin apparently thought of his weapon as being ideal for the Navy, suggesting that his combination piece would be particularly useful in boarding operations in that it would do away with the need for separate firearm and cutlass. It was also suggested that merchant sailors and Army sappers (engineers) would find it useful. In view of the unsettled conditions of the country at that time, most citizens went about fully armed. Elgin reasoned that he ought to have a considerable civilian market for his weapon. Unfortunately, he was doomed to disappointment.

The largest of his sales was to the U. S. Navy for 150 Elgins for use on the Wilkes Expedition to the South Seas. Officially known as the United States South Seas Exploring Expedition, commanded by Lieutenant Charles Wilkes, USN, this expedition departed Hampton Roads, Virginia, on August 18, 1838. After a cruise which took it around the world, it arrived at New York Harbor on July 3, 1842. This expedition performed valuable scientific surveys in both the Atlantic and the Pacific Oceans, as well as in the Antarctic.

Although the Elgins were ordered specifically for this expedition, there is no evidence that they were even taken along in the arms chests of any of the vessels. A few may have been taken along on an individual basis.

The weapons delivered to the Navy were in 54 caliber, all with a box frame and side hammer. The smooth-bore, muzzle-loading barrel is 5 inches long and is fitted with an iron front sight. There is no rear sight. The blade, trigger guard and hand guard are in one piece. This hand guard appears only on the Navy Elgins; all have walnut grips. These Navy Elgins were manufactured by C. B. Allen, of Springfield, Massachusetts, and were delivered to the Navy for $17.50 each, including a leather holster/scabbard which also had provision for carrying a brass-tipped steel ramrod. The blade, trigger guard and hand guard assembly was manufactured by N. P. Ames of Chicopee Falls, Massachusetts, and was attached to the pistol in the Allen shop.

Dimensions of the known Elgins vary, including the lot made for the Navy. There is a Navy Elgin in the Mariners Museum at Newport News, Virginia, with an overall length of 16⅞ inches. The blade, which extends 6³⁄₁₆ inches ahead of the 5-inch barrel, is 11¹¹⁄₁₆ inches long, measured from the tip of the blade to the inside front of the trigger guard. The blade is 2 inches wide. This specimen weighs 2 pounds, 6½ ounces.

The weapon bears the serial number "5." The legend "C. B. ALLEN /SPRINGFIELD /MASS" appears in three lines below the figure "5" at the front of the left side of the frame. The figure "5" appears in the center of the left vertical flat of the octagonal barrel at the breech end and also beneath the breech end of the reinforcing side plates on the left side of the blade. The top flat of the barrel bears the legend, "ELGINS PATENT" and "C.B.A./P.M./1837" in three lines.

The blade of this specimen is held between two

United States Military Academy is another Elgin of yet different dimensions. This Navy cutlass pistol measures 16½ inches long over-all. The barrel is 5 inches long. The blade, 11⁵⁄₁₆ inches long over-all, extends 5⅝ inches ahead of the muzzle. Width of the blade is 2 inches. Weight is 2 pounds, 4 ounces. This weapon bears the serial number "120" on the left flat of the barrel at the breech, on the front left of the box frame, and on the rear of the blade. The markings are indistinct, the top flat of the barrel bearing "ELGINS/P—" and "PM/186—."

Examples of other Navy Elgins, of somewhat different dimensions appear in other museums and in private collections.

It is known that Allen also made Elgins other than those delivered to the Navy. In addition to the cutlass pistol, he made a model with a Bowie knife

Now in the West Point Museum collection, this 54 caliber Navy Elgin, serial number 120, is almost half an inch shorter and over two ounces lighter than serial number 5.

side plates under the barrel by two bolts. The back bow of the trigger guard is attached to the frame by an inside screw, while the hand guard is attached to the butt by a wood screw. This particular method of attaching the blade to the pistol was exclusive with Allen and was used on all Navy Elgins. Three other methods of attaching the blade to the pistol are known. These are noted later.

In the Smithsonian Institution in Washington, D.C., is another Navy Elgin specimen, of slightly different dimensions. It is stamped with the serial number 123/127. This weapon is 17 inches long over-all. The blade is 11½ inches long and 2 inches wide. The blade extends 6¹⁄₁₆ inches ahead of the 5-inch barrel. This Elgin weighs 2 pounds, 4 ounces. The legend "C.B. ALLEN" appears on the left side of the box frame. The address is not legible.

In the West Point Museum collections of the

blade. All Allen-made Elgins have an octagonal barrel, while those produced by other manufacturers most often have a round barrel. The Allen Bowie knife Elgins were for the civilian trade and were without the hand guard. Among the known Allen Bowie knife models, calibers vary from 35 to 64. On some civilian models, the method of attaching the blade to the pistol differs from that employed on the Navy weapons. In these civilian models the top of the blade passing under the barrel is provided at the fore-end with a tongue which fits into a groove or slot under the muzzle. The back of the blade fits into a vertical slot in the front of the box frame and is held fast with screws. The blade is integral with the trigger guard.

The arms firm of Morrill, Mossman & Blair of Amherst, Massachusetts, also manufactured Elgins, these for the civilian trade. In fact, this firm may

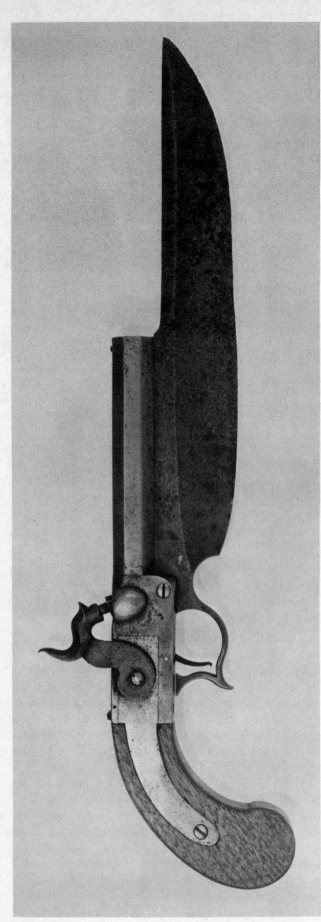

An Allen-made commercial Elgin. Note the different method of attaching the barrel, and the lack of a handguard.

have begun production some months before Allen. It is reported that this concern received a contract for a thousand Elgins, but there is no record that anything even remotely approaching that number was ever produced.

All Elgins manufactured by this maker have a Bowie knife blade and no hand guard. Blade and trigger guard are integral. Calibers vary in known specimens from 32 to 50. Among these examples is a small weapon of 36 caliber which is 10½ inches long overall, with a barrel 3¼ inches long. The blade is 6¾ inches long over-all and extends 3 inches ahead of the muzzle. This blade is 1⅛ inches wide. This Elgin weighs one pound.

In contrast with this weapon is a big item, 18½ inches long over-all, of 44 caliber. This gun has a barrel 5⁵/₁₆ inches long. The blade is 12¹¹/₁₆ inches ahead of the muzzle. The blade is 1⅝ inches wide. This specimen weighs 2 pounds, 3 ounces.

Incidentally, the vast majority of existing Allen made Elgins are smooth-bores, whereas those made by Morrill, Mossman & Blair have rifled barrels.

Morrill, Mossman & Blair utilized the second of the two methods described above to attach the blade to the barrel in most instances. A third method sometimes was used. In this method the blade is not attached to the barrel in any manner. Instead, a portion of the upper rear of the blade fits snugly into a vertical slot in the box frame where it is secured by two screws.

An unmarked Elgin Bowie knife pistol also is known which uses yet a fourth method of attaching the blade to the pistol. In this specimen, a slotted rib extends under the full length of the barrel. The blade rests in this slot and is secured by a screw at the muzzle and a screw in the box frame. This unmarked item has been ascribed to Morrill, Mossman & Blair.

This outfit remained in business for slightly less than a year. During July 1837 Silas Mossman, Jr., retired from the firm and his associates, Henry A. Morrill and Charles Blair, then organized the firm of Morrill & Blair. During its two years of existence, this firm manufactured a limited number of Elgins for the civilian market.

A fourth maker of Elgins also got into the act. This is evidenced by the existence of a large Bowie knife specimen marked on the right side of the blade with the legend "H. Harrington/Cutler/Southbridge/Mass." On the left side of the blade appears "George Elgin's Patent," this in a rectangular block with floral designs.

The combination of the pistol with a blade proved to be impractical for the military and civilian markets alike and the Elgins fell into disuse. Yet at this very minute, some mis-guided genius no doubt is working on an idea every bit as odd. ●

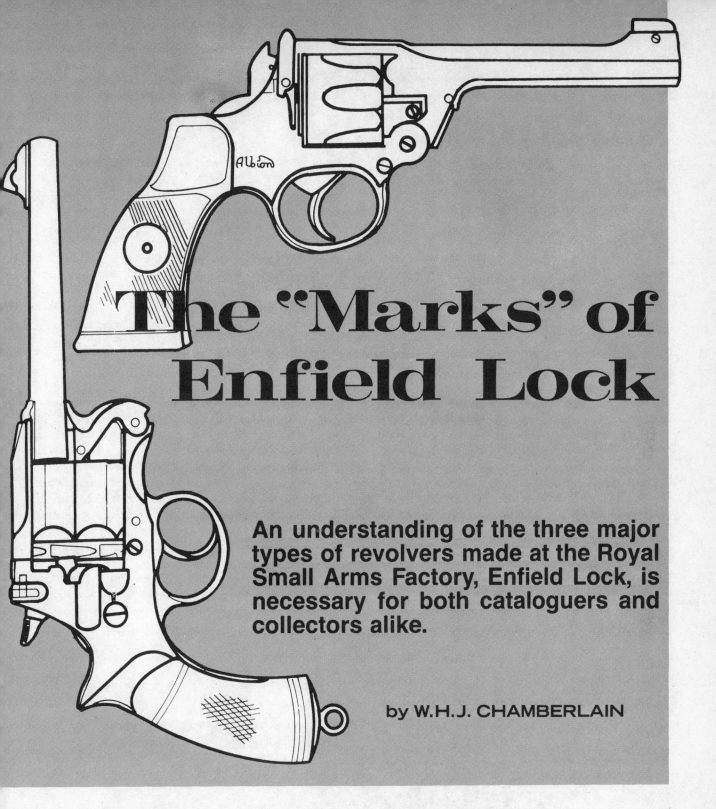

The "Marks" of Enfield Lock

An understanding of the three major types of revolvers made at the Royal Small Arms Factory, Enfield Lock, is necessary for both cataloguers and collectors alike.

by W.H.J. CHAMBERLAIN

LACK OF ADEQUATE background information has led many collectors to lump all British military cartridge revolvers together, without regard for their origins or differences. My purpose here is to distinguish the three major types of revolvers made at the Royal Small Arms Factory, Enfield Lock, Middlesex, England, from the military types of Webley revolvers with which they are so often confused. Collectors and cataloguers will find this useful. If the cataloguers will only pay attention, the collectors will find it *very* useful.

The Enfield revolvers and the military Webley revolvers resemble each other in that they all (a) are top-opening, (b) use a simultaneous opening-extracting mechanism, (c) employ a rebounding hammer as a safety device and (d) have a rather ungraceful shape. There are several interesting questions which can be asked about the revolvers made at RSAF, Enfield Lock. Why, for example, did the government twice abandon contract procure-

Fig. 1—"Pistol, Revolver, Breech-loading (Enfield) Interchangeable, Mk I" as officially designated. This is serial 6686, in caliber 476, and is dated 1881. The Mark Is do not have stamps identifying them as to arsenal, model or date.

ment of revolvers in favor of government manufacture and, twice, abandon that in favor of contract procurement again? What is the history of the process of design for each model—and for their cartridges? What is the relative degree of scarceness of each model and legitimate variation? Without a common knowledge of the identity of these revolvers, it will be difficult at best to arrive at the answers to these and other questions. Deliberately rephrasing myself: my purpose is to identify Enfield revolvers. Therefore, in this article, I shall stick to the facts and the Enfields and let speculation and the Webleys alone.

The first group of Enfield revolvers consists of two "Marks," both made in caliber 476 center-fire at the RSAF during the 1880s. The Mark I (Fig. 1) was authorized in July, 1880, as the "Pistol, Revolver, Breech-loading, Enfield (Mark I) Interchangeable." As first issued, the barrel, frame, lockplate and recoil shield were browned; the cylinder, front sight post and most screws were blued. Nickel plating was applied to the top strap, stock cap, stock cap eyebolt and stock screw, making this one of the very few service revolvers on which even a minor area of nickel plating has any legitimacy. Nickeling was discontinued in February, 1881. The top strap was then browned; the other parts which had been nickeled were now case-hardened and tempered. At some time between August, 1881 and February, 1882, the Mark II

Fig. 2—"Pistol, Revolver, Breech-loading (Enfield) Interchangeable, Mk II" as officially designated. This is serial A3801, dated 1884.

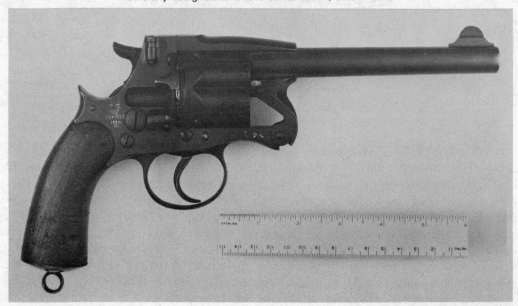

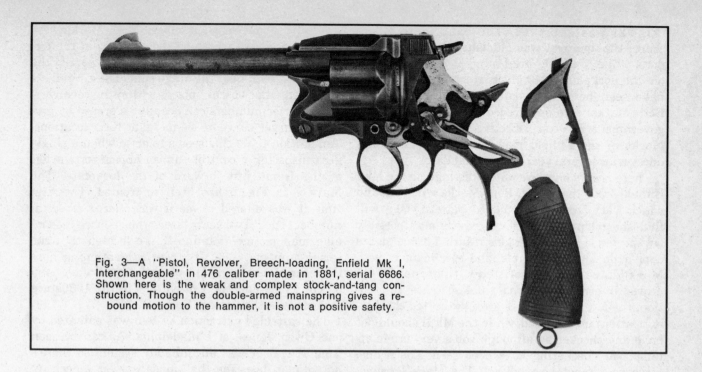

Fig. 3—A "Pistol, Revolver, Breech-loading, Enfield Mk I, Interchangeable" in 476 caliber made in 1881, serial 6686. Shown here is the weak and complex stock-and-tang construction. Though the double-armed mainspring gives a rebound motion to the hammer, it is not a positive safety.

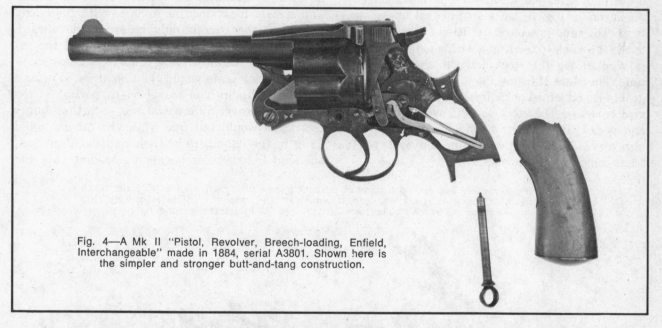

Fig. 4—A Mk II "Pistol, Revolver, Breech-loading, Enfield, Interchangeable" made in 1884, serial A3801. Shown here is the simpler and stronger butt-and-tang construction.

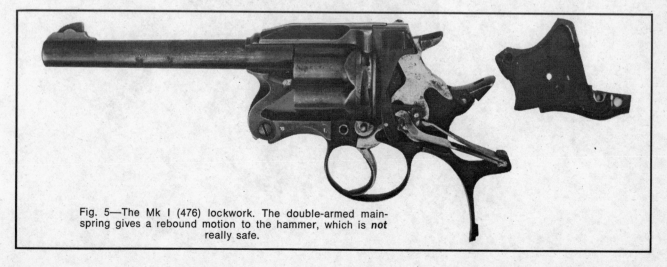

Fig. 5—The Mk I (476) lockwork. The double-armed mainspring gives a rebound motion to the hammer, which is **not** really safe.

(Fig. 2) was approved. The exact date is obscure: the approval was published as of the latter date, while Mark II Serial number 9 is dated 1881 on the lockplate. All Mark II revolvers which I have seen have been dated 1881, 1882 or 1884. Both Marks were superceded by the Webley Mk I government revolver, effective in 1887, and both Marks of the Enfield may have been out of production for several years before that date.

There is only one sure way to distinguish the Mk I Enfield from the Mk II. Both Marks will be found which vary from the standard pattern. One will find short barreled versions, which may possibly be shortened-barrel versions. Mark I front sights appear on Mark II barrels, and specimens of both Marks have been retrofitted with ordnance-approved internal or external safety catches. In addition, the Mk I should have a well executed checkering pattern on the wood, while the Mk II should not have any checkering although some very crude attempts at checkering have been seen. The frame, however, cannot be modified. The Mark I frame, as shown in Fig. 3, lacks an integral upper stock tang. The tang is separately fitted to the stock and hooks the stock to the frame with a long wood screw serving to dog the stock down to the fixed lower tang. The Mark II frame, Fig. 4, has both tangs integral to it and joined at their lower points by an integral crossbar. The stock sockets over this crossbar and is held in place by a solid throughbolt, which also serves as buttcap screw and lanyard eye. It's a less complex arrangement.

A word about serial numbers. Both Marks were numbered at two points on the exterior: at the forward end of the frame and on the lower part of the barrel lug, both near the hinge joint. These numbers are repeated at obscure places within the revolvers. The exterior numbers can readily be erased by giving a sharper curve to the metal at their locations. Temptation to do this seems to arise when a single digit inspector or control number appears on the left of the frame just forward of the lockplate. The Mark I in Fig. 5 has been so treated. The first time it was offered to me it was offered as serial number "one." Two years later, when a more reasonable man let me examine it, we located the true serial number: 6686. It is worth mentioning here that serial numbers "1" of both the Enfield 455 of the 1920s and the Enfield 380 of the 1930s are in custody at the Pattern Room, RSAF.

The cartridge extraction system was patented by one Owen Jones, of Philadelphia. As can be seen from Fig. 6, it was an unhandy system so there's no point in boasting that Jones was an American. The system functioned as follows. With the barrel unlatched the barrel could be swung downward, which would draw both the cylinder and the extractor plate forward along their two piece shaft. The extractor plate would then be arrested after a fraction of an inch of travel on its portion of the shaft. The travel differential was such that empty cartridges would fall free while the others would hang in the chambers by their bullets. After that, one shut the revolver, opened the loading gate and

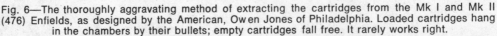

Fig. 6—The thoroughly aggravating method of extracting the cartridges from the Mk I and Mk II (476) Enfields, as designed by the American, Owen Jones of Philadelphia. Loaded cartridges hang in the chambers by their bullets; empty cartridges fall free. It rarely works right.

Fig. 7—A "Pistol, Revolver, No. 1 Mk VI (Enfield)" dated 1926, serial A6599, caliber 455 C.F. The only discernible physical difference between this model and the Webley Mk VI revolvers is that the Enfield has grip-plates which are made in Small, Medium and Large thicknesses, and are so marked.

inserted fresh cartridges one by one. That's the theory. In real life, what usually happens, as verified by my own experience, is that one cartridge will fall thwartwise and jam the whole dratted works. Although the principle of this system is also embodied in the Galand, Thomas, and Merwin & Hulbert revolvers, imitation of a bad idea does not improve that bad idea.

The "Pistol, Revolver, 455 No. 1 Mk VI (Enfield)" of the 1920s, shown in Fig. 7, is a plain copy of the Webley 455 Mk VI of Fig. 8. As far as I can determine, the only discernible difference of design is that grips for this revolver were made in three thicknesses, and marked "S," "M," and "L" correspondingly. Serial number "1" came off the production line on the 31st of August, 1921 and is yet in government custody. The latest Webley Mk VI revolvers with government contract marks on them—as distinct from government open-market purchase marks—date in early 1919. For a short period of time in 1920 the government was purchasing privately owned Webley Mk VI and 455 caliber Colt and Smith & Wesson revolvers if they passed Enfield inspection. One will also find Webley Mk IVs, Vs and VIs with arsenal reconditioning marks dating into the 1930s. On the other hand, dates of production found so far on Enfield 455s don't go beyond 1926. All of this is support for the notion that the Enfield 455 began production merely as a means of keeping the arsenal employed after the Great War and ended by keeping up necessary supply levels while awaiting the development

Fig. 8—A Webley & Scott (Birmingham) 455 revolver, the "Mk VI" as made for the non-government market after World War I. This is serial 446676. It bears the mark, visible, of the Defence Forces of the Irish Free State, and seems earlier to have been on issue to the Royal Irish Constabulary. The Mk VIs made under contract for the British military forces from 1915 through 1919 differ from those made for the civilian market only in details of marking and finish.

Fig. 9—"Pistol, Revolver, No. 2 Mk I" in caliber 380, serial C7286, dated 1934, with issue lanyard. The civilian proof marks on the barrel are irrelevant here. This revolver can give both single-action and double-action fire.

of a newer, smaller, lighter revolver.

That smaller, lighter revolver, when at last approved, became the Pistol, Revolver No. 2 Mark I (Fig. 9) as of June, 1932, the No. 2 MK 1✱ (Fig. 10) as of June, 1938, and the No. 2 MK 1✱✱ (Fig. 11) as of July, 1942. These 380 caliber revolvers resemble the Webley & Scott Company's "Mark IV .38," the basic design offered by Webley for service adoption

Fig. 10—"Pistol, Revolver, No. 2 Mk I✱" in caliber 380, serial G3827 dated 1939. This revolver is double-action only, but still has the internal hammer-safety bar.

Fig. 11—"Pistol, Revolver, No. 2 Mk I**" in caliber 380. This is a contract revolver by Albion Motors, number B1066, dated 1942. This modification has the hammer-safety bar removed.

to replace the 455 revolvers. Chief points of similarity are the famous Webley stirrup latch for the barrel, the cartridge ejection system, the single-piece holster guide/cylinder latch and—of course—their distinctive profile. The chief differences are that the Enfield has a lockplate on the left side and has a trigger guard formed in one piece with the main frame (Fig. 12). Both the Webley & Scott "Mark IV .38" and the Enfield No. 2 Mk 1 series now handle the 38 Smith & Wesson revolver cartridge. The development of the original Enfield cartridge, with its 200-grain unclad lead bullet, is an involved story and outside the bounds of this article. It is sufficient to state that the British were at one time forced to make do with a variety of Enfield, Webley and "other" revolvers in

Fig. 12—A "Pistol, Revolver, No. 2 Mk I*" in 380 caliber, serial G3827. The level extending from the cylinder pawl to the pivot in the butt and borne on by the lower arm of the mainspring is the "mainspring auxiliary" which rebounds and blocks the hammer. The "hammer—safety bar" is visible as a "dot" between the hammer and frame, just above the hinge for the hammer-lifter. Note the integral trigger guard.

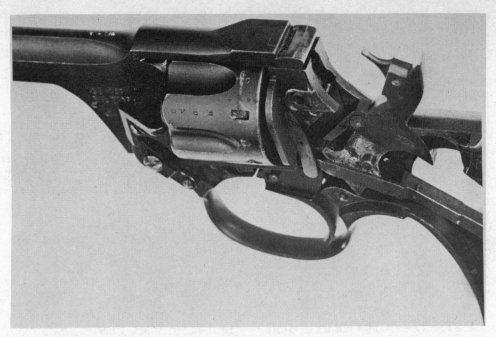

Fig. 13—The hammer-safety bar, its drive rod and its guide groove are visible in the hammer well of this No. 2 Mk I*. The upper end of the bar's guide groove breaches the curve of the frame in front of the hammer at the right.

one or another form of 38 caliber but that whenever the instant cartridge differed from the official "Cartridge, Ball, Revolver, 380 inch," (which is the equivalent of the 38 S&W) an alerting mark of some sort was either stamped or—curse it!—painted on the barrel. The Webley & Scott Mark IV 38 was purchased as a limited standard arm during the Second World War and given military acceptance markings, with the result that the Enfield No. 2 Mk 1**, which has *obscure* markings, is sometimes mistaken for it by beginning collectors.

The differences among the three versions of the Enfield Pistol, Revolver, No. 2 (the Mk 1, MK 1* and Mk 1**) are not complicated in form, although some are hidden from casual view. The basic difference between the No. 2 Mk 1 and Mk 1* is that the Mk 1* can be fired only by pulling the trigger through a cycle; there is no full-cock notch on its hammer. Neither does the Mk 1* have a hammer spur in the regulation pattern, although some private owners have added one. Neither the Mk 1 nor the Mk 1* had a half-cock notch, either. Half-cock wasn't needed with the very solid automatic safety system used in the Enfield's lock-work. The elimination of the hammer spur and full-cock notch occurred in 1939 somewhere between No. 2 Mk 1 number F8064 and No. 2 Mk 1* number G1251.

The No. 2 Mk 1** came into existence by way of a modification to the automatic safety system. The original safety system (Fig. 13) consisted of two elements: a rebound notch on the mainspring auxiliary lever and a safety bar sliding between the revolver frame and the breast of the hammer. The sliding safety bar was eliminated in this modification. When revolvers were made new as No. 2 Mk 1**s, the cor-

responding grooves and camming surfaces in the frame and the linkage hole for the safety bar all were eliminated from the machining sequences (Fig. 14). When earlier models were field-modified after manufacture, those grooves and camming surfaces were, obviously, left untouched. The identification, then, of a No. 2 Mk 1** that began life as a Mk 1* is based on that groove for the safety bar; if the groove's open upper end is visible in the frame at the upper right sector of the hammer well, the revolver was modified after production. The same point can be made for the odd Mk 1 that may have been updated to Mk 1* or Mk 1**, with the additional clue that the serial number should be below the "G"-prefixed series.

Albion Motors, in Scotland, was given the task of producing Mk 1*s and Mk 1**s to supplement those produced at the RSAF and began delivery in 1941. The lowest, dated, Albion serial number in my records is A264/1941. Since W. C. Dowell stated that 684 revolvers were delivered from Albion's shop in 1941, it is possible that their serial numbers begin with the "A" series rather than with zero. The Albion production of No. 2 Mk 1**s does not differ mechanically from the RSAF production, although there are certain readily seen superficial differences: the rear grip strap of the Albion is usually not grooved and its maker's name, the model and the year are *very* plainly stamped on the right of the frame, in contrast to the RSAF Mk 1**. There were other non-RSAF suppliers of the No. 2 Mk 1**, but these general remarks anent Albion Motors' production will serve to introduce the others.

Markings on the 380 Enfield-pattern revolvers are not complicated and those who carefully note the specific combinations of "Mark," maker, year

Fig. 14—A "Pistol, Revolver, No. 2 Mk I**," serial B1066, by Albion Motors. Note the absence of any groove for the hammer safety bar in the area of the right side of the frame in front of the hammer, as well as the lack of the bar.

and serial number will be a long step along the road to making correct assessments of the relative scarcity of any combination thereof. The serial numbers are found in four locations: inside the lock-plate, on the lower front edge of the frame and the lower edge of the barrel lug (both near the hinge), and at the rear edge of the periphery of the cylinder. An inspection mark, consisting of one or more each of letters and numerals, is found on the center of the cylinder's periphery and should not be confused with the serial number. The last two digits of the year of manufacture are on the barrel at the rear and the full date is given on the right rear of the frame. Enfield production of the No. 2 Mk 1 and Mk 1* is indicated by the "Enfield and Crown" symbol seen in Figs. 7, 9 and 10. If the revolver is of Enfield make a monogram consisting of the letters "E" and "D" is found on all metal parts, and this is the only maker's mark found on the RSAF production of the Mk 1**. One will often find the marks of various civilian proof houses, but they were applied after the revolver left the service, without regard to model, and are irrelevant here.

Some general comments based on serial numbers observed or reported: RSAF production of the No. 2 Mk 1 began well before the announced approval date; specimens in the lower 3,000s have been seen dated 1930, in addition to serial number "1." RSAF production of all Marks may have been consecutively numbered; a No. 2 Mk 1** numbered in the WC 8,000s and dated 1943 has been observed. Albion Motors' production was given its own serial number range. The Albion range shows some anomalies, which, with one exception, I'll avoid mentioning here since I don't yet have sufficient data to determine if the anomalies form a factual pattern or are due to cataloguers' errors. It is safe to say, however, that the combined "A" and "B" series for Albion ranges from 1941 through 1943. Next, I have had reported three No. 2 Mk 1**s by Albion in a possible "SS" serial number range: SS16. SS88 and SS93. SS88 was dated 1943. This "SS" series, if part of continuous letter series, signifies a production quantity so far in excess of that usually quoted for Albion Motors' output that one wonders if those revolvers were actually RSAF production misidentified as Albion or if the reporters mistook the cylinder inspection mark for a serial number.

A word about variations. The three types of grips shown in Figs. 9, 10 and 11 are interchangeable among all three Marks of the No. 2 Revolver. It seems proper to keep the styles shown on the specific Marks on which they are shown in the photographs, since that is the sequence in which they first appeared, but there was no bar to replacing any one style with another in the field in case of need. As for so-called "Commando" or "Royal Air Force" variations, I have no information respecting their legitimacy and refuse to legitimize them by speculating upon them in print.

The Enfield No. 2 Mk 1 revolvers are obsolete items once again, having been superceded by a British version of the Browning M1935 9mm semi-automatic pistol. The official date of obsolescence is in the 1950s. The revolvers were made in enormous quantities for a globally-distributed military force and take a cartridge which is still being manufactured; they are yet in service officially and privately. They're good soldiers. •

The Flintlock... Father of Firearms

by LOUIS W. STEINWEDEL

Pennsylvania Flintlocks

A FINGER TIGHTENS around a delicately curved trigger, a jawed hammer rushes forward toward an upright barrier of hardened steel. A flashing brilliance gives birth to a tiny, poofing eruption of fine gunpowder. An imperceptible instant later lock, stock and barrel have moved sharply backward, and a satisfying boom announces the frenzied flight of a leaden ball.

So performed the flintlock, that ingenious little patchwork of steel and springs that crowned three centuries of valiant effort to produce a truly fine gun. To the shooter of modern weapons the flintlock, gripping a piece of raw rock in its vise-like jaws, is hopelessly primitive; yet few realize the unbelievably high degree of perfection the flintlock gun soared to in an age when art and personal skill overshadowed science as an ingredient of gunmaking.

Flint-activated arms went through a maze of development and improvement before they reached their pinnacle of perfection in 18th century England. Three of these stages, the wheel-lock, the snaphaunce and miquelet, are well worth looking at to satisfy ourselves that the "modern" flintlock did not drop from Heaven like the gentle rain.

If you have ever tried to light a firecracker in a rainstorm or high wind you have a vague notion of what faced the pre-flintlock shooter armed with the matchlock, a curious combination of cannon and musket. In its basic form the matchlock was simply an iron barrel mounted on a wooden stock, furnished with a simple mechanism which held a sputtering saltpeter-soaked cord. This "match" was thrust into a priming pan of fine powder when the trigger was pulled. Despite the obvious shortcomings of the matchlock, a respectable number made their way to these shores where their advantage over the native Indian bow was purely psychological. Henry Hudson discovered that fact rather summarily when a band of locals once fell upon his party in the rain. Although the downpour had little effect on the flight of an Indian arrow it thoroughly incapacitated the smouldering matchlock.

About 1517 Johan Kiefuss of Nuremburg made the first really successful application of the flint-plus-steel-equals-fire formula to guns. The result was the wheel-lock, a reliable ignition system composed of a spring-powered serrated wheel which, when the trigger was pulled, spun against a piece of flinty iron pyrites held in a jaw above the wheel. The sparks produced by this device—which operated on the exact principle of the modern cigarette lighter—were directed into a flashpan of priming powder which communicated a small rapid fire or "explosion" to the main charge in the barrel. Although the little spanner wrench that wound the mainspring of the wheel-lock could easily be lost and thus render the whole gun useless, the wheel-lock had a lot to recommend it. No burning match had to be carried,

the gun was not so much at the mercy of the elements, and it fired almost instantaneously. The ignition time of a well-regulated wheel-lock is faster than that of a good flint or percussion lock. There is no hammer fall with a wheel-lock. Nevertheless, the wheel-lock was a complex piece of machinery and frightfully expensive in a day when artisans so skilled as to be able to make one were few and far between. Consequently, most wheel-lock guns were in the hands of nobility or their personal corps of bodyguards, with a few of lesser quality filtering down for military use.

The Snaphaunce

If the wheel-lock was a cousin to the yet unborn flintlock, Holland gave birth to its brother later in the 16th century in the form of the snaphaunce; a flint powered arm that now began to resemble the flintlock of the coming era. The snaphaunce carried the more familiar looking (to us) jawed hammer or "cock" for the serrated wheel of the wheel-lock and placed in front of it a hardened piece of steel (the battery) which the flint smashed against when the trigger was pulled. This showered sparks into the flashpan below which in turn set off the gun. The sliding pan cover of the wheel-lock was retained in the snaphaunce, and was pushed out of the way— to permit the shower of sparks access to the priming powder—by a built-in lever or manually. Whether the wheel-lock or snaphaunce shot better was pretty much a toss-up, depending on the quality of the individual weapons. However, the snaphaunce was a step forward since there was no spanner or winding wrench to lose and, though still not cheap, it could be built far less expensively than the intricate wheel-lock. This last consideration was important, as reliable guns which the less affluent could afford became more and more of a necessity as travel increased along roads where one band of brigands was apt to give battle to another for the privilege of relieving a traveler of his purse and parting his hair with a broad-axe.

Before the gun-prolific 16th century expired, Spain gave to the world the last predecessor of the true flintlock in the guise of the miquelet lock. This bizarre looking contraption, with its right angle hammer and much exposed lockwork, represented a tremendous forward stride, and was to exist in some areas almost totally unchanged for 250 years. The Spanish miquelet was a lock of great strength and reliability; the better examples would perform up to a hundred and fifty times without a misfire; truly a stunning record in the 1600s when the still standard matchlock musket was expected to fail at the very least three out of ten firings. The most noticeable and significant innovation of the miquelet lock was its L-shaped battery, or frizzen, just forward of the cock (or hammer) that cleverly combined a flash-

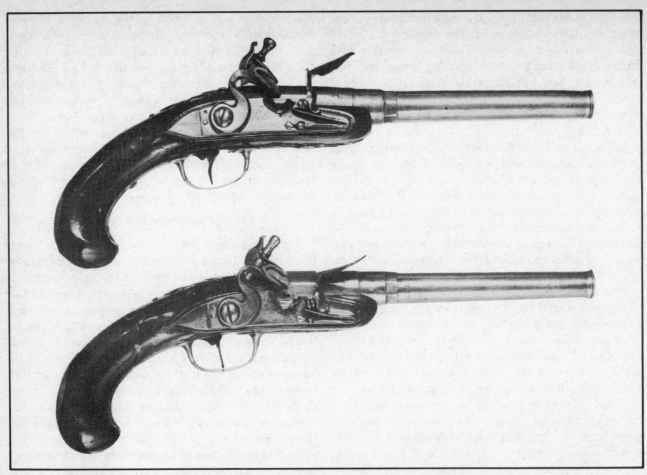

Left: Pistols on which the barrels unscrewed for loading were the first really good breech-loaders, providing superb accuracy with rifled barrels. This silver mounted pair of German specimens was built in 1750.

pan cover with the striker. This was a highly logical piece of invention that further simplified and reduced gun lock cost and, at the same time, steadily improved it.

The prime advantage of the Dutch-invented snaphaunce lock was its totally internal lockwork and better designed hammer, but the device's chief shortcomings were its long-armed frizzen and the use of a separately operated flashpan cover. The striking feature of the Spanish miquelet was its simplified, sure-fire *combination* frizzen and flashpan in one unit; its prime drawback lay in its exposed, vulnerable lockwork. Contemplating these liabilities and assets, Marin le Bourgeoys—King Louis XIII's personal gunsmith—concluded that it was no more than pure logic to marry the Dutch and Spanish efforts. What the royal French gunsmith got for his efforts was the world's first true flintlock which was to remain the standard method of ignition for the next 250 years, a longer life than any other type of firearm. Now, when a shooter pulled the trigger a complex of events occurred that gave him almost ironclad assurance that a perfect shot would instantly follow. The cock sprang forward, its flint striking the frizzen in a shower of sparks and simultaneously knocking the cover off the flashpan to expose the fine priming

powder. The action was so fast that it was now possible to fire a quality pistol *upside down*. The gun had finally come of age.

Despite their vast superiority over the ancient matchlock, the snaphaunce and miquelet never amounted to much as military weapons for the masses because of their comparatively greater cost. The matchlock for all its faults was of utter simplicity, required no great skill to produce, and was extremely cheap. What it lacked in quality could be made up in quantity, and besides tens of thousands were already stacked in various royal arsenals; it would probably have bankrupted most royal treasuries to replace these with more up-to-date arms. But growing industrial prowess and more simplified locks made progress harder and harder to resist. France became the first nation to turn to the flintlock militarily, equipping five regiments with plain but workable models. But it was left to England, up to now conspicuous by her absence in the gun world, to embrace the flintlock most flamboyantly and to build a sprawling empire with its aid.

In the early years of the 18th century there evolved a flintlock musket that bridged the gap between the true ancient arms and the guns of today. This, the first official British army musket, was known more

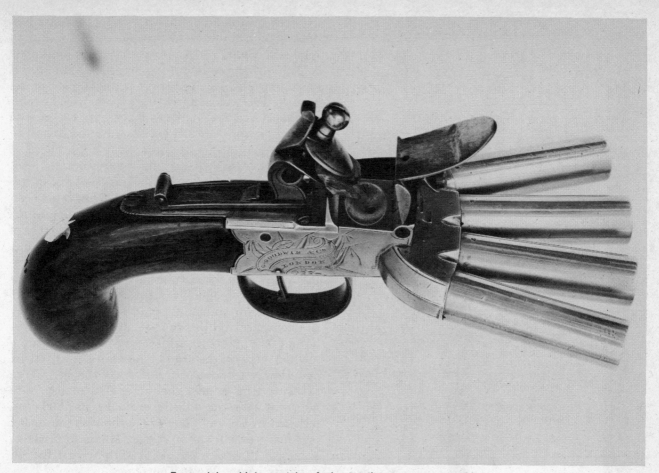

Favored by ship's captains facing mutinous crews was this curious "duck's foot pistol," which is typical of the ingenuity of the flintlock age. This specimen in the Winchester collection also used the screw barrel principle described in the text.

properly as "Her Majesty's Musket" or the "national weapon," but it quickly picked up the nickname of "Brown Bess." The origin of the pseudonym is obscure; a number of historians have explained it by the pickled brown barrel and brownish walnut stock but this explanation seems to ignore the fact that guns had been finished in the same fashion for decades, indeed for centuries, before. But hassles over its title aside, the Brown Bess went forward with the Union Jack to the four points of the compass and quickly became the teeth behind the roar of the British lion.

The Brown Bess

The boast that the sun never set on the British Empire owed a generous measure of thanks to the persuasive qualities of the gun that rapidly became an institution and lingered on, in various forms, for 139 years. Accounting for a bulk of some fourteen pounds and a gangling length of over 60 inches—plus an inhospitable-looking socket bayonet—Bess's facade was nothing less than ferocious. Mechanically, Bess was an aristocrat among military arms which, like the rank and file of the contemporary armies themselves, were frequently the dregs of the market. In contrast to the "national weapons" of

other countries, which could not boast of such refinements until considerably later, the Brown Bess came equipped with a bridle lock which served to firmly hold the lockwork in perfect alignment for sure-fire performance. Further improvements included a reinforced flashpan screw so that the frizzen and pan cover would not be bent out of place by repeated blows of the snapping cock. This greatly increased the longevity of the gun and forever squelched the argument that the flintlock was too fragile for the vicissitudes of military life.

Caliber of the Bess was 76 (11 gauge) which, compared to the tiny bores of today, begins to suggest artillery proportions. However, regulations provided that the piece be loaded with a 71-caliber ball which, as anyone familiar with the ballistics of muzzle loaders will quickly realize, did nothing for accuracy since the powder charge sent the undersized, unpatched ball bouncing erratically down the barrel (with compression escaping around it) to strike unpredictably somewhere in the next few hundred feet. Despite its unpretentious record of inaccuracy, the Bess was child's play to load with such an undersized bullet, so a British regular was able to get off as many as six shots in a minute.

Seizing upon this unequaled speed of fire, John

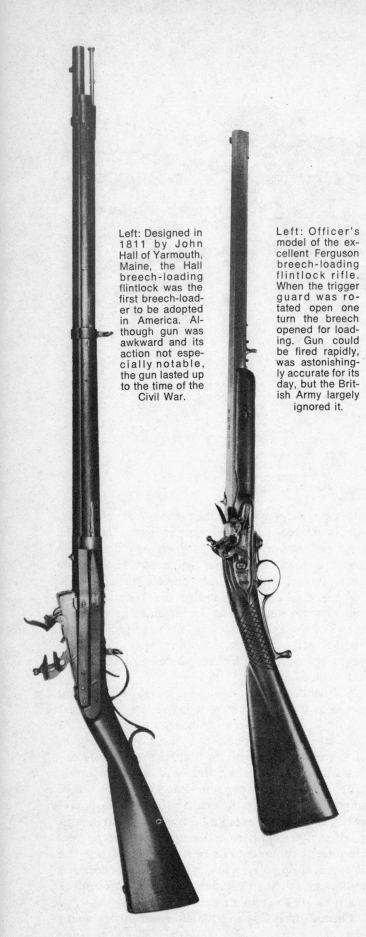

Left: Designed in 1811 by John Hall of Yarmouth, Maine, the Hall breech-loading flintlock was the first breech-loader to be adopted in America. Although gun was awkward and its action not especially notable, the gun lasted up to the time of the Civil War.

Left: Officer's model of the excellent Ferguson breech-loading flintlock rifle. When the trigger guard was rotated open one turn the breech opened for loading. Gun could be fired rapidly, was astonishingly accurate for its day, but the British Army largely ignored it.

Churchill introduced what amounted to mass production into military tactics. Massing a thousand regulars, Churchill could count on almost 6000 rounds of fire per minute issuing forth from a self sustaining sheet of orange flame and bluish smoke. In such a set up obviously the accuracy of the individual gun wasn't overly important, but it was through such tactics, plus the durable sure-fire qualities of the Brown Bess, that a considerable measure of the British Empire was won and held. Quite possibly the same success would have prevailed in the American affair of 1776 had it not been for the more rugged tree-covered terrain, which hindered such strategy, and a sufficient number of backwoodsmen with their slower loading but superbly accurate "long rifles" to make such massing in the open—particularly with scarlet uniforms —a decidedly dangerous business.

The popular notion of the flintlock follows closely the design of the Brown Bess and rarely ventures beyond the more painstakingly made and ornate fowling pieces of the grand seigneurs of the flintlock age. However, the master makers of the day, whose skills were far greater than most of us realize, were not to be satisfied with the ordinary. An 1806 commentary by Colonel Charles Thornton on the almost legendary excellence of Joseph Manton's products serves to illustrate the point with typical British understatement. Wrote Thornton:

"Joseph Manton was of the opinion that he could make a double rifle gun sufficiently stout to carry seven balls in each barrel and that would do more execution than one of my seven barreled guns...

"Great pains were taken in hammering the barrels of the new gun, and when it was finished I went to witness its execution, and resigned to Manton the honour of making the first experiment which was to take place in a passage adjoining his shop. He loaded the piece with the utmost exactness, and judging by his appearance would cheerfully have relinquished the honour to me, but I thought it no more than justice that the inventor should be first gratified. Accordingly, he placed himself and took exact aim but the subsequent concussion was so great, and so very different from the firing of any gun, that I thought the whole shop had blown up. This, however, was not the case. It appeared that the whole force of the powder being insufficient to drive the balls had come out through the touch hole, and what was very extraordinary, the gun was uninjured.

"This circumstance affording indisputable proof of the excellency of the metal, and the firmness of the touch holes, we took out the breech and gently forced out the balls which had moved only six inches."

Early Breechloaders

Despite the skill and artistry lavished upon them, most guns of the flintlock era had one glaring fault in common — they were muzzle-loaders, which meant awkward loading and a loss of compression around a loosely fitting ball, unless the shooter took the time and patience to hammer in a tight ball with a mallet and steel ramrod. This latter method was used with the northern European Jaeger, one of the earliest *rifled* flintlocks, but it was laboriously slow and often deformed the bullet. What if, reasoned some English gunsmiths about the middle of the 17th century, the powder and ball could be loaded into a chamber at the breech that was slightly larger than the bore and then the chamber re-sealed? The answer was the screw barrel gun, which was loaded by unscrewing the entire barrel (frequently brass) which exposed a chamber into which powder and ball were loaded and then the barrel was screwed back into place to form a gas tight seal. When the powder was fired the expanding gases forced the ball forward into the smaller bore for a tight fit without accuracy-destroying "windage" between bullet and bore. The next step was to rifle the bores of the screw barrel guns, which produced a weapon of such superb accuracy that the good specimens compare favorably even with modern pistols.

The story is told of England's Prince Rupert who, for a little divertissement, punctured the head of an iron chanticleer on the steeple of St. Mary's church using a screw barrel pistol with a rifled bore. His uncle, the King, marveled at such accuracy and the steadiness of his nephew's hand, and then decided it was only mere chance. Somewhat offended by his uncle's lack of pride, Rupert drew the mate to his still smoking pistol, and with a cavalier flourish proceeded to lop an iron tail feather off the same target.

Although the screw barrel idea had brought an uncanny accuracy to guns, it had done nothing to obviate the tedious loading process; it had perhaps even complicated it a bit. Therefore, the principle was mostly applied to pistols where it was easier to handle an unscrewed barrel, although some sharp-shooting screw barrel long arms were built and did excellent service. The idea was especially appropriate to tiny pistols which could now be made to throw a ball with far greater force and accuracy than their much bulkier cousins. Screw barrel pistols, particularly the later multi-shot versions, greatly enhanced the likelihood of a gentlemen's survival in the brigand-infested by-ways of London and Paris after dark in the 16- and 1700's.

The screw barrel had admirably proved the worth of both the rifled barrel and breech-loading arms. Now it was left for someone to come up with a breech-loader that could be loaded quickly without the bother of unscrewing the whole barrel. A number of pioneers strove for the honor of producing such a miraculous gun and some highly fanciful ideas emerged; none, it should be noted, more bizarre and

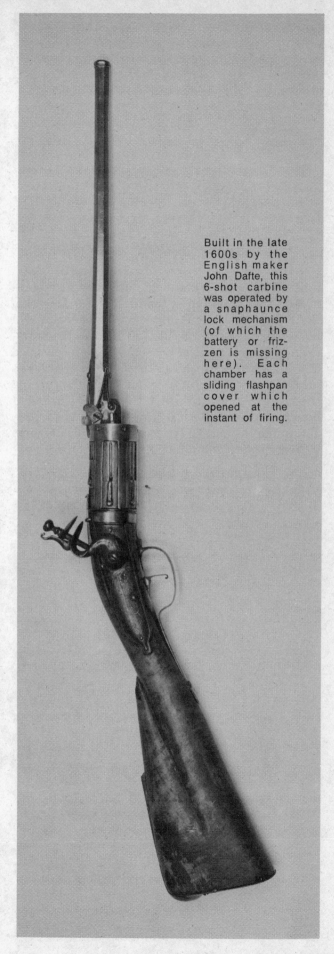

Built in the late 1600s by the English maker John Dafte, this 6-shot carbine was operated by a snaphaunce lock mechanism (of which the battery or frizzen is missing here). Each chamber has a sliding flashpan cover which opened at the instant of firing.

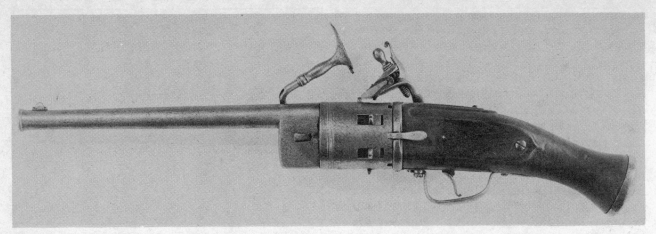

Repeating Snaphaunce revolver marked "J. Pim," built around 1735. Gun is a six-shot.

weird than some of the inane attempts at breechloaders that appeared at the time of the American Civil War. The first flintlock breechloader of real importance appeared about 1720 and was the brainchild of John Warsop of London. His plan consisted of a thick screw which ran through the breech *vertically* and which was lowered for loading by turning the trigger guard to which the coarse-threaded breech-plug was attached. This exposed a chamber, not unlike the ones in the screw barrel pistols some 70 years before, into which first ball and then powder were loaded. Although with its rifled barrel Warsop's gun delivered splendid accuracy, it was subject to the same complaint as the screw barrel pistols; loss of the loose screw and trigger guard combination, which of course rendered the gun totally useless.

The Warsop gun never became more than a curiosity and lay virtually forgotten for over half a century until Patrick Ferguson, a British colonel called the champion shot of the Empire, took notice of the practicality of the design and its obvious superiority

A gunsmith's dream was this 6-shot flintlock pocket pistol with barrels mounted in three layers of pairs. Piece was built by John Brasher for some affluent British buyer who felt the need for more insurance than Lloyd's could provide.

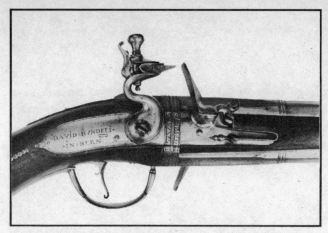

Swiss made flintlock pistol with swivel breech. Barrels are revolved by hand for a second shot.

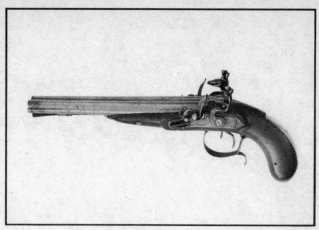

English side-by-side double flinter by Rigby, dating from about 1800.

over the Brown Bess. After some modernizing and streamlining of the Warsop plan, Ferguson came up with a rifle of twelve grooves that could easily be breechloaded by swiveling the trigger guard to one side by a small knob. This lowered the vertical screw and exposed the chamber which could be loaded through a round hole in the top of the barrel. The performance of the Ferguson rifle was no less than magnificent, but an excerpt from an old report on the official tests of the gun gives a good indication of its impressive performance.

Ferguson's Patent

"On the 1st of June, 1776 (Colonel Ferguson) made some experiments at Woolwich, before Lord Viscount Townshend, Lord Amherst, General Harvey, Derangliers, and several other officers with the rifle gun on a new construction, which astonished all beholders. The like had never been done with any other small arms. Notwithstanding a heavy rain and the high wind, he fired during the space of four or five minutes, at a target two hundred yards distant. He next fired six shots in one minute and also fired (while advancing at the rate of four miles an hour) four times in a minute. He then poured a bottle of water into the pan and barrel of the piece when loaded so as to wet every grain of powder, and in less than half a minute he fired with it as well as ever, without extracting the ball. Lastly, he hit the bull's eye lying on his back on the ground, incredible as it may seem to many, considering the variations of the wind and the weather. He only missed the target three times during the whole course of the experiments."

Along with his intense dislike for the American rebels and a hundred of his freshly made rifles, Ferguson was hurried off to the colonies. Later, after the gun had distinguished itself even against the feared American Kentucky or "long rifle"—to which the Ferguson was decidedly superior—another hundred arrived; but such insignificant quantities could only

do so much. Britain largely ignored the Ferguson rifle, depending overwhelmingly on the Brown Bess and John Churchill's massed firepower technique which had served so well in the past. With Ferguson's death at the Battle of King's Mountain in 1780 his gun, too far ahead of its time to be taken seriously by the military, was developed into a sporting rifle and pistol and the British army never again flirted with the breechloader until it adopted the Snider-Enfield in the 1860s.

The breechloader continued to be regarded mainly as a curiosity and toy for the rich up to 1811, when John Hall patented the first important American breechloader. Hall started out as a ship designer, but when the pride of his efforts promptly slid from the launching ways to the briny bottom, he decided that guns might be a safer field. In contrast to the graceful Ferguson, which in appearance was little removed from an ordinary muzzle-loader, the Hall was a cumbersome, awkward looking gun. Its rapid fire qualities, however, sufficiently endeared it to ordnance officials to produce it in quantity as a military weapon. The Hall action—a simplified adaptation of an earlier English design—was far from complex. A small locking lever forward of the trigger guard was first released, which unlocked a breech chamber that sprang up to allow a paper cartridge to be inserted. In theory the idea was impressive, and in practice it was a fast shooter, but the gun was not without the same shortcoming that was to harass breechloaders all the way up to the day of the metallic cartridge; gas leakage at the breech seal. In addition, the releasing lever made the gun difficult to carry on the shoulder in military marching fashion and the center hammer design complicated accurate aiming. Problems or no, Hall and his models were bundled off to the government at Harper's Ferry to produce the breechloader for official use. Despite its disadvantages the gun was popular with Indian fighters because of its firepower, and troops liked it because the action could

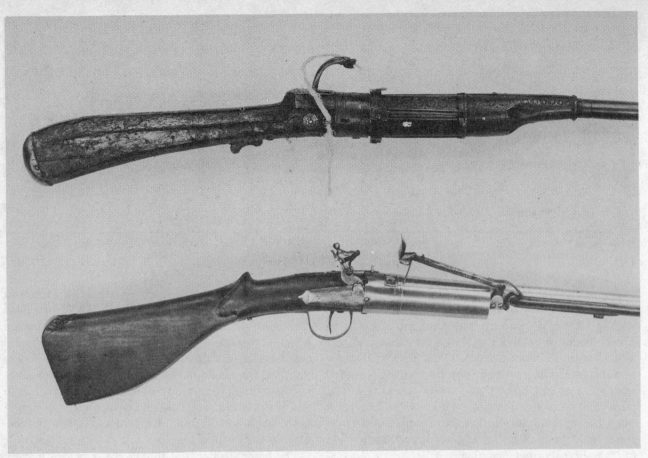

Early multi-shot pieces include this matchlock, top, and flintlock. Both have revolving cylinders. Note the rounded butt, trigger and flash hole covers on the matchlock.

be removed, loaded with a reduced charge, and used as a separate crude but effective little pistol.

It is also interesting to note that the gun was the first quantity-produced weapon to use interchangeable parts. It seems ironic that the surprising early American interest in the breechloader couldn't have been channeled toward a better gun. Fierce Yankee pride aside, it would have been a wiser choice to "borrow" Colonel Ferguson's rifle. Gas leakage was negligible, the design was maneuverable and, in some later models built for private use, the gun could throw its bullet with accuracy up to 500 yards — far beyond the range of the best and most carefully loaded Kentucky rifle.

Early Repeaters

In the logical course of affairs it would seem that the repeating flintlock would follow the breechloader, but actually the reverse was true; the repeater actually *preceded* the more notable breechloaders by a considerable space of time. Probably the earliest of such arms was the Danish-built Kalthoff gun appearing in 1641, which was a *wheel-lock repeating rifle;* a few of these issued to the Danish Royal Guard were used in the siege of Copenhagen, very likely making them the first repeaters ever used in warfare. At around this same time John Dafte, working in Lon-

don, came up with a revolving six-shot carbine activated by a snaphaunce lock. This particular arm so fascinated a later maker of repeaters, one Samuel Colt, that he sought out one for his personal collection. Even in pre-Revolutionary America, craftsmen were capable of producing repeating flintlocks, as evidenced by the highly interesting specimen in the Winchester Collection of a snaphaunce "six shooter" executed by "J. Pim of Bostonne." The gun, built around 1735, is startlingly revolver-like in appearance. Also from "Bostonne" came the amazing John Cookson *magazine* flintlocks which carried a number of charges in the stock, on the principle of the later-day Spencer cartridge repeater of Civil War fame.

But by far the most unbelievable of these ancient repeaters is the Lorenzoni repeater invented in the mid-1600s by Michele Lorenzoni in Florence, Italy. If any gun ever deserved to be called a masterpiece of design this was it. The compartment stock held a supply of powder and balls, and when the shooter wished to load he simply pointed his piece muzzle down and rotated a long lever on the left side of the gun. This simple motion, not unlike that used to activate a modern lever action rifle, pushed one ball into the chamber, measured out a powder charge behind it, sealed off the chamber, primed and closed the flashpan, and finally cocked the flintlock hammer! More amazing yet, this could be kept up for as many as 12 shots. All of this, too, in an age when everyone accepted with a straight face the inevitable truth that invisible demons guided bullets in their flight.

Despite the outrageous cost of the Lorenzoni and the danger that a stray spark might find its way into the powder magazine, about 300 such guns were made. Had they been mass produced by some far seeing prince or potentate, they could have changed the course of history, re-drawn the map of Europe, perhaps made North America an Italian colony.

Probably the most famous of all the repeating flintlocks was the work of a Boston boiler-maker, Elisha Collier, who built the most reliable and most revolver-like of all the multi-shot flintlocks. About 1815, Collier brought to perfection his revolving cylinder repeater only to find an Arctic reception for it. Undaunted, Collier showed up in England with his gun where the climate was sufficiently hospitable for about 400 specimens to be produced, including some rifles and fowlers, but mostly pistols.

Among the notable features of the Collier were an automatic self primer and a breech seal which, upon cocking, pressed the slightly recessed cylinder chambers tightly against the breech of the barrel for a gas-tight seal. This arrangement — used in identical form in the Savage Civil War revolver — served to maintain full compression for a harder hitting shot. Some of these American invented-British built weapons were shunted off to the Indian service, but exceedingly few of these hybrid Colliers of any type survived to the space age.

Forsyth's Fulminates

In the Spring of 1807 the venerable flintlock was dealt a reeling blow by a Scottish minister by profession, and combination sportsman and chemist by avocation, named Alexander Forsyth. With the knowledge that certain fulminate powders exploded by percussion, Forsyth contrived an innocuous-looking little device which applied this principle to setting off the powder charge in a gun barrel. From the Scotsman's discovery the common copper percussion cap soon evolved, and it promptly became apparent that a percussion gun shot faster, because

Invented in 1815 by Elisha Collier, a Boston boilermaker, the Collier revolving flintlock represented the epitome of the multi-shot guns of the flintlock era. Only about 400 such Colliers, including some long arms, were made.

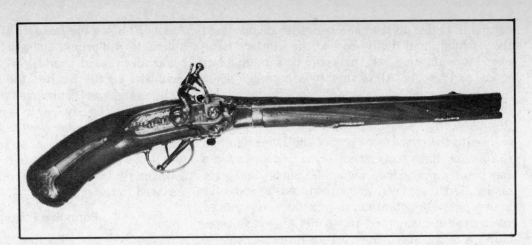

Italian flintlock repeater of the 1690 period.

there was no priming powder that had to fire first, harder because almost all of the compression was trapped behind the ball, and more reliably because the new system was the closest thing to a waterproof lock yet devised. Perhaps it was coincidence or just one of fate's recurring jokes that a Scotsman should be the inventor of the most thrifty type of firearm ever made.

When easy, cheap conversions from flintlock to the new percussion lock became available the flintlock had come to the end of its glorious and ancient road, at least in the sporting world. Military experts of the day found the percussion system fraught with dangers; a few real, most imagined. Although a few percussion guns were in use by the U.S. Government as early as 1833, the flintlock was not officially abandoned in America until 1842; and even then abandonment did not automatically herald its disuse by the military. Thousands of unaltered "firelocks" reposed in Government arsenals and it took the civil conflagration of 1861 to finally sweep the flint gun from active use.

Despite the civilizing influences of the percussion cap, then the cartridge gun, the repeater, the automatic, and so on, the venerable flintlock has never really left us. For instance, Mr. Robert Held in his splendid *Age of Firearms** estimates that there are still about 100,000 Brown Besses alone in use in underdeveloped countries, and hastens to point out that a flintlock (a rare variety at that) was used to defend the Warsaw Ghetto in 1939. In the China Sea region we still find some piratical cut-throats, men who are almost a page out of Captain Kidd, incongruously armed with Lugers and other modern pistols side-by-side with French and British ordnance pieces of the 18th century fired with flintlocks and lanyard cords. The large number of flint guns still in use in deadly earnest is given credulity by the still substantial numbers of quality flints exported from the famous Brandon quarry sites in Suffolk, England. Although in its heyday Brandon's single orders might run as high as two to eleven million flints, even today over 20,000 pieces a week are still

produced, with each "flintknapper" able to account for about 1500 pieces a day. A good flint produces 25 to 50 shots, and in modern America costs around 15 to 25 cents.

Primitive peoples' reasons for continuing to embrace the flintlock are purely pragmatic, but its most enthusiastic fans are American, and now European, muzzle-loaders who have restored, made, or bought recreated guns, and shoot them out of love rather than necessity. Practically every modern firearms innovation, from the breechloader to the repeater to the elevated rib on that best shotgun in your gun case, were first invented in the flintlock age. The venerable flintlock of antiquity has long since become an institution; its esteemed place in the past is assured forever and its present and even its future seem comfortably secure. Flints were still showering spark into their flashpans at the time man set foot on the moon, and probably will still be for a long time to come. ●

*Revised ed., Northfield, Ill., 1970.

Spanish 18th century Miquelet, dated 1796. Note the graceful trigger guard and stock carving.

Some are common...

Some are rare...

All are interesting!

Big Bore Blow-Back Auto Pistols

by DAREL MAGEE

ONE OF THE MORE recently developed areas of gun collector activity has been that of semi-automatic pistols which really began with the Luger frenzy, sparked in the late 1950s by publication of several comprehensive books on Luger Pistols. As Luger popularity (and—as a result—prices) increased, people (the author included) began to look with new interest at the many other types of automatic pistols as a ripe new field with many interesting and unusual varieties to be collected.

By far the largest number of semi-automatic pistols manufactured are of the unlocked-breech, blow-back type. In this system, there is no formal locking mechanism to hold the action securely closed until chamber pressure is reduced to safe levels. Instead, a blow-back action utilizes a breech-block (usually the slide or recoiling portion of the pistol) which has sufficient inertia to seal the action long enough for the chamber pressure to be reduced to tolerable limits. Except for a few notable exceptions, virtually all 22, 25, 32 and 380 caliber pistols are of this type.

Pistols designed for the larger, more powerful cartridges have historically been of the locked breech type to ensure proper closure for safety as well as reliable functioning. However, there have always been some die-hard designers who have insisted on trying to design a high power pistol using a simple unlocked action. One of the interesting things about their "simple" high power pistols was that in the process of simplifying the action, the rest of the pistol sometimes became quite complicated! Let's examine some of these actions, both from a design standpoint and as collector's items. Most of them, with the notable exception of the Astra, were not commercial successes.

Most high-power unlocked blowbacks share the following characteristics:

1. Heavy breechblocks, sometimes with unusual contours, in order to obtain the proper

Fig. 1—One of the earliest and most interesting of all high-power blowback auto pistols, the Danish Schouboe fired a 11.35mm wood bullet with metal jacketing. These two examples, serials 354 (below) and 368 (above) are only 14 numbers apart, but appear quite different. The gun was too radical for its time, or maybe the idea of shooting wood at adversaries didn't appeal to civilian or military customers.

mass (inertia) to hold the breech closed.

2. Powerful recoil springs which delay and cushion the recoiling breechblock. A second buffer spring was sometimes added to take the final shock of the breechblock striking the breechblock stops. (A heavy recoil spring usually makes operation of the slide impossible for women.)

3. Violent recoil due to the high amount of energy imparted to and by the heavy breechblock.

4. Extra-rugged design throughout, as the shock of operation can break delicate parts. Magazine floor plates are usually securely fastened in place for this reason.

5. Large, heavy frame in order to absorb recoil.

6. Usually very dirty inside if they have been fired much, possibly indicating opening of the action and case ejection while powder is still burning in the chamber.

7. Frequently difficult to disassemble, and special care must be exercised so that the heavy recoil spring, (as it departs for parts unknown) can be found again—and that it does not poke you in a sensitive spot as it departs. The second pistol purchased by the author—at age 18—was an Astra Model 400. The instruction booklet accompanying it was in Spanish and not much help. As a consequence the recoil spring and retainer ended up on the floor some 15 feet away.

These large caliber blow-back pistols should be considered collectors items which are potentially dangerous, and (with the possible exception of the Astras) should not be fired.

It is interesting to note that attempts to design and manufacture pistols of this type have covered a long time span, starting in the early 1900s and continuing into the 1950s and early 1960s. Countries of origin include the United States, England, Japan, Spain, China, France, Italy, Germany and Denmark. Cartridges range from 30 U.S. Carbine, 22 Hornet, 7.63 Mauser, 8mm Nambu, 9mm Glisenti, 9mm Bergmann, 9mm Parabellum, 45 ACP, to the unique 11.35 Schouboe with a metal jacket and wood core.

Schouboe

One of the earliest experiments in high-power, unlocked-breech, blow-back pistols was the Schouboe, designed by J. Schouboe and manufactured by Dansk Rekylriffel Syndikat of Copenhagen. Originally patented in 1902 in (apparently) a 32 caliber version, the design, which featured an internal hammer with a striker-type firing pin, was modified and made more massive for use with an 11.35mm bullet (approximately 45 caliber) with a wood core! The bullet was metal jacketed and had a base plug of metal (presumably to prevent ignition of the bullet base). The bullet weighed 4.1 grams (63 grains) and had a reported velocity in

Fig. 2—The evolutionary chain which terminated in the Astra Model 600. From bottom to top: the disassembled Campo-Giro 1904/1913, followed by the Campo-Giro Model 1913/16, which in turn led to the Astra Model 400, which in turn led to the Astra Model 600. The Model 400 was used by the Spanish National Guard. The Model 600 was used in small quantities as a substitute issue arm by the Nazis during WW II. Though it is highly recommended that you do not disassemble the Campo-Giro, the Astras field strip relatively easily.

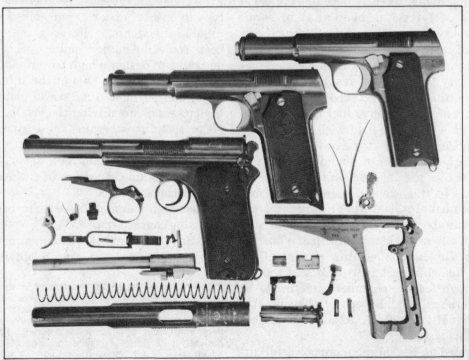

excess of 1600 fps. The pistol was reported to give light recoil with good accuracy and penetration at close range. An intact Schouboe bullet which has been fired is in the author's possession. It appears to have hit base first, leading to the impression that the bullet may have tumbled in flight.

Known variations:

a. 1902/07 as shown in 1907 Schouboe factory pamphlet. Lowest reported serial 300. The lower gun shown in Fig. 1 is a 1902/07, serial 354.

b. 1902/10, the upper gun in Fig. 1. Serial 368. Note that the two guns look completely different even though only 14 numbers apart. Serials 369 and 383 are this style.

c. 1902/12, similar to 1902/10, but with a long safety lever which extends nearer to its smaller trigger guard. No serial numbers reported.

d. 1902/?, similar to 1902/10 but with a sharply angled grip and a longer breechblock. Serial number 366.

Total production was at most only a few hundred pieces, and ceased about the end of World War I. The Schouboe was turned down at least twice in U.S. Government trials, and it was undoubtedly offered to other governments, too.

Campo Giro

The Count of Campo Giro designed a locked-breech pistol for the Spanish Army in 1904. The design was simplified in 1913 to become an unlocked blow-back in 9mm Largo (9mm Bergmann) caliber, and was produced by Esperanza y Unceta in Guernica. Fig. 2 shows a Model 1913, serial 514, disassembled. Even in a "simplified" form it is still very complicated. Note the wedge and buffer spring below the barrel, which softened recoil. A little over 1000 of this model were produced. The assembled pistol is a 1913-16 model, a slightly more simplified version of which just over 13,000 were made. The Astra Models 400 (9mm Largo) and 600 (9mm Parabellum) were derived from the 1913-16 design, and were produced in by far the greatest quantities of all high-power blow-backs.

Beretta

Beretta of Italy produced a military pistol in 9mm Glisenti caliber, the Model 1915, which used an additional buffer spring below the barrel. An example, serial 4183, is shown in Fig. 3. This pistol seems to have been manufactured in limited quantities—probably less than 10,000. A Model 1915-1919-M2-1923 is also shown. This pistol, though similar to the Model 1915, used an external hammer and had a cylindrical fiber buffer instead of a buffer spring. Reported serials are 300,000 to 303,000 range, indicating that approximately 3,000 pistols were produced. Some examples have been cut for a combination shoulder stock/holster.

Fig. 3—Beretta Model 1915 serial 4183 (below), was produced in quantities of less than 10,000. The Model 1915-1919 M2 1923 (above) was probably produced in quantities of about 3,000; serials started around 300,000. Both are very heavy and awkward, and fire the 9mm Glisenti cartridge.

Walther

During World War I Walther produced a large scale version of its very popular Model 4 pocket pistol. The Model 6 in 9mm Parabellum (Luger) was a large, straight blow-back pistol with internal hammer. The highest reported serial number is under 1100, and the Model 6 is considered one of the more desirable Walther Models. The specimen shown in Fig. 4 is serial 754.

Fig. 4—The Walther Model 6 is one of the most desirable Walthers. It is estimated that less than 1100 of these pistols were produced. To the author's knowledge none were German WW I issue weapons, though some were no doubt carried by owners as personal arms. Relatively few seem to have reached the U.S. ➜

Fig. 5—The unusual Spanish Jo-Lo-Ar (above) and the French LeFrancais. Both pistols feature tipping barrels for loading (notice lack of finger serrations on slides). The Jo-Lo-Ar has a cocking lever which allows one-hand slide retraction. The protruding loop on the bottom of the LeFrancais magazine holds one cartridge to permit easy loading when carrying the pistol with chamber empty.

Tarn

The British Tarn, reported to have been produced by the Swift Rifle Company of London, England during World War II, was a straight blow-back chambered for 9mm Parabellum. Production started with serial number 100, which had the safety located between trigger and grip. The gun shown in Fig. 6 is serial 101, which has the safety behind the grip. Production ceased with serial 108 for a total of only 9 guns produced. All 9 pistols were imported and sold by Martin Retting during the 1950s. Some are presently unaccounted for, so start looking!

Fig. 6—The 9mm Tarn, reportedly designed by Free Polish arms technicians early in WW II, was produced in England by the Swift Rifle Company. Only nine examples were made. ➜

Jo-Lo.Ar

The Spanish Jo-Lo-Ar dates from 1924 and is a very unusual pistol. It was made without a trigger guard and has a swing-down manual slide-cocking lever which looks like it should rap the user in the knuckles when the slide recoils. Loading is accomplished by operating a barrel release which allows the barrel to be tipped up without cocking the slide (Notice the example in Fig. 4 [top] which has no slide serrations for fingers to grip!). The pistol illustrated is serial 597. One specimen is reported in 45 ACP, and it was also made in 380, 32 and 25 ACP.

Le Francais

The 1928 model "Type ARMEE" French Le-Francais, caliber 9mm Browning Long, was produced only in limited quantities and was not adopted by the French Army. Like the Jo-Lo-Ar, this pistol also has a barrel release for loading the chamber directly and even has a place to store a single cartridge in a cylindrical protrusion from the magazine bottom. This pistol reloads automatically, but the striker is manually cocked with a trigger bar with an action similar to that of a double action revolver.

Fig. 7—The Japanese "Yato" pistol, produced by the Hamada Arms Shops. A picture of this very scarce Japanese pistol has only been published once before to the author's knowledge. This crudely made but interesting pistol could be the sleeper of a lifetime so watch for it.

Yato

The Japanese "Yato" pistol, caliber 8mm Nambu, was produced at the Hamada Arms Shops. The pistol shown in Fig. 7 is serial 49, and was never finished. Very heavy blue flash marks inside the slide near the chamber would seem to indicate that the slide is opening too soon, allowing gases to escape around the bottleneck Nambu cartridge case. Notice the heavy machined-out area near the rear of the slide, which if left intact would have left it with considerably more mass.

The highest serial number Yato reported to the author is 50. Pistols that are nicely finished and one variation with larger magazine capacity are reported to be in one well-known collector's possession. Very few examples are known: the total production was probably well under 100 pieces.

Fig. 8—This Bernardelli experimental (lower) is believed to have been produced in quantities of less than 100; a few were imported into the U.S. in the early 1950s. Like its Beretta counterparts, it has a recoil-absorbing buffer—in this case, dual springs (inset). The upper pistol is a French MAB imported into the U.S. during 1959-1963; total production appears to have been under 1000.

Bernardelli

Bernardelli of Italy experimented in the 1950s with an unlocked blowback of which a few were reportedly imported by A. F. Stoeger. The pistol was produced in 9mm Parabellum. The following variations are known:

a. Serial 16 and 21 have slide take-down on right side of slide, exposed hammer (Fig. 8).
b. Serial 24 has slide release for take-down on left side of slide, exposed hammer.
c. Serial 47, dated 1957, has concealed hammer (or may be striker fired). It is believed that less than 100 of all variations were produced. The author recalls seeing a consecutively numbered pair at a Disneyland Gun Show in 1964 for $75.00 each.

MAB

The French MAB Model R cal. 380P (9mm Parabellum) was illustrated for sale in the 1959-1963 Gun Digests and then the listing was dropped (probably due to lack of sales). The lowest number known to the author is 1020, and Fig. 8 illustrates serial 1178. This gun is interesting in that the barrel is allowed to recoil with the slide approximately $\frac{3}{16}$" before being stopped by a buffer spring. The gun was probably produced in quantities less than 1000. Some examples between serials 1500 and 1800 have a rotating barrel locking system similar to the MAB Model P-15. This locked-breech model is even scarcer than the unlocked model. Its very existence would indicate that the unlocked model had not proven satisfactory.

Fig. 9—The Kimball automatic pistol manufactured in the 30 U.S. Carbine caliber. This design was an attempt at a friction delay locking system, but could sometimes act as an unlocked pistol. When this happened sufficient stress was sometimes generated to cause slide stops to fail. Firing after lug failure could lead to possible injury to the firer. If you have a Kimball find a collector to sell it to or hang it on your own wall—but don't shoot it! Note differences in chamber walls on two examples discussed (next page).

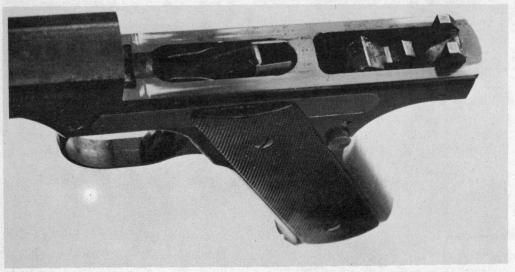

Fig. 10—Kimball pistol, serial #238 with slide removed. The two slide retaining lugs at the rear of the frame have failed on some guns. Cocked hammer appears just ahead of the two lugs.

Kimball

An American semi-locked-breech pistol, this gun was manufactured during the 1955 to 1957 period by the J. Kimball Arms Co. of Detroit, Michigan. This pistol used the 30 caliber Carbine cartridge, and due to the design it sometimes acted as an unlocked gun. The locking mechanism consisted of a grooved or roughened chamber which gripped the expanded cartridge case and thus held the slide locked to the barrel by means of an oversized extractor gripping the rim of the case. The barrel was also free floating, so it could move back about $3/16''$ before separating from the breechblock. Rapid build up of powder crust in the chamber (found in the author's gun when purchased) and possible rim-case separation could sometimes cause the arm to act as an unlocked blowback, resulting in violent enough recoil to cause the slide retaining lugs to fail. The slide could then pass off the rear of the gun, possibly into the firer's face. The author examined one such gun which had failed in this fashion, offered for sale by a collector at a Disneyland Gun Show in 1963 or 1964. The Book of Pistols and Revolvers by W.H.B. Smith, Fourth Edition, Page 667, quotes a test by W.B. Edwards, then Technical Editor of Guns Magazine, on serial 137 in July of 1958. Edwards reported, "The left retaining lug failed and broke off after firing 192 cartridges." This gun should *not* be fired, since it could possibly be dangerous to the user. Production of the Kimball continued through serial numbers well in excess of 150, with higher serial

chased at reasonable prices. The Japanese Yato pistol in the author's collection was purchased from a Luger collector in Phoenix for less than $50.00 with a holster, 2 matching clips and a cleaning rod! Needless to say, the gun is worth many times this amount.

One final word of warning. The Campo Giro is extremely difficult to reassemble. The author has made it a point to disassemble and thoroughly clean all of the guns in his collection, usually finding it relatively easy to reassemble them. The 1913-1916 Campo Giro was disassembled and cleaned first

Fig. 11—Detail of Kimball pistol serial #147 with "roughed-up," very slightly fluted chamber. The roughened area is very difficult to see with the naked eye. The mouth of the chamber is square and the chamber is not stepped.

Fig. 12—Kimball pistol #238 with stepped and slightly fluted chamber. Notice the pronounced step, which extends approximately ¼" from the front of the cartridge case toward the rear of the chamber. The mouth of the chamber is rounded to facilitate feeding.

number guns possibly being assembled from parts. The author's short barrel model (serial 238, shown in Fig. 9) was not completely machined, and some machine work was necessary to make the trigger mechanism function. The author recalls seeing an example with a much longer and larger barrel, marked as being for 22 Hornet caliber, but cannot recall the serial number.

Most of the pistols discussed in this article did not see much use and when found will frequently be in excellent condition. Many people do not know what they are, and quite often examples can be purchased

and—using the disassembly of the 1913 model as a guide—reassembled. Since I don't have a third Campo Giro to disassemble as a guide for the 1913 model I have not felt ambitious enough to reassemble it yet (4 years later). For those brave souls who do disassemble one, be sure to wear gloves; the breech block has razor-like edges which will slice up your fingers in no time at all.

In this article I've made a broad attempt to illustrate just one type of odd and unusual automatic pistols it is possible to collect. Keep your eyes open and you'll be surprised what you will find. ●

Professional equipment and elaborate
setups help, but a good camera plus common
sense will do well for...

GUN & Cartridge Photography

by BOB TREMAINE

THERE ARE a number of very good reasons why every gun collector should also have a collection of photos of the guns in his collection. If there is a theft of a gun, either from your house or while you are attending a gun show or are on your way to one, a picture provides the most accurate description you can give. All guns will have characteristic external marks, scratches, dents or markings that set each one apart from any other gun of the same kind.

A photo that will identify a recovered gun will also show investigating law enforcement officers just what they are looking for. A photo can be used in canvassing hock shops and known fences—a chore that is considerably aided by a well-done 8 x 10 black-and-white photograph. And, of course, swapping pic-

(Above) Gun photography can't be much simpler than this. For good results, area must be flooded with light to kill shadows around trigger guard, grip, backstrap, and hammer. Ideally, gun and film plane should be in straight vertical line, that is, camera should be directly above gun. At shutter speeds slower than 1/60 use a tripod; hand-holding camera is for expert with steady hands.

Although shadows have been washed out by using enough lights to counterbalance each other, camera angle was wrong —note how backstrap is washed out from light that bounces off white background.

tures of your goodies for pictures of other collector's goodies can greatly broaden your collecting enjoyment.

If you are like most amateur photographers, you can make passable prints of Aunt Minnie, the dog, the house and the kids—but when it comes to taking a decent picture of a gun, you are stopped cold. You carefully examine the picture of a scarce gun shown on the cover of a gun magazine. Suddenly you feel that you and your camera are not capable of getting a picture anything like that cover shot—friends, that's hogwash!

Most gun collections should be photographed in black and white. First of all it is less expensive, and

black and white film is more forgiving as far as amateur errors in lighting are concerned. Black and white negatives, if sharp enough, can be enlarged to a considerable degree. While the same can be said for color negatives, the transparency has to be sharper, and if enlarged to the same degree as a comparable b/w negative, it will still tend to "fall apart." This, in photo parlance, means that you will lose definition and the enlarged section will become blurred. If your collection is unusual, a set of color negatives could be made, but for most insurance and police uses the black and white prints will do.

The greatest enemy of good gun photography is shadow. The human eye is so used to shadow that it

This close-up was taken with 35mm SLR. Gun details are in sharp focus, but lights were not balanced, hence the shadows. Exposure was f22 at 1/250 sec. Compare this with next picture.

Lights have been adjusted to wash out some of the shadows, but the increased amount of light also washed out gun details. Same exposure data as previous shot. A spotmeter held directly on the area of serial number would have indicated a different exposure, but wide angle meter did not compensate for added light.

Ross rifle picture was taken with but one floodlight, and white background was not flooded with lights. Long guns can either be suspended by monofilament fishing lines or leaned up against white background. Light was concentrated on "Canada 1905" and light reading with spotmeter was taken only from that area—note how legend "Ross Rifle Co. Quebec" falls away and is barely visible.

simply doesn't note a shadow around a trigger guard or butt plate. Moreover, sad experience has shown that even if you are unaware of a shadow while looking at the gun but not through the camera, one seems to move in the moment you get ready to trip the shutter.

Shadow is nothing more than unequally distributed light. Light is reflected from light surfaces and absorbed by dark surfaces. Let's take a blued gun—a handgun is easier to manage at this stage—and put it down on a dark background such as wood, carpet or a darkly upholstered chair. Now turn on two room lights—see how the shadows form around the gun? Now move the gun away from and toward the background. Note how the intensity of the shadow is reduced as you move the gun away from the background. You will also see how shadows move as you move the gun toward and away from the lights.

Now repeat the experiment by using a sheet of white typing paper as background. Note how the white paper reflects light onto the gun and also how the shadows disappear as the gun is moved away from the background.

Here then is step one: Use a light—preferably white—background. For small guns, a couple of sheets of white bond paper will be adequate; for larger guns, a carefully ironed sheet or a piece of white photographic background paper will do very well. Either move the gun away from the background or move the background away from it. The pros usually use two or maybe three lights—a main, plus one or two fill-in lights which illuminate the background and have it bounce light back on the object being photographed. The main light should be near the camera and at about the same level.

If you have a fair number of gun photos to be taken, and most are handguns, you might want to build a lightbox. If that is beyond your abilities as electrician and cabinet maker, here's a simple photo set-up that can be dismantled easily when you've finished.

Spread several sheets of white typing paper on the floor—but not a carpeted floor, since this will allow tipping of the rest of the set-up. Don't worry about the edges of the paper being visible—the camera lens won't see them. Take four highball glasses, tumblers or tall glass jars and set them, one to each corner, in the form of a rectangle—18" x 24" will do very well. Go to the local hardware shop and buy a plain piece of window glass, 18" x 24" or a bit bigger.

Clean the glass carefully on both sides, then place it over the four tumblers. Two or three photofloods, or even gooseneck lamps with photoflood bulbs, placed on small stands or on stacks of books, will illuminate the gun on the glass and also the background. The white paper reflects enough light upward to wash out any shadows. If the gun is too close to the background, you will pick up shadows. Just place the glass on higher tumblers to kill those shadows.

Now that you have the basic set-up, you must consider the camera. The various Polaroid and Instamatic cameras are not generally suitable for gun photography. They do not offer precise focusing at the reduced ranges required for close-up photos, nor do they have enough mechanical leeway to adjust f-stops and exposure time.

Most of the 35mm single lens reflex (SLR) cameras can be equipped with special close-up lenses or

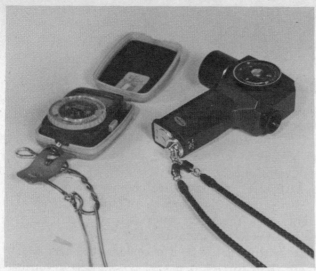

Gossen and Honeywell spotmeter at right. Study this photo, note how shadows intercept and how depth of field tends to dull details. If picture had been shot at f16 or f22, more detail would have become visible on both meters.

Pentax Spotmatic with a set of Vivitar close-up lenses can be used for most of your gun photography. Although strobe lights or ring light can be used, it is best to balance flood lights for maximum control of shadows and details.

bellows attachments. If you use bellows, you must make certain exposure compensations since the lens of the camera is now further away from the film plane. An easier and also less expensive way is to buy a set of close-up lenses, such as the Vivitars. These are available for most 35mm SLRs, and a set of lenses costs less and has greater versatility than the usual close-up attachment.

If you have a twin-lens 2¼" x 2¼", you can also get a set of close-up lenses for it. I have illustrated two entire books with an inexpensive Yashica-Mat and close-up lenses, and have shot color covers for magazines with the same combination. No matter what camera you have, you must mount it on a sturdy

Floodlights in reflectors with plastic shades allow easy control of lights. Crumpled aluminum foil fastened on piece of cardboard makes good reflector for bounce light. Note that Ross rifle is about 2 feet away from white background and only one light is turned on.

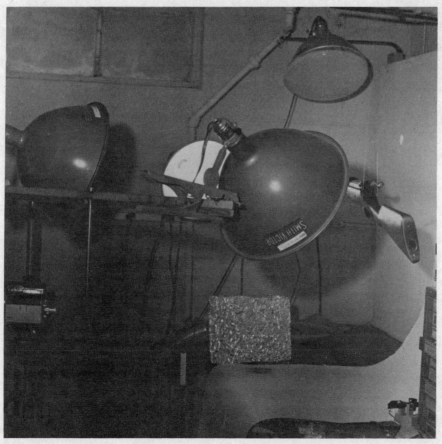

tripod and use a cable release so that you won't jar the camera as you click the shutter.

Even if your camera is one of the more sophisticated models with a built-in light meter, you should investigate a special light meter. The in-camera light meter and the conventional one that you can buy from $25 on up read the light density of a fairly wide arc or angle. They will also pick up some of the reflected light—that is, light bounced off a chromed gun or mother-of-pearl grips. This means that such a meter does not record the actual light conditions on the subject you are about to photograph. A special "spotmeter" takes the light density from but a small arc; therefore the light on the subject is measured more accurately. Spotmeters are expensive, and only if you plan a lot of gun pictures should you invest in a new one. In larger camera stores, however, you can sometimes buy a used spotmeter for less than a conventional light meter. If you should find one, have the salesman check it, install a new battery, and agree to take the meter back should it fail to perform. Run a roll or two of film through your camera while making comparison shots—the spotmeter pitted against either your in-camera meter or a standard light meter, if you have one.

Consider, for instance, a blued gun that has ivory grips. Obviously the light will bounce or reflect off the blue at a different rate than off the yellow-white ivory. A standard light meter will read the available light not only from the light and dark areas of the gun, but also from the background. The spotmeter will read the light for a small area, let's say the loading gate of a single-action Colt. A good rule of thumb is to read and then expose for the dark or shadow areas. If you expose for the light area of the ivory grips the dark areas, such as the cylinder flutes, will come out darker, perhaps even black.

Although I use the same photo setup constantly, I always use a light meter. As bulbs get tired and lights dim, the light meter will still indicate the correct f-stop and exposure time.

In setting up lights, it is seldom necessary to use more than three—at most four—lights. If you use photofloods and will be taking a lot of gun pictures, consider getting light stands, alligator clamps and suitable reflectors. These can be equipped with plastic covers that changes the glare of the photoflood to a non-glare light that makes it easier to balance the light on the object you are photographing.

The matter of depth of field is often confusing. Since you want maximum sharpness and definition for the subject and want the background to fall away,

A simple light box with strobe slaves on side and light coming from box. To kill reflections and hotspots, plastic cover with cutout for camera is used. Note how Derringer on glass appears suspended in mid air. Mamiya press camera can be used with roll film and sheet film, is all-around work-horse of many photogs.

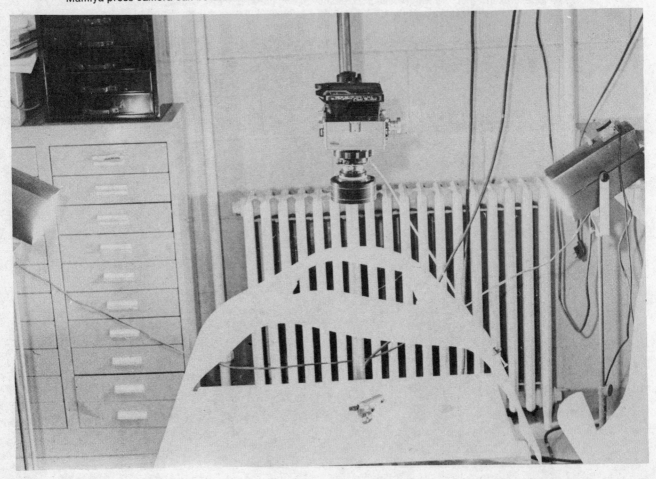

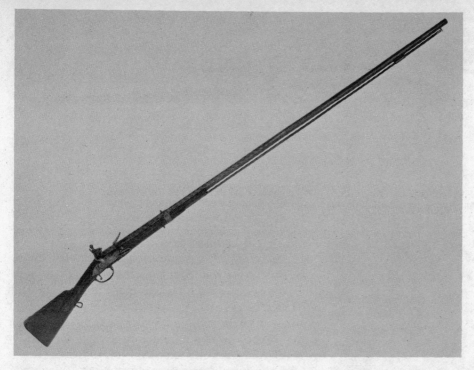

For large collections and museum photography a large light box becomes essential. Standing gun at slant against white background will do in a pinch, but view camera with tilt and swing arrangement of bellows then becomes essential.

take your pictures at the highest possible f-stop—usually either f22 or f16. Remember that the larger the f-stop number, the smaller the aperture in the diaphragm. Therefore, you'll have to expose the film longer, that is, increase the exposure time.

If, for instance, your light meter indicates f8 at 1/125 second is required for your film speed or ASA rating, this would mean that f11 at 1/60 and f16 at 1/30 are going to allow the same amount of light to strike the photosensitive film emulsion. But at f16 your background is still in focus, while at the lower f-stops it becomes a blur.

In selecting your film, much depends not only on the capability of your camera, but also on your skill as photographer. If you do your own developing, you know how to compensate for a fast film—say ASA 400—in your developing and you know how to dodge or burn-in while printing. If you are not doing your own darkroom work, it is best to use a relatively slow film. A slow film is one that is not as sensitive to light as a fast one. Kodak Panatomic-X is a good choice, and enlarges well. ASA 400 film will allow you to take street scene pictures where the photographic image on a slower film would be barely visible, but such faster films, if commercially developed, often show a distressing amount of graininess—

Types of twist barrels are shown here in comparison photo made for leading European arms museum. Note how white the background is and how clear details are on all three barrels. Before snapping shutter, barrels were made level with small supports and levelness of film plane, camera and barrels was checked with carpenter level.

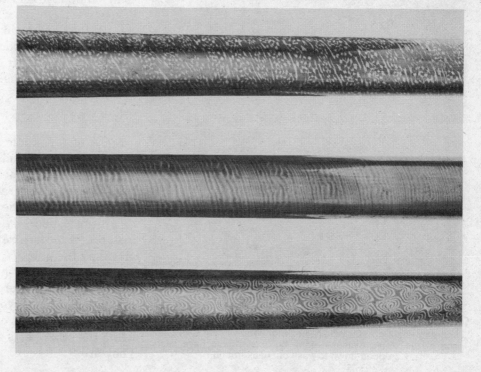

Compare this studio shot with the one where the same gun was photographed outside (the scope was changed between shots). Six photofloods were used with photographic background paper.

Impromptu set-up of a Winchester High-Wall wildcat with Oregon myrtle stock. Available light, but lens should have been stopped down to wash out background.

commonly called golf balls.

Have your prints made by a commercial laboratory. Don't take your film to the local drugstore, since the labs serving such outlets mass-process the film with little regard for solution temperatures or potency of chemicals — and with even less regard for some of the developing steps necessary for quality results from carefully exposed film. If you have ever heard the term "drugstore developing," you know that this is the cheapest and least satisfactory developing job possible.

Custom photo labs — as well as some dedicated amateurs who moonlight to make a few bucks to buy bigger and better equipment — often use a print-making process that is based on specially treated photographic paper. Instead of running the freshly exposed paper through four separate trays of chemicals, the sheet of paper is passed through a special machine and in two seconds you have a finished print. This is a great time saver, but the prints as they come from the machine do not have much of a life span — they fade and turn color in a month or two. If you are having 8 x 10 prints run off, be sure to specify that you need prints with *archival permanence*. It takes a bit longer that way, but your prints will last for a long time if handled correctly. Don't expose them to sunlight, and store them in a dark file or drawer. To prevent curling store prints and negatives flat, with negatives housed in glassine envelopes.

Many of my studio shots are taken with a view camera. Since I often take only one or two photos at a time, the view camera allows me the use of sheet film. The view camera has certain advantages over the 35mm SLR or the twin-lens 2¼" x 2¼", such as in aiding especially critical focusing. Take, for instance, a modern revolver that has a thumb-rest grip. Lay the gun flat, resting it on the thumb-rest. You'll note how the gun tips and doesn't present a perfectly level picture to the camera. At certain critical distances, you will find, especially with close-up lenses, that one part of the gun is in focus while the other parts appear fuzzy and out of focus. They are!

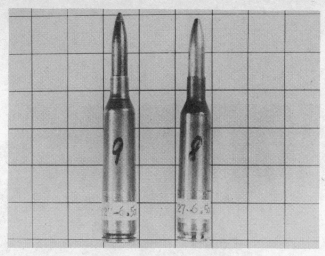

These wildcat rounds were photographed on lightbox. With two strobe slaves and against ¼″ grid, this will give you the desired high and low key lights, especially if set-up is tented.

When properly cropped and printed a shade darker, this would be a passable cartridge picture. Available light, f22, 1/125th sec. on Tri-X rated ASA 400.

To beat this depth of field problem you can keep a small jar of odd small nuts and bolts handy. Prop up the gun with a nut or bolt so that it becomes level, and presto, you will have all parts of the gun in sharp focus. You could do the same thing with the tilt and swing arrangement of a view camera, but don't rush out to buy one. I photographed guns professionally for many years with a 35mm SLR with a set of close-up lenses, and to this date, if I happen to have film in one or the other of my 35mms or my twin-lens reflex camera, I'll use it. You can't ask for better details than those shown on the Ruger Super Blackhawk, and those were shot with a 35mm.

What about taking pictures when you don't have your lights and other refinements available? The first thing to do is avoid shadows around the gun—so remember depth of field, and move the gun about a foot or so away from the light-colored background. A long gun can be held upright by inserting a pencil into the muzzle; Scotch Tape wrapped around the tip of the pencil will prevent it from wobbling around. A long ruler well out of the picture will hold the gun securely enough, and your assistant, unpaid of course, can hold the other end of the ruler. Your dark room man can re-touch the pencil out of the negative, when desired. Use bounce light if at all possible, since it eliminates hard shadows. Another trick is to paint with light. Set the camera on a tripod, open the lens to the smallest opening (highest f-stop) and move a photoflood light, fastened to a broomhandle, back and forth in front of the gun you want to photograph. Avoid blocking the gun with the light—this takes a bit of practice and some luck, but once you have mastered that trick, you are ahead of the game.

In taking pictures of cartridges, follow pretty much the system outlined for long gun pictures taken away from home. Available light will often prove best, since bright floods or a close-up flash will often give you hot spots on the brass. Available light

Somewhat different picture of the same cartridges, same set-up, but rounds have been moved forward to avoid shadow on background. This too is a passable print, although it should be cropped to get rid of extraneous materials such as steps. Here too, turning camera for vertical use of the negative would have been helpful.

means a long exposure time at f16 or f22, so use a tripod. Create a background—even a piece of grey cardboard is better than a dark felt background. Try to avoid too light a background, since the edge of the brass cases might wash out against it.

Now that you are all set to take your first gun pictures, there is just one other point. Camera lenses pick up the dangdest things. I shot a beautiful antique gun picture in an appropriate setting and everything looked perfect. But when the film was developed, I saw that the lens had picked up my fingerprints on the gun! Use a silicone G-66 Gun Mitt to wipe down guns, cartridges and accessories you are about to photograph.

Now that you have all the basic tricks and secrets of no-sweat gun photography, it's time to try them out. Go to it!　　　　　　　　　　　　●

MILITARY BOLT ACTION RIFLES

by MAJ. GEORGE C. NONTE

So YOU WANT to collect guns, but the prices in the popular fields scare you to death? Good Colts are priced as high as late-model used cars, Winchesters as much as central air conditioning for your house, and Lugers the price of a mink coat for your wife or mistress. Such things make you wonder if it's even possible to assemble a meaningful collection without an oil well in the back yard, gushing out dollars? Don't despair.

Actually, there are several collecting fields which have great historical, technological or political meaning in which a large variety of good specimens may still be had reasonably. How about a field in which you can start out by obtaining a new gun each month and not spend more than $25 to $50 per specimen — if you shop astutely? That is the field I'm talking about, and I feel it offers the greatest potential for the neophyte collector — bolt-action military rifles.

Colts and Lugers may be steeped in romance, but when it comes to pure historical significance and the auras of political infighting, the military rifle of the period 1870-1945 (three-quarters of a century of the most tumultuous years of the world) simply can't be beaten. During that period the individual infantry rifle was the dominant arm of war. During that period it made and destroyed countless empires and fought some of the most vicious and bloody battles of history, in places ranging from the tiny village of Ocatal in Nicaragua to the savage siege of Stalingrad. During that same period of time staggering commercial empires were built upon the rifleman, his weapon, and a few handfuls of cartridges — as evidence of which we have the Banana Wars of Central and South America, as well as the vicious infighting for the tremendous natural resources of Africa and Asia. During that period of time countless revolutions rose and fell on the strength of the rifle alone. The names of the revolutionaries who conquered mainly by use of the rifle are legion: Pancho Villa; Fidel Castro; Sun Yat-Sen; Mao Tse-tung — the list is endless.

The machine gun, artillery, aircraft, nuclear weapons, the tank; all of these have played their own crucial part in the history of warfare and the development of mankind and nations — but they have often been secondary to the rifle. The rifle, in the hands of determined men, has been the primary weapon to take and hold ground. Other weapons have devas-

... TRUE COLLECTIBLES

tated nations and virtually continents, but only the rifle has taken and held them and built more than it has destroyed.

Even in today's age of super-sophistication, the military rifle still remains a most efficient weapon. Two or three rifles and a few dollars worth of cartridges have many times proved their ability to clean out an enemy strongpoint which has resisted multi-million dollar bombardment by aircraft and artillery. Even a single well-placed and resolute rifleman can often cripple or destroy resistance where a

tank cannot. The rifle—employed man-on-man—is still the ultimate and the most personal weapon since the Roman short sword.

All of this preamble has been just to point out that the seemingly prosaic military rifle is really one of the most fascinating of all firearms. It has been everywhere; it has done everything; nations have risen and fallen upon it; it has been the instrument of the world's most shining examples of heroism. Even today, no fighting force can exist without it. It is still the weapon of the masses.

Portuguese Kropatscheks, representative of the early military bolt actions, are currently available from Century Arms. From top to bottom: Model 1886 rifle, Model 1886/91 rifle, Model 1886 carbine, Model 1886/91 carbine.

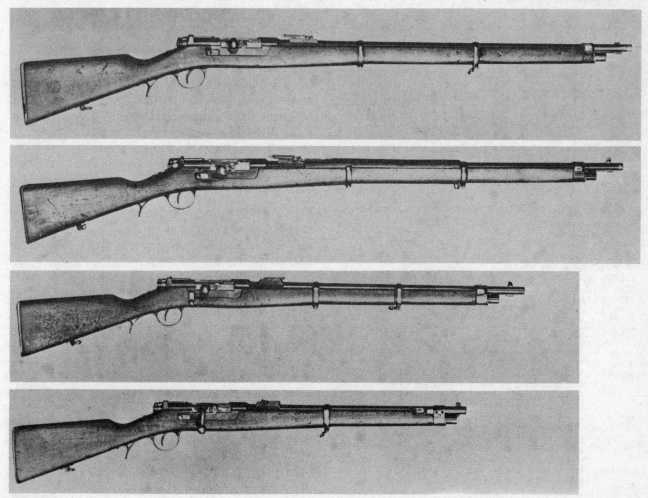

Detail of Kropatschek action (left), markings (right) which indicate Steyr (Austria) manufacture in 1886. Crest is of King Luis I.

TABLE I
Mauser Bolt-Action Military Rifles

Model	Cartridge
M1871 Single-shot (Germany)	11.2x60R
M71/84 Tube magazine (Germany)	11.2x60R
M1889 (Belgium)	7.65x53mm
M1890 (Turkey)	7.65x53mm
M1891 (Argentina)	7.65x53mm
M1892 (Spain)	7x57mm
M1893 (Spain)	7x57mm
M1894 (Brazil, Sweden)	7x57mm; 6.5x55mm
M1895 (Spain, Chile)	7x57mm
M1896 (Sweden)	6.5x55mm
M1898 (Germany)	7.92x57mm
M1898K (Germany)	7.92x57mm
KAR.98a (Germany)	7.92x57mm
KAR.98b (Germany)	7.92x57mm
M1904 Mauser-Vergueiro	6.5x58mm
M1924 (various)	various
M1929 (China, others)	various
M1933/40 (Germany)	7.92x57mm
M1936 (Mexico)	7x57mm
M40K (Germany)	7.92x57mm
M98/40 (Germany)	7.92x57mm
VG (Volksgewehr) (Germany)	7.92x57

These represent only basic models. Numerous variations of stock, sights, barrel length, caliber, and markings exist, even to the extent of having different model designations. These are properly considered simply variations. Often the same rifle will bear different model numbers when made for different countries. In addition, many modifications exist which were performed by Mauser, by the adopting country, or even by subsequent second- or third-hand military owners. One may go as far as he likes in adding variations to a basic collection, but remember that some of the scarcer variations are both costly and difficult to obtain.

Any class of firearms possessing all those virtues and associations can be as interesting to collect as Colts, Lugers, Winchesters, or other popular groups whose influence upon man and his history are not nearly as profound.

But where do you begin to collect bolt-action military rifles, and how much does it cost?

You begin with the 1870s. In that decade the bolt-action rifle, using high trajectory blackpowder cartridges, came into being and literally swept the world. Most significant of these is probably the M1871 Mauser which, with its later M71/84 magazine-fed development, saw use through a large portion of the world. Following it in rapid succession came the various Mannlichers, Lees, Krags and so on. In the decade after 1886 smokeless powder cartridges came to flower, and bolt-action rifle development speeded up. During this period we have the early French Lebel, the Lee and Lee-Metford, more Mannlichers, the Kropatschek, the Berdan, the Commission M1888, the M1889 Mauser, and others listed in our tables. In the following decade of the 90s, development continued to accelerate and we have the Mannlicher-Carcano, more Mannlichers (mainly the M1895 variants), Arisaka, the fabulous M1898 Mauser, the Lee-Enfield, the Krag-Jorgensen, the 91, 94, 96, etc., Mausers, and dozens of major and minor variants of these basic designs.

Mauser Model 1871/84, 11mm rifle was the first bolt action rifle to see wide use. Standard issue rifle had straight bolt handle; some dealers in U.S. turned the bolt handles down.

Mauser Model 1891 Argentine-issue Engineers Carbine, typical of the many Mauser variations used throughout the world.

Following the turn of the century development slowed, consisting mainly of variations of the previous designs. This period includes the M1903 Springfield, the numerous M98 Mauser variations, the Mannlicher-Schoenauer, the Portuguese Mauser Vergueiro, improvements on the French Lebel and — by the beginning of WW I — development of the military bolt-action had stabilized with the British Pattern 13 and Pattern 14 rifles.

During WW I emphasis was mainly upon quantity and variations to suit specific needs rather than new development. In the 20s some work was done which utilized the recent war experience, but it was not until the middle 1930s that a really new design, the French MAS 36, appeared. WW II spelled the death knell for mass use of the bolt-action military rifle, though every major power except the U.S.A. fought that conflict principally with bolt-action rifles that dated from around the turn of the century. In the late 40s and early 50s production of the bolt-action military rifles finally ground to a halt, the Lee-Enfield being produced last in Australia, the M98 Mauser last at the Fabrique Nationale in Belgium and by the Spanish National Armory — and it was then that the last *new* bolt-military rifle was introduced briefly and then passed from the scene. This was the Madsen M47, made in Denmark for the Columbian Navy.

Detail of the action of another run-of-mine Mauser, right? Wrong! It is a Model 1889 Belgian Mauser, which is nothing exciting—except that this example was made in Norwich, Connecticut by Hopkins and Allen!

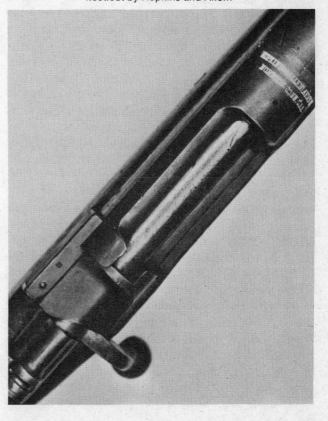

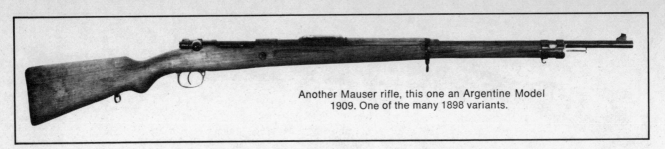

Another Mauser rifle, this one an Argentine Model 1909. One of the many 1898 variants.

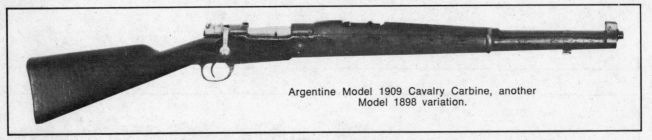

Argentine Model 1909 Cavalry Carbine, another Model 1898 variation.

Like Mausers, Mannlichers were also widely used throughout the world. This is a Greek Mannlicher-Schoenauer Rifle, Model 1903.

If one wishes a collection which chronicles the development of the bolt-action rifle from beginning to end, the entire collection need represent a total expenditure of a relatively few hundred or—at most—thousand dollars. It may contain less than fifty individual specimens, unless one wishes to delve into variations and special-purpose models. We have listed the models we consider most significant in this progression in the table. From an economic standpoint, this field certainly presents an ideal way to begin collecting guns. For less than the cost of one moderately-scarce Colt, you can have a wall full of the most historic firearm developments of our age!

There are a number of other approaches that may be taken. For example, the Mauser and Mannlicher designs having been probably the most important and certainly the most dominant during the period, you might wish to assemble a collection of basic models made under either name. In the case of the Mauser, this would include the M71, M71/84, M1889, M1891, M1892, M1894, M1895, M1896, M1898, and then finally the major variant of the M1898, the Kar.98 and the "small-ring" Mauser. These guns chronicle the complete Mauser evolution. With them you could construct a geneological tree, listing these models in direct succession, after which you might wish to add principal variations—another 15 to 20 specimens. Within the basic list given a reasonably good example of virtually any model may be had for around $50—sometimes a good deal less—with mint specimens ranging to

Detail of crest on Peruvian version of Mauser Model 1898 rifle. A collector could make a career of collecting marking variations on Mausers.

50 or 60% more. The cost of adding the principal variations should be about the same.

A similar collection of Mannlicher rifles could be assembled at about the same cost, but with a bit more work involved in locating good specimens. And, of course, a representative collection of any major designer or manufacturer may be assembled in the

So-called "Manchurian" Mauser, made in China. Note bolt cover.

Ross Model 1905 Mk II (above) and Model 1910 Mk III (below). Though adopted by the Canadian Army, Ross' straight-pull designs proved very unsatisfactory under combat conditions.

same fashion, though none would be quite so extensive as the two just mentioned.

Another collecting approach is to assemble a collection representing a particular historical period or event, or of the rifles of a particular nation or geographical area or combination of nations.

Examples of this would be a collection of the standard military rifles of France (or Germany, or England, and so on) of the period beginning with the first bolt action and ending with the last. The basic collection may also be quite simple, and consist only of major models. In the case of Germany these would be: M71; M71/84; M1888; M1898; Kar.98. Once the major models have all been acquired, one could either add variations, or add *secondary* military rifles in the form of the arms of conquered nations which were pressed into service during the several wars of the period.

Or, you might choose to collect the rifles of the Austro-Hungarian Empire during its relatively short life. Another possibility, and a more extensive one than any of those yet discussed, is a collection of the rifles of a particular war or period of conflict. Those that come to mind first are WW I and WW II. In keeping such a collection simple and straightforward, even these massive conflicts do not require the assembling of a genuinely large number of rifles or a great deal of money. For example, a WW I collection would include: British SMLE and P14; German 1888; M1898, and Kar.98; Italian M1891; Russian M1891; French M1886, M1886M93,

M1890, M1907; Canadian Ross M1905 and M1910; U.S. M1903 and M1917; Rumanian and Dutch M1895 Mannlicher; Austrian M1895 and M1888/90 Mannlichers; and if desired, several Mauser variants manufactured for or by other countries. This isn't a complete list, but gives you an idea of what you would be looking for.

There are many of these collecting areas, each with its own list of required and desired models. As examples we have compiled a Mauser list, a WW I list, and a basic beginning-to-end list of principal models. These will show you some directions to take in selecting a specialty.

Actually, making up your own list isn't at all difficult—once you've chosen an area—using a few references you should already have: *Small Arms of the World,* by Smith (Stackpole); *Mannlicher Rifles and Pistols,* also by Smith (Stackpole); *Mauser Bolt Rifles,* by Olson (Fadco); *The Book of Rifles,* by Smith (Stackpole); *Military Small Arms of the Twentieth Century,* by Hogg and Weeks (Digest Books); *Bolt Action Rifles,* by de Haas (Digest Books); and perhaps a few other more specialized texts you'll encounter if you look around. For a starter, all you'll need is *Small Arms of the World* or *Military Small Arms of the Twentieth Century*—both cover, if briefly, virtually every bolt military rifle made. From them you can select your direction by country, period, maker, designer, or any other criteria that strikes your fancy.

But a word of advice. Resist the temptation—

Lee-Enfield, long standard throughout the British Empire, in an unusual variation converted to 7.62mm NATO at the Enfield arsenal.

Mauser G33/40, another Model 1898 variation of WW II vintage, and a very desirable collector's piece.

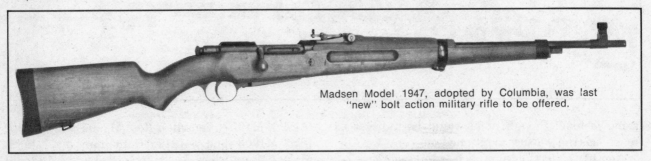

Madsen Model 1947, adopted by Columbia, was last "new" bolt action military rifle to be offered.

The Schmidt-Rubin straight-pull actions were much superior to the Ross, and served the Swiss Army well for many years. Model 1911 carbine (top) and rifle.

after you've gathered a few good specimens—to veer off in pursuit of minor variations. The time for that is *after* you've assembled just the basic models and, if you like, the major variants.

In collecting Mausers, for example, get all the basic models (or nearly all)—then the major variations such as carbines, calibers, etc. In the M1893, for example, get the basic rifle first, then the short rifle and cavalry carbine. After that you can look for marking variations, different manufacturers, conversions and the like.

To the purist collector minor variations are certainly important, but the difference between two makers isn't nearly as important over-all as the differences in basic models. It may, as in France's adoption of M1886 Lebel, have had great technological and political significance, while a difference in makers of the M1886 meant nothing outside of

TABLE II
Key Military Bolt Action Rifles 1870 to Date

Model	Cartridge
M1866 Vetterli (Switzerland)	10.4mm
M1871 Berdan (Russia)	10.5mm
M71 Mauser (Germany)	11mm
M71/84 Mauser (Germany)	11mm
M1874 Gras (France)	11mm
Type 13 Murata (Japan)	11mm
M1886 Lebel (France)	8mm
M1886 Kropatschek (Portugal)	8mm
Type 20 (Japan)	8mm
M1888 Commission (Germany)	8mm
M1888 Lee Metford (England)	303
M1888 Mannlicher (Austria)	11mm
M1889 Krag Jorgensen (Denmark)	8mm
M1889 Schmidt-Rubin (Switzerland)	7.5mm
M1889 Mauser (Belgium)	7.65mm
M1890 Mauser (Turkey)	7.65mm
M1891 Mannlicher-Carcano (Italy)	6.5mm
M1891 Mauser (Argentina)	7.65mm
M1891 Mosin-Nagant (Russia, U.S.S.R.)	7.62mm
M1892 Krag Jorgensen (U.S.A.)	30 U.S. rimmed
M1892 Mauser (Spain)	7mm
M93 Mannlicher (Switzerland)	7.5mm
M1894 Mauser (Sweden)	6.5mm
M1895 Mauser (Spain)	7mm
M1895 Mannlicher Straight Pull (Austria)	8mm
M1895 Mannlicher (Romania, Netherlands)	6.5mm
M1895 Lee (U.S.A.)	6mm
M1896 Mauser (Sweden)	6.5mm
Type 30 Arisaka (Japan)	6.5mm
M1898 Mauser (Germany and various)	7.92mm and others
M1898K Mauser (Germany and various)	7.92mm and others
1902 Lee-Enfield No. 1 (England)	303
M1903 Springfield (U.S.A.)	30 U.S.
M1903 Mannlicher-Schoenauer (Greece)	6.5mm
M1904 Mauser Verguerio (Portugal)	6.5mm
M1905 MKII Ross (Canada)	303
M1910 MKIII Ross (Canada)	303
1914 Pattern 14 (England)	303
Type 38 Arisaka (Japan)	6.5mm
M1917 "Enfield" (U.S.A.)	30
1931 Lee Enfield No. 4 (England)	303
M1931 Schmidt-Rubin (Switzerland)	7.5mm
M1907/15 M34 (France)	7.5mm
M35 (Hungary)	8mm
M1936 MAS (France)	7.5mm
M1936 Mauser (Mexico)	7mm
M1938 Mannlicher-Carcano (Italy)	7.35mm
Type 99 Arisaka (Japan)	7.7mm
M47 Madsen (Colombia)	30 U.S.
M1954 (Mexico)	30 U.S.

TABLE III
World War I Rifles

England

Lee Enfield, SMLE, No. 1	303
Lee-Metford	303
Pattern 14	303

Germany

M1888 Commission Rifle	7.92x57mm
M1898 Mauser	7.92x57mm
K98a Mauser	7.92x57mm

France

M1886M93 Lebel	8.2x50R
M1890 Mannlicher-Berthier	8.2x50R
M1907 Mannlicher-Berthier	8.2x50R

Austria

M1888/90 Mannlicher	8x50R
M1895 Mannlicher	8x50R
M1890 Mannlicher	8x50R

Russia

M1891 Mosin-Nagant	7.62x54R

Italy

M1891 Mannlicher-Carcano	6.5x54mm

U.S.A.

M1903 Springfield	30-06
M1917 Enfield	30-06

Belgium

M1889 Mauser	7.65x53mm

Many others can be added by including small countries or countries that committed only small forces. The list can also be expanded by including obsolete and captured rifles used internally for training and security by various nations, or by their colonial forces not engaged in the main battle areas.

ful and low in cost. Hundreds of thousands of such guns are still to be found in original condition, and can be had for only a few inflated dollars.

The best way to start is to simply figure out how much you want to spend and start looking. Virtually every gun shop has at least a few bolt militaries in its racks and there are plenty more at any gun show. In addition, a number of mail-order houses have pre-1898 models which can be bought freely across state lines because they don't fall under the restrictions of GCA '68. Among these are the historic Kropatschek and German Commission M1888 rifles and carbines from Century Arms, or even the Siamese M98 Mauser which qualifies for free movement because no ammunition is available to fit it.

In any event, there are lots of very interesting military bolt rifles around you. There will never be a better time to start collecting them! ●

someone's profit and loss statement. Then, too, information is plentiful and verifiable on basic models, while facts on minor variations are often vague, controversial, or simply not available. Collecting is more fun when you know what you are doing, or can at least look up the facts before laying out hard cash for an attractive goodie offered at a gun show.

The fact remains that military bolt action rifles remains one field in which specimens are still plenti-

A documentary review of
Christian Sharps'

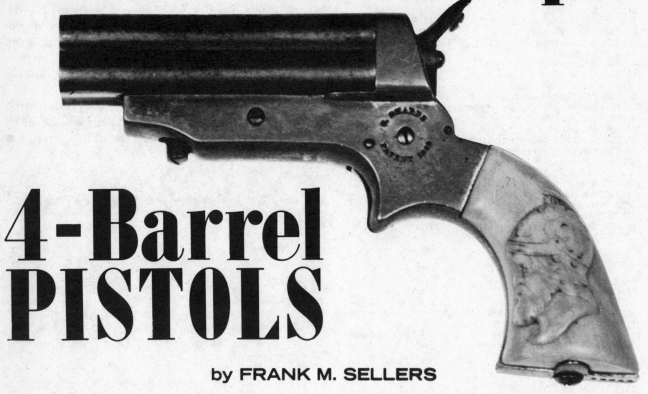

4-Barrel PISTOLS

by FRANK M. SELLERS

THE STORY OF THE Sharps four-barrel pistol begins, officially, on December 18, 1849. On that date the United States Patent Office issued patent number 6960 for a revolver to Christian Sharps, then residing in Washington, D. C.

This "revolver" was, actually, not a revolver at all, but a pepperbox in which the barrels didn't revolve! It was fired by a striker which did revolve, though, on a center post to hit, in sequence, the percussion caps which were placed on nipples on the ends of the barrels. The side hammer served both as a cocking lever and as the force behind the striker.

While it might have proved popular with the people of that time, who were distrustful of all "newfangled" weapons (this pistol retained the shape of the old single shot, which was still much relied on), it was not produced on a commercial basis. Sharps was too involved with the manufacture of rifles under his 1848 patent. According to W. O. Smith, Sharps was in Mill Creek, Pennsylvania at this time (1850-51),[1] and Albert S. Nippes, a resident of Mill Creek, was making the Sharps' patent rifles. The production facilities of the Nippes

shop were limited, however, and Sharps was looking for a larger manufacturer. At first he had considered going into the manufacturing end himself but, unable to raise the money necessary for a factory, he decided to form a corporation for the purpose of making Sharps patent rifles and carbines.[2] The Sharps Rifle Manufacturing Company was incorporated in Hartford, Connecticut, on October 9, 1851. Under the terms of the contract, Sharps was to be a manufacturing consultant and designer. The great, romantic saga of Sharps had begun.

With the exception of a small number of single shots, no pistols were made under Sharps' supervision at either Mill Creek or Hartford. The few pistols made in Hartford were large, caliber 52 single shots. They were advertised in Sharps Rifle Manufacturing Company literature until 1856, but only a relative handful were made. (Three such pamphlets, at least, are known, one of 1851 depicting two shoulder weapons and two single shot, dropping block pistols. The pamphlets of 1855 and 1856 are alike, each showing an 1852 model sporting rifle.) They were unsuccessful in marketing the pistols

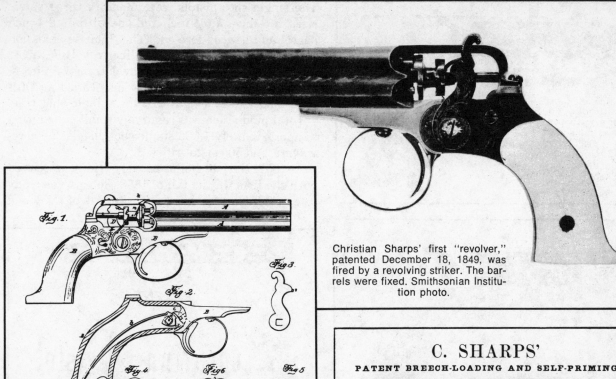

Christian Sharps' first "revolver," patented December 18, 1849, was fired by a revolving striker. The barrels were fixed. Smithsonian Institution photo.

C. Sharps patent, No. 6,960, of December 18, 1849.

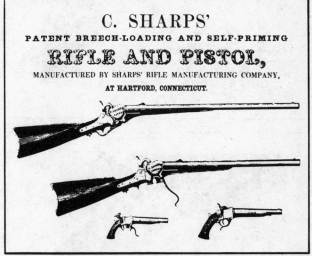

Sharps advertising pamphlet of 1851.

chiefly because of their size and recoil, both of which were extreme. Their weight was 3½ pounds, and the heavy recoil, despite the great weight, was commented on in the trial given these pistols at the Washington Navy Yard.[3]

That Sharps was dissatisfied with the Hartford arrangement is evidenced in various letters written to the two ordnance departments of the government, the Army Ordnance Corps and the Navy Bureau of Ordnance. On August 23, 1851, Sharps wrote to Captain William Manadier, acting Chief of Ordnance, that the company (and especially George H. Penfield, sales agent) wasn't living up to the contract obligations and that he (Sharps) was considering breaking the contract.[4] Again, in November of 1852, Sharps wrote to Springfield Armory looking for a place to make firearms.[5] Although the government did have some facilities available, he was again stymied by a lack of working capital, and the price asked proved more than he could raise. He stayed on with the company at Hartford.[6]

Late in 1853, the situation became unbearable, and Sharps finally made his break with the Sharps Rifle Mfg. Company. Still unable to find suitable manufacturing facilities around Hartford, he returned to Philadelphia, where he established a retail gun store at 336 Frankford Road.[7] Long thought to have been one of the Sharps factories it was, however, only a retail store and warehouse.

On departing from Hartford, Sharps had received 400 rifles and carbines as a settlement for his claims against the company.[8] In less than six months, the entire stock had been sold and he was able to return to the manufacturing business. Sharps was wholesaling a few rifles (obtained in his settlement with the Sharps Rifle Mfg. Company) to John Krider, the well-known gun merchant and gunmaker of Philadelphia, and so was Nippes, who continued to make Sharps rifles of the earlier pattern, it is thought, at this time.

In November of 1854, Sharps went into partnership with Ira B. Eddy, who had already built a rifle factory at the foot of the "Wire Bridge" in the Fairmount section of West Philadelphia. The first gun to be made on a production basis at the Fairmount Rifle Works was a single shot pistol on the same style as the rifles produced at Hartford. During the next four years, all of the facilities of the factory were used to produce this pistol, a revolver, and a pistol-rifle.

Pre-production Sharps, made with pins in the frame—not screws as used later. Caliber 22 rimfire, 2½″ barrel, serial number 27. Marking is standard— C. Sharps & Co. Philada Pa.

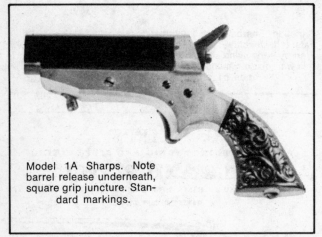

Model 1A Sharps. Note barrel release underneath, square grip juncture. Standard markings.

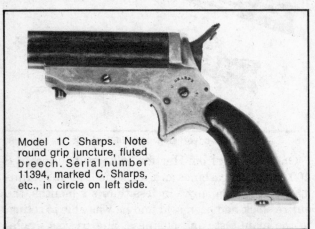

Model 1C Sharps. Note round grip juncture, fluted breech. Serial number 11394, marked C. Sharps, etc., in circle on left side.

Model 2B Sharps. Note square breech and rounded. grip juncture. Caliber 30 rimfire, 3″ barrel, serial number 2244, marked in circle on right side.

The single shot pistols were made in three barrel sizes: a 5-inch, a 6½-inch and one with an 8¼-inch barrel and a wood fore-end. The Sharps percussion revolver was a five-shot 25-caliber revolver almost identical to the first model (oval frame) Smith & Wesson. The pistol-rifle, sometimes called an Officer's Model, was a light (5½ lbs.) single shot rifle.

Total production was relatively small, amounting to approximately 1,000 single shot pistols, 2,000 revolvers, and 500 pistol-rifles.[10]

In 1857, Nathan Bolles became briefly associated with the firm. In the fall of 1858, Sharps was ready to expand. He purchased the interests of Eddy and

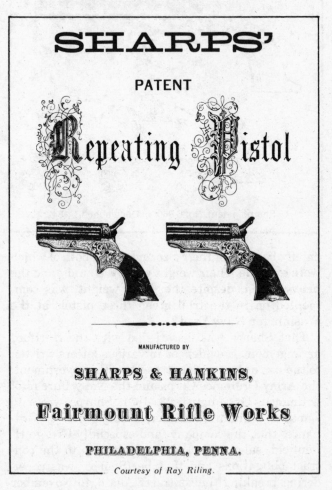

SHARPS'

PATENT

Repeating Pistol

MANUFACTURED BY

SHARPS & HANKINS,

Fairmount Rifle Works

PHILADELPHIA, PENNA.

Courtesy of Ray Riling.

Bolles and thus became the sole owner of the gun factory.[11] Now he could make plans for the production of his four-barrel pistol which, over the years, he had worked on from time to time. With the introduction of the metallic cartridge, he had at last developed it into a practical repeating pistol.

Patent number 22753 was issued to Sharps on January 25, 1859, again for a "revolver." It seems that the patent office was quite stubborn once it set up a classification. At first, pistols made under this patent used pins for all pivot positions, but these pins were soon found to be unsatisfactory. Soon the pins gave way to screws, which would not work loose quite as readily during operation.[12] The first model was 22 caliber. Made with a brass frame, it had a spur or stud trigger, and was a single-action, four-shot repeater. The barrel group was iron, and the grips were hard rubber in a floral design. The first model was made for a longer time than any of the other four-barrel Sharps pistols. Approximately 85,000 of these little pepperboxes were made in the ten years between 1859 and 1868.

The second model, made during the same period as the first version, is basically the same as the former except that it is scaled up to accept the 30 caliber rimfire cartridge. Most of the internal parts are interchangeable between the two.

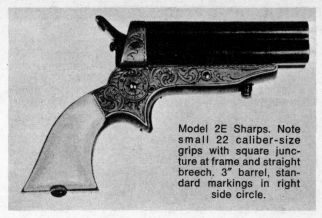

Model 2E Sharps. Note small 22 caliber-size grips with square juncture at frame and straight breech. 3" barrel, standard markings in right side circle.

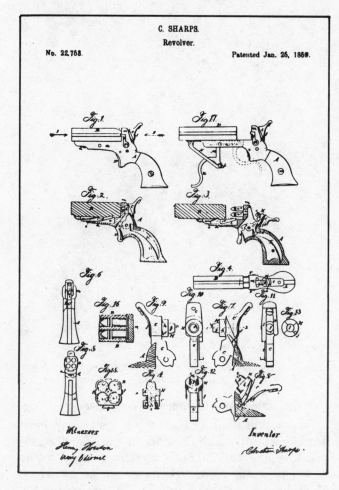

Model 4C Sharps marked C. Sharps Patent Jan. 25, 1859. Serial number 7045, caliber 32 rimfire, 2½" barrel, full nickel plate.

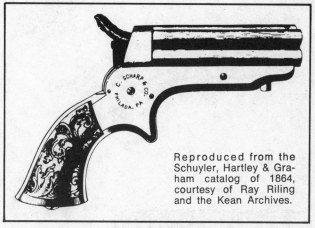

Reproduced from the Schuyler, Hartley & Graham catalog of 1864, courtesy of Ray Riling and the Kean Archives.

In 1862 William Hankins joined the firm and the company became "Sharps & Hankins." Hankins, however, was a woodworker, not a gunmaker,[13] and had little or no authority, apparently, in the running of the company. All correspondence and contracts were handled either by Sharps himself or by Sharps' attorney, William Rogers. In a letter to the Chief of Ordnance, Rogers turned down an order for cartridges, writing that "the company can't complete any business until Mr. Sharps returns. He is out of the city for a few days."[14] With the money brought into the company by Hankins, they were able to acquire a new factory, start producing an iron-frame pistol, and go into the cartridge making business.

The new factory, located at "24th Street above Green,"[15] was first used (in 1864) for the manufacture of metallic rimfire cartridges.[16] Later it was used to make both rifles and pistols.

The pistols made by Sharps & Hankins differed from the first and second models in many ways. They were larger size, were of 32 caliber, and had iron frames. With only one known exception, the Sharps & Hankins (or third model) pistols had the barrel release button on the left side of the frame instead of underneath the frame, as was most common on the earlier pistols. Some are found with the firing pin mounted in the frame instead of on the hammer, a few are also found with extractors.

Because of the war contracts for rifles and cartridges, very little production time could be expended on these pistols. As a result, only about 25,000 of the third model were made. When the partnership was dissolved in 1867, production of this model was stopped entirely.

The fourth, or "birdshead" model, the last of the Sharps pepperboxes produced, was made in the declining years of the company, when Sharps was devoting more and more time to the study of boats and propellers. Fewer than 15,000 of the fourth model four-barrel pistols were made.

Production on all Sharps four-barrel pistols ceased with the death of Christian Sharps in 1874. Although over 150,000 pistols, 150,000 rifles, and 4,000,000 cartridges were made and sold under his patents, he died a relatively poor man. Total cash on hand was only $341.25. Most of the land, buildings and machinery had been previously signed over to his wife and children.[17]

Unusual European copies of Sharps pistol, Belgian (top) and German (bottom).

Classifying the Sharps Four-Barrels

The system used for classifying the Sharps four-barrel pistol, based on a study of over 3,000 specimens, is an extension of the system used by Robert E. Ernst in *The Gun Collector* magazine, issue No. 26 of January, 1949. A table was set up, using the frame sizes as the main identifying feature, then the minor variations were listed for each frame size. From this list, the basic models were picked out. Only major variations are indicated for the basic models (such things as type of finish, grip material, sights, etc., which vary from gun to gun of the same model, were not used in the basic classification).

Of course, there are variations which are not listed here. Over 60 pistol types appeared in the study. Of these, only those types which appeared five or more times are included herein.

Model 1 This model was the smallest of the Sharps four-barrel pistols. It used the 22 caliber

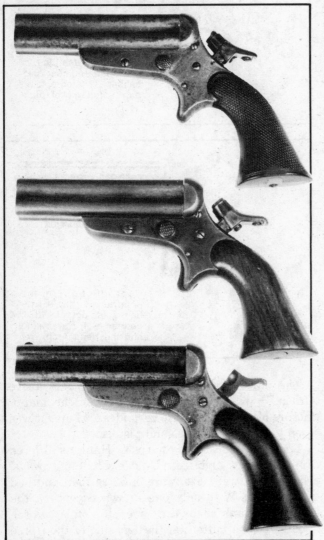

Model 3 Sharps & Hankins variations. Top: Model 3C, 3½″ barrel, has extractor. Serial 5295. Center: Model 3BB, 3½″ barrel, no extractor. Serial 63. Bottom: Model 3D, 3½″ barrel, has plunger-type latch and barrel stop, extractor, large firing pin. Serial 4384.

rimfire cartridge. The barrel block, bored through to make the four barrels, was made of iron, and was 2½ inches long. With the exception of Model 1D, all the frames were brass—1D was iron framed. The face of the breech is recessed for the cartridge heads. A hammer safety is found on some of the earlier pistols. Total production: 85,000.

Model	Breech Shape	Grip Juncture	Barrel Release
1A	Straight	Straight	Under frame
1B	Fluted	Round	Left side
1C	Fluted	Round	Under frame
1D	Fluted	Round	Under frame
1E	Round	Round	Under frame

Model 2 Put in production shortly after the first model and made concurrently with the first model for several years. The demand was not as great for this size pistol and less than half as many were made. Total production was about 35,000. Like the first model, the frame of the Model 2 is brass, with the barrel group of iron. Most internal parts are interchangeable with the corresponding parts of the first model. The barrel length is three inches. The barrel release is under the front of the frame. Some very early models are found with extractors.

Model	Breech Shape	Grip Juncture
2A	Straight	Straight
2B	Straight	Round
2C	Fluted	Round
2D	Fluted	Straight
2E*	Straight	Straight

*Small frame

Model 3 The largest of the four-barrel pistols. The iron barrel block was bored for the 32 rimfire cartridge. The frame was made of iron, not brass as were the first two. A blade-type extractor is found mounted vertically between the barrels on some specimens. Total production about 15,000.

Model	Barrel Release*	Side Plate	Firing Pin
3A	1	Yes	In frame
3AA	1	Yes	On hammer
3B	1-2	No	In frame
3BB	1-2	No	On hammer
3C	2	No	On hammer
3D†	3	No	In frame

*Position of barrel release. "1" indicates release is directly under the face of the breech; "2" indicates that it is slightly forward of the breech face. "3" indicates plunger type release, not lever type.

†Model 3D has a plunger type barrel release instead of the regular type. Otherwise is similar to 3B or 3 BB.

Model 4 The fourth or "birdshead" model of the Sharps four-barrel pistol was the last model made. It also was made in smaller numbers than any other model. Like the third model, the frame and barrel group were made of iron. The caliber was 32 short rimfire. Most of the internal parts were interchangeable with the corresponding parts of the third model. Only about 15,000 of this model were made.

Model	Barrel length	Barrel stop
4A	2½"	Screw under frame
4B	2½"	Pin thru frame
4C	3"	Pin thru frame
4D	3½"	Plunger in frame

Notes and References

[1]Smith, *The Sharps Rifle* (New York, 1943), pp. 23 and 114.
[2]*Ibid.,* p. 24.
[3]National Archives: Section 74; Miscellaneous trials.
[4]*Ibid.,* Section 156; Group 144, letters to the Chief of Ordnance.
[5]*Ibid.,* Group 1. Letter—Ripley to Sharps, November 17, 1852.
[6]*Ibid.,* Group 144. Letter—Sharps to Ripley, December 13, 1852.
[7]The exact date of the move to Philadelphia is not known. An estimate of March, 1854, may be given based on all available information. In all cases herein where exact dates are not given, the information supplied is based on the personal correspondence of Sharps (as preserved in the National Archives), city directories and newspapers of the period.
[8]Two hundred of these carbines, offered to the army at $25.00 each, were turned down by the Chief of Ordnance. National Archives: Section 156; Group 1, letters from the Chief of Ordnance.
[9]Receipt book of John Krider (courtesy of Mr. Ray Riling of Philadelphia).
[10]Production totals are based on observed specimens. High and low range of observed serial numbers are as follows:

Single shot pistols	4 – 827
Revolvers	130 – 1888
Pistol-rifles	10 – 485

[11]This is not, so far, a demonstrable fact. It may, however, be assumed from the fact that both Eddy and Bolles left Philadelphia shortly thereafter, and the firm name once more became "C. Sharps & Co." Before this, various company names had been *Ira Eddy & Co.* (Listed as manufacturers of "Sharp's (sic) firearms"), *Eddy, Sharpe* (sic) *& Co.*
[12]Only about 200 of these pistols were made.
[13]*McElroy's Philadelphia City Directory,* 1862-1863.
[14]National Archives: Section 156; Group 144, letters to the Chief of Ordnance. Letter—Sharps & Hankins to Ramsey, February 16, 1864.
[15]*McElroy's, op. cit.,* 1865.
[16]National Archives: *op. cit.* Letters—Sharps & Hankins to Ramsey, April 26, 1864.
[17]Smith, *op. cit.,* p. 44.

Records in the National Archives

Group 74, Records of the Chief of the Bureau of Ordnance (Navy)

Group 156, Records of the Chief of Ordnance (Army)

Periodicals

The Gun Collector, Madison, Wis., Issue 26
Gopsill's Philadelphia City Directory, 1868-1875
City Directory, Hartford, Conn., 1850-1855
Hartford Courant, 1850-1874
Philadelphia Evening Bulletin, 1854-1874

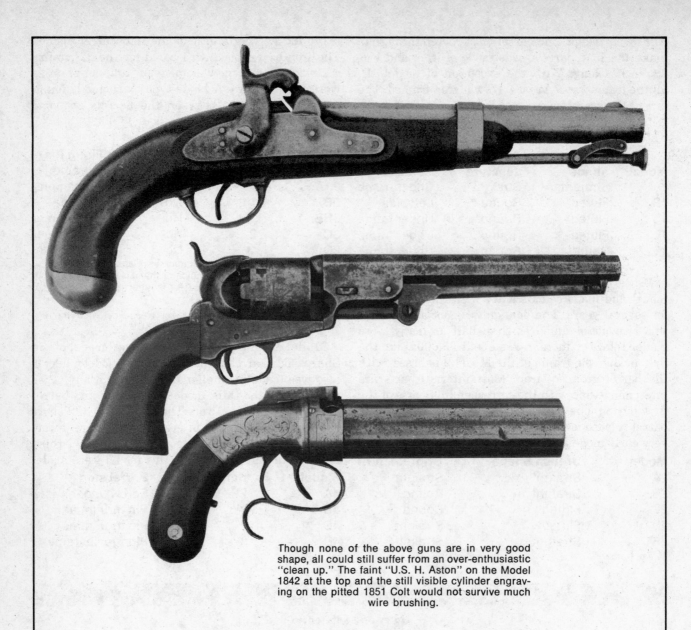

Though none of the above guns are in very good shape, all could still suffer from an over-enthusiastic "clean up." The faint "U. S. H. Aston" on the Model 1842 at the top and the still visible cylinder engraving on the pitted 1851 Colt would not survive much wire brushing.

Mis-directed amateur efforts at "restoration" all too often make the difference between . . .

Collector's Jewel or Collector's Junk

by KINGSLEY P. KARNOPP

ONCE A MAN painted his house at a cost of a few hundred bucks, and got $2,000 more for it than he'd been offered before the paint job. Then he used a little of his profit to start a gun collection. He bought a Civil War revolver at a fair price—the finish was worn off but the mechanism and bore were in good shape. Noticing that the cowboys in the never-never land of Hollywood always had real shiny guns, he spent a few bucks more and had the gun chrome plated. Later on, he got tired of his shiny wonder and took it to a meeting of the Dismal Swamp Gun Collectors Association. "Surely," thought he, "I can make a fast buck on this fine gun over and above my cost and the cost of the plating." He was rudely disappointed when the best offer he got was less than he had paid for the gun when he bought it.

exterior rust and pits, and also the stamped markings and even the shape of the gun had been changed. It is no longer the same gun it used to be, and even with the new gold it seems nearly four ounces lighter. A fresh "paint job" may look good on a house, a car or a woman, but it isn't necessarily the best thing for an old gun.

Modern style rebluing is another common crime. There are few artists in wood and metal who can recondition an old firearm satisfactorily, and these are hard to find and expensive to employ. Modern caustic bluing is commonly used today. The old "rust process" finish takes much longer to apply and is more expensive. The early heat "charcoal blue" is almost a lost art. Since the modern shooter is satisfied with caustic bluing, hardly anyone uses the old

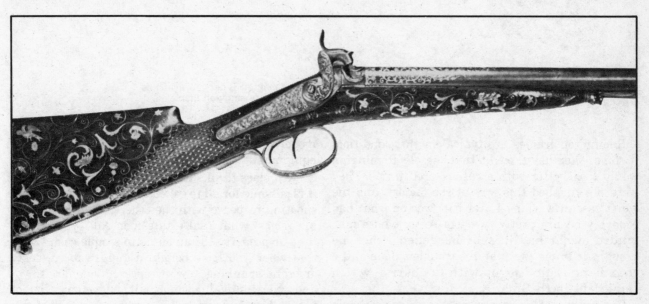

It takes a real craftsman to properly restore a gun with such intricate silver stock inlays as this fine Spanish double-barrel. A gun of this quality is not a good place to learn.

"Look, buster," a critical collector told him, "nobody ever heard of chrome plating before 1928 and on your 1861 pistol it looks as much in place as headlights on a covered wagon. You just loused up a good gun."

"Restoration" like this is a double crime, because it reduces the collector's own value in the gun and reduces the total number of collector's guns by one. Piece by piece unknowing collectors or uncaring dealers have butchered fine old guns to the point where originality ends and faking begins.

At a recent gun collectors meeting I attended, a gold-plated Dragoon Colt was offered for sale. I don't know the price, but there was a hundred dollars worth of gold plating on that gun. It had fallen into the hands of some joker with a buffing wheel, a large supply of coarse polishing paste and lots of muscle, nerve and endurance. By the time this character backed off from the wheel he had removed all the

methods. Even then, restoring involves more than just the right blue. Proper metal preparation is a must.

The gun factories once had men who spent their lives in metal finishing and could put a high polish on a piece without loss of lines and corners, which are inevitably buffed off by the modern 40-hour-week polisher. Few people are working today who can properly "blind polish" a flat side, say of an octagonal Colt cap-and-ball barrel, by using the underside of a leather and grit wheel.

Some gunsmiths can do a nice job of re-casehardening pistol and rifle frames, but the results seldom duplicate the original patterns and colors. The modern cyanide process leaves a wear-resisting "case" but the colors are thin and lack the contrast of old-time bone and leather pack hardening. Also, there is a possibility that the frame will warp and be a complete loss.

The rounded corners on the barrel of this Remington Rider are evidence that it has been worked over by someone with more ambition than skill.

Remington frames are typical in this condition, if some joker has thought that his old Remington would look better with a case-colored frame. They were not finished this way at the factory, and the worst case of warping I ever saw was on what had probably been a pretty good .44 Army whose misguided owner had it color hardened. When he brought it to me to fix up his troubles, none of the chambers would line up with the barrel, which pointed distinctly SE by E.

Generally speaking there are three kinds of people interested in the old guns. The original type is the pure collector. He wants nothing but the finest firearms in the same condition as when they left the factory a century or more ago. He puts his collection under glass and wouldn't dream of shooting any of the guns, although usually guns in fine outside condition are also good shooters.

Then there is the shooter-collector. He likes them in good outside condition but his first demand is that the bore be shootable. He will take a look and the brighter the bore, the brighter his smile. He wants to shoot this piece to see if he can do as well as grandpa did. He sticks to the methods of bygone years and wants the gun just the way it was made years ago.

The last type of collector has sprung up in only the past few years. He likes to shoot targets or game with muzzle-loading firearms but is happy with a brand new modern piece with chromemoly barrel and modern micrometer sights. If he can pick up an old timer in fine shape, he sees no harm in putting new slots in the barrel or screw holes in the tang for modern sights which are usually superior to original equipment.

Each class thinks the other is a trifle tetched, but it is possible for all to collect and enjoy black-powder shooting in peace with the others. There is a unifying factor, what real estate men call "your equity in your property." It amounts to simple cash terms, that when you have bought a gun, restored, rusty, or brand spanking new, it represents dollars to you and a constant value which will not decrease. In fact, it may increase as the years go by. Any collector or shooter hates to take a beating on selling guns. Care and an appreciation of what others find valuable in an old gun may go a long way toward making the difference between a finely restored profit or a chrome-plated loss.

Many interesting guns can still be picked up from junk shops, attics and basements, or from old, long-neglected collections. The rust and dust of scores of years may be on them, or the results of generations of juvenile dry firing all too apparent. What should be done to these pieces in restoring that will satisfy the collector-shooter, or modern muzzle-gun fan?

The beginner's first impulse when he gets a rusty old gun is to rush to the nearest steel power brush and scour the metal parts. Or with coarse emery cloth he scratches away until the surface is bright, although probably not smooth. He then uses lots of muscle and sandpaper on the stock, and on the brass inlays, if any.

When he is through the results are fearful and wonderful to behold, and later he wishes he hadn't done it.

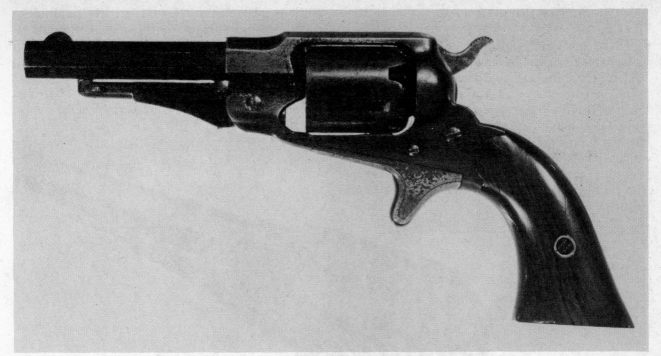

Another Remington, this one a New Model Pocket, shows much original finish and nice sharp edges. Despite pitting on frame, antique gun in this shape should be left alone.

To clean the steel parts of an old gun the best tool is a piece of scrap brass held easily in the hand, with one edge sharpened by filing square. Used like a wood plane or spokeshave, this device simply planes the high rust spots off. The brass will need frequent resharpening but it will not harm the basic finish. It may leave traces of brass on the surface but these can be wiped off with an oily rag. It is amazing how smooth and even the finish can be made without scratching down to bare metal. If the original finish was blue, a pleasant surprise may result, with much more color showing up than one might expect. If brown, the original smooth light color can sometimes be restored.

Very fine 000 or 0000 steel wool with oil on it will help in the final stages, but be careful not to overdo with this. Sometimes even a motor-driven circular steel brush may be used without harm, provided the wire size does not exceed .005″ and *only light pressure* is used. This is particularly useful in cleaning out checkered surfaces such as the thumbpiece of a hammer.

One very common problem is worn and rounded screw-slots. Don't compound the felony by using a screwdriver with a rounded point. See that the point is filed sharp and square. When the screw is out, clamp it gently in a vise with the head resting on the jaws. With a light hammer peen the upset edges back toward the slot. Quite a bit of metal can be pushed back where it belongs in this way. With a knife-edge file widen and deepen the slot a little to square it up.

Do not damage the thread in the frame or other part by trying to force in a screw that "looks about right." Most screws for Colts and Remingtons are available from dealers in antique gun repair parts. These sometimes will fit other makes. Careful study and measurements may make possible re-tapping the hole with a larger standard tap.

On brass or German silver inlays, guards and the like, do not try for a high polish. It will look too new compared with the rest of the gun, and will soon dull anyway. Remove the worst tarnish by rubbing very lightly with fine steel wool. Stop before the bare metal shows. The patina of age is attractive on old brass and has a mellow look that highly-polished metal cannot equal.

Concerning wood, sandpaper is almost never advised. First try washing the stock with thick soap-suds used sparingly on a rag. Sometimes a lot of gummy dirt that has been hiding the original finish comes off this way. If the stock has had an amateur varnish job, try rubbing with a greasy rag and pumice stone to cut through to the basic finish. As a last resort, use varnish-remover sparingly.

The fellow who likes to shoot and yet does not want to reduce the value of his gun in the eyes of the pure collector does not have to butcher a good gun. To take one of the most common situations, let's assume he has acquired a fine Navy Colt. Like all percussion revolvers, the Navy has a front sight that is far too low to group in the black at the shorter pistol ranges. Because of this many Navys are floating around the country with dovetail slots cut in the barrel and a higher front sight installed. On the other hand there are many collectors doing poor shooting because they do not want to alter their guns in this way.

There is a happy solution to this situation. A detachable sight can be made to slip on for shooting and off for collecting and does the gun no harm. A heavy ring of steel or brass can be fitted to the muzzle. It has a blade welded or soldered to the top side. On the opposite side is a *brass* setscrew to tighten it on the barrel. A notch filed on the inside under the blade will accommodate the original front sight and center the temporary one on it. The blade can be filed to correct height, and bent for lateral adjustment.

mechanical perfection. New parts, barrels, cylinders, grips and small parts can be fitted along with adjustable sights. Add a new blue job and the shooter will then have a good gun for blazing at targets. He will not have had to damage a collector's item to get one.

"Who used it" brings up another point. There is a romance to the old guns, which is much of the reason for collecting them.

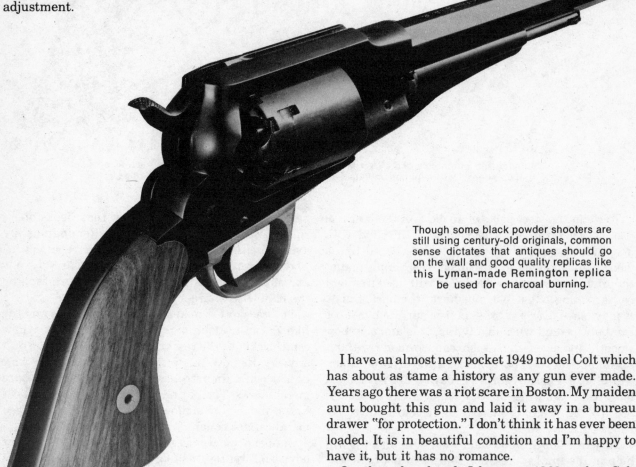

Though some black powder shooters are still using century-old originals, common sense dictates that antiques should go on the wall and good quality replicas like this Lyman-made Remington replica be used for charcoal burning.

The sighting notch on the Colt hammer nose may need to be filed a little to open it up. There is no objection to this if not overdone. The big Remingtons have a reasonably good sighting notch in the frame and can be let alone in this respect, but they can use the higher front sight too. A new sight for a Remington is a little easier proposition. They are big and hefty and can be screwed out. A new sight of the proper height can be made and substituted.

Remingtons offer another advantage for the man who wants a cap-and-ball gun strictly for shooting. A good, solid Remington frame, even if the rest of the gun is in junk condition, can be rebuilt to

I have an almost new pocket 1949 model Colt which has about as tame a history as any gun ever made. Years ago there was a riot scare in Boston. My maiden aunt bought this gun and laid it away in a bureau drawer "for protection." I don't think it has ever been loaded. It is in beautiful condition and I'm happy to have it, but it has no romance.

On the other hand, I have an 1862 pocket Colt with the backstrap engraved with the name of a Union army captain and his organization. Well worn and with its blue rusted to a smooth brown, this gun did not get that way behind a Washington office desk. It travelled the long bloody trail from Bull Run to Appomatox. The really interesting guns were used, saw service, and honest marks of wear should not be removed merely to make the gun look all bright and shiny.

An old gun should be carefully cleaned of the grime of ages, and operating parts restored to good mechanical condition. But no amount of heavy buffing will fool the critic, and it will decrease the value of the gun in a resale. Restoring a gun is not like painting a house, and the "collector" who does not understand that should take up stamp collecting. ●

Spur-Trigger Suicide Specials

by WILLIAM B. FORS

The COLTS are too expensive and the Winchesters are all gone, so there is not much left to collect. Right? Wrong!

There is still a virtually untapped but interesting group of revolvers known as "Suicide Specials" that are gaining in popularity as a collector specialty. Even better, they still fall in a reasonable price range—twenty dollars upwards.

The term Suicide Special was first used in 1948 by Duncan McConnell, writing in the American Rifle-

man. It was used to designate a group of low quality revolvers, usually 22 or 32 caliber, manufactured during the period from 1870 into the early 1900s. The 1870 date coincides with the expiration of the

Top: Allen & Wheelock 22 (upper left), *circa* 1860 and Ethan Allen 22 (lower), *circa* 1868 . . . both distinctive side-hammer models of high quality.

Below: The name "Deringer-Phila." (lower gun) appears on this high-quality revolver made by the originator of the much-copied "derringers." Surviving relative, I.J. Clark, made upper gun of Suicide Special quality after Deringer's death. It is marked "Centennial 1876."

"Empire" model (upper gun), of Suicide Special quality, is by J. Rupertus of Philadelphia and marked with both names. Lower model is "Protector Arms" by Rupertus but without his name on it. Both from the early 1870s.

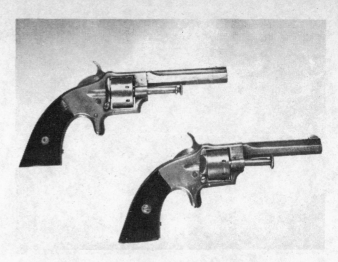

They could be twins, but both are infringements on the basic Smith & Wesson patent. Upper gun is Rollin White 22 marked "Made for Smith & Wesson" . . . lower gun is later Lowell Arms model, also marked "Made for Smith & Wesson." Both companies were licensees and made good quality copies of S&W Model One, 2nd issue. Ejector on side of each is from Ruben Drew patent.

basic Rollin White patent covering a bored-through cylinder for rear cartridge loading. Smith & Wesson held these rights exclusively from 1856 to 1869.

Beginning in 1870, some fifty or more manufacturers began turning out small caliber cartridge revolvers. Workmanship was often poor, tooling crude and the first shot fired using the old black powder cartridge often blew up the gun and injured the holder . . . from this came the name, "Suicide Special."

The immediate popularity of these poor quality revolvers is not surprising in view of the times. During the Civil War many soldiers, especially officers, had carried the small S&W revolver as an "escape gun" or "security symbol." Travel now broadened into the less settled areas as the opening of the west began and the railroad linked both coasts.

Demand for a small revolver continued unabated as the S&W exclusive rights expired and prices dropped from eight dollars for an S&W to one dollar or less for a look-alike model of low quality.

Shop-keepers bought a cheap revolver to keep near the cash box, home-owners kept one in a bedside drawer, and the traveler, by horse, bicycle or train, put one in his pocket. A small revolver was also favored by the gambler and prostitute—the "derringer" fable notwithstanding—as most realized that seven shots was better than one or two. In most cases, these guns were a "security symbol" and were rarely fired . . . which is probably just as well! Little boys mailed away for them to use for firing blank cartridges on the Fourth of July. Mail order restrictions on firearms were virtually unknown then. In

Two "Victor" models, both by Harrington & Richardson. Upper gun is "Victor No. 1," a spur trigger model from the late 1870s. Lower gun, the DA "Victor," helped outmode the other with added trigger guard and double action lockwork.

Otis A. Smith made the upper gun marked "No. 22." Lower model by Maltby-Henley under J.T. Smith patents features double-action, concealed hammer and knurled safety knob on top of frame above grip. The spur trigger models couldn't compete with pistols with such features.

Hopkins & Allen and Iver Johnson companies had a multitude of Suicide Special names . . . Here are four (from lower left to upper right); "Tramps Terror" by H&A, "Smoker No 1" by I.J., "Ranger" by H&A, "Capt. Jack" by H&A.

the middle 1880s, however, both state and local governments began to enact ordinances restricting the purchase of firearms by minors.

From an estimated peak production of 600,000 in 1885, the output of low quality Suicide Special revolvers dropped each year to a low of 100,000 in the year 1890. Explanations are many, so take your choice among: 1) increased legal restrictions; 2) market saturation; 3) depression years; or 4) consumer not happy with poor quality of product. Probably it was a combination of all these factors plus the introduction of new higher quality double-action designs that simply outmoded the single-action spur-trigger models. Thousands of these guns have spent nearly a century stashed away in box or drawer; many can still be found in mint,

unfired condition.

Generally accepted specifications for the basic Suicide Special are:

Blue or nickel finish;
7-shot cylinder (5 in cal. 32);
Birdshead or square-butt handle;
Grips of wood, hard rubber or pearl (rarely);
Barrel of 3 inches or less with three to five groove rifling;
Single-action lockwork on solid frame casting;
Spur or sheath trigger (no guard);
Side-gate loading and removable sideplate;
Cylinder pin removable forward;
Roll-on, poor quality engraving – if any;
Blade front sight; grooved rear sight;
Maximum length: six inches plus.

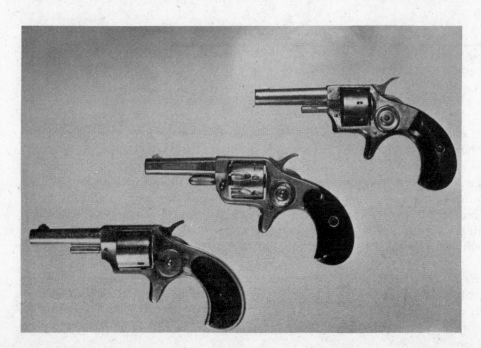

Copying each other's ideas was commonplace. The circular sideplate was popular in the late 1870s. From left to right: Remington "Iroquois," Colt "New Line" and Marlin "OK" models.

These low-quality guns were made to chamber the old black powder cartridges. Don't, repeat *don't*, attempt to fire the modern, more powerful smokeless powder 22 ammo. CB or BB caps have been used, but you are still taking a chance of ruining the piece. Besides, you want these guns as collector's items, not plinkers.

Where can one start collecting Suicide Specials? There are several good sources available:

1) Antique gun lists offered by mail order dealers through advertisements in gun publications. These lists are published about every two months and for one dollar (two, first class mail), you can

tique revolvers. Locate several who do and make your wants known. Dealers visit more shows and can make buys for you. Naturally he needs to make a profit, and the piece may be slightly higher from him than you'd pay at a show—but at least it's now yours!

The days of the rare find in someone's attic or at a rummage sale are pretty much gone. There are just too many of us collectors prowling the country now. Wherever you find them, a Suicide Special revolver will run you from twenty to forty dollars. Better-known maker names, not technically classified as Suicide Specials, can cost you up to one

New double-action models from 1880 on spelled the end for the spur trigger. Clock-wise from upper right: H&R "Victor," Maltby-Henley Hammerless, H&A "XL Double Action" and H&A "XL I."

receive them for a year. First class mail is a good investment, since the better buys go quickly after the lists come out.

2) Gun collectors' shows, also advertised in the gun publications, are held in most areas every few weeks or months. From fifty to one hundred or even more tables will display firearm items for sale. This is the place to meet and trade with other collectors—and make lasting friendships.

3) Advertisements in *Gun Report* Magazine and *Shotgun News* newspaper feature dealer and collector ads offering antique revolvers by mail.

4) Local gun dealers, who may or may not handle an-

hundred dollars—depending upon condition. Prices on both these type pieces are edging upwards year by year.

Be wary, however, of the seller who puts a high asking price for a gun in poor condition. Make certain all parts are intact, the gun operates and fifty percent or more of the finish is present even though aged in appearance. Lesser quality than described above puts the gun in the "junk" class and undesirable to own. Of course, with each succeeding purchase you will become a more discriminating buyer.

Should you select this collecting area for your

Side-gate loading was standard for Suicide Special revolvers because it was cheaper to manufacture. Cylinder pin, released by front or side spring catch, was used to push out spent cartridges, one by one. Swingout cylinders were yet to come with DA models.

specialty, several books should join your gun library. They will save you money as you begin buying. *The Gun Collector's Handbook of Values* by Charles Edward Chapel is a must. Chapel lists prices of Suicide Special type revolvers ranging from ten to twenty-eight dollars value. This author, who is also a contributing editor to Chapel, believes these values are somewhat understated due to the recent many-fold increase of collector interest in the field.

Another book, now out-of-print but sometimes found at gun book dealers, is Donald B. Webster's *Suicide Specials*. Webster deals with our subject in a most authoritative manner and the book is well worth the purchase price—new or used. Enlarging upon Webster's fine start, this author

published a *Collector's Handbook of U.S. Cartridge Revolvers 1856 to 1899*. Listed in this handbook are some 500 brand names of Suicide Specials.

Here are some of the more common names (by maker) that you will encounter on Suicide Specials:

Aetna Arms—(Private brand name, made by Harrington & Richardson).

Bacon Arms—Bonanza, Conqueror, Daisy, Express, Gem, Guardian and Little Giant.

Bliss & Goodyear—American Boy, Challenge, Chieftain, Crescent, Crown, Jewel, Defiance, Excelsior, Non Pareil, Patriot, Penetrator, Spy, True Blue, Veteran.

Continental Arms—Continental No. 1.

Crescent Firearms—Crescent, Elgin Arms, Faultless, Hartford Arms, Hibbard, Howard Arms, Knockabout, Metropolitan, Mohawk, New York Arms, Norwich Arms, Tiger, Victor, Victor Special.

Hood Firearms—Alaska, Alert, Alexis, Boy's Choice, Czar, Jewel, Liberty, Rob Roy, Scout, Union Jack, Victoria, Wide Awake.

Hopkins & Allen—(Over one hundred brand names used)—Acme, Alex, Alexis, Allen 22, American Eagle, Americus, Aristocrat, Automatic, Bang-Up, Bloodhound, Blue Jacket, Blue Whistler, British Bulldog, Capt. Jack, Creedmore, Czar, Despatch No 1, Diamond Arms, Dictator, Double-Header, Dreadnought, Elector, Encore, Expert, Faultless, Garrison, Governor, Half-Breed,

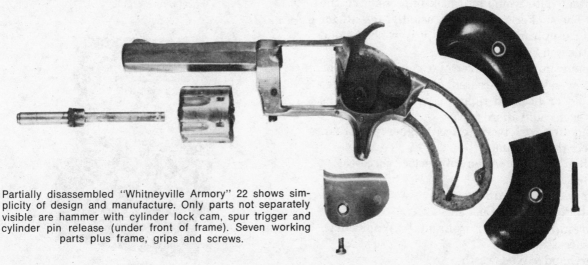

Partially disassembled "Whitneyville Armory" 22 shows simplicity of design and manufacture. Only parts not separately visible are hammer with cylinder lock cam, spur trigger and cylinder pin release (under front of frame). Seven working parts plus frame, grips and screws.

Hard Pan, Imperial, Joker, King Pin, Leader, Life-Long, Little Pet, Little Scott, Marquis of Lorne, Monitor, Monarch, Mountain Eagle, My Companion, Nero. No. 3, Non-XL, Never-Miss, Orient, Paragon, Parole, Pathfinder, Pet, Petrel, Phoenix, Ranger, Red Hot, Reliable, Reliance, Royal, Scott, Spitfire, Striker, Thames Arms, Tramps Terror, Union, Western Bulldog, White Jacket, Wonder, Xpert, You Bet.

Lee Arms— Red Jacket Series; 1, 2, 3, etc.

Meriden Arms—(Subsidiary of Sears Roebuck & Co.)—Aubrey, Senator, Standard, Meriden.

Mohawk Arms—Mohawk.

Norwich Falls Pistol Co.—Bulldozer, Frontier

J. Rupertus Patent Pistol Co.—Rupertus Arms, Empire, Hero, Nero, Terrier, Protector Arms.

T.J. Ryan Pistol Co—Napoleon, Retreiver, Ryan.

Otis A. Smith—No. 22, 32, etc.

U.S. Revolver Co.—(Private brand name of lower quality Iver Johnson models.

Above are, by no means, complete listings but do cover some of the better known and more available names in the Suicide Special category.

Among the manufacturers listed the reader will note some duplication of names. Few companies respected the name rights of another. If a distributor or jobber wanted a certain name on a revolver he was buying in large quantity, he usually got it. Fringe makers were also not above adding a patent date to a gun, even though that patent might have been issued to him for some unrelated other product! The patent date would still look impressive to the buyer. The maker's name was usually absent, for he was rarely connected in any way with the end sale of the gun by the jobber.

In determining the maker of a gun, one must be wary of even legitimate patent dates. Patent holders often sold or licensed rights to several makers as long as each could afford to pay.

Better-quality revolvers (priced higher now than they were then) include:

Ethan Allen Co. (Allen & Wheelock successor)

Allen & Wheelock

American Standard Tool Co.

Colt Pt. F.A. Mfg. Co.

Forehand Arms (Forehand & Wadsworth successor)

Forehand & Wadsworth

Harrington & Richardson

Iver Johnson Arms & Cycle Works

Lowell Arms

Looks authentic? Look again. Box is replica with copy of Manhattan Firearms label on lid. Gun is look-alike to Manhattan but made by American Standard Tool Company at later date. Both were made on the same tooling. Collectors must be wary of home-made replica boxes possibly sold as original.

Another replica box with Colt "Open Top" 22 (first 22 model made by Colt) on velvet pad with catalog sheet reprint inside box lid. Enhance your collection with such a project on those wintry nights.

The "Iroquois" was the only 22 cartridge model put out by Remington Arms circa 1877. Illustration inside box lid is frontispiece page from old catalog.

Early model 22 cartridge boxes by Union Metallic Cartridge Company. Exact dates are not known but believed to be late 1800s. Box at lower left by United States Cartridge Company.

Three early 22 cartridge boxes by Remington Arms-Union Metallic Cartridge Company manufactured after the two companies merged.

Two Winchester Repeating Arms 22 cartridge boxes, old but exact dates not known.

Manhattan Firearms
Marlin Arms
E. A. Prescott
E. Remington & Sons
Rollin White Arms
Smith & Wesson
Whitney Arms

The above models usually bear the company name, patent dates and model name (if any).

Finding Suicide Special revolvers and their better quality competitors involves constant searching, reading of dealer lists and scanning of the gun publication advertisements. I do have a few general rules to follow in making a buying decision... First, buy only those guns in good to very good or excellent condition (according to NRA standards). As stated previously, this means all parts intact, gun operating and fifty percent or more original finish. Junk guns have little value except for parts you may require. If you find a revolver from the low quality list at twenty dollars asking price and in the minimum condition stated above, buy it if only for trading material. A name from the better quality list, same condition and under fifty dollars, again buy

it. Trading and especially trading up is the mark of an advancing collector.

These are my own personal guideposts in collecting. Disagree if you wish, for each individual collector must set his own course, objectives and budget. When my collecting days started, money was a problem—it still is!—but I still get a thrill from holding a compact 22 sheath trigger pistol in my hand, rubbing the grips, and debating whether to add it to my collection for the asking price of twenty-seven dollars. I feel I am holding a piece of history in my hand and price has little to do with my excitement.

You don't have to be a "Colt Connoisseur" to enjoy collecting—those of us in the low-priced field have fun too. ●

Bibliography

Suicide Specials, by Donald B. Webster, Jr.
(Stackpole Books, Harrisburg, Penn.)
"Notes on the Manufacturers of Cheap Pistols," Wm. Paul Smith,
Gun Report, Dec. 1961
"Suicide Specials," by Duncan McConnell
(*American Rifleman,* 1948)
Collectors Handbook of U.S. Cartridge Revolvers 1856 to 1899
by W. Barlow Fors (Barlow Book Co., Northbrook, Ill.)

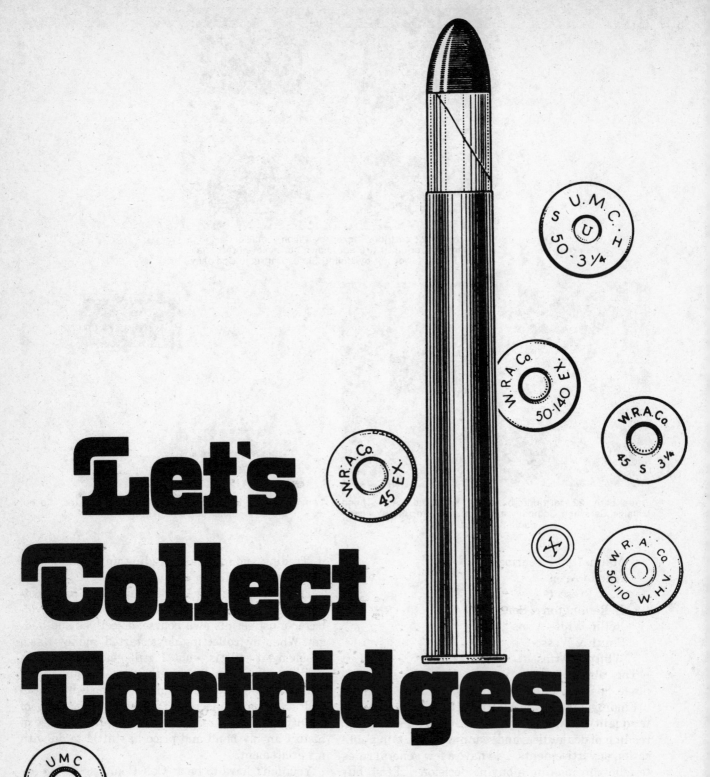

Let's Collect Cartridges!

by STUART MILLER

Collectors' gun prices have skyrocketed in recent years, but
there are still many bargains for the cartridge collector.
Here's how to get started in this burgeoning field, with
tips on what to collect, how to find 'em and price information.

THERE IS still time to climb aboard the cartridge collecting bandwagon, but don't put it off—the fare will go up as time goes on! There is no branch of the broad arms collecting field that has grown more rapidly, since the end of World War II, than this one.

There have been a few cartridge collectors and dealers in this country for the past 50 years or more, but the hobby just didn't spread. It was probably the exposure of millions of people to guns and ammunition in World War II that really aroused their interest. Whatever it was, it worked, for since then the number of collectors and dealers specializing in cartridges has risen rapidly.

Despite the natural rise in prices that this influx of collectors has caused, now is an excellent time to begin this hobby for several reasons. First off, you are no longer alone. Chances are that within driving distance there is some fellow collector that you can talk with, deal with, cooperate with—and compete with! As each new collector starts in, he commences "digging" in some new places and usually comes up with new specimens. There are now enough dealers so that, with sufficient time and money, you can come up with *most* of the items you want. Then, since the war, a number of books have been published with the cartridge collector in mind, so you can now get a good idea of what you have—and have to get! I'll get around to these books later.

Just what are the good and bad features of this comparatively new hobby? The biggest advantage is its interest. There are, no doubt, a few American males who do not have any interest in guns, but they are few! Lately most guns have gone up in price to a point where there isn't much hope of building up a good collection. The guns are just not around any more, and if you do find them, the prices take the fun out of it.

Another thing is the amount of house room that a gun collection takes up. A large collection of cartridges can be easily housed in an attractive cabinet, one that looks like a conventional piece of furniture. This is especially advantageous in the modern compact home or apartment.

As I mentioned, cartridge prices have been going up—just what hasn't?—but you can still assemble an economical collection. There are hundreds of cartridges that may be purchased for 25 cents apiece or less, even from dealers. There are, of course, the much touted "gems" of great rarity that may run over $100 each, but it is the same in any collecting you may do. Look at the rare stamps or coins that are worth thousands of dollars. It is a well-proven fact

Below—Left to right: 12mm Perrin revolver; 44 Henry Flat rimfire; 50 Spencer RF carbine; 56 Spencer Infantry Rifle RF; 50 Maynard carbine perc.; 56 Billinghurst & Requa volley gun; 54 Burnside carbine perc.; 58 Springfield "bite-and-tear" paper cartridge; 50 Gallager carbine perc.

that you can't get them all, so have fun with what you can afford, and hope for the rare ones!

To me, a nice feature of this hobby is its youth. While valuable books have been written on the subject, there is much, much more to be learned. Once you get going on your specialized, perhaps, collection, you'll find entirely new variations and come up with facts unknown to other collectors. Maybe you will write the next cartridge book or article! Anyhow, come on in and learn with us!

There are always disadvantages in anything, and cartridge collecting has its share. The biggest headache is the fact that loaded cartridges, primers and powder *must not be sent through the mails!* The usual method is by Railway Express, with a minimum shipping charge that causes a few venturesome souls to try to send them through the mails. *Don't!* While you might get away with it, it is a federal law you're breaking, and it just isn't worth it. There are, with restrictions, other shipping means available in some areas. Whatever means you have, shipping costs can be cut. Lets figure out how.

First off, you can cut down on the shipping cost per cartridge by ordering as many cartridges as you can afford at one time. The charges will be almost the same whether you have 10 or 100 cartridges shipped, so make it one big order instead of three little ones.

The other practical method is to get some neighboring collector to go in with you and combine your orders. The dealer is usually willing to pack the orders separately, but ship to you as one lot. Thus you can divide the charges and save up to 50% in the process. Many of our customers work it this way and are happy with the results.

Cartridges are, of course, "explosive," and this leads to a natural prejudice against them among the uninformed. This often results in the "Oh, you can't collect cartridges, Junior, you might blow yourself up," routine.

True, there is a certain amount of danger in cartridges—what section of arms collecting doesn't have some?—but with cartridges, it is very slight. If you put the cartridge in a gun, you can shoot yourself with it; if you pound it with a hammer, it will probably go off; if you throw it in the fire, it will scare the "be-junior" out of you, but won't do much more damage.

Probably the biggest fallacy is that if you drop a cartridge, it will surely go off. 'Taint so! I have handled cartridges for years, and dropped my share of them—usually on concrete floors—with the only result being a dented case or bullet. Nor can I remember hearing of any collector having a specimen explode in this manner. Now, don't go throwing them around just to disprove my theory, but I do repeat that with any normal treatment, cartridges just won't explode through handling.

Digging 'Em Up

Now, where are you going to get the cartridges that you want for your collection? Most of them you are going to have to buy, but there is the chance of getting some for free, so let's explore that first. Sit down and make a list of your friends and acquaintances who are 1) cartridge collectors (may you be so lucky!), 2) gun collectors, 3) target shooters, 4) hunters, 5) veterans (they usually brought back a few cartridges and should be tired of them by now), 6) people who have old guns or people who have friends who have old guns. These are all potential sources of cartridges. So, ask them for any old cartridges and you may be surprised at what comes up.

Here is a psychological tip—take any cartridges they want to give you. Chances are they won't be anything special, but by taking them very gratefully, you'll build up your trading stock and they'll keep you in mind should they come across any later.

Most of the cartridges that you buy will have to come from cartridge dealers. They have been combing the country for years and seem to have accumulated most of the available items. Many dealers content themselves with selling at gun shows, but there are a number of us who put out annual catalogs describing and pricing the available cartridges. In the Directory pages of the GUN DIGEST you will find a listing of the well-established dealers. It is important that you get as many of these lists as possible. All dealers do not have the same stock, and their prices vary. It is only by comparing several lists that you can arrive at a fair catalog value of the cartridges.

"Catalog values" for some of the rarer cartridges are printed in the *Gun Report.* Most of the prices given are in line with current selling prices. However in other instances, personal ideas and interests have distorted the prices so that they are not always accurate. Some day everyone hopes that we cartridge collectors will have a catalog something like the stamp catalogs. Such a project will have to be from many sources and is still in the future. Till then, you are going to have to keep on checking the lists.

Because of the cost of printing, envelopes, stamps, etc., dealers are no longer able to give out free cartridge lists. The price of these catalogs will generally run from 25c to $1, depending on size, added data, photographs, etc. Many dealers send complimentary catalogs to their active customers. Even after these catalogs are out of date, they should be filed away for reference. The descriptions and measurements given in these catalogs are usually accurate and helpful.

The traditional place where you should find old cartridges are the hardware stores, the older the better. The only trouble is that someone has no doubt been there first, and the dealers will not break a box of cartridges to sell a single specimen. Many

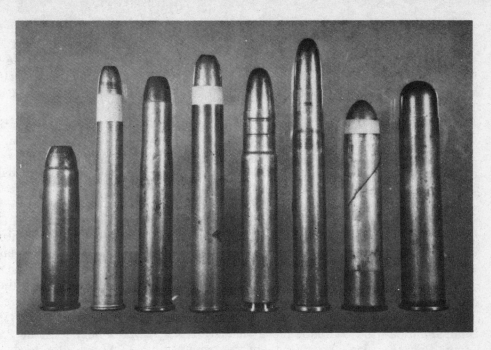

Left to right: 50-115 Bullard, semi-rimmed; 40-85-2⁵⁄₁₆ Ballard; 45-125-3¼ Winchester Express; 50-140-3¼ Sharps; 505 Gibbs magazine rifle; 475 No. 2-3½ Express; 577 Snider, coiled brass type; 600 Nitro Express, the biggest of them all.

of the stores that handle second-hand guns often get in a few rounds of ammunition with each gun and will sometimes part with a specimen or two. Whenever you get a chance at cartridges that you feel are both unusual and reasonable, it's a good idea to get an extra one or two. You are going to find that it is usually much easier to obtain specimens from another collector by trading him something that he needs, than by trying to purchase it.

Besides the hardware and sporting goods stores, always check pawnshops, antique shops, second-hand stores and army surplus stores. Of course if there is an antique gun dealer nearby, keep in contact with him; such shops often get in odd lots of cartridges. If you are on good terms with the sheriff or the police department, either may be able to help you out from time to time.

So much for getting the cartridges — what now?

Care of Cartridges

It used to be that everyone polished and buffed his cartridges till they gleamed, then lacquered or shellacked them to preserve the finish. Lined up on a display board these are very attractive. I don't mind it so much on the modern rifle cartridges, but I don't like to see a cartridge that is perhaps a hundred years old shining brighter than it did when it first rolled out of the factory, perhaps in time for the Civil War. More and more collectors prefer to merely clean the cartridge rather than buff and polish to brilliance.

Be particularly careful in cleaning and polishing plated cartridge cases. This plating is extremely thin and, once it is worn through, the specimen is ruined. The same applies to the lacquered steel military cartridges and those with color identification on case and bullet tip. In working on the paper-patched buffalo rifle cartridges, remember that the paper patch can be easily damaged; these are almost impossible to restore to original condition once the damage is done.

If you are going to fasten the cartridge to display boards, do so in a manner that will not damage the specimen. Some years ago I got a cartridge board with the cartridges fastened to the board by wood screws! Those holes in the rare Crispin, in the big rimfires, the Sharps, etc., made them almost valueless. You may not ever plan to sell your specimens, but someone will some day, so don't spoil it for the next generation of collectors.

This is a hobby that needs but little equipment to successfully pursue it. An accurate micrometer is one thing that you will probably have to buy. Most of the measurements that are so necessary for identification of the unknown cartridges you will find are given in thousandths of an inch. These "mikes," graduated from .0- to 1 inch, can often be found in pawnshops. A good steel ruler, preferably with a sliding bar, and divided into 32nds or 64ths, is also needed, though it need not be longer than 4 or 5 inches. A small but strong magnet is handy for checking for plated steel cases or bullets. For temporary marking of cartridges, a Listo-type wax-pencil, as used for marking glass or china, is just the thing. A handful of small coin envelopes are handy for carrying and identifying cartridges. The only other collecting needs — besides time, money and a little bit of luck — are notebooks and pencils.

As you first begin, you will know every cartridge you have, where you got it, what you paid for it, etc. However, as the collection grows from a handful to several hundred, you will find that you can't possibly remember them all. So, you will either pass up one you need, or else buy some that you already have. The answer is a small loose-leaf notebook listing your collection, giving caliber, headstamp, bullet type, date you got it, source and price. Better work out a code for your source and price, so that you will be able to keep your trade secrets.

Still another notebook that you should keep is your "Data File." You are going to enjoy doing quite a bit of correspondence in this hobby, and in many letters there are going to be a few bits of data that you will want to save.

Rather than ending up with stacks of old correspondence, copy out the special data into another loose-leaf notebook, then ditch the letters. By marking the pages as to calibers or categories, you can combine the data for easy reference. Always give the source and date of the information.

There are two general ways of keeping and displaying the collection; either mount it on boards or keep it in cabinets. If you have the room, skill, and ambition—the boards make a wonderful display. However, don't position them permanently until you are sure you have the whole set; it is difficult to shift the specimens around on the board once they are fastened down. An interesting version of board mounting is to put them in a hanger on the wall so that they resemble the pages of a book, and may be swung back and forth to show the various boards. This is also a good space saver.

Me, I prefer the cabinet method. I am usually short of room, and this method allows me to freely handle and measure the specimens.

Well, that covers why to collect, where to collect, and how to collect—leaving the really big problem. What to collect!

Cartridges to Collect

As in all the rest of this hobby, there are really no set rules; it is primarily a matter of your personal preference. If you are fond of small game hunting, you may go for shotgun shells. Maybe your hitch in the armed forces turned your interest to U.S. and foreign military rounds. Or maybe you have sat through so many TV westerns that your fancy has been turned to buffalo rifle shells. It's strictly up to you. The first thing, though, is to assemble a small general collection. This should come before your specialty collection for several reasons. Most important is that it will give you a good basic idea as to what is available, and a better understanding of the evolution of the cartridge. As you work on this collection, you will automatically pick out the field for your special collection.

This general collection, with its specimens of the weird ignition types such as the combustibles, the teat fires, the lip fires, etc., are going to be far more interesting to your non-collecting audience than your specialty. It is going to be frustrating to discover, as you will, that they'll be far more interested

in a 25 cent pinfire than in a $25 prize specimen!

The basic collection should include a set of the current American rifle and revolver cartridges; a few specimens of the British big game—or "elephant gun"—cartridges; the early patent ignition types as mentioned; a few of the better known Civil War types, and a representative set of U.S. military calibers from the Civil War to date. To these add a few of the foreign military calibers used in WW I and II, and you have a good balanced beginning, one that should please everyone.

Now, how about things from the price standpoint?

I believe that you'll find U.S. sporting rifle cartridges of the last century the most popular field. Because of this popularity, the prices have been steadily moving up, and it is seldom that you get any U.S. paper-patched-bullet cartridges for much less than a dollar, and it's usually up from there. Most of the Winchester 1876, 1886 and 1895 cartridges will still be found in the 35c to 65c price range. The 1873 Winchester loads are, of course, even more reasonable. It is when you get into the Sharps, the Bullards and Ballards; the What Cheers; the "everlastings;" the various models of Maynards, the Creedmoors, etc., that the prices run up into real dollars, in most instances.

As an aftermath of the Civil War Centennial fever, many are still trying to assemble representative collections of the often weird types tried out and used by both sides.

The majority of these will run in the $3 and *up* class. The exceptions to this will be the rimfire Spencers and Henrys, and the inside-primed Perrin revolver cartridges at around $1.00. Next would come the 50 cal. Maynard percussion, often found around a dollar, following this would be the 50 P/L paper and brass case Gallager and the 54 and 58 cal. paper musket at from $1.50 to $3.00. Then comes the 50 Smith and the traditional taper case 54 Burnside—these have risen sharply the past few years, but should be obtainable for less than $5. So, while the Civil War series is fascinating and steeped in history, you have to pay for it.

U.S. military cartridges make a nice bet, especially if you will content yourself with post-Civil War types. With the 58 inside primed, the various 50-70 and 45-70 Springfields, the 30-40 Krags, the 30-03 and 30-06 and, finally, the current 7.62 NATO cartridges, this makes a satisfying special field. In additional to their association to the Indian campaigns, the Spanish-American War and the World Wars, these have the advantages of being accurately described in government publications. While rarities exist by the dozen, most of the more common items can be had in the 20 cent to 50 cent bracket.

The most colorful speciality, one that has not been worked too hard, is shotgun shells. The bright paper cases with the brass heads and the shiny all-brass cases make an interesting color scheme. Because of the many variations in shot and powder load, most collectors content themselves with saving only variations in color, and headstamp. The many small companies that existed briefly in the '80s, the '90s and the very early 1900s, putting out their own special shells, makes this a popular search. American-made shells are far more popular in this country than the foreigners. In this specialty, the factory loaded rounds command the best price, then the unfired primed empties, last the handloaded rounds.

This lack of enthusiasm for foreign cartridges also extends to the military and sporting rifle cartridges. This stems, perhaps, from the lack of information available, and the fact that the cartridges are found in so few places in this country. The most sought

of them and makes the collecting of the rimfires easier and interesting. Here is where headstamp collecting seems particularly popular. The earlier American rimfires were often found with raised headstamps, such as P for the Phoenix Cartridge Co., U for Remington-U.M.C., H for Winchester, etc. Later ones included the sunken headstamps H, P (this time for Peters), U, US, and the diamond of Western Cartridge Co. The idea is to get complete sets of each headstamp. It's an interesting search that will last you for a long time. Prices in the rimfire field are lower than average; the more common variations run under 25 cent and there are not many rimfires that will run much over a dollar.

Another neglected field is the revolver cartridge. This seems to be another case of everyone having

Above—Left to right: 2.7mm Kolibri; 5mm Charola Anitua; 6.5mm Bergmann rimless-grooveless; 6.5mm M1894 Mannlicher (note rim); 9mm Mars; 11.35mm Schouboe (wood-cored bullet); 45 M1923 Thompson; 455 Webley & Scott Navy.

after foreign sporting shells are the British big-game series. The size, length, and power of these shells are always fascinating, even to the non-collector. These are to be found in almost all collections, but few make it their specialty. They are not overly expensive, averaging from $1.00 to $3.00 for the majority.

Foreign military ammo is becoming a more popular field than it used to be. With the interest there is today in the world military situation, it is easy to tie in the small arms ammunition involved. The color identification on base and bullet-tip of many of these adds considerable color and interest to the collection. Again, the drawback is limited sources, and not much hope of completing sets. Prices here generally fall into the 25 cent to 50 cent class.

Since Chuck Suydam wrote his book, *The American Cartridge* covering U.S. rimfires, there has been a burst of energy in that direction. Prior to this, the multitude of case length variations, etc., had discouraged many collectors, myself included. While this book does not have all the answers, it has a lot

some, but no one doing much about it. This seems all the more odd since the revolver is a traditional American weapon. Then, too, there are two excellent books on the subject, so this might be a good specialty for you. There are plenty of variations, they are not expensive, and being small, the collection can be more compact. Most of the lesser specimens may be purchased at from 10 to 35 cents.

Automatic pistol cartridges are more popular and more expensive than the revolver cartridges. Many of the early European versions are much sought after, with resulting high prices. It is here that you find such unusual items as the 5mm and 6.5mm Bergmann, made without rim or groove on the case, and the rare Danish 11.35mm Schouboe with its wood-cored, metal jacket bullet, the high velocity Mars auto pistol series, and the big Bergmanns. Many of these rarities will run $10 or even a lot more, but don't let that scare you off this field. Most of the American auto pistol cartridges and the more common European ones fall into the 15 to 75 cent category. With the current popularity of the sub-machine gun in military tactics, the variations of the pistol cartridge are increasing every year. In fact, I know several men who collect nothing but variations and headstamps of the 9mm Luger auto pistol cartridge, and they're kept very busy and happy.

This brings up still another type of specialty that is fast gaining favor. This is the single caliber collection. You merely have to pick out a caliber that interests you and then try to get every type of bullet, case and headstamp that is made. Of course if you pick out a popular caliber such as 22 rimfire, 30-30, 30-06, 45 ACP, 44-40, 9mm Luger, etc., calibers that are made in foreign countries, too, your collection is that much more interesting. A good feature of this type of collection is that all the car-

you. Just don't pay too much for these types.

One of the most eye-catching collections of ammunition is one of cannon shells. I only know of one or two who collect them, for who has that much room for specimens that may weigh up to a hundred pounds apiece? Also, how are you going to have them shipped to you? Finally, if they are loaded rounds (even the projectiles are loaded in some), a specimen can easily take apart you and your house, too! That is not for me! Many of these cannon loads carry complex, sensitive fuzes, too, a menace in themselves.

I have found that most collectors are interested in strictly small arms ammunition, through 60 caliber, but not the automatic cannon shells that seem to start with 20mm caliber.

Cover design of the Hoxie Bullet catalog of 1910.

tridges are the same size, so the problems of storage and display are simplified. With this kind of collection the notebook mentioned earlier is an absolute necessity.

After all this on what to collect, perhaps a few words on what you shouldn't collect (or what isn't popular) would be in order. Offhand I can think of only three fields that seem to hold little general interest: wildcats, big stuff, and fakes—or "replicas," as they are called by their promoters.

Wildcats—home-designed and made cartridges—hold much interest for the shooter and would-be designers, but not much for collectors. Anyone can sit down and whip up his own cartridge, and it will be the only specimen in existence—how can you hope to make a collection like that! Some of these wildcat cartridges, of course, may turn out to be next season's commercial cartridge, so they do have their interest. Personally, I consider any custom cartridge that has its own headstamp worthwhile, but I can't get enthusiastic over any with merely a formed case, that is, one made from some other caliber case. But, again it's personal choice all through this whole hobby, so don't let me discourage

The final "don't" is about fakes. In any hobby, when the prices start to go up, there is always some skilled and unscrupulous soul who will try counterfeiting. In the beginning, he says, the cartridge is so rare that he'll never be able to get one, so he makes up a replica "...just for my collection." Somehow, though, these often turn up in someone's hands who thinks it is the McCoy. Beware of the rarity at a bargain price. This is a durned nice hobby, so let's keep it clean without this sort of thing!

There are some fine cartridge collecting books available—check the library section in the back of this book. Many of the gun magazines have good cartridge articles, too.

The hobby now has its own club, the International Cartridge Collectors Club, with a good sized membership in this country, and a number of collectors abroad. Further information about the club and its monthly publication may be had from the address listed in the collector's club directory.

Well, that's it—here's hoping I've helped you to join the cartridge clan, and may you enjoy it as much as I have. ●

The Gun Collector's Secret Weapon

by BOB STEINDLER

YOU MUST have seen him—at a gun show, a gun shop, or perhaps at an NRA meeting as he walks through the antique gun displays. He stops here and there, examines the displays and readily talks about the features of this or that gun that differentiate it from such-and-such a model. How did he get that smart? Let me clue you in on his secret.

Let's assume the fellow concentrates on collecting early Colt cartridge revolvers. He studies not only the guns in his own collection but he also examines any Colt that he can find—in private collections, at auctions, at gun shows or maybe in museums. But his real secret weapon is the printed page. He has a comprehensive, though per-

haps small and probably quite select, library of gun books, with most of its contents of course concerning Colt guns.

You would expect him to have Jim Serven's classic *Colt Firearms*, Sutherland and Wilson's monumental *The Book of Colt Firearms;* and of course Haven and Belden's excellent *A History of the Colt Revolver*. Bill Edwards' work *The Story of the Colt Revolver* would be well thumbed, and there would also be a copy of Mitchell's *Colt*. In addition to those, there would have to be a copy of Larry Wilson's *The Rampant Colt*; George Virgines' *Saga of the Colt Six-Shooter* would also be handy; Parsons' *The Peacemaker and its Rivals* shows signs of hard use, as does Dave Brown's

The 36 Calibers of the Colt Single Action Army. As you browse along the shelves, you will find a great many other Colt books, some of them about cap-and-ball Colts. And—there should also be various U. S. Army manuals on Colt military revolvers, and probably Boothroyd's monumental *The Handgun*.

This brings me right to the second secret weapon of the knowledgeable collector. He simply does not stop with books that concern only Colt revolvers. Mathews' recently reissued *Firearms Identification* contains quite a bit of information about Colt cartridge revolvers; W.H.B. Smith's *Book of Pistols and Revolvers* also contains some interesting Colt information, as does Taylerson's excellent three volume work on the history of the revolver. If our collector does not have Loren Smith's *Home Gunsmithing the Colt Single Action Revolvers*, then our learned friend is not as learned as we thought, or he missed the boat somewhere along the line.

The monthly gun magazines often have excellent articles on collecting...especially, of course, *The Gun Report*. In recent years it has become the vogue to clip articles and then heave the rest of the magazine out. However, as a man's interests and activities change, collecting interests can also change. Maybe our imaginary revolver buff

gets bitten by the automatic pistol bug, or perhaps by revolving rifles. If the clipped magazines have been given the heave-ho, that is also where that now-needed precious information is—no longer readily available.

Some 20 years ago, you could pick up instruction manuals for nearly any domestic and many foreign guns in a gun show or shop for pennies. More often than not, the owner would practically beg you to "haul that junk away." If you passed up any such opportunities, and don't feel like kicking yourself now, just let me know—I'll do it for you, and I promise I won't be gentle.

After World War II, when most of the gun companies converted back to making sporting guns, they had to train new salesmen. Many of the companies produced excellent manuals about their products, describing how the guns are taken down and serviced. A great many of these also contained exploded views. The service manuals issued at that time by Winchester, for example, are truly collector's items today. There also was a time when the gun companies issued large posters and special calendars. All of these items, from product brochure to service manual, from advertising broadside to catalog, contain valuable gun information that

One corner of author's library. Here, books are organized by subject such as semi-automatic pistols, revolvers, rifles, shotguns, Colt collecting, etc. Military books are not included in these sections. If you index your magazines and want a permanent file of them, have the issues bound.

Some highly technical German publications require a good knowledge of the language, but others can be read and to some extent understood by anyone with some basic "Bier Halle" German. Whatever your language capabilities, *well-illustrated* foreign publications will always be very useful.

is overlooked by a great many gun buffs and collectors.

There is currently a great deal of interest in catalogs. Some of the scarcer ones have been reprinted, and if it is information you want, the three dollar reprint contains the same material as the original that may sell for ten times as much.

All too few collectors, when attending a gun show, pay not the slightest attention to catalogs, broadsides, brochures and similar material. Much information can also be found in certain almost-forgotten annuals. How many times have you walked past a copy of the now defunct *Official Gun Book?* Browse through a copy, and I'll bet that you will find information that you did not even know existed.

A while back I was at a local gun show where some well-battered older editions of the GUN DIGEST were on display. Among the stack I found a third edition which was in better condition than the one in my library, and I picked it up for the grand sum of two bucks—yet the going price for the earlier Digests in used gun book outlets ranges from $15 to $20. The savvy collector seeks out those needed back issues from the specialty houses—the gun book dealers. More about this aspect of gun books a bit later on.

I already mentioned clipping magazines. Since a great many magazines do not issue an annual index, it is up to the reader to make up his own. Ideally, such an index would be broken down by topic category and by author's name. Of course, the gun collector who also hunts, handloads, and shoots competitively could set up the index to

suit his special interests. Thus, he might classify his specialty in collecting, plus handloading information, plus of course product reports on new match guns and bullets.

Most annuals, such as Amber's GUN DIGEST contain a table of contents. Instead of wading through all 28 issues of it when looking for a specific article, I simply photocopy the table of contents page of each edition and stick those photo copies into a ring notebook. This is much easier to handle, saves a great deal of time, and also decreases wear and tear on those scarce early issues.

I consider my 2000 volume library and my reference files as an integral unit. Thus, whenever I manage to latch on to some reference material that seems to contain new information, or some useful data such as serial numbers, I make a note of this fact on one of my library cards. Much to my regret I did not start such a file card system for my library many years ago, when there were only a couple of shelves to dig through.

Gun books are, in many instances, good investments. I have a number of gun books published in the 1940-1955 period that originally sold for only a few dollars each. Now that they are out of print their value has doubled, tripled, and in some cases even quadrupled. Older books, like old guns, of course bring collector's prices and gun book collecting, especially when combined with gun collecting, provides an ever-appreciating investment that does not depend on the stock market or the world gold situation.

Some 20 years ago old Bannerman catalogs were

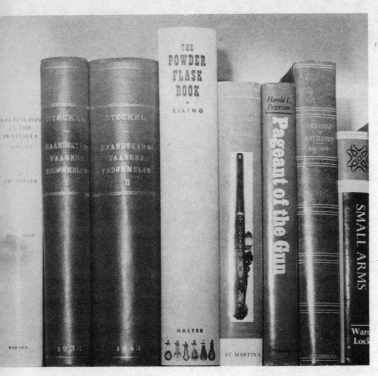

Organization of the library shelves depends on you and your interests. Arrangement can be by type of gun, gun activity, author, or any other system that suits your special interest. After all, you are the man who will be using it.

selling for a buck or two. They are excellent sources of information for gun collectors and, because of their relative scarcity today, some of them sell for a hefty price. Since many of them are now tattered and in imminent danger of falling apart, I had my copies bound. If this is done by an expert book binder the value of the book or catalog will appreciate rather than depreciate. This is not usually the case with restored firearms, however!

While on the subject of collecting books for your library, let me point out a few facts. Even if you buy books merely for the information they contain and not for their monetary or investment value, you will eventually get more than one edition of some of the standard books. Do not discard those obsolete editions! A great many authors delete old information when revising a book, devoting the space to new material. Thus, the older edition may well contain data that won't be in the new edition. Moreover, older editions are very often in demand by gun book collectors. The classic example here is W. W. Greener's *The Gun And Its Development*. The earlier editions are very scarce and valuable, but the final edition, the ninth, has been reprinted. One lucky arms book collector not long ago happened across a gun book in Russian. A closer examination revealed that it was the first edition of Greener translated into Russian! Until that moment the fact that a Russian edition of Greener existed had been only a matter of record in the Library of the British Museum.

I have already mentioned reprints, and would like to add two thoughts to the question of these reproductions. Any reprint is worth having if it concerns a gun, company, ammunition or anything else that you are interested in. For some time I had heard about an RWS ammunition catalog that dated back to 1900, but the only original I could find in Germany was simply too rich for my chronically undernourished checkbook. Then a German arms book dealer had enough foresight to have a very limited edition reprinted in color ($7.25 from C. B. Press), and now 200 lucky cartridge collectors can have a copy of that old RWS catalog.

A few years ago, one set of reprints of scarce books was issued that caused much dismay to arms books collectors. They felt that the reprints would devalue their originals. Since the press run of the reprints was relatively small, before the year was over the reprints had attained collector status; the originals doubled and the reprints tripled in value!

Gun collectors are naturally interested in design variations between models. Major design changes were, and still are, patented. One excellent, but infrequently used, source for design information is the United States Patent Office. If you ever visit Washington, D. C., take the time to pay this veritable treasure trove a visit. Copies of patents can be ordered on the spot or by mail if you know the patent number, and though the service is not overly speedy, the wait will prove worthwhile. Some of the larger municipal and university libraries also have extensive patent collections, and an afternoon researching your collecting specialty in one is a good investment.

Your collecting can, if you have the money, be along the more conventional lines—for instance, guns of the American Revolution, or guns and accoutrements of the Civil War period. You can collect Colt Walkers and Dragoons, or perhaps early S & W revolvers and patent evasions. If that is too rich for you, you can settle on collecting cartridges...although some of the rarer of them can cost you as much as $400! And if that is too much for you, you may want to consider clips and magazines for semi-automatic pistols, or perhaps guns that have a tubular feed mechanism. Whatever your collecting interests, a trip to the Patent Office or a good patent library will enable you to acquire the appropriate patents, those relating to your particular aspect of firearm or ammunition design.

In 1951 Ray Riling published his fabulous arms book bibliography *Guns and Shooting*. In this now out-of-print book, Ray lists and describes 2747 titles. Some of them of course belong in museums in locked glass cases, others are so scarce that only three or four copies are known to exist. Still other titles are in German, French, Italian and three or four other languages.

If you can borrow a copy of this volume, you will discover a virtually endless source of basic reference material—material covering everything from cannons to hunting to polearms to knives to modern handguns.

There is no need to buy every gun book that is published—some are rehashes, others may not fall within your sphere of interest. Some authors perpetuate errors, often drawing material from the source that originated the errors or by following the same erroneous paths that misled earlier writers. Some well-respected sources will even flatly contradict each other—this is where the real collector will begin to dig on his own. And the more you dig, the more expert you will become in that area of gun collecting that is your specialty.

One old-time antique gun dealer always advised the new collectors he met to buy a book for their gun library for every gun they bought for their collections. "Books are what make the difference," he said, "between a *collector* and a *gatherer*." That advice is as good today as it was then! ●

Complete set of The Gun Report appreciates in value every year, is of course also valuable source for collector information. Shelf above contains specialized reference material on forensic medicine and gunshot wounds.

Special Sources for Gun Books

New Books

Rutgers Book Center, 127 Raritan Ave., Highland Park, NJ 08904

Norm Flayderman, Squash Hollow RFD 2, New Milford, CT 06776

Used Books

Angler's and Shooter's Bookshelf, Goshen, CT 06756

Tucek., Roxbury, NY 12474

The Charles Daly Collection, 264 So. Robertson Blvd., Beverly Hills, CA 90211

New & Used Books

Ray Riling, 6844 Gorsten St., Philadelphia, PA 19119

C. B. Press, Box 4087, Bartonville, IL 61607

Paul J. Drabeck, 2886 Roosevelt Ave., Bronx, New York

John Roby, 3703 Nassau Dr., San Diego, CA 92115

Jeff Dykes, Box 38, College Park, MD 20740 Western Americana, new and used books

Walter F. E. Andreas, Jr., D-200 Hamburg 68, Wischhofsteig 5, West Germany, catalogs of used and new books available through C. B. Press, Box 4087, Bartonville, IL 61607, at $1.

James C. Tillinghast, Box 556, Marlow, NH 03450 (Ammo Books & Catalogs)

With seemingly endless variations, a collector could make a career out of collecting the Walther

P.38

by JACK H. BUCHERT

W HY SHOULD I want to collect P.38 pistols? They're all alike, with no variations worth mentioning. Why, the Luger and Mauser pistols are much more interesting with their many variations and fine finishes."

So go the typical comments that a P.38 collector must endure. In reality, few collectors recognize and appreciate the P.38 pistol for what it really is. Mechanically, the P.38 is superior to all previous automatic pistol designs in both design and function. The workmanship and finish on the pre-1942 P.38s can't be matched for precision and beauty. Finally, the P.38 offers an almost infinite number of variations for the collector, and new variations still turn up regularly.

In this article, I will cover some highlights of collecting the P.38 and its commercial version, the HP, and illustrate those variations which are encountered most frequently at gun shows and in trading circles.

Acceptance Stamps and Proof Marks

Before discussing variations of the P.38, it is necessary to discuss the various markings you will encounter. Variations of the P.38 can only be properly identified if the collector is first able to identify the numerous proof marks, Waffenamt (weapons office) marks, and police acceptance marks. These markings, numbered and identified as to their location on the guns, will be referred to throughout the text of the article.

Only two German *commercial* proofs are found on P.38-series pistols, and the only change in commercial proofing occurred in April, 1940. Then the crown-over-N proof (1), established in May, 1891, was replaced by the new eagle-over-N (2), which was used on commercial HPs for the remainder of the war. The standard *military* proof, eagle-over-swastika (3), appears on all military P.38 pistols from 1939 to 1945.

The Waffenamt codes were numbers assigned to a particular weapons acceptance office. The purpose of the codes was to conceal the identity and location of the various Waffenamt offices from the Allies. In this discussion we are concerned only with those which tested and accepted P.38s. It will suffice to say that there were nearly 1,000 individual offices, responsible to 14 regional offices located in Germany, France, Poland, Austria, and Belgium. All parts of

Early **Mod. HP.** This model has rectangular firing pin, is often referred to as the "Swedish Contract HP." (Photos courtesy Joseph Schroeder.)

Right side of early HP. Note crown-over-N commercial proof.

Detail of early HP showing visible extractor, thin rear sight.

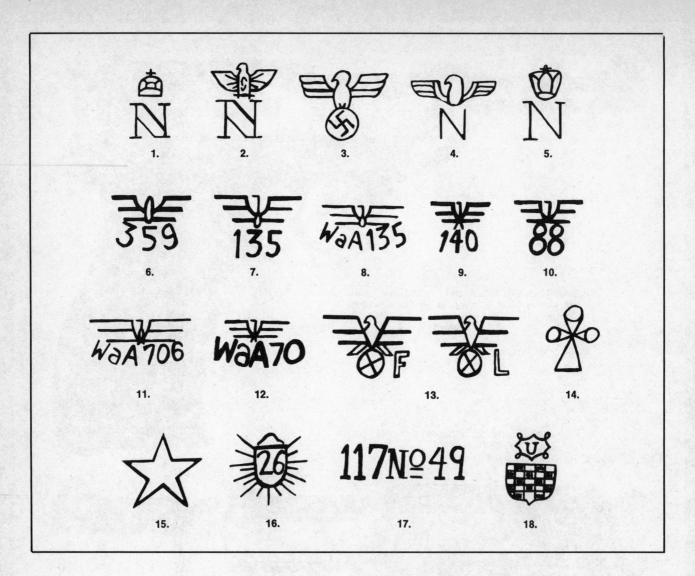

Explanation Of HP & P.38 Proof Markings

1. Found on HPs manufactured before April, 1940. Located on right side of frame in front of serial number, and on right side of barrel block and locking block.

2. Found on HPs manufactured after April, 1940, and on the Mod. P.38 in the positions mentioned for number 1.

3. Proof mark for all variations of the Military P.38 and the ac 45 zero-series. Located on the left side of the barrel block and locking block, and on the right side of the slide between the two Waffenamt stamps.

4. Police Commercial Proof, found on the Walther and Mauser Police models. Found on the left side of the slide by the serial number, and on the barrel and locking block.

5. Variation of the HP commercial proof. This proof used on all barrels manufactured by the East Germans after the war's end. Found on the underside of the barrel.

6. Waffenamt stamp used on all military P.38s manufactured by Walther. Located on the left side of the frame, twice on the right side of the slide, and on the barrel and locking block. On all small parts of P.38s before December, 1941.

7. Waffenamt stamp for Mauser P.38s of 1942 and 1943 manufacture. Located in all places mentioned in number 6.

8. Waffenamt stamp for Mauser P.38s of 1944 and 1945 manufacture. Located on positions mentioned in number 6.

9. Waffenamt stamp for Fabrique Nationale, Leige, Belgium. Located on the frames and slides shipped to Walther. Found on left side of frame, and on right side of slide.

10. Waffenamt stamp for P.38s manufactured by Spreewerke, Berlin, Germany. Located on left side of frame, right side of slide and on barrel and locking block.

11. Waffenamt stamp for Erste Nordboehmische Metallwaren-fabrik, Niedereinsiedel, Czechoslovakia. Manufactured magazines for P.38s. Found on rear of magazines with code jvd.

12. Waffenamt stamp for Boehmische Waffenfabrik, Prague, Czechoslovakia. Found on the front left side of the barrel block on barrels shipped to Walther, used on P.38 reworks.

13. Stamps for the two different police acceptance offices. Found on Walther and Mauser police P.38s on the right side of the slide. Usually acompanied by single Waffenamt stamp.

14. Marking found on the frames of French produced P.38s, usually under the left grip panel.

15. Design of the French Nitro proof. Found on the right side of the slide, and on the barrel block and locking block of French produced P.38s.

16. Typical VOPO rework or acceptance mark. Generally found on the left side of frame, trigger guard, or slide.

17. Swedish military issue number located on either the left or right side of Swedish Contract HPs.

18. Design of Shield found on the right side of slides of the Croatian Contract HP.

Second major HP variation. This example has rare wooden grips, red band painted on thicker rear sight.

the earliest Walther military P.38s are marked with a Waffenamt stamp. However, as the war progressed this practice was discontinued with respect to small parts to facilitate faster production, and only the frame, slide, barrel, and barrel locking-block were marked after 1941. Holsters for P.38 pistols will also bear Waffenamt stamps. For example, the marking WaA195 will be found on holsters made in Köln (Cologne) Germany and on holsters made by different companies in towns surrounding Cologne, since weapons office 195 was located in Cologne and holsters made in that region were sent to that office for inspection and acceptance.

The Walther HP

The commercial forerunner of the P.38 pistol was designated "Die Walther Heeres Pistole," or simply, the *Modell HP*. The Carl Walther plant at Zella-Mehlis (Thuringin) Germany had developed this design, which was accepted in 1938 by the German military as the superior replacement for the Luger. For a short time in 1939 and 1940, some HP pistols were manufactured on a commercial or contract basis along with the military models of the P.38. In 1941 the "Heereswaffenamt" (Army Weapons Office)

began procuring HPs for military use on a limited scale.

The first model of the HP pistol is characterized by a rectangular-shaped firing pin, round lanyard loop, black checkered plastic grips, and crown-over-N (1) proof marks. Early serial number placement was on the right side of the frame, the front of the barrel, and on the *underside* of the left rear side of the slide. The last three digits of the serial appear on the base of the locking block. This variation was discontinued in March, 1940. An earlier model having a "concealed" extractor and wood grips exists, but only two examples have been noted.

The second model HP was nearly identical with the first. The major differences are its round firing pin and eagle-over-N (2) proofs. It was produced through the end of 1940, and checkered wood grips could be ordered as an optional item.

The third model HP differed in that it had a larger rectangular-shaped lanyard loop, ribbed, dark brown, plastic grips, and the slide serial number was moved to the outside upper-right flat portion of the slide. This design became the standard throughout the rest of the war. The commercial-

Detail of right side of military procured HP showing the WaffenAmt stamp on slide. Note eagle-over-N commercial proof.

Slide markings of late **Mod. P.38** manufactured in 1944.

grade blue and polish was dropped in June, 1941, and varying, deteriorating quality of finish became the rule.

In 1941 the German military began procuring HPs in limited numbers. These pieces are identical to the third variation with the addition of one Waffenamt stamp, eagle-over-359 (6), on the right side of the slide.

In 1944 Walther changed the slide legend from "Mod. HP" to "Mod. P.38." In 1945 the commercial slide legend was dropped completely in favor of the standard "ac45" military slide marking. In addition, a zero was placed in front of the commercial serial number on the right side of the frame. All of these 1945 models bear two Waffenamt (6) marks, with the military proof (3) between them on the right side of the slide. These pistols were procured exclusively for military use, hence the military markings. The zero in front of the serial number apparently signified that this model was a non-standard military run.

In addition to the standard 9mm HPs, there was limited production of 7.65mm (Luger) HPs, and some 7.65mm single-action HPs with wood target grips. Some were also made with lightweight alloy frames.

In August and September, 1940, Walther produced the 7.65mm HP models. The exterior appearance of a standard 7.65mm is identical to the early model round-pin HP with the exception that it is marked 7.65mm instead of 9mm on the slide. These pistols fall in the 2990 to 3100 serial range. The single-action 7.65mm HPs with wood thumb-rest grips were very special and were apparently ordered in one lot. These HPs fall in the low 3100 to 3250 serial number range.

In November and December, 1940, Walther produced a lightweight frame model HP. These pistols fall in the mid-6800 to mid-6900 range. They are identical in appearance to the commercially finished HPs of this period, but the frame is a different color due to the alloy metal. There were also machining differences in the frame to give added strength to the alloy.

Some early HPs will be found with a red band on the rear sight. It is correct, and undoubtedly was an optional feature that could be ordered as these pistols were for both commercial or contract purchase.

Lastly, among late 1943- and early 1944-manufactured HPs there are those which exhibit a reddish-color frame or slide. This departure from the normal

Single-action 7.65mm HP. This model has thumb-rest target grips, and the lockwork has been altered so it will not function as a double-action. Photo courtesy Lt. Kenneth Nichols.

blue was caused only by an improper amount of water and temperature in the bluing process. There is no special significance to the red color as far as collectors are concerned.

Walther Military P.38s

Procurement of the Walther P.38 by the Heeres-waffenamt began in late 1939. The progression of early mechanical changes coincide with those of the HP, so for the sake of brevity won't be repeated in detail. All Walther military P.38s manufactured before June, 1941, have a commercial-grade, high-polish blue finish. The grips were serial-numbered to the gun. In addition, the magazines on all P.38s produced prior to December-January, 1941-42 were all numbered to the gun. P.38s that still have the correct matching magazine are worth a premium, as there are fewer P.38s that survived with original magazines than Lugers.

The earliest military P.38 is known as the "First Model Zero-Series." This pistol has its extractor *concealed* in the slide and a rectangular firing pin. The slide has the Walther Banner and "P.38," proofing is the eagle-over-swastika (3) and all small parts are marked with eagle-over-359. This model began with serial 01 and ended with approximately

01500. There is some evidence that the first 30 or so were special test pieces, and may have additional features.

The Second Model Zero-Series is identical to the first with the exception that its extractor is visible from the side of the slide. These pistols are in the 01500 to 04500 serial range and their survival rate has been very low as few are seen.

The Third Model Zero-Series represents the final design change. The rectangular firing pin was changed to the standard round pin. Some of these pistols have a red band on the rear sight, like HPs of the same vintage.

In September, 1940, the Walther Banner on the slide was replaced by the code number "480," which had been assigned to Walther. This variation had a short run, as in October, 1940, Walther was assigned "ac" as their code designation in the new Nazi all-letter system.

The "ac no-date model" was manufactured in October, 1940, and is considered to be the rarest of all military P.38s. About mid-way through October, 1940, the ac no-date reached serial number 10,000 and numbering started over with a suffix letter "a" added to the serial number. With the beginning of the a block, the number 40, for 1940, was added beneath the ac on the slide. This variation is referred to as the "ac40."

Midway through the letter a block a standard ac40 die came into use. From this point on through the end of 1943, the date marking on the slides of military Walther P.38s was standardized.

While collecting P.38s, one notices the scarcity of early Walther military models. More specifically, pre-1942 P.38s in excellent condition are few and are far between. The obvious reasons are: First, the P.38 was the workhorse of the German army during WWII, and the earlier examples were exposed to

wear, weather, and battle for a much longer period. Secondly, vast numbers of this group of pistols saw service on the eastern front which would account for untold thousands being captured and/or destroyed. This explains why such a high proportion of the few that are available bear East German *VOPO* (Volkspolizi) marks and have been reworked and refinished. We'll discuss VOPO-marked P.38s later on.

1941 production ran from the no-letter block through the j block, a total of 110,000 pistols. There were 10,000 pistols in each letter block, and at the beginning of each year a new series was started. For example—December, 1941 was in the j block; Janu-

Very early First Model Zero Series military P.38. Note concealed extractor, thin rear sight.

Early Third Model Zero Series.

ary, 1942 started with the no-letter block, then went into the a block, and so on.

In late 1943 Walther changed from the double-line date markings (stacked) to the single-line slide markings. The 1943 single-line P.38 variation falls in the late m and n letter blocks. The single-line markings used on Walther P.38 pistols was standard from this point until the end of the war.

In 1943 and 1944 there were a couple of blocks of an interesting Walther variation. These pistols have a large lower-case ac etched over the date, a gray finish, and bear either Mauser WaA135 or Fabrique Nationale WaA140 Waffenamt markings on the frame and slide. One possible explanation is that these slides were made and marked at the Belgium FN plant, then shipped to Mauser for assembly and acceptance. This is a variation which is highly desirable to the collector but is rarely offered.

In 1943 and 1944, Fabrique Nationale shipped many frames and slides to Walther for assembly to supplement production. In addition, thousands of barrels, coarse-serration hammers, and stamped slide-release levers were made for Walther by Fabrique Nationale and Boehmishe Waffenfabrik, located in Prague, Czechoslovakia. Boehmishe Waffenfabrik also supplied the coarse-serration

480 code Walther military P.38, manufactured in September, 1940.

Detail of markings on **ac no date.** Rarest of all military P.38 pistols, made in October, 1940.

Early **ac** with "40" added. Another difficult-to-find variation.

Detail of standard **ac 40** marking.

hammers used on late Walther and Spreewerke-made P.38s. FN also supplied other unmarked small parts. In addition P.38 magazines were made by Erste Nordboehmische Metallwarenfabrik, Niedereinsiedel, Czechoslovakia. These magazines are marked "JVD" on the left side and WaA 706 on the rear. They belong with 1944- and 1945-manufactured Walther and Spreewerke P.38s.

The German police procured a number of ac43 and ac44 P.38s in the no-letter range. These guns have a commercial proof (4) on the left side of the slide and the right side of the barrel block and locking block. On the right side of the slide is an eagle-over-L

(13) police acceptance stamp. As with other pistols that bear these police markings, this variation of the P.38 was processed by a commercial proof house for police, political, or para-military organizations. The L has not been identified as to the organization it represents. Walther police-marked P.38s are very scarce.

Mauser Produced P.38s

In 1942 the war was making great demands on the German Army. They were fighting on many fronts and the Allied armies had been striking back in earnest. Small arms of all types were in short sup-

Details of single line marking on late Walther P.38.

Unusual **ac 44** double line variation. Slide was produced by Fabrique Nationale, marked for Walther, and finished and assembled by Mauser. Note the WaA135 acceptance mark.

ply, and the Oberkommando der Wehrmacht (Armed Forces High Command) began to seek new sources and expand small arms production. As a result the Mauser-Werke in Oberndorf received licensing and machinery to begin production of the P.38.

By November, 1942, Mauser had completed tooling and production of the Mauser P.38 began. The code initially assigned to Mauser was byf, changed to svw in 1945. The Waffenamt accepting Mauser P.38s was WaA 135, located at Oberndorf.

Mauser differed from Walther in their serial number lettering blocks, beginning with the a-block in December, 1942, and continuing with part of the a-block into 1943. The first alphabet series continued thru the z-block, which by then was September, 1944. Then they started with 10,000 byf44 P.38s in the no-letter range, and progressed to the f-block (SVW45) in April, 1945.

The first byf42 P.38s had a matte black finish on the slides, which gave them a distinct black appearance, different from the military blue which was used later. None of the byf42s, or later Mauser issues, had serial numbered grips or magazines. Magazines for Mauser P.38s have the Oberndorf WaA 135 stamp on the rear.

The 1943 production P.38 is almost identical to

1944 Walther P.38 with a Fabrique Nationale frame. Note acceptance mark.

the 1942 model. Minor differences include machine marks and finish. The only major difference was the changing of the design of the Waffenamt stamp from eagle-over-135 (7) to eagle-over-WaA 135 (8) in the p-block in late 1943. This new acceptance mark was used on all later Mausers.

In September, 1944, Mauser began looking for a finish that would be a durable but faster to apply substitute for the standard bluing process. The result is what is referred to as the "dual-tone" byf44 Mauser P.38. The finish on these pistols is very distinctive — the barrels usually have a weak blue finish while the slides, frames and small parts range in

Mauser 1943 military P.38. Note early style WaffenAmt stamp on frame.

"Dual-Tone" Mauser-made P.38. Note blued barrel, late acceptance mark.

SVW 45 produced before war ended.

hue from a "gun metal" gray to a heavy dark gray. Mauser used this finish throughout the remainder of their production.

At approximately serial 3000e, Mauser's code was changed to SVW. This was in late December, 1944, though the pistols were dated 1945. These P.38s are interspersed with e-block byf44s in the same serial range so there must have been a quantity of 44 dated slides that had not yet been used. Some of these early SVW45s will show a weak blue finish over the entire pistol; the reason for this brief lapse is not known. Production of the German SVWs ended at about serial 3750f in April, 1945.

As with the Walther pistols discussed earlier, there is a group of Mauser-made P.38s that were procured for police use. In late 1943 — November and December — about 800 pistols in the no-letter block were procured. These are marked byf43 and exhibit the police acceptance stamp, eagle-over-L (13), and have a blue finish. There was some overlapping in December, 1943 of pistols marked byf43 or byf44. From January to September, 1944, Mauser byf44s have a deep blue finish and are marked with police acceptance (13). In September, while Mauser was changing to the dual-tone finish, about 100 P.38s were marked with eagle-over-L. Beginning with serial 4400 the police marking was changed to eagle-over-F (14), and the pistols were dual-toned. Police procurement of SVW45s was limited to approxi-

French-produced **SVW 45.** Note Parkerized finish and steel grip panels.

mately 200 pistols, starting with serial 5600. Unlike Walther, Mauser reserved the no-letter block for commercial proof house (police) acceptance. The first pistols in this block were produced in November, 1943, and only several hundred per month were manufactured and procured until the range ran out in early 1945.

The French took control of the Mauser-Werke after Oberndorf was overrun in April, 1945. Almost immediately they began producing P.38s for their own use. The French were involved in several colonial wars immediately following WW II, particularly in Indochina. Since their own arms industry was in bad shape from the war, they sought other means of obtaining small arms.

The French continued the German serial number sequence, first using up remaining stocks of German-marked and accepted parts. The first French SVW45 P.38s were made of these mixed, left-over parts. They used a gray parkerized finish, though some of their early no-letter range trial pieces have a blue finish. One will also sometimes encounter byf44-marked pistols in the g-block which have the French star (15) nitro proof on the right side of the slide.

In 1946 the French produced approximately 6000 additional pistols, marked SVW46, before they had to abandon the Mauser plant due to loud Soviet protest. Found on the late French-produced SVW45 and SVW46 P.38s are many different acceptance and inspection marks, identified in the marking table.

Spreewerke-Manufactured P.38s

In 1943 personnel from the Mauser-Werke in Oberndorf went to Berlin to set up a government-operated plant to produce P.38s. The identification code assigned to Spreewerke was cyq. Very early cyq P.38s were identical, in finish and manufacture, to Mauser-produced P.38s of this period. However, when the Mauser personnel left the plant in December, 1943, the quality of finish and machine work fell off rapidly. This was because the Spreewerke plant was geared to produce P.38s as fast as possible—it turned out approximately 20,000 pistols per month, an extremely high rate for this time. By December, 1944 the y-block was completed. In January, 1945, the z-block pistols were being produced and here a point of debate and concern occurs. At about mid-z-block, Spreewerke's cyq slide marking becomes *cvq*. One camp of collectors has argued that Spreewerke's code was changed from cyq to cvq, while the opposing view is that the tail on the y in the code die had broken, leaving the *appearance* of a v. After examining several of these cyq P.38s, I must lean toward the latter belief.

In mid-January, 1945, Spreewerke began a new alphabet series. The letter a was added as a prefix to the serial number. By March, 1945, the 3000b-block range had been reached. By this time, due to bomb damage or other problems, Spreewerke seems

SVW 46 manufactured by French. Note RWS proofs on barrel and concentric rings before number on frame.

Late 1944 Spreewerke P.38. Note large serrations on Czech-made hammer, late stamped slide release.

1945-manufactured Spreewerke P.38. Note "cvq" marking and letter prefix.

Very late zero series Spreewerke P.38 made up of inferior parts. Note large "U" acceptance mark on frame.

to have almost completely lost its ability to manufacture new pistols.

A new cyq series was begun, which is referred to as the zero-series cyq. A zero was added in front of the serial number, starting at 1 again, to signify that these were non-standard production. About 4400 of these zero-series pistols were assembled and the collector will encounter this variation with refinished Walther slides on Spreewerke frames, FN-manufactured internal parts, Czech-contract barrels, and so on. These P.38s are proofed with a large capital "U," which stands for Untersuchung, or "tested." Characteristics of this variation are poor fitting parts, badly milled or cracked surfaces, spotty finishes. Pistols of this variation should be thoroughly examined by the collector before shooting.

The Spreewerke factory fell into Soviet hands when Berlin was occupied and the plant and machinery was dismantled and taken elsewhere. Many of the post-war East German-manufactured P.38s exhibit machining marks characteristic of the Spreewerke machinery.

Post-War Reworks

After the Second World War the Soviet-bloc coun-

tries made wide-spread use of the P.38. Very little is known about this use as official information is unavailable. Any variation of P.38 or HP may be encountered which has the so-called "VOPO" markings. These were pistols that were captured during the war and later utilized by East Germany, Poland, Czechoslovakia or any other country that was given aid and arms by the Russians at the war's end. Barrels manufactured by the Soviet-bloc country having the machinery display a large crown-over-N (5) proof mark on the underside of the barrel. Many of this variation are made up of major components of different pistols which were re-serial numbered to match. Some of these combinations are very unusual and highly desirable to the collector. One group of P.38s appears to have been completely manufactured new in the late 1940s or early 1950s and has the characteristics of the Spreewerke manufactured guns. These P.38s are marked with the letters above-9, surrounded by a wreath, located on the left side of the frame above the take-down lever. The serial numbers are preceded by a large capital letter N. Little is known about this variation.

The majority of the VOPO-reworked P.38s have

Walther manufactured P.38 with VOPO marking on trigger guard. Note capital "A" on frame denoting a rework. Inset illustrates crown-over-N marking found on East German manufactured barrels.

been imported with the VOPO marks defaced with a punch. This is believed to have been done by the importers to hide the fact that these pistols came from Soviet-bloc countries. Since the United States government placed an embargo on importing weapons from Soviet countries, the VOPO marks had to be removed or made unidentifiable in order to import them.

Many rare and highly desirable P.38s and HPs are still in the hands of the GIs who brought them back after WW II. Perhaps you should take another look at yours today! ●

East German reworked pre-war HP. The frame is that of a second model zero series, with the HP slide renumbered to match. Note Czech contract barrel and VOPO acceptance mark. An extremely scarce variation.

Value Guide To P.38 Variations

Variation/No. Produced		Scarcity	Value NRA Ex.
Mod. HP	rect. pin, exp. extractor (1,000)	Obtainable/Hard to locate	$ 350
Mod. HP	Swedish Army Marking (unknown)	Difficult to find/scarce	400
Mod. HP	round pin, early ser. no. placement (4,780)	Hard to find in ex. cond.	325
Mod. HP	7.65 mm plastic grips (120)	Very rare	1,800+
Mod. HP	7.65 mm single-action, wood grips (140)	Extremely rare	2,400+
Mod. HP	late ser. no. placement, comm. fnsh. (5,100)	Hard to find in ex. cond.	300
Mod. HP	lightweight frame, comm. fnsh. (100)	Extremely rare	1,200
Mod. HP	Late nos., comm. fnsh., waffen. marked (1,200)	Very scarce in ex. cond.	325
Mod. HP	Croatian Contract (200)	Very rare	No sale figure
Mod. HP	late military grade finish (6,600)	Easy to find	220
Mod. HP	military grade fnsh., waffen. marked (4,100)	Easy to find	230
Mod. HP	Any comm. fnsh./wood optional grips (unknown)	Wood grips very scarce	+$50 any model
Mod. P.38	(1,700)	Easy to find	225
AC 45	Zero Series (1,100)	Easy to find	225
1st. Model	Zero Series Military P.38 (1,500)	Very hard to find/rare	600
2nd. Model	Zero Series Military P.38 (3,000)	Very rare	500
3rd. Model	Zero Series Military P.38 (8,500)	Scarce in ex. cond.	375
480 Code	(7,200)	Extremely rare/ex. cond.	450
AC	(not dated) (2,800)	Extremely rare/any cond. (NRA vg)	400+
AC	(40 added) (5,700)	Very rare/ex. cond.	300
AC 40	(14,300)	Scarce	275
AC 41	ac on frame (25,000)	Scarce	225
AC 41	no ac on frame (35,000)	Scarce in ex. cond.	200
AC 41	Military grade finish (50,000)	Fairly common	150
AC 42	(120,000)	Common	135
AC 43	double line (125,750)	Common	110
AC 43	single line (20,000)	Common/harder to locate	110
AC 43	Police acceptance (250)	Very scarce	300+
AC 43	Accepted Mauser WaA 135 (4,000)	Uncommon/hard to find	150
AC 44	(117,500)	Common	90
AC 44	Police accepted (500)	Very scarce	275+
AC 44	FN WaA 140 frames (5,000)	Uncommon/hard to find	140
AC 44	FN grey fnsh. double line slides (7,000)	Uncommon/scarce	175
AC 45	All factory matching (33,000)	Common	90
AC 45	Factory mismatched, Late c and d block (9,000)	Common/most in new cond.	90
AC 44	or AC 45 with Fnh barrel	Fairly common	100
byf 42	(19,000)	Hard to locate	185
byf 43	(154,300)	Common	90
byf 43	Police accepted (800)	Hard to find/scarce	220
byf 43	Accepted with late WaA 135 (Approx 1,500)	Very hard to find	150
byf 44	Military blue (91,000)	Very common	90
byf 44	Dual tone finish (44,000)	Very common	90
byf 44	Police L blue fnsh. (1,900)	Hard to locate	250
byf 44	Police L dual tone (100)	Scarce/rare	300+
byf 44	Police F dual tone (1,125)	Fairly easy to find	225
SVW 45	German production (14,800)	Fairly common	150
SVW 45	Police F marked (200)	Very scarce/rare	325+
SVW 45	French production all varieties (25,000)	Fairly easy to find	175
SVW 46	All marking variations (6,000)	Hard to find/scarce	275
cyq	(260,000)	Very common	90
cyq	1945 prod. letter prefix (14,000)	Fairly common	125
cyq	Zero Series (4,400)	Fairly easy to find	125

Values are for NRA excellent condition. Experimental and one-of-a-kind models have been excluded purposely. All production figures are an accurate approximate figure. VOPO marked and reworked P.38s with markings intact are worth about 20% more in excellent condition. Late P.38s with fnh marked barrels are worth about 10% more than shown.

Values are average sale figures that author has observed and are intended as a guide only.

Fascinating mechanisms, lots of history... and fun to shoot, too!

SELF-LOADING RIFLES

by DONALD M. SIMMONS, JR.

MANY PEOPLE in the gun collecting game have the feeling that all the goodies have been bought and salted away, leaving only junk to be bought at gun shows. I suppose there is some truth to this but if one strays a little from current vogues in collecting and looks for something still reasonably priced, you will find there are still "cream puffs waiting in the wings." One of the most overlooked collectables is the self-loading rifle. There is plenty of history and adventure tied up in this relatively recent type of firearm. Because of current legal restrictions, it is impractical for most private individuals to collect

U.S. military semi-automatic rifles: Top—The Johnson 30-06, complete with ultra-light bayonet. Middle—U.S. Rifle M-1 (Garand), 30-06. Bottom—U.S. Carbine M-1, 30 Carbine.

machine guns. Since most of the post-WW II assault rifles fall into this category, we'll limit ourselves to guns which can be fired only semi-automatically.

At the end of this article I will discuss some of the scarcer self-loading rifles that have been recently seen for sale at large gun shows and elsewhere. There are still lots of good ones around, and most won't cost an arm and a leg. The Lugers and Mauser Broomhandles, Kentucky rifles, Civil War arms, many Smith & Wessons, Colts and Winchesters are very much sought after, but some of their rarest examples are still not as rare as a Pedersen Device.

The self-loading rifle is about to come into its own as a collector's item, so let's take a look at what there is to collect and consider some of the logical divisions into which this class of arms can be broken down. Let's begin with a taste of the history of these fascinating rifles.

History

The self-loading (or semi-automatic or auto-loading) rifle is a fairly recent invention. Almost as long as there have been firearms, there have been men who dreamed of an arm that would reload itself automatically, leaving only the pulling of the trigger to the shooter. The concept itself is simple, but its implementation took centuries. Consider the flintlock revolver Collier made in 1815 and apply to it the later Webley-Fosbery automatic revolver design. Elisha Collier could easily have leaped forward nearly a century by adding a mechanism by which recoil cocked his flint hammer and indexed the cylinder. Collier could have had such vision, but the arm that resulted would have been a nightmare to keep operating because of its unsealed breech and black powder fouling. Thus we have arrived at two of the steps necessary to develop a practical self-loading weapon, the self-contained cartridge (for sealing) and smokeless powder (for less residue). The last step in the progression was the ability to cheaply mass produce close tolerance parts with machine tools rather than by hand.

Pauli, a Swiss, invented the cartridge, as we know it today, back in the black powder days of 1812. In 1866 Hiram Berdan perfected Pauli's invention so well that Berdan-primed cartridges are still used by most of the world, and in 1885 a Frenchman, Vieille, invented a smokeless powder. Of course, Eli Whitney, of cotton gin fame, had pointed out even before the Civil War the immense advantages of mass production and the ability to interchange gun parts.

Thus it was, by the last decade of the nineteenth century, that all ingredients necessary for the birth of a self-loading rifle were present. Two American geniuses in firearm design each independently took a Winchester lever action repeater and converted it to a self-loader. Hiram Maxim was first, making

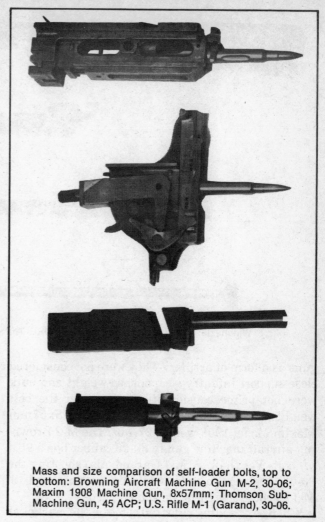

Mass and size comparison of self-loader bolts, top to bottom: Browning Aircraft Machine Gun M-2, 30-06; Maxim 1908 Machine Gun, 8x57mm; Thomson Sub-Machine Gun, 45 ACP; U.S. Rifle M-1 (Garand), 30-06.

a recoil-operated Winchester in 1883. When the Maxim/Winchester was fired recoil pushed the butt against a spring-loaded buttplate which, by linkage, worked a shortened loading lever through its operating arc. In 1892 John Browning came up with an entirely different principle. A small cup with a hole the diameter of the projectile was mounted in front of the gun's muzzle. As the bullet passed through the hole, the gas emerging from the muzzle pushed on the entire cup. The cup then moved forward, and by linkage, reloaded the action for the next shot. Encouraged by these earliest designs, both men went on to design a variety of automatic weapons— starting with machine guns. This was because the current military demand was for a reliable machine gun, with virtually no interest in a self-loading rifle. Thus, it was that the development of a practical self-loading rifle had to wait for the machine gun to be developed, though it had actually preceded the machine gun as a working prototype.

It was a fortunate choice for the designers that they turned to machine gun design first. A reliable high-powered self-loading rifle of reasonable weight is a real challenge. In the late nineteenth and early twentieth centuries the military employed machine

Winchester Model 1903 rifle, stripped, 22 WRF. The second item from the top is the unusually heavy bolt.

guns as a form of artillery. They were not considered close support infantry weapons, so weight and bulk were not prime considerations. Consider the bolt weights of two machine guns. The bolt of the 8x57mm Maxim Model 1908 weighs 27.7 oz. The M-2 Browning aircraft machine gun in 30-06 caliber has a 26.4 oz. bolt. Yet the U.S. M-1 Garand, also shooting the 30-06, has a 5.6 oz. bolt while the bolt on the U.S. M-1 Carbine tips the scale at only 2.9 oz.!

When self-loading rifles did come on the market at the turn of the century, it was the civilian-shooter-hunter, not the military, who first accepted the new breed. Among the first of these self-loading rifles were the carbines derived from the successful Bergmann, Luger, Mannlicher, and Mauser pistols. These carbines, though they utilized pistol actions and ammunition, were true rifles with long barrels and wood fore-ends. As a collectable class these have become very expensive because they appeal to both the semi-automatic long gun collector and the auto-matic pistol collector.

The military were very skeptical of the self-loading rifle as a replacement for the deeply entrenched bolt action repeating rifle. They had seen and experienced battlefield conditions, and were very doubtful that a complex self-loader could hold up in the field. There was also an abiding fear that a rifleman in combat, armed with an auto-loading rifle, would expend his ammunition too quickly and be caught short. I'm sure we agree that the early prototype self-loading rifles would not give as good field service as, for example, the Mauser Model 1898. In fact, I rather doubt that any self-loading rifle ever designed is as durable as a well built bolt action repeater. This "flaw" in the semi-automatic is basic, since there is a fixed amount of energy available to cycle its action after it has been fired. For example, take a self-loading rifle which has been over-lubricated and try firing it at sub-zero temperatures—you'll have trouble. But operate a U.S. Model 1903

Winchester Model 74 (top) and Stevens Model 87, both 22 long rifle. This type of low-priced auto-loader was economical enough that any shooter could afford one.

(Springfield) rifle under the same conditions and, by expending a little more *manual* energy, the bolt can be opened and closed. The U.S. Garand of WW II fame had a propensity for jamming after being soaked in a prolonged rain. This weakness was studied all through the war, yet was only corrected as recently as the Korean conflict. The second argument against the military semi-automatic rifle did not prove valid — troops do not waste ammunition in the initial phases of an engagement. More importantly, when a target does appear, an immense amount of firepower can be brought to bear when the troops have self loaders.

The self-loading rifle made its combat debut in World War I, the war that also saw the machine gun and trench warfare come into their own. Needless to say, the early self loader did not shine in this type of war. The gas-operated Mexican Mondragon Model 1908 was produced by SIG of Switzerland for the Germans, who also used a few Mauser Model 1906/08s. The French used the St. Etienne semi-automatic rifle of 1917. None of these were very successful. At the war's end our troops were ready to sweep the German trenches with the Pedersen Device, a semi-automatic pistol attachment for a modified Springfield rifle. The device was really a replacement bolt which fired a pistol-type cartridge semi-automatically. When the war ended in 1918, 65,000 Pedersen Devices had been produced. Almost all were later destroyed, so they are exceedingly rare today. The modified rifles were later returned to normal service — I was issued one in WW II for training.

World War II was the serious proving ground for the semi-automatic self-loading military rifle, which became — for a very short period — the ultimate in foot-soldier weaponry. Today most nations have obsoleted their semi-automatics, and are using selective fire (semi- and full-automatic) assault rifles. The United States M-14 and M-16, the British and many NATO countries' FN rifle LIA1, and the Communist block AKs are all good examples.

U.S. Rim-Fire Semi-Auto Rifles

Probably no other firearm did more to popularize the self-loading rifle than did Winchester's Model 1903 automatic rifle. This rifle was designed by Thomas C. Johnson, a long time employee of Winchester — not John M. Browning, to whom the design is sometimes attributed. Johnson also had to develop a new 22 rimfire cartridge, the 22 WRF, to go with it, because the 22s of his day had too large a spread

Advertisement for the Bayard single-shot self-ejector from a Sears, Roebuck Catalogue of 1911. Notice the misleading use of the word "semi-automatic," and high cost of ammunition in those bygone days!

in power to operate a self-loading action reliably. The 1903's action was called a "balanced breech bolt recoil operated mechanism" by Winchester when it was announced in 1904 — a grand sounding collection of verbiage which meant simply "blowback action." The Winchester 1903 in 22 Winchester rimfire (WRF) lasted as a favorite until 1933, when it was phased out in favor of an identical action chambered for the conventional 22 Long Rifle rimfire and called the Model 63. In 1939 the 63 gave way, in turn, to the more reasonably priced Model 74, which was made in 22 Long Rifle and, as a separate gun, in 22 Short. The 74 was replaced by the Model 77 in 1959, and it in turn gave way to the Models 290 and 190. The progression of the Winchester line has been described because it shows the acceleration of model changes in recent years, changes not so much predicated on basic design advances as they are on decreasing the manufacturing cost of the rifle. If Winchester were to make the Model 1903 rifle in its original form today, it would cost well over $100 — the "economy" version of the 190 is currently listed at just over half that.

Remington Arms introduced their equivalent of the Winchester 03, the Model 16 auto-loading rifle, in 1914. In 1941 they brought out the Model 550, a real breakthrough which utilized William's floating chamber. With it the Remington was able to fire a mixture of Shorts, Longs and Long Rifles, with no adjustment. In 1960 they introduced their revolutionary Model 66 auto-loading 22 with its bolt sliding in a nylon plastic action. This rifle is well engineered but for some unfathomed reason has not had the sales such an advanced product warrants.

Savage and Stevens both had a self-loading 22 on the market by 1938. Their designs, much simpler to manufacture than the Winchester 1903 or the Remington 16, were therefore much less expensive. The Savage and Stevens, which further popularized self-loaders, were followed by offerings from Mossberg, Marlin, Harrington and Richardson and most recently Ruger. The Ruger is interesting because it uses a detachable rotary magazine like the Mannlicher-Schoenauer and resembles the Savage Model 99 action. Still another recent development is the Armalite AR-7. This unique self-loading 22 rifle can be taken apart and stored in its hollow plastic stock. It is an ideal camping or boat gun because it floats! These U.S. 22 auto rifles with their variety of actions and styles form a very interesting collection and — with the possible exception of the early Winchesters — are very easily found and inexpensive to buy. They also have another big plus — they are fun (and cheap) to shoot!

Foreign Rim-Fire Semi-Auto Rifles

For many years only one make of foreign semi-automatic rifle was commonly seen in the United States. This was Walther with their excellent Model 1 and Model II, which could both be used either as a bolt action repeating rifle or as a single-shot. As a self-loader, they shot 22 Long Rifle, but would handle Shorts or Longs when used as a bolt action.

The Anciens Establissements Pieper of Belgium sold, through Sears Roebuck, the Bayard 22 which automatically ejected and recocked itself, but it had no magazine so was not by our definition a self-loading rifle. This "semi-automatic" was sold here before World War I. In 1959 Winchester brought out their Model 55, also a single-shot auto-ejecting rifle.

Since World War II quite a few foreign self-loading 22 rifles have been imported into the United States. One of the most unusual is the French Unique, sold for a while by Firearms International. It is really a ten shot automatic pistol with a removable barrel. The action is assembled into a stock, complete with long barrel, to make a semi-automatic rifle. Today there are at least ten different — if more conventional — makes being imported. The excellent Browning, Erma, Franchi and Squibman (made in the Philippines) are but a few.

U.S. Commercial Center-Fire Semi-Auto Rifles

For many years the United States led the world in the development of marketable center-fire commercial self-loading rifles. By 1909 three different makes were on the U.S. market. Of these, two lasted in some form until after 1950. These three basic self-loaders each use a different system to accomplish their cyclic action.

The first in order of appearance was the Winchester Model 1905, first offered in August of that year. The 1905 was a logical development from the 22 WRF Model 1903 and was also designed by Thomas C. Johnson. It was chambered for two special cartridges, the 32 and 35 Winchester self-loading (WSL) which were never used in any other type of firearm. These shells, as well as the guns, are now collectors' items. The original cartridges left much to be desired ballistically, so the 1905 was followed by the more powerful Models 1907 (351 WSL) and 1910 (401 WSL). The 1907 was made as late as 1957, but the 1905 was dropped in 1920 and the 1910 in 1936. These Winchesters were all blowback operated; there was no locking of the bolt to the barrel at the moment of firing. They rely on the inertia of a heavy bolt and a relatively low chamber pressure to keep the bolt from opening too quickly. They are well-made rifles and were available in custom grades with special stocks. They had one feature not shared by most of their contemporaries — a detachable box magazine — one of today's prerequisites for an auto-loader.

The next self-loader on the domestic scene was the Remington Model 8, designed by John M. Browning.

Recent innovations in 22 semi-automatics: Top—Armalite Explorer AR 7, which can be disassembled and stored in its stock. Middle—French Unique, a 22 pistol with a long barrel assembled in a wooden stock. Bottom—The revolutionary Remington 66, which uses "nylon" plastic for most of its parts.

Browning, though working at Remington, offered them the manufacturing rights only on a royalty basis. The Model 8 — like the Winchester line — had special cartridges developed for it which were a good bit hotter than Winchester's. These were the 25 Remington (a rimless version of the 25-35), the 30 Remington (like the 30-30), the 32 Remington (like the Winchester 32 special) and the 35 Remington. These cartridges were not only adapted to other Remington products, but were also used by Winchester and Marlin. The 35 Remington, the only surviving family member, is a better hunting round

The threesome of American centerfire auto loaders: Top—Winchester 1905, caliber 35 WSL; Middle—Remington Model 8, caliber 30, Remington; Bottom—Standard Arms Co. Model G, caliber 25 Remington.

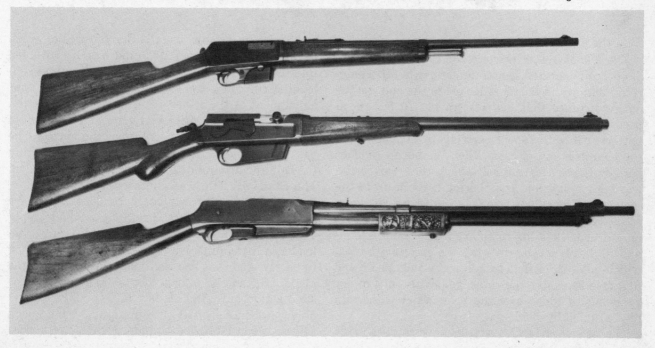

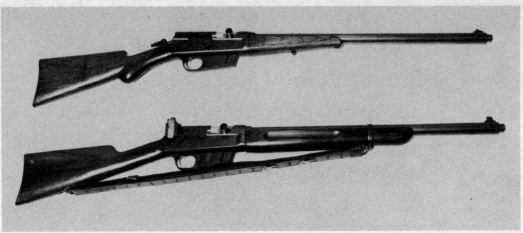

Two Remington Model 8s: Top—The Model 8 sporter in 30 Remington; Bottom—A very rare experimental military Model 8, used by the U.S. Army in the 1920s, in 25 Remington.

U.S. Carbine variations: Top—Early 15 shot "L" sight M-1. Upper Middle—Modified sight and bayonet M-1. Lower Middle—M-1 A-1 with folding stock and flash hider. Bottom—M-2 full machine gun (illegal). Notice the muzzle-mounted compensator, 30 round magazine

than the ever-popular 30-30.

The Model 8 and its successor, the Model 81, are long-recoil-operated semi-automatic rifles. In a long-recoil action the barrel is locked to the bolt for the entire distance that the bolt travels. At full recoil position the barrel then travels forward, back to battery, while the spent cartridge is stripped from the chamber and ejected. When the barrel reaches battery it releases the bolt which then moves forward, stripping and chambering a round from the magazine. The rifle is now ready for firing. The long-recoil system is a very positive locking system. Its only drawback is its complexity. The Remington 8 and 81 have a tube covering the recoiling barrel, which gives the rifle a barrel-heavy look. The 8 and 81 are essentially the same gun with only minor refinements added over the years. They were both discontinued by 1950.

The other early U.S. self-loading sporting rifle was short lived. This was the Standard rifle, which began production about 1909 and was discontinued in 1911 or 1912. The Standard was not only a self-loading rifle, but also could be used—with a minor adjustment by the owner—as a slide action repeater. It is a gas-operated rifle in which a small amount of gas is tapped from the barrel near the muzzle. The gas drives a piston in a cylinder rearward, unlocking the bolt and driving it to the rear to open the action. The Standard rifle was chambered for the 25, 30, and 35 Remington rimless cartridges that were developed for the Model 8. The Standard had a reputation for jamming when being used as an autoloader, a little quirk which was enough to bring on its early demise. The self-loader was called the Model "G," and an almost identical rifle which was slide action only, the Model "M." The "G" is takedown and has a built-in magazine with a quick release floorplate. The Standard rifles were both

KRIEGHOFF HIGH POWERED AUTOLOADING RIFLE

This new, high-powered gas operated semi-automatic rifle, which shoots any high power rimless cartridge is the very first of this type commercially available anywhere in the world. It is, moreover, held shorter and handier than any other repeating rifle and far lighter than a double rifle. The advantages of the Krieghoff Automatic in comparison with any bolt action rifle are . . . .

1. Short action; consequently handier, more pleasing form and better balance.
2. Lighter; the rifle weighs only about 7 lbs.
3. Noiseless automatic loading for no movement of the hands for the second shot, thus eliminating interruption of aiming when shooting at hunted game.
4. Far faster sequence of the second, third, fourth and fifth shots.
5. Pleasant and comfortable shooting with but slight recoil because the power of the gases are utilized for cocking and loading. Consequently only a small part is transmitted into shoulder recoil.

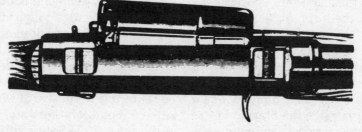

As compared to a double barrel rifle:

1. Much lighter.
2. Rapid possibility of a third shot.
3. Greater accuracy at all distances because cross fire, as in double rifles, not possible.
4. Doubling; that is, simultaneous firing of two shots is impossible.
5. Greater magazine capacity, (4 to 5 shots).
6. Pleasant shooting, (slight recoil).

The Krieghoff automatic is the fulfillment of an ancient hunter's dream and the solution of a problem with which arms designers of all countries labored for decades. Every lover of guns will be impressed with the handy, pleasing contour, the light weight and the pleasant shooting. Every arms expert will recognize the strong lock, the short action, the reliable function, the easy loading and the excellent accuracy. Anyone who has an opportunity to use this gun will experience a new shooting thrill.

Viewed externally, the Krieghoff Automatic gives the impression of a 'racy' Over and Under shotgun inasmuch as under the rifle barrel lies a second tube in which the action rod is located. This rod is activated

 ©

by the powder gases which are forced into the tube by means of a small opening in the barrel just before the muzzle and in this manner the breech is opened, the hammer cocked, and the empty cartridge ejected. A recoil spring then brings the rod back in position and simultaneously places the next cartridge in the chamber and locks the breech.

For the first shot the cocking and loading operation is done by hand by means of pushing back the knob on the side of the breech and releasing same, permitting it to slide forward and load the first cartridge.

The action is a block lock, in principle similar to that of most target rifles. A steel block is pushed up from beneath behind the barrel and cartridge chamber and bolts the barrel so well that even cartridges of the very heaviest type may be used. The breech is so constructed that the cartridge cannot be fired until the breech is perfectly closed and bolted. The action itself is closed on all sides so that it is impossible for dirt and other foreign bodies to get in. After ejection of last cartridge the breech remains open.

The lock is built so short that the distance from the base of the cartridge to the trigger is only 3". (Compare this with the distance in other repeating rifles.) On the side next to the lock lies the cartridge magazine which holds three or four cartridges. If desired the rifle may be delivered with set trigger. The action may be removed without tools and the entire action mechanism may be taken apart likewise without tools.

The safety lies forward in the trigger guard and effectively bolts the lock and trigger.

The stock is so connected with barrel and action that it is practically impossible to break. A steel rod runs through the stock and is fastened under the butt plate. The rifle is regularly supplied with pistol grip and cheek piece, but on special order may be had to any required stock specifications.

Whereas in the ordinary blow-back actions the velocity and therewith the energy of the bullet is reduced, in a gas operated gun such as this in which the gases are utilized after the bullet has left the barrel, exactly the same ballistical results are attained as in a gun with fixed breech.

Price $500.00

The original advertisement for the Krieghoff as it appeared in the 1939 Stoeger's catalogue. This rifle and the Johnson were the first truly high-powered semi-automatic rifles offered to the American shooter.

Two high-powered rarities. If you find either of these you are fortunate indeed! Top—Swiss SK-46, offered in various calibers in the early post WW II years but not adopted by anyone. Bottom—Czech ZH-29 in 8x57mm, made in very limited numbers and evaluated by a number of governments during the early 1930s.

manufactured by the Standard Arms Co. of Wilmington, Delaware. The design was by Morris F. Smith, a Philadelphian who had several patents on gas-operated firearms.

In looking back over the United States' three early center-fire sporting self-loaders, one is struck by several thoughts. First, these three rifles, the Winchester (blowback), the Remington (recoil-operated), and the Standard (gas) represent the gamut of self-loading action types—all by 1909! Second, the Winchesters were mildly successful, the Remingtons were very well accepted, but the Standard was a complete failure. Yet, ironically, the Standard's gas operation is the only system used for semi-automatic rifles today. The gas-operated system that failed with the Standard was relied on by every G.I. who carried a Garand or M-1 Carbine in World War II. The message here is that just *having* a good idea isn't enough—the execution of that idea into reality is the important part!

U.S. Military Semi-Auto Rifles

Even before World War I our military had tested some self-loading rifles on a one or two prototype basis, with never even a small production run. Both Springfield and Rock Island Armories had made such prototypes, and there are also such forgotten names as the Murphy-Manning, the Farquahar-Hill, and the White. None of these ever received serious consideration. In the 1920s, however, there was a resurgence of interest by our armed forces. A number of new self-loading guns such as the Thompson, Berthier and Bang were tested. Like the pre-war semi-automatics, none were successful enough to justify

even limited production. By 1928/1929 the U.S. Army had decided to replace the 30-06 military cartridge, which had been in use since 1906, with the 276 Pedersen round. This cartridge was designed by John Pedersen for his military semi-automatic rifle, which had a toggle-joint action like the German Pistole 1908 (Luger). Though the Pederson was not a success, John Garand designed a 276 rifle of his own which was to become the U.S. M1 rifle. Then General Douglas MacArthur decided that we should retain the 30-06, a fortunate decision which avoided our entering World War II with two different caliber rifles. From a collector's standpoint, if you have one of the rare 276 U.S. test rifles you are a very lucky collector indeed!

In 1936 the Garand was adopted. The M1 proved itself a worthy arm in World War II, and while it may not have been quite as accurate as the 1903 Springfield at long ranges, its fire power endeared it to the heart of every combat G.I.

The U.S. government also wanted a light self-loading rifle that could be carried by officers and non-combatants in place of the difficult-to-master 1911 Colt pistol. After testing a number of designs, Winchester's carbine was adopted. Designed by "Carbine" Williams, its easy handling and fifteen round capacity were great morale builders for rear echelon soldiers. Though officially named the "U.S. Carbine Cal. .30 M1," we always called the Garand-designed arm the "M1" and the Williams arm the "Carbine." Over six million Garands and a like number of Carbines were made.

The last semi-automatic rifle to be adopted by our military was the Johnson, used by the Marine Corps. The Johnson was designed by a Marine—Captain

Russian WW II, semi-automatic rifles: Top—Model 1938 Tokarev, 7.62mm Russian. This example was captured by the Finnish and later sold to a U.S. dealer. Bottom—Chinese 56, copy of the Russian SKS in 7.62x39mm. Notice the attached folding spike bayonet.

Melvin M. Johnson, Jr. Unlike the classic struggling inventor, he was well-to-do and a graduate of Yale University. He studied and wrote on the design of automatic arms, finally designing one so good that it was almost chosen over the Garand rifle. Johnson was always bitter that his design was rejected and the Springfield Armory-sponsored Garand adopted. I don't really think now, looking back thirty years, that he had a case. As stated, the Johnson rifle was used by the Marines, and the Dutch also bought a large quantity for use in the East Indies. It is these Dutch service rifles that most collectors own. The Johnson rifle, unlike the gas operated M1 rifle and carbine, was recoil operated. It is the only recoil-operated military rifle ever used in quantity, because for reliable operation the recoiling barrel must have the same mass at all times. The Johnson had prob-

lems when the barrel-mounted bayonet changed the barrel weight and slowed-up or mistimed the recoil action. Johnson did get around the bayonet weight problem by designing what must be the world's lightest bayonet, but the gun really wasn't rugged enough to take the beating that a military rifle must take. However, Johnson's rifle had some wonderful features—a ten-shot charger-loaded rotary magazine and a quickly detachable barrel.

A U.S. Rifle M1, a U.S. Carbine M1 and a Johnson would make a very interesting nucleus for a semi-automatic military rifle collection.

Foreign Commercial Center-Fire Semi-Auto Rifles

By and large there apparently was even less interest in self-loading rifles abroad than in America. Aside from the various pistol-caliber carbines, both

German WW II semi-automatics: Top—G-41(W), a rather rare early issue—notice the large diameter gas cone at muzzle. 8x57mm. Middle—K-43, 8x57mm. Bottom—G-43, 8x57mm, fitted with telescopic sight for sniping.

Fabrique Nationale (FN) SAFN: Top—7x57mm Venezuelan Army Model with compensator on muzzle. Bottom—30-06 Columbian Army Model.

Mauser and Mannlicher did develop some very early higher-power designs but these guns are extremely rare today. The European military mind was as apathetic to the self-loader as ours, and there seems to have been even less civilian interest than here. This indifference might be explained by the fact that in most of the world only the very rich could afford to hunt and own firearms. Thus it was that one of the first European self-loading high-power sporting rifles offered for sale here was the Krieghoff, a German gas-operated rifle, available briefly from A. F. Stoeger in 1940. Chambered for almost any domestic high-power rifle cartridge, its price was $500—very high for those post-depression days. I doubt if more than a few guns were ever delivered because of the onset of World War II. In the same 1940 Stoeger catalog the Johnson rifle was also offered to the U.S. sportsman. These two guns, on successive catalogue pages, represented the first time that really high-powered auto-loaders were available to civilian shooters.

Foreign Military Semi-Auto Rifles

The eve of World War II found most of the future combatants with some sort of self-loading rifle in hand. The U.S.S.R. had started to design a military self-loading rifle about the same time as the United States, and in 1936 adopted the full- and semi-automatic Simonov (AVS). Their first true *semi*-automatic was the Model 1938 Tokarev (SVT-38), a gas-operated rifle chambering the rimmed 7.62mm Russian service round. While the Tokarev is not in the class of our M1, it is still a very good design—particularly when you consider the fact that it used the archaic Russian rimmed cartridge! The 1938 Model was followed by two later Tokarevs, the Model 1940 which had both semi-automatic (SVT-40) and selective-fire (AVT-40) versions. After World War II,

the Russians adopted their revolutionary SKS, a self-loading rifle which fires a high-performance short rifle cartridge. The SKS was the infantry rifle that faced our M-14 and M-16 in Vietnam—the Chinese and various communist block nations have made thousands of them. The example I have has a chrome-plated bolt and bore and is a first class production in all respects. From a collecting standpoint the SKS is one of the more recently designed foreign military self-loaders available, so it is a very desirable item.

Just prior to World War II the Germans were also working on a self-loading rifle to replace the bolt-action Model 98. Though not as far along as we or the Russians, by 1941 they had two designs which seemed promising. One was from Walther, the G-41(W), and the other from Mauser, the G-41(M). Both were gas operated, and the Mauser even resembled the famous '98 rifle. Both designs used an interesting method for tapping barrel gas—instead of the characteristic hole in the barrel to release gas to the piston, there is a muzzle cone somewhat reminiscent of John Browning's original Winchester semi-automatic. This cone collects the gas at the muzzle and directs it against an unusual ring piston which encircles the barrel. The gas drives the piston to the rear, unlocking the bolt and driving it rearward in the conventional manner.

The two rifles were made and issued in limited numbers to troops for field evaluation. As a result of these tests the Walther was adopted in 1941 and the Mauser discontinued. The muzzle cone was not wholly satisfactory so in 1943 the G-41 was replaced by the more conventional gas-pistoned G-43 and later K-43. These fine weapons, while somewhat crude looking, were very up to date as they were made from sheet metal stampings, some plastic parts, and castings and forgings finished only on operating surfaces. These self-loading rifles repre-

SKETCHES OF DIFFERENT SEMI-AUTOMATIC RIFLE ACTIONS

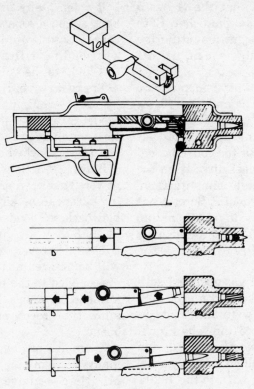

Simple blowback action.

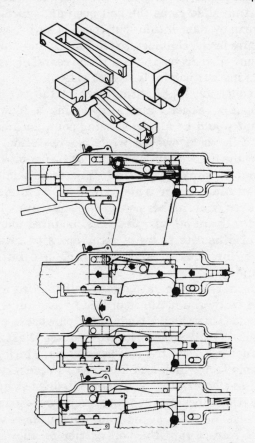

Recoil Operation. Notice basic parts are same as a blowback, but a lock added between the bolt and barrel. A rigid unlocking cam is also added to the receiver.

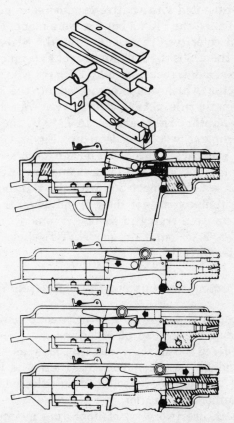

Gas Operation. Similar to recoil action except lock is mounted rigidly to the receiver, and unlocking cam is on a moving gas-operated piston.

sented a real breakthrough, both in function as well as in production cost and material saving. The primary difference that I have found between the G (Gewehr) and K (Karabiner) is that the G has a threaded muzzle to take a grenade launcher. Both guns have a built-in telescopic sight mounting lug on the receiver and, interestingly enough, neither can take a bayonet.

Since World War II the French have adopted two semi-automatics, the Model 1949 and the 49/56. These rifles were combat tested in the French days of Vietnam. The 1949 rifle is unusual in that gas operation is accomplished without the conventional piston—the tapped-off gas impinges directly on the bolt carrier to effect a worthwhile simplification.

For many years the Italian firm of P. Beretta has been taking U.S. M1 rifles and modifying them into a poor man's version of the M14 with detachable box magazine and selective fire. They use the 7.62mm NATO ammunition.

The Swedes have an unusual gas-operated self-loader in the Ljungman, which like the French 1949, has no gas piston. These rifles were also made in Denmark by Madsen and—in 8 x 57mm—by Egypt. The Czechs, although a Russian satellite, still design and manufacture their own excellent military arms with some native designs dating back to the 1920s. A few Czech Model 52s have come back to U.S. collectors from various world hot spots. The Swiss experimented with a native designed semi-automatic rifle called the SK 46, but few were made. They now use a selective-fire assault rifle, the SIG-AMT.

In the 1930s the Belgian firm of Fabrique Nationale had a designer named M. D. Saive who designed an action which was incorporated into the FN semi-automatic rifle, SAFN, shortly after World War II. This military rifle, adopted in 1949 by the Belgian government, was also adopted by Egypt, Columbia, and Venezuela. The Saive design uses essentially the same action as the Tokarev and the SKS. Saive's action was in competition with the Garand-system for a replacement for the Garand when the NATO nations were trying to adopt a common basic rifle. The FN FAL, our T-48, was NATO's choice, but we adopted the M16.

Collecting Self-Loading Rifles By Their Actions

There are many ways in which a collection of semi-automatic rifles can be organized. So far we have considered such basic sub-divisions as military, commercial or national origins. There is at least one more way to classify self-loading rifles and that is by method of operation.

There are two ways of imparting motion to the bolt; recoil or residual gas. Gas operation can be further subdivided into two classes. In the first the gas energy is applied to the cartridge itself and the cartridge becomes a rearward moving piston. This is "blowback" action. In the second the gas is collected and re-directed to both unlock and drive the bolt open. Many firearms engineers consider blowback action a separate class in which case there are three classes: recoil, blowback and gas operated. In self-loading rifles, gas, either blowback or "redirected," is the only method used today.

There are really only two successful recoil-operated semi-automatic rifles, the Remington Model 8 (and its successors) and the Johnson. The Remington uses a long recoil action while the Johnson travels locked only ⅛" before unlocking.

Blowback actions are normally only used on low-powered arms, where the mass (weight) of the recoiling parts can be kept low. Winchester's line of early blowback self loaders almost seem to be exceptions, in that they are hunting rifles for centerfire cartridges. However, heft a Winchester 1910 and you will be amazed at its weight. This unusual weight, mass added to the bolt, is located under the wooden fore-end. It keeps the bolt closed long enough to allow the breech pressure to drop before the bolt opens.

Examples of gas operated self-loading rifles are many. For example, let us look at the U.S. Carbine M1. Here we have an inertia piston which moves only ¼" but drives an operating slide rearward. The operating slide cams the bolt open and starts it to the rear by momentum, but there is still some gas pressure in the chamber, so after unlocking, this gas pressure also drives the bolt to the rear. This is gas-unlocking but partial blowback action.

A collection highlighting each of the two basic self-loading actions and also having a blowback variant would be a good starting point for a beginning collector. However, while gas operation dominates the field of self-loading rifles, do not make the mistake of thinking that it dominates all semi- and full-automatic firearms. Low-power pistols are blowback, but higher-powered pistols are almost universally *recoil* operated. The mounted machine gun also has its share of *recoil*-operated arms, of which the Maxim and Browning are but two examples.

Another way to categorize self-loading rifles would be by the methods of locking and unlocking the bolt. This should begin with blowback, where the bolt is momentarily locked by mass. Next come bolts derived from the bolt action rifle, which have multiple lugs which lock in recesses in the receiver. Multi-lug bolts can be further sub-divided by the method of unlocking. Some are rotated out of engagement—as in the Garand and M1 Carbine—while others retract into the bolt carrier to allow it to unlock. The German G-41W, G-43 and K-43 are good examples of this latter type. Finally, some bolts are canted—either rear or front—and lock in the receiver this way. Rear lockup is characterized by the FN Siave type rifle, while front lock is unusual. One of the few examples is the Czech Model 52 semi-automatic rifle. Front locking is always desirable because there is less opportunity for excessive play in the action.

The world of self-loaders today seems to be divided into two systems; Garand (U.S. Rifle M14) and the Saive (Tokarev, FN, SKS). Both have been fully tested under the most rigorous battle conditions. Both are good—the Garand system is hard to beat for ruggedness with low weight, while on the other hand the Siave is easier to manufacture—so pay your money and take your choice. Happily, as a collector you can get an example of each.

The Collector

I think that a collection of any type of mechanism is interesting—as a personal quirk I like guns, but I could probably get just as much pleasure out of old wind-up phonographs, pocket watches, old cars or player pianos. All interest me, and I have found many other collectors who feel the same way. This makes collecting semi-automatic rifles a challenging hobby. It is fascinating to see how different designers faced with the same problems sometimes found entirely different but equally effective answers. And rifles of this type are still not as sought after as handguns.

At recent gun shows and in periodicals I have seen the following self-loading rifles offered for sale:
1 Standard rifle; 30 Rem.
2 Standard rifles; 25 Rem.
1 Ljungman; 8mm Mauser
1 Japanese M1 copy (very rare)
1 Beretta M-59; 7.62 NATO

1 French M1949; 7.5mm
1 Krieghoff; 8mm Mauser (very rare)
1 Dreyse 32 ACP carbine (rare)
1 Pedersen rifle; 276 (rare)
1 Pedersen device (very rare)
1 Mexican Mondragon; 7mm Mauser
1 German G-42W; 8mm Mauser
1 FN SAFN Egyptian; 8mm Mauser

Prices ranged from a low of $85 for the FN-SAFN and the French Model 1949, up to an asking price of $1,850 for the ultra-rare Pedersen device. Some of these guns are far rarer than the Borchardt or the Luger carbine, yet command a much lower price. One of our best known dealers is still selling FN-SAFN 7mm Venezuelan rifles for $70. This represents the best bargain of all the rifles which are listed above.

While most of today's military rifles are selective fire, there are semi-automatic civilian equivalents for the M14, M16 and Armalite AR-18. These rifles can't be fired as machine guns but otherwise are identical to their military versions so they are interesting to collectors and shooters alike.

The era of the military semi-automatic self-loading rifle came with World War I and ended by the second decade after World War II. In this short period of fifty years many guns were made for both military and commercial markets that are now historically interesting. To the collector this fifty year span can be an intriguing hunting ground for rare semi-automatic rifles. And one of the happiest things about collecting such modern arms is that 90% of them can still be fired, thus adding another dimension to the fun of collecting. With all this in mind who knows—maybe I'll see you at the next gun show, where we'll both be looking at self-loading rifles! ●

Bibliography

Askins, Charles—*Rifles and Rifle Shooting.* The MacMillan Co., 1934.

Barnes, Frank C.—*Cartridges of the World.* Digest Books, Inc., 1965.

Chinn, Lt. Col. USMC, George M.—*The Machine Gun.* U.S. Government Printing Service, Vol. 1, 1951; Vol. 4, 1955.

A History of Browning Guns. Browning Arms Co., 1942.

Guns Annual. Jerome Rakusan, ed. Publishers Development Corp., 1971.

Hackley, F.W., Woodin, W.H., Scranton, E.L.—*History of Modern U.S. Military Small Arms Ammunition,* Vol. 1880-1939. The MacMillan Co., 1967.

Hatch, Alden—*Remington Arms in American History.* Rinehart & Co., 1956.

Held, Robert—*The Age of Firearms.* Harper & Bros.,1957; Digest Books, Inc., 1970.

Jacobs, Charles R.—*The New Official Gun Book.* Crown Publishers, Inc., 6th ed., 1955/1956.

Johnson, George B., Lockhoven, Hans-Bert—*International Armament,* Vols. 1 and 2. International Small Arms, 1965.

Johnson, Melvin M. Jr., Haven, Charles T.—*Automatic Arms.* William Morrow & Co., 1941.

Logan, Herschel C.—*Cartridges.* Bonanza Books, 1954.

Ommundsen, H., Robinson, Ernest H.—*Rifles and Ammunition.* Cassell & Co., Ltd., 1915.

Peterson, Harold L.—*The Treasury of the Gun.* Golden Press, Inc., 1962.

Satterlee, L.D.—*A Catalog of Firearms for the Collector.* Privately printed, Detroit, 1927.

Smith, W.H.B., Smith, Joseph E.—*Small Arms of the World.* The Stackpole Co., 1966.

U.S. Rifle 7.62mm M14. Army Field Manual, 1959.

U.S. Rifle Caliber .30, M1. Dept. of the Army Field Manual, 1951.

United States Martial Arms. Dordco Verlag, 1967.

Wahl, Paul—*Carbine Handbook.* Arco Publishing Co., Inc., 1964.

Wahl, Paul—*Gun Trader's Guide.* Shooter's Bible, Inc., 1964.

Watrous, George R.—*Winchester Rifles and Shotguns.* Winchester Repeating Arms Co., 1950.

Multi-barrel signal pistols are not a new idea, but few have seen as wide use as...

THE SIGNAL PISTOL MODEL 'L'

by
LT. VAGN G. B. CHRISTENSEN

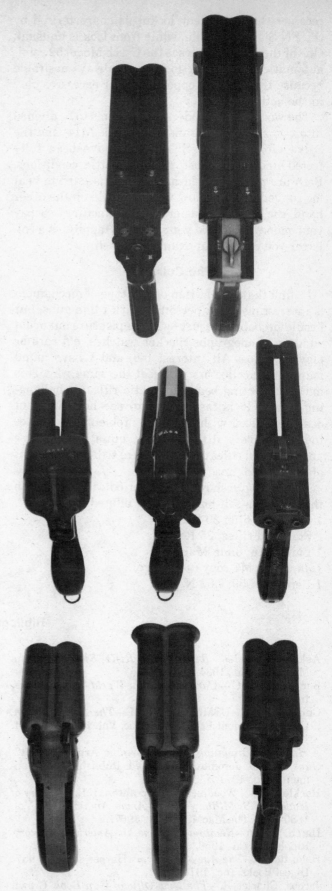

Top views of most of the world's multi-barreled signal pistols.

Top: German WW II
Center: Japanese
Bottom: German WW I

SIGNAL PISTOLS have been known and used for several hundred years, but strangely enough, signal pistols with more than one barrel have only been used in the period from World War I to the end of World War II. It is also worth noting that only Germany and Japan have made and used such pistols, though Sweden and Denmark produced experimental models.

The advantages of using signal pistols with more than one barrel are very obvious, because shooting more flares at one time will have the effect of greatly increasing the number of letters in the signal codes.

Germany was the first country to produce two-barrel signal pistols. Fig. 1 shows some World War I German brass Navy signal pistols. At the end of World War I demand for signal pistols with more that two barrels must have existed, because a 4 barrel model (Fig. 2) was also made for the German Navy. This pistol is double-action, making it possible to send 4 signals in a rather short period of time.

Fig. 1—German WW I Models. Top, bronze submarine pistol; center, modified submarine pistol; bottom, AWW-37.

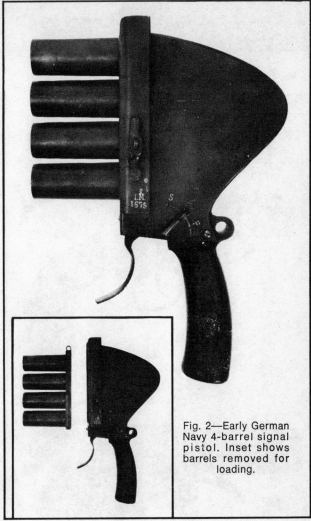

Fig. 2—Early German Navy 4-barrel signal pistol. Inset shows barrels removed for loading.

It must have been a doubtful pleasure to fire the top barrel, however, because the recoil is extremely heavy.

It seems that Japanese firearms designers had been aware of this recoil problem, since nearly all Japanese 2- and 3-barrel signal pistols have a recoil reducing mechanism to minimize the reaction. Fig. 3 shows different types of Japanese 2- and 3-barrel signal pistols.

In this article we will discuss only the famous double-barrel German signal pistol, Model L. "Signal Pistole Modell L" is the very brief nomenclature which disguises rather than describes this historically interesting and technically complicated series of German World War II pistols.

While we do not know the original designer of this pistol, the arms factory of Emil Eckoldt in Suhl stamped one of their earlier models "pat.gesch." (patent protected). Unfortunately, destruction of the buildings that housed the German patent offices during World War II has rendered it impossible to locate the patent that was issued for this design.

From analysis of the rather large number of these pistols that are known, they can be classified into four major types: Model L, original type (Fig. 4), Model L, FL type (Fig. 6), Model L, LN type (Fig. 7), Model L, F1 type (Fig. 9).

Although it is not known whether the German government officially recognized these four distinct types, this classification is the result of the examination of hundreds of pistols of each type; details of functioning, markings, form, surface finish, and materials are uniformly constant within each group.

The year of introduction of the Model L is unknown; the earliest year marking recorded is 1936. The last year noted is 1944, which may well be the last year of manufacture.

Data: Model: L. Action: single (hammerless). Bore: 26.65mm (4 ga.). Weight: 1210 grams. Over-all length: 280mm. Barrel length: 165mm. Width: 70mm. Height: 167mm. Barrel and frame: aluminum. Grips: wood. Total number of parts: 83. Extractor: automatic. Surface finish: anodized (black).

As Fig. 4 shows, the original model differs from later versions in that it has wood grips and no left-side retaining screws for the barrel pin and opening lever pin. However, these pins are held by retaining screws on the right side of the pistol frame; since

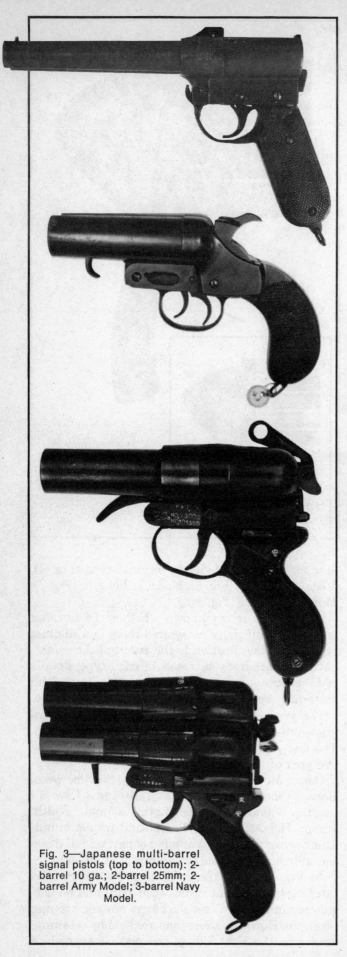

Fig. 3—Japanese multi-barrel signal pistols (top to bottom): 2-barrel 10 ga.; 2-barrel 25mm; 2-barrel Army Model; 3-barrel Navy Model.

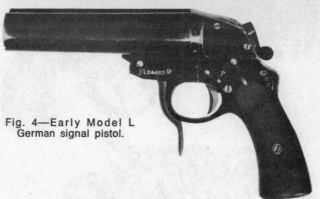

Fig. 4—Early Model L German signal pistol.

Fig. 5—Model L completely disassembled. With 83 parts, the Model L is unusually complex.

these screws are placed in the middle of the pins, and since the diameter of the screw head is slightly larger than that of the pins, they are still secured.

As Fig. 5 shows, these pistols have an unusually large number of parts (the FL type has 83), and it is correspondingly difficult to disassemble and even more so to assemble, since most of the components must be assembled in a specified sequence. Moreover, special tools are required for complete disassembly. Most components are marked either R or L (right or left), which eases, somewhat, the assembly of the pistol.

In spite of the unusual number of parts, and their complicated functioning, the pistol has proven to be exceptionally free from functional failures. However, it must be admitted that when firing (for example) old stocks of original ammunition it has happened that the barrel locking lug is broken off, and the frame has broken at the junction of the standing breech and the forward portion of the frame. Even though the pistol is designed to fire either of the barrels singly, or both barrels simultaneously,

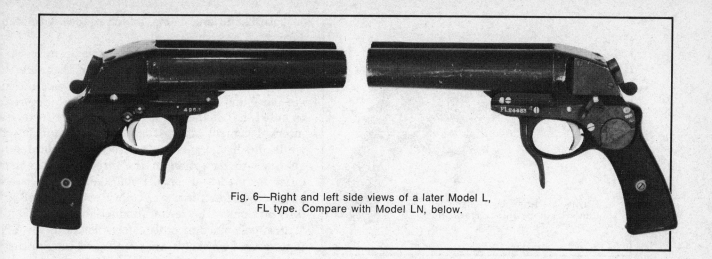

Fig. 6—Right and left side views of a later Model L, FL type. Compare with Model LN, below.

the latter method can scarcely have been used very frequently. The relatively light weight of the pistol renders its recoil particularly severe even on single fire.

A number of distinct differences can be noted between the FL and LN types (Figs. 6 and 7). These are:

1. A trigger safety is found only on the FL-type pistol.
2. The rearmost part of the frame is curved on the FL type, but straight on the LN-type pistol.
3. The screw that retains the barrel selector lever is located on the side of the lever on the FL-type, while it is located on the top center of the lever on the LN-type.
4. The upper edge of the standing breech is curved on the FL-type, and straight on the LN-type.
5. The shape of the safety lever and opening lever differs between the two types.
6. The rear end of the safety lever spring housing is level with the frame on the FL-type, but depressed below the surface on the LN-type.
7. The cartridge indicator pins, safety lever, barrel selector lever, firing pin retainers, stop pin for barrel selector, opening lever, extractor, and the "boltbefaestigelse" (bolt nuts) are of brass in the FL-type, and iron for the LN-type.
8. Surface finish on the FL-type is a shiny black anodizing, while the LN-type has a gray matte anodized finish.

To load any of the Model L pistols the opening lever is pushed down and forward. When this is done the following things happen: 1. Barrel tips up for loading; 2. Fired cases, if any, are extracted; 3. Safety lever moves to 'safe' position; 4. Barrel lever moves to 'common' position—that is, to fire both barrels; 5. Hammer is cocked; 6. Signal pins indicate 'cocked.'

Fig. 7—Model L, LN type. Compare with FL type, above.

The meaning of the letter markings "FL," "LN," and "F1," stamped on nearly all types, is not explained. A catalog of the Emil Eckoldt arms factory in Suhl, dated February 12, 1939 and intended for the Danish Army Ordnance Office, has the phrase "Fur den Flugbetrieb" (for the Air Service) stamped on the front cover.

"FL" may be an abbreviation of this phrase, and "LN" could be an abbreviation of "Luft Nachrichte," but the fact is that German Air Force crews used the name "Fridolin" for the "FL" signal pistols, and "Lina" for the "LN" types. The number 24483, which always follows the "FL," "LN" or "FL," also remains unidentified. It may be the patent number.

The serial number always appears on the right side of the frame, while the factory-identifying stamp is found at the rear of the left side of the frame.

Aside from these letters and figures, the pistols dated before 1939 bear the following proof marks: "U" and "B," of course, stand for "Untersuchungs-stempel" and "Beschussstempel," or inspection proof and firing proof. The figure 4 in a circle indicates that the pistol was submitted to a 4-gauge shotgun proof. The "U" and "B" stamps are found

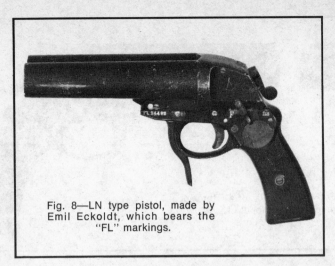

Fig. 8—LN type pistol, made by Emil Eckoldt, which bears the "FL" markings.

on both barrel and frame, in accordance with standard proof procedure.

Proof regulations for signal pistols seem to have been suspended after 1940, and from that date on these proof stamps (except for caliber designation) are not found on signal pistols. It is furthermore to be noted that as the war neared its end the factories internal control stamps became fewer and fewer while finish and surface treatment deteriorated in quality. An exception to the foregoing statement must be made for pistols marked "GBW," since pistols made in Bittner's factory even in 1943 are fully on a par with pre-war production.

Strangely enough only a few pistols of the LN type made by Eckoldt are found, and though these

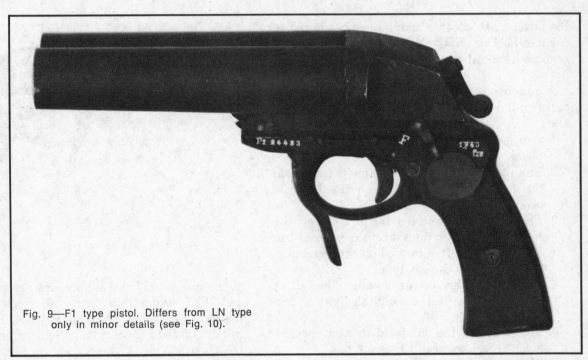

Fig. 9—F1 type pistol. Differs from LN type only in minor details (see Fig. 10).

Fig. 10—Top views (left to right) of F1, LN and FL types, and Bottom view of FL (left) and F1 loading levers.

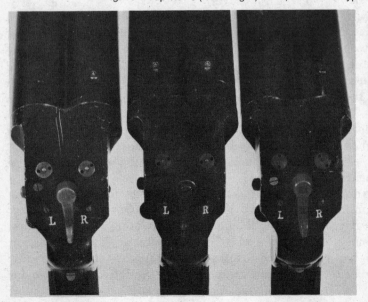

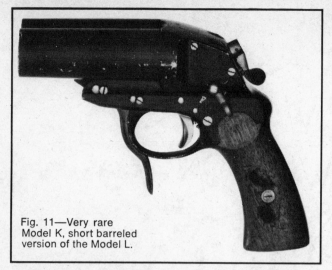

Fig. 11—Very rare Model K, short barreled version of the Model L.

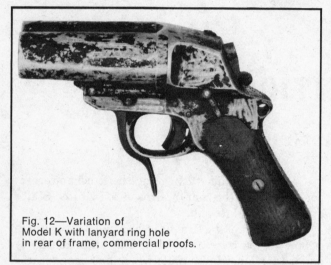

Fig. 12—Variation of Model K with lanyard ring hole in rear of frame, commercial proofs.

The following firms are known to have produced model "L" signal pistols.			
Firm	Code	Type	Year Marking
Emil Eckolt, Waffenfabrik Suhl	Ecko	FL	1936-1937-1938 1940-1941-1942
Emil Eckolt, Waffenfabrik Suhl	Ecko	LN	no marks
Heinrich Krieghoff, Waffenfabrik Suhl	fzs	FL	1941-1942-1943 1944 and no marks
Heinrich Krieghoff, Waffenfabrik Suhl	fzs	F1	1943-1944
Heinrich Krieghoff, Waffenfabrik Suhl	fzs	LN	1943
Heinrich Krieghoff, Waffenfabrik Suhl	H.K.	FL	1940
Gustav Bittner, Waffenfabrik Weipert (in occupied Czechoslovakia)	gpt	LN	1943-1944
Gustav Bittner, Waffenfabrik Weipert	GBW	LN	1941-1942-1943
Gustav Bittner, Waffenfabrik Weipert	GBW	FL	1941
Unknown	ojr	LN	no marks
Unknown	MA/AM*	FL	no marks

(*intertwined letter logo)

pistols are of the LN-type, they are all marked "FL" in front of the 24483 number.

The firms known to have produced Model L signal pistols are listed in the table.

The pistol illustrated in Fig. 9 is of the F1-type. It is almost identical to the LN-type illustrated in Fig. 7, but as shown in Fig. 10 it differs in the width of the upper part of the opening lever; 11.8mm for the F1-type, as opposed to 18mm for the FL-type. The grips also differ slightly, enough so that they are not readily interchangeable. The designation "F1" was in all likelihood given to this pistol to avoid confusion in the identification of replacement parts that were not interchangeable between the two models. Recorded serial numbers of the F1 pistol range from 3118 to 8042.

In the previously-mentioned Eckoldt catalog the original model pistol is shown with a barrel length of 100.5mm. This pistol, designated Model K, is illustrated in Fig. 11. Only this one example, without any proof or makers marks, has been reported.

Data: Model K. Action: single (hammerless). Bore: 26.65 mm (4 ga.). Weight: 950 grams. Overall length: 210mm. Barrel length: 100.5mm.

Width: 70mm. Height: 167mm. Barrel and frame: aluminum. Grips: wood. Total number of parts: 83. Extractor: automatic. Surface finish: anodized (black).

The pistol shown in Fig. 12 bears a strong resemblance to the Model K pistol in functioning as well as appearance. It differs in that it has a lanyard hole at the rear of the frame.

Production of this pistol was probably also extremely limited, since only two pistols of this type have been reported—both, interestingly enough, from Norway.

Data: Action: single (hammerless). Bore: 26.65mm (4 ga.) Weight: 995 grams. Overall length: 218mm. Barrel length: 100mm. Width: 69.2mm. Height: 162mm. Barrel and frame: aluminum. Grips: wood. Extractor: automatic. Surface finish: anodized (black). Markings: on barrel and frame: under a crown, B; U; S. On barrel: "Sander."

Though signal pistols have thus far received relatively little collector notice, they are as interesting and offer as much variety as most other types of firearms. Our research on the Model L, still far from complete, demonstrates this very well indeed! ●

Pioneer in Cartridge Pistols

by JAMES E. SERVEN

IT WAS A COOL January day on the Nebraska prairie. The year was 1872, and one of the best publicized buffalo hunts in history was about to begin. Red Willow Creek had suddenly taken on the appearance of the old-time rendezvous. Traveling down from North Platte had come the large entourage of the Grand Duke Alexis of Imperial Russia. He was escorted by United States cavalrymen and two of the frontier's most colorful personages. Lt. Col. George A. Custer and W. F. "Buffalo Bill" Cody.

A short distance from the tents of the Grand Duke's party were the buffalo-hide tepees of a band of currently docile Sioux Indians led by Chief Spotted Tail. The responsibility for managing this royal hunt had been passed on to General Sheridan and he wanted to give the titled Russian guest all the thrills and western drama possible. The Indians were a sort of window-dressing—they were to appear in resplendent costumes, whoop up some dances, and give demonstrations of their various skills, especially with the bow.

All this was very good, but the Duke was more interested in having a go at the buffalo with a new Smith & Wesson pistol which had been presented to him during a visit to the Smith & Wesson plant a month past. This pistol was truly a fancy weapon and the Duke carried it in his belt with great pride. It was a big six-shot top-break pistol in the 44 caliber developed for pistols the Smith & Wesson company was currently manufacturing for the Imperial Russian government. The metal parts were engraved and inlaid with gold; the stocks were of pearl and bore the coat-of-arms of the United States and of Imperial Russia.

The big day of the first hunt had dawned clear and crisp. Horses were saddled and the hunting party headed for a herd of buffalo which had been located by guide Charley Reynolds.

Alexis appeared in a heavy gray uniform trimmed in green, with shiny buttons bearing the Imperial coat-of-arms; a cloth turban topped the royal head. Custer and Cody were both dressed in buckskin. Cody had a few comments to make about Custer's sealskin cap and possibly Custer thought as little of Cody's old black slouch hat. Cody's long hair tumbled down from under the wide hat-brim to his shoulders—a sight that doubtless gave some of the Sioux furtive thoughts contrary to the friendly spirit of the occasion.

At length the herd was sighted and the Grand Duke and Custer excitedly spurred forward, closely followed by the calmer and more experienced Cody. Coming within range of a buffalo cow the Duke triggered six shots from his new revolver. The result? The buffalo galloped on! This may look pretty bad, and of course it is not the way the story was then given to the public. However, Alexis' record was actually better than Custer's. On Custer's first buffalo hunt he had not only missed the buffalo but in the process had shot his horse in the head!

In fairness, it must be added that the Duke was a

GRAND DUKE ALEXIS KILLING HIS FIRST BUFFALO.

Above—The Smith & Wesson No. 3 New Model single action, cal. 44-40 "Frontier" 6-shot revolver. Below—The big 6-shot double action Smith & Wesson, cal. 44 Russian, sometimes called the "Navy Model."

Left—Smith & Wesson's first double action revolver, the 38 Double Action, was first produced in 1880. Later variations had some minor changes. Right—The 44 American Model, which was introduced in 1869, was first to utilize interchangeable parts.

good horseman and a bold hunter; he soon acquired the skill necessary to kill several buffalo and everybody was happy—especially Smith & Wesson, who reaped a good publicity dividend on the $400 the Duke's deluxe six-shooter had cost them.

Top-break Pistols

The Smith & Wesson top-break pistol, similar in general style to that given to Alexis, was the first big metallic cartridge handgun to appear on the American market which was absolutely new and borrowed nothing from the older caplock pistols. Colt's Single Action Army 45 followed closely but Smith & Wesson took the lead in manufacturing a true metallic cartridge six-shooter. Up to this time, however, Smith & Wesson production had been limited to ineffective volcanic type pistols and small tip-up pistols in the relatively weak 22 and 32 rimfire sizes.

Beginning in 1870 and during the following half century Smith & Wesson top-break pistols enjoyed a good share in firearms purchases for military, police, and civilian use; they won high honors on the target range. Hundreds of thousands were sold; they found their way to Russia, Turkey, Mexico and many other countries.

You will have noticed that the word pistol is used here in its generic sense. Thus it embraces all handguns whether they may be the revolvers which make up the great bulk of Smith & Wesson production in this period or the single-shot top-break pistols.

Every worthwhile product is imitated, and so it was with Smith & Wesson's automatic ejecting top-break pistols. The market eventually was flooded with cheap pot-metal of this style, especially in the pocket sizes. For this reason, the top-break pistol as a class has been regarded with some disdain by shooters and collectors of today. But let us center our attention on Smith & Wesson, the originators of this type of firearm, a firm that to my knowledge has never put out a shoddy product. I would like to tell you some of the highlights in the colorful history of the Smith & Wesson top-break—who designed it, how the models evolved, some of the records it achieved.

Smith & Wesson's 32 rimfire tip-up pistol (called No. 2 Army), had seen some service in the War Between the States, one of the first metallic cartridge pistols so employed. The small cartridge was not well suited for military service; the Colt and Remington 44 cap and ball models then in use had far greater range and power. These facts being very clear, Smith & Wesson set as its mission the development of a 44 pistol which would have the advantages of metallic ammunition—with automatic ejection. The success of the 44 Henry rifle and the Winchester Model 1866 had shown that these features were desirable and successful in a rifle—why not in a pistol?

The development of radically different mechanical systems does not take place at the flash of an idea—it takes time and trial, but by 1869, Smith & Wesson was ready with a big 44 pistol of novel design. This pistol, continuing their previous system of designating models by numerals, was called the "No. 3." I hope I shall not confuse you with names as we take a look at the different models. While Smith & Wesson has certainly made some of the finest handguns the world has ever seen,

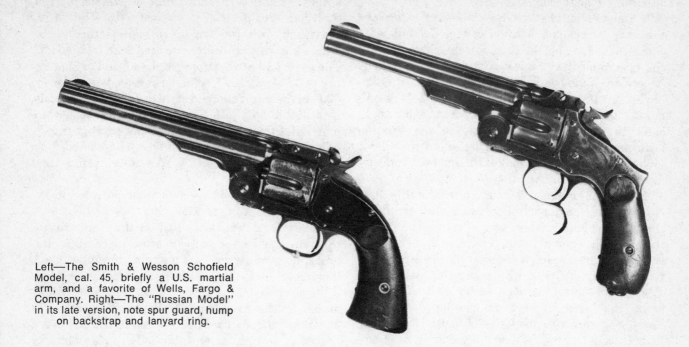

Left—The Smith & Wesson Schofield Model, cal. 45, briefly a U.S. martial arm, and a favorite of Wells, Fargo & Company. Right—The "Russian Model" in its late version, note spur guard, hump on backstrap and lanyard ring.

none of this skill seems to have been devoted to devising an easily understood system of naming their various new products. The Smith & Wesson pistol designated as "New Model" soon became the "Old Model;" different catalogs call the same pistol different names, but we'll sort them out and put them in proper perspective.

The first big No. 3 Smith & Wesson employed a centerfire brass cartridge known as the 44 American. This pistol has an 8" ribbed barrel, wood stocks and could be had in blue or nickel finish. Rollin White's troublesome cylinder patent having expired, a greater freedom in design was now possible.

Ideas born in several inventive minds went into the design of this new pistol. Among these men were Abram J. Gibson, Louis C. Rodier and Chas. A. King, superintendent at the Smith & Wesson plant. Perhaps the most significant contribution was in the patent purchased in the spring of 1869 from W. C. Dodge. Dodge, a former examiner in the U.S. Patent office, had turned his attention to breech-loading arms. He had assumed two things to be of prime importance in designing a pistol— the extraction of all shells simultaneously with neither cylinder nor any other part becoming detached in attaining this simultaneous ejection.

Starr and other pistol manufacturers had used the principle of a tip-down barrel, so there was no great novelty in Smith & Wesson's going from a tip-up hinged barrel to a tip-down or top-break system for its big pistols. The principal novelty was in the automatic simultaneous ejection. There were other advantages, too, including more rigid barrel latching and easier inspection of cylinder chambers and barrel. Significant also were the improvements in manufacture of the centerfire ammunition.

When the first No. 3 pistol (American model) came off the Smith & Wesson workbenches in 1870, sample pistols were sent to the U.S. Ordnance department, to government agents in other countries and to prominent dealers like Schuyler, Hartley & Graham of New York City. Uncle Sam finally decided to order a trial lot of 1000 and these pistols, stamped U.S. on top of the barrel rib near the breech, were delivered in the spring of 1871.

The Russian Model

In Hartford, about 25 miles down the Connecticut River from the Smith & Wesson plant at Springfield, Russia's military attaché to the United States, Maj. Gen. Alexander Gorloff, was in the process of taking final delivery of 30,000 Berdan rifles manufactured by Colt. The new Smith & Wesson pistol was shown to General Gorloff and he liked what he saw.

To make a long story short, General Gorloff signed the first of ten contracts with Smith & Wesson on May 1, 1871. All in all, Smith & Wesson was to make approximately 145,000 of the big top-break pistols for the Russian Imperial government, and these orders provided welcome funds for the development of Smith & Wesson arms.

One of the results of consultations between Smith & Wesson executives, General Gorloff, and the chief Russian inspector, Capt. Kasavery Ordinetz, was the development of an improved reloadable 44 centerfire cartridge which we know today as the 44 Russian, ballistically one of the truly outstanding pistol cartridges.

The pistols for the first Russian order resembled the long barrel No. 3 American model but were chambered for the 44 Russian cartridge. Pistols chambered for the 44 Russian caliber and sold to the American trade were generally marked "Russian Model" on the rib in addition to Smith & Wesson's name, address, and the assorted patent dates applicable to the pistol. Pistols sold to the Russian government were stamped in letters of the Slavic alphabet, a jumble that makes little sense to one unfamilar with Cyrillic writing.

Some minor changes occurred after the first 5000 No. 3 American model pistols had been manufactured. The hammer was notched across the face so that it might engage a stud projecting from the barrel catch, thus making it necessary to draw the hammer to half cock before breaking the pistol open. There was a swell provided around the trigger pin along the lower frame bevel for added strength. Shorter barrels were available if desired. Some pistols, especially for the Mexican trade, were chambered for 44 rimfire cartridges. Thus persons using the popular Henry or Model 1866 44 rimfire Winchester rifles might employ the same ammunition for pistol and rifle. Turkey was another country which favored the 44 rimfire, having previously purchased Model 1866 Winchester muskets in that caliber.

By the end of 1874 all the No. 3 American pistols had been sold and their manufacture had ceased. In their brief span of manufacture, they had, however, made quite a name for themselves, paving the way for ready acceptance of the top-break models which immediately were to succeed them.

In 1873 rather radical design changes were made in the Russian contract pistols, giving us the first truly distinctive Russian pattern. This new design retained the ribbed top-break barrel but the length was reduced at first to 7" and later to 6½". A larger, saw-handle type of grip was provided, with a knuckle or swell in the frame at the rear above the stocks. A finger rest or spur was added to the bow of the trigger guard, and a lanyard ring was attached to the butt. The "feel" and balance were quite different. Smith & Wesson production was then limited to this one model.

The western trade expressed their dislike for the big saw-handle grip of the Russian design in no uncertain terms, although it was not long before they were to have a new big Smith & Wesson top-break model more to their liking.

Bvt. Col. Geo. W. Schofield of the 10th Cavalry, stationed at Fort Leavenworth, took a keen interest in the development of military hand arms. He saw, in the big Smith & Wesson top-break pistol, excellent potential as a cavalry weapon. Col. Schofield had an inventive turn of mind, and went to work on

several changes in the Smith & Wesson design. Smith & Wesson was impressed with some of his ideas and soon was set up to manufacture a new model known to collectors as the "Schofield Model." The government was impressed, too, and in September of 1874, Smith & Wesson received an order for 3000 of the new Schofield style pistols. These pistols, identifiable by the U.S. stamped in the butt, were more like the old American model in appearance, had a 7" ribbed barrel, and were chambered for a newly designed 45 Smith & Wesson centerfire brass cartridge.

The Schofield model was a little sturdier in appearance and construction than its predecessors. The barrel catch was pivoted on the frame rather than on the barrel section; some mechanical improvements were made as manufacture progressed, including a different barrel latch, these changes being specified in a second order for 3000 pistols placed by the Army in 1875. In addition to the 7" barrel pistol, a 5" barrel size was offered; this pistol proved quite popular with Wells Fargo & Company and western users generally. However, like the confusion which sometimes resulted from the production of the 44 American and the similar but different 44 Russian cartridge, the 45 Smith & Wesson caliber created problems for the military and others where the 45 Colt had become standard. The Schofield model survived but a few years. Along with the departing Russian models, it was superseded by the real gem among the big top-breaks, Smith & Wesson's "No. 3 New Model."

In review, we have now had a look at the No. 3 American 44 made in 1870-71 and the slightly different second model made in both 44 American and 44 Russian calibers during 1871-73. For some reason the factory referred to the No. 3 American model chambered for the 44 Russian cartridge as the "Old Old Russian Model." The Russian model (saw-handle grip) made in 1873 and 1874 with a 7" barrel was called the "Old Model Russian." To confuse things a little further, the pistols of same general appearance, but with 6½" barrels and incorporating certain mechanical improvements devised by Capt. Ordinetz and Smith & Wesson, were called the "New Model Russian." These were referred to sometimes as cavalry models and were manufactured during 1875, 1876, and 1877, with the last shipment going off to Russia in January, 1878.

Having concentrated their efforts on the big No. 3 holster pistols, Smith & Wesson had fallen a few steps behind Colt in the pocket pistol field. They decided something must be done to regain a share of this trade, so in the spring of 1876 there appeared a 38 top-break five-shot pocket pistol, single action of course, as were all Smith & Wesson pistols thus far produced. For this smaller

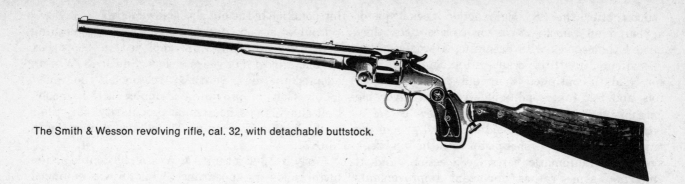

The Smith & Wesson revolving rifle, cal. 32, with detachable buttstock.

weapon Smith & Wesson designed a new cartridge (38 S & W), following their successful principle of using a bullet without a shoulder.

The pioneer 38 pocket pistol had a rather long ejector housing under the barrel, a sheath trigger and, for the first time on Smith & Wesson pistols, rubber stocks were available. Except for its lack of a bow trigger guard, the pistol looked somewhat like a small edition of the big "New Model Russian" and consequently earned for itself the popular name "Baby Russian."

After a short time the long ejector housing of this first design was eliminated and other mechanical improvements were made, but the pistol underwent little change in general appearance. In this second form it is sometimes called the Model of 1880. It was also identified in some literature as "New Model 38" to distinguish it from the "Baby Russian" which became the "Old Model 38." When the third major set of improvements was employed, including a bow trigger guard, it became known as the "Model of 1891," in which form it remained on the scene until 1911. A unique fea-

ture of the 1880 and 1891 pistols was that they could be supplied with an interchangeable single shot barrel to use alternately with the regular barrel and cylinder normally employed. These single shot barrels became available in 22 rimfire, 32 S & W centerfire and 38 S & W centerfire.

This brief review of Smith & Wesson's history in the top-break pistol field could not provide a definitive, detailed recital of all the minor changes in various models, for that would take book-length space. For those interested in pursuing such details there is John E. Parsons' excellent book *Smith & Wesson Revolvers** which provides detailed facts and figures through all the single action models. For the double action models and other types as well, interesting material will be found in McHenry & Roper's book *Smith & Wesson Hand Guns†*, and in the excellent *Smith & Wesson 1857-1945††* by Robert Neal and Roy Jenks.

---

*New York, 1957.
†Huntington, W. Va., 1945.
††New York, 1966.

This cased set contained a Smith & Wesson Model 1891 single action revolver, cal. 38, a 22 rimfire single shot barrel, interchangeable target stocks, a hollow, brass-handled screwdriver with four blades and a brush wiper. The case was leather covered and was lined with chamois skin.

Soon after the 38 single action pocket pistol appeared on Smith & Wesson's price lists, they busied themselves with designing a single action 32 caliber centerfire pocket pistol. Smith & Wesson had discontinued their old 32 rimfire pistols and felt that conditions were now favorable for a pistol smaller than the 38. The new 32 S & W pocket pistol retained the old bird-head grip of the rimfires. It was a five-shot pistol with the top-break system of automatic cartridge ejection, and it embodied some rather important improvements including the rebounding hammer patented by D.B. Wesson and James H. Bullard in 1877. Like its bigger brother, the 38, this pocket model was turned out in standard barrel lengths from 3″ to 6″ and employed a sheath trigger.

These were busy days on the Smith & Wesson drawing boards, for they not only were developing two completely new pocket pistols but, the Russian contracts now out of the way, they were burning the midnight oil working on new designs for a big top-break pistol that would have none of the handicaps of the previous models but which would embody all the improved features gained through almost ten years of experience. How well they did this may be found in the outstanding record of their No. 3 New Model, which became available to the trade in 1878.

The No. 3 New Model

At the time of its introduction, the No. 3 New Model was chambered for the 44 Russian cartridge. The cylinder had the six chambers customary for the big 44 and 45 pistols; the standard barrel was 6½″ long.

Among the improvements, other than its more streamlined appearance and smaller, more comfortable grip, was a simple rebounding lock which prevented the hammer from striking the cartridge except at the act of firing. The cylinder could not be rotated while the trigger was in the safety notch position, and the cylinder was provided with a stronger hexagonal extractor stem — the cylinder could be removed without a tool. There were fewer parts.

Smith & Wesson's dark blue finish is famous; it is a result of extra care in the polishing room and a special skill and "know-how" in producing a velvet-smooth finish. The blued pistols were fitted with plain or checked wood stocks while plated pistols were fitted with contrasting black hard-rubber stocks.

Having expressed the opinion that the No. 3 New Model single action Smith & Wesson was the cream of the crop among all top-break pistols, I shall give you reasons for this view. First, however, I would like to describe briefly the few top-break models which were manufactured subsequent to

introduction of the big No. 3 New Model.

Double action pistols were certainly nothing new; this principle was employed in pepperbox pistols almost 50 years before Smith & Wesson adopted the idea. Smith & Wesson felt they must follow Colt in providing a double action model, Colt having gained some popularity for their double action "Lightning Model" pistol, introduced in 1877.

Early in 1880 a Smith & Wesson 38 double action pistol made its appearance. This 38 was equipped with a straight-back bow trigger guard. A rather unsightly double row of grooves was milled into the periphery of the cylinder toward the rear, necessitated by the rocker type of cylinder stop; customary flutes, as on all top-break Smith & Wesson cylinders were found toward the front. Like the preceding 38 single action, the double action model had a five-shot cylinder and employed the same 38 S & W centerfire cartridge.

It is claimed that over 500,000 pistols of this general design were manufactured before it was discontinued in 1911. During the 30 years of its production, five modifications of mechanical significance were made, including elimination of the extra cylinder grooves. Pistols with the grooves were subsequently described as the "Old Model DA 38," while pistols of the later type were "New Model DA 38." Along with the new cylinder design were changes in the side plate, bow guard, hammer, trigger and other small parts. The ribbed barrels were available in lengths from 3¼″ to 6″.

Not many months after the 38 double action was introduced, Smith & Wesson had a double action 32 on the market. This pistol closely resembled the early 38 except for size, having the bow guard, double grooves in the cylinder and other features. During the course of its manufacture from 1880 to 1919, over 300,000 were sold. Barrel lengths were available from 2″ to 6″.

The least popular in Smith & Wesson's triumvirate of double actions in the 1880's were their six-shot 44 models. These were an enlarged version of the 38, having the same general characteristics. Introduced in the spring of 1881, the first model was chambered for the 44 Russian cartridge; it lasted until 1913, during which time a little over 50,000 were produced.

They were tried by several nations as a naval weapon and consequently have been called the "Navy Model." A variety of barrel lengths, from 4″ to 6½″, were available.

A similar weapon, designed to attract western trade and chambered for the 44 WCF cartridge, was on the market from 1886 to 1910. This was called the "Frontier Model," the Winchester 44 WCF cartridge (44-40), then very popular for either rifle or pistol, having become generally

Left, from the top—M1899 military 38 with lanyard ring; M1917 military, 45 ACP; New Century or "triple lock," cal. 44; double action 38 "Navy Model;" Perfected Model, 22 target. Right, from the top—Safety Hammerless 38; another in 32; M1902 "Lady Smith," 22 rimfire; 35 cal. auto pistol; "Straightline" single shot 22 rimfire.

regarded as the "frontier" caliber. This cartridge, being longer than the 44 Russian, required a cylinder ⅛" longer than that in the so-called "Navy Model." A few pistols were made to accommodate the 38 WCF cartridge.

These 44 double action pistols, along with the revolver-rifle I shall next describe, were probably the least successful of any Smith & Wesson top-break models.

During the same flurry of activity which brought along the development of Smith & Wesson's double action pistols, imaginative minds were at work on the idea of producing a smallbore sporting rifle that could be easily and inconspicuously carried. Stevens and F. Wesson pistols with attachable shoulder stocks had attained some degree of popularity, which led Smith & Wesson to introduce a revolver-rifle that was little more than a No. 3 New Model pistol with a long 16", 18", or 20" ribbed barrel. To this long-nosed pistol was added an attachable walnut shoulder stock; a short fore-end of mottled red hard rubber was installed under the barrel; stocks were of the same material. Smith & Wesson called this weapon its "New Repeating Rifle." These so-called new repeating rifles were nicley put up in a cloth-covered carrying case along with accessories which often included Smith & Wesson's special bullet mould and reloading tool. A special cartridge was designed. It was 320 caliber, employing a 1½" brass shell in which the bullet was wholly encased, thus no part of the bullet could touch the cylinder wall.

As in most attempts to employ a revolving cylinder principle to rifles, the escape of gas at the junction of cylinder and barrel, close to the shooter's face, made the weapon unpleasant to shoot. The first Smith & Wesson revolver-rifles became available in 1880 and, after very poor sales, manufacture was discontinued seven years later. A little less than 1000 were made. Despite its relative uselessness as a weapon, this piece today has a high value as a collector's item. The revolver-rifles were beautifully made. Their unusual appearance and the small production have contributed to their high specimen value.

The Safety Hammerless

Now we turn from those few models that did not catch the public's fancy to a double action model which was one of the most popular pocket and house pistols ever produced. This is Smith & Wesson's concealed hammer model put out in January of 1887 and variously called the "Safety Hammerless" and "New Departure." It was indeed a departure from the standard ideas of a visible hammer pistol, and it had safety features of great value. Daniel B. Wesson provided the ideas for a squeeze bar at the back of the grip, making it impossible

to fire the pistol unless it were held firmly in the hand and squeezed at the moment of pressing the trigger. Many thousands were sold during the many years this model was manufactured; it was produced in a 32 centerfire model as well as the 38. Quite a few improvements found their way into the construction as time went by. Collectors count five distinct variations, the most obvious of which are in the forms of the barrel catch.

Even the United States government became a little excited over this model. Col. Elmer Otis of the 8th U.S. Cavalry requested 100 of the 38 caliber "Safety Hammerless" arms with 6" barrels for trials. These pistols were shipped from Springfield in July of 1890. The 38 S & W caliber as a military weapon, however, was found lacking in stopping power. Smith & Wesson's hopes of a large government order were not realized.

The ultimate in Smith & Wesson top-break pocket pistols with a visible hammer came off the workbenches late in 1908 and was ready for the trade by January, 1909. In outer appearance this pistol was not very different from the 38 double action model introduced in 1880, but it had built into it all the improvements developed over almost 30 years of manufacture. The lockwork had been simplified and improved; spiral springs replaced the old flat springs; a thumb latch on the left side of the frame provided extra, positive locking. Smith & Wesson called this their "Perfected" model and it was about as perfect as a pocket or belt pistol of this style could be—but the day of the top-break was nearing its end and by 1920 the "Perfected" model gave way to newer ideas of design.

One other top-break pistol deserves our attention before we turn back to those fine big No. 3 New Model holster and target pistols—this is the small group of top-break single shot target pistols offered by Smith & Wesson beginning in May of 1893. The first model was merely an alternate single shot barrel to be used with the 38 single action revolver. However, by 1905 Smith & Wesson found it advisable to produce a pistol of this type designed solely for the 22 target barrel, eliminating hand- and stop-slots and removing the projecting flanges normal for a cylinder revolver. By 1909 further improvements had been made and the Smith & Wesson single shot became elevated to the title "Perfected Target Pistol." It was indeed a very excellent pistol and far superior to the straight-line 22 single shot, shaped like an automatic pistol, which replaced the "Perfected" model in 1923.

Smith & Wesson had by this time become quite conscious of the possibilities in selling pistols designed for competitive shooting. Thus they developed a style of long target stocks which could

A, Safety Lever.
B, Safety Catch.
C, Hammer.
D, Trigger.
G, Safety Latch Spring.

Above—The Smith & Wesson Perfected Model, a 22 rimfire single shot target pistol. Inset—Mechanism of the Safety Hammerless, showing concealed hammer and action of the grip safety.

be used on any of their pistols and which encased the metal frame of the grip, being held in place by two screws rather than one. Persons with large hands often preferred these stocks for the pocket or belt pistols as well as for target models.

I have described in some detail the big No. 3 American and the No. 3 Russian models, but have touched only briefly on the No. 3 New Model. I mentioned earlier that I would explain why I have such a profound admiration for this model. My high regard comes from having owned a number of specimens, from shooting them, and from studying the records they have made.

At the time the No. 3 New Model was introduced, A. C. Gould (who sometimes wrote under the name Ralph Greenwood) was one of America's most respected authorities on weapons and the shooting sports. The revised edition of his book *Modern American Pistols and Revolvers* (1894)* contains much first-hand information about handguns of the period, and, regarding Smith & Wesson's top-break system, he wrote: "While the advantages of a solid frame revolver with fixed barrel are admitted for certain uses, it seems generally admitted that for fine work, where accuracy is the chief

object, no revolver is equal to one which permits an inspection of the inside of the barrel."

This opinion was shared by most of the top shooters of the day including Chevalier Ira Paine, Walter Winans, the Bennett brothers, and Dr. Louis Bell.

Prominent westerners liked the No. 3 New Model, too. Bill Cody, having greatly admired the beautiful Smith & Wesson pistol the Grand Duke Alexis had brought to the West in 1872, had become a Smith & Wesson user. His show business partner, Texas Jack Omohundro, long a user of the big top-break pistols, ordered a pair of the "New Model" design. It was my good fortune to acquire Texas Jack's big "American Model" some years ago when I purchased a firearms collection in Portland, Oregon. My friend Herschel Logan ended up with this pistol, and it proved to be so interesting to Herschel that he sat down and wrote *Buckskin and Satin,* a fascinating story about the adventures of Texas Jack and Texas Jack's celebrated actress wife, Mlle. Morlacchi, originator of the cancan in America.

The No. 3 New Model was a multipurpose arm. It was offered as an army pistol, a frontier pistol, and a target pistol. More calibers and different loads were available than in any other model. At first there was the 44 S & W Russian, the 44 S &

*Reprinted 1946 by Samworth, but now out of print.

Prices for Revolver, either Blue Finish or Nickel Plated

CALIBER	Length of Barrel, In Inches	MODEL	With Rubber Stock	With Ivory Stock	With Pearl Stock
32	3 or 3½	Double Action	$10.75	$12.00	$12.25
32	6	Double Action	11.75	13.00	13.25
32	3 or 3½	Safety Hammerless	11.75	13.25	13.50
32	2	Safety Hammerless, Bicycle Pattern	11.75	13.25	13.50
32	6	Safety Hammerless	12.75	14.25	14.50
32	6½	32-44 Target, Single Action	15.50	18.00	19.50
38	3¼	Single Action	10.75	12.25	12.50
38	4	Single Action	11.00	12.50	12.75
38	5	Single Action	11.25	12.75	13.00
38	6	Single Action	11.75	13.25	13.50
38	6½	38-44 Target, Single Action	15.50	18.00	19.50
38	3¼	Double Action	11.75	13.25	13.50
38	4	Double Action	12.00	13.50	13.75
38	5	Double Action	12.25	13.75	14.00
38	6	Double Action	12.75	14.25	14.50
38	3¼	Safety Hammerless	12.75	14.25	14.50
38	4	Safety Hammerless	13.00	14.50	14.75
38	5	Safety Hammerless	13.25	14.75	15.00
38	6	Safety Hammerless	13.75	15.25	15.50
38	4	Single Action, W.C.F.Ctg.	12.75	15.25	16.75
38	5	Single Action, W.C.F.Ctg.	13.00	15.50	17.00
38	6½	Single Action, W.C.F.Ctg.	13.50	16.00	17.50
38	4	D'ble Action, W.C.F.Ctg.	13.75	16.25	17.25
38	5	D'ble Action, W.C.F.Ctg.	14.00	16.50	17.50
38	6½	D'ble Action, W.C.F.Ctg.	14.50	17.00	18.00
44	4	Single Action, R.M. or W.C.F.	12.75	15.25	16.75
44	5	Single Action, R.M. or W.C.F.	13.00	15.50	17.00
44	6 or 6½	Single Action, R.M. or W.C.F.	13.50	16.00	17.50
44	8	Single Action, R.M.	14.50	17.00	18.50
44	6½	Single Action, Target	15.50	18.00	19.50
44	8	Single Action, Target	16.50	19.00	20.50
44	4	Double Action, R.M. or W.C.F.	13.75	16.25	17.25
44	5	Double Action, R.M. or W.C.F.	14.00	16.50	17.50
44	6 or 6½	Double Action, R.M. or W.C.F.	14.50	17.00	18.00
32	3¼	Hand Ejector	10.50	12.00	12.25
32	4¼	Hand Ejector	10.75	12.25	12.50
32	6	Hand Ejector	11.25	12.75	13.00
32	4	Military and Police, W.C.F.	13.75	16.25	17.25
32	5	Military and Police, W.C.F.	14.00	16.50	17.50
32	6½	Military and Police, W.C.F.	14.50	17.00	18.00
38	4	Military and Police	13.75	16.25	17.25
38	5	Military and Police	14.00	16.50	17.50
38	6½	Military and Police	14.50	17.00	18.00

CALIBER	Length of Barrel	MODEL	6 inch	8 inch	10 inch
22	6, 8, 10	Single Shot Target	$12.00	$13.00	$14.00
32	6, 8, 10	Single Shot Target	12.00	13.00	14.00
38	6, 8, 10	Single Shot Target	12.00	13.00	14.00
		Combination Revolver and Single Shot Pistol complete, with case	24.00	25.00	26.00

PRICES.

SUNDRIES.	For 32 Revol.	For 32-44 and 38-44 Revol.	For 38 Revol.	For 38 Mil. Revol.	For 44 Revol.	For Single Shot Pistol	For 32 H.E. Revol.
Reloading Tools, per set	$2.00	$2.25	$2.00	$2.25	$2.25		$2.00
Leather Holster and Belt	.75	1.00	.75	1.00	1.00	$1.00	.75
Rubber Pocket Holster	.75		.75				.75
Chamois Revolver Pockets	.75		.75				.75
Extension Stock, For 44 Single Action Revolver only					3.50		
Full Silver Plating	2.25	4.00	2.50	4.00	4.00		2.25
Full Gold Plating	4.00	6.00	4.75	6.00	6.00		4.00
Nickel Plating or Bluing	1.50	2.00	1.75	2.00	2.00		1.50
Adjustable Rear Sights, Adapted to 38 Single and Double Action, 32-44, 38-44, 44 Target and Single Shot Target Models.		1.75					
"Paine" Front Sight, For 38 Single and Double Action, 32-44, 38-44, 44 Target and Single Shot Target Models.		.60					
Lyman Front Sight, For 38 Single and Double Action, 32-44, 38-44, 44 Target and Single Shot Target Models.		.75					
Lyman Rear Sight Slide.		1.00					
Target Sights, For Military and Police Revolver, per set.					1.50		
Target Sights, For 32 Hand Ejector Revolver, per set.							1.75
Mailing and Registration of Revolvers	.28	.61	.33	.50	.57	.41	.35
Mailing and Registration of Loading Tools	.34	.30	.35	.38	.38		.34
Mailing and Registration of Holster and Belt	.15	.18	.15	.18	.18	18	.15

Engraving, per Revolver, from $1.50 upwards, according to quality and quantity.

Brass Handled Screw Driver, four blades, $0.60.

Revolver Cases, $2.50 up.

Extra Barrels, Complete For Interchanging	32 D.A.	32 Safety	32 Hand Ejec.	38 S.A. D.A. and Safety	38 Mil.	44 S.A.	44 D.A.	32-44 38-44 S.A. includ. Target Sights	Single Shot Pistol.
3 or 3½ in.	$2.50	$2.50							
3¼ inch			$1.25	$2.75					
4 inch				3.00	$1.50	$3.50	$3.50		
4¼ inch			1.25						
5 inch				3.25	1.50	3.75	3.75		
6 inch	3.50	3.50	1.25	3.75		4.00	4.00		$6.00
6½ inch					1.50	4.00	4.00	$6.00	
8 inch						5.00			7.00
10 inch									8.00
Special Stocks									
Pearl	1.50	1.75	1.75	1.75	3.50	4.00	3.50	4.00	10.00
Ivory	1.25	1.50	1.50	1.50	2.50	2.50	2.50	2.50	10.00
Black Rubber Target									.75

Smith & Wesson Automatic Revolvers.

NEW MODEL 44, No. 3.

BLUED OR PLATED.

Central Fire, Double Action, Six Shot, weight 2¼ lbs., Cal 44-100. length of barrel 4-inch, **$17.50;** 5-inch, **17.81;** 6-inch **$18.12**

Extra, Pearl Stocks, **5.00;** Ivory, **2.18.**

NEW MODEL, 32, No. 1½.

BLUED OR PLATED.

Central Fire, Double Action **$11.68**

Extra, Pearl Stocks, **$1.87;** Ivory, **$1.25.**

Five Shot, Weight 14 oz., Calber 32-100. 3 and 3½ in. only made.

NEW MODEL, 38, No. 2.

BLUED OR PLATED.

Central Fire, Double Action, Five Shot, Weight 13 oz. Caliber 38-100, length of barrel 3¼ inch, **$13.00;** 4 inch, **13.31;** 5 inch, **13.75.**

Extra, Pearl Stocks, **$2.50;** Ivory, **$1.56.**

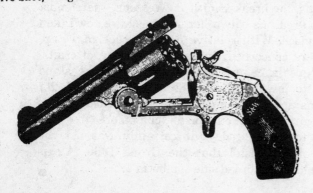

BLUED OR PLATED.

Single-Action, Cal. 32-100, Central-Fire, length of barrel 3½ inch, Five Shot. weight 12½ oz., Rebounding **$10.43**

Extra, Pearl Stocks, **1.87;** Ivory, **1.25.**

Single-Action, Cal. 38-100, Central-Fire, Five Shot, weight 16 oz., length of barrel 3¼ in., **$11.75;** 4in., **12.06;** 5-in. **12.50**

Extra, Pearl Stocks, **2.50;** Ivory, **1.56.**

Single-Action, Cal. 44-100, Central-Fire, Six Shot, New Russian Model, weight 2½ lbs., lengths of bar'l, 6 & 6½ in., Reb'd'g, **16.25**

Extra, Pearl Stocks, **5.00;** Ivory, **2.18.**

W Russian Gallery and the 450 Webley. Then for the frontier model there was the 44 WCF, requiring the long 1⁹⁄₁₆″ cylinder and the long barrel strap. A very few were made in the 38 WCF caliber. Some were made for Turkey and other buyers in 44 rimfire.

Ira Paine is said to have suggested the 38/44 chambering, this pistol using special 38/44 Gallery or 38/44 Target cartridges in which the bullet was seated inside the case flush with the mouth as in the 320 revolver-rifle cartridges.

A round ball 38 gallery cartridge was also developed, the ball seated deeply in the case over 20 grains of black powder. A similar round ball load, using 10 grains of black, was offered for the 32/44 revolver.

The smallest bore was the 32/44, using the same style of cartridge employed for the 38/44. This caliber is claimed to have been suggested by F. E. Bennett and his brother W. W. Bennett, American pistol champions. Two cylinder lengths were available in the 38/44 and the 32/44 (1⁷⁄₁₆″ and 1⁹⁄₁₆″). These two target model pistols were introduced in 1887 and manufactured up to 1910.

Smith & Wesson made a total of 4333 single action revolvers chambered for the 38/44 and 32/44 cartridges. In 38/44, 1023 had 1⁷⁄₁₆″ chambers and 390 had 1⁹⁄₁₆″; in 32/44, 2621 had chambers 1⁷⁄₁₆″ while 299 had 1⁹⁄₁₆″ chambers. The longer chambers were possible only on those revolvers that S & W had made with a longer cylinder and top strap to accomodate the 44/40 cartridge, which were intended to compete with the Colt Frontier revolver.

The standard barrel length for the No. 3 New Model pistols was 6½″, but barrel lengths of 4″, 5″, 6″ and 8″ were also available. Old Smith & Wesson catalogs list a good variety of optional sights, stocks, finishing, and accessories.

Smith & Wesson's new No. 3 Army Model did not stir up much enthusiasm in ordnance circles. Although a few were ordered at the time of the Spanish-American War, no top-breaks were actually delivered and the specifications of the contract were changed to require a solid frame 38 pistol which became known as the "Military and Police" model, and with it was developed the 38 S & W Special cartridge.

The 32 and 38 caliber pocket pistols had not sold well west of the Mississippi, but the Far West was a logical market for the big No. 3 New Model 44s. Smith & Wesson engaged a young artist who had been doing some accurate and interesting western illustrations in *Harpers* and *Century* magazines. His name was Frederic Remington. Remington's illustrations did much to bring attention to the big top-break pistols. But pistols were going out of style as a part of men's attire in

the West and the trade quieted down.

Some orders from law enforcement agencies were received. Several hundred pistols were shipped to Australia where they were issued to the colonial police. These pistols were accompanied by attachable walnut shoulder stocks, the metal yoke being shaped with a shorter curve at the base than the yoke on revolving-rifle stocks. Some years ago, with the help of an old-timer among Smith & Wesson workmen, I found 200 walnut shoulder stocks for the No. 3 New Model in a dark corner of a storeroom at the plant. These stocks, some with blued metal coupling and others nickeled, were packed individually in attractive green cartons. The cartons were in sturdy wood boxes, about 50 cartons to the box, the lids fastened with square-cut nails. They had been slumbering a long time.

Bearded Walter Winans, author of *The Art of Revolver Shooting,* had this to say about shoulder stocks: "I do not care much for detachable stocks for revolvers. They turn a revolver into an inferior carbine, and the revolver is not meant for a long range weapon." Walter Winans had a lot more to say about Smith & Wesson firearms. After a year or two of experimenting with them, he shot with no other make of pistol. For military competition at Bisley which required a 45 caliber pistol, Winans used the 450 Eley. In other shooting he used either the 44 Russian or the 32/44 S & W.

Among the reasons that Winans, Gould, Gastine Renette of Paris, and many other shooting perfectionists around the turn of the century preferred the Smith & Wesson top-break target arms were these: The efforts of Smith & Wesson firm were devoted exclusively to making high quality hand arms. The barrels, cylinders and small parts were shaped from finest quality cast steel; Gould tells us the framework was of Bessemer steel made in Troy, N.Y. Fine machinery, precise gauging, close tolerances, skilled workmen, strict inspection —all these things were factors.

Shooters were especially pleased with the perfect alignment of the barrel and cylinder. This was assured by inlaying a piece of very hard steel at the stop notch and thus preventing wear.

It is obvious that, as fine as were those carefully made, handsomely finished and smooth working top-break Smith & Wessons, there must be good reasons why other systems have now taken their place. With relative merits in design we are not here concerned; in relative quality of craftsmanship the Smith & Wesson top-breaks stand equal to any. In the hands of Ira Paine, Walter Winans and the Bennetts they established records in accuracy that our pistol champions find difficult to match today. It certainly was not the fault of the pistol that the Grand Duke Alexis couldn't hit the broad side of a buffalo. ●

10cm Automatics

by JAMES B. STEWART

T HE PATENTING in September 1905 and subsequent production of the Model 1906 automatic pistol by the Fabrique Nationale d'Armes de Guerre of Herstal, near Liege, Belgium, ushered in both the 25 caliber auto pistol cartridge and the vest-pocket automatic. With the fantastic commercial success of this arm came a host of imitators and copiers, each vying to produce the smallest, lightest, and the cheapest personal defense firearm.

Because of a combination of factors, including the ability to be held and pointed effectively as well as the power and physical dimensions of the cartridge, 10cm (3^{15}/$_{16}$ in.) in over-all length seemed to be the lower limit for this class of weapon. The initial FN offering was over 11cm long, but by the early teens several firms had applied for patents for designs which would allow reduction of the over-all size to about 10.5cm (4¼ in.). One of the first of these to be marked as "10cm long" was the Walther Model II, which became available in 1914. Aside from it and the Spanish "Martian" apparently no others of this size were put into production before the outbreak of the First World War.

Commencing almost immediately after the cessation of hostilities a veritable flood of patent applications for super-small 25 caliber automatics appeared. Probably the first of these to actually see production and be advertised as 10cm long was the German Mann, of 10.5cm length. This unusual design was not popular. However, almost simultaneously Walther introduced a much updated version of their Models II and V which they designated the Model IX. This arm was not only the first truly 10cm long automatic but its great popularity caused it to be copied by manufacturers both in and outside of Germany.

Although many of the precursors and copies of the Walther IX were advertised as being 10cm long, in reality only four other 25 caliber vest-pocket automatics were actually this small. Of these three were German, the two versions of the Sauer Model 1928 and the Model II Schmeisser of the C. G. Haenel Company, and one Belgian, the complex Melior "Baby."

Germany was by far the largest producer of the super-vest-pocket automatic. One of the first copies of the Walther IX was the 10.5cm "Liliput" of August Menz, which was also later sold under the *Bergmann Erben* tradename. The odd automatics of Hugo Helfricht were slightly larger, except for his final and more conventional looking Model 4. The earliest of the Sauer vest-pocket series, the Model 1924, was larger than its later brothers by half a centimeter, but it too was advertised as 10cm long. Strangely enough Walther's largest domestic competitor, Mauser, waited until the mid-30s to replace their first vest-pocket model,

with its over 11cm length, with the WTP II at a scant 10.5cm.

As might be expected, that hotbed of automatic pistol manufacture, Spain, became the second largest producer of true vest-pocket automatics. In addition to the pre-war Martian, vest-pocket versions were made of several of the better-selling larger Spanish 25 caliber automatics. Bonifacio Echeverria made the Star Model E, which was a diminutive version of his Model CO. This exposed-hammer design scaled about 10.5 cm long. Although examples are extremely rare, there were also 10.5cm versions made of the unusual Sharpsooter tipping-barrel automatic and the odd and famous Jo.Lo.Ar. with its spur trigger and pivoted slide-cocking lever.

In addition to these scaled-down models there was a Spanish direct copy of the Walther Model IX called the SEAM Pocket Model, and several small copies of the Browning 1906 such as the Debatir and the Vulcain. Like most copies of the Walther IX and the Browning, these were actually 10.5cm long. All of these Spanish automatics were produced prior to the 1936 Spanish Civil War. The earliest were probably the Sharpsooter and the Vulcain, dating from the early 20s, followed by the SEAM, Debatir, Jo.Lo.Ar. and Star in the late 20s.

For some unknown reason Belgium, the country that was the second largest manufacturer of automatic pistols in Europe, was late to introduce the "10cm" automatic. This is doubly unusual since the vest-pocket arm had originated in Belgium. Finally FN itself designed a reduced-size version of its original "Standard" Browning pistol which it named the "Baby" Browning. This arm looks superficially like the Walther Model IX, but has considerable in-

Walther Model IX. The first *truly* 10cm-long auto, this arm went into production in 1921. It was very popular and was much copied. Many thousands were made before the Second World War halted production. Fancy versions were available with high relief engraving and plating in nickel or gold. A favorite WW II souvenir, it is much sought by collectors and shooters.

Pre-World War 1 "Martian." This 25 caliber Spanish 10.5cm automatic, manufactured by Martin A. Bascaran about 1912, may well have been the first to be advertised as "10cm long." The unusual pivoted-trigger-guard-type takedown was similar to that used on the Webley & Scott and Harrington & Richardson automatics. The pistol also had a "pop-up" rear sight to indicate a loaded chamber—apparently prior to Walther's use of the device. The indicator will work, unlike the Walther, only on a loaded round, not on an empty shell.

FN "Baby" Browning. The belated first attempt by the originator of the 25 caliber auto to meet the 10cm competition, this 10.5cm long pistol was introduced by the Fabrique Nationale d'Armes de Guerre of Belgium about 1936. Aside from the enclosed barrel it was quite similar to the Walther IX. One innovation was the use of dual, concentric recoil springs to increase reliability in this small size. The design is still in production but, because of the 1968 Gun Control Act, is not importable into the U.S. It was marketed here previously by the Browning Arms Co. of St. Louis.

Sharpsooter Vest Pocket. Another exposed-hammer design, the Sharpsooter (sic) also featured a tip-up barrel. This combination made it unnecessary to pull back the slide to load, so no finger grooves were furnished. The small 10.5cm long five-shot model of this arm, made by the Hijor de Calixto Arrizabalaga, is quite rare; most were seven or eight shot, and larger. The same firm also made a 10.5cm-long version of the famous Jo.Lo.Ar., which is similar but has no trigger guard and has a lever pivoted to the right side of the slide which can be used to cock the pistol.

Walther Model II, 10.5cm-long 6.35mm automatic. This arm has a "pop-up" rear sight which serves as a loaded-chamber indicator. It was manufactured by Carl Walther in Germany during 1914 and 1915. Like almost all "10cm" autos, this one has a five-round magazine. It is one of the scarcest Walther pistols.

ternal differences. However, it did not go on the market until about 1934 or 1935, nearly fifteen years after Walther had pioneered in this area.

The second diminutive Belgian vest-pocket automatic was patented by the firm of Fabrique d'Armes F. Delu et Cie and put into production early in the 1930s. Though 10.5cm in length, this automatic was unusually thin—as thin as the Walther. Manufactured under the "Delu" name, this pistol was also sold under the "Bayard" tradename by Anciens Etablissements Pieper as their Model 1936.

The most complicated of the vest-pocket automatics was made by Robar et Cie, one of the most prolific automatic pistol producers of all time. This arm, sold under their "Melior" tradename,

Star Model E. Made by the famous Spanish firm of Bonifacio Echeverria, the Model E was a 10.5cm version of its bigger brother, the Model CO (later called CU, then "Starlett"). The design was introduced about 1926. The pistol illustrated is dated 1928. Few examples of this survive, the only Spanish design from a still existing company. Note the exposed hammer.

Mauser WTP II. This was the final German 10cm design to be produced prior to World War II. Waffenfabrik Mauser scaled down their WTP I (Westentaschen Pistole I) to 10.5 cm long and offered it on the world market in 1936. It was very popular and, despite the short time it was available, many thousands were sold. When the French occupied the Mauser plant at the close of World War II they assembled nearly a thousand WTP IIs from spare parts.

Melior "Reduit" or "Baby." This final Belgium contribution is the fifth true 10cm 25 caliber auto, and is the most complex. The design has a concealed hammer and grip, magazine, and manual safeties. The Walther IX has only a manual safety, and is striker fired. Made by Robar et Cie, this design appeared about 1938 and few were made; it is also known in catalogs as the "Model I." Interestingly, all known examples have a cloisonne monogram inlay in the left grip and a plain molded monogram in the right.

was variously called the "Baby," the "Model 1," and the "Reduit," or "reduced." Not only is this amazing pistol only 10cm long, it has, unlike the extremely simple striker-fired Walther IX, an internal hammer and—in addition to a manual safety—a magazine safety and a grip safety! It apparently did not fare well in the market place, as examples are extremely scarce.

Two other European countries made super-small firearms prior to the Second World War. Czechoslovakia was early in the game, producing in 1921 two different 10.5cm automatics which were, incidentally, also the only two folding-trigger automatic pistols to ever be marketed, the "Fox" and the Praga. Both are well known to collectors but the "Fox," being made in very limited numbers by Alois Tomischka, is extremely rare.

Unique "Mikros." This French copy of the Walther IX was made in the 1930s by the Manufacture d'Armes des Pyrenees in Hendaye, just across the border from Spain. Only a few thousand were made. The internal construction was modified just enough to avoid infringing Walther's patents.

Praga Vz. 21. This rare Czech auto is quite familiar to collectors. One of the two folding trigger designs among 25 caliber automatic pistols (the other being its contemporary, the Czech "Fox" by Alois Tomischka), it was made in 1921 by the short-lived firm of Zbrojovka Praga. Only a few thousand of these 10.5cm-long pistols were marketed. The folding trigger was intended to be used as a manual safety; the arm can be cocked with one hand.

Mann Model 1921. This German 10.5cm-long 6.35mm auto, like its earlier variation the Model 1920, is of unusual internal-breech-bolt design and does not have a slide. The arm's odd looks and tendency of the bolt to pinch the web of the thumb against the frame kept it from being popular.

The Praga, made by a relatively short-lived company, is itself scarce.

France, like Belgium, did not enter the super-vest-pocket category until quite late, and then produced only three examples. The Manufacture d'Armes des Pyrenees produced, under their "Unique" tradename, the pistol known as the "Mikros" which was an almost exact—but slightly larger—duplicate of the Walther Model IX. The Manufacture d'Armes Bayonne produced under the MAB tradename another Model IX copy named the Model B. The third manufacturer in France was M. Seytres of St. Etienne, who produced a vest-pocket version of his well-known Browning-copy "Union" automatic both under his own tradename and for Verney-Carron, the cartridge makers, under the tradename Vercar.

The holocaust of the Second World War virtually destroyed the European arms industry and when it was rebuilt economic conditions were not favorable to re-establishing the many small shops that had specialized in the vest-pocket automatic. In addition, the lessons of the war resulted in consumer interest shifting to larger, more powerful calibers and to double-action lockwork which could not be accommodated in the "10cm" size. As a result, with the exception of some limited production of the MAB Model B and the re-introduction of the Browning "Baby" (which is still being made) only two other 10cm autos have since been produced.

One of these, the stainless steel Bauer currently made in the United States, is an exact under-license copy of the Browning "Baby" and indeed, the parts are even interchangeable with the

Sauer WTM 1928 (a). The second true 10cm-long automatic, this modernized version of the 1924 model is somewhat more conventional in design but still has an unusual disassembly. Sauer products were of uniformly fine construction and excellent finish and were among the highest-quality arms of pre-World War II Germany.

Right-side view of Sauer WTM(a) showing the patent marking and top ejection. The WTM designation stands for "Westentaschen Modell"—"vest-pocket model."

Menz "Liliput." This 10.5cm-long Walther IX look alike was produced by August Menz of Germany from about 1924 until sometime early in the 1930s. It was sold under the "Bergmann Erben" tradename in very limited quantities. Like the Walther, the 6.35mm Liliput and its novelty little brother, the 4.25mm Liliput, were much sought after by G.I.s as war souvenirs.

Bayard Model 1936. Originally marketed by the manufacturer, Fabrique d'Armes F. Delu et Cie, the majority of these pistols were sold under the Bayard tradename of the Anciens Etablissements Pieper of Belgium. While 10.5cm long, the Delu (or Bayard) is one of the thinnest 25 caliber automatics ever sold. It is scarcely ¾" thick, equal to the smaller Walther IX. Apparently no large quantity was marketed under either tradename as examples are scarce.

Sauer WTM. This 1924 model was the first of J. P. Sauer & Sohn's line of 25 cal. vest pocket autos. The conventional appearance of this 10.5cm-long arm conceals a unique design and an unusual takedown system. Note the lack of grip securing screws and the extra front-end finger grooves needed during disassembly.

Right-side view of Sauer WTM 1928(b) showing the alteration to side ejection. Note the serial number in comparison to the earlier model. Model 1928(b) guns were numbered in the general Sauer handgun serializing system rather than in the separate sequence which had been stablished for the earlier vest-pockets. Only a few thousand of each model/type were actually made.

Sauer WTM 1928(b). This, the third true 10cm pocket auto, as a further refinement and simplification of the earlier Sauers. Although it resembles the (a) variation, virtually no parts are interchangeable except the grips and magazine.

Debatir. This rare Spanish 10.5cm long 25 caliber arm is a modified 1906 Browning design. Unusual features are the "disc" manual safety, the grip safety, and the spring-loaded claw to retain the grips. Only two or three examples survive. Manufacturer is unknown.

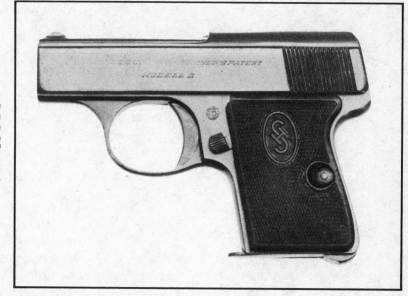

Schmeisser Modell II. This fine German-made Walther IX look-alike, the fourth true 10cm auto, was made by the C. G. Haenel firm to the patents of Hugo Schmeisser—who also designed the famed submachine gun of World War II. This 1929 model is unusual in that it must be manually put on "safe" before the magazine can be removed. Apparently very few were made.

Helfricht Model 4. Fractionally smaller than its earlier brethren, this German-made 1928 model scales just 10.5cm. It also becomes the "large capacity" champ of the list because of its six-shot magazine. The make was the product of the firm of A. Krausser and is based on the patents of Hugo Helfricht. Some were tradenamed Helkra.

Browning. The only new contribution to the super-vest-pocket automatic came from a country which had not previously manufactured this sized arm, Italy. This pistol, in production from late 1945 until sometime in the 50s, was manufactured by the firm of V. Bernardelli and—like so many of its competitors—was referred to as the "Baby." It was unusual in being available in more than one caliber. Although initial production was for the 25 ACP cartridge it was later made in 22 Long and 22 Short calibers. Thus this beautifully-constructed and finished pistol is the smallest arm ever to chamber these two calibers, a fitting footnote to the super-vest-pocket pistol story. ●

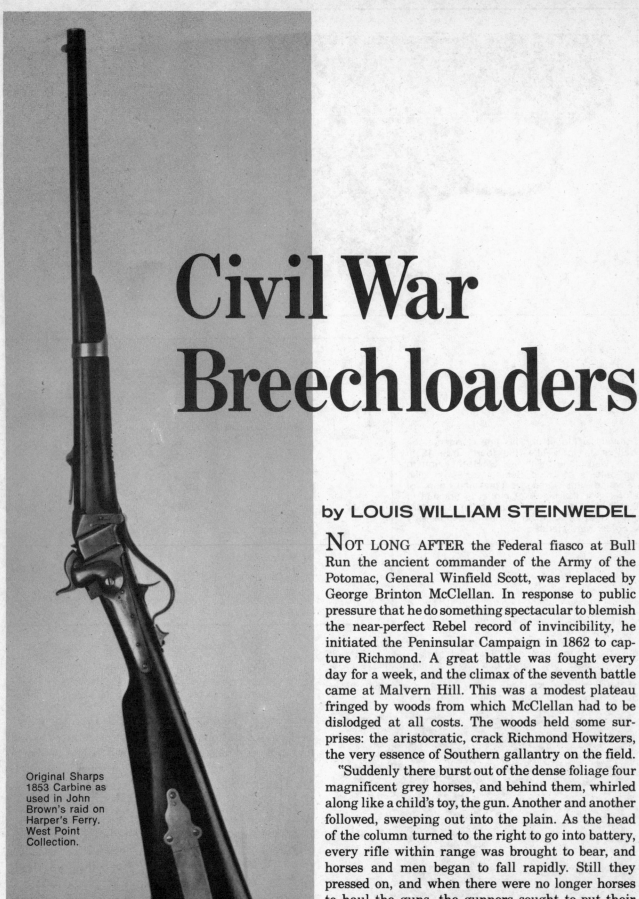

Original Sharps
1853 Carbine as
used in John
Brown's raid on
Harper's Ferry.
West Point
Collection.

Civil War Breechloaders

by LOUIS WILLIAM STEINWEDEL

NOT LONG AFTER the Federal fiasco at Bull
Run the ancient commander of the Army of the
Potomac, General Winfield Scott, was replaced by
George Brinton McClellan. In response to public
pressure that he do something spectacular to blemish
the near-perfect Rebel record of invincibility, he
initiated the Peninsular Campaign in 1862 to cap-
ture Richmond. A great battle was fought every
day for a week, and the climax of the seventh battle
came at Malvern Hill. This was a modest plateau
fringed by woods from which McClellan had to be
dislodged at all costs. The woods held some sur-
prises: the aristocratic, crack Richmond Howitzers,
the very essence of Southern gallantry on the field.

"Suddenly there burst out of the dense foliage four
magnificent grey horses, and behind them, whirled
along like a child's toy, the gun. Another and another
followed, sweeping out into the plain. As the head
of the column turned to the right to go into battery,
every rifle within range was brought to bear, and
horses and men began to fall rapidly. Still they
pressed on, and when there were no longer horses
to haul the guns, the gunners sought to put their
pieces into battery by hand; nothing however could
stand before that terrible storm of lead, and after

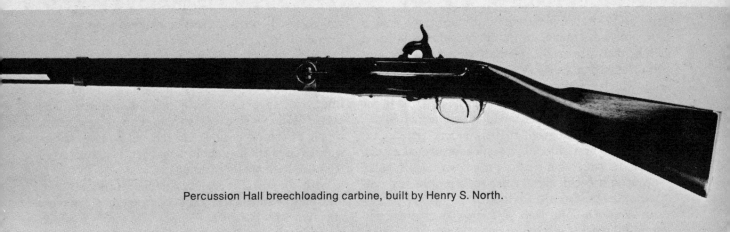

Percussion Hall breechloading carbine, built by Henry S. North.

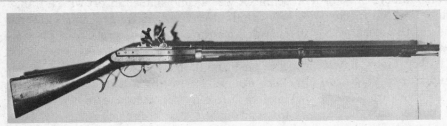

The Hall flintlock rifle, designed in 1811, was the first American breechloader. Never popular, the Confederates referred to the Hall as "a wretched apology."

ten minutes of gallant effort the few survivors, leaving their guns in the open field, took shelter in the friendly woods." After the holocaust one of the shaken survivors was moved to say: "We went in a battery and came out a wreck. We staid (sic) ten minutes by the watch and came out with one gun, ten men, and two horses, without firing a shot."

Much of "that terrible storm of lead" came from a comparatively small number of extraordinary rifles in the hands of an unorthodox assemblage of soldiers. The rifles were Sharps breechloaders, and the men were Hiram Berdan's "Sharpshooters." They formed a formidable combination: rifles which were accurate up to 1500 yards and men with shooting eyes which could make them effective even at that range.

Together, they would help re-write the rules of warfare. Superbly accurate, rapid fire breechloaders could not only break up classic infantry charges at close range, but could harass artillery crews so intensely as to drive cannon completely out of its customary place in the infantry line. Strategically placed corps of breechloader-armed riflemen, such as Berdan's men in the Peach Orchard at Gettysburg, could singlehandedly turn the tide of great battles.

The American Civil War firmly established the breechloader as the ultimate martial arm for years to come; within a short time after the war no major government in the world would continue to rely on muzzleloaders. Union cavalrymen, who used both, often preferred a good breechloader over complex or fragile repeaters. One officer compared the two weapons and wrote, "The Spencer carbine was latterly in very general use, superseding Sharps. There was little to choose between them as I have fired as many rounds out of Sharps' in the course of twenty minutes, as out of Spencer. The latter fired seven shots pretty rapidly, but it takes some time to reload."

The breechloading rifle did not spring onto the Civil War scene "whole and full grown" but was preceeded by at least a century and a half of creative

Rare Confederate copy of (right) of Sharps gun by "S. C. Robinson Arms Mfg. Co., Richmond, Va."

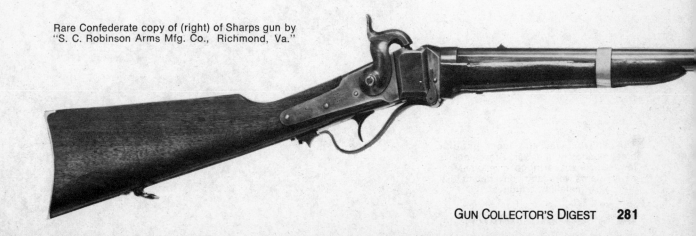

trial-and-error development. Although even earlier attempts were made, the first practical breechloader can be traced to an Englishman named John Warsop who devised a coarsely threaded vertical breechplug which could be unscrewed by swiveling off the trigger guard. A charge could then be inserted in the breech. Fifty years later the idea was picked up and refined by a flamboyant British major, Patrick Ferguson, who brought 200 breechloader-armed special troops to the colonies to "put down the Rebels." Ferguson breechloading rifles were marvelously accurate, the best weapon of the 18th Century.

In America John Hall of Yarmouth, Maine, patented a breechloading flintlock smoothbore musket in 1811 which used a simple tip-up breech mechanism. A release on the underside of the stock activated the hinged breechblock which tilted up to allow the insertion of powder and ball or, later a paper cartridge. The Hall was manufactured at Harper's Ferry Arsenal and, despite its awkward center-hammer "boxlock" design, it remained current for many years. In fact, percussion versions of this obsolete piece of engineering, built by Henry S. North, were still being issued during the Civil War.

Early breechloaders were beset with their share of troubles. The most common was that all of them leaked gas at the breech. But pioneer designers were willing to work around the problems to get to the great advantages offered by breechloading rifles. The first to score a major breakthrough was Christian Sharps, a pupil of John Hall, who patented his basic breechloader in 1848. From this prototype was destined to come perhaps the most dreaded small arm of the Civil War and certainly the most famous big game rifle ever built on the North American continent. Throughout the entire Civil War the Sharps rifle was one of the very few "patent" arms for which the crotchety U.S. Chief of Ordnance, General James W. Ripley, had any great respect.

Sharps' rifle went through several stages of development, including the famous slant breech "John Brown" model and the "New Model 1859." The design was blessed with enduring, classic simplicity. A toggle link mechanism connected the vertically mounted breechblock to the combination lever-trigger guard which dropped the breechblock below barrel level to expose the chamber for loading with a linen cartridge containing powder and ball. The breechblock was fitted with a normal percussion nipple at the right side, and the cap flame was carried through the breechblock to a "jet" which directed it to the base of the cartridge.

With the aid of a designer named Hezekiah Conant, Sharps solved the gas leak problem in the most effective way possible. Mounted in the face of the breechblock was a cone shaped insert with a flange, loosely fitted into a recess in the breechblock. When the powder charge was fired, gas under pressure rushed back around this cone and was directed forward to push the flange tightly against the breech. In effect, Conant was trying to equalize the pressure pushing back to effect an instantaneous gas seal by means of an opposite reaction.

Captain Minié's famous hollow-base Minié ball for muzzleloading rifle muskets added great accuracy but did not resolve any of the other problems of muzzleloaders. Sharps, however, used the hollow-base ball in his breechloader to even greater effect. When the powder fired, the pressure expanded the base of the bullet to fill the rifling grooves completely for excellent accuracy. Also, since the bullet was breech-loaded, there was no chance of bullet deformation because it did not have to be rammed down the barrel, and fouling problems were less crucial than in muzzleloaders. The marriage of the Minié ball to the breechloader produced a weapon of superb accuracy, plus speed, convenience, and greater safety.

In February of 1860 a test was conducted at the Washington Marine barracks between a Sharps and a regular issue musket at ranges of 100 to 450 yards. The Sharps fired 67 rounds with 53 hits; the musket fired 60 shots and recorded 20 hits, none of them on target at maximum range. This was a nice parade

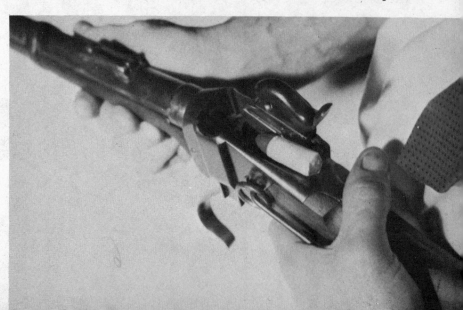

The Sharps was the most popular breechloader of the war. Breechlock is lowered, linen cartridge inserted. Most early Sharps were later converted to take metallic cartridges.

This unusual specimen is a standard muzzle-loading musket made in 1862 which has been converted to breechloader by Millbank system. The movable breechblock was turned to the side by means of visible handle so a metal cartridge could be inserted. Method was awkward.

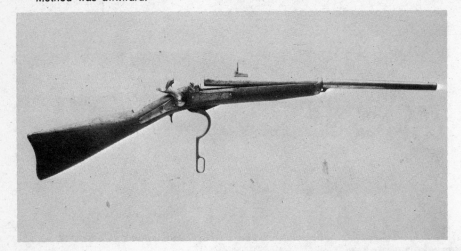

The Gibbs carbine used a tip-up barrel similar to shotgun action. 52 caliber paper cartridge was inserted in the breech and fired by an ordinary percussion cap. Marked "Wm. F. Brooks, Mfr., New York," the government bought 1,052 Gibbs carbines.

This big 69 caliber musket, designed by G. W. Morse, was one of few breechloaders used by Confederacy. The gun is a conversion from muzzle loader.

ground demonstration, but a better test of the Sharps presented itself during the Wilderness Campaign. Union movements were being watched from a Confederate observation tower on the other side of the Po River, and the nearest a rifleman could get was 1500 yards. Even Sharps-armed sharpshooters were perplexed; their rifles were only sighted to 1000 yards. Then one fellow came up with the idea of elongating the leaf sight with a whittled wooden strip. Trial and error revealed the right length, and within a few minutes the Sharpshooters had cleared the tower three quarters of a mile away.

Although the Sharps was the best and most popular of the Civil War breechloaders, it was by no means the only one. The Grand Army of the Republic threw more than 20 different kinds of breechloaders into the field, mostly carbines, and there was about double that number available to select from. Running the gamut of them all is a capsule course in human inventiveness and perserverence; it is amazing how many answers there could be to the problem of designing a simple, single shot breech-loading rifle. The study of Civil War carbines is one of the most fascinating, and challenging, fields in all gun collecting.

Next in numerical popularity to the Sharps was a carbine designed by General Ambrose Burnside, a military man who also had practical experience as a firearms manufacturer. Burnside had sold about 1,000 of his offbeat looking rifles to the Government even before the war, and before it was over the Ordnance Department had purchased 55,000 more plus nearly 22 million of the special cartridges. The wartime Burnsides were operated by pressing down and forward on a lever-trigger guard assembly which caused the breechblock to slide back and down, exposing a chamber into which the tapered, ice cream cone shaped cartridge was inserted. The brass cartridge had a hole at the base covered with bee's wax and was fired by a separate, exterior percussion cap.

Despite a fine piece of public relations work early in the war, Frank Wesson's 44 rimfire breechloader remained largely ignored, with only 151 U.S. purchases. In June of 1861 Union forces were being bothered by sporadic fire from across the Potomac and a "Harper's Weekly" reporter covered the indident with flowery Victorian prose. "One afternoon Major Knipe of General Williams Staff spied a trio of Virginians preparing to pepper (our) position, and the major deemed the gay cavaliers of the Old

The 56 caliber Starr breech-loading carbine, patented in 1858, was manufactured at Yonkers, N.Y. The Starr looks very much like the Sharps, and action was also similar. The government bought 25,603 of these guns.

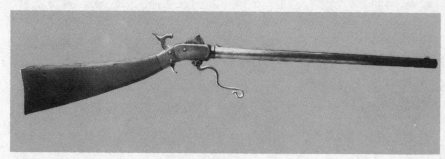

A rare specimen at Smithsonian Institution is this unusual Confederate attempt at a breechloading carbine. Marked "C.S.&P.," the gun is 54 cal.

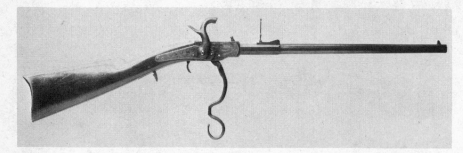

The weird 50 cal. "Cosmopolitan" carbine was commonly nicknamed the "grapevine" or "monkeytail" because of its odd shaped lever trigger guard. The U.S. bought 9,342 of them.

Dominion fair game for his steady hand and finely wrought Wesson rifle. Springing from his saddle he drew a bead on Mr. Secessionist. A report, a thin cloud of white curling upward, and in an instant like a wounded bird, the doomed figure was seen to fall off his steed." If the story is true, it certainly must have been the luckiest shot of the war, because the little 44 rimfire, similar to the Henry repeater cartridge, simply didn't have the carrying power to be accurate at the ¾-mile range mentioned.

Details of the score of Civil War carbines would fill a volume, but some highlights are interesting. The Smith carbine, of which over 30,000 were bought, used a 50 caliber rubber-cased cartridge fired by a separate percussion cap. The cartridge must have smelled rather odd in a hot barrel. The Palmer carbine, made by E. G. Lamson at Windsor, Vt., used the Spencer 56-50 self-contained metal cartridge and had the distinction of being the first bolt action arm ever used by the U.S. Government. The Jenks percussion breechloader, built by Remington on contract, used a unique "mule ear" side hammer intended to deflect the breech gas away from the shooter's face. Some specimens were later re-designed by James Merrill of Baltimore to use a regular side-lock hammer. Gwyn & Campbell's percussion carbine had a grooved, tilt-down breechblock resembling the

later Martini action, and the gun was nicknamed the "monkey tail carbine" for its weird shaped lever trigger guard.

But perhaps the prize for non-conformity should go to Lt. Colonel J. Durell Greene for his 54 caliber percussion carbine. His design used a pair of nearly identical triggers, and to load you first pulled the front trigger which released the button-pinned barrel so that it could be swiveled to the left. The barrel could then be pushed forward a little, out of its breech housing, and rotated to the right to finally expose the breech for loading. A Maynard tape primer mechanism was tacked on to complete the complexity. Both the U.S. and British Governments bought Greene carbines before the Civil War. There is an unsubstantiated story that the British disliked the complex Greenes and sold them back to the Americans.

Because the Civil War came at a time of intense innovation and development in firearms, wartime small arms—in all their vast variety—were a Chinese puzzle to the ordnance officers who had to choose among them and nothing less than a nightmare to the logician who had to keep them supplied and functioning. But for the collector of a century later, the individualistic inventors of long ago left a fascinating heritage. ●

The Gun Control Act of 1968

THE GUN CONTROL ACT of 1968 has importance to every person in the United States who possesses a gun, but its provisions are vitally important to every active gun collector. On the following pages we have reproduced those portions of the Treasury Department regulations set up to enforce GCA'68 that are most important to the average collector. However, these selected portions represent just over a tenth of the total material in the Part 178 and Part 179 regulations, and we recommend that you examine a complete copy of Title 26, Code of Federal Regulations, at your local dealer's so you will be aware of all the provisions. Better yet, why not procure your own copy from your District or Regional Bureau of Alcohol, Tobacco and Firearms Office or from the Bureau's headquarters in Washington, D.C. — it's free.

Since these are the provisions as originally written, they are subject to interpretation and revision. In case of question, your local Bureau of Alcohol, Tobacco and Firearms office is the best place to go for assistance.

Part 179 applies to machine guns and other regis- terable weapons. Please note the difference in the meaning of the word *firearm* between Part 178 and Part 179. The Part 178 definition encompasses all firearms (Title I), while a Part 179 "Firearm" is a machine gun, sawed-off rifle or other registerable weapon (Title II) — but not a conventional pistol, rifle or shotgun! Why this confusion has to exist is not known, but be aware and beware of it!

At the conclusion of this chapter there are lists of guns whose status has been clarified or changed as a result of various Revenue Rulings (known as ATF Rulings). Rulings on additional guns and ammunition are continually under consideration, so these lists should not be considered complete or final. Guns that appear on these lists are still *guns* under the law; those classified as "Curios and Relics" can now be acquired interstate by a licensed collector, while those removed from the National Firearms Act no longer require registration. Note: If you have a gun that was registered during the 1968 Amnesty and is one of those that does not now require registration, write the BATF and ask that it be "de-registered."

Title 26 — INTERNAL REVENUE

Chapter I — Internal Revenue Service, Department of the Treasury
SUBCHAPTER E — ALCOHOL, TOBACCO, AND OTHER EXCISE TAXES
PART 178 — COMMERCE IN FIRE-ARMS AND AMMUNITION

In order to implement the provisions of Title I, State Firearms Control Assistance (18 U.S.C., chapter 44), of the Gun Control Act of 1968 (82 Stat. 1213), and Title VII, Unlawful Possession or Receipt of Firearms (82 Stat. 236; 18 U.S.C., Appendix), of the Omnibus Crime Control and Safe Streets Act of 1968 (82 Stat. 197), as amended by Title III of the Gun Control Act of 1968 (82 Stat. 1236), the following regulations are hereby prescribed as Part 178 of Title 26 of the Code of Federal Regulations:

Subpart B — Definitions
§ 178.11 Meaning of terms.

Ammunition. Ammunition or cartridge cases, primers, bullets, or propellent powder designed for use in any firearm other than an antique firearm. The term shall not include (a) any shotgun shot or pellet not designed for use as the single, complete projectile load for one shotgun hull or casing, nor (b) any unloaded, non-metallic shotgun hull or casing not having a primer.

Antique firearm. (a) Any firearm (including any firearm with a match-lock, flintlock, percussion cap, or similar type of ignition system) manufactured in or before 1898; and (b) any replica of any firearm described in paragraph (a) of this definition if such replica (1) is not designed or redesigned for using rim-fire or conventional centerfire fixed ammunition, or (2) uses rimfire or conventional centerfire fixed ammunition which is no longer manufactured in the United States and which is not readily available in the ordinary channels of commercial trade.

Business premises. The property on which firearms or ammunition importing, manufacturing or dealing business is or will be conducted. A private dwelling, no part of which is open to the public, shall not be recognized as coming within the meaning of the term.

Collection premises. The premises described on the license of a collector as the location at which he maintains his collection of curios and relics.

Collector. Any person who acquires, holds, or disposes of firearms or ammunition as curios or relics.

Commerce. Travel, trade, traffic, commerce, transportation, or communication among the several States or between the District of Columbia and any State, or between any foreign country or any territory or possession and any State or the District of Columbia, or between points in the same State but through any other State or the District of Columbia or a foreign country.

Curios or relics. Firearms or ammunition which are of special interest to collectors by reason of some quality other than is ordinarily associated with firearms intended for sporting use or as offensive or defensive weapons. To be recognized as curios or relics, firearms and ammunition must fall within one of the following categories:

(a) Firearms and ammunition which were manufactured at least 50 years prior to the current date, but not including replicas thereof;

(b) Firearms and ammunition which are certified by the curator of a municipal, State, or Federal museum which exhibits firearms to be curios or relics of museum interest; and

(c) Any other firearms or ammunition which derive a substantial part of their monetary value from the fact that they are novel, rare, bizarre, or because of their association with some historical figure, period, or event. Proof of qualification of a particular firearm or item of ammunition under this category may be established by evidence of present value and evidence that like firearms or ammunition are not available except as collector's items, or that the value of like firearms or ammunition available in ordinary commercial channels is substantially less.

Dealer. Any person engaged in the business of selling firearms or ammunition at wholesale or retail; any person engaged in the business of repairing firearms or of making or fitting special barrels, stocks, or trigger mechanisms to firearms; or any person who is a pawnbroker.

Firearm. Any weapon, including a starter gun, which will or is designed to or may readily be converted to expel a projectile by the action of an explosive; the frame or receiver of any such weapon; any firearm muffler or firearm silencer; or any destructive device; but the term shall not include an antique firearm. In the case of a licensed collector, the term shall mean only curios and relics.

Firearm frame or receiver. That part of a firearm which provides housing for the hammer, bolt or breechblock, and firing mechanism, and which is usually threaded at its forward portion to receive the barrel.

Licensed collector. A collector of curios and relics only and licensed under the provisions of this part.

Licensed dealer. A dealer licensed under the provisions of this part, and a dealer licensed under the Federal Firearms Act if such license is deemed valid under section 907

of the Omnibus Crime Control and Safe Streets Act of 1968 (82 Stat. 235).

Machine Gun. Any weapon which shoots, is designed to shoot, or can be readily restored to shoot, automatically more than one shot, without manual reloading, by a single function of the trigger. The term shall also include the frame or receiver of any such weapon, any combination of parts designed and intended for use in converting a weapon into a machine gun, and any combination of parts from which a machine gun can be assembled if such parts are in the possession or under the control of a person.

Rifle. A weapon designed or redesigned, made or remade, and intended to be fired from the shoulder, and designed or redesigned and made or remade to use the energy of the explosive in a fixed metallic cartridge to fire only a single projectile through a rifled bore for each single pull of the trigger.

Short-barreled rifle. A rifle having one or more barrels less than 16 inches in length, and any weapon made from a rifle, whether by alteration, modification, or otherwise, if such weapon, as modified, has an overall length of less than 26 inches.

Short-barreled shotgun. A shotgun having one or more barrels less than 18 inches in length, and any weapon made from a shotgun, whether by alteration, modification, or otherwise, if such weapon as modified has an overall length of less than 26 inches.

Shotgun. A weapon designed or redesigned, made or remade, and intended to be fired from the shoulder, and designed or redesigned and made or remade to use the energy of the explosive in a fixed shotgun shell to fire through a smooth bore either a number of ball shot or a single projectile for each single pull of the trigger.

State. A State of the United States. The term shall include the District of Columbia, the Commonwealth of Puerto Rico, and the possessions of the United States (not including the Canal Zone).

State of residence. The State in which an individual regularly resides, or maintains his home, or if such person is on active duty as a member of the United States Armed Forces, the State in which his permanent duty station is located: *Provided,* That an alien who is legally in the United States shall be considered to be a resident of the State in which (a) he is residing and has

so resided for a period of at least 90 days prior to the date of sale or delivery of a firearm or ammunition, or (b) his embassy or consulate is located if the principal officer of such embassy or consulate issues a written statement to such alien authorizing his acquisition of a firearm or ammunition. Temporary sojourn in a State does not make the State of temporary sojourn the State of residence.

Example 1. A maintains his home in State X. He travels to State Y on a hunting, fishing, business or other type of trip. He does not become a resident of State Y by reason of such trip.

Example 2. A maintains a home in State X and a home in State Y. He resides in State X except for the summer months of the year and in State Y for the summer months of the year. During the time that he actually resides in State X he is a resident of State X, and during the time that he actually resides in State Y he is a resident of State Y.

Unserviceable firearm. A firearm which is uncapable of discharging a shot by means of an explosive and is incapable of being readily restored to a firing condition.

Subpart C—Administrative and Miscellaneous Provisions
§ 178.23 Right of entry and examination.

Any internal revenue officer may enter during business hours the premises, including places of storage, of any licensed importer, licensed manufacturer, licensed dealer, or licensed collector for the purpose of inspecting or examining any records or documents required to be kept by such importer, manufacturer, dealer, or collector under this part, and any firearms or ammunition kept or stored by such importer, manufacturer, dealer, or collector at such premises.

§ 178.26 Curio and relic determination.

A licensed collector who desires to obtain a determination whether a particular firearm or ammunition is a curio or relic shall submit a written request, in duplicate, for a ruling thereon to the Assistant Regional Commissioner. Each such request shall be executed under the penalties of perjury and shall contain a complete and accurate description of the firearm or ammunition, and such photographs, diagrams, or drawings as may be necessary to enable the Assistant Regional Commissioner to make his determination. The Assistant Regional Commissioner may require the submission to him, or to an officer designated by him, of the firearm or ammunition for examination and evaluation. If the submission of the firearm or ammunition is impractical, the licensed collector shall so advise the Assistant Regional Commissioner and designate the place where the firearm or ammunition will be available for examination and evaluation.

§ 178.29 Out-of-State acquisition of firearms by nonlicensees.

No person, other than a licensed importer, licensed manufacturer, licensed dealer, or licensed collector, shall transport into or receive in the State where he resides (or if a corporation or other business entity, where it maintains a place of business) any firearm purchased or otherwise obtained by such person outside that State: *Provided,* That the provisions of this section (a) shall not preclude any person who lawfully acquires a firearm by bequest or intestate succession in a State other than his State of residence from transporting the firearm into or receiving it in that State, if it is lawful for such person to purchase or possess such firearm in that State, (b) shall not apply to the transportation or receipt of a rifle or shotgun obtained in conformity with the provisions of §§ 178.30, 178.96, and 178.97, and (c) shall not apply to the transportation of any firearm acquired in any State prior to the effective date of the Act.

§ 178.30 Out-of-State disposition of firearms by nonlicensees.

No nonlicensee shall transfer, sell, trade, give, transport, or deliver any firearm to any other nonlicensee, who the transferor knows or has reasonable cause to believe resides in any State other than that in which the transferor resides (or if a corporation or other business entity, where it maintains a place of business): *Provided,* That the provisions of this section shall not apply to (a) the transfer, transportation, or delivery of a firearm made to carry out a bequest of a firearm to, or any acquisition by intestate succession of a firearm by, a person who is permitted to acquire or possess a firearm under the laws of the State of his residence, and (b) the loan or rental of a firearm to any person for temporary use for lawful sporting purposes.

Subpart D — Licenses
§ 178.41 General.

(c) Each person seeking the privileges of a collector licensed under this part shall file an application, with the required fee (see § 178.42), with the District Director for the internal revenue district in which his collec-

tion premises are to be located, and, pursuant to § 178.47, receive from the Assistant Regional Commissioner the license covering the collection of curios and relics. A separate license may be obtained for each collection premises, and such license shall, subject to the provisions of the Act and other applicable provisions of law, entitle the licensee to transport, ship, receive, and acquire curios and relics in interstate or foreign commerce, and to make disposition of curios and relics in interstate or foreign commerce to any other person licensed under the provisions of this part, for the period stated on the license.

(d) The collector license provided by this part shall apply only to transactions related to a collector's activity in acquiring, holding or disposing of curios and relics. A collector's license does not authorize the collector to engage in a business required to be licensed under the Act or this part. Therefore, if the acquisitions and dispositions of curios and relics by a collector bring the collector within the definition of a manufacturer, importer, or dealer under this part, he shall qualify as such. (See also § 178.93 of this part.)

§ 178.50 Locations covered by license.

The license covers the class of business or the activity specified in the license at the address described therein. Accordingly, a separate license must be obtained for each location at which a firearms or ammunition business or activity requiring a license under this part is conducted; however, no license is required to cover a separate warehouse used by the licensee solely for storage of firearms or ammunition if the records required by this part are maintained at the licensed premises served by such warehouse: *Provided,* That a licensed collector may acquire curios and relics at any location, and dispose of curios or relics to any licensee, or to other persons who are residents of the State where the collector's license is held and the disposition is made.

Subpart F — Conduct of Business
§ 178.91 Posting of license.

Any license issued under this part shall be kept posted and kept available for inspection on the premises covered by the license.

§ 178.93 Authorized operations by a licensed collector.

The license issued to a collector of curios or relics under the provisions of this part shall cover only transac-

tions by the licensed collector in curios and relics. The collector's license is of no force or effect and a licensed collector is of the same status under the Act and this part as a nonlicensee with respect to (a) any acquisition or disposition of firearms or ammunition other than curios or relics, or any transportation, shipment, or receipt of firearms or ammunition other than curios or relics in interstate or foreign commerce, and (b) any transaction with a nonlicensee involving any firearm or ammunition other than a curio or relic. (See also § 178.50.)

Subpart H — Records
§ 178.121 General.

(a) The records pertaining to firearms transactions prescribed by this part shall be in permanent form, and shall be retained on the licensed premises in the manner prescribed by this subpart. The records pertaining to ammunition prescribed by this part shall be retained on the licensed premises in the manner prescribed by § 178.125.

(b) Internal revenue officers may enter the premises of any licensed importer, licensed manufacturer, licensed dealer, or licensed collector for the purpose of examining or inspecting any record or document required by or obtained under this part (see § 178.23). Section 923 (g) of the Act requires licensed importers, licensed manufacturers, licensed dealers, and licensed collectors to make such records available for such examination or inspection at all reasonable times.

(c) Each licensed importer, licensed manufacturer, licensed dealer, and licensed collector shall maintain such records of importation, production, shipment, receipt, sale, or other disposition, whether temporary or permanent, of firearms and ammunition as the regulations contained in this part prescribe. Section 922(m) of the Act makes it unlawful for any licensed importer, licensed manufacturer, licensed dealer, or licensed collector knowingly to make any false entry in, to fail to make appropriate entry in, or to fail to properly maintain any such record.

§ 178.124 Firearms transaction record.

(a) A licensed importer, licensed manufacturer, or licensed dealer shall not sell or otherwise dispose, temporarily or permanently, of any firearm to any person, other than another licensee, and a licensed collector shall not sell or otherwise dispose of any curio or relic to any person, other than another licensee, unless he records the transaction on a firearms transaction record, Form 4473: *Provided,* That a firearms transaction record, Form 4473, shall not be required to record the disposition made of a firearm delivered to a licensee for the sole purpose of repair or customizing when such firearm is returned to the person from whom received.

...The format required for the record of receipt and disposition of firearms or firearms curios and relics is as follows:

FIREARMS ACQUISITION AND DISPOSITION RECORD

Description of firearm						Receipt			Disposition
Manufacturer and/or Importer	Model	Serial No.	Type of action	Caliber and gauge	Date	From whom (name and address or name and license number)	Date	Name	Address or license No. if licensee, or Form 4473 Serial No. if Forms 4473 filed numerically

§ 178.146 Deliveries by mail to certain persons.

The provisions of this part shall not be construed as prohibiting a licensed importer, licensed manufacturer, or licensed dealer from depositing a firearm for conveyance in the mails to any officer, employee, agent, or watchman who, pursuant to the provisions of section 1715 of title 18, U.S.C., is eligible to receive through the mails pistols, revolvers, and other firearms capable of being concealed on the person, for use in connection with his official duties.

§ 178.147 Repair of firearm.

A person not otherwise prohibited by Federal, State or local law may ship a firearm to a licensed importer, licensed manufacturer, or licensed dealer for the sole purpose of repair or customizing, and notwithstanding any other provision of this part, the licensed importer, licensed manufacturer, or licensed dealer may return in interstate or foreign commerce to that person the repaired firearm or a replacement firearm of the same kind and type.

§ 178.148 Ammunition loading for personal use.

The licensing provisions of this part shall not apply to any person who engages only in hand loading, reloading, or custom loading ammunition for his own firearm, and who does not hand load, reload, or custom load ammunition for others.

Subpart J—Penalties, Seizures, and Forfeitures
§ 178.161 False statement or representation.

Any person who knowingly makes any false statement or representation with respect to any information required by the provisions of the Act or this part to be kept in the records of a person engaged in firearms or ammunition business, or in applying for any license, exemption, or relief from disability, under the provisions of the Act, shall be fined not more than $5,000 or imprisonment not more than 5 years, or both.

§ 178.166 Seizure and forfeiture.

Any firearm or ammunition involved in, or used or intended to be used in, any violation of the provisions of the Act or of this part, or in violation of any other criminal law of the United States, shall be subject to seizure and forfeiture, and all provisions of the Internal Revenue Code of 1954 relating to the seizure, forfeiture, and disposition of firearms, as defined in section 5845(a) of that Code, shall, so far as applicable, extend to seizures and forfeitures under the provisions of the Act.

Title 26—INTERNAL REVENUE
Chapter I—Internal Revenue Service, Department of the Treasury
SUBCHAPTER E—ALCOHOL, TOBACCO, AND OTHER EXCISE TAXES
PART 179—MACHINE GUNS, DESTRUCTIVE DEVICES, AND CERTAIN OTHER FIREARMS.

In order to implement the provisions of Title II, Machine Guns, Destructive Devices, and Certain Other Firearms (U.S.C., Title 26, Chapter 53), of the Gun Control Act of 1968 (Public Law 90–618, 82 Stat. 1213), the following regulations are hereby prescribed as Part 179 of Title 26 of the Code of Federal Regulations:

Subpart B—Definitions
§ 179.11 Meaning of terms.

Antique firearm. Any firearm not designed or redesigned for using rim fire or conventional center fire ignition with fixed ammunition and manufactured in or before 1898 (including any matchlock, flintlock, percussion cap, or similar type of ignition system or replica thereof, whether actually manufactured before or after the year 1898) and also any firearm using fixed ammunition manufactured in or before 1898, for which ammunition is no longer manufactured in the United States and is not readily available in the ordinary channels of commercial trade.

Any other weapon. Any weapon or device capable of being concealed on the person from which a shot can be discharged through the energy of an explosive, a pistol or revolver having a barrel with a smooth bore designed or redesigned to fire a fixed shotgun shell, weapons with combination shotgun and rifle barrels 12 inches or more, less than 18 inches in length, from which only a single discharge can be made from either barrel without manual reloading, and shall include any such weapon which may be readily restored to fire. Such term shall not include a pistol or a revolver having a rifled bore, or rifled bores, or weapons designed, made, or intended to be fired from the shoulder and not capable of firing fixed ammunition.

Firearm. (a) A shotgun having a barrel or barrels of less than 18 inches in length; (b) a weapon made from a shotgun if such weapon as modified has an overall length of less than 26 inches or a barrel or barrels of less than 18 inches in length; (c) a rifle having a barrel or barrels of less than 16 inches in length; (d) a weapon made from a rifle if such weapon as modified has an overall length of less than 26 inches or a barrel or barrels of less than 16 inches in length; (e) any other weapon, as defined in this subpart; (f) a machine gun; (g) a muffler or a silencer for any firearm whether or not such firearm is included within this definition; and (h) a destructive device. The term shall not include an antique firearm or any device (other than a machine gun or destructive device) which, although designed as a weapon, the Director finds by reason of the date of its manufacture, value, design, and other characteristics is primarily a collector's item and is not likely to be used as a weapon. For purpose of this definition, the length of the barrel on a shotgun or rifle shall be determined by measuring the distance between the muzzle and the face of the bolt, breech, or breechlock when closed and when the shotgun or rifle is cocked. The overall length of a weapon made from a shotgun or rifle is the distance between the extreme ends of the weapon measured along a line parallel to the center line of the bore.

Fixed ammunition. That self-contained unit consisting of the case, primer, propellant charge, and projectile or projectiles.

Frame or receiver. That part of a firearm which provides housing for the hammer, bolt or breechblock and firing mechanism, and which is usually threaded at its forward portion to receive the barrel.

Machine gun. Any weapon which shoots, is designed to shoot, or can be readily restored to shoot, automatically more than one shot, without manual reloading, by a single function of the trigger. The term shall also include the frame or receiver of any such weapon, any combination of parts designed and intended for use in converting a weapon into a machine gun, and any combination of parts from which a machine gun can be assembled if such parts are in the possession or under the control of a person.

Muffler or silencer. Any device for silencing or diminishing the report of any portable weapon, such as a rifle, carbine, pistol, revolver, machine gun, submachine gun, shotgun, fowling piece, or other device from which a shot, bullet, or projectile may be discharged by an explosive, and is not limited to mufflers or silencers for "firearms" as defined.

Pistol. A weapon originally designed, made, and intended to fire a small projectile (bullet) from one or more barrels when held in one hand, and having (a) a chamber(s) as an integral part(s) of, or permanently aligned with, the bore(s); and (b) a short stock designed to be gripped by one hand and at an angle to and extending below the line of the bore(s). The term shall not include any gadget device, any gun altered or converted to resemble a pistol, any gun that fires more than one shot, without manual reloading, by a single function of the trigger, or any small portable gun such as: Nazi belt buckle pistol, glove pistol, or a one-hand stock gun designed to fire fixed shotgun ammunition.

Revolver. A small projectile weapon, of the pistol type, having a breechloading chambered cylinder so arranged that the cocking of the hammer or movement of the trigger rotates it and brings the next cartridge in line with the barrel for firing.

Rifle. A weapon designed or redesigned, made or remade, and intended to be fired from the shoulder and designed or redesigned and made or remade to use the energy of the explosive in a fixed cartridge to fire only a single projectile through a rifled bore for each single pull of the trigger, and shall include any such weapon which may be readily restored to fire a fixed cartridge.

Shotgun. A weapon designed or redesigned, made or remade, and intended to be fired from the shoulder and designed or redesigned and made or remade to use the energy of the explosive in a fixed shotgun shell to fire through a smooth bore either a number of projectiles (ball shot) or a single projectile for each pull of the trigger, and shall include any such weapon which may be readily restored to fire a fixed shotgun shell.

Transfer. This term and the various derivatives thereof shall include selling, assigning, pledging, leasing, loaning, giving away, or otherwise disposing of.

Unserviceable firearm. A firearm which is incapable of discharging a shot by means of an explosive and incapable of being readily restored to a firing condition.

Subpart C — Administrative and Miscellaneous Provisions
§ 179.25 Collector's items

The Director shall determine in accordance with section 5845(a), I.R.C., whether a firearm or device, which although originally designed as a weapon, is by reason of the date of its manufacture, value, design, and other characteristics primarily a collector's item and is not likely to be used as a weapon. A person who desires to obtain a determination under that provision of law shall follow the procedures prescribed in § 179.24 relating to destructive device determinations, and shall include information as to date of manufacture, value, design and other characteristics which would sustain a finding that the firearm or device is primarily a collector's item and is not likely to be used as a weapon.

Subpart F — Transfer Tax
§ 179.91 Unserviceable firearms.

An unserviceable firearm may be transferred as a curio or ornament without payment of the transfer tax. However, the procedures for the transfer of a firearm as provided in § 179.90 shall be followed in a tax-exempt transfer of a firearm under this section, except a statement shall be entered on the transfer application, Form 5 (Firearms), by the transferor that he is entitled to the exemption because the firearm to be transferred is unserviceable and is being transferred as a curio or ornament. An unapproved transfer, the transfer of a firearm under the provisions of this section which is in fact not an unserviceable firearm, or the transfer of an unserviceable firearm as something other than a curio or ornament, may subject the transferor to civil and criminal liabilities. (See sections 5811, 5852, 5861, and 5871 I.R.C.)

Subpart G — Registration and Identification of Firearms
§ 179.101 Registration of firearms.

(a) The Director shall maintain a central registry of all firearms in the United States which are not in the possession of or under the control of the United States. This registry shall be known as the National Firearms Registration and Transfer Record and shall include:

(1) Identification of the firearm as required by this part:

(2) Date of registration; and

(3) Identification and address of person entitled to possession of the firearm as required by this part.

(b) Each manufacturer, importer, and maker shall register each firearm he manufactures, imports, or makes in the manner prescribed by this part. Each firearm transferred shall be registered to the transferee by the transferor in the manner prescribed by this part. No firearm may be registered by a person unlawfully in possession of the firearm except during an amnesty period established under section 207 of the Gun Control Act of 1968 (82 Stat. 1235).

(c) A person shown as possessing firearms by the records maintained by the Director pursuant to the National Firearms Act (Chapter 53, I.R.C.) in force on October 31, 1968, shall be considered to have registered the firearms in his possession which are disclosed by that record as being in his possession on October 31, 1968.

(d) The National Firearms Registration and Transfer Record shall include firearms registered to the possessors thereof under the provisions of section 207 of the Gun Control Act of 1968.

(e) A person possessing a firearm registered to him shall retain proof of registration which shall be made available to any internal revenue officer upon request.

(f) A firearm not identified as required by this part shall not be registered.

Commemorative Firearms Classified As Curios And Relics Under 18 U.S.C. Chapter 440*

COLT—

1. Abercrombie & Fitch, "Trailblazer", .45 New Frontier
2. Alabama Sesquicentennial, .22
3. Alamo, .22 & .45
4. Abilene, .22 (Kansas City—Cow Town)
5. Appomattox Court House Centennial, .22 & .45
6. Arizona Territorial Centennial, .22 & .45
7. Arkansas Territory Sesquicentennial, .22
8. Belleau Wood, .45 Automatic (World War I Series)
9. California Bicentennial, .22
10. California Gold Rush, .22 & .45
11. Carolina Charter Tercentenary, .22 & .22/.45
12. Chamizal Treaty, .22 and .45
13. Chateau Thierry, .45 Automatic (World War I Series)
14. Cherry's Sporting Goods 35th Anniversary, .22/.45
15. Chisholm Trail, .22 (Kansas Series—Trails)
16. Civil War Centennial Single Shot, .22
17. Coffeyville, .22 (Kansas Series—Cow Town)
18. Colorado Gold Rush, .22
19. Colt, Colonel Samuel, Sesquicentennial, .45
20. Colt's 125th Anniversary, .45
21. Columbus (Ohio) Sesquicentennial, .22
22. Cook, H., "1 of 100", .22/.45
23. Dakota Territory, .22
24. Des Moines, Reconstruction of Old Fort, .22 and .45
25. Dodge City, .22 (Kansas Series—Cow Town)
26. Earp, Wyatt, Buntline Special .45 (Lawman Series)
27. Earp, Wyatt, .22 & .45 (Lawman Series)
28. European Theater, .45 Automatic (World War II Series)
29. Forrest, General Nathan Bedford, .22
30. Fort Findlay (Ohio) Sesquicentennial, .22
31. Fort Hays, .22 (Kansas Series—Forts)
32. Fort Larned, .22 (Kansas Series—Forts)
33. Fort McPherson (Nebraska) Centennial Derringer, .22
34. Fort Scott, .22 (Kansas Series—Forts)
35. Fort Stephenson (Ohio) Sesquicentennial, .22
36. Forty-Niner Miner, .22
37. Garrett, Pat., .22 & .45 (Lawman Series)
38. Genesco (Illinois) 125th Anniversary Derringer, .22
39. Gettysburg, Battle of Centennial, .22
40. Golden Spike Centennial, .22
41. Hickok, Wild Bill, .22 & .45 (Lawman Series)
42. Hood, General Tennessee Campaign Centennial, .22
43. Idaho Territorial Centennial, .22
44. Indiana Sesquicentennial, .22
45. Kansas Centennial, .22
46. Maine Sesquicentennial, .22 & .45
47. Masterson, Bat, .22 & .45 (Lawman Series)
48. Meade, George, Pennsylvania Campaign, .22 & .45
49. Meuse Argonne, .45 Automatic (World War I Series)
50. Montana Territory Centennial, .22 & .45
51. Missouri Sesquicentennial, .22
52. Morgan, General John Hunt, Indiana Raid, .22
53. Murrieta, Joaquin, "1 of 100", .22/.45
54. Nebraska Centennial, .22
55. Nevada Centennial, .22 & .45
56. Nevada Centennial "Battle Born", .22 & .45
57. New Jersey Tercentenary, .22 & .45
58. New Mexico Golden Anniversary, .22
59. Oklahoma Territory Diamond Jubilee, .22
60. Oregon Trail, .22
61. Pacific Theater, .45 Automatic (World War II Series)
62. Pawnee Trail, .22 (Kansas Series—Trails)
63. Pony Express, Russell Majors and Waddell, Presentation Model, .45
64. Pony Express, Centennial, .22
65. Rock Island Arsenal Centennial Single Shot, .22
66. St. Augustine Quadricentennial, .22
67. St. Louis Bicentennial, .22 & .45
68. Santa Fe Trail, .22 (Kansas Series—Trails)
69. Second (2nd) Marne, .45 Automatic (World War I Series)
70. Shawnee Trail, .22 (Kansas Series—Trails)
71. Sheriff's Model, .45
72. Texas Ranger, .45
73. West Virginia Centennial, .22 & .45
74. Wichita, .22 (Kansas Series—Cow Town)
75. Wyoming Diamond Jubilee, .22

Harrington and Richardson—

1. Abilene Anniversary, .22 Revolver
2. Centennial Officer's Model Springfield Rifle, .45–70 Govt.
3. Centennial Regular Model Springfield Rifle, .45–70 Govt.

High Standard—

1. Supermatic Trophy, Model 107, .22 Pistol

Ithaca—

1. St. Louis Bicentennial, Model 49, .22 Rifle

Marlin—

1. Marlin 90th Anniversary, Model 39–A, .22 Rifle
2. Marlin 90th Anniversary, Model 39–A, .22 Carbine

Remington—

1. Canadian Territorial Centennial, Model 742, Rifle
2. Montana Territorial Centennial, Model 600, Rifle

Winchester—

1. Alaskan Purchase Centennial, Model 1894, Carbine
2. Buffalo Bill, Model 1894, Carbine
3. Buffalo Bill, Model 1894, Rifle
4. Canadian 1967, Centennial Model 1894, Carbine
5. Canadian 1967 Centennial Model 1894, Rifle
6. Golden Spike, Model 1894, Carbine
7. Illinois Sesquicentennial, Model 1894, Carbine
8. Nebraska Centennial, Model 1894, Carbine
9. Theodore Roosevelt, Model 1894, Carbine
10. Theodore Roosevelt, Model 1894, Rifle
11. Winchester Centennial, Model 1866, Carbine
12. Winchester Centennial, Model 1866, Rifle
13. 150th Anniversary Texas Ranger Commemorative, Model 1894 Carbine

Ruger—

1. Canadian Centennial, Matched No. 1, Rifle Sets, Special Deluxe
2. Canadian Centennial, Matched No. 2, Rifle Sets
3. Canadian Centennial, Matched No. 3, Rifle Sets
4. Canadian Centennial, Model 10/22, Carbine

Smith & Wesson—

1. 150th Anniversary Texas Ranger Commemorative, Model 19 Revolver

See footnote

Other Firearms Classified as Curios or Relics Under 18 U.S.C. Chapter 44.*

Astra M400, semiautomatic pistol, German Army Contract, caliber 9mm Bergmann Bayard, Serial Number range 97351–98850.

Astra M600, semiautomatic pistol, caliber 9mm Parabellum, marked with German Waffenamt acceptance stamp, 1939–1945.

Astra M300, semiautomatic pistol, calibers 7.65mm and 9mm "Kurz", marked with German Waffenamt acceptance stamp, 1939–1945.

Austrian Kolibri, semiautomatic pistol, calibers 2.7mm and 3mm Kolibri.

Bannerman Model 1937, Springfield rifle, caliber 30–06.

Belgian Clement, semiautomatic pistol, caliber 5mm Clement.

Bergmann-Bayard M1908, semiautomatic pistol, caliber 9mm Bergmann-Bayard.

Beretta M1951, semiautomatic pistol, Egyptian Contract, caliber 9mm Parabellum.

Beretta M1951, semiautomatic pistol, Israeli Contract, caliber 9mm Parabellum.

Browning M1935 Hi-Power, semiautomatic pistol, Canadian, Congolese, Indian and Nationalist China Contract, caliber 9mm Parabellum.

Browning "Baby" Model, semiautomatic pistol, Russian Contract, caliber 6.35 mm.

Browning M1910 and M1922, semiautomatic pistol, Contract pieces; M1910 Dutch Navy; M1922 Dutch or French Navy and M1922 Yugoslavian Army, calibers 7.65mm and 9mm Kurz.

Browning M1922, semiautomatic pistol, caliber 7.65mm bearing German Navy acceptance stamp.

Browning M1935 Hi-Power, semiautomatic pistol, caliber 9mm Parabellum, bearing German Navy acceptance stamp.

Browning M1935 Hi-Power, semiautomatic pistol, cut for stock and with tangent sight, caliber 9mm Parabellum, bearing German Waffenamt acceptance stamp, 1939–1945.

Browning M1922, semiautomatic pistol, caliber 9mm "Kurz", bearing German Waffenamt acceptance stamp, 1939–1945.

Colt Model 1911, semiautomatic pistol, English Contract, caliber .455.

Colt Pocket Model 1903 and 1908, hammerless, semiautomatic pistol, U.S. Government Contract, calibers .32 ACP and .380 ACP, marked U.S. Property.

Chicom Types 51 and 54, Tokarev semiautomatic pistol, caliber 7.62mm.

Czechoslovakian CZ50, semiautomatic pistol, caliber 7.65mm.

Czechoslovakian CZ52, semiautomatic pistol, caliber 7.62mm.

Czechoslovakian CZ38, semiautomatic pistol, caliber 9mm "Kurz".

Czechoslovakian CZ27, semiautomatic pistol, caliber 7.65mm, with flanged barrel for silencer and bearing German Waffenamt acceptance stamp, 1939–1945.

Czechoslovakian CZ38, semiautomatic pistol, caliber 9mm "Kurz" bearing German Waffenamt acceptance stamp, 1939–1945.

Danish M1910/1921 Bayard, semiautomatic pistol, caliber 9mm Bergmann-Bayard.

Finnish Lahti L–35, semiautomatic pistol, caliber 9mm Parabellum.

French MAB Model D, semiautomatic pistol, caliber 7.65mm bearing German Navy acceptance stamp.

French M1935, semiautomatic pistol, caliber 7.65mm French Long, bearing German Waffenamt acceptance stamp for period of 1939–1945.

French Unique Model 17, semiautomatic pistol, caliber 7.65mm bearing German Waffenamt acceptance stamp for period of 1939–1945.

French Unique Kriegsmodell, semiautomatic pistol, caliber 7.65mm, bearing German Waffenamt acceptance stamp for period 1939–1945.

French MAB Model D, semiautomatic pistol, caliber 7.65mm, bearing German Waffenamt acceptance stamp for period 1939–1945.

German Menz Liliput, semiautomatic pistol, caliber 4.52mm.

German P38, caliber 9mm Parabellum, Mauser or Walther manufactured and dated 43, 44 or 45 and marked with the Third Reich police acceptance stamps of Eagle C, F, K or L.

Italian Brixia M1906, semiautomatic pistol, caliber 9mm Glisenti.

Italian Glisenti M1910, semiautomatic pistol, caliber 9mm Glisenti.

Japanese Type 26, revolver (1893), 9mm rimmed.

Japanese Type 94 (Model 1934), semiautomatic pistol, caliber 8mm Nambu (8x21mm cartridge), manufactured in Japan 1934–1945.

Japanese "Grandpa" Nambu, Model 1904, semiautomatic pistol, caliber 8mm Nambu.

Japanese "Baby" Nambu, semiautomatic pistol, caliber 7mm Nambu.

Japanese Type 14 (1925), semiautomatic pistol, caliber 8mm Nambu.

Japanese Type 1 (1941), semiautomatic pistol, caliber 7.65mm.

Japanese Type II Hamada, semiautomatic pistol, caliber 7.65mm.

Luger Model P08, semiautomatic pistol, caliber 9mm Parabellum, Mauser manufactured 1936 through 1942 and marked with the Third Reich police acceptance stamps of Eagle C, F, K or L and all serial numbers followed by suffix letters U, X or Y.

Luger DWM Swiss, semiautomatic pistol, M1899–1900, caliber 7.65mm Luger.

Luger DWM "GL", semiautomatic pistol, M1900–1910, marked presentation, calibers 7.65mm Luger and 9mm Parabellum.

Luger DWM, semiautomatic pistol, M1900, American Eagle and Commercial, caliber 7.65 mm Luger.

Luger DWM, M1902, semiautomatic pistol, American Eagle, Cartridge Counter and Commercial, caliber 9mm Parabellum.

Luger DWM, M1902–1904, semiautomatic, prototype in the 10,000B to 10,999B serial number series, calibers 7.65mm Luger and 9mm Parabellum.

Luger DWM, M1903, semiautomatic pistol, transitional, employing functional components of both the old and new model series in calibers 7.65mm Luger and 9mm Parabellum.

Luger DWM, M1904 semiautomatic pistol, Navy, altered or unaltered, caliber 9mm Parabellum.

Luger DWM, M1906, semiautomatic pistol, Russian, caliber 9mm Parabellum.

Luger DWM, M1906–1908, semiautomatic pistol, Portuguese Navy, caliber 9mm Parabellum.

Luger DWM, M1900–1906, semiautomatic, Bulgarian, altered or unaltered in calibers 7.65mm Luger and 9mm Parabellum.

Luger DWM, M1906, semiautomatic pistol, French, caliber 7.65mm Luger.

Luger DWM, M1906 Abercrombie & Fitch, calibers 7.65mm Luger and ·9mm Parabellum.

Luger Vickers Commercial, semiautomatic pistol, caliber 9mm Parabellum.

Luger, M1934, semiautomatic pistol, Mauser Dutch, caliber 9mm Parabellum.

Luger, semiautomatic pistol, Krieghoff Commercial, calibers 7.65mm Luger and 9mm Parabellum.

Luger, semiautomatic pistol, Persian (Iranian) standard and artillery variations, caliber 9mm Parabellum.

Luger, M1923 DWM or Mauser, semiautomatic pistol, Stoeger marked, all barrel lengths, calibers 7.65mm Luger and 9mm Parabellum.

Luger, M1934, semiautomatic pistol, Mauser Latavian, caliber 7.65mm Luger.

Makarov, semiautomatic pistol, Russian and East German, caliber 9mm Makarov.

Mannlicher, semiautomatic pistol, M1900, M1901, M1903 and M1905, caliber 7.63mm Mannlicher.

Mauser M1910, semiautomatic pistol, caliber 7.65mm marked with German Navy acceptance stamp, World War I through World War II.

Mauser M1910/34, semiautomatic pistol, caliber 7.65mm, marked with German Navy acceptance stamp.

Mauser M1934, semiautomatic pistol, caliber 7.65mm marked with Third Reich police acceptance stamps of Eagle C, F, K or L.

Mauser HSc, semiautomatic pistol, caliber 7.65mm, marked with Third Reich police acceptance stamps of Eagle C, F, K or L.

Mauser M1934, semiautomatic pistol, caliber 7.65mm, marked with German Navy acceptance stamp.

Mauser HSc, semiautomatic pistol, caliber 7.65mm, marked with German Navy acceptance stamp.

Mauser HSc, semiautomatic pistol, caliber 7.65mm NSDAP marked (SA).

See footnote

Mexican Obregon, semiautomatic pistol, caliber .45 ACP.

North Korean Type 1964, semiautomatic pistol, caliber 7.62mm, Tokarev.

Norwegian M1914, semiautomatic pistol, caliber .45 ACP.

Phoenix (U.S.A.), semiautomatic pistol, caliber .25 ACP.

Polish FM "VIS", M1935 (Radom), semiautomatic pistol, caliber 9mm Parabellum, marked with German Navy acceptance stamp.

Rifle, English, Esser-Barratt, slide action, caliber .303.

Rifle/Shotgun, U.S., Standard Arms Co., Model "Camp", slide action, caliber .50 (approx.).

Rifle, U.S., Standard Arms Co., Model G, slide action or gas operated, caliber unknown.

Rifle, U.S., Standard Arms Co., Model M., slide action, calibers .25–.35, .30 Rem. & .35 Rem.

Rifle, German, Mauser, DSM 34, bolt action, caliber .22 rimfire (training rifle).

Rifle, German, Mauser, K98K, bolt action, with side rail for attaching ZF41 telescope and mount, 7.92mm.

Roth Steyr 1907, semiautomatic pistol, caliber 8mm.

Sauer 38 (H), semiautomatic pistol, caliber 7.65mm, marked with Third Reich police acceptance stamps of Eagle C, F, K or L.

Smith & Wesson, Mercox Dart Gun, caliber .22 rimfire, blank.

Smith & Wesson, semiautomatic pistol, caliber .35, all eight variations.

Smith & Wesson, 2nd Model, single shot pistol, calibers .22 rimfire, .32 S & W and .38 S & W.

Smith & Wesson, 3rd Model, single shot pistol, calibers .22 rimfire, .32 S & W and .38 S & W.

Smith & Wesson 1st Model, Ladysmith revolver, caliber .22 rimfire long.

Smith & Wesson 2nd Model, Ladysmith revolver, caliber .22 rimfire long.

Smith & Wesson 3rd Model, Ladysmith revolver, caliber .22 rimfire long.

Smith & Wesson Model 39–1 (52–A), semiautomatic pistol, caliber 9mm Parabellum.

Smith & Wesson Model 39, steel frame, semiautomatic pistol, caliber 9mm Parabellum.

Smith & Wesson, semiautomatic pistol, caliber .32 ACP.

Smith & Wesson Model Straight Line, single shot pistol, caliber .22 rimfire long rifle.

Steyr-Hahn M1912, semiautomatic pistol, caliber 9mm Steyr.

Steyr-Hahn M1912, semiautomatic pistol, caliber 9mm Parabellum, marked with Third Reich Police acceptance stamps of Eagle C, F, K or L.

Tokagypt 58, semiautomatic pistol, caliber 9mm Parabellum.

Walther Model 6, semiautomatic pistol, caliber 9mm Parabellum.

Walther PP, semiautomatic pistol, caliber 7.65mm bearing both German "NSKK" and "NSDAP" markings.

Walther PP, semiautomatic pistol, calibers 7.65mm and .22 rimfire, NSDAP marked SA, RFV, FJ, RRZ and PDM.

Walther PPK, semiautomatic pistol, caliber 7.65mm NSDAP marked PDM.

Walther PPK, semiautomatic pistol, caliber 7.65mm, Political Leader variations, bearing NSDAP markings:
  a. RZM control mark.
  b. Hoheitsabzeichen (party insignia eagle and swastika) on right and left side of grip.
  c. RZM control mark and Hoheitsabzeichen on same gun.

Walther PP, semiautomatic pistol, caliber 7.65mm, marked with Third Reich police acceptance stamps of Eagle C, F, K or L.

Walther PPK, semiautomatic pistol, caliber 7.65mm, marked with Third Reich police acceptance stamps of Eagle C, F, K or L.

Walther PP, semiautomatic pistol, caliber 9mm "Kurz", marked with German Waffenamt acceptance stamp, 1939–1945.

Webley & Scott, M1913, Navy or Commercial, self-loading pistol, caliber .455.

Winchester Model 54, rifle, speed lock variation, caliber .270.

Firearms removed from the National Firearms Act (26 U.S.C. Chapter 53) as collectors' items which are also classified as Curios or Relics under 18 U.S.C. Chapter 44.*

Belgian Cane Gun, 41 caliber rimfire.

Bergmann Bayard Pistol, Model 1908, 9mm Bergmann—Bayard with shoulder stock and 4 inch barrel.

Bergmann Model 1897, caliber 7.65mm (7,8mm) pistol with accompanying shoulder stock.

Bergmann self-loading pistol, Mars Model 1903 with accompanying shoulder stock.

Borchardt Model 1893, caliber 7.63mm pistol with accompanying stock.

Browning Pistol, Model 1903, 9mm Browning Long, with shoulder stock and 5 inch barrel.

The Chicago palm pistol, caliber .32 rimfire extra short.

Colt Pistol, Model 1905, .45 rimless, with leather shoulder stock-holster and 5 inch barrel.

Frank Wesson Bicycle Rifle with accompanying shoulder stock.

Gaulois palm squeezer, 8mm short.

German (Nazi) Belt Buckle Gun, .22 rimfire, marked "D.R.P. Ausl. Pat., Louis Marquis, W. Elberfeld."

German (Nazi) Belt Buckle Gun, 7.65mm, marked "D.R.P. Angem."

Greener Cattle Killer (Original Model)— No. B1201, .310 caliber.

Greener Cattle Killer (Pocket Pattern)— No. B1203, .310 caliber.

Greener Safti Killer—No. B1216, .22 caliber.

Greener Universal Safti Killer—No. B1217, .310 caliber.

Hamilton Rifle Model 7.

Hamilton Model 11.

Hamilton Model 15.

Hamilton Model 19.

Hamilton Model 23.

Hamilton Model 27 and 027.

Hamilton Model 31.

Hamilton Model 35.

Hamilton Model 39.

Hamilton Model 43.

Heal Rifle, No. 10, caliber .22.

"JGA" (J. G. Anchutz, Ulm, Germany), .22 caliber Flobert single shot pistol.

J. Stevens "hunters pet" pocket rifles with accompanying shoulder stock (except those chambered for shotgun ammunition).

The "Little All Right" palm pistol, .22 caliber rimfire patented by Edward Boardman and Andrew Peavey, January 18, 1876.

Luger Pistol-Carbine, Model 1902, 7.65mm Luger with original commercial type shoulder stock and forearm and 11¾ inch barrel.

Mannlicher Pistol-Carbine, Model 1896, 7.63mm Mannlicher, with rifle type shoulder stock and forearm and 11¾ inch barrel.

Manville, 18 shot drum, 25mm, semiautomatic Tear Gas Gun.

Mauser Pistol-Carbine, Model 1896, 7.63mm, with shoulder stock-holster and 11¾ inch to 16 inch barrel.

Mauser Pistol, Model 1912/14, 9mm Mauser short or .45 ACP, with shoulder stock-holster and 5 inch barrel.

The Merveilleux squeezer, 8mm short and 6mm.

Military type Nambu pistol, Model 1904, caliber 8mm Nambu (Riku Shiki Nambu Kenju) with an accompanying shoulder stock.

O S S, "Liberator" Pistol, .45 ACP or 9mm.

Peavey, A. J., Knife Gun, .22 short rimfire.

The Protector palm gun, .32 rimfire, extra short patented by Jacques Turbiaux, Patent No. 732644.

Quackenbush Bicycle Rifle with telescopic wire stock, .22 caliber.

See footnote

Remington Flare (Very) Pistol, Mark III, 10 gauge.

Remington Cane Gun, Model 1, .22 rimfire.

Remington Cane Gun, Model 2, .32 rimfire.

The Shatuck "Unique" palm gun in .22 and .32 caliber rimfire manufactured by O. F. Mossberg.

Stevens Rifle, No. 20, with smooth bore barrel for .22 and .32 rimfire shot cartridges.

The Taylor "Fur Getter" manufactured by F. C. Taylor Fur Company, St. Louis, Missouri, .22 caliber rimfire.

The Tribuzio "Squeezer" invented by Catallo Tribuzio of Turin, Italy, caliber 8mm short.

Walther Pistol, Model 1937 "Armee Pistol", 9mm Parabellum, with shoulder stock and 4.9 inch barrel.

Webley & Scott Pistol, Mark I, No. 2, .455 caliber, with shoulder stock.

Luger DWM Pistol, Model 1900, 1902, or 1906, in 7.65 Luger or 9mm Parabellum caliber, having the American Eagle chamber crest, and barrel lengths of either 4 inches or 4¾ inches with original detachable Ideal shoulder stocks and Ideal frame grips.

National Firearms Act Firearms Classified as Curio or Relics Under 18 U.S.C. Chapter 44.

Machine Gun, Maxim (German manufacture), Models MG08 & MG08/15, all calibers.

Thompson Submachine Gun, Model 1921, all calibers.

Thompson Model 1927, Semiautomatic Carbine, caliber .45 ACP.

Rifle, German, Model 1918, Anti-tank, (PzAGew 1918), caliber 13.25mm.

These National Firearms Act weapons classified as curios or relics are still subject to all the controls under the National Firearms Act. However, licensed collectors may acquire, hold or dispose of them as curios or relics subject to the provisions of 18 U.S.C. Chapter 44, and the regulations in 26 CFR Part 178. They are still "firearms" as defined in the National Firearms Act and 18 U.S.C. 921(a)(3).

Note: These lists of guns which have been reclassified because of their status as collector's items are complete as of press time. However, additions to these lists are continually being concidered and properly supported. Suggestions for additions may be submitted to the Bureau of Alcohol, Tobacco and Firearms at any time.

---

*The determination that a firearm is a curio or relic means that licensed collectors may acquire, hold or dispose of them as curios or relics subject to the provisions of 18 U.S.C. Chapter 44, and the regulations in 26 CFR Part 178. They are still "firearms" as defined in 18 U.S.C. 921(a)(3).

Gun Collector's Groups & Shows

This list is probably the most complete directory of gun collector's groups, meetings and shows ever compiled. Use it to find groups or shows in your vicinity—write the address shown for membership information, show dates and guest policies (some shows are closed except to members and invited guests).

Don't limit yourself to nearby shows—the monster Ohio Gun Collectors shows (closed) attract thousands of members from throughout the United States and even overseas! And don't overlook the national groups either—they offer an outstanding opportunity to get to know the top collectors in your field.

*Clubs and shows identified with an asterisk did not confirm our listing as of press time, but the addresses are current and believed accurate. All other U.S. and Canadian listings have been confirmed by an officer of the group.

Though great effort went into compiling this directory, some errors and omissions are bound to occur. Please bring these to our attention for further editions.

NATIONAL COLLECTING GROUPS

American Society of Arms Collectors, Inc.
Robert F. Rubendunst, Secty-Treas.
6550 Baywood Lane
Cincinnati, OH 45224
(2 shows)

Armor & Arms Club
c/o J.K. Watson
25 Broadway
New York, NY 10004
(2 shows)

Colt Commemorative Gun Coll. Assn. of Amer.
P.O. Box 5206
Beverly Hills, CA 90210
(annual)

International Cartridge Collectors Assn., Inc.
4065 Montecito Ave.
Tucson, AZ 85711
(annual)

National Automatic Pistol Collectors Assn.
P.O. Box 15738
Tower Grove Station
St. Louis, MO 63163
(annual)

COLLECTOR'S GROUPS AND SHOWS, BY STATE

ALABAMA
Alabama Gun Collectors Assn.
P.O. Box 20021
Birmingham, AL 35216
(3 shows)

North Alabama Gun Collector's Assn.*
P.O. Box 564
Huntsville, AL 35804

ARIZONA

Arizona Gun Collectors Assoc.*
Curtiss Todd
912 W. Monte Way
Phoenix, AZ 85041

ARKANSAS

Arkansas Searcy Rotary Club Gun Show*
Larry James
Box 1104
Searcy, AR 72143
(1 show)
Hot Springs Gun Show*
Jim Thorwarth
120 King Arthur Lane
Hot Springs, AR 71901
Ft. Smith Dealers and Collectors Assn.*
Tony Smith
1407 57 Terrace
Ft. Smith, AR 72901

CALIFORNIA

Arcadia Elks Gun Show*
John Lessard
18147 NewBurgh Street
Azusa, CA 91702
California Arms Collectors*
G. Robert Lawrence
P.O. Box 1777
Santa Ana, CA 92701
California Historical Arms Assoc.*
Norm or Ann Ferrando
P.O. Box 5101
Vallejo, CA 94590
Calif. Hunters & Gun Owners Assoc.*
V.H. Wacker
2309 Cipriani Blvd.
Belmont, CA 94002
California-Nevada Arms Collectors
P.O. Box 214955
Sacramento, CA 95821
(4 shows)
Glendale Gun & Artifact Show*
Mike's Sport Shop
3516½ Ocean View Blvd.
Glendale, CA 91208
Greater California Arms Collectors Assn.
8291 Carburton St.
Long Beach, CA 90808
Los Angeles Gun & Ctg. Collectors Assn.*
F.H. Ruffra
20810 Amie Ave.
Torrance, CA 90503
Nevada Arms Collectors*
P.O. Box 214955
Sacramento, CA 95821
Northern California Historical Arms Coll. Assn.*
Julia Lundwall
25 Mizpah St.
San Francisco, CA 94131
San Bernardino Valley Arms Collectors, Inc.*
F. Schaperkotter
2697 Acacia Ave.
San Bernardino, CA 92405
Southern California Arms Collectors Assn.*
Frank E. Barnyak
4204 Elmer Ave.
No. Hollywood, CA 91602

COLORADO

Arapahoe Gun Collectors*
Bill Rutherford
2968 S. Broadway
Englewood, CO 80110
Colorado Antique Gun Collectors Assn.
1348 S. Yates
Denver, CO 80219
(monthly)
Colorado Gun Collectors Assn.*
Arnie Dowd
5970 Estes Ct.
Arvada, CO 80002
Manitou Springs Gun Show
Charles Cell
406 E. Unitah St.
Colorado Springs, CO 80903
(1 show)

CONNECTICUT

Antique Arms Coll. Assn. of Conn.*
A. Darling
35 Stanley St.
New Haven, CT 06511
Cornwall Bridge Gun Show*
Bob Harris
P.O. Box 67N
Cornwall Bridge, CT 06754
Stratford Gun Collectors Assn., Inc.*
P.O. Box 52
Stratford, CT 06497
Ye Connecticut Gun Guild, Inc.*
Larry Kaufman
75 N. Sheffield Drive
Windsor, CT 06095

DELAWARE

Delaware Antique Arms Collectors
C.S. Landis - Secty.
2408 Duncan Rd.
Wilmington, DE 19808
(monthly)
Legion of Honor Gun Club
Henry M. Sipple
117 Karlyn Dr.
New Castle, DE 19720

FLORIDA

Florida Gun Collectors Assn.*
Bob Marvin
P.O. Box 470
Jasper, FL 32052
Haines City Gun Show*
M.B. Smith
P.O. Box 1167
Haines City, FL 33844
St. Petersburg Gun & Edged Weapons Show*
Don Upchurch
501 66th Avenue
St. Petersburg, FL 33705
Tampa Bay Gun Collectors Assn.*
Col. Emmet M. Jeffreys
401 49th St. N.
St. Petersburg, FL 33710

GEORGIA

Cherokee Gun Club*
Guy Stancil
P.O. Box 42
Gainesville, GA 30501

Georgia Arms Collectiers Assn., Inc.
P.O. Box 450
Atlanta, GA 30301
(monthly meetings, 2 shows)
Griffin Gun Club*
Lamar Conner
P.O. Box 390
Griffin, GA 30223
Laurens County Sportsmen Gun Club*
Paul Johnson
217 Lassiter Dr.
Dublin, GA 31021

IDAHO
Idaho Falls Civitan Club, Inc.
P.O. Box 2131
Idaho Falls, ID 83401
(1 show)

ILLINOIS
Central Illinois Gun Collectors Assn., Inc.
Donald E. Bryan, Secty-Treas.
R.R. #2
Jacksonville, IL 62650
(4 shows)
Fort Dearborn Frontiersmen*
Al Normath
8845 Pleasant Ave.
Hickory Hills, IL 60457
Fox Valley Arms Fellowship, Inc.
P.O. Box 301
Palatine, IL 60067
(6 shows)
Illinois Gun Collectors Assn.*
P.E. Pitts
P.O. Box 1524
Chicago, IL 60690
Little Fort Gun Collectors Assn.
Ernie Robinson, Exec. Secty.
P.O. Box 194
Gurnee, IL 60031
(6 shows)
Midwest Gun Collectors Assn.
Gene Jordan
1505 Sunset Dr. - Spring Beach
East Peoria, IL 61611
(4 shows)
Mississippi Valley Gun & Cartridge Coll. Assn.*
Mel Sims
Box 426
New Windsor, IL 61465
Pioneer Valley Gun Assn.*
Jim Florence
P.O. Box 66
Glen Ellyn, IL 60137
Sauk Trail Gun Collectors, Inc.
L.D. Carlock, Secty-Treas.
RT. 1 Box 169
Prophetstown, IL 61277
(4 shows)
Tri-County Gun Club, Inc.*
Dale Hartle
501 W. Dixon Street
Polo, IL 61064
Wabash Valley Gun Collectors Assn., Inc.
Betty J. Baer, Secty.
1002 Lincoln Park Ave.
Danville, IL 61832
(4 shows)

INDIANA
Central Indiana Gun Coll. Assn.*
Paul E. Daughterty
421 E. Washington St.
Hartford City, IN 47384
Crawfordsville Gun Club Inc.*
Robt. J.K. Edmonds
R.R. 2
Crawfordsville, IN 47933
Hartford City Gun Show
Bruce W. Davis
2412 Chippewa Lane
Muncie, IN 47302
(6 shows)
Midwest Gun Traders, Inc.
c/o Glen Wittenberger
4609 Oliver St.
Ft. Wayne, IN 46806
(monthly)
Northern Indiana Gun Collectors Assn.
16150 Ireland Rd.
Mishawaka, IN 46544
(monthly)
Southern Indiana Gun Collectors Assn.
509 N. Third St.
Boonville, IN 47601
(4 shows)
Tippecanoe Gun & Cartridge Club*
Leonard Ledman
RR 12, Box 212
Lafayette, IN 46202

IOWA
Cedar Valley Gun Collectors
R. L. Harris
Rt. 1
Marion, IA 52302
(2-3 shows)
Central States Gun Collectors Assn.*
Avery Gile
1104 So. 1st Avenue
Marshalltown, IA 50158
Clear Lake Gun Show*
Lloyd Ashland
100 5th Ave. North
Clear Lake, IA 50428
Council Bluffs Rifle & Pistol Club
E.D. File
372 Harrison St.
Council Bluffs, IA 51501
(1 show)
Des Moines Area Collectors Show
1422-48th St.
Des Moines, IA 50311
(2-3 shows)
Eastern Iowa Gun And Cartridge Coll. Assn.*
F. Fitzpatrick
305 N. Eliza St.
Maquoketa, IA 52060
Mid-America Gun Collectors Show*
Tom Myers
YMCA
Davenport, IA 52801
Quad City Arms Coll. Assn.*
A. Squire
1845 W. 3rd St.
Davenport, IA 52802

Wildlife Club of Ellsworth College
Sujit Dhar
Ellsworth College
Iowa Falls, IA 50126
(monthly)

KANSAS

Chisholm Trail Antique Gun Assn., Inc.*
Carney Pace
P.O. Box 13093
Wichita, KS 67213

Colby Gun & Coin Show
Box 572
Colby, KS 67701

Four State Collectors Assn.*
M.G. Wilkinson
915 E. 10th
Pittsburgh, KS 66762

Kansas Cartridge Collectors Assn.
Jack Saunders
Catherine Route
Hap, KS 67601
(monthly, 1 show)

Missouri Valley Arms Collectors Assn.
P.O. Box 8204
Shawnee Mission, KS 66208
(monthly, 1 show)

Solomon Valley Gun Collectors
c/o Frank Wheeler
Box 230
Osborne, KS 67473
(annual)

Ulysses Gun Show
Jerry D. Anderson
Box 52
Ulysses, KS 67880

Valley Falls Lions Club*
Roy Reichart
Valley Falls, KS 66088

Wichita Gun Show*
Ken Cinotto
P.O. Box 13093
Wichita, KS 67213

KENTUCKY

John Hunt Morgan Gun Collectors, Inc.
P.O. Box 525
Paris, KY 40361

Kentuckiana Arms Collectors Assn., Inc.
P.O. Box 1776
Louisville, KY 40201
(monthly)

Kentucky Gun Collectors Assn.
P.O. Box 64
Owensboro, KY 42301
(monthly, 3 shows)

LOUISIANA

Ark-La-Tex Gun Collectors Assn.*
Harry G. King
414 Mohawk Trail
Shreveport, LA 71107

Bayou Gun Club Inc.*
David J. Seibert Jr.
2820 Ramsey Drive
New Orleans, LA 70114

Pelican Arms Collectors Assn.
8681 Sharon Hills Blvd.
Baton Rouge, LA 70811
(monthly)

Thibodaux Gun Show*
William S. Binnings, Sr.
Box 540 R.F.D. No. 1
Thibodaux, LA 70301

MARYLAND

Baltimore Antique Arms Assn.
Stanley I. Kellert
R.D. 1, Box 256
Lutherville, MD 21093
(2 shows)

Cumberland Valley Arms Collectors Assn.*
Mrs. S. Naylor
Rt. 2
Hagerstown, MD 21740

Eastern Area Firearms & Militaria Coll.
Charles Snyder
3520 Mullin Lane
Bowie, MD 20715
(6-7 shows)

Maryland Arms Collectors*
Mrs. Allen P. Karr
Broadmoor Road.
Baltimore, MD 21212

Penn-Mar-Va Antique Arms Soc.*
T. Wibberley
54 E. Lincoln Ave.
Hagerstown, MD 21740

Potomac Arms Collectors Assn.*
P.O. Box 4066
Silver Spring, MD 20904

MASSACHUSETTS

Bay Colony Weapons Collectors Inc.
47 Homer Road
Belmont, MA 02178
(monthly)

Massachusetts Arms Collectors*
John J. Callan, Jr.
15 Montague St.
Worcester, MA 01630

MICHIGAN

Lower Michigan Gun Collectors*
8639 Donna Dr.
Westland, MI 48185

Michigan Antique Arms Collectors, Inc.
W.E. Heid - Secty.
8914 Borgman Ave.
Huntington Woods, MI 48070
(3-4 shows)

Royal Oak Historical Arms Collectors, Inc.*
Mrs. Chester Parker
13143 Borgman Ave.
Huntington Woods, MI 48070

Sterling Heights Gun and Coin Show*
Rodger Crooks
5451 Meadowview
Sterling Heights, MI 48077

MINNESOTA

Minnesota Weapons Collectors Assn., Inc.
P.O. Box 662
Hopkins, MN 55343
(6 shows)

Twin Ports Weapons Collectors*
Jack Puglisi
6504 Lexington St.
Duluth, MN 55087

MISSISSIPPI

Dixie Arms Collectors*
Ruth Creecy
1509 W. 7th
Hattiesburg, MS 39401
Mississippi Gun Collectors Assn.*
Mrs. J.E. Swinney
Box 1332
Hattiesburg, MS 39401

MISSOURI

Bagnell Dam Gun Show*
C. T. Williams
Lake Ozark, MO 65049
Edwardsville Gun Show*
A.W. Stephensmeier
317 North Grand Blvd.
St. Louis, MO 63103
Meramec Valley Gun Collectors*
L.W. Olson
Star Route
St. Clair, MO 63077
Mineral Belt Gun Coll. Assn.*
G.W. Gunter
1110 E. Cleveland Ave.
Monett, MO 65708
Shepard Mountain Gun, Coin & Artifacts*
Larry Nelson
Rt. 1
Morningside Lane
Ironton, MO 63650
St. Louis Antique Arms Assn.*
Joseph E. Heneberry
7400 Pershing Ave.
St. Louis, MO 63130

MONTANA

Montana Arms Collectors Assn.
John Byrd
Canyon Ferry Museum
York Route
Helena, MT 59601
(various)
Mon-Dak Collectors
Jim Huff
311 Colorado Ave.
Laurel, MT 59044
(1 show)

NEBRASKA

Nebraska Gun & Cartridge Collectors*
E. M. Zalud
710 W. 6th St.
North Platte, NB 69101
Nebraska Muzzle Loading Rifle Assn.*
P.O. Box 241
Grand Island, NB 68801
Pine Ridge Gun Collectors
Loren Pickering
509 Elm St.
Crawford, NB 69339
(monthly, 1 show)
Red Cloud Gun & Hobby Show*
Bob Bohrer
705 N. Jefferson
Red Cloud, NB 68970

NEW HAMPSHIRE

Maple Tree Gun Coll. Assn.*
E.P. Hector
Meriden Rd.
Lebanon, NH 03766
New Hampshire Arms Collectors Inc.
James Tillinghast
Box 5
Marlow, NH 03456
(monthly)
New Hampshire Collectors Assn.
Box 148
Nashua, NH 03060

NEW JERSEY

Fort Lee Arms Collectors Assn.*
Gil Frankhuizen
P.O. Box 264
Franklin Lakes, NJ 07417
Jersey Shore Antique Arms Collectors*
Bob Holloway
1755 McGallard Ave.
Trenton, NJ 08610
New Jersey Arms Collectors Club*
Clifford Fox
P.O. Box 331
Gladstone, NJ 07934

NEW MEXICO

New Mexico Gun Collectors Assn.*
P.O. Box 14145
Albuquerque, NM 87111
(monthly, exc. summer)

NEW YORK

Empire State Firearms Assn.
Frank Knapp
P.O. Box 2328
Rochester, NY 14623
(1 show)
Fort Lee Arms Collectors*
W.E. Sammis R.D.
776 Brookridge Dr.
Valley Cottage, NY 10989
Hudson-Mohawk Arms Collectors Assn., Inc.*
Bennie S. Pisarz
108 W. Main St.
Frankfort, NY 13340
International Militaria Collectors Society
Sydney B. Vernon
P.O. Box 387
Baldwin, NY 11510
Iroquois Arms Collectors Assn.*
Dennis Freeman
12144 McNeeley Rd.
Akron, NY 14001
Long Island Antique Gun Collectors Assn.*
Frank Davison
8 Johnson Place
Baldwin, NY 11510
Mid-State Arms Coll. & Shooters Club*
Bennie S. Pisarz
108 W. Main St.
Frankfort, NY 13340
New York State Arms Collectors Assn., Inc.
Marvin K. Salls
R.D. 1
Ilion, NY 13357
(6 shows)

Northeastern Arms Collectors Assn., Inc.
P.O. Box 253 M
Bayshore, NY 11706
(monthly)
Westchester Arms Collectors Club, Inc.*
F. E. Falkenbury, Jr., Secy.
75 Hillcrest Rd.
Hartsdale, NY 10530

NORTH CAROLINA
Cape Fear Gun Collectors*
David Blalock, Jr.
Rt. 1
Linden, NC 28356
Carolina Gun Collectors Assn.
Joe G. Mashall
P.O. Box 5881
Winston Salem, NC 27103
(4 shows)

NORTH DAKOTA
Minot Rifle & Pistol Club, Inc.
E. F. Bolte
Box 414
Minot, ND 58701
(monthly)

OHIO
Barberton Gun Collectors Assn.*
R.N. Watters
1108 Bevan St.
Barberton, OH 44203
Central Ohio Gun & Indian Relic. Coll. Assn.*
Coyt Stookey
134 E. Ohio Ave.
Washington Court House, OH 43160
Lakeshore Gun Collectors*
R.N. Watters
1108 Bevan St.
Barberton, OH 44203
Maumee Valley Gun Collectors Assn.*
J. Hennings
3450 Gallatin Rd.
Toledo, OH 43606
Ohio Gun Collectors Assn., Inc.
P.O. Box 3824
Columbus, OH 43214
(6 shows)
Ohio Valley Military Society
Mr. Wolfgang Sell
OVMS P.O. Box 36188
Cincinnati, OH 45236
(bi-monthly)
The Stark Gun Collectors Inc.*
Russ E. McNary
147 Miels Ave. N.W.
Canton, OH 44708
Tri-State Gun Collectors, Inc.*
Steve Gamble
1115 N. Main Street
Lima, OH 45801

OKLAHOMA
Claremore Gun Club*
Jack L. Chandler
121 N. Lynn Riggs
Claremore, OK 74017

Indian Territory Gun Collectors Assn.*
P.O. Box 4491
Tulsa, OK 74104
Midwest City Optimist Club
Chief John Ferrish
Box 10422
Midwest City, OK 73110
(2 shows)

OREGON
Jefferson State Arms Collectors*
Art Chipman
2251 Ross Lane
Medford, OR 97501
Oregon Cartridge Collectors Assn.
c/o Dick Hamilton
P.O. Box 152
Junction City, OR 97448
(monthly)
Willamette Valley Arms Collectors Assn.
Murry Brooks
2110 W. 20th St.
Eugene, OR 97405
(monthly)

PENNSYLVANIA
Central Penn Antique Arms Assn.
549 West Lemon Street
Lancaster, PA 17603
(monthly)
Colonial Valley Gun Show*
Dennis D. Smith
Colonial Valley
Menges Mills, PA 17346
Curry Run House Gun Show
Zenas H. Hoover
P.O. Box 1
Indiana, PA 15701
(3 shows)
Forks of the Delaware Weapons Assn., Inc.
John F. Scheid - Secty-Treas.
348 Bushkill St.
Easton, PA 18042
(monthly)
Four Mile Range Gun Club*
Carl Malizia
604 East Allegany Avenue
Emporium, PA 15834
Lancaster Muzzle Loading Rifle Assn.
James H. Fredrick, Jr.
Box 447, R.D. 1
Columbia, PA 17512
(monthly)
Mideastern Antique Gun Collectors
Box 445
Gettysburg, PA 17325
(4 shows)
Northern Tier Antique Gun Collectors*
Cliff Breidinger
Trout Run, PA 17771
Pennsylvania Antique Gun Collectors Assn., Inc*
Ray Petry
801 N. Jackson Street
Media, PA 19063
Pennsylvania Gun Collectors Assn.
Arch Waugh, Sr.
37 Woodside Drive
Washington, PA 15301
(4 shows)

Presque Isle Gun Collectors Assn.
J.C. Welch
156 E. 37th Street
Erie, PA 16506
(bi-monthly, 1 show)
Somerset Rifle & Pistol Club*
J. Richard Ross
2 Stein Bldg.
Somerset, PA 15501
Two Lick Valley Gun Collectors Assn., Inc.
1410 Washington St.
Indiana, PA 15701
(4 shows)
Winchester and Colt Collectors Assn.
T.R. Weber, Jr.
P.O. Box 313
Plymouth Meeting, PA 19462
(2 shows)

SOUTH CAROLINA

Belton Gun Club, Inc.
P.O. Box 605
Belton, SC 29627
South Carolina Arms Collectors Assn.*
J. W. McNelley
3215 Lincoln Street
Columbia, SC 29201

SOUTH DAKOTA

Dakota Territory Gun Collectors Assn.
Jim Aplan
Box 474
Onida, SD 57564
(6 shows)

TENNESSEE

Cleveland Gun & Knife Show*
Fred Bullard
1725 25th Street
Cleveland, TN 37311
Memphis Antique Weapons Assn.
Nelson T. Powers
4672 Barfield Road
Memphis, TN 38117
(monthly)
Memphis Gun Show*
C.F. Manton
2247 Lovitt Drive
Memphis, TN 38138
Smoky Mountain Gun Collectors Assn.*
P.O. Box 22
Oak Ridge, TN 37830
Tennessee Gun Collectors Assn., Inc.
3556 Pleasant Valley Rd.
Nashville, TN 37204
(2 shows)

TEXAS

Alamo Gun Collectors, Inc.
P.O. Box 1328
Seguin, TX 78155
(monthly)
Brazoria County Gun Collectors Assn.*
Calvin Vernor
35 Cypress Ct. St.
Clute, TX 77531
Brownsville Tip-O-Texas Wildcat Show*
1350 W. Elizabeth Street
Brownsville, TX 78520

Corpus Christi Antique Gun Collectors Assn.*
Jerry Murphey
10701 Timbergrove Lane
Corpus Christi, TX 78410
Dallas Gun Collectors Assn., Inc.
Richard Shea
P.O. Box 538
Duncanville, TX 75116
(monthly, 3 shows)
Houston Gun Collectors Assn.*
C. Mc Kim
5454 Stillbrooke
Houston, TX 77035
Paso Del Norte Gun Collectors Inc.
Ken Hockett
1216 Mescalero
El Paso, TX 79925
(6 shows)
Permian Basin Rifle & Pistol Club, Inc.
E.L. Good
P.O. Box 459
Midland, TX 79701
(monthly)
Sabine Gun Collectors Inc.
P.O. Box 6137
Beaumont, TX 77705
(2 shows)
Sweetwater Gun & Coin Show*
Claude Wilson
Sweetwater, TX 79556
Texas Gun Collectors Assn.
Mrs. Taska Clark
3119 Produce Row
Houston, TX 77023
(2 shows)
Waco Gun Collectors*
C.V. Pruitt
4021 N. 26th Street
Waco, TX 76708
West Texas Gun Collectors
R.B. Morris
613 West 2nd St.
Odessa, TX 79761
(4 shows)

UTAH

Utah Gun Collectors Assn.
S. Gerald Keogh
875 20th St.
Ogden, UT 84401
(6 shows)

VIRGINIA

North-South Skirmish Assn.
P.O. Box 114
McLean, VA 22101
(4 shows)
Peninsula Kiwanis Club
102 W. Mercury Blvd.
Hampton, VA 23669
(Weekly)
Portsmouth Gun Show*
Jack Staylor
1604 Golf Road
Chesapeake, VA 23321

Roanoke Valley Gun Show
P.O. Box 6323
Roanoke, VA 24017
(3 shows)

Shenandoah Valley Gun Collectors Assn.
P.O. Box 926
Winchester, VA 22601
(monthly, 2 shows)

The Greater Richmond Gun Show*
Bert Dodd or Jack Staylor
1604 Gaff Road
Chesapeake, VA 23321

Virginia Arms Collectors Assn., Inc.
Robert C. Whitaker
P.O. Box 354
Dahlgreen, VA 22448
(monthly, 1 show)

WASHINGTON
Washington Arms Collectors
Don Zwicker-Sec/Treas.
446 Pelly Ave. North
Renton, WA 98055
(monthly)

WISCONSIN
Central States Gun Collectors*
Mrs. Caryl Molzahn
427 So. 23rd St.
La Crosse, WI 54601

Chippewa Valley Weapons Collectors*
J.M. Sullivan
504 Ferry St.
Eau Claire, WI 54701

Great Lakes Arms Collectors Assn., Inc.
1811 North 73rd Street
Wauwatosa, WI 53123
(6 shows)

Wild River Gun Collectors Show*
Herman Menke
St. Croix Falls, WI 54024

Wisconsin Gun Collectors Assn., Inc.*
Rob Zellner
W180N8996 Leona Lane
Menomonee Falls, WI 53057

WYOMING
Wyoming Gun Collectors
224 No. 2 West
Riverton, WY 82501
(1 show)

CANADA

Alberta
Canadian Historical Arms Society
P.O. Box 901
Edmonton, Alberta, Canada
(monthly)

Ontario
Ontario Arms Collectors Assn.*
P. Peddle
174 Ellerslie Ave.
Willowdale, Ont., Canada

Oshawa Antique Gun Collectors Inc.
c/o Gordon J. Dignem (Pres.)
613 Rosemere St.
Oshawa, Ontario Canada
(5 shows)

Quebec
Lower Canada Arms Collectors Assn.*
Secretary
P.O. Box 1162
St. B
Montreal 101, Quebec, Canada

EUROPE

England
Arms & Armour Society of London
F. Wilkinson
40 Great James St.
Holborn, London N. 3HB W.C.1.

France
Les Arquebusiers de France
Mme, Marckmann
70 Rue des Chamtiers
78-Versailies, France

SOUTH AFRICA
Historical Firearms Soc. of South Africa
"Minden" 11 Buchan Rd.
Newlands, Cape Town, South Africa

ASSOCIATIONS WITH PUBLICATIONS OR ACTIVITIES OF INTEREST TO COLLECTORS
National Rifle Assn.
1600 Rhode Island Ave.
Washington, DC 20036

National Muzzle Loading Rifle Assn.*
Box 67
Friendship, IN 47021

National Bench Rest Shooters Assn., Inc.*
Bernice McMullen
607 W. Line St.
Minerva, OH 44657

American Single Shot Rifle Assn.
Dennis Hrusosky
411 David Ave.
Joliet, IL 60433

American Ordnance Assn.
819 Union Trust Bldg.
Washington, DC 20005

PERIODICALS for COLLECTORS

The American Rifleman (M)
National Rifle Assn., 1600 Rhode Island Ave., N.W., Wash., DC 20036. $7.50 yr. Firearms articles of all kinds.

Arms Gazette
Wallace Beinfeld Publications, Inc., P.O. Box 35154, Los Angeles, CA 90035. $8 yr. U.S., others $15 yr. Articles for the collector.

Army (M)
Assn. of the U.S. Army, 1529 18th Ave. N.W., Wash., DC 20036. $10.00 yr. Occasional articles on small arms.

Canadian Journal of Arms Collecting (Q)
Museums Restoration Service P.O. Box 2037, Sta. D. Ottawa, Ont., Canada. $4.00 yr.

The Classic Collector (Q)
Intrigue Publications, Inc., 711 So. St. Asaph St., Alexandria, VA 22314. $5 yr. For serious collectors, investors and hobbyists.

Deutsches Waffen Journal
Journal-Verlag Schwend GmbH, Postfach 340, D7170 Schwabisch Hall, Germany. $11.50 yr. Antique and modern arms, their history, technical aspects, etc. German text.

The Gun Report
World Wide Gun Report, Inc., Box 111, Aledo, IL 61231. $7.00 yr. For the gun collector.

Gunsport & Gun Collector
The Clark Bldg., Suite 2100, Pittsburgh, PA 15222. Md. 20637. $5.00 yr.

Gun Week†
Amos Press, Inc., P.O. Box 150, Sidney, Ohio 45365. $5.00 yr. U.S. and possessions; $6.00 yr. Canada; $7.00 yr. foreign. Tabloid paper on guns, hunting, shooting.

Gun World
Gallant Publishing Co., 34249 Camino Capistrano, Capistrano Beach, CA 92624. $7.50 yr. For the hunting, reloading and shooting enthusiast.

Guns & Ammo
Petersen Pub. Co., 8490 Sunset Blvd., Los Angeles, CA 90069. $7.50 yr. Guns, shooting, and technical articles.

Guns
Guns Magazine, 8150 N. Central Park Ave., Skokie, IL 60076. $7.50 yr. Articles for gun collectors, hunters and shooters.

Guns Review
Ravenhill Pub. Co. Ltd., Standard House, Bonhill St., London E.C. 2, England. $10.20 yr. For collectors and shooters.

The Journal of the Arms & Armour Society (M)
F. Wilkinson (Secy.), 40 Great James St., Holborn, London WC1, England. $4.00 yr. Articles for the collector.

The Luger Journal
Robt. B. Marvin, Publ., P.O. Box 326, Jasper, FL 32052. $6.00 yr.

Ordnance* (M)
American Ordnance Assn., 819 Union Trust Bldg., Wash., DC 20005. $8.00 yr. Occasional articles on small arms and related subjects.

The Rifle Magazine*
Dave Wolfe Publishing Co., Box 3030, Presott, AZ 86301. $5.00 yr. Journal of the NBRSA.

Shooting Times
PJS Publications, News Plaza, Peoria, IL 61601. $5.85 yr. Guns, shooting, reloading; articles on every gun activity.

The Shotgun News‡
Snell Publishing Co., Box 1147, Hastings, NB 68901. $5.00 yr. Sample copy 75¢. Gun ads of all kinds.

*Published bi-monthly
†Published weekly
‡Published twice per month.

M Membership requirements; write for details.
Q Published Quarterly.
All others are published monthly.

The Collector's Bookshelf

Accoutrements

Accoutrement Plates, North and South, 1861-1865, by Wm. G. Gavin. Geo. Shumway, York, PA, 1963. 236 pp., 220 illus. $12.00.

The 1st detailed study of Civil War belt buckles and cartridge box insignia. Dimensions, materials, details of manufacture, relative and dollar values given.

American Engraved Powder Horns, by Stephen V. Grancsay. Originally published by The Metropolitan Museum of Art, at NYC, 1945. The 1st reprint publ. by Ray Riling Arms Books Co., Phila., PA, 1965. 96 pp. plus 47 full-page plates. $15.00.

A study based on the J. H. Grenville Gilbert collection of historic, rare and beautiful powder horns. A scholarly work by an eminent authority. Long out of print and offered now in a limited edition of 1000 copies.

Badges & Emblems of the British Forces 1940, Arms and Armour Press, London, 1968, 64 pp. Paper, $3.00.

Reprint of a comprehensive guide to badges and emblems worn by all British forces in 1940, including Welfare, Aux. Services, Nursing Units, etc. Over 350 illus.

Buttons of the British Army 1855-1970, by Howard Ripley, Arms & Armour Press, London, 1971. 64 pp. $5.00.

Guide for collectors with over 650 buttons illus.

Early Loading Tools and Bullet Molds, by R. H. Chamberlain. The Farm Tribune, Porterville, GA, 1971. 75 pp., illus. Paper covers, $3.00.

An excellent aid to collectors.

Insignia, Decorations and Badges of the Third Reich and Occupied Countries, by R. Kahl, Military Collectors Service, Kedichem, Holland, 1970. 135 pp., $9.95.

Handbook of regalia with descriptive text and over 800 line illus.

The Leather Jacket Soldier, by O. B. Faulk. Socio-Technical Pub., Pasadena, CA, 1971, 80 pp., illus. $10.00.

History of such Spanish military equipment of the late 18th century as lances, horse accoutrements, guns, uniforms, etc.

Metal Uniform Insignia of the US Army in the Southwest, 1846-1902, by S. B. Brinckerhoff, Arizona Pioneers Hist. Soc., Tucson, Ariz., 1972, 28 pp., illus. Paper covers. $2.50.

Monograph on buttons, badges, buckles, and other uniform insignia.

Militaria, by Frederick Wilkinson. Hawthorn Books, New York, NY, 1969. 1st U.S. ed. 256 pp., well illus. in halftone. $5.95.

Introduction to military items of interest to collectors, including prints, medals, uniforms, military miniatures, weapons, badges, etc.

New England Militia Uniforms and Accoutrements, by J. O. Curtis and Wm. H. Guthman. Old Sturbridge Inc., Sturbridge, MA, 1971. 102 pp. Paper covers. $4.

An identification guide which illustrates uniforms, epaulettes, helmets, helmet plates, belt buckles and cartridge pouches.

The Powder Flask Book, by Ray Riling. Bonanza Books, NY 1968. A reprint. 520 pp., large format, profusely illus. First re-issue of the 1953 original ed. $9.95. A limited number of the originals are available for inscription and autograph at $35.00.

Covers the literature on flasks, their makers, and users —hunters, shooters and the military—as well as showing the arms, cased or not, short and long. A relative price listing for collector advantage is included.

Cartridges

Cartridge Headstamp Guide, by H. P. White and B. D. Munhall. H. P. White Laboratory, Bel Air, MD, 1963. 263 pp., illus. $10.00.

An important reference on headstamping of small arms ammo, by manufacturers in many countries. Clear illus. of 1936 headstamps of every type.

Cartridges, by Cyril Waterworth. Farleigh Press, Lindfield, N.S.W. 2070, Australia, N.D. 80 pp., illus. $1.50.

Rifle, handgun and collectors cartridges are shown and briefly described, but no prices are given.

Cartridges for Collectors, by Fred A. Datig. Borden Publishing Co., Alhambra, Calif., Vol. I (Centerfire), 1958; Vol. II (Rimfire and Misc.) Types, 1963; Vol. III (Additional Rimfire, Centerfire, and Plastic,) 1967. Each of the three volumes 176 pp., well illus. and each priced at $7.50.

Vol. III supplements the first two books and presents 300 additional specimens. All illus. are shown in full-scale line drawings.

Cartridges of the World, by Frank C. Barnes, John T. Amber ed., Digest Books, Inc., Northfield, IL, 1972. 8½"x11", 378 pp. Profusely illus. Paperbound. $6.95.

The third edition of a comprehensive reference for hunters, collectors, handloaders and ballisticians. Covering over 1000 cartridges, loads, components, etc., from all over the world.

Centerfire American Rifle Cartridges, 1892-1963, by Ray Bearse, A. S. Barnes & Co., S. Brunswick, NJ, 1966. 198 pp., illus. $6.98.

Identification manual covering caliber, introduction date, origin, case type, etc. Self-indexed and cross-referenced. Headstamps and line drawings are included.

Centerfire Pistol and Revolver Cartridges, by H. P. White, B. D. Munhall and Ray Bearse. A. S. Barnes, NY, 1967. 85 pp. plus 170 pp., illus. $10.00.

A new and revised edition covering the original Volume I, Centerfire Metric Pistol and Revolver Cartridges and Volume II, Centerfire American and British Pistol and Revolver Cartridges, by White and Munhall, formerly known as Cartridge Identification.

Manual of Pistol and Revolver Cartridges, Vol. I, by H. A. Erlmeier and J. H. Brandt. C. D. Associates, Wiesbaden, Germany, 1967. 268 pp., illus. $21.50.

Both English and German text on centerfire and metric calibers.

Metallic Cartridges, T. J. Treadwell, compiler. The Armoury, NYC, 1959. Unpaginated. 68 plates. Paper, $2.95. Cloth, $5.95.

A reduced-size reproduction of U.S. Ordnance Memoranda No. 14, originally publ. in 1873, on regulation and experimental cartridges manufactured and tested at Frankford Arsenal, Philadelphia, Pa.

Price List of the U.S. Cartridge Company's Ammunition, a 1969 reprint of the 1891 original, publ. by J. C. Tillinghast, Marlow, N.H. 29 pp., illus., paper covers. $2.50.

Displays many of the now hard-to-find cartridges.

G. Roth Aktiengesellschaft. Horn Co., Burlington, Vt., 1968. 28 pp., illus., paperbound. $2.50.

Reprint of a German cartridge catalog of 1913, with drawings and dimensions.

Shotgun Shells: Identification, Manufacturers and Checklist for Collectors, by F. H. Steward. B. and P. Associates, St. Louis, Mo., 1969. 101 pp., illus., paper covers. $4.95.

Historical data for the collector.

Small Arms Ammunition Identification Guide. Normount Tech. Pub., Forest Grove, OR, 1971. 151 pp., illus. Paper, $3.00.

A reprint of the guide originally published as FSTC-CW-07-02-66, revised.

Small Arms Ammunition Identification Guide, An Army Intelligence Document, Paladin Press, Boulder, CO, 1972. 254 pp., illus. Paper, $5.00.

An exact reprint of FSTC-CW-7068, 1969 updated. An identification guide for most countries.

General

The Age of Firearms, by Robert Held. Digest Books, Inc., Northfield, IL, 1970. New, fully rev. and corrected ed., paper covers. 192 pp., fully illus. $4.95.

A popular review of firearms since 1475 with accent on their effects on social conditions, and the craft of making functional/artistic arms.

Air Gun Batteries, by E. G. Wolff. Public Museum, Milwaukee, WI, 1964. 28 pp., illus., paperbound. 75¢.

Study of discharge mechanisms on reservoir air guns.

Air Guns, by Eldon G. Wolff. Milwaukee Public Museum, Milwaukee, WI, 1958. 198 pp., illus. Paper, $6.00.

A scholarly and comprehensive treatise, excellent for student and collectors' use, of air gun history. Every form of arm is described, and a list of 350 makers is included.

Air Guns and Air Pistols, by L. Wesley. A. S. Barnes Co., NY, 1964. 210 pp., illus. $5.00.

Latest, enlarged ed. of a standard work.

Ancient Armour and Weapons in Europe, by John Hewitt. Akademische Druck- u. Verlagsanstalt, Graz, Austria, 1967. 3 vols., 1151 total pp., illus. $50.00.

Reprint of a renowned British work first published 1855-1860; covers armour, weapons, military history and tactics through the 17th century.

Antique Arms Annual, ed. by R. L. Wilson, S. P. Stevens, Texas Gun Coll. Assn., Waco, Texas. 1971. 262 pp., profusely illus. $15.00.

A magnificent work showing hundreds of fine color photographs of rare firearms. Decorated paper covers.

Antique European and American Firearms in the Hermitage Museum, by L. Tarassuk. Arco Pub. Co., NY, 1972. 224 pp., 130 pp. of illus., 54 pp. in full color. $20.00.

Selections from the museum's 2500 firearms dating from the 15th to 19th centuries, including the magnificently decorated Colt rifle and pistols presented by Samuel Colt to Tzars Nicholas I and Alexander II.

Antique Firearms, by Frederick Wilkinson. Guinness Signatures, London. 1st ed., 1969. 256 pp., well illus. $15.00.

Sixteen monographs on important aspects of firearms development from the 14th century to the era of the modern repeating rifle. Shows museum-quality arms, many in full color.

Antique Firearms: Their Care, Repair and Restoration, by Ronald Lister. Crown Publ., New York, 1964. 220 pp., 66 plates, 24 figs. $2.98.

A workshop manual for collectors and gunsmiths, giving correct procedures for every step in preserving firearms.

Antique Weapons, A-Z, by Douglas J. Fryer. G. Bell & Sons, London, 1969. 114 pp. illus. $7.50.

A concise survey of collectors' arms, including firearms, edged weapons, polearms, etc., of European and Oriental design, classified by types.

Antique Weapons for Pleasure and Investment, by R. Akehurst. Arco Pub. Co., N.Y., 1969. 174 pp., illus. $5.95.

Reprint of an English book covering an extensive variety of arms, including Japanese and Hindu edged weapons and firearms.

Americans and their Guns, compiled by Jas. B. Trefethen, ed. by Jas. E. Serven, Stackpole Books, Harrisburg, Pa., 1967. 320 pp., illus. $9.95.

The National Rifle Association of America story through nearly a century of service to the nation. More than a history—a chronical of help to novice and expert in the safe and proper use of firearms for defense and recreation, as well as a guide for the collector of arms.

The American B.B. Gun, by A. T. Dunathan, A. S. Barnes, S. Brunswick, NJ, 1971. 154 pp., illus. $10.00.

Identification reference and a price guide for B.B. guns, plus a brief history and advertising plates.

Arco Gun Book, ed. by Larry Koller. Arco Publ. Co. Inc., NYC, 1962. 397 pp., illus. $7.50.

A concise encyclopedia for arms collectors, shooters and hunters.

Les Armes Americaines 1870-1871 de las Defense Nationale, by P. Lorain and J. Boudriot. Librarie Pierre Petitot, Paris, France, 1970. French text, 96 pp., illus. $12.50.

Covers all U.S. weapons bought by the French government a century ago.

Armes a Feu Francaises Modeles Reglementaires, by J. Boudriot. Paris, 1961-1968. 4 series of booklets; 1st and 2nd series, 5 booklets; 3rd and 4th, 6 booklets. Each series, $6.75, $9.75, $10.75, $11.75, resp.

Detailed survey of all models of French military small arms, 1717-1861, with text in French and fine scale drawings. Each series covers a different period of development; the last covers percussion arms.

Armi e Armature Italiane, Fino al XVIII Secolo, by Aldo Mario Aroldi. Bramante Editrice, Milan, Italy, 1961. 544 pp., profusely illus. (Much in color). In slip case, $65.00.

A luxurious work on the golden age of Italian arms and makers through the 18th cent., emphasizing body and horse armor, edged weapons, crossbows, early firearms. Italian text. Beautiful and scholarly work for the advanced collector.

Le Armi da Fuoco Portatili Italiane, dalle Origini al Risorgimento, by Gen. Agostino Gaibi. Bramante Editrice, Milan, Italy, 1962. 527 pp., 320 illus. (69 in color), in slip case. $65.00.

A magnificently produced volume covering Italian hand firearms from their beginning into the 18th cent. Italian text. Superb illus. of historic weapons, engraving, marks, related equipment. A companion book to *Armi e Armature Italiane.*

Armi e Armature Orientali, by Gianni Vianello, Bramante Editrice, Milano, Italy, 1966. 423 pp. Magnificently illustrated, mainly in full-color tip-ins. $56.00 with slip case. Ed. ltd. to 1600 copies.

A new addition to a notable series of fine books in the arms and armor field. The introduction is 68 pp., 105 pp. of commentary on the 250 pp. of illus.

Arming the Troops, by Paul C. Boehret. Publ. by the author at Chalfont, Pa., 1967. 39 pp., illus. $7.50. The same in paper wrappers $5.00.

A catalog of arms makers of the early years of U.S. history, from 1775 to 1815.

The Armourer and his Craft, by Charles ffoulkes. Frederick Ungar Publ. Co., N.Y., 1967. 199 pp., illus. $18.50.

Standard British reference on body armor, 11th-16th cent.; covering notable makers, construction, decoration, and use. 1st ed. 1912, now reprinted.

Armourers Marks, by D. S. H. Gyngell. Thorsons, Ltd., England, 1959. 131 pp., illus. $10.00.

Some of the marks of armourers, swordsmiths and gunsmiths of almost every foreign country.

Arms Archives, by H. B. Lockhoven, International Small Arms Publ., Cologne, W. Germany, 1969. Unpaginated but coded. Illus. English and German text, loose-leaf format. Available in 4 series; "A" Handguns, "B" Automatic Weapons, "C" Longarms, "D" Antique Arms. Each series in 4 installments at $10 per installment. Binders for each series $5.50.

A major breakthrough in arms literature. Scaled photographs of guns and their cartridges, fully described. Only 1st installment now available in series "D".

Arms and Armor in Colonial America, 1526-1783, by H. L. Peterson. Crown, New York, reprinted ed., 1964. 350 pp., illus. $3.95.

Well-organized account of arms and equipment used in America's colonization and exploration, through the Revolutionary period.

Arms and Armor Annual, edited by Robert Held. Digest Books, Inc., Northfield, IL, 1973. 320 pp., illus. Paper covers. $9.95. Cloth, $19.95.

Thirty outstanding articles on weaponry by leading arms and armor historians of the world.

Arms and Armour, 9th to 17th Century, by Paul Martin, C. E. Tuttle Co., Rutland, Vt., 1968. 298 pp., well illus. $15.00.

Beautiful illustrations and authoritative text on armor and accessories from the time of Charlemagne to the firearms era.

Arms and Armour of the Western World, by B. Thomas, O. Gamber & H. Schedelmann, McGraw Hill, N.Y.C., 1964. 252 pp., illus. (much in color), $27.50.

Museum quality weapons and armor shown and described in a magnificent book, which gives the association of specimen arms with the men and events of history. Superb photographs in color. Pub. 1963 in German as "Die Schonsten Waffen . . ." price $25.00.

Arms and Equipment of the Civil War, by Jack Coggins, Doubleday & Co., Inc., NY, 1962. 160 pp., $5.95.

Tools of war of the blue and the grey. Infantry, cavalry, artillery, and navy: guide to equipment, clothing, organization, and weapons. Over 500 illus.

Arms Making In the Connecticut Valley, by F. J. Deyrup. George Shumway Publ., York, Pa., 1970. Reprint of the noted work originally publ. in 1948 by Smith College. 290 pp., line maps, $10.00.

A scholarly regional study of the economic development of the small arms industry 1798-1870. With statistical appendices, notes, bibliography.

Arms of the World—1911, ed. by Joseph J. Schroeder, Jr., Digest Books, Inc., Northfield, IL, 1972, 420 pp., profusely illus. $5.95.

Reprint of the 1911 Adolph Frank ALFA 21 catalog, in 4 languages—English, German, French, Spanish.

Author and Subject Index to the American Rifleman Magazine 1961-1970, by W. R. Burrell, Galesburg, MI, 1971. 64 pp. $6.50.

Alphabetical listing by author, title and subject.

The Bannerman Catalogue 1903, Francis Bannerman Sons, New York, N.Y. Reprint released in 1960. 116 pp., well illus., $3.50.

A reprint in facsimile of this dealer's catalog of military goods of all descriptions, including weapons and equipment.

The Bannerman Catalog 1965, Francis Bannerman Sons, Blue Point, N.Y. The 100th anniversary ed., 1966. 264 pp., well illus. $5.00.

Latest dealer catalog of nostalgic interest on military and collector's items of all sorts.

Bannerman Military Goods Catalog, 1907. Benchmark Publ. Co., NY, 260 pp., illus. Paper, $3.95.

Exact reprint of original catalog with thousands of items listed.

A Bibliography of Military Books up to 1642, by Maurice J. D. Cockle. A new reprint of the Holland Press, London, 1965. 320 pp., illus. $15.00.

Describes the important military books from the invention of gunpowder to subject date. A standard reference.

Blades and Barrels, by H. Gordon Frost. Walloon Press, El Paso, TX, 1972. 298 pp., illus. $16.95.

The first full-scale study about man's attempts to combine an edged weapon with a firearm.

British and American Infantry Weapons of World War II, by A. J. Barker. 1st ed., 1969, Arco Publishing Co., New York, N.Y. 76 pp., illus., $3.50.

A British officer's survey that includes numerous specialized weapons, all illustrated and described.

British Military Firearms 1650-1850, by H. L. Blackmore. Arco Publ. Co. Inc., New York, 1962. 296 pp. and 83 plates of photographs, line drawings, appendices and index. $10.00.

This excellent work admirably and authoritatively covers the subject in every detail. Highly recommended.

British Pistols and Guns, 1640-1940, by Ian Glendenning. Arco Publ. Co., NY, 1967. 194 pp., photos and drawings. $7.50.

Historical review of British firearms, with much data and illustration of furniture and decoration of fine weapons.

The British Soldier's Firearm, 1850-1864, by C. H. Roads. Herbert Jenkins, London, 1964. 332 pp., illus. $14.50.

Detailed account of development of British military arms at the acme of the muzzle-loading period. All models in use are covered, as well as ammunition.

The Canadian Gunsmiths 1608-1900, by S. James Gooding. Museum Restoration Service, Canada, 1962. 322 pp., illus. $17.50.

Comprehensive survey of the gunmakers of Canada and the products of their skill, from early settlement to the age of the breech-loader.

The Chi-Com Series, by Granville Rideout, Yankee Publ. Co., Ashburnham, MA, 1971. 246 pp., illus. $12.95.

New definitive reference work on Chinese Communist weapons in Southeast Asia. Limited and numbered ed.

Civil War Collector's Encyclopedia, by Francis A. Lord, Stackpole Books, Harrisburg, PA, 1963, 384 pp., 350 illus. $17.95.

A reference work on Civil War relics, for museums, students, writers, and collectors of Union and Confederate items. Identifies arms, uniforms, accoutrements, ordnance material, currency, postage, etc. Many patent drawings. Lists of manufacturers and vendors, North and South, are given.

Civil War Guns, by Wm. B. Edwards, Stackpole Books, Harrisburg, PA, 1962. 464 pp., over 400 illus. $5.95.

Comprehensive survey of Civil War arms, identification data, procurement procedures, and historical data. Important information on replicas, imitations, and fakes.

The Collecting of Guns, ed. by Jas. E. Serven. Stackpole Books, Harrisburg, PA, 1964. 272 pp., illus. $24.50.

A new and massive compendium of gun lore for serious collectors by recognized experts. Separate chapters cover major categories and aspects of collecting. Over 600 firearms illus. Handsomely designed, deluxe binding in slip case. Reprinted 1966, by Bonanza, no case, $5.95.

Colt Commemorative Firearms, by R. L. Wilson. Chas. Kidwell, Wichita, KS, 1969. 108 pp., $10.00.

A chronological listing and a precise description of all Colt commemoratives from 1961 through 1969.

The Complete Book of the Air Gun, by G. C. Nonte Jr. Stackpole Books, Harrisburg, PA, 1970. 288 pp., illus. $7.95.

From Plinking to Olympic competition, from BB guns to deluxe rifles, pistols, the air shotgun.

The Complete Book of Gun Collecting, by Charles E. Chapel. Coward-McCann, Inc., N.Y.C., 1960. 222 pp., illus. $5.95.

Answers hundreds of questions for the beginner, and is a reference for the advanced collector and student of firearms. It covers hand cannon of the 14th century to arms of the present day.

Confederate Arms, by Wm. A. Albaugh III, and E. N. Simmons. Stackpole Books, Harrisburg, PA, 1957. 278 pp., illus. $3.95.

Contains much heretofore unpublished information on the arms and associated material of the Confederacy.

The Complete Rehabilitation of the Flintlock Rifle and Other Works, by T. B. Tryon. Limbo Library, Taos, NM, 1972. 112 pp., illus. Paper covers. $6.95.

A series of articles which first appeared in various issues of the *American Rifleman* in the 1930s.

Deanes' Manual of the History and Science of Fire-arms, by J. Deane. Standard Publications, Huntington, WV, 1946 facsimile reprint of the rare English original of 1858. 291 pp., three folding plates. $6.00.

A history of firearms, plus design and manufacture of military and sporting arms.

Digest of Patents Relating to Breech-Loading and Magazine Small Arms (1836-1873), by V. D. Stockbridge, WA, 1874. Reprinted 1963 by E. N. Flayderman, Greenwich, Conn. 180 pp., 880 illus. $12.50.

An exhaustive compendium of patent documents on firearms, indexed and classified by breech mechanism types, valuable reference for students and collectors.

Early Firearms of Great Britain and Ireland from the Collection of Clay P. Bedford. The Metropolitan Museum of Art, NY, 1971. 187 pp., illus. $17.50.

Authoritative account of an exceptional body of historic firearms, and a detailed survey of three centuries of gunmaking.

Early Percussion Firearms, by Lewis Winant, Wm. Morrow & Co., Inc., N.Y.C., 1959. 292 pp., illus. $2.98.

A history of early percussion firearms ignition—from Forsyth to Winchester 44-40, from flintlocks of the 18th century to centerfires. Over 230 illus. of firearms, parts, patents, and cartridges—from some of the finest collections here and abroad.

Encyclopedia of Firearms, ed. by H. L. Peterson. E. P. Dutton, N.Y.C., 1964. 367 pp., 100 pp. of illus. incl. color. $14.95.

Fine reference work on firearms, with articles by 45 top authorities covering classes of guns, manufacturers, ammunition, nomenclature, and related topics.

Encyclopedia of Modern Firearms, Vol. 1, compiled and publ. by Bob Brownell, Montezuma, IA, 1959. 1057 pp. plus index, illus. $22.50. Dist. by Bob Brownell, Montezuma, IA 50171.

Massive accumulation of basic information of nearly all modern arms pertaining to "parts and assembly." Replete with arms photographs, exploded drawings, manufacturers' lists of parts, etc.

English, Irish and Scottish Firearms, by A. Merwyn Carey. Arco Publishing Co., Inc., NY, 1967. A reprint. 121 pp., illus. in line and halftone. $6.50.

Out-of-print since 1954, this work covers the subject from the middle of the 16th century to the end of the 19th.

European & American Arms, by Claude Blair, Batsford, London, and Crown Publ., N.Y.C., 1962, 192 pp., 9″x12″. Profusely and magnificently illus. $6.95.

A complete visual encyclopedia on all sorts of arms of Europe and America with over 600 photographs of pieces from nearly all the major collections of Western Europe, America, and Russia, from about 1100 to 1850. A splendid text describes historical and technical developments.

European Armour in the Tower of London, by A. R. Dufty. H. M. Stationery Office, London, England, 1968. 17 pp. text, 164 plates, $12.60.

Pictorial record of almost 400 pieces of armor, helmets, and accoutrements in the famous Tower of London collection.

European Arms & Armour, by Chas. H. Ashdown, Brussel & Brussel, NY, 1967. A reprint, 384 pp., illus. with 42 plates and 450 drawings. $5.95.

Historical survey of body armor up to the era of gunpowder, with some coverage on weapons and early firearms.

Famous Guns from the Smithsonian Collection, by H. W. Bowman. Arco Publ. Co., Inc., NY, 1967. 112 pp., illus. $3.50.

The finest of the "Famous Guns" series.

Famous Guns from the Winchester Collection, by H. W. Bowman. Arco Publ. Co., NYC, 1958 and later. 144 pp., illus. $3.50.

The gems of the hand and shoulder arms in the great collection at New Haven, CT.

Die Faustfeuerwaffen von 1850 bis zur Gegenwart, by Eugene Heer, Akademische D.-u. V., Graz, Austria, 1972. 234 pp. of German texts, 215 pp. of illus. $30.00.

First volume in a series which will cover the history of Swiss firearms from 1800. The handguns issued between 1850 and 1950 are described and illustrated in considerable detail.

Feuerwaffen von 1300 bis 1967, by Hans-Bert Lockhoven. International Small Arms Publ., Cologne, W. Germany, 1969. 96 pp., illus. $6.95.

Review of the principal developments in military small-arms from early times, German text.

Firearms, by Walter Buehr. Crowell Co., N.Y.C., 1967. 186 pp., illus. $5.95.

From gunpowder to guided missile, an illustrated history of firearms for military and sporting uses.

Firearms Blueing and Browning, by R. H. Angier. Stackpole Books, Harrisburg, PA, 151 pp., illus. $5.00.

A useful, concise text on chemical coloring methods for the gunsmith and collector interested in restoration.

Firearms Curiosa, by Lewis Winant, Ray Riling, Philadelphia, PA, 2nd and deluxe reissue 1961, 281 pp., well illus. $5.00.

Reissue publ. by Bonanza Books, N.Y.C., 1965. $2.98.

An important work for those with an interest in odd, distinctive and unusual forms of firearms.

The Firearms Dictionary, by R. A. Steindler. Stackpole Books, Harrisburg, PA, 1970. 256 pp., nearly 200 illus. $7.95.

A super single-source reference to more than 1800 English and Foreign gun-related words, phrases and nomenclature, etc. Highly useful to all armsmen—collectors, shooters, hunters, etc.

Firearms in England in the Fourteenth Century, by T. F. Tout. Geo. Shumway, York, PA, 1958. 58 pp., illus., paper covers. $4.00.

Reprint of a 1911 monograph on the history and manufacture of early British firearms, by a distinguished historian.

Firearm Silencers, by D. B. McLean. Normount Armament Co., Forest Grove, OR, 1968. 123 pp., illus., paperbound. $4.00.

The history, design, and development of silencers for U.S. military firearms.

Firearms, Traps & Tools of the Mountain Men, by Carl P. Russell. A. A. Knopf, NY, 1967. 448 pp., illus. in line drawings. $15.00.

Detailed survey of fur traders' equipment in the early days of the west.

The Fireside Book of Guns, by Larry Koller. Simon & Schuster, N.Y.C., 1959. 284 pp., illus. in artistic photography and full-color plates. $12.95.

On all counts the most beautiful and colorful production of any arms book of our time, this work adequately tells the story of firearms in America—from the first explorers to today's sportsmen.

The Flintlock, Its Origin and Development, by Torsten Lenk; J. T. Hayward, Editor, Holland Press, London, 1964. 192 pp., 134 illus. $6.95.

First English-text version of the 1939 Swedish work termed "the most important book on the subject." Original illus. are reproduced, and a new index and bibliography complete this valuable book.

Forsyth & Co.—Patent Gunmakers, by W. Keith Neal and D. H. L. Back. G. Bell & Sons, London, 1st ed., 1969, 280 pp., well illus. $12.95.

An excellent study of the invention and development of the percussion system by the Rev. Alexander Forsyth in the early 19th century. All Forsyth types are covered, plus a diary of events from 1768 to 1852.

Four Studies on the History of Arms, by Arne Hoff, et al. Tojhusmuseet, Copenhagen, 1964. 145 pp., illus., paperbound. $6.75.

A Danish museum publication containing in English text scholarly monographs on arms topics of historic interest.

French Military Weapons, 1717-1938, by James E. Hicks. N. Flayderman & Co., New Milford, CT, 1964. 281 pp., profusely illus. $9.50.

A valuable reference work, first publ. 1938 as *Notes on French Ordnance,* this rev. ed. covers hand, shoulder, and edged weapons, ammunition and artillery, with history of various systems.

French Pistols and Sporting Guns, by A. N. Kennard. Transatlantic Arts, Inc., Levittown, NY, 1972. 63 pp., illus. $2.95.

Traces the technical evolution of French pistols and sporting guns from matchlock to breechloader.

Gamle Danske Militaervaben, by Th. Moller. Host & Sons, Denmark, 1st reprinting, 1968. 64 pp., well illus. in line. Heavy paper covers. $4.00.

Old Danish military weapons, with Danish and English text, covering weapons from 1771 to 1832, plus accoutrements.

Gas, Air and Spring Guns of the World, by W. H. B. Smith. Stackpole Books, Harrisburg, PA, 1957. 279 pp., well illus. $4.98.

A detailed, well-documented history of the air and gas gun industry throughout the world. It includes ancient and modern arms, and it devotes a chapter to accurate velocity tests of modern arms.

The Gatling Gun, by Paul Wahl & D. R. Toppel. Arco Publ., N.Y.C., 1971. 168 pp., illus. $5.95.

History of the famed rapid-fire weapon used by many of the world's armies and navies from 1861.

German Infantry Weapons, ed. by D. B. McLean. Normount Armament Co., Forest Grove, OR, 1966. 191 pp., illus., paperbound. $3.00.

World War II German weapons described and illustrated, from military intelligence research.

German Infrantry Weapons of World War II, by A. J. Barker. Arco Publ. Co., New York, NY 1969, 76 pp., illus. $3.50.

Historical and statistical data on all types of the subject weapons, ammunition, etc.

German Secret Weapons of World War II, by I. V. Hogg. Arco Pub. Co., NY, 1970. 80 pp., illus. $3.50.

Compact, comprehensive account of Germany's secret weapons, eccentric and brilliant. Includes plans and technical details.

German Weapons-Uniforms-Insignia 1841-1918, by Maj. J. E. Hicks. J. E. Hicks & Son, La Canada, CA, 1958. 158 pp., illus. $6.00.

Originally published in 1937 as *Notes on German Ordnance 1841-1918,* this new edition offers the collector a wealth of information gathered from many authentic sources.

Die Geschichtliche Entwicklung Der Handfeuerwaffen, by M. Thierbach, Akademische Druck, Graz, Austria, 1965. Vol. 1, 590 pp., German text; Vol. II, 36 Plates. $37.00.

The famous German work on history and development of firearms, accessories and ammunition, first published in 1886 in Dresden.

A Glossary of the Construction, Decoration and Use of Arms and Armor in all Countries and in all Times, by Geo. C. Stone, Jack Brussel, NY, 2nd reprint, 1966, 694 pp., illus. $9.95

The outstanding work on its subject, authoritative and accurate in detail. The major portion is on oriental arms.

Great American Guns and Frontier Fighters, by Will Bryant, Grosset & Dunlap, NY, 1961. 160 pp., illus. $3.95.

Popular account of firearms in U.S. history and of the events in which they played a part.

The Great Guns, by H. L. Peterson and Robt. Elman. Grosset & Dunlap, NY, 1972. $14.95.

Basic and general history with 70 full color illustrations and 140 photos of some of the finest guns from American collections. A well written text.

Great Weapons of World War I, by Com. G. Dooly, Walker & Co., NY, 1969, 340 pp., illus. $14.50.

Describes all the important weapons and system developments used during WWI.

The Gun Collector's Handbook of Values, by C. E. Chapel. Coward-McCann, Inc., NY, 1972. 398 pp., illus. $12.50.

10th rev. ed. of the best-known price reference for collectors, with values for 1973-74.

The Gun and its Development, by W. W. Greener. Bonanza Books, NY, 1967. A reprint. 804 pp., profusely illus. $5.95.

A facsimile of the famous 9th edition of 1910. Covers history and development of arms in general with emphasis on shotguns.

Gun Digest Treasury, ed. by J. T. Amber, 4th ed., 1972. Digest Books, Inc. Northfield, IL. 352 pp. illus. Paper, $5.95.

The best from 25 years selected from the annual editions.

The Gun, 1834, by Wm. Greener, with intro. by D. B. McLean. Normount Technical Publ., Forest Grove, OR, 1971. 240 pp., illus. Paper, $4.95.

Reprint of the 1835 British ed. on various small firearms.

Gunmakers of Indiana, by A. W. Lindert. Publ. by the author, Homewood, IL, 1968, 3rd ed. 284 pp., illus. Large format. $15.00.

An extensive and historical treatment, illus. with old photographs and drawings.

Guns, by Dudley Pope. Delacorte Press, N.Y.C., 1965. 256 pp., illus. $9.98.

Concise history of firearms, stressing early museum-quality weapons. Includes small arms as well as artillery, naval, and airborne types. Fine photographs, many in color.

Guns, by F. Wilkinson, Grosset & Dunlap, NY, 1971. 168 pp., $3.95.

From the discovery of gunpowder to the complex weapons of today. Over 100 photos in color.

Guns and Gun Collecting, by De Witt Bailey; et al. Octopus Books, London, Eng., 1972. 128 pp., illus. $5.95

A new look at the world of firearms, including not only the historical aspects but hunting and sporting guns and 19th and 20th century weapons of war. Nearly 180 photos, 78 in full color.

The Guns of Harpers Ferry, by S. E. Brown Jr. Virginia Book Co., Berryville, VA, 1968. 157 pp., illus. $12.50.

Catalog of all known firearms produced at the U.S. armory at Harpers Ferry, 1798-1861, with descriptions, illustrations and a history of the operations there.

Guns of the Old West, by C. E. Chapel. Coward-McCann Inc., N.Y.C., 1961. 306 pp., illus. $6.95.

A definitive book on American arms that opened the frontier and won the West. Shows arms, rare pictures, advertisements, and pertinent associated material.

Guns and Rifles of the World, by Howard L. Blackmore, The Viking Press, NY, 1965. 290 pp. 1042 halftone and line illustrations. $9.98.

One of the finest books to come out of England. Covers firearms from the handgun to air, steam, and electric guns.

Guns Through the Ages, by Geoffrey Boothroyd. Sterling Publ. Co., N.Y.C., 1962, 192 pp., illus. $1.69.

A detailed illustrated history of small arms from the invention of gunpowder to today. Covers ignition methods, proof marks, fakes, ammo, etc. Bibliography.

Guns of the Wild West, by Elsie Hanauer. A. S. Barnes & Co., NY 1973. 112 pp. $12.

History and development of the gun, the early frontiersmen who needed firearms to survive, and the early outlaws who used guns as part of their trade. Nearly 100 pages of full-color illus.

Haandskydevaabens Bedommelse, by Johan F. Stockel. Udgivet Af Tojuhusmuseet, Copenhagen, Denmark, 2nd limited reprint, 1966. Vol. I, 397 pp., plus 6 plates, Vol. II, 1080 pp. illus. Both $35.00.

Printed in Danish but considered by scholars to be the finest and most complete source for the "marks" and "touches" of gunmakers. Both are well illus.

Handbuch Der Waffenkunde, by Wendelin Boeheim. Akademische D.U.V., Graz, Austria, 1966, 694 pp., illus. $14.00.

One of the famous works of 1890—long out-of-print. Now in a new printing, German text. Historical weapons and armor from the Middle Ages through the 18th century.

Handfeuerwaffen, by J. Lugs, Deutscher Militarverlag, Berlin, 1956. 2 Vol., 315 pp., illus. German text, $40.00

Noted reference on small arms and their development in many nations. All types of weapons are listed, described and illustrated, with data on manufacturers.

Die Handfeuerwaffen, by Rudolf Schmidt, Vienna, Austria, 1968, Vol. I, text 225 pp., Vol. II, 76 plates. $20.00.

Reprint of an important 1875 German reference work on military small arms, much prized by knowledgeable collectors. The fine color plates in Vol. II show detailed and exploded views of many longarms and handguns.

Die Handwaffen, by Werner Eckardt and Otto Morawietz. H. G. Schulz, Hamburg, 1957. 265 pp., 15 plates, 175 illus. $10.00.

An important work (in German) on German Service arms from their beginnings through World War II. A symposium on the subject—ancient, obsolete, semi-modern and modern.

Hatcher's Notebook, by Maj. Gen. J. S. Hatcher. Stackpole Books, Harrisburg, Pa., 1952. 2nd ed. with four new chapters, 1957. 629 pp., illus. $11.95.

A dependable source of information for gunsmiths, ballisticians, historians, hunters, and collectors.

Hibbard, Spencer, Bartlett & Co. Catalog. American Reprints, St. Louis, MO, 1969. 92 pp., illus. Paper, $5.00.

Reprint of 1884 catalog on guns, rifles, revolvers, ammo, powder flasks, etc. Descriptions and contemporary prices.

A History of Firearms, by W. Y. Carman. Routledge & Kegan Paul Ltd., London, England, 1955. 207 pp., illus. $4.50.

A concise coverage, from earliest times to 1914, with emphasis on artillery.

A History of Firearms, by H. L. Peterson. Chas. Scribner's Sons, N.Y.C., 1961. 57 pp., profusely illus. $4.95.

From the origin of firearms through each ignition form and improvement to the M-14. Drawings by Daniel D. Feaser.

A History of Shooting, by Jaroslav Lugs, Spring Books, Feltham, England. 1st printing, 1968. 227 pp., well illus., with contemporary drawings and photographs. $4.98.

Historical survey dealing mainly with marksmanship, duelling and exhibition shooting in Europe and America.

A History of Spanish Firearms, by James D. Lavin. Arco Co., NY, 1965. 304 pp., illus. $9.95.

This history, beginning with the recorded appearance of gunpowder in Spain, traces the development of hand firearms through their golden age—the eighteenth century—to the death in 1825 of Isidro Soler. Copious reproductions of short and long arms, list of gun makers and their "marks", a glossary, bibliography and index are included.

A History of Weaponry, by Courtlandt Canby, Hawthorne Books, Inc., NY, 1963, 112 pp., illus. $2.98.

From the caveman's club to the M-14 rifle, from Greek fire to the ICBM.

The History of Weapons of the American Revolution, by Geo. C. Neumann. Harper & Row, NY, 1967, 373 pp., fully illus. $15.00.

Collector's reference covering long arms, handguns, edged and pole weapons used in the Revolutionary War.

Hopkins & Allen Gun Guide and Catalog (ca. 1913). Wagle Publ., Lake Wales, FL, 1972. 32 pp., illus. Paper covers. $3.75.

Facsimile of the original catalog. Shows the firms rifles, shotguns and pistols, and includes prices. Full color cover painting by Dan Smith.

Illustrated British Firearms Patents 1714-1853, comp. and ed. by Stephen V. Grancsay and Merrill Lindsay. Winchester Press. NY, 1969. Unpaginated. $15.00.

Facsimile of patent documents with a bibliography. Limited, numbered ed. of 1000, bound in ¾ leather and marbled boards.

Ironmaker To The Confederacy, by C. B. Dew. Yale Univ. Press, New Haven, 1966. 345 pp., illus. $10.00.

History of Joseph R. Anderson's Tredegar Iron works in Richmond, VA, which produced weapons and military equipment essential to the Confederacy's armed forces.

Japanese Infantry Weapons, ed. by D. B. McLean. Normount Armament Co., Forest Grove, OR, 1966. 241 pp., well illus., paperbound. $3.50.

Survey of World War II Japanese weapons, based on military intelligence research.

Lock, Stock and Barrel, by R. H. McCrory. Publ. by author at Bellmore, NY, 1966. Paper covers, 122 pp., illus. $4.00.

A handy and useful work for the collector or the professional with many helpful procedures shown and described on antique gun repair.

Mauser-Gewehre & Mauser-Patente, by R. H. Korn. Akademische Druck Graz, Austria, 1971. 440 pp. German text, most completely illustrated with copious line drawings, charts, many of them folding plates. $30.00.

Fine reprint of the extremely-rare original. Truly a must for every Mauser buff, it has never been surpassed.

Mauser, Walther & Mannlicher Firearms, by W. H. B. Smith, with an intro. by John T. Amber. Stackpole Books, Harrisburg, PA, 1971. 673 pp., illus. $14.95.

W. H. B. Smith's three classics, now in one convenient volume.

Mexican Military Arms, The Cartridge Period, by James B. Hughes Jr. Deep River Armory, Inc., Houston, TX, 1967. 135 pp., photos and line drawings. $4.50.

An interesting and useful work, in imprinted wrappers, covering the period from 1866 to 1967.

Military Arms of Canada, by Upper Canada Hist. Arms Soc. Museum Restoration Serv., West Hill, Ont., 1963. 43 pp., illus. $1.50.

Booklet cont. 6 authoritative articles on the principal models of Canadian mil. small arms. Gives characteristics of each, makers, quantities produced.

Military Small Arms of the 20th Century, by Ian V. Hogg & John S. Weeks. Digest Books, Inc., Northfield, IL, 1973. 256 pp. Paper covers. $7.95.

Weapons from the world over are meticulously examined in this comprehensive encyclopedia of those military small arms issued since 1900. Over 500 illus.

Miniature Arms, by Merrill Lindsay. Winchester Press, New York, NY, 1970. 111 pp., illus. $5.95.

A concise study of small-scale replicas of firearms and other weapons of collector interest. Fine color photographs.

Modern Breech-Loaders, Sporting and Military, by W. W. Greener, with intro. by D. B. McLean. Normount Tech. Publ., Forest Grove, OR, 1971. 256 pp., illus. Paper covers. $3.50.

Reprint of the 1870 ed. Covers rifles, carbines, and the "new" breech-loading pistols.

Same title, this is a reprint of the 1871 ed. Lujac Publ., Pueblo, CO, 1972. 275 pp., illus. $4.95.

Reprint of original 1870 ed. Covers rifles, carbines, and the "new" breech-loading pistols.

Monographie der K. K. Osterr.-Ung: Blanken und Handfeuer-Waffen, by Anton Dolleczek. Akademische Druck, Graz, Austria, 1970. 197 pp., illus. $10.00.

Facsimile reprint of a standard 1896 German work on military weapons. In German text, illus. with line drawings and color plate of regimental colors.

Montgomery Ward & Co. 1894-1895, reproduction of a 600-page catalog, ed. by Jos. J. Schroeder, Jr., Digest Books, Inc., Northfield, IL, 1970. profusely illus. $4.95.

A nostalgic look at the past, and for the gun enthusiast a look at models and prices prevailing in the late 19th century.

The NRA Collector's Series, Digest Books, Inc., Northfield, IL, 1971, 84 pp. paper covers $2.95.

Reprint of the three predecessors of *American Rifleman* magazine and the first edition of *American Rifleman.*

The NRA Gun Collectors Guide, by staff members of NRA. National Rifle Assn., Washington, D.C., 1972. 256 pp., well illus. $4.50.

A wealth of information on collecting and collectors arms, with 64 major and 41 short articles, selected from the last 18 years of in "The American Rifleman."

Notes on U.S. Ordnance, Vol. II, 1776-1941, by James E. Hicks. Modern Books & Crafts, Greens Farms, Conn., 1971. 252 pp., illus. $8.00.

Updated version of a standard work on development of military weapons used by U.S. forces, from handguns to coast artillery and aerial bombs. This is not to be confused with Hicks 1940 United States Ordnance, referring mainly to Ordnance correspondence as Vol. II.

One Hundred Great Guns, by Merrill Lindsay. Walker & Co., NY, 1967. 379 pp., fine color illus. $9.95.

Deluxe illus. history of firearms, covering all principal types of small arms and their makers. Bibliography.

A super-deluxe edition is available at $75.00.

Ordnance Memoranda No. 22. The Fabrication of Small Arms for the U.S. Service, by Lt. Col. James G. Benton. Benchmark Pub. Co., Glendale, NY, 1970. 229 pp., 35 plates. $9.50.

Reprint of an 1878 War Dept. pub. on U.S. production of military firearms and edged weapons.

An Outline of the History and Development of Hand Firearms, from the Earliest Period to About the End of the Fifteenth Century, by R. C. Clephan [Original ed., 1906]. A reprint in 1946 by Standard Publications, Inc., Huntington, W.Va. 60 pp., illus. $4.00.

A worthy facsimile of a very scarce, concise and scholarly work.

Pageant of the Gun, by Harold L. Peterson. Doubleday & Co., Inc., Garden City, NY, 1967. 352 pp., profusely illus. $3.95.

A storehouse of stories on firearms, their romance and lore, their development and use through 10 centuries. A most satisfying history of firearms chronologically presented.

Remington Arms in American History, by A. Hatch, Rinehart & Co., NY, 1956. 359 pp., illus. $6.50.

Collector's guide with appendix of all Remington arms, ballistics tables, etc.

Remington Catalog [Price List] of 1885, a reprint in facsimile, by The Wyoming Armory, Inc., Cheyenne, Wyo., 1969. 48 pp., well illus., paper covers. $2.50.

All rifles, handguns, cane gun, sights, cartridges, shotguns, accessories, etc. A priced catalog.

The Remington Historical Treasury of American Guns, by Harold L. Peterson. Thomas Nelson & Sons, N.Y.C., 1966. 199 pp., illus. $2.95.

A historical saga woven into first-rate Americana through the facts and details of the Remington firm and their products.

Rifled Infantry Arms, by J. Schon; trans. by Capt. J. Gorgas, USA. Dresden, 1855; facsimile reprint by W. E. Meuse, Schuylersville, NY, 1965. 54 pp., illus. $2.50.

Reprint of classic essay on European military small arms of the mid-19th century. Paper covers.

Russian Infranty Weapons of World War II, by A. J. Barker and John Walter, Arco Publ. Co., NY, 1971. 80 pp., $3.50.

History and development of World War II infantry weapons used by the Red Army. Each weapon is fully described and illus.

Schuyler, Hartley & Graham Catalog, publ. by Norm Flayderman, Greenwich, Conn., 1961. 176 pp., illus. $9.50.

A reprint of a rare 1864 catalog of firearms, military goods, uniforms, etc. An extensive source of information for Civil War collectors.

Sears, Roebuck & Co. Catalogue No. 117, J. J. Schroeder, ed. A reprint of the 1908 work. Digest Books, Inc., Northfield, Ill., 1969, profusely illus., paper covers. $3.95.

This reprint of a famous catalog brings to all arms collectors a treasured replica of the collectibles and prices of yesteryear.

Second World War Combat Weapons, by Hoffschmidt & Tantum. WE, Inc., Old Greenwich, CT, 1968. 212 pp., illus. $7.95.

German weapons, vehicles, and projectiles illustrated and described. First of a 7-vol. series.

Secret Weapons of the Third Reich, by L. E. Simon, WE, Inc., Old Greenwich, CT, 1971. 248 pp., illus. $8.95.

Review of German World War II military research and its products.

Shooter's Bible Gun Trader's Guide, by Paul Wahl. Stoeger Arms Corp., So. Hackensack, NJ, 1973. 254 pp., 6th rev. ed. Paper covers. $4.95.

Fully illus. guide to identification of modern firearms, plus current market values.

Silencers. Paladin Press, Boulder, CO, 1971. 205 pp., illus. $9.95.

Reprint of Frankford Arsenal Report R-1896. The functional and physical details on foreign and domestic silencers, including patent drawings, engineering data, manufacture, etc.

Silencers, Snipers & Assassins, by J. David Truby, Paladin Press, Boulder, CO, 1972. 209 pp., illus. $15.95.

Traces development of silencers from their invention by Hiram Maxim in 1908 to American snipers' use during the Korean conflict.

Small Arms, by Frederick Wilkinson, Hawthorne Books, Inc., New York, 1966. 256 pp., illus. $4.95.

A history of small firearms, techniques of the gunsmith, equipment used by combatants, sportsmen and hunters.

Small Arms and Ammunition in the United States Service, 1776-1865, by B. R. Lewis. Smithsonian Inst., Washington, D.C., 1968. 338 pp. plus 52 plates. $12.50.

2nd printing of a distinguished work for historians and collectors. A limited number of deluxe, signed and numbered copies (1st reprinting 1960) are available in full leather and gilt top at $25.

Small Arms Identification and Operation Guide—Eurasian Communist Countries, by Harold E. Johnson, Inco., 1972. 218 pp., illus. Paper covers. $4.00.

Reprint of 1970 U.S. Army manual FSTC-CW-07-03-70.

Small Arms Lexicon and Concise Encyclopedia, by Chester Mueller and John Olson. Stoeger Arms, So. Hackensack, NJ, 1968. 312 pp., 500 illus. $14.95.

Definitions, explanations, and references on antiques, optics, ballistics, etc., from A to Z. Over 3,000 entries plus appendix.

Small Arms of the Sea Services, by Robt. H. Rankin. N. Flayderman & Co., New Milford, CT, 1972. 227 pp., illus. $14.50.

Encyclopedic reference to small arms of the U.S. Navy, Marines and Coast Guard. Covers edged weapons, handguns, long arms and others, from the beginnings.

Small Arms of the World, by W. H. B. Smith and J. E. Smith. 9th ed., 1969. Stackpole Books, Harrisburg, PA. 786 pp., profusely illus. $17.95.

A most popular firearms classic for easy reference. Covers the small arms of 42 countries, clearly showing operational principles. A timeless volume of proven worth.

Spanish Military Weapons in Colonial America, 1700-1821, by S. B. Brinckerhoff & P. A. Chamberlain. Stackpole Books, Harrisburg, PA, 1972. 160 pp., illus. $14.95.

Spanish arms and armaments described and illustrated in 274 photographic plates. Includes firearms, accoutrements, swords, polearms and cannon.

Springfield Armory, Pointless Sacrifice, by C. L. Dvarecka. Prolitho Pub., Ludlow, Mass., 1968. 177 pp., illus. Paper covers. $1.00.

Story of the armory's closing; contains names, particulars and the quantities made of Springfield arms.

Stevens Pistols and Pocket Rifles, by K. L. Cope, Museum Restoration Service, Ottawa, Can., 1971. 104 pp. $8.50.

All are shown, identified, detailed, variations, listings of dates, etc.

Stoeger's Catalog & Handbook: New York World's Fair 1939 Jubilee Issue, Stoeger Arms, NY, 1970. 512 pp., illus. Paper, $4.95.

Reprint describing pre-W.W. II sporting arms.

Superimposed Load Firearms 1360-1860, by D. R. Baxter. Privately printed for the author in Hong Kong, 1966. $22.00. Foreword by Keith Neal. Ltd. ed., 500 copies only.

Excellently illustrated with photographs, diagrams, figures and patent drawings. Covers over-under arms of all countries, and a list of gunmakers and inventors is included.

Technical Dictionary for Weapon Enthusiasts, Shooters and Hunters, by Gustav Sybertz. Publ. by J. Neumann-Neudamm, 3508 Melsungen, W. Germany, 1969, 164 pp., semi-soft covers. $7.50.

A German-English and English-German dictionary for the sportsman. An excellent handy work.

Treasury of the Gun, by H. L. Peterson, Crown Publishing Co.'s reprint, NYC, 1965. 252 pp. profusely illus., some in color. $7.95.

A beautiful production, presenting a new high in authoritative text. Virtually every significant type of firearm of the past 650 years is shown.

A Treatise on Ancient Armour and Weapons, by F. Grose, Benchmark Publ., Glendale, NY, 1970. Irreg. pagination, illus. $12.50.

Reprint of a 1786 monograph from the collection in the Tower of London and other sites.

U.S. Cartridge Co. Collection of Firearms, WE, Inc., Old Greenwich, CT., 1970. 142 pp., illus. $6.00.

Describes each arm in detail as to manufacture, action, period of use, function, markings, patents, makers, etc.

U.S. Firearms: The First Century, 1776-1875, by D. F. Butler. Winchester Press, NY, 1971. 320 pp., illus. $15.00.

A rich mine of carefully researched information and data on American firearms of this period. Illustrated with photos, schematics and historical documents.

U.S. Martial and Collectors Arms, by D. Verlag. Military Arms Research Service, San Jose, CA, 1971. 83 pp. Paper covers. $2.50.

Complete listing of U.S. arms inspectors: names, initials used, types of guns inspected circa 1790s through 1964. Detailed tabulations of guns bought by U.S.; quantities; serial number ranges; contractors.

U.S. Military Firearms, 1776-1956, by Maj. Jas. E. Hicks. J. E. Hicks & Son. La Canada, Calif., 216 pp., incl. 88 pages of fine plates. $12.50.

Covering 180 years of America's hand and shoulder weapons. The most authoritative book on this subject. Packed with official data.

U.S. Military Small Arms 1816-1865, by R. M. Reilly. The Eagle Press, Inc., Baton Rouge, La., 1970, 275 pp., illus. $22.50.

Describes and superbly illustrates every known type of primary and secondary martial firearm of the period 1816-1865. Limited, numbered ed.

U.S. Weapons Development 1920-25. An abridged reprint from official sources, this Section 1 covering rifles, pistols and some miscellaneous items. Design Publ., Inc. Hyattsville, Md. [circa 1968]. 57 pp., illus., paper covers. $5.00.

Dependable material for the collector and shooter.

A Universal Military Dictionary, by Captain George Smith. The rare original book was published at London in 1779. This facsimile reprint was released in 1969 by Museum Restoration Service, Ottawa, Ontario, Can. 336 pp., 16 fold-out plates. $27.50.

A most useful reference. Offered only in a numbered, limited issue of 700 copies.

Weapons of the American Revolution, and Accoutrements, by Warren Moore. Funk & Wagnalls, NY, 1967. 225 pp., fine illus. $10.00.

Revolutionary era shoulder arms, pistols, edged weapons, and equipment are described and shown in fine drawings and photographs, some in color.

Weapons of the British Soldier, by Col. H. C. B. Rogers. Seeley Service & Co., London, 1960. 259 pp., illus. in line and halftone plus full color frontis. $8.75.

The story of weapons used by the British soldier throughout the ages and the many developments in personal arms during the course of history.

The Whitney Firearms, by Claud Fuller. Standard Publications, Huntington, W. Va., 1946. 334 pp., many plates and drawings. $12.50.

An authoritative history of all Whitney arms and their maker. Highly recommended. An exclusive with Ray Riling Arms Book Co.

The World of Guns, by Richard Akehurst. Crown Publ., NY, 1972. 127 pp., illus. $3.95.

Many full color plates tell the story of guns from the first simple handguns: guns in warfare, sporting guns, rifles, the American West, duelling pistols, etc.

Handguns

American, British & Continental Pepperbox Firearms, by Jack Dunlap. H. J. Dunlap, Los Altos, CA, 1964. 279 pp., 665 illus. $15.00.

Comprehensive history of production pepperpots from early 18th cent. through the cartridge pepperbox. Variations are covered, with much data of value to the collector.

The American Percussion Revolver, by F. M. Sellers and Sam E. Smith. Museum Restoration Service, Ottawa, Canada, 1970. 200 pp., illus. $15.00.

All inclusive from 1826 to 1870. Over 200 illus., with profuse coverage on lesser-known arms.

Antique Pistols, by S. G. Alexander, illus. by Ronald Paton. Arco Publ. Co., New York, 1963. 56 pp., 12 color plates. $15.00.

The large 8-color plates show 14 examples of the pistol-maker's art in England and U.S.A., 1690-1900. Commentary on each by a knowledgeable English collector.

Arms Collection of Colonel Colt, by R. L. Wilson. Herb Glass, Bullville, N.Y., 1964. 132 pp., 73 illus. Lim. deluxe ed., $16.50; trade ed., $6.50.

Samuel Colt's personal collection is well-described and photographed, plus new technical data on Colt's arms and life. 51 Colt guns and other revolving U.S. and European arms are included.

Artistry in Arms. The R. W. Norton Gallery, Shreveport, LA., 1970. 42 pp., illus. Paper, $2.50.

Automatic Firearm Pistols, by Elmer Swanson, Wesmore Book Co., Weehawken, NJ. 1st (and only) ed. 1955, 210 pp., well illus. $15.00.

A veritable catalog exclusively on automatic handguns for collectors, with many line drawings and descriptions, plus then-market market values of each.

Automatic Pistols, by H. B. C. Pollard, WE Inc., Old Greenwich, CT, 1966. 110 pp., illus. $5.95.

A facsimile reprint of the scarce 1920 original. Covers historical development of military and other automatics, shooting, care, etc.

The Book of Colt Firearms, by R. Q. Sutherland and R. L. Wilson. Privately printed, Kansas City, Mo., 1971. 604 pp. 9x12", profusely illus. $50.00.

This exhaustive large work, highly informative and scholarly, contains 40 color plates showing 420 Colt firearms, plus 1258 black and white photographs.

Book of Pistols & Revolvers, by W. H. B. Smith. Stackpole Books, Harrisburg, PA, 1968. 758 pp., profusely illus. $6.00.

Rev. and enlarged, this encyclopedic reference, first publ. in 1946, continues to be the best on its subject.

Browning Hi-Power Pistols, Normount Armament Co., Forest Grove, OR, 1968. 48 pp., illus., paperbound. $1.50.

A handbook on all models of Browning Hi-Power Pistols, covering their use, maintenance and repair.

Collector's Guide to American Cartridge Handguns, by Dewitt E. Sell. Stackpole Books, Harrisburg, PA, 1963, 234 pp., illus. $3.98.

Catalogs the important U.S. makers in its field, with histories of the firms and their production models. Photos, descriptions and features of many older and current handguns are included.

Collector's Guide to Luger Values 1972-73 Edition, by Michael Reese. Pelican Pub. Co., Gretna, LA, 1972. 10 pp., paper covers. $1.00.

Collector's guide to top prices.

Colt Commemorative Firearms, by R. L. Wilson. Charles Kidwell, Wichita, Kans., 1969. Unpaginated, well illus., paper covers. $5.95. In hard deluxe covers, limited issue of 1000 copies, each numbered. $10.00.

Description and fine color photographs of commemorative handguns issued by the Colt company, 1961-1969, all replicas of famous earlier models.

Colt Firearms from 1836, by James E. Serven. New 7th ed. Foundation Press, La Habra, CA, 1973. 398 pp., illus. $19.95.

Excellent survey of the Colt company and its products. Updated with new SAA production chart and commemorative list.

Sam Colt: Genius, by Robt. F. Hudson, American Archieves Publ. Co., Topsfield, MA, 1971. 160 pp., illus. Plastic spiral bound. $6.50.

Historical review of Colt's inventions, including facsimiles of patent papers and other Colt information.

Sam Colt and His Gun, by Gertrude H. Winders. John Day Co., NY, ca. 1959. 159 pp., illus. $4.50.

Concise biography of the "inventor" of the revolver.

Colt Tips, by E. Dixon Larson. Pioneer Press, Union City, TN, 1972. 140 pp., illus. Paper covers. $3.95.

Comprehensive, discriminating facts about Colt models from 1836 to 1898.

Colt's Variations of the Old Model Pocket Pistol, 1848 to 1872, by P. L. Shumaker. Borden Publishing Co., Alhambra, CA 1966, a reprint of the 1957 edition. 150 pp., illus. $6.00.

A useful tool for the Colt specialist and a welcome return of a popular source of information that had been long out-of-print.

Samuel Colt's New Model Pocket Pistols, by S. G. Keogh. Priv. publ., 1964. 31 pp., 20 illus., paperbound. $3.00.

"The story of the 1855 Root model revolver," with detailed classification data and descriptions. Well illus.

Combat Shooting for Police, by Paul B. Weston. Charles C. Thomas, Springfield, IL, 1967. A reprint. 194 pp., illus. $10.00.

First publ. in 1960 this popular self-teaching manual gives basic concepts of defensive fire in every position.

Confederate Handguns, by Wm. A. Albaugh III. Hugh Benet Jr., and Edw. N. Simmons. Geo. Shumway, York, PA, 1963. 272 pp., 125 illus. $5.95.

Every known true Confederate pistol and revolver is described and illus., with the story of its maker and procurement by the C.S.A. Much new information includes listing of C. W. makers and dealers, information on replicas and fakes. Indispensable to the collector and student of these arms and their period.

The Encyclopedia of the Third Reich, Book 1, by R. B. Marvin. Universal Research, Inc., Fort Lauderdale, Fla., 1969, from offset typewritten copy. 37 pp., very clear and sharp illustrations, paper covers. $4.00.

This volume considers only handguns, but is a concise collector's guide to the main types of W.W. II German pistols and revolvers.

English Pistols & Revolvers, by J. N. George. Arco Publ. Co., Inc., N.Y.C., 1962, 256 pp., 28 plates, $6.50.

The 2nd reprinting of a notable work first publ. in 1938. Treats of the historical development and design of English hand firearms from the 17th cent. to the present. A much better book than the former reprint, particularly as to clarity of the tipped-in plates.

European Hand Firearms of the 16th, 17th, and 18th Centuries, by H. J. Jackson and C. E. Whitlaw. Bramhall House, New York, NY. A reprint of the noted original. 108 pp., fine photographic plates. $5.95.

A work for scholars and collectors, including a list of arms makers. Not without error.

The Evolution of the Colt, by R. L. Wilson, R. Q. Sutherland, Kansas City, MO, 1967. 54 pp., illus. $3.00.

Pictures the fine Colt arms of the publisher from percussion to cartridge. Includes a Colt bibliography.

Die Faustfeuerwaffen von 1850 bis zur Gegenwart, by Eugen Heer. Graz, Austria, 1971. 457 pp., illus. $30.

Historical treatment of Swiss military pistols and revolvers of the last half of the 19th century. German text.

'51 Colt Navies, by N. L. Swayze. Gun Hill Publ. Co., Yazoo City, MS, 1967. 243 pp., well illus. $15.00.

The first major effort devoting its entire space to the 1851 Colt Navy revolver. There are 198 photos of models, sub-models, variations, parts, markings, documentary material, etc. Fully indexed.

Flintlock Pistols, by F. Wilkinson. Stackpole Books, Harrisburg, PA, 1968. 75 pp., illus. $4.95.

Illustrated reference guide by a British authority, covering 17th-19th century flintlock pistols.

Georgian Pistols; The Art and Craft of the Flintlock Pistol, 1715-1840, by Norman Dixon, Geo. Shumway, York, PA, 1971. 184 pp., illus. $14.00.

The art of the Georgian gunmaker, describing the evolution of the holster pistol and the duelling pistol, with the parallel changes in style of the turn-off pistol.

German Pistols and Holsters 1934 to 1945, by R. D. Whittington III. Brownlee Books, College Station, Tex., 1969. 1st ed., limited to 2000 numbered copies, 223 pp., well illus., in halftone. $15.00.

A manual for collectors on subject items issued to the military, police and NSDAP. Covers all models of various designs, including those of foreign manufacture.

German Pistols and Revolvers 1871-1945, by Ian V. Hogg, Stackpole Books, Harrisburg, PA, 1971. 160 pp. $12.95.

Over 160 photos and drawings showing each weapon, plus exploded views of parts, including markings, firms, patents, mfg. codes, etc.

The Handbook of Handgunning, by Paul B. Weston. Crown Publ., NYC, 1968. 138 pp., illus. with photos. $4.95.

"New concepts in pistol and revolver shooting," by a noted firearms instructor and writer.

Handbuch der Faustfeuerwaffen, by Gerhard Bock and W. Weigel. J. Neumann-Neudamm, Melsungen, Germany, 1968. 4th and latest ed., 724 pp., including index. Profusely illus. $21.00.

A truly encyclopedic work in German text on every aspect of handguns. Highly recommended for those who read German.

The Handgun, by Geoffrey Boothroyd. Crown Publishers, Inc., New York, NY, 1970. 564 pp., profusely illus., plus copious index. $19.95.

A massive and impressive work, excellently covering the subject from matchlocks to present-day automatics. Many anecdotes, much comment and pertinent data, including ammunition, etc.

Handguns Americana, by De Witt Sell. Borden Publ. Co., Alhambra, CA, 1972. 160 pp., illus. $8.50.

The pageantry of American enterprise in providing handguns suitable for both civilian needs and military purposes.

A History of the Colt Revolver, by C. T. Haven and F. A. Belden, Bonanza Books, NY, 1967. A reprint. 711 pages, large format, profusely illus. in line and halftone. $8.95.

A great and massive work, including details on other Colt arms from 1836 to 1940. A must for every Colt collector.

Home Gunsmithing the Colt Single Action Revolvers, by Loren W. Smith, Ray Riling Arms Books Co., Phila., PA, 1971. 119 pp., illus. $7.95.

Detailed information on the operation and servicing of this famous and historic handgun.

The Identification and Analysis of Luger Proof Marks, by Robt. B. Marvin. R. B. Marvin, Jasper, FL, 1972. 88 pp., illus. Paper covers. $7.50.

Shows Luger pistol markings and their use in identifying the type of pistol. Complete cross index.

The Identification and Registration of Firearms, by Vaclav "Jack" Krcma, C. C. Thomas, Springfield, IL, 1971. 173 pp., illus. $17.50.

Analysis of problems and improved techniques of recording firearms data; many rare handguns illus.

Japanese Hand Guns, by F. E. Leithe, Borden Publ. Co., Alhambra, CA, 1968. Unpaginated, well illus. $8.50.

Identification guide, covering models produced since the late 19th century. Brief text material gives history, descriptions, and markings.

Japanese Military Handguns and Holsters 1893-1945, by John C. Van Lund. J. C. Van Lund, Donelson, TN, 1972. 467 pp., illus. $15.

A help in identifying Japanese handguns and holsters. Gives variations, serial ranges, and production totals. Limited ed. Signed by the author.

L'Aristocratie Du Pistolet (Handgun Aristocracy), by Raymond Caranta & Pierre Cantegrit. Balland, Paris, France, 1971. 357 pp., illus. $25.00.

Covers the most glamorous handguns made during the industrial period, 1847 to date, with references to the men who designed or used them. French text.

Law Enforcement Handgun Digest, by Dean Grennell and Mason Williams. Digest Books, Inc., Northfield, IL, 1972. 320 pp., illus. Paper covers. $5.95.

Written especially for law enforcement officers and handgun-enthusiasts. From selection of weapon to grips, ammo, training, etc.

The Luger Pistol (Pistole Parabellum), by F. A. Datig. Borden Publ. Co., Alhambra, CA, 1962. 328 pp., well illus. $8.50.

An enlarged, rev. ed. of an important reference on the arm, its history and development from 1893 to 1945.

Lugers at Random, by Charles Kenyon, Jr. Handgun Press, Chicago, IL. 1st ed., 1970. 416 pp., profusely illus. $15.00.

An impressive large side-opening book carrying throughout alternate facing-pages of descriptive text and clear photographs. A new boon to the Luger collector and/or shooter.

Lugers Unlimited, by F. G. Tilton, World-Wide Gun Reports, Inc., Aledo, IL, 1965. 49 pp., illus. Paper covers. $2.00.

An excellent monograph about one of the most controversial pistols since the invention of hand firearms.

Manhattan Firearms, by Waldo E. Nutter, Stackpole Books, Harrisburg, PA, 1958. 250 pp., illus., in halftone. $7.95.

Complete history of the Manhattan Firearms Mfg. Co., and its products. Excellent specialized reference.

Mauser Pocket Pistols 1910-1946, by Roy G. Pender, Collectors Press, Houston, TX, 1971. 307 pp. $14.50.

Comprehensive work covering over 100 variations, including factory boxes and manuals. Over 300 photos. Limited, numbered ed.

The Mauser Self-Loading Pistol, by Belford & Dunlap. Borden Publ. Co., Alhambra, CA. Over 200 pp., 300 illus., large format. $12.50.

The long-awaited book on the "Broom Handles," covering their inception in 1894 to the end of production. Complete and in detail: pocket pistols, Chinese and Spanish copies, etc.

Military Pistols and Revolvers, by I. V. Hogg. Arco Pub. Co., NY, 1970. 80 pp., illus. $3.50.

The handguns of the two World Wars shown in halftone illus., with brief historical and descriptive text.

The Modern Handgun, by Robert Hertzberg. Arco Publ. Co., New York, NY, 1965. 112 pp., well illus. $3.50.

Pistols and revolvers of all types are traced from their beginnings. Data on modern marksmanship included.

The NRA Firearms Assembly Guidebook to Handguns. National Rifle Assn., Wash., D.C., 1973, 206 pp. Paper covers. $4.

Illus. articles on the takedown of 101 pistol and revolver models.

Simeon North: First Official Pistol Maker of the United States, by S. North and R. North, Rutgers Book Center, Highland Park, NJ, 1972. 207 pp., illus. $7.95.

Exact reprint of the original. Includes chapters on New England pioneer manufacturers and on various arms.

The "Parabellum" Automatic Pistol, the English version of the official DWM handbook on Luger pistols. Normount Armament Co., Forest Grove, OR, 1968. 42 pp., illus. Paper wrappers. $1.25.

A user's handbook, a reference work for collectors. A reprint of the original detailed instructions on use, disassembly and maintenance. Includes three folding plates.

The Peacemaker and Its Rivals, by John E. Parsons. Morrow, NYC, 1950. 140 pp., illustrated. Appendix, bibliography, and index. $7.50.

Detailed history and development of the Single Action Army Colt, with an over-all study of the six-shooter's significance in American history.

Percussion Revolvers of the United States, by R. Thalheimer. Von Hoffman Press, St. Louis, MO, 1970. 224 pp., illus, $7.95.

Reference work on U.S. and Confederate percussion revolvers, plus a history of firearms from the hand-cannon to percussion revolvers.

Pistolen Atlas, by Karl R. Pawlas, Nuremberg, Germany, 1970. Arranged alphabetically by maker and model in loose-leaf binding. Each vol. $10.00.

Carefully planned and researched for the "automatic arms buff," shooter and collector, depicts hundreds of auto. pistols of all nations and of all calibers with excellent illus. and descriptive text in English, French, German and Spanish. 13 volumes projected, of which vols. 1, 2, 3, 5, 6, 7 and 8 are now ready.

Pistols of the World, by Claude Blair, Viking Press, NYC, 1968. 206 pp., plus plates, $9.98.

Authoritative review of handguns since the 16th century, with chapters on major types, manufacture, and decoration. Fine photographic illustrations.

Pistols, Revolvers, and Ammunition, by M. H. Josserand and J. Stevenson, Crown Publ. Co., NY, 1972. 341 pp., illus. $7.50.

Basic information classifying the pistol, revolver, ammunition, ballistics and rules of safety.

Pistol and Revolver Guide, by George Nonte. Stoeger Arms Corp. So. Hackensack, NJ, 1967. 192 pp., well illus. Paper wrappers. $3.95.

A history of the handgun, its selection, use and care, with a glossary and trade directory.

The Rampant Colt, by R. L. Wilson. Thomas Haas, Spencer, Ind., 1969. 107 pp., well illus. $10.00.

Study of Samuel Colt's coat-of-arms and the rampant colt figure used on Colt firearms and in advertising.

Report of Board on Tests of Revolvers and Automatic Pistols. From *The Annual Report* of the Chief of Ordnance, 1907. Reprinted by J. C. Tillinghast, Marlow, NH, 1969. 34 pp., 7 plates, paper covers. $3.00.

A comparison of handguns, including Luger, Savage, Colt, Webley-Fosbery and other makes.

The Revolver, 1818-1865, by Taylerson, Andrews & Frith. Crown Publ., NYC, 1968. 360 pp., illus. $7.50.

Noted British work on early revolving arms and the principal makers, giving production data and serial numbers on many models.

The Revolver, 1865-1888, by A. W. F. Taylerson. Crown Publ., NYC, 1966. 292 pp., illus. $3.49.

Detailed study of 19th-century British and U.S. revolvers, by types and makers, based on study of patent records.

The Revolver 1889-1914, by A. W. F. Taylerson. Crown Pub., NY, 1971. 324 pp., illus. $7.50.

The concluding volume of this definitive work deals with Continental arms, American rimfire and centerfire, British centerfire, and obsolescent arms in use.

The Revolver, Its Description, Management, and Use, by P. E. Dove. Arms and Armour Press, London, 1968. 57 pp., 6 engravings, stiff paper wrappers. $3.75.

A facsimile reprint of a rare classic, dealing principally with the Adams revolver compared to the qualities of the Colt.

Revolving Arms, by A. W. F. Taylerson, Walker and Co., New York, 1967. 123 pp., illus. $8.50.

A detailed history of mechanically-rotated cylinder firearms in Europe and the U.S. Primarily on handguns, but other types of revolving guns are included.

Russian Pistols in the 17th Century, by L. Tarassuk. Geo. Shumway, York, Pa., 1968. 35 pp. plus plates. $4.00.

Monograph on museum quality Russian handguns of the 17th century. Fine, detailed photographs.

Saga of the Colt Six-Shooter, and the famous men who used it, by G. E. Virgines. Frederick Fell Co., New York, NY, 1969. 220 pp., well illus. $7.95.

History of the Colt Single-Action Army revolver since 1873, with much information of interest to collectors and shooters.

Savage Automatic Pistols, by James R. Carr, Publ. by the author, St. Charles, Ill., 1967. A reprint. 129 pp., illus. with numerous photos. $6.50.

Collector's guide to Savage pistols, models 1907-1922, with features, production data, and pictures of each. A reprint of the circa 1912 Savage promotional instructive booklet titled *It Banishes Fear* is recommended to accompany the above. Paper wrappers, 32 pp. $1.50.

Sixguns by Keith, by Elmer Keith. Stackpole Co., Harrisburg, PA, 1968 (reprint of 1961 edition). 335 pp., illus. $4.95.

Long a popular reference on handguns, this work covers all aspects, whether for the shooter, collector or other enthusiasts.

Smith and Wesson 1857-1945, by Robert J. Neal and Roy J. Jenks. A. S. Barnes and Co., Inc., NYC, 1966. 500 pp., illus. with over 300 photos and 90 radiographs. $25.00.

A long-needed book, especially for knowledgeable enthusiasts and collectors. Covers an investigation of the series of handguns produced by the Smith and Wesson Company.

Smith and Wesson Catalog of 1901, a reprint facsimile by The Wyoming Armory, Inc., Cheyenne, WY, 1969. 72 pp., well illus., paper covers. $2.25.

All models, engraving, parts and break-down lists, etc.

Southern Derringers of the Mississippi Valley, by Turner Kirkland. Pioneer Press, Tenn., 1971. 80 pp., illus., paper covers. $2.00.

A guide for the collector, and a much-needed study.

The Story of Allen and Wheelock Firearms, by H. H. Thomas. C. J. Krehbiel, Cincinnati, OH, 1965. 125 pp., illus. $6.50.

Brief history of the Allen & Wheelock guns produced in mid-19th century, and their maker. Well illus. with descriptions of specimens.

The Story of Colt's Revolver, by Wm. B. Edwards, Castle Books, NY, 1971. 470 pp. $9.98.

Biography of Samuel Colt and his invention. Hundreds of photos, diagrams, patents and appendix of original advertisements.

System Mauser, a Pictorial History of the Model 1896 Self-Loading Pistol, by J. W. Breathed, Jr., and J. J. Schroeder, Jr. Handgun Press, Chicago, IL, 1967. 273 pp., well illus. Hardbound. $12.50.

10 Shots Quick, by Daniel K. Stern. Globe Printing Co., San Jose, CA, 1967. 153 pp., photos. $8.50.

History of Savage-made automatic pistols, models of 1903-1917, with descriptive data for collectors.

The 36 Calibers of the Colt Single Action Army, by David M. Brown. Publ. by the author at Albuquerque, NM, new reprint 1971. 222 pp., well illus. $15.00.

Edited by Bev Mann of *Guns Magazine*. This is an unusual approach to the many details of the Colt S.A. Army revolver. Halftone and line drawings of the same models make this of especial interest.

U.S. Martial and Semi-Martial Single-Shot Pistols, by C. E. Chapel, Coward-McCann Inc., NYC, 1962. 352 pp., over 150 illus. $7.50.

Describes in detail all single shot martial pistols used by the US armed forces and by military units of the states. A definitive guide.

United States Single Shot Martial Pistols, by C. W. Sawyer, WE, Inc., Old Greenwich, CT, 1971. 101 pp., illus. $5.00.

History of pistols used by the U.S. Armed Services 1776-1871.

U.S. Test Trials 1900 Luger, by Michael Reese II. Coventry Publ. Co., Gretna, LA, 1970. illus. $7.00.

For the Luger Pistol collector.

Use and Maintenance of the Browning "Hi-Power" Pistol, (No. 2 MK 1 and Commercial Models), by D. B. McLean. Normount Armament Co., Forest Grove, OR, 1966. 48 pp., illus., paperbound. $1.50.

Covers the use, maintenance, and repair of various Browning 9mm parabellum pistols.

The Webley Story, by Wm. C. Dowell, Skyrac Press, Leeds, Eng. 337 pp., profusely illus. $21.00.

Detailed study of Webley pistols and revolvers, covering over 250 specimens. This important reference also gives detailed listing of English small arms cartridge patents through 1880.

The Webley-Fosbery Automatic Revolver. A reprint of the original undated booklet pupl. by the British makers. Deep River Armory, Houston, TX, 1968. 16 pp., illus., paper. $3.00.

An instruction manual, parts list and sales brochure on this scarce military handgun.

Long Guns

The American Shotgun, by David F. Butler. Winchester Press, NY, 1973. 256 pp. $15.

Authoritative and profusely illus. Traces the entire evolution of the American shotgun and modern American shotshells.

Automatic and Repeating Shotguns, by R. Arnold. Barnes & Co., N.Y.C., 1960. 173 pp., illus. $2.95.

Their history and development, with expert professional advice on choosing a gun for clay target shooting, game shooting, etc.

Ballard Rifles in the H. J. Nunnemacher Coll., by Eldon G. Wolff. Milwaukee Public Museum, Milwaukee, Wisc., 2nd ed. 1961. Paper, 77 p. plus 4 pp. of charts and 27 plates. $2.50.

A thoroughly authoritative work on all phases of the famous rifles, their parts, patent and manufacturing history.

Basic Documents on U.S. Martial Arms, commentary by Col. B. R. Lewis, reissue by Ray Riling, Phila., Pa., 1956 and 1960.

Rifle Musket Model 1855. The first issue rifle of musket caliber, a muzzleloader equipped with the Maynard Primer, 32 pp. $2.50.

Rifle Musket Model 1863. The Typical Union muzzleloader of the Civil War, 26 pp. $1.75.

Breech-Loading Rifle Musket Model 1866. The first of our 50 caliber breech-loading rifles, 12 pp. $1.75.

Remington Navy Rifle Model 1870. A commercial type breechloader made at Springfield, 16 pp. $1.75.

Lee Straight Pull Navy Rifle Model 1895. A magazine cartridge arm of 6mm caliber. 23 pp. $3.00.

Breech-Loading Rifle Musket Model 1868. The first 50-70 designed as such. 20 pp. $1.75.

Peabody Breech-Loading Arms (five models)—27 pp. $2.75.

Ward-Burton Rifle Musket 1871—16 pp. $2.50.

Springfield Rifle, Carbine & Army Revolvers (cal. 45) model 1873 including Colt and Smith & Wesson hand arms. 52 pp. $3.00.

U.S. Magazine Rifle and Carbine (cal. 30) Model 1892 (the Krag Rifle) 36 pp. $2.50.

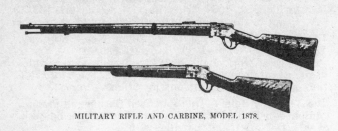

MILITARY RIFLE AND CARBINE, MODEL 1878.

Bilderatlas zum Grundriss der Waffenlehre, by K. T. Von Sauer. Pawlas, Nurnberg, Germany, 1968. Paper folder containing 28 pp. text and 26 plates. $7.50.

Facsimile of an 1869 set of plates depicting military rifles of Germany, with explanatory pamphlet in German text.

Blunderbusses, by D. R. Baxter. Stackpole Books, Harrisburg, Pa., 1970. 80 pp., 60 illus. $4.95.

Traces blunderbuss development from the 16th century, covering basic designs, firing systems, the double blunderbuss and revolving pepperbox design.

Bolt Action Rifles, by Frank de Haas, ed. by John T. Amber, Editor of GUN DIGEST. Digest Books, Inc., Northfield, IL, 1971. 320 pp., illus. Paper, $6.95.

The definitive work, covering every major design since the Mauser of 1871.

The Book of Rifles, by W. H. B. Smith. Stackpole Books, Harrisburg, PA, 1963 (3rd ed.). 656 pp., profusely illus. $6.00.

An encyclopedic reference work on shoulder arms, recently up-dated. Includes rifles of all types, arranged by country of origin.

Boy's Single-Shot Rifles, by Jas. J. Grant, William Morrow & Co., Inc., NY, 1967. 608 pp., illus. $10.00.

A wealth of important new material on an ever-popular subject, authoritatively presented. By the author of *Single Shot Rifles and More Single Shot Rifles.*

The Breech-Loader in the Service, 1816-1917, by Claud E. Fuller, N. Flayderman, New Milford, Conn., 1965. 381 pp., illus. $14.50.

Revised ed. of a 1933 historical reference on U.S. standard and experimental military shoulder arms. Much patent data, drawings, and photographs of the arms.

A voluminous work that covers handloading—and other things—in great detail. Replete with data for all cartridge forms.

British and American Flintlocks, by Fred. Wilkinson. Country Life Books, London, 1971. 64 pp., illus. $2.95.

Historical and technical aspects of flintlock firearms, in military and civilian use.

British Military Longarms 1715-1815, by D. W. Bailey, Stackpole Books, Harrisburg, PA, 1971. 80 pp. $4.95.

The Regulation service longarms of the British Army and Navy during a century of conflict in Europe, America and India, are fully described and illus.

British Military Longarms 1815-1865, by D. W. Bailey. Stackpole Books, Harrisburg, PA, 1972. 79 pp., illus. $4.95.

Concise account, covering muskets, carbines, rifles and their markings.

Browning Automatic Rifles, Normount Armament Co., Forest Grove, OR, 81 pp., illus. Paper, $2.00.

Reprint of Ordnance Manual TM 9-1211, on all types of caliber 30's.

Carbine Handbook, by Paul Wahl. Arco Publ. Co., N.Y.C., 1964. 80 pp., illus. $6.00. Paperbound, $3.95.

A manual and guide to the U.S. Carbine, cal. .30 M1, with data on its history, operation, repair, ammunition, and shooting.

Carbines Cal. .30 M1, M1A1, M2 and M3, by D. B. McLean. Normount Armament Co., Forest Grove, OR, 1964. 221 pp., well illus., paperbound. $3.00.

U.S. field manual reprints on these weapons, edited and reorganized.

Civil War Carbines, by A. F. Lustyik. World Wide Gun Report, Inc., Aledo, IL, 1962. 63 pp., illus., paper covers, $2.00.

Accurate, interesting summary of most carbines of the Civil War period, in booklet form, with numerous good illus.

Complete Book of Rifles and Shotguns, by Jack O'Connor, Harper & Bros., N.Y.C., 1961, 477 pp., illus. $6.95.

A splendid two-part book of encyclopedic coverage on every detail of rifle and shotgun.

Description and Instructions for the Management of the Gallery-Practice Rifle Caliber .22—Model of 1903. Inco., 1972. 12 pp., 1 plate. Paper, $1.00.

Reprint of 1907 War Dept. pamphlet No. 1925.

Description of U.S. Military Rifle Sights, by Edw. A. Tolosky, E. A. Tolosky, Publ., 1971. 117 pp. Paper, $8.50.

Covers period from 1861 to 1940. New and excellent work for collectors and fans of the U.S. Military. Definitive text, full-size line drawings.

Early Indian Trade Guns—1625 to 1775, by T. M. Hamilton. Museum of the Great Plains, Lawton, Okla. 1969. 34 pp., well illus., paper covers. $2.50.

Detailed descriptions of subject arms, compiled from early records and from the study of remnants found in Indian county.

English Sporting Guns and Accessories, by Macdonald Hastings. Ward Lock & Co., London. 1st ed., 1969. 96 pp., well illus. $4.00.

A delightful monograph on shotguns and accessory equipment for hunting from 1800 to the advent of the breechloader, including historic arms and ammunition.

Fifteen Years in the Hawken Lode, by John D. Baird, The Buckskin Press, Chaska, MI, 1971. 120 pp., illus. $10.00.

Complements "The Hawken Rifle" by the same author. Collection of thoughts and observations over many years on the famed Hawkens.

The First Winchester, by John E. Parsons. Winchester Press, New York, NY, 1969. 207 pp., well illus., $8.95.

This new printing of *The Story of the 1866 Repeating Rifle* (1st publ. 1955) is revised, and additional illustrations included.

Flintlock Guns and Rifles, by F. Wilkinson, Stackpole Books, Harrisburg, PA, 1971. 80 pp., $4.95.

Illus. reference guide for 1650-1850 period showing makers, mechanisms and users.

.45-70 Rifles, by J. Behn, Rutgers Book Center, Highland Park, NJ, 1972. New ed., 150 pp., illus. $5.95.

Covers the official U.S. Army small arms cartridge and the weapons for its use.

The Fuller Collection of American Firearms, by H. L. Peterson. Eastern National Park & Monument Assn., 1967. 63 pp., illus. $2.50.

Illustrated catalog of principal military shoulder arms in the collection. Decorated paper wrappers.

Garand Rifles M1, M1C, M1D, by Donald B. McLean. Normount Armament Co., Forest Grove, OR, 1968. Over 160 pp., 175 illus., paper wrappers. $3.00.

Covers all facets of the arm: battlefield use, disassembly and maintenance, all details to complete lock-stock-and-barrel repair, plus variations, grenades, ammo., and accessories; plus a section on 7.62 mm NATO conversions.

German Machineguns, by D. D. Musgrave & S. H. Oliver, Mor Associates, Wash., DC, 1971. 472 pp., $17.50.

Covers aircraft and ground types, including rare and little-known weapons, plus information on ammunition, accessories, and mounts. Over 500 illus.

German Mauser Rifle—Model of 1898, by J. E. Coombes and J. L. Aney. A reprint in paper covers by Francis Bannerman Sons, New York, NY, of their 1921 publication. 20 pp., well illus. $1.50.

Data on the subject weapon and its WWI development. Bayonets and ammunition are also described and illus.

German Submachine Guns and Assault Rifles. WE, Inc., Old Greenwich, CT, 1967. 161 pp. $5.95.

Aberdeen Proving Ground reports on over 50 models of World War II German rapid-fire weapons are reprinted.

The Golden Age of Shotgunning, by Bob Hinman, Winchester Press, NY, 1971. 175 pp., illus. $8.95.

The story of American shotgun and wingshooting from 1870 to 1900.

The Gun that Made the Twenties Roar, by W. J. Helmer, Macmillan Co., NY 1969. 286 pp. illus. $7.95.

Historical account of John T. Thompson and his invention, the Thompson submachine gun. Includes virtually a complete manual in detail.

The Hall Carbine Affair; An Essay in Historiography, by R. Gordon Wasson. Privately printed, Danbury, CT, 1971. 250 pp., illus. Deluxe slip-cased ed. of 250 copies. $75.00.

Based on the original work (limited to 100 copies) of 1941 and a 1948 revised ed. of only 750 copies. This issue, enlarged and re-researched, relates to sales and purchases of Hall carbines in the Civil War, in which J. Pierpont Morgan was involved.

Hall System Military Firearms and Conversions in the Museum Collection. Veteran Association of the First Corps of Cadets Museum, Boston, MA, 1973. 20 pp., illus. Paper covers. $1.00.

Illustrates and describes various models, including several Confederate conversions.

Hall's Breechloaders, by R. T. Huntington. Geo Shumway, Publ. 1972. 369 pp., illus. $15.00. Paper, $12.00.

Definitive treatise on John H. Hall and his inspectors. Shows all known models of the Hall rifle, appurtenances and pistol.

Handfeuerwaffen System Vetterli, by Hugo Schneider, et al. Stocker-Schmid, A. G. Dietikon-Zurich, Switzerland, 1972. 143 pp., illus. $26.00.

Describes and illustrates the many models of Vetterli rifles and carbines, the bayonets and ammunition used with them. Many large clear illustrations. German text.

Hawken Rifles; The Mountain Man's Choice, by John D. Baird, The Buckskin Press, Chaska, MI, 1971. 95 pp., illus. $10.00.

History and collector's reference on Hawken rifles, developed and used in the West in the fur trade.

Hints to Riflemen, by H. W. S. Cleveland. Distributor, Robert Halter, New Hope, PA, 286 pp., illustrated. $10.00.

A reprint of the original 1864 edition, to which *Practical Directions for the use of the Rifle* has been added.

The History of Winchester Firearms 1866-1966, ed. by T. E. Hall and P. Kuhlhoff, Winchester-Western Press, New Haven, CT, 1966. 159 pp., illus. $10.00.

Called the collector's item of the century, this 3rd ed. of Geo. R. Watrous' work rises to new glory in its scope and illustrations, beautifully produced, with a slip case showing old hunting scenes by A. B. Frost and Frederic Remington. Limited ed.

Identifying Old U.S. Muskets, Rifles & Carbines, by Col. A. Gluckman. Stackpole Books, Harrisburg, PA, 1973. 487 pp., illus. $2.98.

Collector's guide to U.S. long arms, first publ. 1959. Numerous models of each type are described and shown, with histories of their makers.

Johnson Rifles and Light Machine Guns, ed. by D. B. McLean. Normount Armament Co., Forest Grove, OR, 1968. 55 pp., illus., paperbound. $2.00.

Manual on the only recoil-operated auto-loading rifle issued to U.S. forces.

Johnson Semi-Automatic Rifle, Rotary Feed Model, 1941 Instruction Manual, by the Johnson Arms Co. Design Publ., Hyattsville, Md., 1969. 72 pp. illus., paper covers. $4.00.

A reprint of the original instruction manual.

The Kentucky Rifle, by J. G. W. Dillin. Geo. Shumway, York, PA, 1967. 5th ed. 202 pp., illus. $20.00.

A respected work on the long rifles developed in colonial days and carried by pioneers and soldiers. Much information of value to collectors and historians. Limited ed.

The Kentucky Rifle: A True American Heritage in Picture, compiled by Philip Cowan, et al. The Kentucky Rifle Assn. Wash., D.C., 1967. 110 pp., illus. $15.

Presents an outstanding group of Kentucky Rifles, most of them never before pictured.

The Kentucky Rifle, by Merrill Lindsay. Arma Press, NY/ The Historical Society of York County, York, PA, 1972. 100 pp., 81 large colored illustrations. $15.

Presents in precise detail and exact color 77 of the finest Kentucky rifles ever assembled in one place. Also describes the conditions which led to the development of this uniquely American arm.

Kentucky Rifle Patchboxes & Barrel Marks, by Roy F. Chandler, Valley View Offset, Duncannon, PA, 1971. 400 pp., $20.00.

Reference work illustrating hundreds of patchboxes, together with the mark or signature of the maker.

The Lee-Enfield Rifle, by E. G. B. Reynolds. Arco Publ. Co., NY, 1968. 224 pp., drawings and photos. $9.50.

New U.S. edition of a standard reference on models and modifications of the famous British military rifle.

Lewis Automatic Machine Gun, publ. originally by Savage Arms Co., Utica, NY. A reprint by L. A. Funk, Puyallup, WA, 1969. 47 pp., illus., paper covers. $1.50.

This facsimile covers the Model 1916 gun, explaining all features of operation, action, nomenclature, stripping and assembly.

Longrifles of North Carolina, by John Bivins, Jr. Geo. Shumway, York, PA, 1968, 200 pp., profusely illus. $24.00.

Historical survey of North Carolina gunmakers and their production during the 18th and 19th centuries. Over 400 gunsmiths are included. Fine photographs.

Longrifles of Note, by Geo. Shumway, Geo. Shumway, York, PA, 1967. 90 pp., illus. Paper covers, $3.95.

A review of 35 fine American long rifles, with detailed illustrations showing their art work, plus descriptive material.

The Machine Gun, Vol. II, Part VII, by Lt. Col. G. M. Chinn. Paladin Press, Boulder, Col., n.d. 215 pp., illus. $15.00.

Reprint of a 1952 Navy publication of Soviet WW II rapid fire weapons.

Marlin Catalog of 1897. A reprint in facsimile by the Wyoming Armory, Inc., Cheyenne, WY, 1969. 192 pp. Well illus., paper covers, $3.50.

All models are covered, cartridges, sights, engraving, accessories, reloading tools, etc.

Marlin Catalog, 1905, Wyoming Armory, Inc., Cheyenne, WY, 1971. 128 pp. Paper, $4.00.

Reprint. Rifles, shotguns, pistols, tools, cartridge information, factory engraving and carving illustrated and described.

Maynard Catalog of 1880, a reprint in facsimile by the Wyoming Armory, Inc., Cheyenne, WY, 1969. 32 pp., illus., paper covers. $2.25.

All models, sights, cartridges, targets, etc.

Military Sharps Rifles and Carbines, by R. E. Hopkins. Hopkins, Campbell, Calif., 1967. 141 pp., illus. $11.50.

A guide to the principal types, with photographs, patent data, technical details, etc.

The NRA Firearms Assembly Guidebook to Shoulder Arms. National Rifle Assn., Wash., D.C. 1973. 203 pp. Paper covers. $4.

Text and illus. explaining the takedown of 96 rifles and shotguns, domestic and foreign.

The Northwest Gun, by Chas. E. Hanson Jr. Nebraska State Historical Society, Lincoln, NB, 1970. 85 pp., illus. Paper covers. $4.50.

The corner-stone of collecting Indian trade guns.

The Original Mauser Magazine Sporting Rifles. Shooter's Bible, S. Hackensack, NJ, 56 pp., illus., paperbound. $1.00.

Facsimile reprint of a Mauser firearms brochure, with English text.

Parker, America's Finest Shotgun, by P. H. Johnson. Outlet Book Co., Inc., NY, 1968. 260 pp., illus. $2.95.

An account of a great sporting arm—from post Civil War until 1947, when it was sold to Remington. Values, models, etc.

Parker Brothers Gun Catalog, 1869. B. Palmer, Tyler, TX, 1972. 14 pp., illus. Paper covers. $4.

Facsimile of Charles Parker's first issued catalog on "Parker Breech-Loading Shot Guns."

The Pennsylvania-Kentucky Rifle, by Henry J. Kauffman. Bonanza Books, NY, 1968. A reprint. 374 pp., illus. $4.95.

A classic work first publ. in 1960 on early long rifles. Makers descriptions, and manufacturing methods are covered.

Percussion Guns & Rifles, by D. W. Bailey, Stackpole Books, Harrisburg, PA, 1972. 79 pp., illus. $5.95.

A guide to the muzzle-loading percussion guns and rifles of the 19th century.

Pictorial History of the Machine Gun, by F. W. A. Hobart. Drake Publ., Inc., NY, 1972. 256 pp. $9.95.

Text is enhanced by over 240 photos and diagrams and a table of machine gun data giving essential details on a large number of guns—some of which never got beyond the prototype stage.

Pictorial History of the Rifle, by G. W. P. Swenson. Ian Allan Ltd., Shepperton, Surrey, England, 1971. 184 pp., illus. $9.50.

Essentially a picture book, with over 200 rifle illustrations. The text furnishes a concise history of the rifle and its development.

Red Coat and Brown Bess, by Anthony D. Darling. Museum Restoration Service, Ottawa, Ontario, Can., 1970. Paper covers, 63 pp., very well illus., in line and halftone. $3.00.

An unusually excellent treatise on the British Army in 1774-1775. Includes detailed text and illus. of various models of the "Brown Bess," plus "Records of the Battles, Sieges and Skirmishes of the American Revolution."

Remington Arms Revised Price-List, 1902. Arthur McKee, Northport, NY, n.d. 64 pp. Paper covers. $3.50.

Reprint, fully illustrated.

Remington Firearms, 1906 Catalog, Arthur McKee, Northport, NY, n.d., 48 pp., illus. Paper covers. $3.50.

Reprint. Guns, parts, ammo., prices, etc.

The Rifled Musket, by Claud E. Fuller. Stackpole Books, Harrisburg, Pa., 1958. 302 pp., illus. $4.95.

The authoritative work of the late Claud E. Fuller and basically an account of the muskets whose model dates fell within the Civil War years—1861, 1863 and 1864. Part Two treats the contract muskets. Some reproduced material, notably Bartlett & Gallatin's "Digest of Cartridges," is almost wholly illegible, as is much of an 1860 Ordnance Dept. report.

Major Ned H. Roberts and the Schuetzen Rifle, by Gerald O. Kelver, G. O. Kelver, Publ., Mentone, IN, 1972. 99 pp., illus. $4.00.

Selected writings on old single shot rifles, sights, loads, etc.

Sir Charles Ross and His Rifle, by Robt. Phillips and J. J. Knap, Museum Restoration Service, Ottawa, Canada, 1969. 32 pp., illus. Paper covers. $2.00.

The story of the man who invented the "Ross Model 1897 Magazine Sporting Rifle," the 1900 under the name of Bennett, and many others.

Royal Sporting Guns at Windsor, by H. L. Blackmore, H. M. Stationery Office, London, England, 1968. 60 pp. text, 52 plates. $9.54.

Catalog of the most decorative and interesting guns in the Royal Armoury collection at Windsor Castle.

Schuetzen Rifles, History and Loading, by Gerald O. Kelver, Gerald O. Kelver, Publisher, Brighton, CO, 1972. Illus. $4.00.

Reference work on these rifles, their bullets, loading, telescopic sights, accuracy, etc. A limited, numbered ed.

Scloppetaria, by Capt. H. Beaufroy, Richmond Publ. Co., Richmond, England, 1971. 251 pp. $11.00.

Reprint of the 1808 edition written under the pseudonym "A Corporal of Riflemen." Covers rifles and rifle shooting, the first such work in English.

Sharps Firearms, *v. 3, Pt. 3, Model 1874 Rifles,* by Frank M. Sellers and Dewitt Bailey II. Frank M. Sellers, Denver, Colo., 1969, 20 pp., illus., paper covers. $7.50.

A separately printed section of a continuing comprehensive collector's reference. This current work shows and describes the known M1874 variations.

The Sharps Rifle, by W. O. Smith. Morrow, NYC, 1943, reprinted 1965. 138 pp., illus. $10.00.

Study of America's first successful breech-loader patented 1848, with information on its history, development, and operation.

Shotguns by Keith, by E. Keith. Stackpole Books, Harrisburg, PA, 1967. 307 pp., illus. A new edition, $2.98.

Guns and their accessories from history to ornamentation, their ammunition, and the practical use of American, English and European arms.

Single-Shot Rifles, by James J. Grant. Wm. Morrow & Co., NYC, 4th printing 1964. 385 pp., illus. $8.50.

A detailed study of these rifles by a noted collector.

Single Shot Rifles and Actions, by Frank de Haas. Ed. by J. T. Amber. Published by Digest Books, Inc., Northfield, IL, 1969. 342 pp., illus. paper bound. $7.95.

A definitive book on over 60 single shot actions and rifles, their use, repair, remodeling, etc.

Sniper Rifles of Two World Wars, by W. H. Tantum IV. Museum Restoration Service, Ottawa, Can., 1967. 32 pp., illus. $1.50.

Monograph on high-accuracy rifles used by troops in World Wars I and II and in Korea. Paper wrappers.

Sporting Guns, by Richard Akehurst. G. P. Putnam's Sons, New York, NY, 1968. 120 pp., excellently illus. and with 24 pp. in full color. $5.95.

One of the noted Pleasures and Treasures series. A nostalgic tracing of the history of shooting, and of the guns and rifles used by the sportsman.

Springfield Muzzle-Loading Shoulder Arms, by C. E. Fuller, F. Bannerman Sons, NYC, reprinted 1968. 176 pp., illus. $12.50.

Long-awaited reprint of an important 1930 reference work on weapons produced at Springfield Armory, 1795-1865, including ordnance reports, tables, etc., on flintlock and percussion models.

Springfield Rifles, M1903, M1903A1, M1903A4, compiled by the publ. Normount Armament Co., Forest Grove, OR, 1968. Over 115 pp., illus., paper wrappers. $2.50.

Routine disassembly and maintenance to complete ordnance inspection and repair; bore sighting, trigger adjustment, accessories, etc.

The '03 Springfields, by Clark S. Campbell, Ray Riling Arms Books Co., Phila., PA, 1971. 320 pp., illus. $16.50.

New, completely revised, enlarged and updated ed. based on the 1957 issue.

The Story of Pope's Barrels, by Ray M. Smith. Stackpole Books, Harrisburg, PA, 1964., 211 pp., illus. $10.00.

Detailed account of the achievements and life of Harry M. Pope, master rifle bbl. maker.

Submachine Guns Caliber .45, M3 and M3A1, U.S. FM23-41 and TM 9-1217. Normount Armament Co., Forest Grove, OR, 1967. 141 pp., illus., paperbound. $3.00.

Reprint of two U.S. Army manuals on submachine guns.

The Thompson Gun, publ. by Numrich Arms, West Hurley, NY, 1967, 27 pp., illus., paper covers. $1.95.

A facsimile reprint, excellently done, of a 1923 catalog of Thompson sub-machine guns.

Thompson Submachine Guns, compiled from original manuals by the publ. Normount Armament Co., Forest Grove, OR, 1968. Over 230 pp., well illus., many exploded views. Paper wrappers. $4.00.

Five reprints in one book: Basic Field Manual, Cal. 45, M1928AI (U.S. Army); Cal. 45, Model 1928 (for British); Cal. 45 (U.S. Ordnance); Model M1, Cal. 45 (U.S. Ordnance) and Ultra Modern Automatic Arms (Auto-Ordnance Corp.).

Thoughts on the Kentucky Rifle in its Golden Age, by Joe Kindig, Jr. George Shumway, York, PA, 1970. A facsimile reprint of the 1960 original. 561 pp., replete with fine arms and data on many makers. $14.50.

Covers mainly the arms and their makers in the Lancaster area of Pennsylvania. An authoritative work.

Underhammer Guns, by H. C. Logan. Stackpole Books, Harrisburg, PA, 1964. 250 pp. illus. $4.98.

A full account of an unusual form of firearm dating back to flintlock days. Both American and foreign specimens are included.

United States Rifle, Cal. .30, Model of 1917, a reprint of an official government booklet by Normount Publ. Co., Forest Grove, OR, 1969. 80 pp., line illus., paper covers. $2.00.

A training manual issued by the War Department in 1918. A much-wanted and useful booklet.

Westley Richards Modern Sporting Rifles and Cartridges. A reprint of an original undated catalog of the British makers. Safari Outfitters, Richfield, Conn., 1968. 60 pp. illus., paper. $4.95.

Facsimile of issue, covers big game rifles and ammunition.

Winchester—The Gun That Won the West, by H. F. Williamson, Combat Forces Press, Washington, D.C., 1952. Later eds. by Barnes, NY. 494 pp., profusely illus. $5.95.

A scholarly and essential economic history of an honored arms company, but the early and modern arms introduced will satisfy all but the exacting collector.

The Winchester Book, by Geo. Madis. Art & Reference House, Lancaster, Texas, 1971. 542 pp., illus. $20.00.

First release of 1,000 autographed deluxe copies at this special price. After these are sold only a standard ed. will be available, the price the same. $20.00.

Winchester '73 & '76, the First Repeating Center-Fire Rifles, by D. F. Butler. Winchester Press, New York, NY, 1st ed., 1970. 95 pp., well and tastefully illus. in line, halftones and photos. Color frontispiece. $7.95.

A complete history of the subject arms and their then-new ammunition, plus details of their use on America's western frontiers.

The World's Assault Rifles (and Automatic Carbines), by D. D. Musgrave and T. B. Nelson. T. B. N. Enterprises, Alexandria, VA, 1967. 546 pp., profusely illus. $19.50.

High velocity small-bore combat rifles are shown and described in much detail, arranged by type and nationality. A companion volume to *The World's Submachine Guns,* by Nelson and Lockhoven.

The World's Submachine Guns (and Machine Pistols), by T. B. Nelson and H. B. Lockhoven. T. B. N. Enterprises, Alexandria, VA, 1962. 739 pp., profusely illus. $15.50.

The 2nd printing (1964) of the first work with descriptive data on all significant SMGs to date, arranged by national origin. A glossary in 22 languages is included. It is a companion volume to the *The World's Assault Rifles* by Musgrave and Nelson.

Lightner Reprints

The following titles come from the Lightner Library Coll., Cocoa Beach, Fla. All have paper covers, all were publ. in 1973.

Browning Arms Co. Catalog, 1935. 188 pp., illus. $4.

Facsimile reprint showing first superposed models and grades.

Charles Daly (Prussian) Catalog, ca. 1930. 24 pp., illus. $4.

Facsimile catalog showing Regent and Diamond grades, over-unders, 3-barrel trap models.

A. H. Fox Gun Co. Catalog, 1923. 40 pp., illus. $4.

Facsimile of the 1923 catalog. All models and grades including single barrel trap models, and information on the Fox-Kautsky single trigger.

A. H. Fox Gun Catalog, 1934. 23 pp., illus. $4.

Facsimile showing all models, parts, prices, of Fox guns made by Savage Arms Corp., Utica, NY.

Ithaca Gun Co. Catalog, 1915. 25 pp., illus. $4.

Facsimile reprint of a large format catalog. Shows hammerless models.

Ithaca Gun Co. Catalog 51-F, 1930. 22 pp., illus. $4.

Facsimile of a large format catalog. Shows new lock models, gives prices.

Lefever Arms Catalog, 1892. 32 pp., illus. $4.

Facsimile of a very rare catalog.

The Parker Gun Catalog, 1934. 15 pp., illus. $3.

Facsimile of the last catalog issued by the original Parker Bros. Company.

The Parker Gun Catalog, 1937. 34 pp., illus. $5.

Facsimile of the 1937 catalog, publ. by the Parker Gun Works, Remington Arms Co., Inc. Their largest, most beautiful and last regular catalog issued. The only one displaying all Parker trap and Skeet models.

The Parker Gun Dealer's Illustrated Price Catalog, 1940. 8 pp., illus. $2.

Last wholesale and retail price catalog issued by Parker Gun Works, Remington Arms Co. Shows all models and accessories.

Remington Arms Co. Catalog, 1910. 62 pp., illus. $4.

Facsimile showing all double barreled models, including special 750 grade, autos, rifles, parts.

L. C. Smith (Hunter Arms Co.) Catalog, 1907. 34 pp., $5.

Facsimile of a large, beautifully illus. catalog. Shows early hammerless models, parts and prices.

L. C. Smith (Hunter Arms Co.) Catalog, 1928. 28 pp., illus. $4.

Facsimile reprint showing all models—trap, Skeet, eagle, etc.

L.C. Smith (Hunter Arms Co.) Catalog, 1918. 24 pp., illus. $4.

Facsimile reprint showing all hammerless models and prices.

L. C. Smith (Hunter Arms Co.) Catalog, 1939. 24 pp., illus. $4.50.

Facsimile of the Golden Anniversary Issue. Separate anniversary brochure included.

L. C. Smith (Hunter Arms Co.) Catalog, 1945. 24 pp., illus. $4.

Facsimile of the last L. C. S. catalog. Shows most modern models.

Swords and Knives

The American Bayonet, 1776-1964, by A. N. Hardin, Jr. Geo. Shumway, York, PA, 1964, 252 pp., profusely illus. $20.00.

First comprehensive book on U.S. bayonets of all services, a standard reference for collectors. All bayonets made for long arms and described in full detail, with outstanding photographs, and historical development of principal types. Full references and bibliography.

American Knives, the First History and Collectors' Guide, by Harold L. Peterson. Scribner's, N.Y.C., 1958. 178 pp., well illus. $6.95.

A timely book to whet the appetite of the ever-growing group of knife collectors.

American Polearms, 1526-1865, by R. H. Brown. N. Flayderman Co., New Milford, Conn., 1967. 198 pp., 150 plates. $14.50.

Concise history of pikes, spears, and similar weapons used in American military forces through the Civil War.

American Socket Bayonets, 1717-1873, by D. B. Webster, Jr. Museum Rest. Service, Ottawa, Can. 1964. 48 pp., 60 illus., paperbound. $1.50.

Concise account of major types, with nomenclature, characteristics, and dimensions. Line drawings.

The American Sword 1775-1945, by H. L. Peterson. Ray Riling Arms Books Co., Phila., PA, 1973. 286 pp. plus 60 pp. of illus. $16.50.

1973 reprint of a survey of swords worn by U.S. uniformed forces, plus the rare "American Silver Mounted Swords." (1700-1815).

American and European Swords in the Historical Collections of the U.S. National Museum, by T. T. Belote. Benchmark Pub. Co., Glendale, NY, 1970. 163 pp., illus. $7.50.

A reprint of Smithsonian Institution Bulletin 163, first published in 1932.

Arts of the Japanese Swords, by B. W. Robinson. Chas. E. Tuttle Co., Rutland, Vt., 1961. 110 pp. of descriptive text with illus., plus 100 full page plates, some in full color. $15.00.

An authoritative work, divided into 2 parts—the first on blades, tracing their history to the present day; the second on mounts and fittings. It includes forging processes; accounts of the important schools of swordsmiths; techniques employed plus a useful appendix on care and cleaning.

Basic Nazi Swords & Daggers, by Peter Stahl. Die Wehrmacht Military Publ., Stanford, CA, 1972. 30 pp., illus. Paper covers. $2.

Pictures and identifies Nazi swords and daggers.

Bayonets Illustrated, by Bert Walsh, Bashall Eaves, Ireland, 1970. 49 pp., illus. $5.00.

162 detailed line drawings of bayonets from many countries and periods.

Bayonets, an Illustrated History and Reference Guide, by F. J. Stephens. Arms and Armour Press, London, 1968. 76 pp., stiff paper wrappers, 134 photographs. $5.00.

A general historical survey of all categories of the weapon, from the U.S. and many other countries.

Bowie Knives, by R. Abels. Pub. by author, NYC, 1960. 48 pp. profusely illus. Paper covers. $2.00.

A booklet showing knives, tomahawks, related trade cards and advertisements

Bowie Knives From the Collections of Robert Abels and the Ohio Historical Society, by Wm. G. Keener and D. A. Hutslar. The Ohio Historical Society, 1962. 124 pp., profusely illus. Paper covers. $4.50.

Limited ed. of an original Museum Catalog of a special exhibit by the Ohio Historical Sociery.

British Cut and Thrust Weapons, by John Wilkinson-Latham. Charles E. Tuttle Co., VT, 1971. 112 pp., illus. $7.50.

Well-illustrated study tracing the development of edged weapons and their adoption by the British armed forces. Describes in detail swords of cavalry and mounted troops, infantry, general officers, yeomanry, militia, the navy and air force.

British Military Bayonets from 1700 to 1945, by R. J. W. Latham. Arco Publ. Co., N.Y.C., 1969. 94 pp., illus. $8.50.

History and identification catalog of British bayonets, with fine illustrations, marks, dimensions, and equipment of various British army units.

British Military Swords, From 1800 to the Present Day, by J. W. Latham, Crown Publishers, NY, 1967, 91 pp., illus. $3.95.

Survey of British swords used by various branches of the Army, with data on their manufacture, specifications, and procurement.

The Canadian Bayonet, by R. B. Manarey, Century Press, Alberta, Can. 1970. 51 pp. $5.00.

Illustrated history of the Canadian bayonet.

Classic Bowie Knives, by Robert Abels. R. Abels, Inc., NY, 1967. 97 pp., illus. with numerous fine examples of the subject. $7.50.

A nostalgic story of the famous blades, with trade advertisements on them, and photos of users.

A Collector's Pictorial Book of Bayonets, by F. J. Stephens, Stackpole Books, Harrisburg, PA, 1971. 127 pp., illus. $5.95.

Instant identification of bayonet types, plus their history and use.

Cut and Thrust Weapons, by E. Wagner, Spring Books, Longdon, 1967. 491 pp., line drawings. $17.50.

English translation of a survey of European edged weapons, their traditions, manufacture, and use.

Daggers, Bayonets & Fighting Knives of Hitler's Germany, by John R. Angolia. James Bender Pub. Co., Mountain View, CA. 1st ed. 1971. 334 pp., profusely illus. $14.95.

An exceptionally fine, useful compilation for collector, historian and student.

The Daggers and Edged Weapons of Hitler's Germany, by Maj. J. P. Atwood. Publ. privately for the author in Berlin, Germany, 1965. 240 pp. illus. New edition, 1967. $15.00.

Lavishly illus. with many plates in full color, this is an outstanding production, easily the best information (for the collector) on the subject.

Daggers and Fighting Knives of the Western World: From the Stone Age Until 1900, by Harold L. Peterson, Walker and Co., New York, 1967. 256 pp., illus. $2.98.

The only full-scale historical and analytical work on this subject, from flint knives of the stone age to British and American naval dirks.

Early Japanese Sword Guards, by Masayuki Sasano. Japan Pub. Trading Co., San Francisco, CA, 1972. 256 pp., illus. $12.50.

220 of the finest open-work sword guards, dating from early periods and representing most of the major schools.

Edged Weapons, by Fred Wilkinson. Guinness Signatures, London, 1970, 256 pp., plus 14-page index. Excellently illus., many in full color. $12.95.

Scholarly treatment of all kinds of blades—from flint to steel, rapiers, smallswords, knives, daggers, hunting weapons, polearms, etc., plus construction and decoration.

A Guide to Oriental Daggers and Swords, by Michael C. German. M. C. German, London, Eng., 1967. 59 pp., illus. Paper covers. $3.95.

Excellent, inexpensive guide for identifying and classifying hundreds of different Oriental daggers.

Italian Facist Daggers, by Fred. J. Stephens. Militaria Pub. Ltd., London, England, 1972. 25 pp., illus., some in color, Paper covers. $5.

First publ. devoted to collecting the daggers of Fascist Italy.

Japanese Sword Blades, by Alfred Dobree, George Shumway, York, PA, 1967. 39 pp., illus., in paper wrappers. $4.50.

A two-part monograph, reprinted from a notable work.

The Japanese Sword and Its Fittings, by members of the Japanese Sword Society of New York. Cooper Union Museum, N.Y.C., 1966. Paper covers. 26 pp. of text plus many illus. $3.50.

The authoritative text in the form of a catalog describing the illus. of items in the possession of members of the society.

Kentucky Knife-Traders Manual, compiled by R. B. Ritchie. R. B. Ritchie, Hindman, KY, 1971. 66 pp., illus. Paper covers. $5.75.

Lists some 2000 pocket knives and their values by brands, pattern and condition, plus a listing of about 400 collectible razors.

Robert Klaas Sword and Dagger Catalog, Robt. Klaas, Solingen-Ohligs, W. Germany 1938. 32 pp., illus. Paper, $5.00.

Reprint of the original 1938 catalog. A rare reference work. 16 pp. of swords and daggers with original prices.

Military Edged Weapons of the World, 1880-1965, by H. A. Mauerer, College Pt., NY, 1967. 151 pp., illus. $4.50.

Various swords, blades, etc., in a private collection are dimensioned, described, and photographed. A guide for collectors. Paper wrappers.

Photographic Supplement of Confederate Swords, by Wm. A. Albaugh III. Wm. A. Bond, Vernon, TX, 1963. 205 pp., 300 photos. $6.95.

Over 200 specimens of C. W. edged weapons are shown with data on their owners and makers. Useful for collectors and students.

A Primer of World Bayonets. G. Hughes, London, 1969. Unpaginated, illus. Paper, $5.00.

A comprehensive (2 vol.) manual on the bayonet.

Rapiers, by Eric Valentine. Stackpole Books, Harrisburg, Pa., 1968. 76 pp., 58 photos., 3 drawings. $4.95.

A desirable monograph, first on its subject, to be publ. in English. Covers methods of authentication, renovation, cleaning and preservation.

Regulation Military Swords, by J. Wilkinson-Latham, Star Products, London, 1970. 32 pp., illus. Paper, $4.00.

Survey of military swords of U.S., England, France and Germany.

Romance of Knife Collecting, by Dewey P. Ferguson, Dewey P. Ferguson, Fairborn, OH, 1970. 100 pp., illus. Paper covers, spiral binding. $5.00.

From stone to steel knives, care, patterns, counterfeiting, history of knife companies, etc.
Price Guide to above title, by D. P. Ferguson, same place, 1972. 60 pp., illus. Paper covers. $4.00.

Russian Military Swords, 1801-1917, by E. Mollo, Historical Research Unit, London, Eng., 1969. 56 pp., illus. $7.50.

First book in English to examine and classify the various swords used by the Russian Army from Alexander I to the Revolution. 42 photos, 27 line drawings, 10 in color.

The Samurai Swords, by J. M. Yumoto. Tuttle Co., Rutland, Vt., 1958. 191 pp., illus. $4.50.

Detailed information on evaluation of specimens, including origin and development of the Japanese blade.

Scottish Swords and Dirks, by John Wallace. Stackpole Books, Harrisburg, Pa., 1970. 80 pp., illus, $4.95.

An illustrated reference guide to Scottish edged weapons.

Scottish Swords from the Battlefield at Culloden, by Lord Archibald Campbell, Mowbray Co., Providence, RI, 1971. 63 pp., illus. $5.00.

Modern reprint of an exeedingly rare 1894 limited private ed.

Shosankenshu, by H. L. Joly. Holland Press, London, 1963. Unpaginated. $12.50.

List of Japanese artists' names and kakihan found on sword furniture by the late European authority. Completed in 1919, previously unpubl., this is a facsimile of Joly's MS and line drawings. Lists nearly 3,000 names.

Sword, Lance and Bayonet, by Charles ffoulkes and E. C. Hopkinson. Arco Publishing Co., NY, 1967. 145 pp., well illus. in line and halftone. $7.50.

A facsimile reprint of the first attempt at a consecutive account of the arms, both general and official use, since the discarding of armor.

The Sword and Same, by H. L. Joly and I. Hogitaro, Holland Press Ltd., London, 1971. 241 pp., plates and line drawings. $18.00.

New printing of Arai Hakuseki, "The Sword Book in Honcho Gunkiko" and "The Book of Same Ko Hi Sei Gi of Inaba Tsurio."

Swords & Blades of the American Revolution, by Geo. C. Neumann. Stackpole Books, Harrisburg, PA, 1973. 288 pp. well illus. $24.95.

An encyclopedia of 1,600 bladed weapons—swords, bayonets, spontoons, halberds, pikes, knives, daggers, and axes—used by both sides, on land and sea, in America's struggle for independence.

Swords & Daggers, by Frederick Wilkinson. Hawthorn Books, NY, 1968. 256 pp., well illus. $5.95.

Good general survey of edged weapons and polearms of collector interest, with 150 pp. of illustrations and descriptions of arms from Europe, Africa and the Orient.

Swords for Sea Service, by Commander W. E. May, R. N. & P. G. W. Annis, H. M. S. O., London, 1970. 398 pp. in 2 volumes, $30.00.

Study based on the swords, dirks and cutlasses in the National Maritime Museum in Greenwich, plus many other outside weapons, and information on the British sword trade, industry, makers and retailers. 140 black and white plates, 3 color plates and many other illus.

Swords of Hitler's Third Reich, by Major J. R. Angolia, F. J. Stephens, Essex, England, 1969. Over 100 pp., well illus. $8.95.

A comprehensive work on the swords of the German Army, Navy, Air Force, SS, Police, Fire Dept., and many other government departments—plus belts, hangers, and accoutrements—all described and illus.

U.S. Sword Bayonets, 1847-1865, by R. V. Davis, Jr. Priv. prt., Pittsburgh, PA, 1963. 36 pp., 17 pl., paper. $4.00.

Histories, production data, and good photos of U.S. military sword bayonets of Civil War era.

Though many of these books will be available from local gunshops or bookstores, others will be very hard to find. We suggest that you contact Ray Riling Arms Books, 6844 Gorsten St., Philadelphia, PA 19119; Rutgers Book Center, 127 Raritan Ave., Highland Park, NJ 08904; Norm Flayderman & Co., RFD 2, Squash Hollow, New Milford, CT 06776, or other sources mentioned in the article "The Gun Collector's Secret Weapon," by Bob Steindler in this volume.